Understanding Industrial Relations

Understanding Industrial Relations

Third Edition

DAVID FARNHAM
Principal Lecturer in Industrial Relations, Portsmouth Polytechnic

JOHN PIMLOTT
Lecturer in Industrial Relations, University of Southampton

HOLT, RINEHART AND WINSTON

London · New York · Toronto · Sydney · Tokyo · Hong Kong

Holt, Rinehart and Winston Ltd: 1 St Anne's Road,
Eastbourne, East Sussex BN21 3UN

British Library Cataloguing in Publication Data

Farnham, David
    Understanding industrial relations.—
    3rd ed.
    1. Industrial relations—Great Britain
    I. Title   II. Pimlott, John, *1934–*
    331′.0941   HD8391
ISBN: 0-03-910694-2

First published by Cassell 1979
Second Edition 1983
Third Edition published by Holt, Rinehart and Winston 1986

Typeset by Phoenix Photosetting, Chatham
Printed and bound in Great Britain by Mackays of Chatham Ltd.

Last digit is print no: 9 8 7 6 5 4 3 2 1

Contents

Preface to First Edition

The purpose of this book is to provide a comprehensive introduction to British industrial relations in its wider contexts. Whilst it is aimed primarily at students of industrial relations whether they are managers or trade unionists, this book can be used by practitioners of industrial relations, by those reading for degrees and professional qualifications, and by anyone who wants an understanding of the principles and practices of contemporary industrial relations. This text should also be useful to the lay public and specialist groups, such as the teaching profession, who would like a broad appreciation of how those involved in industrial relations regulate and conduct their business together. In this way, we hope, our readers will obtain a better knowledge and awareness of the multiplicity of factors influencing employment practices and the ways in which industrial relations decisions are made in Britain today.

We have written this book for three main reasons. First, our experience as teachers of industrial relations over a number of years has made us increasingly aware that there is a need for an introductory book in this field. In it, we seek not only to explain British industrial relations practices and to put them into their wider social perspectives, but also to examine them through explicit descriptive, analytical and conceptual frameworks. Second, with the increasing volume of labour law, the debate about worker participation in managerial decision making, and the variety of industrial relations changes which have taken place in Britain since the early 1970s, we consider that the time is now right to attempt a synthesis of some of the recent literature and principal research findings in the field. Third, in undertaking this task, we believe that our complementary academic and teaching backgrounds – in addition to our previous industrial experiences – give some degree of balance to our study of industrial relations.

David Farnham
John Pimlott

July 1979

Preface to Second Edition

Political and economic events have moved very rapidly since we completed the first edition of this text three years ago. These events, in turn, are having a profound impact on the practices and patterns of industrial relations in Britain, as the country moves towards the second half of the 1980s. In 1979, with the Labour Party in office, trade union power seemed to have reached its peak, while some managements appeared to have lost confidence in their 'right to manage'. Three years later, a radical Conservative Government, led by Margaret Thatcher, is having a major influence in altering the economic, legal and social contexts in which industrial relations between employers and trade unions, and between trade unions and their members, take place.

Unemployment, for example, is over the three million mark; productivity per man-hour has increased, while total output has drastically fallen; new labour laws, namely the Employment Acts 1980 and 1982, have been enacted; trade union bargaining power has been drastically weakened by the impact of the economic recession; the influence of both the Trades Union Congress and the Confederation of British Industry on governmental policy-making has been effectively neutered; and employers are generally taking a much harder line on employment issues such as pay negotiations and manpower cutbacks, which they would not have done a short time ago. It is these events and their consequences which we have attempted to incorporate in this edition. We have also updated the descriptive and background material where necessary. In doing this, we would like to thank Ron Hodrien, Information Officer at Portsmouth Polytechnic, for kindly reading the proofs of this edition. Any remaining errors are ours alone.

David Farnham
John Pimlott

November 1982

Preface to Third Edition

Since the first edition in 1979, the climate of British industrial relations has altered radically, new labour laws have been enacted, new research has been published and the balance of bargaining power between employers and organized employees has shifted significantly towards employers and management. We tried to incorporate some of these developments in our second edition, published in 1983, as we have thoroughly revised and updated this new edition to take account of the main empirical and contextual changes of the 1980s.

This has been done in three ways. We have restructured the text, reordered its content, omitted four previous chapters and introduced three new ones – Chapters Two, Seven and Twelve. We have rewritten and updated the remaining chapters and added new material, such as recent employment law and research findings, where appropriate. Finally, we have used figures, tables and section subheadings for the first time, as well as putting bibliographical references at the end of each chapter rather than at the end of the book. With all these changes we believe our text will continue to be an attractive and useful source book for students and teachers alike.

This book could not have been completed and published without the help and support of a number of people. We would particularly like to thank and acknowledge the help provided by our editor, Simon Lake, Ron Hodrien and Sylvia Horton of Portsmouth Polytechnic and Felicity Farnham, Frances Farnham and Robina Pimlott. Any errors of fact or judgement remain ours alone.

David Farnham
John Pimlott

June 1986

Introduction

This book provides a comprehensive introduction to British industrial relations. Its aim is to put British industrial relations practices, and the contexts in which they take place, into satisfactory descriptive and analytical frameworks. It is an approach, we hope, which not only is rigorous in its method but also relates the realities of British industrial relations to a sound conceptual base. Our purpose throughout is to describe and outline those empirical findings and analytical tools which help to explain the complex nature of industrial relations between employers and employees in their many contrasting, often contradictory, and sometimes confusing aspects. We hope that in using this book, our readers will gain some insights into the rich diversity and yet underlying coherence of British industrial relations.

Because of this complexity, our objective is to achieve some degree of balance between being comprehensive in our coverage and selective in the use of material; between considering common practices and theoretical principles; between providing concrete examples and abstract concepts; and between discussing past experience and present controversy. We are not seeking to produce an industrial relations handbook or an instant kit of industrial relations tools which can be mechanically applied to solve industrial relations problems, even if this were possible. We seek, rather, to provide a book which is informative, thought-provoking and balanced in its views, but which demonstrates the uniqueness of British industrial relations and encourages its readers to be sceptical about simplistic explanations of industrial relations phenomena and behaviour.

We start from three basic assumptions about the nature of industrial relations in Britain. The first is that the focus of industrial relations is how individuals and groups, the organizations representing their interests and wider institutional forces determine decisions affecting employment relationships. These include the contractual relationships between employers and employees and the power relationships between employers and trade unions. Implicit in our approach is the view that managers, employees, trade unions and government all have interests in industrial relations decision making in our sort of society. Industrial relations is not the sole prerogative of management or the trade unions: it is an activity in which all these groups are vitally concerned.

Our second assumption is that industrial relations practices are indivisible from their concepts, principles and theories. What happens in industrial relations and how it happens are its *practices*. They are essentially empirical phenomena and are best identified by the descriptive method. Arising out of such practices is a language of industrial relations. These are its *concepts*. Although these concepts are abstract and analytic, they are useful in describing and classifying industrial relations phenomena. Closely related to the concepts of industrial relations are its *principles*. They centre on the patterns of order, systematization and regularity which are discernible within industrial relations practices and situations. They identify and separate out the essential characteristics and general conventions of industrial relations. They have to be under-

stood by students of industrial relations and applied by industrial relations practitioners.

At a higher level of abstraction still, why certain practices happen in industrial
relations are its *theories*. These are explanatory in nature although if they are used
prescriptively theories can have a 'normative' character. When used normatively,
industrial relations theories depend on an individual's value judgements and perceptions of the world, suggesting what 'ought to be' in given social situations. Compared
with the practices, concepts and principles of industrial relations its theories are more
likely to be the subject of greater speculation, whether by academics, practitioners, or
others. Nevertheless, theories are essential since without theories of behaviour, people
can neither act out their own social roles nor understand the roles of others and their
social environments. Ultimately a social theory is a way of perceiving, understanding, and predicting people's actions in practical, real-life situations. Those 'practical'
people who insist that they are immune from abstract 'theory' are usually unaware of
the preconceptions or prejudices which determine their own views of the world in which
they live. As John Maynard Keynes commented many years ago: 'practical men, who
believe themselves to be quite exempt from any intellectual influences, are usually the
slaves of some defunct economist.'[1]

Collective bargaining, for example, is now a common industrial relations practice.
What it is, how it operates and its results can be observed and described in specific cases.
In general terms, collective bargaining is also an industrial relations concept and it can
be described and analysed as such. Its basic principles, such as the conditions necessary
for its existence, its main elements, its structure, and its strengths and weaknesses, for
instance, can then be abstracted and compared with other industrial relations practices
and so on. Ultimately, through the processes of reasoning, observation, and empirical
investigation, the essential nature of collective bargaining, its fundamental purposes,
and why it exists can be examined and discussed in their theoretic contexts. Some
commentators, for example, explain collective bargaining in economic terms, some as a
political process, and others as a reflection of class relations in capitalist economies. In
short, by using the appropriate conceptual, analytic and theoretic tools, we are better
able to describe, analyse and understand the practices of collective bargaining or of any
other industrial relations activity.

Our third assumption derives from the second. It is that different people perceive
industrial relations in different ways and from different theoretical positions. This is one
of the problems in teaching and in learning about industrial relations: there is no
approach to the subject which satisfies everyone. Some people view industrial relations
in terms of class conflict between the owners of private capital and the working class
with wage labour to sell. Others see it in terms of industrial conflict between employers
and employees and their representative organizations. Others see conflict of any kind
at work as being abnormal, unnecessary and anti-social. For these reasons, industrial
relations becomes both an academic and a political arena where the opposing ideologies
and different value systems of individuals and groups compete against one another and
for the minds and actions of the uncommitted.

These three fundamental assumptions are the cornerstones upon which this book is
based. Our method and the descriptive and explanatory frameworks which we have
arrived at and use stem from these assumptions. It is an approach, we believe, which
describes, analyses and explains the complex nature of industrial relations in advanced
market economies like that of Britain.

Our approach is essentially an *institutional* one which we believe to be useful for
students new to the subject. This does not deny the validity of other approaches
deriving from behavioural systems or Marxist assumptions. However, our starting
point in trying to understand industrial relations is that it comprises a *network of*

institutions or a 'patterned set of social relationships directed towards a definable set of social objectives.'[2] Institutions of all kinds, whether they are political, economic, social or industrial relations, have an existence beyond the particular persons involved in them at any one time and, within certain limits, they establish the patterns of social behaviour amongst their participants by institutionalizing them. In other words, the behaviour of people within institutions is constrained within certain expected social norms and parameters. Individual and group behaviour which is institutionalized is largely conditioned by the expectations both of others within the institution and of society generally as to how its participants *should* behave. It seems to be tautological but trade unionists, for example, behave as trade unionists precisely because they are members of trade unions. It is unions as organizations and trade unionists as people bound together by a set of common values which make up the institution of trade unionism.

In addition to trade unionism, there are other major industrial relations institutions considered in this book. These include collective bargaining, employers, the law, management, and the state's role in industrial relations. A knowledge of these institutions and the individual participants is important if we are to understand everyday industrial relations situations. It is these institutions which largely pre-determine the broad limits within which industrial relations practitioners and participants, such as managers, trade unionists and third-party representatives, act in practical situations. We repeat, because of their involvement in industrial relations, the behaviour of its participants becomes institutionalized within certain expected norms and parameters. Although industrial relations institutions are broadly compatible with one another there are nevertheless conflicts between and within them. The norms and values associated with an institution like trade unionism, for example, may be directly contrary to some of those associated with the institution of management, the principles of shop steward organization or those of the state.

The institutions of industrial relations subsume four subsidiary social networks. These are a *network of organizations*; a *network of participants*; a *network of processes*; and a *network of decisions*: all of which interact and inter-relate together within the industrial relations environment and beyond it. The main industrial relations organizations existing in Britain include, for example, the Advisory Conciliation and Arbitration Service; the Central Arbitration Committee; employers' associations; firms and other work enterprises acting as employers; industrial tribunals; shop stewards committees; and trade unions. In turn, the industrial relations participants operating within and among these organizations include arbitrators, conciliators and mediators; union branch officers; full-time trade union officers; personnel officers; managers; officials of employers' associations; shop stewards; trade union members; and employees who are not members of trade unions.

Similarly, there are a number of industrial relations processes through which industrial decisions are made and implemented. These include conciliation; dispute settlement; grievance handling; industrial tribunals; negotiation; joint consultation; managerial prerogatives; trade union policy making; strikes; lock-outs; conflict avoidance procedures and so on. Finally, industrial relations decisions can be found in a variety of sources including arbitration awards; case law; collective agreements; courts of inquiry; custom and practice at the workplace; the findings of industrial tribunals; Parliamentary statutes; union rule books; works rules and so on. It is this network of institutions, with their subsidiary networks of organizations, participants, processes and decisions, which provides the core of industrial relations and the main elements of this book.

The book is divided into five parts. Part One gives the general background to industrial relations. First we examine and compare the main theories of industrial relations to provide a framework for analysing industrial relations institutions, practices and activities throughout the text (Chapter One). We then identify and describe the principal contexts within which industrial relations take place – especially their historical, labour market and technological contexts (Chapter Two).

Part Two focuses on the main institutional and organizational features of British industrial relations. Initially we analyse the nature of employers and management and the ways in which they manage industrial relations with unions, employees and their representatives (Chapter Three). We then consider the roles of employers' associations as representatives and agents of employer interests (Chapter Four). This leads on to an examination of trade unions as bargaining agencies, their structures and internal organization, and how they conduct their internal and interunion affairs (Chapter Five). This is followed by an outline of the nature, structure and results of collective bargaining in both the private and public sectors (Chapter Six).

Part Three is concerned with the state and industrial relations. First we describe and analyse the relationships between employers and the Conservative Party, the unions and the Labour Party and the roles of the Confederation of British Industry and the Trades Union Congress (Chapter Seven). We then discuss the principles underlying state intervention in industrial relations including minimum wage regulation, pay and economic policy, third party settlement of industrial disputes and industrial tribunals (Chapter Eight). Next the elements of individual labour law and collective labour law are outlined. We look at, for example, the contract of employment, the job protection rights of employees, trade unions and the law, and the law regulating closed shops, union ballots and trade disputes (Chapters Nine and Ten).

In Part Four, we examine industrial relations practices at workplace or establishment level. The right to manage and other managerial practices are explored as well as the non-union firm (Chapter Eleven). We then turn to the personnel management function within enterprises outlining its scope, activities, tasks and relationship to line management (Chapter Twelve). The importance of shop stewards and workgroup representation is also considered, with the workplace relationships between stewards and managers outlined and accounted for (Chapter Thirteen). In the final chapter of Part Four, we examine the central part which negotiating and consultative machinery play in regulating relations between employers and employees and employers and trade unions at enterprise level (Chapter Fourteen).

In Part Five, we focus on the problem of power sharing in industrial relations. We also draw some tentative conclusions about the changing nature of industrial relations and the issues emerging in it in the 1980s (Chapter Fifteen).

REFERENCES

1. J. M. Keynes, *The General Theory of Employment, Interest and Money*, Macmillan, London, 1936, p. 383.
2. D. Martin (ed.), *50 Key Words: Sociology*, Lutterworth Press, Guildford, 1970, p. 35.

PART ONE

The Background to Industrial Relations

1

Theories of Industrial Relations

The social sciences examine, explain and try to predict the behaviour of individuals and groups in those institutionalized activities which are not biologically determined. There are, however a number of difficulties in studying humans in their social situations. One is the inherent complexity of the task. For example, to what extent is it possible to separate out the psychological, economic, social and political aspects of people's behaviour in society? Secondly, there is the difficulty of constructing abstract concepts, models, and theories of human actions from observed behaviour and then to articulate these images, whether verbally or in writing, in language which is rigorous to the specialist on the one hand, but comprehensible to the interested non-specialist on the other. The ultimate problem for the student of the social sciences is how to be objective about essentially subjective social phenomena. Indeed, some social philosophers argue that there is no such thing as a truly objective social science. Social reality at any given time, by this view, is dependent upon the particular paradigm being used by the social scientist or human actor.

What is true for the social sciences generally is true for the study of industrial relations particularly. We do not intend to evade these and other related issues in this book. Our purpose in this chapter is to outline and to compare the main academic theories by which industrial relations institutions, structures and processes are analysed by different social theorists. Secondly we suggest a framework by which the complex phenomena of industrial relations institutions and activities may be conceptualized and categorized. The purpose of having a theory of industrial relations is not an arid academic exercise nor unrelated to the real world. All social actions in life and all the decisions preceding them are based on people's theoretical appraisals of particular social situations, even if they are not manifestly aware of them. This applies, in particular, to the emotive and political area of industrial relations. Every social act people make is a combination of theory, experience, social conditioning and practice. In other words, the theories which individuals develop about industrial relations are attempts to construct logically consistent ways of understanding and explaining social behaviour and real-life activities in this complex field of human interest.

It soon becomes clear in real-life situations, however, that people can examine the same industrial relations issue from quite different viewpoints. Consequently each of them behaves as if he or she were in different social situations. An example of this would be the contrasting perceptions which a personnel manager and a shop steward might have of a pay dispute in the company in which they work. One of them might perceive the issue in managerial, corporate and middle-class terms, the other in union and working-class terms and each will act in accordance with his or her beliefs about the situation but in different ways. In this chapter, we examine phenomena such as this and what we consider to be the major theories of industrial relations. We then outline the main theoretical assumptions around which we have based this book.

1.1   UNITARY THEORY

The following quotation is taken from the evidence submitted to the Donovan Commission by the then Chairman and Managing Director of the Rugby Portland Cement Company, Halford Reddish, who, perhaps without realizing it, was putting forward an essentially unitary and human relations view of industrial organization and industrial relations to the Commissioners:

1. I am asked 'how good relations are achieved in a company which does not negotiate with trade unions'.
2. Our thinking proceeds as follows . . .
   Modern industrial organization is in effect a partnership between the labour of yesterday (which we call capital) and the labour of today (all of us who work for wages and salaries) . . .
4. We deplore the use of the terms 'industrial relations' and 'labour relations'. We prefer 'human relations', by which we mean a recognition of the essential human dignity of the individual . . .
5. An employee, at whatever level, must be made to feel that he is not merely a number on a pay-roll but a recognized member of a team . . .
6. We reject the idea that amongst the employees of a company there are 'two sides' meaning the executive directors and managers on the one hand and the weekly-paid employees on the other. Executive directors are just as much employees of the company as anyone else. We are all on the same side, members of the same team . . .
8. We recognize that the tone of any organization depends primarily on one man, on the executive head of it: on his philosophy, on his outlook, on the standards which he sets, on his example: in short, on his leadership.
9. Leadership is surely the key to good human relations – leadership at all levels. It must embrace, *inter alia*: . . . Maintenance of strict discipline, as firm as it is fair . . .
   A conviction that loyalty must be a two-way traffic. I expect every employee to be loyal to the company and to me as the temporary captain of the team: he has an equal right to expect loyalty from me . . . Communication – in the widest sense of the term . . . [1]

The essence of a unitary theory of industrial relations, held by Halford Reddish and others, is that every work organization is an integrated and harmonious whole existing for a common purpose. They assume that each employee identifies unreservedly with the aims of the enterprise and with its methods of operating. By this view, there is no conflict of interest between those supplying financial capital to the enterprise and their managerial representatives, and those contributing their labour skills. By definition the owners of capital and labour are partners to the common aims of efficient production, high profits and good pay in which everyone in the organization has a stake. It follows that there cannot be 'two sides' in industry. Indeed managers and managed alike are merely parts of the same 'team'. This team, however, is expected to be provided with strong leadership from the top to keep it working and to ensure commitment to the tasks to be done and to its managerial office-holders.

This requires, on the part of management, at the minimum a paternalistic approach towards subordinate employees or, at the extreme, a more authoritarian one, together with a suitable communication structure to keep employees informed of managerial decisions. Conversely, employees are expected to remain loyal to the organization and to its management in deference to the common problems facing managers and subordinates alike. Thus the unitary theory of industrial relations emerges from a belief that work enterprises, whether privately or publicly owned, are very much like a professional football team: 'Team spirit and undivided management authority co-exist to the benefit of all.'[2] Work organizations, in short, are viewed as unitary in their structure and unitary in their purposes, and as having a single source of authority and a set of participants which is motivated by common goals. Consequently industrial relations is assumed to be based on mutual co-operation and harmony of interest between management and managed within the enterprise.

One implication of unitarism is that factionalism within the enterprise, or in a part of it, is seen as a pathological social condition. Subordinate employees are not expected to challenge managerial decisions or the right to manage, while trade unionism is viewed as an illegitimate intrusion into the unified and co-operative structure of the workplace. More than this, it is suggested, trade unionism competes almost malevolently with management for the loyalty and commitment of employees to their employer. In other words, the unitary theory denies the validity of conflict at work whether between management and employees, between management and unions, or even between the organization and its customers. The concepts of common purpose and harmony of interests further imply:

> that apparent conflict is either (a) merely frictional, e.g. due to incompatible personalities or 'things going wrong', or (b) caused by faulty 'communications', e.g. 'misunderstandings' about aims or methods, or (c) the result of stupidity in the form of failure to grasp the communality of interest, or (d) the work of agitators inciting the supine majority who would otherwise be content.[3]

Collective bargaining and trade unions are therefore perceived as being anti-social mechanisms, since acceptance of two opposed and competing interest groups within the enterprise in the persons of management and union representatives only precipitates and crystallizes unnecessary and destructive industrial conflict between what in effect are viewed as two non-competing, co-operative parties.

It soon becomes evident that the unitary theory of industrial relations is predominantly managerially oriented in its inception, in its emphasis and in its application. Indeed it is a theoretical perspective with which many managers identify because it reassures them of their roles as organizational decision makers and legitimizes the acceptance of their authority by subordinate employees. A number of American-based companies in Britain, for example, are unitary organizations and carry over this perspective from the United States, as illustrated by their preference neither to deal with nor to negotiate with trade unions. Even where such companies have been forced into conceding trade union recognition to their manual employees, they are often very reluctant to extend equivalent rights to their white-collar counterparts. However, it would be wrong to associate unitarism with American firms alone. Many British companies, large and small, are also directed by boards and managed by executives with basically unitary views. Some of these organizations, while reluctantly negotiating with trade unions, nevertheless continue to direct their industrial relations policies along unitary lines by limiting, for example, the subject matter about which they are prepared to bargain with trade union representatives to a narrow range of issues.

Some employees also hold unitary theories of work and of industrial relations. It seems likely, for example, that the Churches and the armed services have traditionally tended towards unitary structures and consensus values which have generally been accepted by their managerial cadres and their subordinates alike. Whether these circumstances will continue, however, is debatable in the light of European developments. The growth of unionization has already substantially proceeded within some of the armed forces in west Europe, for example, whilst both the Anglican and Catholic Churches have become internally factionalized in recent years.

In summary, unitary theory in its purest form stresses the harmonious nature of work enterprises and of industrial relations within them. To what extent it represents consistent and compatible viewpoints amongst different status groups within particular organizations depends upon two main factors: first, their internal social structures; and, second, whether their predominant value systems are accepted by subordinate personnel within them. The latter is, perhaps, the linchpin around which unitary theory of industrial relations is accepted or rejected.

1.2   CONFLICT THEORY

Conflict theory is based on two interrelated views of society and of industrial relations between employers and employees. The first is that although Britain and western industrialized societies are still class-based, they are essentially 'post-capitalist' in the sense that political and industrial conflict are institutionally separated within them and that 'industrial conflict has become less violent because its existence has been accepted and its manifestations have been socially regulated'.[4] The second view is that work organizations are microcosms of society. Since society comprises a variety of individuals and of social groups, each having their own social values and each pursuing their own interests and objectives, it is argued, those controlling and managing work enterprises similarly have to accommodate the differing values and competing interests within them. It is only by doing this that private or public enterprises can function effectively. Industrial relations between employers and unions and between managers and trade unionists, by this view, are an expression of the conflict and the power relations between organized groups in society generally. As such, it is argued, industrial conflict between managers and their subordinates has to be recognized as an endemic feature of work relationships and managed accordingly.

A major element in post-capitalist theories of contemporary society and industrial relations is the proposition that the nature of class conflict has substantially changed from that suggested by Marx in his nineteenth-century analysis. In Marxist theory class conflict is perceived as being synonymous with industrial conflict and political conflict. Under capitalism, Marxists argue, the capitalists or the owners of the means of production are identical with the ruling class in industry and politics, whilst wage earners, owning only their labour, are relatively powerless in industrial relations and in politics. Capitalists are the social elite and the proletariat are the socially weak. What, then, has changed according to post-capitalist analysis? First, they argue, we now live in a more open and socially mobile society compared with the class-based social divisions associated with nineteenth-century capitalism. The widening of educational opportunity, the democratization of politics, and the growth of public-sector industry, for instance, have opened up recruitment to a whole range of sought-after roles in society, including those within industry, politics, education, the professions, the arts and so on, which would have been inconceivable a hundred years ago. Moreover, the creation of the welfare state, it is suggested, has mitigated the worst effects of social deprivation, economic inequality and abject poverty.

Second, the post-capitalists argue, the distribution of authority, property and social status in society is now more widely diffused than in the past. The positions which individuals occupy in the authority structure of industry, for example, do not necessarily correlate with their positions in the political structure or with their social standing in the community. The village postman can become the local councillor, the schoolteacher a Member of Parliament and the trade unionist a Justice of the Peace. Similarly the convener of shop stewards within a factory might have potentially more industrial power than the senior management with which he or she negotiates. Such individuals may also have more political power if they are on the selection panel of the local constituency Labour Party responsible for selecting the prospective Parliamentary candidate in a safe Labour seat. In other words, post-capitalists take the view that the dominant and subordinate classes within industry need no longer necessarily correspond with the political or social classes in society generally.

Above all, these theorists believe, the institutionalization of conflict in industry not only has decreased in intensity but also has changed its form. Several changes seem to be of particular importance in this respect:

> (1) the organization of conflicting interest groups itself; (2) the establishment of 'parliamentary' negotiating bodies in which these groups meet; (3) the institutions of mediation and arbitration; (4) formal representations of labor within the individual enterprise; and (5) tendencies towards and institutionalization of workers' participation in industrial management.[5]

Thus, it is argued, the emergence of trade unionism, employers' organizations and collective bargaining, together with shop steward representation at enterprise and workplace level, now effectively regulate the inevitable social conflicts arising between management and subordinates at work. Even where these conflicts seem irresolvable, third-party intervention, usually through state agencies providing conciliation and arbitration services, is now available to provide workable remedies. By this analysis, extending worker participation in managerial decision making is seen as a logical progression in institutionalizing the power relations between managers and subordinates at work. Post-capitalist society, in short, is viewed as an open society in which political, economic and social power is increasingly dispersed and in which the regulation of industrial and political conflict are of necessity dissociated.

A second theoretical concept closely related to that of post-capitalism, and of central importance in the conflict theory of industrial relations, is 'pluralism'. According to Clegg one of its major apologists:

> Pluralism emerged as a criticism of the political doctrine of sovereignty – that somewhere in an independent political system there must be a final authority whose decisions are definitive. Not so, said the pluralist. Within any political system there are groups with their own interests and beliefs, and the government itself . . . depends on their consent and co-operation. There are no definitive decisions by final authorities: only continuous compromises.[6]

A plural society, in other words, is relatively stable but not static. It has to accommodate to different and divergent pressure groups to enable social and political changes to take place constitutionally. This is achieved through negotiation, concession and compromise between pressure groups, and between many of them and government.

It is from this analysis of political pluralism that industrial relations pluralism is derived. Just as society is perceived as comprising a number of interest groups held together in some sort of loose balance by the agency of the state, so work organizations are viewed as being held in balance by the agency of management. The pluralist concepts of political sovereignty and of managerial prerogative have much in common. Trade unions are viewed as the legitimate representatives of employee interests at work with the right to challenge the right to manage. There are also, it is suggested, similarities between the processes of political concession and compromise, on the one hand, and of collective bargaining and consultation on the other. Above all, the pluralist argues, 'greater stability and adaptability is given to industrial relations by collective bargaining than by shackling and outlawing trade unions'.[7] According to pluralist theory the central feature of industrial relations is the potential conflict existing between employer and employed and between management and managed within work enterprises. Unlike unitary theory however, trade unionism is accepted as having both a representative function and an important part in regulating this conflict, rather than in causing it. Similarly, collective bargaining is recognized as being the institutional means by which conflict between employers and employees is regularized and resolved.

Industrial conflict, therefore, is accepted by pluralists not only as being inevitable but also as requiring containment within the social mechanisms of collective bargaining, conciliation and arbitration.

There is little doubt that the post-capitalist and pluralist analyses of industrial relations, with their emphasis on the twin virtues of parliamentary democracy and collective bargaining as separate but conflict-resolving and rule-making processes, have been the predominant academic orthodoxy in Britain since the early 1960s. Initially they were strongly associated with the thinking of a small group of University of Oxford academics. Their individual and collective views, for example, had an important impact on the deliberations and findings of the Royal Commission, chaired by Lord Donovan between 1965 and 1968, and on its final Report. The so called 'Oxford' approach to industrial relations has influenced not only public policy and a generation of scholars in the field but also industrial relations practitioners.

Yet industrial relations pluralists are not without their critics. The latter believe, for instance, that those working within the pluralist framework implicitly accept the institutions, principles and assumptions of the social and political *status quo* as unproblematic.

> In doing so they add their professional status, personal prestige, and influential involvement in public policy making to the forces and influences which lead subordinate groups to continue seeing the *status quo* as legitimate, inevitable, unchangeable, 'only to be expected', subject only to changes at the margin.[8]

Others, such as Goldthorpe, have argued that the liberal pluralist approach to industrial relations is fundamentally conservative. Indeed:

> the changes which it seeks to promote are ones designed to bring about the more effective integration of labour into the existing structure of economic and social relations, in industry and the wider society, rather than ones intended to produce any basic alteration in this structure.[9]

Nevertheless, industrial conflict theory remains a major theoretical approach to industrial relations in Britain.

1.3   SYSTEMS THEORY

If conflict theory has dominated British thinking in the field, then so called 'systems theory' has been the major American contribution to industrial relations theorizing. Systems theory has also influenced British and European students of industrial relations, including those supporting conflict theory. Systems theory was first articulated by John Dunlop in his seminal book *Industrial Relations Systems*, published in the United States in 1958. Its purpose was to present a general theory of industrial relations and 'to provide tools of analysis to interpret and to gain understanding of the widest possible range of industrial-relations facts and practices.'[10] An industrial relations system is not, for Dunlop, part of a society's economic system but a separate and distinctive subsystem of its own, partially overlapping economic and political decision making systems with which it interacts. In his view systems theory provides the analytical tools and the theoretical basis to make industrial relations an academic discipline in its own right.

According to Dunlop:

> An industrial-relations system at any one time in its development is regarded as comprised of certain actors, certain contexts, an ideology which binds the industrial-relations system together, and a body of rules created to govern the actors at the work place and work community.[11]

It is this network or web of rules, consisting of procedures for establishing the rules, the substantive rules themselves, and the procedures for deciding their application to particular situations, which are the products of the system. 'The establishment and administration of these rules is the major concern or output of the industrial-relations subsystem of industrial society.'[12] These rules are of various kinds and may be written, oral or custom and practice. They include managerial decisions, trade union regulations, laws of the state, awards by governmental agencies, collective agreements, and workplace traditions. Furthermore, they cover not only pay and conditions but also disciplinary matters, methods of working, the rights and duties of employers and employees and so on. It is the 'rules' of industrial relations which have to be explained by the 'independent' variables of an industrial relations system.

As can be seen in figure 1.1 there are three sets of independent variables or factors in an industrial relations system: the 'actors', the 'contexts', and the 'ideology' of the

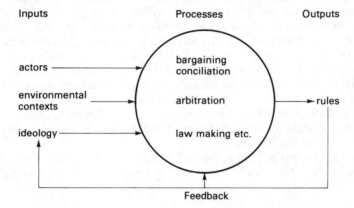

Source: J. T. Dunlop, *Industrial Relations Systems* (Southern Illinois University Press 1958)

Figure 1.1 A simple model of an industrial relations system.

system. The actors or active participants comprise: first, a hierarchy of managers and their representatives; second, a hierarchy of non-managerial employees and their representatives; and third, specialized third-party agencies whether governmental or private. Dunlop argues that managerial hierarchies need not own the capital assets of production and may be located in either private or public enterprises. He also suggests that although employees may not necessarily be formally organized, they usually are. Indeed, they may be organized into a number of competing or complementary organizations. In his view, however, totalitarian societies may have governmental agencies which are so powerful that they override managers and employees on almost all matters.

Dunlop also describes three environmental contexts that play a decisive part in shaping the rules of an industrial relations system and with which these actors interact. These are:

(1) the technological characteristics of the work place and work community, (2) the market or budgetary constraints which impinge on the actors, and (3) the locus and distribution of power in the larger society.[13]

He regards particular technologies as having far-reaching consequences in determining industrial relations rule making. Technology, for example, affects the size of the workforce, its concentration or dispersion, its location and proximity to the employees' places of residence, and the duration of employment. It also influences the proportions of skills in the workforce, the ratio of male to female workers, and health and safety at the place of work. An industrial relations system also has to adapt to the product markets or to the budgetary constraints of the enterprise. Although these impinge on management initially, they ultimately concern all the actors in a particular system. Such constraints may be local, national or international. Dunlop considers, for example, the balance of payments to be a form of market constraint for national systems of industrial relations. Furthermore, in Britain voluntary organizations like charitable trusts and also nationalized industries are no less constrained by budgetary forces, for example, than private businesses. These constraints are no less operative in planned economies than in market economies.

By the locus and distribution of power in the larger society, Dunlop means the distribution of power *outside* the industrial relations system which is given to that system. This is important because the relative distribution of power in society tends to be reflected within the industrial relations system itself. Yet it need not necessarily determine the behaviour of the actors in industrial relations. It is, rather, a context which helps to structure the industrial relations system itself. The distribution of power within the larger society is particularly likely to influence the state's specialist industrial relations agencies. National industrial relations sytems reflect such societal power. This helps to explain the differences which exist, he argues, between the American, British, Spanish, Swedish and Russian systems of industrial relations. Equally, a plant level system of industrial relations which is part of a highly centralized, industry-wide structure, as in Britain, differs significantly from one which is formally decentralized to plant level as in the United States.

The final element in the Dunlopian systems theory is the ideology or set of ideas and beliefs held by the actors which binds the system together. More precisely, in Dunlop's words:

> The ideology of the industrial-relations system is a body of common ideas that defines the role and place of each actor and that defines the ideas which each actor holds towards the place and function of the others in the system.[14]

The ideology of an industrial relations system, he says, must be distinguished from that of the wider society. Nevertheless, they would be expected to be similar or at least compatible with each other. Each of the main sets of actors in an industrial relations system might even have its own ideology. But the hallmark of a mature industrial relations system is that its constituent ideologies are sufficiently congruent to allow the emergence of a common set of ideas which recognize an acceptable role for each in the system. In this respect, Dunlop quotes the ideology of voluntarism, or legal abstentionism, as being traditionally accepted by the parties in the British system of industrial relations.

These, then, are the main concepts described by Dunlop in his systems theory of industrial relations. The ideas have been refined and developed by other writers but they have not radically changed Dunlop's model. As Wood and his colleagues argue the 'rules' approach to industrial relations does not and need not focus upon rules *per se* 'but also on both rule-making and application, and their links with behaviour.'[15] Systems theory, however, has its critics. On the one hand, supporters of the systems approach have criticized its lack of analytical rigour and its static view of industrial relations. They have suggested that the model requires refinement and development. For example, they have argued that Dunlop's systems theory uses the term 'system' in a too loose and undefined manner. They also consider that in concentrating on the structural or static features of industrial relations Dunlop has omitted to provide a framework for analysing the processes or dynamics of industrial relations decision making. There are other criticisms of systems theory, first, its inability to give sufficient weight to 'influenced action, and actors' definitions' of industrial relations, second, its notion of a unifying ideology and, third, the difficulties in analysing change and conflict. Its major weakness, however, is that little emphasis is placed upon the actors' definitions of social structure 'and how the interaction between structure and definition influence [social] action.'[16]

Marxist critics, on the other hand, view systems theory, like pluralist theory with which it is closely identified, as being too concerned with defending the political and economic *status quo*. For them the real significance of pluralism and systems thinking is that:

> It provides a plausible explanation of reality in that it recognizes conflicts which are visibly apparent yet it is as protective of the *status quo*, and as unquestioning about existing relationships, as the purely static unitary approach.[17]

Notwithstanding these points systems theory like conflict theory has had a major impact on industrial relations theorizing and research work among non-Marxist thinkers in the field since the 1960s. As such, it needs to be understood by students and practitioners of industrial relations so that they can assess its relative strengths and weaknesses for themselves.

1.4   SOCIAL ACTION THEORY

Social action theory in industrial relations contrasts with systems theory. Whilst systems theory suggests that behaviour in an industrial relations system is explicable in terms of its structural features, social action theory emphasizes the individual responses of the social actors such as managers and union representatives to given situations. Social action theory is pre-eminently associated with the studies of Max Weber. According to Weber, action is social 'by virtue of the subjective meaning attached to it by the acting individual . . . it takes account of the behaviour of others and is thereby oriented in its course.'[18] He insists that in order for social actions to be explained they must be interpreted in terms of their subjectively intended meanings, not their objectively valid ones. If only observable behaviour is examined, it is argued, the significance and value which individual actors place upon their behaviour are likely to be misinterpreted.

Social action, then, is behaviour having subjective meaning for individual actors, with social action theory focusing on understanding particular actions in industrial relations situations rather than on just observing explicit industrial relations behaviour. This contrasts with systems theory which regards behaviour in industrial relations as reflecting the impersonal processes external to the system's social actors over which they have little or no control. In emphasizing that social action derives from the personal meanings which individuals attach to their own and other people's actions, social action theorists are suggesting that social actors are constrained by the way in which they construct their own social reality. 'On the one hand, it seems, Society makes man, on the other, Man makes society'.[19] Individual actors, however, do not share the same value systems which 'means that individuals attach different meanings to their interactions.'[20] Managers and shop stewards, for example, do not come together because they have the same goals and values 'but because, for a while at least, their differing ends may be served by the same means.'[21]

Figure 1.2 indicates the main influences affecting individual choice and social action in given situations. The fundamental point is that social action emerges out of the meanings and circumstances attributed by individuals to particular social situations,

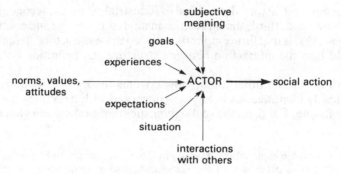

Figure 1.2   The main influences on individual social action.

thereby defining their social reality. Through interaction between actors, such as that between personnel managers and shop stewards, line managers and personnel specialists and stewards and their members, individuals as well as having an element of choice in interpreting their own roles, and in acting out their intentions, also modify, change and transform social meanings for themselves and others. The major difference between a social action approach in examining behaviour in industrial relations and a systems approach is this: action theory assumes an existing system where action occurs but cannot explain the nature of the system, 'while the Systems approach is unable to explain satisfactorily why particular actors act as they do.'[22] The first views the industrial relations system as a product of the actions of its parts, the other aims to explain the actions of its parts in terms of the nature of the system as a whole.

   Social action theory also has its critics. Marxists argue, for example, that those supporting the action frame of reference neglect the 'structural influences of which the actors themselves may be unconscious.' Whilst the consciousness of individual actors in the industrial relations system towards its politico-economic structures can be to some extent autonomous, it is limited in practice. This is because:

> Definitions of reality are themselves socially generated and sustained, and the ability of men to achieve their goals is constrained by the objective characteristics of their situation.[23]

Perhaps the most useful feature of social action theory in industrial relations is the 'way in which it stresses that the individual retains at least some freedom of action and ability to influence events.'[24] Although the structures of the industrial relations system may influence the actions of its actors, these in turn also influence the system as a whole including its outputs.

1.5   MARXIST THEORY

Marxist interpretations of industrial relations are not strictly theories of industrial relations *per se*. Marxism is, rather, a general theory of society and of social change with implications for the analysis of industrial relations within capitalist societies. Marxist analysis, in other words, is essentially a method of social enquiry into the power relationships of society and a way of interpreting social reality. It is not a definitive political creed. Indeed there are a number of different schools of Marxist scholarship, social thought and political action. This means that Marxist thinking is neither necessarily dogmatic nor monolithic, although it can be sectarian. Hence it is not strictly accurate to refer to *a* Marxist theory of industrial relations. To understand the relevance of Marxist theory to industrial relations it is necessary to separate out those main features of general Marxist analysis which contribute to its special character as a means of interpreting relations between the capitalist class and wage earners. Further, Marx himself wrote comparatively little about trade unionism and collective bargaining, basically because neither of these institutions was firmly established in Britain when he was studying nineteenth century capitalist development. Thus the application of Marxian theory as it relates to industrial relations derives indirectly from later Marxist scholars rather than directly from the works of Marx himself.

The starting points for the Marxist analysis of society are the assumptions that: social change is universal; class conflict is the catalytic source of such change; and these conflicts, which arise out of differences in economic power between competing social groups, are rooted in the structures and institutions of society itself. Relations between social groups, in other words, are perceived as being not only dominated by pressures for change but also encompassed by inevitable internal contradictions which must eventually transform the class based nature of pre-capitalist and capitalist societies. The conceptual method by which Marxists examine the dynamic character of social relations is described as 'dialectical materialism'.

> When reality is viewed dialectically it is seen as a process involving interdependent parts which interact on each other. When reality is also viewed materialistically it is seen as phenomena predominantly influenced by economic factors. The dialectical relationship between economic factors, therefore, provides the prime motivation for change. This briefly is what Marxism in the first instance is about.[25]

Dialectical materialism, in other words, assumes that a society's social and political institutions grow out of its economic infrastructure or power base, and that it is from the dialectical conflict between social classes with opposed economic interests that social change takes place.

For Marxists, as can be seen from figure 1.3, the capitalist or bourgeois state is only one stage in the evolution of human society. The first stage is primitive communism. Feudalism emerges out of this and from feudalism capitalism develops. The significance

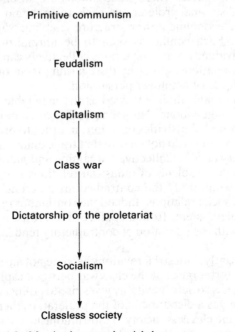

Primitive communism

↓

Feudalism

↓

Capitalism

↓

Class war

↓

Dictatorship of the proletariat

↓

Socialism

↓

Classless society

Figure 1.3 Marxist theory and social change.

of capitalism, in the Marxist view, is that it too is a changing phenomenon which has not done away with class antagonisms but has given rise to new social conflicts within society, those between the 'Bourgeoisie' and the 'Proletariat'.

> By bourgeoisie is meant the class of modern Capitalists, owners of the means of social production and employers of wage labour. By proletariat, the class of modern wage-labourers who, having no means of production of their own, are reduced to selling their labour power in order to live.[26]

The contradictions which persist between those who privately own the means of production in the pursuit of profit, on the one hand, and those who have to sell their labour for wages to survive, on the other, are thus perceived as being irreconcilable in the context of a class based bourgeois society.

For Marxists moreover, unlike pluralists and unitarists, political and class conflict are synonymous with industrial conflict since 'the capitalist structure of industry and of wage-labour is closely connected with the pattern of class division in society.'[27] Thus the conflict taking place in industrial relations between those who buy labour and those who sell it is seen as a permanent feature of capitalism, merely reflecting the predominant power base of the bourgeoisie and the class relations of capitalist society generally. By this view

> Class conflict permeates the whole of society and is not just an industrial phenomenon. In the same way trade unionism is a social as well as industrial phenomenon. Trade unions are, by implication, challenging the property relations whenever they challenge the distribution of the national product. They are challenging all the prerogatives which go with the ownership of the means of production, not simply the exercise of control over labour power in industry.[28]

There are both short-term and long-term implications in the Marxist analysis of bourgeois society and of the class-based structure of capitalist industrial relations. Within society, for example, the class struggle between capital and labour is regarded as being continuous – even where trade unions are absent. It takes place, it is argued, because capitalists and proletarians seek to maintain and to extend their relative positions in the economic power structure enabling 'surplus value' to be distributed between them. Such conflict is seen to be unremitting and unavoidable. Neither employees individually nor trade unions collectively can be divorced from the realities of these power relations, either by disregarding them or by succumbing to the manipulative techniques of employer persuasion.

Trade union organization is viewed as the inevitable consequence of the capitalist exploitation of wage labour. The vulnerability of employees as individuals invariably leads them to form collectivities or unions in order to protect their own class interests, although many Marxists do not believe that trade unions in themselves provide the basis for revolutionary action. Collective bargaining and militant trade unionism, however, cannot resolve the problems of industrial relations in capitalist society. They merely accommodate temporarily the contradictions inherent within the capitalist mode of production and social relations. Indeed the continuous relationship of conflict, whether open or concealed, 'stems from a conflict of interests in industry and society which is closely linked with the operation of contradictory tendencies in the capitalist economic system.'[29]

More significantly, industrial relations become not an end in themselves, but a means to an end – the furtherance of the class war between capital and labour, for by Marxist analysis, bourgeois society inevitably gives rise to political revolution by the proletariat. Out of this emerges a dictatorship of the proletariat, then socialism and ultimately the communism of the classless society. Trade unionism and industrial relations conflict are merely symptoms of the inherent class divisions within capitalism. They are, Marxists contend, a main element in the working-class struggle against capitalist exploitation, and in the eventual emergence of a socialist economy, followed by utopian communism. It is out of trade union consciousness and industrial conflict, they suggest, that working-class consciousness and political revolution can be precipitated. As such, these conflicts are instrumental in the 'formation of the proletariat into a class, overthrow of bourgeois supremacy, conquest of political power by the proletariat'[30] and in acting out the materialist conception of history. To Marxists, industrial relations are essentially politicized and part of the class struggle. They become overtly political when either class seeks to influence the state to intervene on its behalf. They become potentially revolutionary when working-class organizations, including trade unions, seek to abolish the power base of the bourgeois class within capitalism and to establish a socialist society.

1.6 METHODOLOGICAL INTERACTION

What, therefore, are industrial relations? What sense can be made of this area of human activity which appears to have at least five theoretical perspectives – the unitary; the conflict; the systems; the social action and the Marxist – each of which is based on its own assumptions about human behaviour, and none of which seems to relate substantially to the others? Is there, indeed, only *one* valid theory of industrial relations, or are there elements in more than one of these theories which put industrial relations in contemporary Britain into appropriate analytical and descriptive frameworks?

In the first place, unitary theory provides an image of the ideal world in which there is industrial stability and no industrial conflict. Its interpretation of the nature of society with its emphasis on an orderly and stable community, imbued with common purpose and a value consensus, bears little relation to the reality of everyday social relations. Further, it fails to recognize the competition and conflict which occur in advanced industrial societies among those seeking the control and allocation of limited economic and social resources. Moreover, our experiences and observations of industrial relations in a market economy like Britain do not lead us to believe that the purpose of industrial relations is to advance the common goals of management and subordinate employees through mutual co-operation whilst, at the same time, allowing management exclusive or predominant decision making authority within work organizations. It is at most a paternalistic view of industrial relations and at its least a justification for unchallenged managerial prerogative at work. Moreover, it is inconsistent. It is hardly possible to stress the commonality of interests in industrial relations between management and subordinates and to justify, simultaneously, the usually considerable inequalities in income, status and power which exist between most managers and non-managerial employees in our sort of society. Unitary theory, nevertheless, provides a major source of support and authority for many managers and employees who identify with its underlying assumptions of conflict-free industrial relations.

A more realistic view of industrial relations is that deriving from conflict and pluralist theories. It is empirically obvious, for example, that diverse pressure groups, pursuing their own self interest through intergroup negotiation and compromise, are a basic feature of our society. In this context, the main purpose of its industrial relations institutions is to resolve conflict within and between different interest groups. This is not to deny the class based structure of British society or the economic and social inequalities which persist in industrial relations. But it suggests that the Marxist stress on the inevitable and polarized class struggle in industry and society between capitalists and proletariat, whilst probably a valid interpretation of nineteenth century Victorian capitalism, does little to explain the complex political, economic, and social conflicts of late twentieth century Britain. In our view, the existence of the mixed economy, the welfare state, social democracy, advancing prosperity, and wide-based trade unionism have radically transformed the lives of ordinary citizens, at home, at work and politically, compared with their position in the heyday of market capitalism which ceased to exist, in effect, after 1939.

Despite its critics pluralism neither inherently views social relations statically, nor morally justifies the political, economic and social *status quo*. Indeed a pluralist theory is just as useful a method of perceiving social behaviour and industrial relations practices in dynamic terms, as is the Marxist analysis. It is a pragmatic interpretation of society and of its power relations but it does not necessarily justify them. A pluralist can also accept that 'within the existing form of society . . . a disordered state of industrial relations may best be understood not as a pathological, but as a normal condition.'[31] Perhaps the weakest and strongest element in the industrial conflict and pluralist position is, somewhat paradoxically, its attempt to avoid absolute moral value judgements. On the other hand, both unitary theory and Marxist theory are essentially value laden – but from diametrically opposed political and moral viewpoints.

Systems theory also has something to offer the student of industrial relations. Its emphasis on the diverse forms of industrial relations rules which exist, the different rule-making methods, and the ways in which rules are applied is a useful contribution to industrial relations theorizing, and to understanding industrial relations practices. One of the most valuable insights which systems theory provides is its identification of the variety of industrial relations variables and the complex ways in which they interact. By focusing on the 'outputs' or rules of industrial relations systems, on their 'processes' such as collective bargaining and other types of rule making, and on their 'inputs' such as the actors involved in rule-making, systems theory provides a useful framework for classifying and describing the elements within any industrial relations structure. For example, it can be used to compare different industrial relations systems at workplace, enterprise, national or international levels.

The major disadvantage of systems theory as an analytical tool is its concentration on the structural features of industrial relations at particular points in time. In other words, it is a static theory from which it is difficult to explain industrial relations change. Its harsher critics argue that by concentrating on the structure of social order and on highlighting the mechanisms of social control within industrial relations, the systems theory – like that of conflict theory – is politically biased towards the *status quo*. In our view, however, although systems theory focuses upon structure rather than upon change, it does not necessarily justify the existing social order when it is used as a tool to analyse and describe an industrial relations structure.

The key contribution which social action theory provides in industrial relations is the importance attached to individual meanings and actions in work relationships. These include inter-managerial relationships, relationships between managers and union representatives, amongst union representatives, and between union representatives and their members. It is the industrial relations actors' own definitions of their work situations which are taken as the basis for explaining their behaviour and relationships. The obverse to systems theory it emphasizes the relevance of individual actors in perceiving the nature of their work, in making personal choices, in interacting with others, and in taking industrial relations decisions. The actions of industrial relations participants, in other words, are not viewed as being determined solely by the structural constraints within which they operate, but by the expectations and values of individual actors and the meanings *they* assign to particular industrial relations situations.

One of the strongest features of the Marxist theory is its dynamic approach to industrial relations and its explanations of its 'inner logic' and of social change. With its strong moral condemnation of capitalist values and its rejection of the ethics of liberal political economy, Marxist theory is overtly subjective and critical about industrial relations in what it describes as capitalist societies. In practical terms the strength of

Marxism as a means of interpreting industrial relations is that it provides a theoretical perspective which not only analyses what is perceived as social reality, but also rejects it on moral grounds and suggests means for changing it. Is there, then, anything in Marxist theory which can be utilized in an attempt to understand industrial relations in contemporary society?

An essential element, in our view, is the endemic nature of class conflict in liberal democracies which is highlighted by Marxist theory. This is not to argue that class conflict and industrial conflict are necessarily identical. They clearly overlap but they are not always synonymous. Experience in Britain suggests that the institutional means for resolving political and industrial conflict arising from social class differences have become largely, but not always, separated. Moreover, the 'capitalist-class' and 'working-class' dichotomy appears to be too simplistic an explanation of the class structure in contemporary Britain. There is neither an integrated capitalist class nor an integrated working class. The so-called capitalist and working classes have never been either homogeneous or exclusive. Social stratification, in short, is multidimensional. It incorporates both individual and collective differentials in income, wealth, status, education, occupation, power, quality of life and social values. However, in so far as the Marxist theory focuses on the inherent class nature of liberal democracies – which is partially reflected in their industrial relations institutions – it provides a useful analytical tool for understanding those conflicts in industrial relations deriving from competing class and power interests at work and in society.

Having examined the main theories analysing industrial relations, we would argue that a methodological interactive approach largely based on the conflict and pluralist analyses, but incorporating systems, social action and Marxist theories where appropriate, provides the most convincing theoretical framework. In this way, more than one methodology can be used to explain sometimes conflicting phenomena by providing a coherent synthesis of institutional, structural, action and class theory. Conflict theory, for example, accounts for two apparently irreconcilable elements in industrial relations. There seem to exist, that is, at one and the same time, a degree of order, stability and moral legitimacy within and between industrial relations institutions, on the one hand, and considerable impetus for change, coercion and ideological conflict within and between them, on the other. In short, consensus and equilibrium in industrial relations appear to coexist with conflict, instability and power relations. Yet this should not be surprising for consensus and agreement, whether between union and management, or between union and union, or even between a union and its membership, are but complementary processes to conflict and dissent between them. Clearly, consensus and accommodation between the competing parties and their representatives in industrial relations can only emerge, by a process of negotiation and compromise, out of initial conflict between them. Similarly, industrial relations conflict usually results from a breakdown in industrial relations consensus.

As can be seen in figure 1.4 a set of agreed industrial relations rules, for example a collective agreement between an employer and a union, only comes about from a consensus between the parties. This temporarily resolves the conflict between them. Such a consensus only continues until one of the parties attempts to move away from the established rules, either by breaching them or by trying to create new rules. This results in industrial conflict and in the use of power by one of the parties against the other so as to achieve its own goals by force. A new consensus can only then be obtained after a period of bargaining, concession and compromise between them. If a new consensus does not emerge either through negotiation, conciliation or arbitration this induces either a breakdown in relations between the parties or a unilateral enforcement of the stronger party's rules on the other. Such decisions, however, are affected by the industrial relations structures and contexts within which the actors operate.

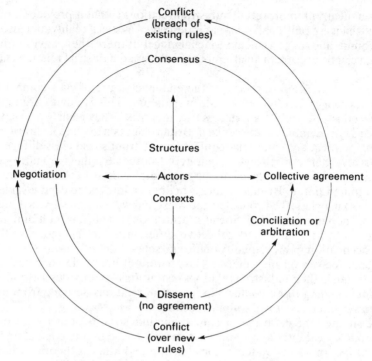

Figure 1.4   Conflict and concensus in collective bargaining.

In using the device of methodological interaction students of industrial relations are able not only to account for conflict and consensus in industrial relations but also to demonstrate how the two processes can obtain at the same time. They are also able to apply those elements of systems, social action and Marxist theories to particular industrial relations situations. Nevertheless, whilst recognizing the class based nature of British society, those using a methodological interactive approach to industrial relations do not necessarily have to accept industrial and political conflict as being conterminous as suggested by Marxist theory. Further:

> there is no *a priori* inconsistency between pluralism and the pursuit of . . . egalitarian social and economic policies . . . But the absence of an *a priori* inconsistency between the pluralist ethic and . . . egalitarian policies does not demonstrate that, if the test was made, there would in practice be no conflict between them.[32]

1.7   SUMMARY

This chapter advances a series of complex arguments and introduces its readers to some difficult concepts in industrial relations. However, we believe it necessary that students should be aware that there are a number of different theories by which industrial relations can be understood and interpreted. The ways in which individuals perceive the reality and practices of industrial relations, for example, derive from the views which they have of society, from their own personal experiences, and from their perceptions of the purposes of industrial relations, institutions and practices. We would suggest that a methodological interactive theory of industrial relations is best suited to provide a framework which relates structure and process, conflict and change and systems and action in industrial relations. This contrasts with unitary theory which emphasizes the co-operative nature of work and work relations, its static structure, and its distaste for industrial conflict.

Industrial conflict theory sees the institutions of industrial relations as conflict-resolving social mechanisms, whilst systems theory focuses on industrial relations 'systems' as the institutional means by which the rules of employment are established and administered in industrial societies. Social action theory emphasizes the importance of individual responses to industrial relations situations, as mediated by people assigning meanings to the structures within which they operate and the actions of others. Marxist theory, in contrast, highlights the class nature of the employment contract and the continuous class struggle between those representing capital and labour within capitalist societies. Whilst accepting the limitations of systems, social action and class conflict theories, we believe that there are elements within each of them which can be integrated into industrial conflict and pluralist theory. In our view, methodological interaction provides an empirically and conceptually useful framework for understanding the complexities of industrial relations actions, structures, processes and institutions.

We do not regard methodological interaction in industrial relations, however, as justifying the existing political, economic and social orders within modern capitalism. Equally, those using it need not deny that social, economic and industrial relations injustices continue to exist in our type of society. The implication, however, is that although it is possible to diagnose the nature of such problems, it is much more difficult in practice to devise measures to resolve them adequately. It is a pragmatic approach, not a prescriptive ideology. Despite its weakness, methodological interaction has three major merits in industrial relations theorizing. First it takes into account, in systems and consensus terms, that existing industrial relations institutions, structures and processes influence industrial relations actions and hence ensure institutional stability. Second, it also takes into account, in social action and conflict terms, that the activities of industrial relations participants influence these institutions thereby inducing industrial relations change. Third, whilst acknowledging class conflict in societies like Britain, those attempting methodological interaction can analytically distinguish class conflict from industrial conflict and are at the same time provided with both a static and a dynamic interpretation of industrial relations practices in their wider societal contexts.

1.8 REFERENCES

1. H. Reddish, Written memorandum of evidence to the Royal Commission on trade unions and employers' associations, in B. Barrett, E. Rhodes, and J. Beishon (eds.), *Industrial Relations and the Wider Society*, Collier Macmillan, London, 1975, p. 298f.
2. A. Fox, *Royal Commission on Trade Unions and Employers' Associations Research Papers. 3. Industrial Sociology and Industrial Relations*, HMSO, London, 1966, p. 2.
3. *Ibid.*, p. 12.
4. R. Dahrendorf, *Class and Class Conflict in Industrial Society*, Routledge and Kegan Paul, London, 1959, p. 257.
5. *Ibid.*
6. H.A. Clegg, Pluralism in industrial relations, *British Journal of Industrial Relations*, November 1975, p. 309.
7. *Ibid.*, p. 311.
8. A. Fox, Industrial relations: a social critique of pluralist ideology, in J. Child (ed.), *Man and Organization*, Allen and Unwin, London, 1973, pp. 219ff.
9. J.H. Goldthorpe, Industrial relations in Great Britain: a critique of reformism, *Politics and Society*, 1974, vol. 4(4).

10. J.T. Dunlop, *Industrial Relations Systems*, Southern Illinois University Press, Carbondale, 1958, p. vii.
11. *Ibid.*, p. 7.
12. *Ibid.*, p. 13.
13. *Ibid.*, p. 9.
14. *Ibid.*, pp. 16f.
15. S.J. Wood, A. Wagner, E.G.A. Armstrong, J.F.B. Goodman and J.E. Davis, The 'industrial relations system' concept as a basis for theory in industrial relations, *British Journal of Industrial Relations*, 13(3), 1975, p. 305.
16. D. Fatchett and W.M. Whittingham, Trends and developments in industrial relations theory, *Industrial Relations Journal*, 1976, pp. 51f.
17. V.L. Allen, Marxism and the personnel manager, *Personnel Management*, December 1976, p. 21.
18. M. Weber, *Economy and Society*, vol. 1, Bedminster Press, NY 1896, p. 4.
19. D. Silverman, *The Theory of Organizations*, Heinemann, London, 1970, p. 141.
20. P, Kirkbride, Industrial relations theory and research, *Management Decision*, vol. 17(4), 1977, p. 333.
21. D. Silverman, *op. cit.*, p. 137.
22. *Ibid.*, p. 142.
23. R. Hyman, *Strikes* (2nd ed.), Fontana, London, 1977, p. 72.
24. M.P. Jackson, *Industrial Relations* (2nd ed.), Croom Helm, London, 1982, p. 27.
25. V.L. Allen, *op. cit.*, p. 22.
26. K. Marx and F. Engels, *The Communist Manifesto*, Penguin, Harmondsworth, 1967, p. 79.
27. R. Hyman, *Industrial Relations*, Macmillan, London, 1975, p. 21.
28. V.L. Allen, *The Sociology of Industrial Relations*, Longmans, London, 1971, p. 40.
29. R. Hyman (1975), *op. cit.*, p. 31.
30. K. Marx and F. Engels, *op. cit.*, p. 95.
31. J.H. Goldthorpe, *op. cit.*, p. 452.
32. H.A. Clegg, *op. cit.*, p. 316.

2

The Contexts of British Industrial Relations

In order to understand present day British industrial relations, it is necessary to examine the major forces which have helped to shape it and continue to shape it today and the contexts within which it has grown. The institutions, practices, beliefs and characteristics of British industrial relations are the result of many social, economic, political and legal forces which have exerted their pressures within British society for nearly two hundred years. The sheer volume of historical evidence, research, statistics and descriptive writing dealing with British industrial relations require some form of contextual analysis, in order to facilitate understanding and awareness. The contextual approach we use in this chapter provides, we believe, the best available tool for understanding the bewildering volume of information available on British industrial relations. It is a mistake, however, to see the contexts we have chosen as necessarily internally coherent and tightly constructed analytical devices. They are, we believe, broad general categories which, taken together, permit insights and understanding of industrial relations phenomena.

The contexts chosen deal in turn with: historical evidence; political forces, ideas and beliefs; economic forces, theories and policies; the nature of constantly changing labour markets; and the impact of technological change. These five vital contexts provide, when seen together, a broad explanation of the main forces which have fashioned British industrial relations. They also provide the informed contemporary observer with useful constructs for understanding the forces which continue to shape today's industrial relations, its institutions and practices.

2.1 THE HISTORICAL CONTEXT

It is commonplace to state that any understanding of present events and circumstances depends heavily upon a sound knowledge of history. It is as true of modern medicine and law as it is of politics, education or local government. Perhaps, though, in no other area of human activity is history used so intensively to explain present circumstances as in industrial relations. The volume of academic and popular history dealing with trade unionism and the British Labour Movement is now very extensive. There is also a considerable literature dealing with the political influence of the trade unions and working-class organizations. By comparison, academic researchers have shown relatively less interest in the history of firms and employers' organizations, though not in the evolution of management theory and practice.

The most important reason for using the history of industrial relations as a vital element in understanding the present system lies in the force of tradition within both trade unions and employers' organizations themselves. By following and enforcing traditional methods and values the major participants in industrial relations are mutu-ally enabled to maintain solidarity of purpose, shared values, and familiar routines and practices. Tradition serves as a moral defence against external criticism and attack: it is the handmaiden of insularity. Appeals to tradition allow both employer and employee organizations to reject uncomfortable facts and rapidly changing circumstances. Tradi-tion in industrial relations is particularly strong in the belief and attitudes of trade unionists; the reverence for established crafts, skills and working practices; 'win–lose' collective bargaining and in legal abstentionism. As Alan Flanders observed,

> no one who knows trade unionism from the inside could possibly doubt that the appeal to tradition is a very telling argument and that there are grounds for concluding that trade unions 'are especially prone to take tradition as their principal guide on industrial and social behaviour.'[1]

It would be a mistake, however, to believe that other British institutions do not attach great importance to the identity and security offered by tradition – the legal profession, the armed forces and even Parliament are notable for their adherence to it. Indeed, it might be said that tradition is a national characteristic of the British and is particularly marked in the field of industrial relations.

The historical context within which British industrial relations developed and matured comprised three dominating strands. First, there was the growth and development of private enterprise capitalism and the use of *laissez-faire* markets to determine incomes, prices and economic priorities. Second, was the emergence and growth of trade unionism and collective bargaining as the principal means of protecting workers from the vicis-situdes of free market capitalism. Third, was the response of the British ruling class in the nineteenth century to the twin threats to their power presented by organized workers and the growth of parliamentary political democracy. It is these three major strands of capitalism which largely created the institutions and practices characterizing British industrial relations since the early years of the twentieth century. It is necessary to describe each strand in turn to see this development clearly in its historical context.

The industrial revolution in Britain was based upon private capital, steam-power and the belief in an unfettered free market for determining both labour wages and other prices. This marked a clear break with the past when land and agriculture were under the control of a powerful aristocracy and formed the basis of wealth and political power. In a process of rapid change a complicated pattern of long-established social rankings and mutual social obligations gave way to class relationships based largely upon those earning wages or making profit and market forces. A clearly identifiable if incoherent working class emerged. Initially it was unorganized, fragmented and without political power.

The essential ideology underpinning the new industrial capitalism was the belief in leaving enterprising individuals and firms alone to pursue their own interests through private investment in factories and machine technology. Efficiency and business ability, it was felt, would emerge through competition and the need for inventiveness. A vital element in the new economic system was the belief that the market was the only means of determining prices, wages, profits and the value of corporate shares. The role of the state was confined to preventing disruptive forces emerging which would act in 'restraint of trade' and to provide naval protection for foreign trade. This new economic order slowly transformed Britain during the nineteenth century into the richest and most powerful nation in the world. It also created a new industrial working class which gradually developed economic and political objectives and its own representative institutions.

The path to political influence was initially blocked for this new working class did not possess the franchise. Parliament was dominated by the aristocracy still and increasingly by the representatives of the new capitalism. Radical elements in the working class first campaigned for political power by supporting the democratic claims of the Chartists. When that movement failed in the 1840s, attention concentrated upon the more moderate and less overtly political objectives of trade unionism. The history of the British trade union movement is complicated, complex and diverse and can only be summarized here. In essence, its growth was uncertain and faltering in the nineteenth century, and only embraced a minority of employees by the beginning of the twentieth century. It was largely confined to skilled workers with relatively secure employment and earnings such as printers, textile workers and skilled artisans. Unions catering for the semi-skilled and the unskilled such as coalminers, dockers and gasworkers also emerged though. The steady growth and development of the trade unions forced the employers to respond in kind by forming their own organizations which then either suppressed the unions through lockouts or recognized and accommodated them.

The principal aims of trade unionism were clearly established by the end of the nineteenth century. The first objective was to seek and obtain recognition from employers. The second was to enter into collective agreements on terms and conditions of employment covering union members. The third was to seek legislation on such matters as compensation for injury at work, state benefits when unemployed and old age pensions. All three objectives had been secured, to varying degrees, by 1914. The main structure of British industrial relations was quite apparent by this date. It constituted national trade unions, a few powerful employers' organizations, a complex pattern of collective bargaining and the use of well-understood procedures. These remain its essential features today.

The third strand in the historical context of British industrial relations is the methods used by the ruling groups in nineteenth century Britain to neutralize the threat of trade union power and to accommodate the unions within the constitution. There were two likely political responses to the emergence of trade unions and pay bargaining: the first was employer intransigence and legal suppression; the second was employer accommodation and legal abstentionism. Parliament, dominated by landed and capitalist interests, chose the second path – though some individual employers chose the first.

By the late nineteenth century the leaders of Victorian capitalism had decided that trade unionism was acceptable as long as it did not challenge the main economic structures of private enterprise, open competition and the free market. The unions also had to accept the unfettered right of employers or 'masters' to do what they wanted in their factories and mines. In exchange trade unions were recognized and collective bargaining was entered into with them on a limited range of matters. In short, the price to be paid for establishing trade unionism and collective bargaining was acceptance by the trade union movement of all the major economic, social and political structures of industrial capitalism of the nineteenth century. Out of this rather one-sided accommodation of labour to capital grew the belief that the working-class movement had to be divided into its 'political' and 'industrial' wings. The political wing was to concentrate on parliamentary representation and the industrial wing on the ostensibly non-political activity of collective bargaining.

> The system to which the unions had adapted was one of competitive economic liberalism, and although they wanted this modified they still needed a loose-jointed economic system and space within which to exercise their negotiating functions and methods, just as they needed political space within which to extend their activities and interests.[2]

By 1914 the basic pattern had been established. Both the industrial relations system and the political system survived the economic and political vicissitudes of the 1920s and 1930s. It was not until the 1950s and 1960s, in conditions of full employment and economic prosperity, that the traditional system of industrial relations was to be challenged from above by government and from below by workplace bargaining.

2.2   THE POLITICAL CONTEXT

The emergence in the nineteenth century of trade unionism as the natural challenge or countervailing power to industrial capitalists presented those controlling the British State with a set of political difficulties which they sought to resolve in line with an evolving democracy. Similarly, the British State has also had to resolve political and economic problems which the economic system has produced despite the historical dominance of just one system – liberal capitalism. These have included unemployment, unacceptably low wages, refusal to accept the collective bargaining role of trade unions and dangerous working conditions. It has, therefore, been the major role of the State to seek to limit the excesses of those representing either labour or capital in the economic and political systems. This is not an even-handed exercise, for the State unavoidably reflects the differences in power between labour and capital and favours the side whose political influence is greatest; it is not neutral, though it often strives to be.

The State, in broad terms, incorporates the collective power and authority of the law, the legal system, the armed forces, the police and the executive arm of government. Its basic role is to uphold the established norms, values and culture of society.

> The State concerns itself with maintaining the culture in being, both by providing for the reproduction of culture through successive generations and the mechanisms of enforcement of the formal rules (as in law) which uphold it.[3]

If that culture is dominated by the beliefs and values of liberal capitalism then the State upholds it. If the State were to uphold the beliefs and values of socialism or any other political ideology, it would be the political task of those supporting socialism in a democratic society to convince the electorate that they should form a government through the democratic processes of elections to Parliament. Such a process of fundamental cultural and political change within a democratic framework is extremely slow.

One of the central features of the British political system has been, and remains, the absorption by a State dominated by capitalist and propertied interests of the demands of working-class and trade union organizations for power and representation. Where those demands have been based on non-violent and orderly political activities and ideas and are democratically pursued they have been acknowledged and the way to power cautiously opened. Where they have been based upon revolutionary seizure of power and the overthrow of property, they have been unremittingly opposed and invariably defeated. It has, therefore, been an essential feature of British politics, and to accommodate the moderate demands of organized labour providing they are constitutional, respectful of the legal rights of property and non-violent for the parties and governments representing those social classes with the greatest interest in upholding the values of liberal capitalism, the success of this political strategy, slowly developed by the British ruling classes since the early nineteenth century, is self-evident. It has largely neutralized the ideological challenge of revolutionary socialism, separated the Labour Movement into its industrial and political wings and maintained widespread working-class electoral support for parties representing the values and beliefs of liberal capitalism. It has also enabled working-class interests to obtain important political, economic and legal advantages and to build a major political party which has governed the country several times in the twentieth century.

During the nineteenth century the political issues presented by the growth of trade unionism were: their right to exist legally; their right to take industrial action without being subjected to either criminal or civil court actions; and the right to engage in collective bargaining with employers on their members' terms and conditions of employment. All these rights were effectively denied to the growing trade union movement not only by employers but also by judicial interpretation of the common law doctrine of 'restraint of trade'. Parliament, however, eventually took the view that the line being pursued by the judges was unreasonable and unfair, given the nature of the society rapidly developing under industrial capitalism and the unavoidable extension of the right to vote to the majority of adult males. In keeping, therefore, with the ruling-class strategy of steady absorption of legitimate working-class demands on the constitution, nineteenth century Parliaments – which had almost negligible working-class representation – reformed the old Master and Servant laws and passed the Trade Union Act 1871 and the Conspiracy and Protection of Property Act 1875. These Acts largely freed trade unions from all but perverse legal judgements in respect of their right to legal existence, the protection of union funds and property, and the freedom to strike and picket peacefully. This legislation was completed by the Trade Disputes Act 1906 which prevented employers from obtaining civil damages from unions conducting industrial action in 'contemplation or furtherance of a trade dispute'.

Though this legislation was eagerly sought by the trade unions of the time they did not have the direct political power to demand it of either the Conservative or Liberal Parties which dominated Parliament in the nineteenth century. The only explanation of why Parliament made legal concessions to the trade union movement of its own volition must be the belief that moderate and constitutional trade unionism should be encouraged by showing that reasoned argument and 'fair play' would prevail, whereas extremism and violence would not. By such a strategy the working class was to be gradually admitted to political power and influence – as long as its members embraced constitutionalism, the rights of private property and the economic supremacy of industrial capitalism.

> Union leadership rarely wavered in its constitutionalism. While the unions were born out of labour's defensive responses to the British version of economic liberalism, their leaders exploited the British version of political liberalism to secure legal protections and a foothold in both industrial and political decision making. Their commitment to the institutions and the ideology of political liberalism therefore followed directly from their needs.[4]

The strategy of defending capitalism from the mild challenges of the trade unions in the late nineteenth and early twentieth centuries was further bolstered by legislation which, whilst helping to meet specific and limited working-class aspirations, did little to hinder the operations of free market capitalism. In 1897 Parliament passed the Workmen's Compensation Act giving limited protection and compensation in the event of industrial injury. It also approved Fair Wages Resolutions in 1891 and 1909, which were intended to ensure that firms receiving government contracts observed terms and conditions of employment no less favourable than those generally applying in the trade or industry concerned. The Unemployed Workmen's Act 1905 provided State unemployment benefits for the first time. Poverty in old age amongst the working class was partially relieved by the provision of limited State pensions in 1908. Another important measure was the passing of the Trade Boards Act 1909 which secured legally enforceable minimum wages for the lowest paid and those in 'sweated trades'. The fact that the trade boards covered workers who were rarely trade union members, and who possessed negligible political influence, reinforces the view that the ruling strategy of the capitalist class, expressed through Parliament and the State, was the pursuit of liberal democracy by policies of social and economic amelioration. This strategy succeeded in encouraging moderate and constitutional trade unionism and in isolating militants, syndicalists and political extremists.

The severest political test of the institutions, beliefs and industrial practices of this liberal economic strategy, which had reached a relatively advanced state of development by 1914, was the desperate social and economic conditions created by the depression of the 1920s and 1930s and the trauma of the General Strike of 1926. The fact that Britain survived the intense political difficulties of this period without widespread disorder or social upheaveal was largely owing to the stability and consensus which had been established by the strategy of economic liberalism, the encouragement of constitutional and moderate trade unionism and the passing of ameliorative employment and social legislation. In the 1920s this political tradition found its supreme advocate in the Conservative Prime Minister, Stanley Baldwin. By successfully appealing for an 'English' way of solving severe social problems, and by expressing strong disapproval of extreme solutions and violent political language and making appeals to commonsense, he was able to end the General Strike of 1926 after only nine days. He did so on terms which left the power of the State intact and, indeed, strengthened, without imposing savage peace terms upon the defeated trade union movement.

> The general strike, apparently the clearest display of class war in British history, marked the moment when class war ceased to shape the pattern of British industrial relations.[5]

The politics of industrial relations, which had evolved during the nineteenth century, to reach comparative maturity by 1914 and withstand the strains of the General Strike and the depression of the 1930s faced further severe tests in the different political and economic climate which followed the end of the second world war, when in 1945 a Labour government was elected to power with a massive majority. Such was the force of the industrial relations traditions which had been forged over the previous century that, in combination with the relatively low expectations and aspirations of most trade unionists, the unaccustomed conditions of full employment, rising living standards and improved welfare state provisions more than satisfied those trade union leaders and members whose working lives had started in the 1920s and 1930s. Moreover, they wanted to help 'their' Labour government. There was therefore a period of 'cultural delay' until post war prosperity became accepted as the norm and until a new generation of workers reached maturity under the very different economic and political conditions of the 1950s and 1960s.

The political problems facing Britain in the post war period emanated mainly from the new economic situation. Pay, profits and prices rose appreciably faster than productivity giving rise to steadily increasing rates of inflation. Shop stewards began to dominate pay bargaining at local level and took advantages of labour shortages created by full employment. Economic growth and consumer-led booms gave rise to continual balance of payments and sterling crises. The performance of British industry was impeded by strikes, low investment, out of date technology, restrictive working practices and inefficient management. The result was a lower rate of economic growth than that of major industrial competitors, inexorable increases in the rate of inflation, a high level of unofficial strike activity, skill shortages, a poor export performance, ever increasing volumes of imports, and sterling crises leading to damaging devaluations.

The politics of industrial relations in the post war period, therefore, were the result of Britain's persistent and apparently irreversible economic weaknesses. The strategy of economic liberalism, founded upon the great strength of nineteenth century British capitalism and imperialism and the weakness of trade unionism and working-class political organizations, became increasingly irrelevant. The British people began to forget their past subsistence level existence and seek ever increasing standards of living. The undeniable roots of the crisis in post-war industrial relations politics lay in the failure of the economy to meet the material aspirations of the British people. These aspirations were fed by the promises of prosperity made by all political parties at general elections and upon the persuasive power of the advertising industry. The situation was aggravated by the promises made by political parties to increase public expenditure on welfare provisions, higher pensions, more houses and improved national health services, without resort to greatly increased taxation. The inevitable failure of governments to square these economic circles led to a series of political dilemmas.

In the 1960s and 1970s, the solutions sought by successive governments were at first voluntary and then legally enforceable incomes policies to restrain pay, prices and profits and thereby to reduce inflation. The management of the national economy was dependent upon the tripartite agreement of government, the Trades Union Congress (TUC), and the Confederation of British Industry (CBI) to ensure the co-operation of labour and capital. Use was also made of social contracts between 1975 and 1979, whereby the Government promised high levels of public expenditure and full employment along with rising social security benefits and pensions in exchange for acceptance by the TUC and CBI of an effective and enforceable prices and incomes policy. Both these policies failed to work or to arrest the comparative failures of the British economy.

By the late 1970s there was a general disillusionment with tripartitism and with government interventionist policies aimed at solving Britain's economic problems. The emergence of Margaret Thatcher as Leader of the Conservative Party after their defeat in the 1974 General Election, and the subsequent election of a Conservative Government in 1979, marked the rejection of incomes policies and many forms of major government intervention in the economy. Instead the Conservatives promised a return to a more *laissez-faire* approach to economic policy relying upon strict monetarist measures to control inflation. They left prices, incomes, profits and investment to be determined by market forces and sought the privatization of public assets to raise financial revenue and the enactment of new legislation to curb trade union power and to 'return the unions' to their members. By the mid 1980s, these policies had greatly reduced inflation but at the very heavy cost of persistently high unemployment, a reduced manufacturing capacity and excessively high rates of interest. Legislation was passed in 1980, 1982 and 1984 which effectively narrowed trade union immunities against civil actions arising out of trade disputes, imposed greater controls over unlawful picketing, limited the practice of closed shops and required trade unions to ballot their members on a wide range of issues. This legislation, combined with high unemployment and loss in their membership, greatly reduced the power of trade unionism.

The history of industrial relations politics in Britain suggests that there are three main frameworks for political control. The first is that of the classical period of liberal capitalism in the nineteenth and early twentieth centuries, but which had run its course by 1945. This framework can be best described as 'economic and political liberalism' or 'collective *laissez-faire*'. Its essential features were strong and confident capitalism, rampant imperialism, weak trade unionism and a tradition of non legal or 'voluntary' industrial relations practices and collective bargaining.

The second framework, which can best be described as 'bargained corporatism', emerged after the end of the second world war. Its essential features were the tripartite sharing of policy making power amongst government, TUC and CBI, national economic weakness, strong trade unions, incomes policies and social contracts, and legislation largely favourable to the trade unions. This political framework failed to solve Britain's economic problems and for many people had become largely discredited by the late 1970s.

The third political framework, which emerged with the election of the first Thatcher Conservative Government in 1979, marked a return to the values, beliefs and practices of 'classical' capitalism. It is perhaps best described as *neo-laissez-faire*; its essential features a resurgence of capitalist values and confidence, reliance on market forces to allocate economic resources – including labour, greatly reduced trade union power, abandonment of tripartism, high unemployment and reduced reliance on the welfare state. At its heart lay a belief in economic individualism and a rejection of employee collectivism and state economic interventionism.

> Overall, the *laissez-faire* option means pushing back trade-union strength by means other than compromises and agreements, neutralizing various democratic pressures on economic policy and cutting back severely on public services.[6]

2.3   THE ECONOMIC CONTEXT

Trade unions and the industrial relations practices which they have developed operate mostly within the confines of the British economy. Trade union aspirations, policies and actions must take into account the nature of the economic system and the realities of financial and industrial life. Trade unions, therefore, have inevitably developed as reactive rather than proactive organizations. They adjust pragmatically to existing economic circumstances and structures seeking always to protect their members' immediate work interests, including reasonable pay, adequate conditions of employment and job security. They are rarely capable of reshaping in a fundamental way the economic structures and forces which determine their members' lives. This does not mean that sections of the trade unions do not hold long-term aspirations for the replacement of capitalism with socialism but, in their judgement, such a transformation of society is best pursued through the Labour Party, leaving the trade unions to work the best they can within existing economic circumstances.

By acting as pressure groups, either as individual unions or collectively through the TUC, unions seek to influence government in order to achieve advantages for their members or economic advancement for Britain as a whole. For example, the unions normally urge measures upon government which, they believe, are likely to reduce unemployment, generate economic growth, assist whole industries or individual sectors of employment, prevent employers imposing unacceptably low wages on their members, increase investment, improve training and raise standards of health and safety at work. All these measures have some effect upon the British economy. Similarly, collective bargaining, closed shops, manning agreements, control over the introduction of new technologies and opposition to changes in working practices also affect the performance and efficiency of the economy. It is, however, extremely difficult either to estimate or measure the degree to which trade union power and practices affect or change the British economy.

> The fact is that what the public is interested in, and what politicians want to know about, is the overall or general impact of unions. They want an answer to the question: how far have unions been responsible for inflation and unemployment since, say, the mid-sixties? And if the answer is 'quite a lot' what can be done about it? The tragedy has been that the specialists, at their present level of knowledge, find it very difficult to answer questions of this kind; except to say that it is all very complex and hand round a book list.[7]

Despite the absence of hard factual evidence and measurements, those on the political Right argue that the trade unions are responsible for most of the failings of the British economy, whilst those on the Left claim that workers and their organizations are blamed for the crises created by a decayed and dying capitalist system. In other words:

> undue attention and credence has been given to the answers of those who have mistaken faith and conviction for the patient accumulation of all the relevant data.[8]

The economic framework within which industrial relations operates in the mid 1980s can best be described like the political framework as *neo-laissez-faire* capitalism. Since 1979, a determined attempt has been made by Government to reduce state intervention in the economy by leaving prices, incomes and employment to be determined largely by market forces, by reducing the public sector through expenditure cuts and privatization, and by cutting overall public expenditure in real terms. Trade union power has also been undermined by legislation passed since 1980. Compared with the loss of membership and high unemployment, though, its effects have probably been marginal at the collective bargaining table. The protagonists of the new spirit of private enterprise and market capitalism argue that only by breaking free from state intervention in the economy, and trade union 'monopoly power' in the labour market, can the British economy become more efficient, competitive, innovatory and resourceful. But many fear the social and political strains imposed by such a regime:

> The circumstances bearing upon the nation now may prove too severe a test on its ability to preserve its familiar shape. It may fail either to break through to dynamic growth or to resume its halting liberal movement towards a less divided society. It may become embedded instead in a texture of politics and industrial relations more harsh, vengeful and embittered than any it has known before . . .[9]

The question which needs to be asked is: why did it become necessary in the late 1970s for a popularly elected government to embark upon such painful and divisive economic and social policies? The straightforward and simple answer to this question is because of the persistent and seemingly irreversible decline of the British economy by comparison with its major industrial competitors. Equally, increases in living standards expected by the majority of the people had not been fulfilled. Neither had their expectations for improved public services, national health provision and welfare state benefits reached levels of general satisfaction. Between 1945 and the late 1970s a succession of different governments tried to plan, stimulate, or cajole the economy and its major decision makers into greater output, but with little lasting effect. The radical right-wing economic policies pursued with apparent popular support since the election of the first Thatcher Government in 1979 were a clear break with all previous post-war policies, based largely upon political consensus and powerful government economic intervention.

> For more than thirty years every British Government has had a different answer to the question of economic and industrial decline. The Thatcher administration has adopted a novel approach. It has tried to change the question. Instead of the Government being regarded as primarily responsible for solving Britain's problems, the onus has shifted to the people. In the process the post-war consensus about economic management has been challenged. [But] . . . has the Government created sufficient widespread consent, as opposed to acquiescence, to promote a new 'settlement' about how the economy and society should be run to match that of the previous thirty years?[10]

In order to understand the consensus economic policies which dominated economics for the previous thirty years it is necessary first briefly to describe the forces which shaped the economy before 1945.

Britain was the first country to pass through the industrial revolution. That revolution was based upon steam-power, machine manufacturing and an increasingly sophisticated banking and financial system. The overriding economic philosophy was to leave economic decisions to entrepreneurs, capitalists and bankers – a *laissez-faire* philosophy. The 'hidden hand' of the market, it was believed, would determine prices and costs as well as rewarding enterprise and efficiency and punishing sloth and inefficiency. The role of government was to be residual; confined to ensuring a sound money system based upon the gold standard and the Bank of England. The courts were to play their part by upholding the common law doctrine of 'restraint of trade'. The problems resulting from movements in the trade cycle and the resultant fluctuations in unemployment were not seen to be in any way the responsibility of government. The adherents of the 'new' capitalist economic order believed that left to its own devices the market system would prove to be self-correcting through the price mechanism and the flow of gold reserves. It was against this economic background and set of beliefs that the British trade unions emerged and matured. Their main concerns were membership growth, legal protection, organizational consolidation and adaptation – albeit piecemeal – to this confident and dynamic economic order.

The British economy, whilst it began to lose its impetus and to be challenged by the United States and Imperial Germany in the late nineteenth century, did not begin to reveal its deep-seated weaknesses until the Great Depression of the 1920s and 1930s. In those decades the basic industries of coal, iron and steel, textiles, agriculture and railways contracted severely. Unprecedentedly high levels of unemployment ensued which did not begin to fall substantially until after the beginning of the second world war. During the 1930s serious challenges were made to the belief in *laissez-faire*, free trade and the self-correcting forces of free market capitalism. The most persuasive analysis came from the Cambridge economist, John Maynard Keynes, whose seminal book *The General Theory of Employment, Interest and Money* published in 1936, was to acquire economic orthodoxy for almost 30 years after 1945.

Keynes argued that the economy could well persist at high levels of unemployment for long periods and that the self-correcting mechanism of the market was largely a delusion. If the existing economic order was to be preserved, as well as the liberal democracy it supported, he argued, it would be necessary for governments to stimulate demand though budgetary and public works measures. Thereby the level of economic activity would be raised which by a multiplier effect would increase business transactions and lower levels of unemployment. The white paper on full employment supported by the wartime Coalition Government in 1944 was heavily influenced by Keynesian ideas and became politically and morally binding upon successive British governments for the next three decades. This gave rise to a consensus on government managing of the economy, with both Labour and Conservative Governments manipulating aggregate demand, public spending and budget deficits in order to achieve full employment. During this period the TUC was fully consulted on economic policy, was continually involved in national economic bodies and played an important role in national economic management.

Whilst the Keynesian revolution had apparently solved the political problems and human miseries associated with high unemployment, it soon became obvious that new economic difficulties followed in its train. These difficulties though small at first were to lead eventually to the break up of the Keynesian consensus in the late 1970s. The first problem was the emergence of a steadily growing and persistent rate of inflation. This inflation was, and still is, largely attributed, by some, to the power of trade unions to force up money wages through collective bargaining and industrial action. The answer of Keynesian economists and politicians was to advocate an agreed prices and incomes policy. Such a policy, it was argued, would require trade unions and employees in general to limit pay demands, and firms to control price increases. In exchange for such promises and agreements from the TUC and the CBI, government would continue to pursue full employment policies, to assist industrial expansion and to improve welfare state benefits. A succession of incomes policies both voluntary and legally enforceable were pursued in the 1960s and 1970s but their permanent benefits were extremely limited as inflation continued to be a major economic and social problem:

> incomes policies can reduce the rate of wage inflation in the short run but no more. Once the policy is off, catch-up increases occur with the result that incomes policies affect the *path* but not the level of wage inflation over time.[11]

The failure of incomes policy, social contracts and tripartite management of the economy by government, the TUC and CBI led to radically new economic policies after the election of the Thatcher Conservative Government in 1979. Incomes policies were abandoned in favour of strict monetarist policies aimed at reducing inflation. The Thatcher Government believed that inflation was the result of excessively high levels of government spending, an ever growing public sector borrowing requirement and government facilitated expansions of the money supply. It was, the Government believed, these factors which caused inflation. Trade unions merely added to the price spiral, they were not the cause of inflation. Monetarism replaced Keynesianism as the Treasury orthodoxy. Whilst there is some evidence that strict monetarist policies played a part in the reduction in inflation, it was at the cost of high interest rates which discouraged investment and resulted in high unemployment and falling output. Thatcherite economic policies also resulted in:

> . . . a Britain divided between haves and have nots, between north and south, between 'new' industries and 'traditional' manufacturing and between owner occupiers and council tenants. Unemployment has risen considerably; standards of provision in the social services have been increasingly squeezed; sizeable parts of manufacturing industry have disappeared; and relations between central and local Government have been a financial and constitutional mess. [Moreover] . . . the losers have been in the main the trade unions and the least well off, the unemployed and the poor . . .[12]

Against such a background the trade unions and the TUC became dispirited, uncertain of their national role and resentful of the new legislation which they believed threatened their hard-won collective freedoms. Their pay bargaining power was weakened by considerable membership losses, persistently high unemployment and a resurgence of managerial confidence. TUC inspired campaigns and so called 'days of action' against Government policy achieved little. The return of the Thatcher Government to power at the 1983 General Election, with one of the largest majorities this century, continued and consolidated monetarist economic policies and forced the TUC to rethink its position.

> The trade unions themselves are in a difficult position: they are aware of their weakness not only in the industrial arena but also politically since Labour's crushing defeat at the 1983 election . . . Overall, the union movement was, at national level, in its weakest position for fifty years.[13]

Despite these developments and the obvious loss of trade union power after 1979, there is no clear evidence that management in general took unreasonable advantage of the shift in power to attack trade union rights at the workplace or to impose harsh new working practices. A survey of workplace industrial relations carried out in 1984 by the Industrial Relations Research Unit at Warwick University found that:

> The evidence does not, then, support the view that the emerging trend of industrial relations is based on an aggressive managerial attack on established unions or that industrial relations and personnel issues have waned in importance . . . [but] It should not be assumed that an entirely new atmosphere of industrial relations has been created.[14]

The force of tradition and long-established relationships and practices are powerful and enduring elements in British industrial relations.

Any discussion on the economic context of industrial relations must take account of the argument that trade union bargaining power 'prices workers out of jobs' by pushing up real wages faster than productivity. In 1984 the Chancellor of the Exchequer, Nigel Lawson, said:

> The evidence suggests that in Britain, a 1 per cent change in the average level of real earnings will, in time, make a difference of between 0.5 per cent and 1 per cent on the level

of employment – that will mean in all probability between 150,000 and 200,000 jobs.[15]

Central to this statement is the belief that if real wage levels can be held constant or even reduced, the number of jobs will hold steady or even expand. The logic of this position is that trade union power to raise real wages results in fewer jobs. The facts, however, do not appear to support this argument. For it is a well-established fact that trade union membership density is much more marked among manual workers than it is among nonmanual employees. Yet between 1979 and 1983 the real wages of nonmanuals increased by 19 per cent in terms of output prices, 'compared to only 10 per cent for the manual group. It seems clear from this that those who cannot call up the "big battalions" do not appear to need them.'[16]

In the same period, employment in the nonmanual sector rose whilst employment in the manual sector fell. This suggests that it is labour market forces rather than trade union power which are responsible for relative changes in real wages and employment levels.

> The picture over the last decade, therefore, is one of considerable variation in wage increases across different groups in the workforce, with those who have done worst also being the most hard hit by rising unemployment. The notion of 'pricing into jobs' would appear to be much more complicated than it is widely represented to be.[17]

If real wage increases cause unemployment then over the decade 1975–85 employment should have fallen in nonmanual occupations and remained stable or risen in manual occupation. This did not happen. Obviously, the economic, social, union and market forces, which along with other factors determine pay levels, also determine unemployment levels. To single out pay increases as the prime or sole cause of increases in unemployment suggests the search for a politically convenient explanation of the phenomenon.

2.4   THE LABOUR MARKET CONTEXT

There are markets for labour in the same way that markets exist for products, services, company shares and money: but because the commodity being bought and sold is the physical and intellectual labour of human beings, labour markets are extremely complex and qualitatively different from other markets. In broad terms, the national labour market and its subsidiary local and specialist labour markets mainly operate according to forces determined by the demand for labour and its supply. Labour markets are, therefore, a very important part of the general framework within which British industrial relations operate and have evolved. The free play of labour market forces, however, is moderated to varying degrees by the collective bargaining power of trade unions, by taxation policies, by income thresholds provided by state unemployment and welfare benefits, and by government schemes and legislation which seek to protect people from the unacceptably harsh conditions which would prevail if free labour market forces were left fully unrestrained.

If any market is to work efficiently and fairly, participants must possess considerable knowledge of the forces operating within and upon the market, as well as detailed understanding of what it can provide and at what prices. There is considerable evidence to suggest that many employers and employees possess at best an imperfect knowledge of labour market conditions and of labour market prices or pay rates. Employers are often at a loss in estimating what pay and conditions they should offer in order to secure certain types of labour, as well as where and how to find it. Similarly, many employees have only a vague idea of what wage and salary levels are paid elsewhere for their types of skills, educational qualifications and experience. Even when they are aware that higher wages could be obtained elsewhere, they often do not act upon it:

. . . when people change jobs or decide not to move, a complex of social and psychological factors affect their choice much more than differences in pay . . . the knowledge that workers have of alternative employment opportunities, and their ability to respond to them by moving house, or travelling longer distances to work, are severely limited. In all these ways the labour market differs from what is supposed to happen in the product market, or the market for money.[18]

Obviously, despite the vital role they play in allocating and deploying labour amongst different employers, labour markets are hedged about with all sorts of practical limitations and restrictions.

Labour force trends

The civilian labour force in Britain consists of people aged 16 or over with jobs, excluding those in the armed forces, together with those in that age group seeking work. In 1984, the labour force numbered about 26.5 million people, comprising of 15.5 million men and 11 million women of whom over three million were unemployed. Despite existing high levels of unemployment, the labour force grew by about half a million people between 1983 and 1984. Assuming unemployment remains broadly at the 1984 level, the labour force could grow by a further three quarters of a million by 1991. Two-thirds of this growth will be females coming onto the labour market. The overall size of the labour force is determined by two fundamental factors. First, there is the population effect, that is the numbers in the population in each age group. Second, there is the activity rate effect, that is the proportion of the population in different age and sex groups in the labour force. The overall size of the population of working age has been growing since 1975, as shown in figure 2.1, and this trend is projected to continue until 1989. For the rest of the century it is expected to remain relatively stable. The labour force activity rate has for some time been upwards for women and downwards for men. This increase in the female activity rate is expected to continue into the early 1990s, whilst the rate for men is likely to remain relatively unchanged as indicated in figure 2.2.

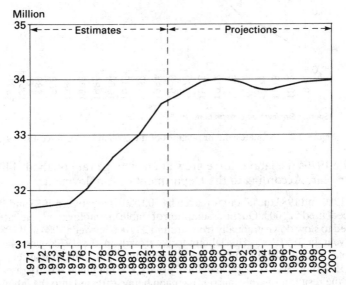

Source: *Employment Gazette* (July 1985)

Figure 2.1 Population of working age 1971–2001.

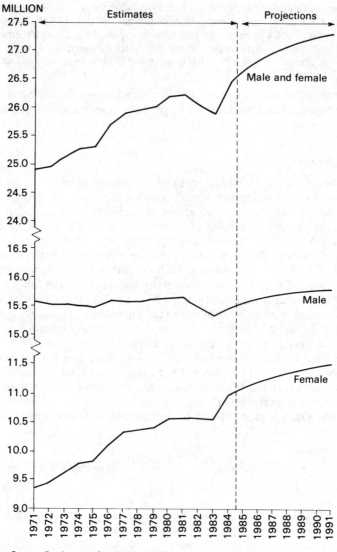

Source: *Employment Gazette* (July 1985)

Figure 2.2   Estimates and projections of the civilian labour force 1971–91.

During the 1970s the labour force grew at an average rate of about 140 000 or half a per cent per year. According to the Department of Employment:

> Between 1980 and 1983 the labour force fell by 300 000, but between 1983 and 1984 grew by an unprecedented 510 000. On the assumption of stable unemployment, the rate of increase is projected to slow down gradually from around 230 000 between 1984 and 1985 to around 40 000 a year in 1991 . . . The labour force growth in the 1970s was almost entirely attributable to the increased numbers of women entering the labour market . . . Between 1983 and 1984 there was an unprecedentedly sharp rise in female activity rates, thought to be chiefly the result of (mainly married) women being attracted into the labour market by the increasing number of part-time job opportunities.[19]

This long-term relative decline in male employment – especially manual male employment – and the growth in female part-time and to a lesser degree full-time employment have obvious implications for industrial relations in terms of the movement towards lower paid part-time jobs and reduced trade union recruitment. This is because trade union density has been and remains markedly low among part-time female employees. By the end of the 1980s, however, labour force fluctuations will have lost much of their volatility and a more stable labour force will contain a high proportion of people who have adjusted to the economic conditions prevalent since the late 1970s.

Table 2.1 *Percentage employment by major economic sectors 1955 and 1984 – Great Britain.*

Sector	1955 %	1984 %
Agriculture, forestry and fishing	5	1.5
Manufacturing	40	26
Services	45	65
Others	10	7.5
All	100	100

Source: Employment: The challenge for the Nation (CMND 9474) *Employment Gazette*

The main trends in employment in major economic sectors have been apparent for many years. As shown in table 2.1 employment has shifted substantially from the manufacturing sector to the service sector during the last 30 years, with agriculture, forestry and fishing also shrinking as an employment base. In examining employment shares between the private and public sector, we observe that in the mid 1980s out of an estimated employed labour force of 23.7 million some 16.8 million (71 per cent) were in the private sector, with the remaining 6.9 million (29 per cent) of the labour force in the public sector. Of these 1.7 million (seven per cent) were employed in public corporations, 2.4 million (9.9 per cent) by central government and 2.9 million (12.5 per cent) by local authorities. Figure 2.3 breaks down public sector employment by industry group, showing that education and the National Health Service comprise almost 40 per cent of the public sector employment. Whilst the public sector employed about 30 per cent of all employees in the mid 1980s, further privatization programmes could well reduce both absolutely and relatively those employed in public sector enterprises.

The occupational structure of the labour force is also constantly changing because of the way industries decline and new ones emerge. Outdated technologies give way to new ones and the demand for occupational skills changes. Table 2.2 illustrates some of the more noticeable changes in the occupational structure between 1971 and 1981. It is likely that many of these trends will continue. The rapid growth in managerial and administrative jobs, for example, probably reflects the growing importance attached to the management function, particularly in the public sector and other of the larger scale enterprises. At the same time the number of supervisors has expanded sharply. Employment in health and welfare services and in education has grown markedly but is now probably in slight decline due to more restrictive public expenditure policies. The number of engineers and scientists in employment has grown along with technicians, mainly in mechanical and aeronautical engineering. The most obvious areas of falling labour demand indicated in the table are engineering and construction craft workers, and for skilled and unskilled operatives. This trend reflects the overall decline in male manual employment in the manufacturing, construction and mining sectors in the last two decades. The continuing decline for male manual employees will continue to affect total trade union membership which has tended to be high in these occupations.

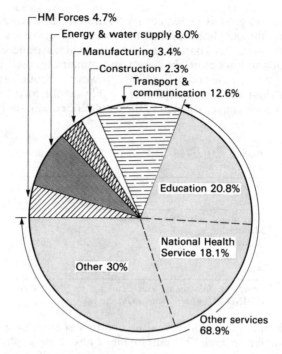

HM Forces 4.7%

Energy & water supply 8.0%

Manufacturing 3.4%

Construction 2.3%

Transport & communication 12.6%

Education 20.8%

National Health Service 18.1%

Other 30%

Other services 68.9%

Source: *Economic Trends* (March 1984)

Figure 2.3   Public sector employment by industry group (1983).

Table 2.2 *Main occupational changes 1971–81.*

Occupation	1971 (000s)	1981 (000s)	Percentage Change 1971–81 %
Managers and administrators	555	706	+27
Education professions	703	863	+23
Health and welfare	656	955	+46
Other professions	829	997	+20
Engineers and scientists	451	578	+28
Clerical occupations	2 584	2 538	−2
Supervisors	213	295	+39
Engineering craft occupations	1 916	1 724	−10
Construction craft occupations	812	762	−6
Skilled operatives	851	643	−24
Other operatives	4 767	3 782	−21
Security occupations	229	283	+23
Other personal services	1 775	1 779	0

Source: *Employment Gazette* (October 1985)

One of the most clearly observable trends in the labour market in recent decades has been the growth of part-time employment. According to one study:

Almost five million of the employees in employment in Britain work part-time, constituting 24 per cent of the total workforce . . . Between 1951 and 1981 there has been a fall in the number of full-time employees of 2.3 million (1.9 million men and 0.4 million women), while the number of part-timers has risen by 3.7 (0.7 million men and 3 million women). The latest employment estimates indicate that these trends are continuing in the 1980s, confirming that the growth in job provision is being achieved through the creation of part-time jobs.[20]

The group most directly affected by these developments are women. Increasingly their employment opportunities appear to be being provided from part-time work where job security is notoriously poor, pay is low and trade unions are not recognized or are weak.

From this brief survey of the national labour force a number of characteristics are discernible. Against a backcloth of rising unemployment, the British labour force has been growing rapidly and will continue to grow, but at a slower rate, until the early 1990s. Much of this growth is due to the increasing number of females, mainly married women, entering the labour market. Most of the jobs which have been created in recent years have been for part-time female employees in the service sectors of the economy. This trend is likely to continue. The number of men in full-time employment in the labour force, which was stable in the 1970s, declined sharply between 1981 and 1983, with most of the job losses occurring amongst male manual employees. Full-time manual employment for men is expected to decline further. After several decades of rapid growth in public sector employment the number employed has begun to fall slightly. Privatization policies are likely to cause public sector employment to fall further, with the private sector growing as a proportion. Employment by industry shows a marked long-term decline in manufacturing, mining and quarrying, construction and agriculture. The service sector of the economy has increased by three million employees between 1961 and 1981 and will continue to expand largely through providing work on a part-time basis for female employees.

The trade union and industrial relations consequences of these changes are apparent. Trade union density is likely to fall as the number of manual male-dominated jobs declines in areas where trade union membership is traditionally strong. The growth of part-time employment of women is unlikely to provide sufficient new union members to offset that fall unless female attitudes to unionization change radically. The general effect of these employment and trade union membership trends, along with continuing high unemployment, could well weaken the impact of collective bargaining on pay and conditions of employment.

Influences on pay determination

It has long been contended by some politicians as well as by labour market economists that pay levels are largely determined in the long term by movements in the demand for labour and its supply, by the level and duration of unemployment, by trade union bargaining strength and, to a lesser degree, by the provision of state unemployment benefits. It is improbable, however, that changes in any one of these four factors have an immediate effect upon the price paid for labour in general. In highly specific areas of the labour market, though, for computer specialists say, rapid changes in labour demand which cannot be matched by supply in the short term can lead to high pay increases. In the labour market, therefore, it is probable that changes in any of these factors are likely to take some time to work through the market. For example, there is no clear evidence of what effect the substantial increase in unemployment since the late 1970s has had upon pay levels in general. The fact that average pay has risen faster during the 1980s than has inflation suggests that the 'unemployment effect' on pay levels is generally rather weak.

Pay settlements, on the other hand, have been at appreciably lower levels than in most of the 1970s, when unemployment was much lower and trade union density and bargaining power was greater. This does not mean that once higher unemployment and lower rates of inflation have persisted for some time, and are seen as relatively permanent features of the economy, that the result will not be progressively lower increases in pay settlements. Historical evidence suggests that 'new' economic circumstances have to persist for several years before long-established attitudes and behaviour change, and before institutions, such as trade unions and employers' associations, adjust their bargaining policies and practices. Those who believe, however, that high unemployment reduces pay settlements and 'prices people into work' stress that:

> Unions cause unemployment to be higher than it need be when they cause the real union wage to be above its 'full employment level' and encourage government to set rates of unemployment compensation at relatively high levels . . . it is the taxpayer, the consumer and the economically inactive who finance the excessive real wages of employed union labour.[21]

Those who oppose such views insist that trade unions possess relatively little power compared to the power possessed by the owners and managers of companies and capital. They point to the fact that, compared with taxation, the unions have had little influence over the redistribution of national income from wealth and profits to pay and state benefits. Trade union strength is largely confined, they argue, to preventing downward movements in pay, to securing job control and preventing dismissals. In short, trade unions are too weak rather than too strong.

> An analysis of economic power reveals a very different state of affairs to the frequently expressed opinion that unions are too powerful. Such an opinion focuses upon symptoms and ignores causes. In reality, unions are weaker than employers, whose possession of the means of production enables them to command decision-making procedures . . . For the most part unions remain insecure bodies reacting to, rather than initiating, labour market developments and possessing little ability to influence wider economic events.[22]

2.5   THE TECHNOLOGICAL CONTEXT

Changes in technology affect industrial relations by creating new products, new materials, new production systems and by changing the occupational structure of the labour market. All these forces compel employers, employees and trade unions to alter working methods, job content, pay differentials and skill protection practices. When technological change is fundamental, for example the introduction of steam-power or electricity, whole industries and many occupations eventually disappear taking with them long-standing working practices and even whole trade unions. The process, however, is usually extended over comparatively long periods of time allowing people and institutions to adjust to changing circumstances slowly.

The history of industrialization and of capitalist development is largely the history of technological change.

> The fundamental impulse that sets and keeps the capitalist engine in motion comes from the new consumers' goods, the new methods of production or transportation, the new markets, the new forms of industrial organisation that capitalist enterprise creates.[23]

This process of innovation is continuous and involves acceptance of change by people and institutions. In order to create greater wealth it is necessary not only to accept change but also to foster and encourage it regardless of its attendant insecurities and social upheavals. Those individuals, companies and nations which do not embrace and foster technological change are left behind unable to compete in producer and consumer markets and become destined to lower standards of living. If they stick to outdated technologies they eventually lose either their jobs, or markets or both on massive scales. For industrial exporting nations, such as Britain, the choice is either to pursue and accept new technologies or to suffer absolute decline as an industrial nation. This technological imperative imposes itself upon employers and trade unions alike.

> Technology of course has always been changing. In an economy like ours which is dominated by the need to make profits, every manufacturer must continually improve methods of production in order to stay ahead of the competition. If this doesn't happen, the goods don't sell.[24]

It is, however, dangerous to believe in a crude form of technological determinism, since whilst technology is a powerful force it is not an overwhelming one. New technologies can be rejected or ignored and the consequences of either move, though hard, accepted and lived with. They can be left entirely to market forces for their implementation, or their effects can be planned for and people protected. Trade unions can blindly oppose the use of new technologies, or consider the long-term advantages associated with them and bargain to ensure that they are introduced with proper concern for everyone involved.

> The real problem is not whether technological development by itself is good or bad. That is a misleading way of looking at it. The important issue is the control of technological development . . . the way to ensure that scientific knowledge can benefit the workforce is by careful but firm negotiation through the union machinery.[25]

In short, organized workers normally oppose new technologies unfeelingly imposed by employers and harsh market forces which will result in heavy job losses, loss of occupational status and skill, and deterioration in terms and conditions of employment for those remaining in work. Conversely, they often accept them where the introduction can be negotiated and the worst social consequences eliminated or ameliorated.

The economic history of Britain since the early nineteenth century has been largely the history of the exploitation of new technologies on which whole new industries and product markets were subsequently based. These industries then gave rise to a long upward cycle of economic activity before going into decline and being replaced by new technologies which repeated the process. The Russian economist, Kondratiev, writing in the early years of this century, believed that long business cycles of expansion, boom and decline were related to fundamentally new technologies. The American economist, Schumpeter, argued that the capitalist system was dependent for its dynamism and prosperity upon the 'creative destruction' of new technologies. Renewed interest in these ideas has been expressed in the 1980s by writers such as Toffler who seek to understand the consequences of the microelectronics revolution or the 'third wave' of rapid economic, social and technological change.

Briefly, there have been three fundamental technological revolutions which have shaped human civilization. The first was the *agrarian revolution* which produced food and clothing by crop growing and animal husbandary and led to permanent human settlements. This basic economic system, whilst undergoing considerable development and refinement, remained essentially unchanged for several thousand years until the *second agrarian revolution* and the first *industrial revolution*, based on the steam-engine, took place in England in the late eighteenth and early nineteenth centuries. Subsequent technological developments fed the momentum of the industrial revolution. These included the development of electricity, gas, the internal combustion engine, motor vehicles, chemicals, petroleum, aeroplanes, synthetic fibres, plastics, radio, television and many other inventions. The third great phase of economic and social development effectively started in the 1970s with computers and the advent of microelectronics, biotechnology, robotics and information technology. It is believed that the *electronics revolution* which we are now experiencing is as fundamental and as all pervasive as the previous agrarian and industrial revolutions. It will, in time, transform social, cultural, economic and political life. It is argued, for example, that the microelectronics revolution will:

> profoundly affect the industrial structure, performance and attitude of the developed countries. These are not just marginal effects . . . they are deep and widespread and collectively signal a fundamental and irreversible change in the way the industrialised societies will live.[26]

The practical applications of the new technology of microelectronics are almost endless. Cheap microcomputers and microprocessors are revolutionizing office work, banking and financial services, warehouse and stock control systems, customer retailing, data handling of all types, printing methods, domestic appliances, vehicle instrumentation, industrial processes and quality control to name but a few areas of application. Information technology is providing immense banks of electronically stored and retrievable data which can be transmitted and received via satellite communications systems. Visual Display Units and computer terminals are becoming as commonplace as the spanner or ballpoint pen. Robotic engineering is replacing human employment in what was often extremely dirty, unhealthy and repetitive work. In 1983 there were 1 753 robots in Britain an increase of over 50 per cent in a year. This could rise to 'between 6,000 and 10,000 by 1991.'[27] The use of computerised numerical controlled machine tools is also expanding in the engineering industry and by 1990 could account for 15 per cent of all machine tools. Biotechnology is creating a:

> social and economic revolution in genetic engineering, the pharmaceutical industry, the production of vaccines, agriculture and the food-processing industry.[28]

A whole range of new materials is also emerging, including ceramics which are stronger and more durable than many steels, composite fibre materials of which carbon fibre is the best known, and low porosity cements of great strength. 'Materials science and technology are radically transforming our environment.'
The overall impact of these new technologies is immense.

> First, these technologies are capable of application to a wide variety of economic tasks in all regions of the world. Second, their development and dissemination are proceeding at a considerably faster pace than has been usual for technological advances in the past. Third, no phase of deceleration is in sight for any of them. And fourth – a characteristic deriving from the previous three – they have the power to reshape social relationships and to alter the structure of the global economy.[29]

The factor which probably influences trade union attitudes more than any other when considering the new technologies is the number of job losses which might be caused. On this issue there are two schools of thought. The pessimists argue that job losses will be very considerable and result in permanent structural unemployment.

> This quantum leap in technology will accelerate the structural changes in the pattern of employment which have been steadily advancing over the past decade and will exert an immensely destructive impact on both existing jobs and the future supply of work.[30]

The optimists, on the other hand, believe that in the longer term the new technologies will create more jobs than they destroy but they also recognize that in the short term high levels of structural unemployment might take place.

> The overall conclusion is that, when the wider effects are taken into account, the introduction of new technology offers the prospect of greater wealth and the possibility of increased employment opportunities in the economy as a whole . . . it is now estimated that, in Scotland, there are more jobs in microelectronics than there are in steel and coal . . . Failure to capture the cost and quality advantages associated with new technology will lead

to job losses. In contrast, firms introducing the new technology may avoid job losses altogether.[31]

The Institute of Employment Research at the University of Warwick has stated that whilst about 340 000 jobs could be lost due to new technology by 1990 more than 420 000 new jobs would probably be created. However, this process of job destruction and job creation will give rise to serious mismatches between the skills possessed by the job losers and those required for work in the new growth areas of the economy.

It has been the general policy of the TUC that the introduction of new technology need not lead to unemployment providing government increases public sector investment, helps private industry to survive recession, accepts the need for tripartite planning for the manufacturing sector, provides more training opportunities and improves social security benefits. The Thatcher Governments have provided few of these things. Having expressed these broad national requirements for the rapid introduction of new technology the TUC has issued specific guidelines to affiliated unions on how to negotiate the introduction of new technology in firms and at the workplace. The TUC report *Employment and Technology* was issued in 1979 as a guide to unions and trade union officials negotiating new technology agreements with employers and managers. The TUC guide contains in summary form, a ten-point plan for new technology agreements:

- No new technology to be introduced unilaterally by management; status quo clause recommended – agreement before change; establishment of procedures for consultation.

- Inter-union collaboration in negotiations; build up of technical expertise by unions.

- Unions guaranteed access to information before decision taken.

- Aim to maintain and improve employment and living standards; no redundancies, or good redundancy payments; planned approach to redeployment and relocation of staff.

- Adequate provision for training and retraining; use redundancy period for retraining.

- Reduction of working hours and eventual elimination of systematic overtime.

- Avoid polarisation of workforce and disruption of existing pay structures; share benefits of technology among all employees.

- Unions should have a say in systems design and reprogramming; procedures established to cover personal data on workforce; no computer-gathered information to be used in work performance measurement.

- Stringent standards established on health and safety, particularly in use of visual display units.

- Joint union/management team to monitor developments and review progress.[32]

The TUC has also mounted an ambitious training programme for union representatives required to negotiate new technology agreements, as well as supplying them with information in the form of workbooks and case studies. Individual trade unions have produced their own specialist training materials and guides. The unions most concerned with the impact of new technology are those with white-collar and technician memberships such as the Association of Scientific Technical and Managerial Staffs, the clerical workers, local government officers and the Technical and Supervisory Section of the engineering workers. To a lesser degree, a number of blue-collar unions are taking a keen interest in negotiating new technology agreements. They include the transport workers, public employees and the Post Office and Engineering Union. Both the white-collar and blue-collar unions stress that there should be no compulsory redundancies, full union participation in planning and implementing technological change, improved pay, holidays and a shorter working week, retraining, access to company information and health and safety protection. Since about 1980 the trade unions have negotiated hundreds of, often quite complex, new technology agreements with employers as diverse as Imperial Chemicals, Lucas Aerospace, Vickers Shipbuilding, Rolls Royce, Cadburys, National Bus Company, British Telecom and Ford Motors.

There is a tendency, however, to confuse new technology agreements with more old-fashioned productivity agreements, which many unions experienced in the 1960s and 1970s.

> Productivity agreements, with which incentive schemes may be bracketed, clearly swamp those over technology . . . Most unions have responded to technological change in terms of maintaining, if not improving, real wages, reducing working hours, and achieving the best possible agreement on redundancy where that appears unavoidable. The employers' response has usually forced these demands into a productivity framework.[33]

It would also appear that union achievements have fallen far short of the TUC policy on new technology. And 'most unions have been slow to realise the challenges posed by new technology.'[34] Many unions have had little choice but to accept the introduction of new technology with few safeguards for their members. This has been because of the superior bargaining power of the employer against a background of high unemployment and deep anxieties on the part of the union membership about the possible costs of militant opposition:

> in Britain's economic circumstances, many unions have had little choice but to adopt a defensive position, or to accept management's productivity initiatives.[35]

It would also appear that the ability to negotiate higher redundancy payments, plus the fact that many noncraft employees can obtain job upgradings when new technology is introduced, has fragmented and weakened union bargaining strength. It is an important fact that a few white-collar unions have dominated the negotiation of successful new technology agreements:

> the pre-eminence of white-collar unions in technology bargaining also reflects the nature of the unions and their membership. White-collar workers face some of the greatest effects of technological change, and have the greatest aspirations to be treated as equals in consultation with management.[36]

In general, however, it would appear that the new technology can be successfully introduced by determined employers who realize that failure to do so will result in their inability to compete commercially. Even where trade unions are powerfully entrenched, as in printing and mining, it has only proved possible to delay and not to prevent the introduction of new technology. Much more important than trade union opposition is the failure of some employers either to realize the vital importance of the new technology or to provide the capital required to invest in it.

2.6   SUMMARY

The aim of this chapter has been to place British industrial relations in a fivefold contextual framework in order to understand the forces which have shaped it and continue to shape it. The categories used are not rigidly separate, neither are they analytically exclusive. They are, however, sufficiently self-contained areas to allow a clear picture of the forces which have shaped British industrial relations to emerge. The fact that the contexts we have chosen often overlap and are interrelated reveals the true, and singular nature of the industrial relations system; an inextricably connected with all the main aspects of British historical, political, economic, occupational and techno-logical development.

The historical context is of particular importance because of the deep attachment of British trade unionism to their old traditions and to the debt which they owe to their early leaders' struggles for survival and legitimacy. Whilst tradition and historical loyalties engender a sense of social purpose and cohesiveness, they also breed a conservatism and introspection which makes modernization and the ability to change very difficult. The British system of industrial relations has been shaped by three historical forces. These are: first, the economic and labour market needs of *laissez-faire* market capitalism; second, the growth and development of trade unionism, collective bargaining and job protection practices; and third, the long-established British ruling-class policy of softening the political and economic power of capitalism in order to accommodate the constitutional and law abiding objectives of trade unionism and working-class politics.

This latter policy permitted a combination of aristocrats with land-owning interests and industrial capitalists to rule nineteenth century Britain without revolution, by absorbing slowly and judiciously the moderate demands of the industrial working classes into the constitution. This ruling-class tradition became a central philosophical feature of both the Conservative Party and the governing establishment until the British economy began to seriously decline in the 1960s. Since then the policy of judicious accommodation to labour's demands has been challenged by the 'new right'. The post war consensus, they argued, resulted in economic stagnation, excessive trade union power and was a major obstacle to the revival of the British economy. The consensus, according to the new right, had to be broken, therefore.

Perhaps the central feature of British politics which has shaped British industrial relations has been the challenge, first by trade unions and then by the Labour Party, to the political domination of Parliament and to law-making by the supporters of free market private enterprise. The common law decisions of judges which rendered trade unions illegal, left their funds unprotected and made striking a criminal or civil offence, were reversed by parliaments dominated by ruling-class interests and deemed as necessary in order to accommodate working-class power rather than to meet it head on. Under this ruling-class policy of judicious accommodation, and with the protection of legal immunities, the trade unions were able to grow and develop and to establish collective bargaining as the main method of advancing the economic interests of their members. It also enabled the trade unions, in time, to establish and finance the Labour Party. The extension of the franchise also led to legislation in the early years of this century and onwards, to give specific protection and advantages to workers and which laid the foundations of the Welfare State.

The greatest test to this political consensus came in the post-war era when the British economy failed to provide the rising living standards and expanding Welfare State provisions which all political parties promised at general elections. The election of the Thatcher Conservative Government in 1979, and its re-election in 1983, presented a marked change of direction. Much of the old ruling-class policy of judicious accommo-dation to working-class demands was jettisoned. Some trade union immunities were ended by legislation. Tripartite economic management involving government, the TUC and CBI was abandoned in favour of strict monetarist policies and market forces. Determined efforts were made to curb public expenditure and public sector employment and to insist that the maintenance of full employment was the responsi-bility of employers, employees and the market rather than of government. The conse-quences of this abrupt change in direction are not yet clearly determined.

Changes in economic policy, structural changes in the economy and the second industrial revolution created by the new technology of microelectronics have played a considerable part in reshaping British industrial relations in the 1980s. The decline of the 'smoke-stack' industries and of the manufacturing sector of the economy and the growth in the service sector have resulted in a decline in traditionally male manual occupations and a rise in white-collar, managerial and female employment. The growth of female employment, particularly part-time work, is very evident and will probably be the main employment growth area for the rest of the 1980s. There is considerable evidence to suggest that levels of unemployment will remain comparatively high for some time, largely because of population, structural and technological forces which even greatly increased public expenditure might not reduce.

What part these changing economic, political, labour market and technological forces will eventually exert over the British system of industrial relations is uncertain. For example, it is far from clear what is the long-term relationship between higher unemployment and upward movements in real wages and salaries. It is also doubtful that reductions in real wages will slow down the rate of job losses. Similarly, the impact on employment levels of the new technologies is uncertain. It appears however that those who forecast massive job losses are unduly pessimistic, since in the long term whole new industries and labour markets are being created. Probably the changes which have occurred since the late 1970s have had their most marked impact on the deep-seated attitudes of managers, trade unionists and employers which were formed in the immediate post-war period. Both employers and trade unions have shown a willingness to accept change and cautiously to reform collective bargaining practices in order to improve job security, introduce new technologies, reduce manning requirements, improve competitiveness and raise efficiency.

The key question, however, is whether or not the new economic, political and industrial relations order introduced after 1979, and the resulting changes in relations between employers, unions and employees, will provide the basis for a long-term settlement, similar to that which followed the 30 years after 1945. Alternatively it could prove to be no more than an abortive and ruthless attempt to change the whole direction of British post-war economic, industrial relations and social history which failed.

2.7   REFERENCES

1. A. Flanders, *Management and Unions*, Faber and Faber, London, 1975, p. 280.
2. A. Fox, *History and Heritage*, Allen and Unwin, London, 1985, p. 436.
3. G. Thomason, *A Textbook of Industrial Relations Management*, Institute of Personnel Management, London, 1984, p. 66.
4. A. Fox, *op. cit.*, p. 435.
5. A.J.P. Taylor, *English History, 1914–1945*, Oxford University Press, London, 1967, p. 250.
6. C. Crouch, *The Politics of Industrial Relations*, Fontana/Collins, Glasgow, 1979, p. 185.
7. W.E.J. McCarthy (Ed.), Introduction in *Trade Unions*, Penguin Books, Harmondsworth, 1985, p. 18.
8. *Ibid.*, p. 18.
9. A. Fox, *op. cit.*, p. 451.
10. P. Riddell, *The Thatcher Government*, Basil Blackwell, Oxford, 1985, pp. 1–2.
11. J.L. Fallick and R.F. Elliott, *Incomes Policies, Inflation and Relative Pay*, Allen and Unwin, London, 1981, p. 260.
12. P. Riddell, *op. cit.*, p. 230.
13. *Ibid.*, p. 191.
14. P. Edwards, The myth of the macho manager in *Personnel Management*, April, 1985, p. 35.
15. Hansard, 30 October 1984. Quoted in D. Metcalf and S. Nickell, Jobs and pay, *Midland Bank Review*, Spring, 1985, p. 8.
16. *Ibid.*, p. 10.
17. *Ibid.*, p. 11.

18. W.E.J. McCarthy, *op. cit.*, p. 15.
19. Labour force outlook, *Employment Gazette*, July 1985, p. 259.
20. O. Robinson, The changing labour market: the phenomenon of part-time employment in Britain in *National Westminster Bank Quarterly Review*, November 1985, p. 19.
21. C. Mulvey, *The Economic Analysis of Trade Unions*, Martin Robertson, Oxford, 1978, p. 147.
22. B. Burkitt, Excessive trade union power: existing reality or contemporary myth? in McCarthy, *op. cit.*, pp. 386–7.
23. J.A. Schumpeter, *Capitalism, Socialism and Democracy*, Unwin University Books, London, 1943, p. 83.
24. Transport and General Workers' Union, *Microelectronics, New Technology, Old Problems, New Opportunities*, TGWU, 1979, p. 2.
25. *Ibid.*, pp. 3–4.
26. I. Maddock, Beyond the Protestant ethic in *New Scientist*, November, 1978, p. 594.
27. V. Williams, Employment implications of new technology, *Employment Gazette*, May 1984, p. 211.
28. F. Blanchard, Technology, work and society: some pointers of ILO research in *International Labour Review*, vol. 123, No. 3, May–June, 1984, p. 268.
29. *Ibid.*, p. 268.
30. C. Jenkins and B. Sherman, Preface, *The Collapse of Work*, Eyre Methuen, London, 1979.
31. Williams, *op. cit.*, pp. 210-12.
32. M. Peltu, In place of technological strife, in *New Scientist*, 13 March 1980, p. 823.
33. R. Markey, New technology, the economy and the unions in Britain, in *The Journal of Industrial Relations*, December 1982, p. 573.
34. *Ibid.*, p. 575.
35. *Ibid.*, p. 576.
36. *Ibid.*, p. 577.

PART TWO

The Institutional Framework

3

Employers and Management

There are many thousands of producer and service enterprises in Britain. They vary in size, type of ownership, method of finance, what they produce, who works in them and how they are internally structured but all of them – other than the relatively small number of one-person businesses and working partnerships – have two main institutional features in common. Each of them is an employer of people and each of them has to be managed by specialist managerial employees to achieve its objectives. It is the role of organizations as employers, and the function of management within them, which provide the connecting themes of this chapter.

3.1 EMPLOYING ORGANIZATIONS

Organizations produce those goods and services demanded by individuals or corporate consumers who are prepared to pay for them either directly in the market-place or indirectly through taxation and public funding. A wide variety of producer or service organizations exist in Britain today. They are found in the extractive, manufacturing, distributive, financial, educational and welfare sectors and incorporate a diverse range of enterprises and establishments including farms, factories, offices, schools, universities, hospitals, banks, insurance companies and so on. Some are large organizations, others are small; some are privately owned, others are public bodies.

A useful way of classifying organizations is by their orientation and ownership, as can be seen in figure 3.1. An organization's orientation reflects the primary goals it seeks to

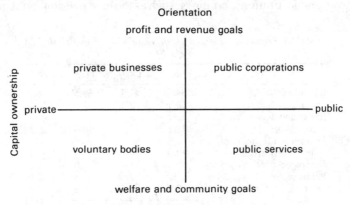

Source: D. Farnham, *Personnel in context* (IPM 1984)

Figure 3.1 Organization typology by orientation and ownership.

achieve. The basic goals of private businesses are to satisfy consumer demand in the market-place, whilst those of the public services are to satisfy citizens' needs within the community 'regardless of whether the citizen can translate that need into effective demand or of whether any means can be found of charging directly for the service.' Private and public organizations are distinguishable 'by the terms demand and need and their derivative objectives are characterized differently.'[1]

Private businesses

Private businesses employ about 13 million people, about half of these in the large-market sector, the rest in the small-market sector. Although large numbers of small, unincorporated businesses exist – often employing very few or only temporary or part-time staff – the most common form of business organization is the registered company. There were about 900 000 registered companies in Britain in 1985.

As can be seen from table 3.1, there are two main types of business corporation, the private limited company and the public limited company. Private companies are required to have at least two shareholders and a maximum of 50 and are precluded from issuing shares to the general public. A public limited company (PLC) is required to have a minimum of seven shareholders but there is no upper limit on either the number of shareholders or its share transactions; its shares are bought and sold on the Stock Exchange.

Table 3.1 *Number of companies on British registers 1980–84.*

	1980	1981	1982	1983	1984
Public companies	9 163	8 018	5 324	5 335	5 407
Private companies	751 642	780 828	802 493	850 375	889 517
All companies	760 805	788 846	807 813	855 710	894 924

Source: Department of Trade, *Companies in 1984* (HMSO 1985)

A major feature of the corporate sector is its concentration into a small number of very large PLCs, including multinationals, and a substantial and expanding number of much smaller private firms. One reason for the concentrated size of PLCs is the amalgamations and mergers which have taken place amongst large and medium-sized firms in recent years. Another feature of PLCs is their pattern of share ownership. Table 3.2 shows that institutional holdings, such as those of pension funds and insurance

Table 3.2 *Percentage distribution of shareholdings in British PLCs 1963–81.*

	1963	1969	1975	1981
Individuals	54.0	47.3	37.5	28.2
Charities	2.1	2.1	2.3	2.2
Banks and insurance companies	11.3	13.8	16.6	20.8
Pension funds, unit and investment trusts	19.0	22.3	31.4	37.1
Companies	5.1	5.4	3.0	5.1
Public sector	1.5	2.5	3.6	3.0
Overseas	7.0	6.6	5.6	3.6
	100.0	100.0	100.0	100.0

Source: *The Observer* (13 October 1983)

companies, are proportionally increasing whilst individual shareholdings are decreasing. These changes reflect the continued divorce of corporate ownership and managerial control in PLCs and the consolidation of a professional managerial élite within them, responsible for their financial profitability, corporate effectiveness and control of resources, including people.

Public corporations

Public corporations employ about two million people in Britain and are defined as public trading bodies having 'a substantial degree of financial independence of the public authority which created them.'[2] They include nationalized industries such as coal, electricity, steel and the railways, and other public bodies such as the Bank of England, National Film Finance Corporation and the Property Services Agency. In 1985 there were some 17 nationalized industries and about 30 other public corporations.

Public corporations have five main features. First, their capital is publicly owned and they are managed by government appointed executives. Second, they are not subject to company law and have a different legal status from private businesses. Third, they obtain their current revenue, or part of it, from selling their goods or services; their capital expenditure is raised by borrowing from the Treasury or the general public. Fourth, they are exempt from the normal parliamentary financial scrutiny exercised over government departments. Fifth, their boards are usually appointed by a secretary of state and their employees are not civil servants.

Public services

The major public services are the civil service, the National Health Service (NHS) and the local authority services, including the police services. They employ about five million people who provide a wide range of services to individuals, their families, the community and private businesses. Funds are provided collectively through national insurance, taxation and local rates. The civil service, which is the administrative arm of central government, comprises over 20 government departments and a number of departmental and non-departmental agencies such as the Manpower Services Commission, the Advisory Conciliation and Arbitration Service and the Equal Opportunities Commission. It employs two main categories of civil servants, industrial civil servants and non-industrial civil servants.

The NHS is based on the principle that medical and health care should be readily available, largely free of charge at the point of use, by anybody normally resident in Britain. It uses the services of a wide range of staff including doctors and nurses, administrative and clerical groups, and ancillary staff such as porters, domestics, gardeners and cooks. The local authorities are divided into two organizational tiers, with the upper tier providing largely strategic services over wide geographical areas and the lower tier providing essentially local services. They employ a wide range of personnel in manual and non-manual grades including skilled and less skilled trades as well as technical and professional staff such as engineers, surveyors, accountants, lawyers, architects and teachers.

Voluntary bodies

Voluntary bodies are usually small, privately owned organizations providing specialized services to their own members or special interest groups. Examples include professional bodies, trade unions, employers' associations and political pressure groups. Being small scale organizations, and as they often have social rather than economic objectives, voluntary bodies do not usually have major industrial relations problems. Nevertheless, they employ people, their managers manage employees, and where trade unions are recognized their managerial representatives negotiate with union representatives. An emerging element in the voluntary sector is worker or producer co-operatives where the enterprises are owned and managed by their members. Larger co-operatives are more likely to employ professional managers, though, responsible for implementing the policies determined by their memberships and management boards.

3.2   THE EMPLOYER – EMPLOYEE RELATIONSHIP

For centuries the common law has referred to the two parties to the employment relationship as that of 'master' and 'servant'. Freedom of contract between the parties became the predominant legal doctrine in the early and mid nineteenth century, in theory. In practice this was not the case. Until 1875, for example, manual workers were in certain circumstances liable to criminal prosecution for breaching their contracts of service. The social gap between master and servant was even greater than the differences between them contractually, and the economic balance of power was severely weighted in favour of the masters.

During the last hundred years, the legal, social and economic contexts of the employment relationship have altered radically. For example, although the contract of employment is still commonly referred to as a contract of service, modern legal usage has slowly replaced the terms 'master' and 'servant' with the more egalitarian terms 'employer' and 'employee'. Further, employees now have a number of significant statutory employment protection and trade union rights. The social and economic circumstances of the workplace have also generally improved to the advantage of employees through, in the main, more enlightened employment policies, trade union organization, improved working conditions and the welfare state.

In the days of the master and servant relationship and in a free labour market, the master was invariably an individual person contracting other individuals, his servants, to render personal services to him in return for some consideration either in cash or in kind. Even with the emergence of the first factories, the master who owned the capital of the business was a 'natural person' whom all could see and physically identify. Slowly, small family firms replaced individual proprietors as employing authorities and these, in turn, gave way to the modern corporate employer of today.

Apart from very small businesses, the typical employer is now a private or public corporate body – PLCs, private companies, the Crown, health authorities, local authorities, water authorities, public corporations and so on. Such organizations are not only large scale but also abstract, legal entities. They have been created by Parliament and the law to provide, amongst other things, a convenient identity on one side of the employment contract. 'Furthermore, when that person is a legal fiction, the rights and duties of the employer are assumed by a variety of managers who act as the agent of the employer.'[3] The archetypal employer today is, in other words, an organization whose 'corporate personality' is a legal creation, determined largely by what the law prescribes.

The concept of the employer, then, has evolved from that of the master as an identifiable natural person in the early days of the industrial revolution to that of a legal entity today. The principle of incorporation in one form or another:

> makes the employer a corporate body or a corporation, which means in the eyes of the law the employer has a legal, if fictional or artificial personality or existence, which is separate and distinct from the personality and existence of anyone who happens to be a member of the organization at the time.[4]

Although work organizations are tangible and real enough for those working in them, they are also legal and fictional bodies which employ people, own property and enter into commercial contracts. The contract of employment between an employer and an employee, for example, is now usually drawn up by the managerial agents of the employer, acting on behalf of the principal or legal entity which they represent, rather than by the employer as a person.

The legal duties of employers, like those of employees, depend upon the terms of the contract between them, although in the absence of any specific agreement certain common duties apply. These include, for example, the duty of the employer to pay its employees for their services, although remuneration is only payable where it has been agreed, whether expressly or implied. If the contract provides for payment, but the amount has not been specified, the employer has to pay a 'reasonable' amount or 'the customary rate' for the job. Generally, the remuneration payable is determined by the collective agreement negotiated between employer and union representatives whose terms become incorporated into the personal contracts of employment of individual employees. In other cases minimum remuneration may be fixed statutorily by wages councils or wages boards. Other common law duties of the employer include: providing the opportunity to earn remuneration; taking reasonable care of the employee's safety; indemnifying employees for any loss sustained in performing their duties; and not exposing employees to grave danger of health or person.

In turn, the major common law duties of employees include: being ready and willing to work; rendering personal service to their employer; respecting the employer's trade secrets; and taking reasonable care of the employer's property. More importantly, employees also have the common law duties of obeying all reasonable and legitimate instructions given to them by their employers and their managerial agents, and of avoiding wilful disruption of the employer's undertaking. The duty of reasonable obedience, for example, requires that employees, once employed, agree to submit to the reasonable authority of an employer in all those matters falling within the scope of the work to be done. This means in practice that the contractual relationship between the parties is a dependent and a subordinate one for the employees, not a coequal one with the employer. Also encompassed within the duty of obeying lawful and reasonable employer commands, there is the common law right of employers to discipline employees who are unsatisfactory in the performance of their job tasks. Finally, by requiring employees to co-operate with their employers, and not to disrupt their businesses wilfully, the common law upholds the power to manage of employers and of their managerial agents. The duty to co-operate also means there is no provision for common law legal protection for those employees engaging in industrial action against their employers in a trade dispute.

In retrospect, the history of the employer–employee relationship is embodied in the development of the employment contract. In practice there has been a progressive liberalization of the relationship, especially in the last 20 years, with a steady restriction of the employer's absolute freedoms and prerogatives at work. These have been effectively constrained by the growth of trade unionism and collective bargaining, and by state interventionism in industrial relations, although the specific impact of these factors on particular employers varies by sector, industry, enterprise and establishment. Nevertheless, changes in the balance of power between employer and employees should not be exaggerated, especially since the recession after 1979. As Jack Jones, former general secretary of the Transport and General Workers Union put it:

There is no doubt about it: power lies with the employer, but with the growth of the unions, there is a more balanced relationship, with give and take on both sides. And that is how it should be.[5]

3.3   THE ROLE OF MANAGEMENT IN ENTERPRISES

All three major sectors of the economy, the large corporate sector, the small corporate sector and the public sector, employ large numbers of managers. It is estimated, for example, that in 1981 there were at least 2.5 million managers in Britain, comprising over 10 per cent of the labour force.[6] These professional managers, most of them employees themselves, are not a homogeneous group. But it is their responsibility to ensure the efficient and effective managing of the organizational resources for which they are accountable, including subordinate employees. It is their task 'to organize the use of resources (including the work of others) towards the objectives of an enterprise.'[7] Managers are, in short, accountable to those owning the organization's capital assets for its economic viability or success; agents of organizational efficiency; custodians of employer interests.

Managerial work

Classical management theorists, such as Fayol, view managers as rational decision makers whose main activities are planning, organizing, directing, co-ordinating and controlling organizational resources. Other theorists believe managers to be neutral intermediaries in the decision making process who take into account in their decision making role the competing needs of employees, consumers or customers, the community, government and, in the case of private industry, shareholders. Recent studies of the managerial role, however, present a somewhat different picture. Mintzberg, for example, classifies managerial behaviour into three sets of roles, common to all levels of management.[8] He describes these as 'interpersonal', 'informational' and 'decisional' roles. In their interpersonal roles managers act as figureheads, leaders and liaison persons; in their informational roles as monitors, disseminators and spokespersons; in their decisional roles as entrepreneurs, disturbance handlers, resource allocators and negotiators. The importance of Mintzberg's work is that it highlights the uncertainty within which most managers operate. Managers are not normally reflective thinkers, they are 'doers' coping with unexpected events and unforeseen circumstances.

Other research shows that managers typically switch every few minutes 'from one subject or person to another, rarely completing one task before being involved in another.'[9] In this sense managing is a responsive rather than an analytical activity. Other documented features of managerial work include: its verbal nature, managers are talkers and listeners rather than readers and writers; its dependence upon other people, involving reciprocal relationships based on trading and exchange; its political nature; and its uncertainty. In short, managerial work 'is one of fragmented activity, incomplete tasks, interruptions, variety and unpredictable events.'[10]

Management, ownership and control

In the public sector the functions of managing, owning and controlling enterprises are generally more clearly delineated than in the private sector. Those managing public enterprises and establishments are appointed to run them in ways likely to achieve the objectives and purposes for which they were created. Ownership rests with the appropriate public authorities, with ultimate control vested in government or other decision taking bodies. Clearly, policy differences can emerge between the political controllers such as secretaries of state, local councillors, or governing bodies and professional managers such as chief executives, heads of institutions and directors of services. But conflicts of these sorts are usually avoidable and avoided.

In the private sector, with the expansion in size and influence of the joint stock company, some writers argue that the control function of ownership is replaced by that of top management, with shareholders becoming less influential in corporate affairs. The logic behind the argument of the 'managerialists' is that if the largest shareholder or group of shareholders in large companies do not have a sufficient proportion of votes in company affairs 'then those companies are managerially rather than owner controlled.'[11] Managerialism is not an homogeneous theory, however, and some authors suggest that since the modern managerial élite has a different relationship to private property than did the old capitalist class, it pursues significantly different business policies than did its predecessors. Hence, they claim, conflicts between management and subordinate employees no longer exist. Other managerialists such as Dahrendorf do not accept this view, believing that what separates management from employees is not property but the authority to make distributional decisions within industrial, commercial and other enterprises.

Non-managerialists either do not accept that a divorce of ownership from control exists, or at least minimize its effects. They argue that ownership is still sufficiently concentrated to ensure owner control. It is further reinforced, they suggest, by interlocking directorates and by the identification of top management with the owning class. Recent research, however, indicates that in terms of shareholdings there has been a divorce of ownership from control in larger private enterprises. And for managers generally 'the interests of owners are seen to take precedence over other groups who have claims on the resources of the enterprise.'[12] Management as a group, it seems, must of necessity co-operate in corporate policy making with those representing shareholder interests at board level. Also, if management is collectively responsible for business efficiency and corporate effectiveness, 'then it cannot be neutral in its contractural relationships with employees.'[13] Ultimately business enterprises are evaluated by the economic criteria of the market-place. It is management's collective responsibility to ensure that these market criteria are satisfied on behalf of owner interests. This requires, amongst other things, the effective managing of the enterprise's capital, physical and human resources.

Management structures

The term 'management' is used in two main senses. First, it is used to describe managers as a group within enterprises: 'the management'. Second, it is used to describe in general terms what managers do, that is managing organizational resources or 'management' as an activity. In the group sense, management may be viewed: as an economic resource, performing a series of technical functions including organizing and administering human and other resources within enterprises; as a system of authority through which corporate policies are translated into activities and tasks by subordinate managers and employees; and as a social élite. Management as a group, in other words, is a technical function, a political activity and a social cadre.

In undertaking its technical and political functions, management is stratified vertically by power and status and horizontally by task and specialism, especially as organizations increase in size. Vertically, there is a separation of decision taking from action taking 'so that vertical jobs are distinguished on the basis of the amount of discretion to decide,'[14] with management operating within its own structure and hierarchy of power and authority. According to a study by Chandler and Daems, one in five industrial workers in Europe and the United States was employed by companies with hierarchies of at least six vertical levels by the mid 1970s. Similar managerial hierarchies exist in public sector enterprises. In both cases 'the invisible hand of market mechanisms' in co-ordinating flows and allocating resources in major industries has been replaced by 'the visible hand of managerial direction.'[15]

Vertical managerial roles may be classified into three main levels of power and influence: corporate, administrative and executive or policy making, programming and interpretive. More simply, the terms corporate or senior management, middle or executive management and first line or supervisory management are often used. Senior management is the relatively small managerial group whose main task is developing and reviewing corporate objectives and policies. Middle management implements corporate objectives and policies and manages subordinate managers. First line management supervises the activities and tasks of non-managerial employees, with relatively little job or role discretion.

Horizontally managerial jobs and work roles are differentiated according to their operational, functional or departmental responsibilities, with individual managers heading specific subunits. The main managerial functional groupings are production (or operations), marketing, finance, research and development, administration and personnel. In small enterprises the horizontal division of managerial work is frequently minimal, with generalist management skills often more important than specialist ones. In larger enterprises, by contrast, general management is mainly a senior managerial task, necessitating the co-ordination and integration of functional specialisms towards stated corporate goals and objectives.

The personnel function

A standard definition of personnel management is that it is 'that part of management concerned with people at work and with their relationships within an enterprise.' According to the Institute of Personnel Management, the professional personnel management association in Britain, it is the aim of personnel management to bring together and to develop into effective organizations those men and women working in them, having regard to the well-being of individuals and of working groups 'to enable them to make their best contribution to [organizational] success.'[16] From a managerial viewpoint the major personnel management problem in any organization is how the efforts of workpeople can be organized and co-ordinated 'in order to attain the highest levels of efficiency, adaptability and productivity.'[17] The underlying issue is how organizational and managerial objectives can be integrated with individual and workgroup aspirations, without generating destabilizing intraorganizational conflict. It is a difficult balance to achieve.

In practice the personnel management function within enterprises is an ambiguous and complex one. First, personnel management is the responsibility of both line managers and personnel specialists. Line managers are responsible for 'managing people', their subordinates. Personnel managers do not normally manage people, except within their own functional specialism, but are responsible for 'managing the people systems' within enterprises. There is therefore some degree of uncertainty regarding which aspects of personnel management should be left to line managers and what should be the responsibilities of personnel specialists. 'Ambiguities in definition generate confusion at the operational level about the nature and locus of personnel management responsibilities.'[18]

Second, the personnel management function within organizations incorporates, to varying degrees, both a management-centred control role and an employee-centred welfare role. The management control role is rooted in managerial concern for efficiency and effectiveness at work and puts managing people firmly into the mainstream of managerial activity. The welfare role, in contrast, is concerned with the well-being of individual employees or workgroups and how they are treated by the organizations employing them. It derives from the activities of the 'welfare movement' which was introduced into some factories by a few altruistic and humane employers at the beginning of the century. Clearly, conflicts of accountabilities can emerge within the personnel function between personnel's concern with efficiency and organizational effectiveness, on the one side, and its aims to seek justice, fair terms and satisfying work conditions for employees on the other. The one assumes pluralistic work enterprises whilst the other emphasises their more unitary features. Also, in furthering corporate and enterprise goals, personnel is clearly identified with employer objectives. In concerning itself with employee equity and fairness, however, personnel is seeking a more independent professional role, midway between employer and employee interests.

Third, there are degrees of role specialization within the specialist personnel function itself. For example, personnel professionals in charge of personnel departments and personnel units normally undertake a large number of tasks ranging across personnel work. They are more properly described as 'personnel generalists'. In this capacity they are more likely to be involved in personnel policy determination and industrial relations than are their subordinates. Personnel subordinates, on the other hand, are sometimes described as 'personnel specialists' to distinguish their role from the roles performed by personnel generalists or personnel managers. This is because, directed by personnel managers, they normally undertake a much narrower range of personnel tasks and activities. Principal areas where personnel subordinates have duties include recruitment and selection, payment administration and personnel information and records.

The specialized personnel management function in enterprises, therefore, and the personnel management function of line managers, play key roles in enabling organizations to achieve their corporate objectives through the people working in them. Co-operation and mutual understanding between professional personnel managers and hard-pressed line managers are necessary to this end, even if in practice the relationship can be problematic. In addition to how personnel activities and tasks might be allocated between personnel managers and line managers, there is the extent to which the work of personnel managers has line or staff authority. There is also the problem of co-ordinating personnel management activities across enterprises. There is no general agreement as to how these issues are best resolved. A contingency approach dependent upon organizational and contextual circumstances is sometimes recommended as the most appropriate personnel strategy.

3.4 MANAGING INDUSTRIAL RELATIONS

How managements handle the complex organizational and human resource problems arising in industrial relations is a debatable and contentious issue. On the one side, in small scale enterprises for example, a relatively unstructured and *ad hoc* approach may be adopted. On the other hand, there is a tendency for industrial relations and employment matters to be standardized and administered bureaucratically in larger private and public enterprises even if, as one early study concludes, strike incidence appears to be linked with standardization and formalization of management practices, especially with 'both "formalisation in industrial relations" and "facilities for shop stewards"'.[19] It also seems possible, according to another study, that 'if personnel managers foster steward organisation and centralise decisions, then they may well stimulate industrial action.'[20]

Whatever the evidence relating to the organizational impact of professionalizing the industrial relations function, and it would appear to point in both directions, there is little doubt that senior managements in many enterprises now view the managing of industrial relations with their employees and representative bodies as both a necessary and a vital managerial task. It has not always been the case. Indeed, the Donovan

Commission claimed unofficial strikes at that time to be the result of the inadequate conduct of industrial relations at company and plant level between managements and unions. The Commission believed that this would persist so long as companies paid 'inadequate attention to their pay structures and personnel policies', and workplace negotiations remained 'in their chaotic state.'[21] The Commission implied that the prime responsibility for this chaos rested with management generally and top management in particular. Accordingly, it strongly recommended that in order to promote the orderly and effective regulation of industrial relations within firms and factories 'the boards of companies [should] review industrial relations within their undertakings.'[22]

In the Commission's view, this required appropriate corporate strategies and policies on industrial relations, with management negotiating comprehensive procedural agreements with trade union representatives at company and plant level regulating their collective bargaining arrangements, methods of grievance handling, disciplinary practices, redundancy schemes, facilities for shop stewards, and health and safety at work. The Royal Commission's prognosis was that company boards and senior management needed to initiate the reconstruction of workplace industrial relations by the promotion of positive personnel policies, by the creation of orderly collective bargaining machinery, by the formalization of industrial relations procedures and, in conjunction with the trade unions, by the regularization of the role of shop stewards in the negotiating process.

These themes were subsequently taken up in the industrial relations code of practice, published by the Department of Employment in 1972. It maintained, for instance, that good industrial relations are the joint responsibility of management, employees and the trade unions representing them. 'But the primary responsibility for their promotion rests with management. It should therefore take the initiative in creating and developing them.' It recommends that managers at the highest level should give, 'and show that they give, just as much attention to industrial relations as to such functions as finance, marketing, production or administration.'[23]

The traditional approach of management has been to accord a low priority to the managing of industrial relations. Because of this, and its consequences, the Donovan Commission and other industrial relations reformists have advocated that managerial initiative in the formalization of effective policies, procedures and practices in industrial relations is a necessary condition for improving the quality and the effectiveness of industrial relations decision making, and in reducing the incidence of industrial conflict at work. In the past especially, the classical response to the trade union presence and to the exigencies of collective bargaining by the boards of many enterprises was at its best reactive and, at its worst, defensive. It was rarely predictive. As one piece of research concluded:

> where the directors' role in industrial relations was concerned . . . What was found was purposive inaction, influential non-participation, a very active form of unconcern . . . and instrumental inconsistency.

In short, 'directors literally do not want to know about industrial relations.'[24]

The reasons for this are not hard to identify. First, even today many managements, especially in the private sector, continue to view the prospect of power sharing with trade unions as threatening their decision-making authority and organizational legitimacy. Even where trade unions are recognized, much managerial time is spent in attempting to preserve its traditional prerogatives rather than in developing new areas of joint regulation with the trade unions with which it negotiates. By this view, trade unionism is seen as an unwarranted challenge to the right to manage. Second, industrial relations is only part of the overall management function. Most managements can probably never be totally expert in the field of industrial relations since, unlike the trade unions, it is not the very essence of their organizational role. For these reasons, there continues to be considerable difficulty in obtaining total commitment and attention to the managing of industrial relations at board or top management level in some enterprises. 'First, industrial relations matters are not readily quantifiable,'[25] second, until recently it was relatively rare for boards to appoint, as a consistent practice, directors of personnel or industrial relations. Even today board and senior managerial appointments continue to be dominated by accountants, lawyers and other of the more traditional groups. Such persons, whether by training, experience or inclination, are rarely imbued in the nuances, subtleties and culture of industrial relations decision making and problem solving.

A third factor giving rise to reluctance by many managers to become deeply involved in industrial relations derives from the practice of concluding industry-wide or national collective agreements in certain industries. Where these operate there is little incentive for line managers to be involved in day to day industrial relations. In other instances, especially where large personnel departments have become established, line managers often prefer to delegate their industrial relations role to personnel managers rather than cope with it themselves. This is often encouraged by the personnel and industrial relations specialists themselves, since it provides added status, power and prestige to their own roles within their employing organizations. For these reasons, therefore, industrial relations – certainly until recently – has had a fairly low priority within the overall corporate strategy of many enterprises, especially in small and medium-sized private sector ones. Industrial relations have also been poorly managed because many managements have often lacked the skills, confidence and commitment for dealing with the trade unions effectively at plant or operational levels.

It is very difficult in practice to determine by objective criteria whether an organization's industrial relations activities and outputs are 'good' or 'bad', 'effective' or 'ineffective', 'satisfactory' or 'unsatisfactory'. Much depends on how these terms are defined and measured and by what criteria they are evaluated. However, partly because of the Donovan Commission's influence, the impact of public policy, the extension of employment legislation and more powerful trade unions, many managements, especially in large scale private corporations, have adopted a more structured and strategic approach to managing industrial relations in recent years. In manufacturing industry, at least, few major multiplant companies employing more than 5 000 employees 'are now likely to be without a main board director with head office responsibility for employee relations.'[26]

In a survey of manufacturing firms conducted for the Confederation of British Industry in 1980, Arthur Marsh found that a 'substantial proportion' of single establishment firms and a 'preponderance' of multiplant firms saw their employee relations 'as having become more formal, either institutionally, procedurally or in relation to the setting down of rules',[27] thus narrowing the gap between public sector and private sector practices. He, nevertheless, concludes that although the boards of these companies believe it proper to have a general philosophy enshrining their managerial style, they often continue to prefer an informal ' "action" frame for their employee relations' rather than a more structured approach.[28] As one writer comments, many managements in Britain have abandoned the old 'formal system' of industrial relations embodying national bargaining. 'But they do not as yet appear to have found an adequate model to replace it.'[29]

3.5   MANAGERIAL APPROACHES TO INDUSTRIAL RELATIONS

Managerial approaches to industrial relations have traditionally been characterized by inconsistency, informality, and lack of structure. Managers have also tended to be reactive in industrial relations situations rather than proactive. There is some evidence to suggest, however, that some employers are beginning to think of themselves 'as adopting a more participative and consultative style of management than was once the case', with a proportion considering 'that they are more "proactive" than "reactive".'[30] In analysing the ways in which management approach industrial relations we need to examine three key concepts: managerial styles, strategies and policies.

Managerial styles

Managerial style in industrial relations is related to a number of organizational and managerial variables and different classificatory systems have been used to analyse them. Fox, for example, puts forward six patterns of industrial relations between management and employees varying according to the degree of legitimacy afforded by each side to the other. He describes these as: the 'traditional', 'classical conflict', 'sophisticated modern', 'standard modern', 'continuous challenge' and 'sophisticated paternal' patterns.[31]

The approach of traditionalist employers is to oppose trade unions and not to recognize them. This is normally characterized by unitary frames of reference by both management and employees, with management often adopting an authoritarian style of dealing with employees. In the classical conflict pattern, unions exist to challenge managerial control and are normally recognized but management is likely to impose decisions unilaterally upon its workforce, either without prior discussion or by forcing decisions through the negotiating and consultative machinery to its own advantage. The sophisticated modern style is where management legitimizes the union role in defined areas of joint decision making because it sees this role 'as conducive to its own interests as measured by stability, promotion of consent, bureaucratic regulation, effective communication or the handling of change.'[32]

In seeking union collaboration and support for corporate goals and objectives a management using the sophisticated modern approach considers a number of key elements. According to Purcell, these are:

1. the encouragement of union membership and support for the closed shop where appropriate;
2. the encouragement of membership participation in trade unions;
3. the encouragement of inter-union co-operation and the development of shop steward committees;
4. the institutionalization of irreducible conflict;
5. the minimization of areas of avoidable conflict;
6. the maximization of areas of common interest;
7. the reduction of the power of strategic groups;
8. the development of effective control systems.[33]

In short, by institutionalizing industrial conflict and by legitimizing trade union power, managements adopting the sophisticated modern style aim to achieve managerial control within the workplace through appropriate collective bargaining strategies.

The standard modern style, which is the dominant approach, is essentially pragmatic, with employers changing and modifying their industrial relations styles in response to internal and external changes. These include managerial preferences, market forces and governmental policies. Oscillations between different approaches to industrial relations, however, 'undermine stability and continuity and more especially place major limitations on the extent to which trust can be generated and maintained.'[34] This can result in confusion and uncertainty 'caused by a mixture of unitary and pluralistic perspectives.'[35]

Where employees, workgroups and unions refuse to legitimate management's right to manage, we have the continuous challenge pattern, with 'periods of uneasy truce as each side licks its wounds and watches the enemy for signs of a weak spot in its defences.'[36] Sophisticated paternalist employers, by contrast, do not normally recognize trade unions and management is able to pursue its organizational policies without internal challenges. Further, most sophisticated paternalists put a great deal of time and energy into managing their employees in professional and skilled ways. For example, they pay a lot of attention to progressive personnel policies, stressing the importance of individual employee contributions within the enterprise. They often have sensitive recruitment and selection procedures, ensuring that only employees with 'correct' attitudes are employed, high pay and attractive fringe benefits, and appropriately designed and implemented management training programmes. They also have relatively high ratios of personnel specialists working for them, providing key services and advice to line management.

Another typology of managerial styles relates employer frames of reference to levels of employee involvement, as shown in figure 3.2. This provides four major managerial styles in industrial relations: 'participative', 'paternalistic', 'consultative' and 'authoritarian'. The participative style, for instance, incorporates pluralistic employer frames of

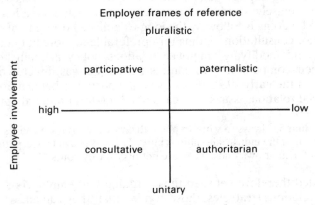

Figure 3.2 Managerial styles.

reference and relatively high levels of employee involvement. Authoritarian managerial styles, on the other hand, are related to unitary frames of reference and low employee involvement. Consultative and paternalistic styles, in turn, are connected with unitary frames of reference and high employee involvement, and pluralistic frames of reference and low employee involvement respectively. As in all typological classifications these are 'pure' or 'ideal' types. In practice, managerial styles in industrial relations can vary within enterprises between different operational areas, locations or time. Each has specific implications for the ways employers manage industrial relations.

Finally, Purcell proposes four 'generic types of industrial relations' within organizations 'combining the two scales of formalisation and trust together.'[37] The four patterns he identifies are 'cooperative constitutionalism', 'adaptive cooperation', 'antagonistic constitutionalism' and 'uninhibited antagonism'. Co-operative constitutionalism combines high formalization of industrial relations and high trust between the parties; adaptive co-operation low formalization and high trust; antagonistic constitutionalism high formalization and low trust; and uninhibited antagonism low formalization and low trust.[38] Each pattern is, again, an 'ideal' type and patterns can vary over time. Each pattern results in differences in behaviour of the parties and in the industrial relations structures within which they operate. These include 'bargaining, consultation and communication, the operation of procedures, union organisation and attitudes, and management organisation and attitudes.'[39]

Strategies

Industrial relations strategies are defined as long-term goals developed by management *'to preserve or change the procedures, practice or results of industrial relations activities over time.'*[40] That some organizations have such strategies is based on a number of assumptions, for example: that corporate management usually determine overall strategies to achieve their corporate goals; that strategic thinking is necessary for corporate success; that corporate leaders have some choice in the matter; and 'that choosing their industrial relations policies rationally implies they be linked to other objectives and policies.'[41]

In practice, of course, this may not always be the case. As Marsh concludes in his study of British manufacturing industry, there is considerable evidence indicating that boards of directors and top management prefer to react to industrial relations issues rather than producing explicit guidelines serving as 'a guide to day-to-day decision making both for themselves and for other levels of management.' What these managements appear to be doing is following the long-established tradition of *ad hoc* decision making after prior consultation, finding this 'preferable to more bureaucratic methods of determining and modifying employee relations policy at main board level and elsewhere in their companies.'[42] In contrast, when he was director of personnel at British Leyland in the early 1980s, Pat Lowry is reported as being a firm supporter of tackling industrial relations issues by means of a long-term rational approach:

> the important thing is always to work to plan, always know your objectives. You have to plan your way out of the industrial relations mire. Then you have to accept that the unions are in business for their own ends. They are not necessarily yours.[43]

Opinion is divided therefore between those arguing that employers do not generally have industrial relations strategies, those arguing that 'they can and should have such strategies and those who believe that, even if their managers do not recognize it, all organizations do have strategies.'[44]

Those managements developing strategic approaches to industrial relations appear to be influenced by a number of factors. These include: union strength; price competitiveness of their products; ratios of labour to capital costs; labour market trends; technology; and union policy and organization. It is argued, moreover, that strategic thinking in industrial relations is only credible:

- if the industrial relations strategy is justifiable by its relationship to a clear and acceptable business strategy;
- if there exists an effective organizational capacity for study and analysis of conditions, monitoring of effects of actions and explaining the rationality of the strategy in question;
- if there is considerable acceptance of the legitimacy of management and its control systems by employees;
- if top management have the educational training to allow them to attack problems in a systematic, detached, 'rational' fashion.

Given the structure of many large scale British organizations, however, these writers believe that it is difficult to develop strategic approaches within such enterprises. It is much easier doing it successfully, they argue, 'in a "green-field site" situation.'[45]

Policies

One of the first formal definitions of industrial relations policy was provided by the Commission on Industrial Relations (CIR). The CIR argued that a corporate industrial relations policy should form an integral part of the total strategy through which enterprises pursue their corporate objectives.

> In this way it will define the company's course of action with regard to particular industrial relations issues; it will also reflect the interaction of industrial relations with policies in other areas, such as production, marketing or finance.[46]

The CIR believed that since industrial relations takes account of all aspects of the relationship between employer and employees, a corporate policy on industrial relations should be conceived in the broadest possible way. Accordingly it recommended that such policies should cover trade union recognition, collective bargaining, grievance procedures and consultative arrangements 'and the broad range of employment policies all of which impinge on industrial relations.'[47]

Another definition of industrial relations policy is provided by Brewster, Gill and Richbell. They define it as:

> a set of proposals and actions which establishes the organization's approach to its employees and acts as a reference point for management. These proposals and actions are selected, either consciously or unconsciously, by those with formal authority in the organization.[48]

They distinguish between 'espoused policy' and 'operational policy'. Espoused policy incorporates the proposals, objectives and standards that top management state that they hold for dealing with employees and employment matters. Operational policy is the way senior management are seen to order industrial relations policies *vis à vis* other policies 'through the mechanisms of restrictions, control and direction' which they impose on line management. Operational policy, they claim, is the way that senior management control the organization 'and, crucially, through the control, reward and punishment of line management.'[49]

Espoused policy and operational policy can differ. Espoused policy, for example, is narrower and more dynamic than operational policy. Moreover, where they differ, it is argued, 'line management will in effect follow the operational policy.' This means in practice that it is operational policy which is experienced by the workforce 'and it is that and their response to it that determines industrial relations, not the espoused policy.' It is operational policy which has the 'greater long-term effect on the quality of industrial relations, while the espoused policy tends to have less effect.'[50]

Brewster and his colleagues also distinguish between the roles performed by different managerial groups in creating and executing industrial relations policies. The 'instigators' determine industrial relations policy and are normally a small core of senior managers which may or may not include personnel specialists. They determine not only espoused policy but also operational policy, though they are rarely aware of doing the latter. It is their values which are indicated to those down the managerial hierarchy 'by the control systems, the areas which are monitored and the kinds of performances that are rewarded or punished.' In practice, lower managers 'adapt their behaviour to conform with their perception of the operational policy, rather than the espoused policies.'[51]

The 'implementers' are the main body of the managerial hierarchy 'and it is their actions, or lack of action, which reflect the operational policy'. Operational policy, it is claimed, develops largely in response to line management's assessments of the wishes of their superiors. Line managers gain an understanding of operational policy as they are 'rewarded, punished, well thought of, or reprimanded'. There is a third group, the 'facilitators', who are industrial relations specialists. They advise and assist in the implementation of industrial relations policy but are also members of one or other of the two main groups. Where the instigators are involved in decisions implementing major change in industrial relations policy, 'the facilitators may become more visible and active as a small group.' Also differences between their functions and those of the people who will implement the policy 'may become more visible and obvious'[52] in relation to it.

3.6   MOTIVATION AND EMPLOYEE INVOLVEMENT

Managers have continuously sought a legitimation of their work role by subordinate employees and a degree of employee commitment to the processes of work, consistent with high output, low costs and the absence of industrial conflict.

> At various times and places they have asserted that compliance was owed to the superior social status of masters, the absolute rights of property ownership, the inherent prerogatives of the managerial function, or to the businessman's special skills and initiative in the production of goods and services.[53]

To secure such compliance by their subordinates, management has adopted a variety of strategies. These range from coercion and force, on the one hand, to more subtle and manipulative methods of work control on the other.

The latter include, for example, scientific management techniques, the development of social skills associated with the so called 'human relations' movement and the 'industrial welfare' school. The welfare approach for example, although not extensively used today except by sophisticated paternalist employers, is concerned with the comfort and attractiveness of working conditions, canteen facilities, employee counselling, sports and social clubs, low-cost housing and so on. More recently, in the 1960s and early 1970s, a few managements were influenced by the ideas and methods of the behavioural sciences, for instance in the use of participative styles of management and in the application of job enlargement and job enrichment techniques, many of which were imported from the United States. Motivating and controlling subordinate employees, however, remain major problems for management today.

Motivating employees

A central feature of all managers' jobs is to improve the work performance of their subordinates. The objective of improving work performance lies in the goals of the department, the work location or the organization. These goals may include reducing labour costs, improving a service of increasing the quantity or quality or work output. Although the problem of improving work performance is mainly a line management task, the personnel specialist usually has the training and the background to guide the line manager in this complex area. As shown in figure 3.3, this concern with performance improvement may be viewed from three linked but relatively discrete vantage points. First, work performance may be improved by developing the ability of employees to do their jobs better. This necessitates, in the first instance, finding and allocating the most suitable people to do the work. It is the purpose of an organization's recruitment, selection and personnel allocation procedures to do these tasks. Improving the knowledge and skills of those already employed is the purpose of its training and development programmes.

Second, work performance may also be improved by altering the content of the job, the methods employed to do it, or the immediate work environment in which the job is

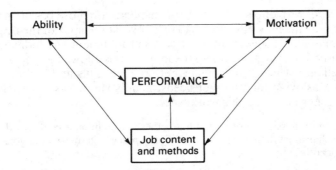

Figure 3.3 Factors influencing performance improvement.

done. The techniques of job design associated with work simplification, ergonomics and human factor engineering, for example, are directed towards these ends. The third major factor affecting work performance is the motivation or commitment of employees towards their job tasks. The essence of the problem from the employer's and the manager's viewpoint is how to identify and manage those factors which cause individuals and workgroups to increase or decrease the effort put into their work.

Early theories of employee motivation viewed the problem in uni-dimensional terms. The scientific management movement, for example, saw motivation in essentially economic terms: select the most efficient work methods, its supporters claimed, and this will secure the maximum economic prosperity for employer and employees alike. Scientific management had at its very foundation the firm conviction 'that it is possible to give the workman what he most wants – high wages – and the employer what he wants – a low labor cost – for his manufactures.'[54] The human relations school, on the other hand, believed social factors within the workgroup to be the major determinants of employee motivation.

> The study of the bank wiremen showed that their behaviour at work could not be understood without considering the informal organization of the group and the relation of this informal organization to the total social organization of the company.[55]

One result of the human relations approach was the concentration of organizational research upon the social dynamics of small group behaviour at work. Because of this, it tended to neglect the effects of technology, pay structures and the interaction of organizations with their external environments on employee motivation and work performance.

It was not until the 1940s and 1950s that it became widely recognized that the problems of human motivation generally, and of employee motivation specifically, were more complex than those which earlier theorists had believed. Abraham Maslow, an American psychologist, for example, argued that people's behaviour is centred around a series of psychological needs arranged in a hierarchy of intensity. 'There are at least five sets of goals, which we may call basic needs. These are briefly physiological, safety, love, esteem, and self-actualization.'[56] The satisfaction of one set of needs at a given level, he argued, leads to attempts to satisfy additional needs at the next higher level and so on. Once a need is attained, it no longer remains a major motivating force, although if it ceases to be satisfied it re-emerges. In the workplace, for example, 'safety' or 'security' needs are concerned with security of employment, a fair level of payment and freedom from arbitrary action from management.

Once such safety needs have been adequately satisfied, Maslow suggested, an individual's 'love' or 'social' needs are released and these too require to be satisfied. These are based on the need to affiliate with others, to communicate with them and to interact at a personal level with one's fellows. 'Esteem' needs are those based on the desire for an acceptable self-image, whilst 'self-actualization', at the apex of the needs hierarchy, is related to a person's concern for emotional self-fulfilment and individual creativity. These are satisfied, it is argued, where the individual is allowed to perform at a level of personal excellence which brings his or her creative skills and abilities into play. In short, by the Maslovian hierarchy of needs, man is viewed as a perpetually wanting animal, both generally and in his work roles.

> Any thwarting or possibility of thwarting of these basic human goals, or danger to the defenses which protect them, or to the conditions upon which they rest, is considered to be a psychological threat.[57]

The theory of a hierarchy of needs forms the basis of the motivation–hygiene analysis of Herzberg. The latter's research found the motivating factors or 'satisfiers' in a job to be those elements deriving from the job content and offering intrinsic rewards at work. The factors which are extrinsic and do not motivate employees, he suggested, derive from the job context. These are the hygiene factors which he saw as potential 'dissatisfiers'. Whilst their absence causes dissatisfaction, he argued, their presence does not act as a positive motivating force on individual workers. In further developing the ideas of Maslow, Herzberg not only gave emphasis to the personal, egotistical and self-actualization needs of people at work, but also saw work as a means of individual fulfilment, personal growth and goal achievement for employees.

By the 1960s, the behavioural sciences had become firmly established as important sources of managerial thinking on the problems of motivation and of employee commitment to work, especially in the United States. Douglas McGregor, for example, in line with the views of human behaviour developed by social scientists like Maslow, found it difficult to accept the traditional assumptions held by management about employee orientation to work. He believed that it is managerial assumptions about controlling labour resources which determine the climate of organizational relationships. He argued that the traditional concept of management is based on the assumption that the direction and control of an organization and its employees should be determined by management alone. This approach reflects a set of assumptions about human motivation which McGregor called 'Theory X'. These include, he said, assumptions that the average human being dislikes work, will avoid it if he or she can, prefers to be directed rather than self-directed at work and has relatively little occupational ambition. Theory X also assumes:

> *Because of this human characteristic of dislike of work, most people must be coerced, controlled, directed, threatened with punishment to get them to put forth adequate effort towards the achievement of organizational objectives.*[58]

McGregor proposed an alternative theory, 'Theory Y'. This is based on quite different assumptions about human behaviour which he felt were more in accord with behavioural science knowledge about human activity. These assumptions were that people do not inherently dislike work and that they welcome self-direction and self-control in the service of work objectives to which they are committed, providing that there are adequate rewards associated with their achievement. The most significant of these rewards, he believed, is the satisfaction of ego and self-actualization needs. Theory Y further assumes that the average human being not only accepts but also, in the right conditions, seeks job responsibility and that the capacity to exercise ingenuity and creativity in solving organizational problems is widely distributed throughout the working population. Unfortunately. 'the conditions of modern industrial life give only limited opportunity for these relatively dormant human needs to find expression.'[59]

In McGregor's analysis, the central principle of management and motivation deriving from the assumption of Theory X is that the direction and control of employees and of their work situations should be exercised through managerial authority alone. The assumptions of Theory Y, on the other hand, point to the principle of integrating individual and organizational needs at work. This suggests that individuals can best achieve their own goals within an organization by directing their work efforts towards the achievement of organizational objectives. In postulating Theories X and Y, however, McGregor was merely identifying a range of ideas about people and motivation at work and appropriate managerial styles for handling them. He did not see these theories as managerial strategies in themselves, but as underlying beliefs about the nature of humankind which influence managers in adopting a particular strategy when managing subordinates.

Another American behavioural scientist who has taken up the theme of integrating individual and organizational needs at work is Chris Argyris. His main focus has been on the effect of the work environment on the personal development of the individual. In his view, most organizations are run in ways which inhibit the realization of the individual's full potential at work. He sees the importance of developing individuals to their highest levels of psychological maturity. In this way, the total potential of their psychological energies can be released to the benefit of the organization and the individual's self-image. Unfortunately interpersonal incompetence amongst individuals in work organizations together with their organizational characteristics, he argues, prevent people becoming mature in outlook. Argyris insists that effective management must aim at the full development of the individual and at authentic interpersonal relationships and coherent organization. He advocates, for example, organizational structures which are flexible and project based and where managerial relationships are as between peers rather than hierarchical.

It is apparent from what has been said about the motivational theories described so far that at least two common themes seem to run through them. The first is that if management wants to achieve a realistic balance between meeting the needs of the individual and those of the organization which it manages, it is necessary to develop an appropriate organizational climate. This implies the necessity of structuring organizations so that employees can develop and mature as individuals and as members of groups, whilst at the same time working for the success of the enterprise itself. Related to this theme is another: although a number of factors determine the climate within an organization, the prevailing influence is the way in which people behave individually and in groups as leaders and followers. An example of this is to be found, for instance, in the writings of the American social psychologist, Rensis Likert. In his view, the behavioural patterns of managers and their approach to their relationships with the employees whom they control are fundamental to job performance and job satisfaction. In other words, the motivation of people at work is directly related to leadership styles and to the organizational environment.

Likert's researches have sought to establish the nature of the relationship between management styles, work performance and job satisfaction in the managed group. His findings have shown that departments which are low in efficiency tend to be run by managers who are 'job centred' and exert constant pressure on subordinates to achieve high output. Departments which attain high performance levels, on the other hand, tend to be run by managers who are 'employee centred'. These managers concentrate on building effective workgroups which are set high achievement goals. Such managers are more concerned with work targets rather than with work methods. They also allow maximum participation to their subordinates in the decision making process. In his researches, Likert identified four main styles or 'systems' of management. Of these, he suggests, 'System 4' – 'Participative Group Management' – generally produces higher productivity, greater involvement of individuals and better labour-management relations than the other three systems. He maintains that this leadership style should provide the following: adequate economic rewards for employees; decision-making through group processes; open communication channels; and close personal understanding between superiors and subordinates. To facilitate this, Likert argues, organizations should be structured as a series of overlapping groups linked by people who are members of more than one group.

Having outlined some of the principal 'psychologically universalistic' or neo-human relations theories of work, we should point out that these behavioural interpretations of work and employee motivation are to a large extent managerially orientated in their analyses. However, from the industrial relations viewpoint and from the sociological perspective, they are somewhat limited in their explanations of certain types of employee behaviour and some aspects of employer–employee relations. First, human relations theorists take a relatively narrow view of the nature of industrial conflict. Although contemporary theorists adopt a more realistic view of industrial conflict compared with the early human relations writers like Mayo and his colleagues, they continue to emphasize that conflict should be dealt with on a problem solving pattern within enterprises rather than on a distributive bargaining basis. By this analysis, conflict resolution at work between management and employees is still viewed in terms of improving interpersonal relations and the importance of collective bargaining is rarely acknowledged.

Second, most of the behavioural theories which have been described are prone to underplay the importance of organizational variables, like workplace culture, trade union organization and social class differences which are not directly amenable to change by management.

> As a consequence they tend to underrate the intractability of industrial conflict and take a correspondingly optimistic view of the prospects for achieving intra-organizational harmony and unity of purpose.[60]

In short, behavioural theories fail to consider power and ideology in industrial relations. Third, the prescriptions of the neo-human relations approach also underestimate the role of technology as a determinant of workplace behaviour. The general conclusions of behavioural research suggest that employees seek greater involvement in their work tasks and good relations among themselves and with management, irrespective of the technology involved. Amongst other things, however, the Luton studies by Goldthorpe and his colleagues concluded that certain types of technology preclude the possibility of job enrichment and increased participation in the job. Accordingly, such workers have a purely calculative and instrumental attitude towards their jobs and become preoccupied with high financial rewards and pay incentives at work. The growing recognition amongst other social scientists of the importance of technology on workplace behaviour has far reaching implications for managerial industrial relations policies. Production line technologies, for instance, may give little scope for enriching jobs or improving the quality of human relations at plant level.

The human relations approach to improving industrial behaviour and efficiency also 'makes a series of assumptions about motivation which cannot objectively be either proved or disproved.'[61] Such phrases as 'good communications', 'job enrichment', 'participative management', 'sensitivity training', and 'team leadership' have become an integral part of the vocabulary of influential areas of British management in recent years. But their long term beneficial effects in reducing industrial conflict, improving employee morale, and raising organizational productivity have yet to be proved.

If these theories are taken in isolation, they are unlikely to contribute to our understanding of employee motivation. In focussing on the job context and on the intrinsic rewards of work, they ignore the bargaining context between management and unions and the role of extrinsic rewards at work. Some British research indicates that human relations theories and the instrumental orientation approach of the 'action theorists' like Goldthorpe and his colleagues can *both* contribute to a better understanding of the complexities of employee behaviour and of job motivation within the workplace. By this view, it has been suggested, it is only when attention is focused on both the job contexts and the bargaining contexts at work, together with the different priorities and attitudes characteristic of each, that workgroup behaviour can be adequately analysed. Although the contexts vary according to managerial styles, organizational structures, payment systems and different technologies, for instance, it is claimed that there is a spectrum of attitudes towards management and job motivation. Certain employees are in the middle of that spectrum and seek both extrinsic and intrinsic rewards from work, 'with the one becoming salient in one context and the other in another. Equally they see both areas of common and conflicting interests with management in different contexts.'[62] Whether in these circumstances a rise in demand for greater intrinsic rewards in their work by employees can abate the demand for higher material rewards for their work or for more power sharing with management has yet to be demonstrated.

Such findings accord with the view that the strength and intensity of employee motivation at work is strongly related to the rewards which people expect from attaining desired goals in their jobs. Obviously the choice of these goals and the value placed on a particular set of rewards are highly individual. Furthermore, they are not always amenable to employee control. They depend upon the nature of the work tasks, the organizational structure and the technology involved. But the important point which 'expectancy theory' makes is that any movement towards improved performance by employees is influenced by two main factors. The first is the probability that work rewards depend on effort and that effective performance by employees will result in given rewards. The second is the value of the rewards perceived by individual workers. A job's intrinsic rewards are seen to be those stemming from the performance of the job or from its tasks by individual employees, whilst its extrinsic rewards are regarded as those external to individuals and are found in the job situation. These are often determined collectively, such as pay, payments systems, working conditions and so on.

Effort and improved performance at work are viewed by 'expectancy' theorists, then, as being related to the rewards in work, the rewards for working, and the likelihood that these rewards derive from contributing a certain level of effort by the employees concerned. Such an approach is compatible with the possibility that some employees will seek collective means to maximize their extrinsic rewards in performing their job tasks, and will contribute a certain level of work effort to achieve these. But there is no reason to expect that these employees will not seek to optimize their job satisfaction at work, through also demanding appropriately structured working methods where this is possible.

Employee involvement

Another managerial approach aimed at developing the work commitment of employees is the device of 'employee involvement'. This is defined as the various means used 'to harness the talents and co-operation of the work-force in the common interests they share with management.'[63] Employee involvement must be distinguished from 'industrial democracy' and 'worker participation'. The aim of industrial democracy, for example, is normally the extension of managerial power sharing in enterprises by a strengthening of the trade union organization and by widening the scope of collective bargaining. Employee participation goes still further. It aims at changing the basic authority structures of enterprises, especially private ones, by legislating for employee representation on company boards as practised in some parts of west Europe.

In outline, employee involvement, industrial democracy and worker participation provide contrasting perspectives on the nature of work enterprises and their systems of managerial control and employee commitment. Together they provide the interface between three areas of enterprise authority and decision making. These are: those where employers and management are prepared to share decisions with or devolve them to employees or their representatives; those where employees expect to influence or share decisions with employers; and those where the law gives rights to employees or places restrictions on managerial power and authority. Employee involvement, by aiming to get the support and commitment of all employees in an organization to managerial objectives and goals, thereby reinforcing a sense of common purpose between management and employees, is essentially unitary in its purposes and its methods. It is defensive of the right to manage and the organizational status quo. It is, however, a set of industrial relations practices which some managements have turned to in the 1980s, in response to economic recession and the relative weakness of trade unionism.

There are a number of employee involvement practices. The main ones are: financial involvement, job involvement and employee communication and information. Financial involvement, for example, though not widespread in Britain, but more common in west Europe, is limited to the private sector. It takes the form of profit sharing or share options, aiming to give employees a capital stake in the enterprises in which they work. With profit sharing, distribution of surpluses is in cash or in shares, normally cash. With share option schemes, employees are authorized to buy shares at a fixed price, at some future period, or can allow their option to lapse.

One of the more common forms of employee involvement is job involvement. The main aim of job involvement is to enable subordinate employees to contribute to the ways in which their job tasks are organized and performed. In this way the job satisfaction of individual employees is raised and organizational effectiveness is enhanced. Various job involvement techniques are used. These include suggestion schemes, attitude surveys, job enlargement, job enrichment, job rotation, quality circles and autonomous workgroups. In practice, no single method of job involvement guarantees employee commitment or increased efficiency. Further, in implementing appropriate job involvement techniques, management needs to take account of a number of factors. These include

> managerial style, the effectiveness of the communications system, the adequacy of industrial relations procedures, the quality of supervision, the quality of the working environment and so on.[64]

Effective systems of employee communication and information are crucial to any scheme of employee involvement in order to increase trust between management and subordinates and improve industrial relations. Employees cannot be genuinely involved in any enterprise where communication and information channels are weak or non-existent. As the code of industrial relations practice states: 'management needs both to give information to employees and to receive information from them. Effective arrangements should be made to facilitate this two-way flow.'[65] An effective communication and information strategy normally requires a positive lead being given by policy level management. A wide variety of information can be communicated. The most basic information relates to the employee's immediate job, since a number of surveys show that information affecting the job tasks of employees are usually considered to be their most important priority. A comprehensive and integrated communication and information strategy, however, requires other corporate information to be made available to all employees, including supervisory and managerial staff.

This includes general, marketing and financial information, whilst the Confederation of British Industry stresses the importance of information relating to 'progress, profitability, plans, policies and people.' Further, whatever the form of communication used, it is recommended that it is 'provided regularly and systematically in a readily understandable form.'[66]

When employees enter into consultative and negotiating arrangements with management through their representatives, employee involvement shifts imperceptibly into employee representation. Although employee representation is a separate and different process from employee involvement in style and in content they are nevertheless related and are not necessarily incompatible with each other. Whereas employee involvement is unitary in its purposes and is normally centred on the interests and activities of individual employees or small workgroups, the major characteristics of consultation and negotiation are their pluralistic and collective nature. They normally take place at higher levels of enterprise decision making than do employee involvement practices.

Where management introduces or changes methods of employee involvement and employee representation in an enterprise, it needs to take a number of organizational factors into consideration. These include its history, managerial style, enterprise culture, technologies, size and type of workforce, union membership, market position, ownership, geographical location and so on. In general, involvement practices are largely directed towards maximizing consensus, trust and employee commitment in organizational goals. Whilst this can be true of consultative practices also, employee representation usually has different purposes and its impact on enterprises varies. Normally it aims at reconciling differences of interest between employers, employees and their representatives and is distributive and power based. Employee involvement, by contrast, is integrative and task centred.

3.7 SUMMARY

There is a wide variety of employing organizations in Britain producing the goods and services demanded by individuals, citizens and enterprises. Some have profit and revenue goals, others welfare and community ones. In some of them capital is owned privately, in others it is vested in public authorities. Enterprises may be classified as private businesses, public corporations, public services and voluntary bodies. In both the corporate and public sectors, there is a tendency for large scale enterprises to develop, employing considerable numbers of employees whose relationships with their employers are generally impersonal and bureaucratically controlled and administered.

Today the employment relationship between employer and employee, although more liberalized than that between master and servant in the past, remains in essence one of power and subordination. Increasingly employers are abstract legal entities and corporate bodies providing one party to the employment contract which itself remains rooted in the common law, even though employees now have a series of important statutory employment and job protection rights provided by Parliament.

The effective and efficient managing of modern complex enterprises is the responsibility of professional managers who are themselves employees. Although managerial work has traditionally been viewed as rational, planned and, by some, value free, recent research suggests that managerial tasks and activities are fragmented and reactive rather than cohesive and proactive. It is also apparent, with the growth in size of private enterprises and the diffusion of their capital ownership, that it is senior managers who direct and control them, not enterprise shareholders. In the public sector too, managerial cadres generally control and deploy the human and physical resources for which they are responsible in order to fulfil corporate objectives, though their accountability is more clearly regulated by their political paymasters.

Managerial roles are differentiated by vertical status and horizontal specialism. Vertically there is a hierarchical separation of decision taking and action taking, whilst horizontal tasks and activities are segmented by a managerial division of labour based on functional expertise and skills. General management is a senior managerial task which co-ordinates and integrates functional specialisms within enterprises.

In managing industrial relations management's key function is the personnel one, the central personnel objective being to incorporate the labour or human resource co-operatively into the enterprise. The personnel function, however, is a problematic and ambiguous managerial area. First, it is split between line management and the specialist staff function with no general agreement about which tasks have line or staff responsibility. Second, personnel management incorporates both a welfare and a control role within enterprises, with role conflict within the personnel function sometimes generated because of this ambivalence. Third, there are differences within the professional personnel role itself, with senior personnel 'generalists' having strategic and analytical tasks and junior personnel 'specialists' more instrumental and passive ones.

The managing of industrial relations has become increasingly standardized and regularized in larger private and public enterprises in comparison with when the Donovan Commission reported. The Royal Commission was generally critical of the way in which company boards and senior management tended to neglect industrial relations management and personnel policy. For a number of reasons, some managements are now adopting a more proactive approach to industrial relations management and employment matters; but not all of them.

In dealing with industrial relations in a professional and skilled manner, employers and management evolve and develop particular styles, strategies and policies affecting subordinate managers and other employees. Managerial styles are classified in a number of ways such as 'traditional', 'classical conflict', 'sophisticated modern', 'standard modern', 'continuous challenge' and 'sophisticated paternal' patterns. Each one has its implications for managerial, union and employee behaviour. Another typology identifies four major managerial styles in industrial relations based on employer frames of reference and levels of employee involvement. These are described as the participative, paternalistic, consultative and authoritarian modes.

Managerial industrial relations strategies are defined as long-term plans aimed at influencing industrial relations activities over time. Although the evidence about managerial commitment to strategic thinking in industrial relations is contradictory, some company boards and managerial leaders now accept the critical relationship between business success, corporate strategy and industrial relations planning. Shorter term industrial relations policies, aimed at defining courses of action on particular employment issues, have been distinguished as espoused policy and operational policy respectively. Espoused policy states managerial intentions in dealing with employees and employment matters. Operational policy, which can differ from espoused policy, is the way that senior management actually control the organization and reward and punish line management when they implement policy decisions through their subordinates.

A distinction is also made between policy instigators, implementers and facilitators. Instigators determine espoused and operational policy, implementers are the main body of the managerial hierarchy whose actions reflect operational policy, whilst the facilitators or industrial relations specialists advise and assist in the implementation of policy. They are also members of one or other of the two main groups.

A major problem for management within large-scale organizations is how to motivate subordinate employees towards greater effort and commitment to managerial objectives. Early theories of motivation were both simplistic and reductionist in their approach. More recently, a series of complex behavioural theories have been proposed. They argue, first, the need to integrate individual and organizational goals at the workplace; second, the importance of participative leadership styles of management; and third, the necessity to gear job rewards to the effort and expectations of employees. The behaviouralists take an optimistic and a narrow view of industrial conflict and they underestimate the impact of technology and of collective bargaining on employee and workgroup behaviour. But there are some workers who are satisfied with purely instrumental ends at work. There is also evidence to suggest that certain employees seek both high job satisfaction and high extrinsic rewards in performing their job tasks.

Another approach which management adopt to control and motivate subordinate employees is employee involvement. Employee involvement, as distinct from power sharing or participatory practices, aims to solicit the maximum support and commitment of all employees to managerial goals and objectives and to reinforce a sense of common purpose between employer and employees. There are various types of involvement including financial involvement, job involvement and employee communication and information. These employee relations practices shade into employee representative systems such as consultation and negotiation but have different aims and objectives. Employee involvement is integrative, unitary and task based, whilst employee representation tends to be distributive, pluralistic and power based.

3.8 REFERENCES

1. G. Thomason, *A Textbook of Personnel Management*, 4th ed., Institute of Personnel Management, London, 1981, p. 9.
2. D. Butler and A. Sloman, *British Political Facts 1900–1979*, 5th ed., Macmillan, London, 1980, p. 363.
3. G. Thomason, *A Textbook of Personnel Management*, Institute of Personnel Management, London, 1975, p. 75.
4. *Ibid.*, p. 87.
5. J. Jones, the Dimbleby lecture 1977, 'The human face of labour', *The Listener*, 8 December 1977, p. 742.
6. Office of Population Censuses and Surveys, *Census 1981. National Report. Great Britain Part 2*, HMSO, London, 1983, p. 6.
7. A. Crichton, *Personnel Management in Context*, Batsford, London, 1968, p. 49.
8. H. Mintzberg, *The Nature of Managerial Work*, Prentice Hall, New Jersey, 1973.
9. R. Stewart, The nature of management? A problem for management education, *Journal of Management Studies*, vol. 21(3) 1984, p. 326.
10. J. Hunt, *Managing People at Work*, Pan, London, 1981, p. 173.
11. D. Farnham, *Personnel in Context*, Institute of Personnel Management, London, 1984, p. 22.
12. R. Mansfield, M. Poole, P. Blyton and P. Frost, *The British Manager in Profile*, British Institute of Management, London, 1981, p. 116.
13. Farnham, *op. cit.*, p. 23.
14. Thomason (1981), *op. cit.*, p. 17.
15. A.D. Chandler and H. Daems (eds.), *Management Hierarchies*, Harvard University Press, London, 1980, p. 1.
16. Institute of Personnel Management, *The Institute of Personnel Management*, IPM, London, 1980, p. 1.
17. D. Barber, *The Practice of Personnel Management*, Institute of Personnel Management, London, 1982, p. 8.
18. K. Legge, *Power, Innovation and Problem Solving in Personnel Management*, McGraw-Hill, London, 1978, p. 26.

19. H.A. Turner, G. Roberts and D. Roberts, *Management Characteristics and Labour Conflict*, Cambridge University Press, Cambridge, 1977, p. 71.
20. E. Batstone 'What have personnel managers done for industrial relations?' *Personnel Management*, June 1980, p. 39.
21. Royal Commission on Trade Unions and Employers' Associations, *Report*, HMSO, London, 1968, p. 120.
22. *Ibid.*, p. 45.
23. Department of Employment, *Industrial Relations Code of Practice*, HMSO, London, 1977, p. 4.
24. J.T. Winkler, The ghost at the bargaining table: directors and industrial relations, *British Journal of Industrial Relations*, July 1974, pp. 193 and 201.
25. A. Marsh, *Managers and Shop Stewards*, Institute of Personnel Management, London, 1973, p. 172.
26. A. Marsh, *Employee Relations Policy and Decision Making*, CBI, London, 1982, p. 62.
27. *Ibid.*, p. 187.
28. *Ibid.*, p. 219.
29. K. Sisson, 'Changing strategies in industrial relations', *Personnel Management*, May 1984, p. 27.
30. A. Marsh (1982), *op. cit.*, p. 203.
31. A. Fox, *Beyond Contract: Work, Power and Trust Relations*, Faber and Faber, London, 1974 pp. 297–310.
32. *Ibid.*, p. 302.
33. J. Purcell, 'Management control through collective bargaining: a future strategy' in K. Thurley and S. Wood (eds.), *Industrial Relations and Management Strategy*, Cambridge University Press, Cambridge, 1983, p. 53.
34. J. Purcell, *Good Industrial Relations*, Macmillan, London, 1981, p. 82.
35. Fox, *op. cit.*, p. 308.
36. *Ibid.*, p. 311.
37. Purcell (1981), *op. cit.*, p. 61.
38. *Ibid.*
39. *Ibid.*, p. 68.
40. K. Thurley and S. Wood 'Business Strategy and Industrial Relations Strategy' in K. Thurley and S. Wood (eds.), *op. cit.*, p. 198.
41. *Ibid.*, p. 199.
42. A. Marsh (1982), *op. cit.*, p. 219.
43. Quoted in *The Guardian*, 10 July 1980.
44. K. Thurley and S. Wood, 'Introduction' in K. Thurley and S. Wood (eds.), *op. cit.*, p. 2.
45. *Ibid.*, p. 223.
46. Commission on Industrial Relations, *Report No. 34. The Role of Management in Industrial Relations*, HMSO, London, 1973, p. 4.
47. *Ibid.*, p. 5.
48. C.J. Brewster, C.S. Gill and S. Richbell, Industrial relations and policy: a framework for analysis in K. Thurley and S. Wood (eds.), *op. cit.*, p. 62.
49. *Ibid.*, p. 64.
50. *Ibid.*, p. 71.
51. *Ibid.*, p. 70.
52. *Ibid.*, pp. 70f.
53. A. Fox, *Man Mismanagement*, Hutchinson, London, 1974, p. 35.
54. F.W. Taylor, *Scientific Management*, Harper and Row, London, 1964, p. 10.
55. F.J. Rothlisberger and W.J. Dickson, *Management and the Worker*, Harvard University Press, Cambridge, 1939, p. 551.
56. A.H. Maslow, A theory of human motivation, *Psychological Review*, May 1943, p. 394.
57. *Ibid.*, p. 395.
58. D. McGregor, *The Human Side of Enterprise*, McGraw-Hill, New York, 1960, p. 34.
59. *Ibid.*, p. 39.
60. T. Kempner, K. MacMillan and K. Hawkins, *Business and Society*, Allen Lane, London, 1974, p. 73.

61. K. Hawkins, *Conflict and Change*, Holt, Rinehart and Winston, London, 1972, p. 38.
62. W.W. Daniel, Understanding employee behaviour in its context: illustrations from productivity bargaining, in J. Child (ed.), *Man and Organization*, Allen and Unwin, London, 1973, p. 61.
63. Granada Guildhall Lectures, *The Role of Trade Unions*, Granada, London, 1980, p. 23.
64. Institute of Personnel Management, *Practical Participation and Involvement. 3 The Individual and the Job*, IPM, London, 1982, p. 189.
65. Department of Employment, *op. cit.*, p. 14.
66. Confederation of British Industry, *Communication with People at Work*, CBI, London, 1977, pp. 12 and 22.

4

Employers' Associations

Just as employees join trade unions to protect their collective interests against employers and management, so employers have formed and join their own organizations to defend their collective interests, not only against trade unions but also for more general purposes. These bodies, being collectivities of organizations rather than of people, are often described as employers' associations. Like trade unions they are diverse institutions. A few are concerned solely with industrial relations issues, whilst others engage only in trading and commercial matters. Many of them participate in both industrial relations and trading activities to varying degrees. The Trade Union and Labour Relations Act 1974 defines employers' associations as any body which:

> consists wholly or mainly of employers or individual proprietors of one or more descriptions and is an organisation whose principal purposes include the regulation of relations between employers of that description or those descriptions and workers or trade unions . . .

Employers' associations also consist of 'constituent or affiliated' associations, or their representatives, where their purposes include regulating relations between employers and their workers or trade unions.[1]

4.1   ORIGINS AND GROWTH

Employers' associations, like trade unions, have a long history. Although it is difficult to specify the first informal groupings of employers which were created, there is some evidence to indicate that formal organizations of employers, or 'masters' as they were then described, were established in certain trades as early as the eighteenth century. There were some early associations or combinations among master printers, master shipwrights and cotton employers, for example. Other examples of early organization amongst employers include the London Master Builders in the 1830s, the Mining Association of Great Britain, formed in 1854, the North of England Ironmasters of the 1860s, and the Amalgamated Weavers Association in the cotton industry after 1884. These employers' associations, certainly until the last years of the nineteenth century, had two main characteristics. First, they were invariably small scale local bodies limiting their activities to particular regions or towns. Second, they were frequently unstable organizations which emerged to deal with a specific industrial relations problem facing their members, such as an industrial dispute, and then lying dormant again when this had been resolved.

It was not until the growth of the new unionism after 1889, and the impact which this had on the activities of certain trade unions, that the first national employers' associations were formed. These included the Shipbuilding Employers Federation in 1889, the Shipping Federation in 1890, the Federated Association of Boot and Shoe Manufacturers in 1891, the Federation of Master Cotton Spinners Associations, also in 1891, and the Employers Federation of Engineering Associations in 1896. This last named association, after enforcing a national lock-out which started over a union claim for an eight-hour day in London during 1897, became the Engineering Employers Federation (EEF) in 1899. These national associations had similar goals to those of the earlier local associations. Their main object was 'to keep a common line and help one another in resisting the unions, particularly to help one of their number who was singled out for union attack.'[2] The shipowners, for example, were particularly active against the closed shop.

These national associations were more securely based and more permanently established than their earlier, locally based predecessors. On the other hand, their emergence was somewhat surprising for British employers combined only reluctantly with one another and under pressure, uneasy in co-operation with their trading competitors. By 1914, however, a number of important associations in the staple trades had become firmly established, their main purpose being to constitute the employers' side of joint boards. The bargaining unit for wages and hours was 'generally delimited by district and occupation, but on grievance procedure and working practices there were some near industry-wide agreements.'[3]

By 1936, with the growth and extension of national collective bargaining in a number of key industries such as engineering, shipbuilding and building construction, it is estimated that there were about 270 national employers' associations dealing with employment matters and 'approximately 1,550 other employers' organizations consisting for the most part of local or regional branches of the national federations.'[4] In other words there were over 1 800 associations dealing with industrial relations issues between employers and unions at that time. By the late 1950s, the Ministry of Labour concluded that there were some 1 600 employers' associations in Britain, although it could not say precisely what proportion of these were national as distinct from local bodies. It did not believe, however, that the proportion had changed significantly since the mid 1930s.[5]

When the Donovan Commission reported in 1968, the Department of Employment and Productivity listed some 1350 employers' associations, ranging from the EEF covering 4 600 establishments and over two million employees to some very small associations in a section of an industry, in one locality. All of them were concerned directly or indirectly with negotiating wages and conditions of employment and many of them had trade association activities. At that time, according to the Confederation of British Industry, in many major industries federated firms employed some 80 per cent of the labour force, though in some industries the proportion was less than 50 per cent.[6]

From what has been described so far, it is clear that industrial action by trade unions has been a major factor persuading employers to create their own collective associations. Certainly in the late nineteenth century, employers' associations were established to protect the right of employers to manage and to organize production in their own enterprises without interference from the unions. More recently they have aimed, amongst other things, at preventing wage cutting in the labour market among competing employers. For some employers, multiemployer bargaining through employers' associations has been a protection against leap-frogging negotiating tactics by militant trade unions. Even today, in some relatively compact and uniform industries like footwear, furniture and shipping, for example, 'homogeneity in respect of technology, location, product market and labour market is very important'[7] in determining collective organization amongst employers. In short, a variety of historical, structural, institutional and economic factors has given rise to the need for employers' associations in different industries.

4.2   TYPES OF EMPLOYERS' ASSOCIATIONS

Table 4.1 shows that employers' associations are found in a wide variety of manufacturing and service industries throughout Britain. In 1983 there were 312 known employers' organizations, compared with 340 in 1979, with a total membership of 338 872 employers or local associations of employers. Some guide to the density of organization amongst employers is provided by the 1980 workplace industrial relations survey. This study of some 2 000 private and public establishments employing 25 or more employees shows that 27 per cent of all the establishments surveyed, including those in the public sector, were members of employers' associations. This comprised 56 per cent of all manufacturing establishments and 65 per cent of those in the construction industry. Membership in distributive and service sector establishments was much lower, varying between 11 and 33 per cent.[8]

Table 4.1 *Major employers' associations: number of members 1979–83.*

Association	1979	1980	1981	1982	1983
Engineering Employers Federation	18	19	18	19	19
West Midland Engineering Employers	1 210	1 227	1 125	958	886
Engineering Employers London Association	850	804	1 147	1 023	911
Engineering Employers West of England Association	454	443	404	387	361
Thirteen other Engineering Employers Associations	3 369	3 158	3 013	3 045[1]	2 808[1]
National Farmers Union	125 856	121 118	125 162	123 056	121 494
National Federation of Building Trades Employers	10 146	10 193	10 000	10 000	9 465
General Council of Shipping/ British Shipping Federation	229	219	213	205	177
Freight Transport Association	15 890	15 869	15 038	14 226	13 566
Test and County Cricket Board	19	19	19	19	19
Electrical Contractors Association	2 193	2 248	2 232	2 251	2 162
Chemical Industries Association	339	341	339	199	164
British Printing Industries Federation	3 178	2 801	2 650	2 508	2 606
Newspaper Society	293	288	282	281	277
Motor Agents Association	*	*	15 444	14 545	14 264
National Federation of Retail Newsagents	28 367	28 669	28 669	29 202	29 638
Road Haulage Association	15 045	14 117	12 732	11 726	11 277
Heating and Ventilating Contractors Association	1 185	1 211	1 193	1 194	1 192
British Paper and Board Industry Federation	109	99	84	74	69
Federation of Civil Engineering Contractors	518	508	481	467	444
Federation of Master Builders	20 328	20 251	20 118	20 087	20 059
National Pharmaceutical Association	*	*	*	*	6 977

Table 4.1 *continued*

Association	1979	1980	1981	1982	1983
National Association of British and Irish Millers	46	47	48	49	50
Dairy Trade Federation	4 400	4 500	4 500	4 500	4 100
Newspaper Publishers Association	10	12	12	12	11
Publishers Association	257	253	289	244	243
British Jewellery and Giftware Federation	2 035	2 027	1 951	1 715	1 661
National Farmers Union of Scotland	*	*	*	16 272	15 837
Cement Makers Federation	*	6	6	*	3
National Organization of Employers of Local Authorities professional staff	*	*	*	36	36
National Association of Master Bakers	*	*	*	*	3 949
Scottish Building Employers Federation	*	*	*	*	29
Builders Merchants Federation	*	*	*	*	911
Total of above associations	[25] 236 344	[26] 230 546	[27] 248 679	[28] 258 300	[33] 265 665
Total of other associations	[315] 56 759	[320] 113 675	[302] 105 095	[299] 81 113	[379] 73 207

[1] Fourteen in 1982 and 1983
* Figures not available
Source: *Annual Report of the Certification Officer*, (HMSO 1980–84)

The relatively high density of organization amongst manufacturing employers and establishments is confirmed by the University of Warwick's survey of manufacturing establishments in the winter of 1977–78. (The Warwick Survey 1977–78). This investigation, covering 970 establishments with 50 or more employees, showed that 75 per cent of the establishments surveyed were members of employers' associations. This varied between 71 per cent for mechanical and electrical engineering establishments to 82 per cent for textile establishments. Interestingly, foreign ownership appears only to have a slightly inhibiting effect, with '69 per cent of foreign-owned establishments being in employers' organisations compared with 75 per cent of the British.'[9] In the private sector, at least, establishments and employers are substantially more likely to be members of employers' associations where trade unions are recognized for manual employees.

Employers' associations differ widely in structure and organization in different industries. A useful classification is to categorize them into three main types. First, there are national federations to which local employers' associations, based on geographical areas, are affiliated. The Engineering Employers Federation, for example, consists of 19 local associations, each with its own member firms, covering over a million manual and staff employees in thousands of establishments. The largest local associations in the Federation are the London district, with about 1 000 member firms; the West Midlands, with over 900; and the West of England Association, with over 300. Similarly, the National Federation of Building Trades Employers, with about 10 000 member firms is organized into local associations and regions.

The second type of association is that having a single national body, like the Electrical Contractors Association, with local branches throughout the country. The Electrical Contractors Association has over 2 000 member firms, representing about 80 per cent of the companies and employees in the industry. These companies are organized into a number of branches and regions in England, Wales and Ireland. The third type of employers' association is the single association with a national coverage. These include the Co-Operative Employers Association, the Multiple Shoe Retailers Association, and the Multiple Food Retailers Employers Association. Other examples include the Federation of London Clearing Banks, the Federation of London Wholesale Newspaper Distributors, the Council for Local Education Authorities (CLEA), the Association of Metropolitan Authorities, and the Local Authorities Conditions of Service Advisory Board (LACSAB).

Of these, LACSAB is probably the most outstanding example of an employers' association operating in public industry. It is both a servicing agency and a negotiating agency, working on a variety of manpower and industrial relations issues on behalf of local government employers and is funded mainly through the rate support grant and the local authority provincial councils. In practice, its work and activities also extend to a number of other public organizations and charitable bodies outside local government. It is a somewhat unusual organization since other public sector industries rely heavily on small industrial relations secretariats to service their employer representatives rather than on a specialized employers' association like LACSAB. It was formed at the end of the second world war as a company limited by guarantee. Currently the Board comprises a number of leading local authority representatives, including those from the Association of County Councils (ACC), the Association of District Councils and the Association of Metropolitan Authorities (AMA). There are now some 30 negotiating bodies covered by its activities. These range in size from the local authorities national joint council for manual workers covering about a million employees to the joint council for coroners covering under 200. Other local authority negotiating groups using the services of LACSAB include those covering: chief executives; professional, technical and clerical staff; social workers; the police and fire services; and school teachers.

Besides LACSAB, CLEA, ACC and AMA, there are a number of other representative employers' associations in the local authority services. Examples include: the National Organization of Employers of Local Authorities Administrative Professional and Technical Services, one for manual workers and another for employers of new towns staff. There are also representative organizations of provincial employers, such as the South Western Provincial Employers of Local Authorities Services (manual workers) and that representing Northern Provincial Employers (manual workers).

4.3   ACTIVITIES

Employers' associations undertake three main activities on behalf of their members. First, they represent employers in their dealings with trade unions. Second, they give specialist assistance to their members by providing advisory and other services to their constituent enterprises and establishments. Third, employers' associations act as political and economic pressure groups *vis à vis* government, departments of state and the general public.

Industrial relations functions

In representing employer interests in their relations with trade unions, employers' associations take part in two activities: negotiating terms and conditions of employment with trade union representatives and the processing of disputes between employers and trade unions. This function is clearly set out, for example, in the objects of the National Federation of Building Trades Employers. It seeks, amongst other things:

To promote the formation of regularized methods of procedure in regard to:
    i. The negotiation and conclusion of agreements relating to wages, hours and other conditions of employment.
    ii. The adjustment of any differences arising out of the operation of such agreements.
    iii. The prevention of cessations of work pending such adjustment.
    iv. The adjustment of differences involving demarcation of work.
To settle any questions arising with trade unions or other labour organizations in connection with building works.[10]

Before 1914 collective bargaining, where it existed, took place mainly at district or regional level between local employers' associations and district union committees. During the first world war bargaining shifted to industry level, with some workplace bargaining. During the interwar period, industry-wide collective bargaining between national employers' associations and national trade unions became normal practice. In the period since 1945, initially workplace bargaining and more recently single employer bargaining have become common practices in parts of private industry, especially in the manufacturing sector. To some extent this has weakened the traditional bargaining role of some employers' associations. However, substantive agreements on pay and conditions and procedural agreements on negotiating arrangements between employers and trade unions continue to be concluded in some cases on an industry-wide basis in the first instance. Employers' associations, therefore, continue to play a part in these activities. Apart from the public sector, these substantive agreements largely determine minimum rates of pay rather than actual earnings. Individual employers, therefore, negotiate additional payments at company or workplace level with shop stewards, although even some elements of enterprise or workplace earnings – such as shift allowances, holiday payments, overtime premia and so on – are calculated on the basic rates laid down in national agreements. It is mainly non-pay conditions such as the length of the working week and holiday entitlements which are still standard elements, and these are often determined by national agreements between employers' associations and trade unions, with district agreements of virtually no importance.

National agreements on pay may be classified into three categories. First, there are minimum agreements where employers' associations and trade unions determine a decreasing proportion of enterprise or workplace earnings. In these industries, the gap or 'drift' between national agreements and local earnings is high. The second category is the comprehensive agreement. These agreements provide relatively little opportunity for earnings drift to occur. They also enable employers' associations and trade union officers – rather than managers and shop stewards – to play a substantial part in pay determination. Third, there are partial agreements. These are intermediate between minimum and comprehensive agreements, where nationally determined basic rates still have an important influence on employee earnings and on additional payments made at company or workplace level.

Industries where minimum multiemployer agreements apply include chemicals, engineering, hosiery and knitting, and rubber manufacturing. In the engineering industry, for example, the Engineering Employers Federation and the Confederation of Shipbuilding and Engineering Unions negotiate minimum rates, overtime and shift-work premia, holiday pay, minimum piecework standards and a framework of conditions for manual workers, covering length of the working week and holidays. Minimum conditions and procedural agreements are also negotiated for technicians, draughtsmen and clerical workers. In recent years, Federation policy has been to oppose across-the-board pay increases and to negotiate national minimum rates and standard conditions for manual workers, serving as safety nets around which member companies conclude their own enterprise or plant agreements with shop stewards and the unions. In the hosiery and knitting industry, it was the practice until the early 1960s to negotiate industry-wide piecework price lists. Since then management and union representatives have bargained piece rates and work loads at company and mill level. This is largely due to the changing economic and technological conditions of the industry. The policy of the Knitting Industries Employers Federation is to encourage mill bargaining and to confine national agreements to determining basic rates and standard conditions of employment in the industry.

Employers' associations continue to play a major part in the negotiation of comprehensive agreements in industries such as electrical contracting, port transport, and shipping. For many years, for instance, the joint industry board (JIB) in electrical contracting, comprising the Electrical Contractors Association and the Electrical Electronic Telecommunication and Plumbing Union, has graded the industry's manual workforce and determined standard wages rates. The reasons for these tightly controlled centralized agreements include: the labour intensive nature of the industry; the need for its firms' fixed labour costs to be known in advance; the practice of having long-term, fixed price contracts in the trade; and the large number of small firms in the industry which, without such agreements, might be subjected to leap-frog pay bargaining by the union. Because of these factors, the Electrical Contractors Association needs to have fairly strict centralized control over its members' pay negotiations and predicted labour costs. The traditional links between JIB rates and electrician's pay in related industries, however, appears to be weakening as recession and unemployment amongst electricians have reduced pay pressures 'and increased the influence of "economic factors" on earnings and settlements.'[11]

Industries having partial national agreements, which are neither as limited as minimum agreements nor as tight as comprehensive agreements, include cotton textiles, printing, construction and footwear manufacturing. In the footwear industry, a main agreement is negotiated between the British Footwear Manufacturers Federation and the National Union of the Footwear Leather and Allied Trades (NUFLAT) nationally. First, the National Joint Conference establishes minimum wage rates (traditionally index linked), hours of work and holiday entitlements. Second, at local level manufacturers and NUFLAT settle the framework for piecework prices in local boards of conciliation and arbitration for the many different operations in footwear manufacture. Additionally, some larger firms conclude enterprise or workplace agreements on job evaluation, shiftwork, productivity, sick pay and pensions.

The ways in which employers' associations handle disputes on behalf of their members vary between industries and associations. Cases fall into two categories, 'namely those disputes which concern the interpretation of a national agreement and those which arise out of domestic negotiations in the individual firm'.[12] From their earliest days, district and national procedures for avoiding disputes and resolving conflicts between employers and unions were negotiated in order to provide a framework of rules aimed at regulating relations between the parties. They were an attempt at resolving industrial conflict between employers and unions through conciliatory methods although, by the end of the nineteenth century, some procedures contained a quasi-judicial element too.

As they have developed, there are now usually three main levels in most national disputes procedures. First, there is the domestic level which often has a number of preliminary stages. The second level is the initial external stage, either through local or district machinery, although this too may have some substages. At this level, the employer is more likely to be represented by officers of its employers' association than by internal management. Finally, there is the highly formalized national level of the procedure, or the 'court' of last resort, where senior officers of the employers' association and the unions represent the parties. In some industries, there may be final recourse to external and binding arbitration if the dispute is not resolved between the parties at national level. In the paper and board industry, for example, the British Paper and Board Industry Federation regards the operation of the industry's external disputes procedure as so important to its member firms that more than 50 per cent of its time is devoted to maintaining the procedure on their behalf.

Advisory and other services

In their research for the Donovan Commission, Munns and McCarthy claim:

> Although the major effort of employers' associations' staff in their industrial relations activities is directed towards the negotiation of agreements and the settling of disputes in conjunction with trade union officials, there is present in all . . . an element in their service to members in which they act as consultants about individual problems.[13]

In the intervening years, the function of providing industrial relations advice to members is an aspect of employers' association activity which has expanded rather than declined. One reason is the development of enterprise and plant bargaining which has detracted from the traditional role of employers' associations as multiemployer negotiators at industry level. Another factor is the growing impact of employment legislation, especially since the 1970s. In these circumstances, and with their officers' specialist knowledge of industrial relations generally and of their own industries particularly, employers' associations are ideally placed to service their members' industrial relations requirements at employer and workplace level. This is particularly the case for smaller employers without the resources to employ their own personnel and industrial relations specialists, and even for larger enterprises which do have personnel specialists.

The services provided fall into two main categories: general and diagnostic. Most of their activities relate to requests by member firms for immediate help in their routine industrial relations problems or 'fire-fighting' activities. But some associations such as the Engineering Employers Federation and the Newspaper Society, for example, have specialist 'fire prevention' services for their members. The general services provided are wide-ranging. They include interpreting national agreements, introducing new payment systems, applying work study techniques, and setting up job evaluation schemes. Many associations also provide comprehensive statistics on earnings and manpower in their industries, although because of market pressures some employers are reluctant to share statistical information with their trading competitors. Other services provided by employers' associations include supervisory, management and industrial relations training, especially for small and medium sized employers. Advice on health and safety at work has also expanded in importance recently. Most employers' associations are obviously well placed to collect accident figures, disseminate safety information, and provide training for safety officers. Finally, answering legal inquiries and providing legal advice in employment matters are also a major activity of most employers' associations. In some industries, representation of their members before industrial tribunals is an important facility provided to member firms too.

Some useful evidence of the relative importance to private manufacturing establishments of the advisory services provided by employers' associations in the late 1970s is included in the Warwick Survey 1977–8. Table 4.2 suggests that the most common services obtained from these associations were legal advice, information on local pay levels and how to interpret government incomes policy. The next grouping centred around education and training and redundancy policy, with advice on recruitment, work study or bonus schemes, and job evaluation constituting a third cluster. It is also significant that most services were used more by large establishments than by small ones.

Table 4.2 *Utilization of employers' associations advisory services by industry and size. (As a percentage of establishments in association membership)*

	Recruitment information	Education and training	Labour legislation	Work Study or bonus schemes	Job evaluation	Redundancy policy	Local pay levels	Incomes policy
Engineering Employers	6	35	76	8	11	32	62	59
Other Engineering	2	41	51	28	16	47	30	41
Chemical Industries Association	5	11	31	17	8	46	28	29
Any Food etc.	1	16	37	9	10	24	33	33
Any Textiles	21	26	79	10	10	14	82	72
Any Clothing	12	45	65	48	36	43	52	52
Any Paper/Printing	24	45	72	32	23	36	62	64
Any Other	6	19	49	2	3	6	45	36
Number of 50–99	4	15	51	5	5	19	47	38
100–199	16	31	58	16	12	26	48	43
Full-time 200–499	9	37	61	11	11	22	56	52
500–999	7	49	72	13	15	17	54	59
Employees 1000+	14	42	75	13	15	24	62	68
ALL	9.0	27.1	57.4	9.9	9.2	21.6	50.4	44.8

Source: W. Brown (ed.), *The Changing Contours of British Industrial Relations* (Blackwell, 1981)

Representation

Employers' associations also fulfil representative functions. The National Farmers Union, for example, is possibly one of the most effective representative lobbies in Britain; it has representation in Parliament and the European Parliament and maintains strong links with agricultural policy makers in Whitehall and the European Economic Community. In general, employers' associations aim to influence the creation and application of social and economic policy affecting their members' interests at local, industry and central levels. Central government and local government are obvious targets, but so too are trade unions – especially in issues opposing employer interests and influencing public opinion. Representing employer interests collectively takes a variety of forms including telephoning and corresponding with government officials and other public servants, political lobbying, fund raising and political campaigns.

Employers' associations are also important sources of recruitment for individuals serving as employer representatives on various tripartite bodies created by governments in the post-war period. These include industrial tribunals, wages councils, the National Economic Development Council, Sector Working Parties and 'little Neddies'.

4.4 INTERNAL STRUCTURES AND ADMINISTRATION

Employers' associations are, like trade unions, diverse in their structure but, at the same time, have certain common features. One thing which they share is their low key approach in carrying out their functions. Employers' associations and their officers rarely seek publicity for their organizations or for themselves when working for their members. With few exceptions, they engage in their day-to-day activities as negotiators, conciliators, advisers and representatives, without courting public attention or attracting the media. In this way, they maintain their members' private interests without allowing them to become public issues. It is not always possible to do this as, for example, when their members are in dispute with the unions with which they negotiate. But nevertheless their preference is to run their internal affairs and to advance the interests of their members privately rather than publicly, confidentially rather than openly. For these reasons, it has been suggested that there is a certain 'clubbishness' surrounding the activities of employers' associations and their internal operations. In that this is derived from an identity of interest based on common goals and shared values among their members, together with an often narrow network of stable personal relationships with one another, this is probably true.

In their internal affairs, the structure of employers' associations is influenced by a number of factors, 'such as the geographical dispersion of the industry, the size distribution of member firms, and their product markets'.[14] It has to be remembered, for example, that many employers' associations originated as district and regional bodies among local employers. The employers' associations in building, construction, engineering and printing are typical examples of this. Their present organizational structures, like those of the unions with which they deal, are considerably influenced by their historical antecedents and local roots. Indeed some 75 per cent of present day employers' associations are local associations. Although national policies are formulated, agreed and implemented by members, there is also scope for local associations to deal with specific problems facing them and to take local initiatives in matters particularly affecting their members. In practice, the commitment of individual employers to 'association' or 'federation' policy is far less forcibly applied than in the trade unions. If one of the larger associations in the Engineering Employers Federation has the resources to develop an advisory service on work study for its members, for example, it does so without an agreement that all affiliated associations in the Federation should take the same action. Similarly, because of the relatively high levels of trade union organization and of local labour market pressures in certain of its areas, some regions of the National Federation of Building Trades Employers are more autonomous than others.

In other cases, the geographical location of an industry has a major influence on employer association structure and administration. In geographically concentrated industries like cotton textiles and furniture manufacturing, for example, the structural features of employers' associations differ widely from those found in more geographically dispersed industries like building construction and engineering. Similarly where an industry consists of a relatively small number of medium sized and large firms, employer co-operation in industrial relations is better organized nationally rather than locally, as in banking through the Federation of London Clearing Banks and in rubber manufacturing through the British Rubber Manufacturers Employers' Association. In other words, the relative importance of local and national associations, and the ways in which they are organized, varies considerably between industries. The autonomy of local associations varies greatly too, with local bodies affiliated to national federations having greater freedom and autonomy than the local branches of national associations. Finally, some employers' associations are organized on product lines which makes them, in effect, confederations of associations. An example of this is the Multiple Shops Federation which comprises a number of small specialist associations covering some sectors of the retail trade, although its industrial relations functions are fairly limited.

Employers' associations, then, are diversely structured. Each varies in the number of establishments it covers, the number of employees in member firms, and the ways in which it runs its affairs. Whilst it is likely that many employers are organized in those industries which have employers' associations, there are some important exceptions. It seems likely, for example, that employers which do not become members are usually very large or very small firms. Very large firms, like the car manufacturers in the engineering industry, often do not affiliate or federate because they have sufficient resources of their own to develop industrial relations expertise. In other cases, they either do not wish to be constrained by national agreements or they prefer to develop their own industrial relations policies. In recent years, for example BL Cars, Philips, the General Electric Company and the Rank Group have all left the EEF in order to disentangle themselves from direct involvement in national bargaining. Very small firms, on the other hand, frequently do not federate because they are non-unionized, or because they feel that they do not require the services provided by an employers' association. In other cases they do not join because they claim that they cannot afford the membership subscriptions involved.

Employers' associations usually obtain their main income from membership subscriptions rather than from investments. There is usually a small initial membership fee and subsequent annual subscriptions. A few have a flat rate subscription, with others basing subscriptions on the number of workers employed, the size of their wage bill or, in rare cases, capital employed. Rarely do subscriptions exceed 0.5 per cent of corporate wage bills. The main costs are staff and administration. Like trade unions, subscription income varies with the size and activities of an association, although it is probable that federations have the highest income. In some cases, as in engineering, electrical contracting and road haulage, employers' associations maintain special indemnity or strike funds out of which payments can be made to member organizations involved in industrial action. These are rarely used nowadays.

The structure of decision making within employers' associations is analogous to that within trade unions, although representing a firm is clearly different from representing trade unionists. 'It is a representative structure in which power to act is delegated to elected individuals from the ranks of the membership.'[15] In the larger associations, ultimate power is vested in the annual general meeting of members. However, a national council is often elected to determine policy, an executive committee or management board to support the main office holders – such as the association president and treasurer – and a number of standing committees concerned with particular aspects of the association's business. The individuals on these bodies are usually company directors or senior members of management within their firms. Employers' associations generally differ from trade unions, however, in the way in which decisions are taken within their meetings or committees. The preferred method is to arrive at a decision by consensus rather than by voting. It is considered that if policies have to be generally acceptable, majority voting can result in a substantial minority being dissatisfied. But there are exceptions to consensus taking, and membership voting is sometimes used to obtain a direct expression of views on crucial issues like the decision to lock out, for example. On these occasions when votes are taken, voting power is related to a member firm's wages and salary bill – as in engineering – not to the number of employees, or to its volume of output. But the general aim is to obtain a consensus of opinion within associations rather than to take a vote. Such decisions often serve as policy recommendations rather than being mandatory for all the employers in membership.

All the larger employers' associations employ full time officers with varying titles. Some of them mainly service internal committees and their elected office holders, whilst others principally act as professional representatives in dealings with member firms, the trade unions or public authorities. The number of full time officers employed by different associations depends on the range of activities and services provided by the organization. Many smaller associations often do not employ full time staff at all, they rely instead on the services of local firms of chartered accountants or solicitors to run them. Similarly, a number of locally based clothing, footwear, and provincial newspaper associations are serviced by their member firms, sometimes on a voluntary basis.

In the larger local and national associations, the executive staff is usually organized into specialist departments under the ultimate control of a Director or Director-General. There might be, for example, an industrial relations division, a legal section, an establishment department, an education and training department, and an economics division, with the association being headed by a Director and/or Secretary. Apart from specialized professional staff such as solicitors, accountants, economists and statisticians, large associations also employ specialist industrial relations officers. They come from a wide variety of backgrounds including management, the civil service, the local authority administration.

> In general, experience and qualifications are regarded as desirable rather than essential attributes of an applicant for employment; the essential thing is that he should be 'the right man for the job' in terms of personal qualities and mental, physical and intellectual capacity.[16]

4.5   SUMMARY

Some employers' associations, like some trade unions, have a long history and emerged in the nineteenth century on a district-by-district basis in response to trade union pressure. Most have been created and organized in reaction to trade union growth and activity; either to protect the right to manage; or to prevent wage cutting amongst employers; or to stop leap-frog pay bargaining by the unions.

nal and local employers' associations are found across a wide spectrum
ncluding some in the public sector. National associations may be
tional federations, national associations with branches, and single
Their activities include negotiating collectively for employers on pay,
ι dispute settlement. They also provide a range of specialist industrial
ιεlations services to their members. In negotiating multiemployer agreements with
trade unions, some employers' associations are concerned mainly with establishing
minimum agreements on pay and standard agreements on conditions. In other cases,
either comprehensive or partial agreements on pay are negotiated. The disputes arising
between employers and trade unions can be disputes of interpretation arising out of
national agreements between employers' associations and trade unions, or disputes of
interest arising out of local negotiations between managers and shop stewards at
enterprise or workplace level. Once a dispute is external to the firm, employers'
associations have an important role in processing them on behalf of their member
organizations. Such dispute settlement contains conciliatory, judicial and power
elements in the decision making process.

The advisory functions of employers' associations are becoming increasingly important especially regarding legal matters, pay issues and training. Associations also play
an important role in political lobbying and representing employer interests in wider
national and economic matters. In carrying out these activities, employers' associations
are essentially 'low key' organizations. They seek neither the limelight nor unnecessary
publicity in fulfilling their duties on behalf of member firms. Their internal structures
vary considerably according to the industry in which they are organized, their geographical location, the size of firms which they represent, and the products which their
members sell. It is generally very large and very small firms which tend not to join
employers' associations. As representative bodies, employers' associations prefer to
make decisions by consensus rather than by voting. When voting takes place, voting
power is usually related to a member's pay bill rather than to the number of workers it
employs. The policies of employers' associations, however, tend to act as guidelines for
members, compared with the more rigidly applied policy decisions of trade unions.

4.6   REFERENCES

1. Trade Union and Labour Relations Act 1974, c. 52, ss. 28(2).
2. E.H. Phelps Brown, *The Growth of British Industrial Relations*, Macmillan, London, 1965, p. xxvi.
3. *Ibid.*
4. Department of Employment and Productivity, *Industrial Relations Handbook*, (revised edition), HMSO, London, 1970, p. 14f.
5. *Ibid.*
6. Royal Commission on Trade Unions and Employers' Associations 1965–1968. *Report.* (Chairman Lord Donovan), HMSO, London, 1968, pp. 7 and 21.
7. Commission on Industrial Relations, *CIR Study 1. Employers' Organizations in Industrial Relations*, HMSO, London, 1972, p. 8.
8. W.W. Daniel and N. Millward, *Workplace Industrial Relations in Britain*, Heinemann, London, 1983, p. 120f.
9. W. Brown (ed.), *The Changing Contours of British Industrial Relations: a Survey of Manufacturing Industry*, Blackwell, Oxford, 1981, p. 18f.
10. Quoted in CIR, *op. cit.*, p. 5.
11. Incomes Data Services, *Report 430*, August 1984, p. 25f.
12. V.G. Munns and W.E.J. McCarthy, *Royal Commission on Trade Unions and Employers' Associations Research papers 7. Employers associations*, HMSO, London, 1967, p. 9.

13. *Ibid.*, p. 51.
14. CIR, *op. cit.*, p. 15.
15. Munns and McCarthy, *op. cit.*, p. 64.
16. *Ibid.*, p. 70.

5

Trade Unions

In this chapter we examine the formal aspects of trade union organization, rather than its informal aspects such as shop steward organization and workplace bargaining which are considered in Chapter Thirteen. Our main purpose here is to explore the diversity of trade union types, structures and activities in Britain but, at the same time, to demonstrate the essential similarity of trade unions as organizations and institutions.

5.1 THE CHARACTERISTICS OF TRADE UNIONISM

According to the Webbs, a trade union 'is a continuous association of wage earners for the purpose of maintaining or improving the conditions of their working lives.'[1] This classical definition of trade unionism remains true in substance, since it is the status of a person's work as an employee in present day society which determines his or her potential eligibility for trade union membership. It needs to be recognized, however, that:

> Trade Unionism is not an 'all or nothing' quality, but one which can exist in varying degree. The 'amount' of unionization can therefore be measured along a continuum, though not a simple one. The position is complicated by the fact that any given level of unionization can be represented by varying proportions of unionateness and completeness.[2]

By this view, the degree of 'unionization' amongst any group of employees is a compound of a union's levels of 'unionateness' and 'completeness'. Unionateness is a qualitative concept, while completeness is a quantitative measurement. Completeness is more usually referred to as 'union density' or 'density of union membership' and it expresses the actual union membership of an employee group, divided by its potential union membership, as a percentage. It is thus a numeric expression of trade union membership amongst a given group of employees.

The concept of unionateness, on the other hand, is a useful tool for analysing trade union behaviour and it suggests that unions have a number of characteristics which vary according to their policies and activities as organizations. Unionateness is used as a measure of the commitment of a body to the general principles and ideology of trade unionism. It has seven elements:

1. Whether a given body declares itself a trade union
2. Whether it is registered as a trade union
3. Whether it is affiliated to the T.U.C.
4. Whether it is affiliated to the Labour Party
5. Whether it is independent of employers for purposes of negotiation
6. Whether it regards collective bargaining and the protection of the interests of members, as employees, as a major function

7. Whether it is prepared to be militant, using all forms of industrial action which may be effective.[3]

The above can, in effect, be reduced to five criteria: those relating to collective bargaining; independence; militancy; affiliation to the Trades Union Congress (TUC); and Labour Party affiliation. In essence, a trade union may be conceptually defined as any organization of employees which, first, has as one of its main objectives negotiating with employers in order to regulate the pay and conditions of its members and, second, is independent of the employers with which it negotiates or seeks to negotiate. Whether it is prepared to be militant, whether it is a TUC affiliate, and whether it is a Labour Party affiliate are merely additional measures of unionateness. The fact that some organizations of employees continue to call themselves 'Associations', 'Guilds' or 'Institutions' is not a major determinant of unionateness nowadays. For example, even though it describes itself as an 'association', the Transport Salaried Staffs Association has most of the other characteristics of unionateness. It can hardly be described as being non-unionate. The Civil and Public Services Association, the Institution of Professional Civil Servants, and the National Association of Teachers in Further and Higher Education, for example, whilst not affiliated to the Labour Party, are highly unionate in most other respects.

The criteria of 'registration' as a trade union and of 'independence' as separate determinants of unionateness are no longer strictly tenable. Under the Employment Protection Act 1975, the functions of the former Chief Registrar of Friendly Societies and the Registrar of Trade Unions and Employers' Associations, established under the Industrial Relations Act 1971, were taken over by the Certification Officer. It is this Officer's main duty to determine whether a trade union is 'independent' as defined by Section 30 of the Trade Union and Labour Relations Act 1974. Certification as an independent trade union, with the legal rights provided under labour law, is only granted to those organizations of employees not under the domination or control of an employer and not liable to interference in their activities by an employer. A number of banking and insurance staff associations such as the Lloyds Bank Group Staff Union and the Sun Life Staff Association have been certified as independent trade unions but other 'company unions', such as the Alumsac Employees Association, have not obtained certificates from the Certification Officer. In other words in order to be 'registered' or issued with a certificate as a trade union under current legislation, a union must by definition be independent of the employers with which it either negotiates or seeks negotiating rights.

By these criteria it is possible to categorize trade unions according to their degrees of unionateness. Thus unions like the National Union of Mineworkers, the National Union of Railwaymen, the Union of Construction Allied Trades and Technicians, and the Electrical Electronic Telecommunication and Plumbing Union, like most well known trade unions, would be considered as highly unionate bodies since they satisfy all five main criteria of unionateness. However, at the other end of the spectrum, there are a number of organizations of employees which, while partially satisfying the collective bargaining criterion, have a fairly low level of unionateness on the four other criteria. These include bodies like the Balfour Beatty Group Staff Association, the Britannic Field Staff Association, the Sun Alliance and London Staff Association and so on. These organizations of employees, or staff associations as they are more generally described, are not bona fide trade unions in the accepted sense of the term.

In some cases, staff associations develop into embryonic trade unions, either by becoming more unionate bodies by amalgamation and merger, or by opening up their membership base later. A number of unionate organizations such as the National Union of Teachers, the National and Local Government Officers Association, the Banking

Insurance and Finance Union, and the Engineers and Managers Association, originated as staff associations and evolved into bona fide unions. It is arguable that for any union to survive and to grow as an organization over time, it has to become increasingly unionate. It took many years, for example, for the school teachers, local government officers, the professional engineers and managers, and even the Association of University Teachers, to accept the logic and necessity of affiliation to the Trades Union Congress.

Between the lowly unionate staff associations and the highly unionate bodies, there is a range of unions exhibiting intermediate levels of unionateness. These include the Police Federations, the Merchant Navy and Airline Officers Association, the National Association of Head Teachers and so on. The Institute of Health Service Administrators, the Royal College of Nursing, the Royal College of Midwives and other such bodies in the National Health Service, some of which have negotiating rights on the appropriate Whitley Councils, are also trade unions in that they independently represent employee interests through collective bargaining, as do bodies like the British Medical Association and British Dental Association. Nevertheless, they are dual purpose organizations because they also have functions as professional associations.

The major purposes of professional bodies are the education and certification of practitioners and the maintenance of professional standards amongst members. These aims derive from the traditional model of the independent fee paid practitioner contracting his or her services to personal clients in the private sector. It is only with the growth of employee status among professional groups in the economy, especially in the public sector, that such organizations have had to take on a trade union and collective bargaining role in addition to their professional one. This has frequently led to conflicts within such bodies between those supporting the professionally conscious image of their organization and those coming to terms with the reality of a trade union consciousness brought about by the nature of their employment.

It is clear in practice that different unions exhibit contrasting degrees of commitment to the principles of trade unionism and to the ideological implications of collective representation, joint negotiation and industrial relations. Traditional craft type unionism differs from non-craft unionism. Similarly, the social and industrial solidarity associated with trade unionists like mineworkers and dockers, who often live and work in closely knit working-class communities, contrasts vividly with the more instrumental trade unionism of most white-collar employees who commute to their employment from more diffuse middle-class suburbs. These comments, however, do not modify the views, first, that the essence of independent trade unionism is collective bargaining for its members; second, that the concept of unionateness is a useful tool for analysing the basic characteristics of trade unionism; and third, that trade unions exhibit differing degrees of unionateness amongst each other and within themselves at particular points in time.

5.2   MEMBERSHIP GROWTH AND DISTRIBUTION

Size and density

It is commonly claimed that there are too many trade unions in Britain, and that many industrial relations problems are seriously exacerbated by multiunionism and inter-union conflicts. Envious eyes are cast at the small number of industrial unions in West Germany and in some other countries. A closer examination of British unions, however, reveals that there is a very high proportion of union membership concentrated in a comparatively small number of trade unions. In 1900, there were 1 323 trade unions reduced to 393 by 1983. Until 1976 the Department of Employment recorded all organizations of employees which were known to include in their objects that of negotiating with employers. The effect of this definition was to record many small professional organizations which had very limited industrial relations functions. Evidence supporting this view comes from the fact that by 1983 only 274 trade unions had certificates of independence from the certification officer. Trade union membership statistics are now effectively limited to those organizations appearing to satisfy the statutory definition of a trade union under Section 28 of the Trade Union and Labour Relations Act 1974.

Further reductions in the number of trade unions have been accomplished by amalgamations which have concentrated large memberships into a small number of unions. This is a trend which is likely to continue. In 1960 for example, as shown in table 5.1, some 17 unions with 100 000 members or more accounted for 67 per cent of total union membership. By 1983 there were 22 unions of this size with a membership which accounted for 80 per cent of all trade union members in Britain. Similarly, whilst TUC affiliates accounted for only 25 per cent of the total number of unions in the early 1980s, the combined membership of TUC unions amounted to almost 90 per cent of overall union membership at that time. Despite the persistence of multiunionism in British industry, the trend in the post-war period has been one of a rapid reduction in the number of small unions with the vast majority of members belonging to a relatively small number of unions affiliated to the TUC.

Trade union strength is often measured in terms of total membership size. Absolute membership figures, however, indicate very little unless expressed as a percentage or density of potential trade union membership, either of the overall labour force or of total employment in particular industries or occupations. Union membership in coalmining in the late 1970s, for example, was 97 per cent of the labour force in that industry, or 297 000 out of 306 000 employees. In the distributive trades, on the other hand, only 15 per cent of the labour force was unionized. Yet that 15 per cent represented a unionized workforce of 428 000 out of a total employed labour force of almost three million. In purely numerical terms, union membership in the distributive trades exceeded the total number of unionized coalminers. But union strength in coalmining far exceeds that in retail and wholesale distribution. The concept of union density, therefore, is an extremely useful indicator of potential trade union power.

Throughout the nineteenth century, overall density of unionization was rarely higher than 10 per cent, with trade unionism confined to a small number of trades and industries. The first decade of the twentieth century saw a sharp rise in union growth with density reaching 23 per cent in 1913. Membership growth continued during the first world war and in the short post-war economic boom, so that 45 per cent of the labour force was unionized by 1920. This density peak was soon eroded, as the inter-war economic depression brought its toll of unemployment and economic distress. By 1933, union density had fallen to its pre-war level of 23 per cent. But it recovered slowly after the gradual economic expansion which began in the late 1930s, and total union density rose to 45 per cent by 1948. Because membership density between 1948 and 1969 varied between 45 per cent and 43 per cent, some observers believed that trade union membership had reached a natural plateau of absolute size and relative density. In the period after 1970, trade union membership made rapid increases once again. In 1974, for example, overall density had reached the 50 per cent mark for the first time, with a total trade union membership of 11.75 million. This represented a gain of over 500 000 members in only four years. By 1979, total union membership had risen to over 13 million out of an employed labour force of about 25 million. In 1980 union membership began to fall again and by 1983 had fallen sharply to a density of about 50 per cent at 11.33 million. Under adverse economic conditions the unions lost nearly two million members in three years.

Table 5.1 Size and number of British trade unions 1960 and 1983.

Number of members	[1960]				[1983]			
	Number of unions	Total membership (in 000s)	% of all unions	% of all membership	Number of unions	Total membership (in 000s)	% of all unions	% of all membership
Under 500	308	51	47.4	0.5	173	27	43.9	0.2
500–9 999	249	661	38.3	6.7	149	343	37.9	3.0
10 000–24 999	44	718	6.8	7.3	21	424	5.3	3.7
25 000–99 999	32	1 782	4.9	18.2	28	1 507	7.1	13.3
100 000–249 999	10	1 742	1.5	17.8	11	1 878	2.8	16.6
250 000 and above	7	4 848	1.1	49.5	11	7 158	2.8	63.1
Total	650	9 803	100.0	100.0	393	11 338	100.0	100.0

Source: *Employment Gazette* (various)

Total union density figures tell very little about actual union membership which varies among industries and occupations. Neither do they reveal anything of the continually changing patterns of employment amongst industries, occupations and major sectors of the economy. During the century of trade union development up till the end of the second world war, employment was concentrated in manual work in the basic industries of coal, steel, textiles, transport and engineering, where trade unionism was traditionally strong. Throughout the inter-war years, and especially after 1945, these industries contracted, causing the loss of millions of jobs. In the same period, employment expanded rapidly in other sectors of the economy where trade unionism was relatively weak. These included: education; the professional services; health; government employment; insurance; banking and finance; distribution; and parts of manufacturing industry. In some of these employment areas the number of white-collar and female employees grew rapidly, but relatively few new trade union memberships occurred. In density terms union membership was sometimes comparatively low.

By 1979 union density was 82 per cent in the public sector, 70 per cent in manufacturing, 23 per cent in agriculture, forestry and fishing, and 17 per cent in private sector services. Clearly, the 20 year period of union membership stability after 1948 had been one during which important changes had taken place in the structures of industry and employment. It had produced, however, an environment which had 'been basically unfavourable to trade union growth.'[4] Conversely, the period between 1969 and 1979 was one of rapid union growth with new members coming from the public sector and more white-collar and female employees joining unions.

The growth of public sector employment after 1945, where governmental policy was to encourage union membership and collective bargaining, helped to offset the loss of union membership in the basic industries. The position is clarified if we examine some of the density variations in major industries during that period. By the late 1970s, for example, out of 35 major industries in Britain only fishing, construction, distribution, leather goods, post and inland water transport, and wood and furniture showed a decline in union density since 1948. Others such as gas, electricity, engineering, water, road transport, air transport, education, health, local government, national government, and the pottery, tobacco and chemicals industries made large membership and density gains. Overall in the post-war period, there has been a steady decline in union density in the strongly unionized manual industries and trades, and a considerable growth in areas white-collar and female employment. Also, there has been a considerable expansion in the number of public sector employees. Due to these shifts in employment, white-collar employees increased from 19 per cent of the occupied population in 1911 to 48 per cent in 1982, whilst manual employment fell from 74 per cent to 52 per cent over the same period. This trend was reflected in union membership growth among white-collar employees where density increased from 15 per cent in 1968 to 44 per cent in 1979.

In recent decades, one of the most rapidly expanding sectors of the labour market has been for female employment. In 1911, females constituted 30 per cent of the labour force compared with about 40 per cent in the mid 1980s. Much of this expansion coincided with the growth of white-collar employment and with the demands for routine clerical work and for the growing labour requirements of the service industries. Over a similar period, the percentage of women in manual occupations revealed a marginal reduction from 30 per cent to 28 per cent of the total labour force, compared with a substantial growth, from 30 per cent to 46 per cent, in female white-collar work. These trends were reflected in female union membership density which increased from 24 per cent in 1948 to 39 per cent in 1979. In the same period male union density rose from 55 per cent to 63 per cent.

Structural changes in industry have obvious implications for union membership and relative densities. It has long been recognized that declining industries result in declining union membership, without necessarily affecting density levels – these might actually increase. Evidence from a wide range of countries suggests that the larger the employing establishment the more likely it is to be unionized. It is also clear that one of the most marked tendencies in the British economy in recent decades has been towards larger economic units in both the private and public sectors. The Bullock Committee of Inquiry on Industrial Democracy produced clear evidence in 1977 to suggest that the larger the company, the higher on average is union density:

> When employment in establishments with less than 100 workers is excluded, the density figure for manufacturing rises from about 62 per cent to 77 per cent; and when employment in establishments with less than 200 workers is excluded, the density figure rises to about 89 per cent.[5]

It would appear, therefore, that the tendency for employment establishments to increase in size for economic and technological reasons is matched by the tendency for employees in these establishments to join trade unions.

Some influences on unionization

Historical evidence appears to indicate that unemployment adversely affects union membership, although time lags are frequently involved. Unemployed members often eventually drop their membership, though most unions retain them in nominal membership. Economic depression also reduces the ability of unions to protect their members' interests. Empirical research also indicates that rapidly rising prices, increasing unemployment and falling living standards constitute a 'threat effect' encouraging employees to join trade unions in an attempt to defend their living standards. Such research suggests:

> that price rises generally have a positive impact upon union growth because of the 'threat effect' – the tendency of workers to unionise in an attempt to defend their standard of living against the threat posed by rising prices – and that wage rises will have a similar impact because of the 'credit effect' – the tendency of workers to credit wage rises to unions and to support them in the hope of doing as well or even better in the future.[6]

This view is further supported by the evidence

> That the behaviour of earnings and prices during the period 1969–79 encouraged large numbers of workers, particularly those in white-collar jobs, to unionise in an attempt to defend or to improve their standards of living.[7]

There is also clear evidence from several studies that employees are more likely to be union members if they live in the north of England, Scotland and Wales and less likely to be union members if they live in the south east. In those regions with high union membership there has been a concentration of manual workers and heavy industry which favours high union density. Also, men as an aggregate are more likely to join unions than are women. This is particularly true for male white-collar employees. There is little evidence to suggest, however, that factors such as marital status and family responsibilities influence unionization amongst either men or women. Empirical research shows that the widespread belief that married women employees are less likely to join unions than are other women is unfounded.

In general, those whose education extends beyond the minimum school leaving age and those who obtain formal qualifications are less likely to join trade unions than are those who leave school at the legal minimum age without any formal educational qualifications. The main exceptions are teachers and nurses who belong to highly unionized professions. Not surprisingly, research evidence shows that white-collar employees, and those in higher status occupations, are significantly less likely to join trade unions than are manual employees. The most important exceptions are the civil service, the health service and other areas of white-collar employment in the public sector. Research in both Britain and America also indicates a positive relationship between the age of the individual, the length of work experience and trade union membership. The longer an individual has been at work the more likely it is that he or she has been exposed to work situations encouraging them to join unions. This again is more true of manual workers than it is for white-collar employees.

Turning to the influence of earnings levels on union membership, it appears to be uncertain whether high earnings lead to unionization or whether unionization leads to high earnings. Where employees believe that there is a causal relationship between high earnings and union membership, they are likely to join unions. It is, however, equally well known that many strongly unionized occupations and industries are characterized by low pay as, for example, local government manual work and textiles. In general unionization is not strong among either the low paid or the highly paid. What the empirical evidence seems to suggest, therefore, is that in general:

> an individual who is self employed, who works part-time, who is a member of a white-collar occupation, or who possesses a degree or related professional qualification is generally less likely to be a union member, whereas a person who is male, who left school before the age of sixteen, who concurrently holds more than one job, who works in Wales or the North of Britain, or who is employed in industries characterised by labour intensity or product concentration is generally more likely to be a union member. The probability of an individual being a union member also generally increases, but at a decreasing rate, with size of establishment, work experience, and level of earnings.[8]

5.3   UNION STRUCTURE

Table 5.2 shows the major trade unions affiliated to the TUC with over 100 000 members each in 1983 and 1960. In 1960 there were 17 TUC affiliates with more than 100 000 members each, including the National Union of Agricultural Workers (NUAW), the Iron and Steel Trades Confederation (ISTC) and the National Union of Tailors and Garments Workers (NUTGW). By 1983 there were 21 such unions within the TUC but by this time the NUAW had merged with the TGWU and both the ISTC and the NUTGW now had under 100 000 members each. Another union, the Royal College of Nursing, had over 100 000 members in 1983 but was not a TUC affiliate. Some important unions such as NALGO, NUPE, ASTMS, BIFU and the NAS/UWT had achieved substantially higher memberships and very rapid rates of growth in the intervening years. Other unions such as the TGWU, EEPTU, UCATT, SOGAT and the CPSA achieved more moderate but steady rises in membership and rates of membership growth, partly by amalgamations and mergers with other unions. Two unions, the NUR and the NUM, had membership decreases of some 57 per cent and 46 per cent respectively between 1960 and 1983, reflecting the contraction in employment of these industrial sectors, whilst the NUT's membership increased by only two per cent during the same period.

Classification and structural determinants

Classifying unions is not just a scholastic exercise. It is partly to separate the elements in a situation that would otherwise appear confused and chaotic. 'But as such, it is also an essential preliminary to the understanding of any order of events, and to useful generalizations.'[9] The classical analytical tool for probing the structure of British trade

Table 5.2 *TUC affiliated unions with over 100 000 members in 1983 and 1960.*

Union	Membership	
	1983	1960[1]
Transport and General Workers Union (TGWU)	1 547 000	1 302 000
Amalgamated Union of Engineering Workers (AUEW)	1 224 000	973 000
General Municipal Boilermakers and Allied Trades Union (GMBATU)	875 000	796 000
National and Local Government Officers Association (NALGO)	780 000	274 000
National Union of Public Employees (NUPE)	689 000	200 000
Association of Scientific Technical and Managerial Staffs (ASTMS)	410 000	—
Electrical Electronic Telecommunication and Plumbing Union (EEPTU)	405 000	243 000
Union of Shop Distributive and Allied Workers (USDAW)	404 000	355 000
National Union of Mineworkers (NUM)	318 000	586 000
Union of Construction Allied Trades and Technicians (UCATT)	260 000	192 000
National Union of Teachers (NUT)	251 000	245 000
Confederation of Health Service Employees (COHSE)	223 000	—
Society of Graphical and Allied Trades (SOGAT)	217 000	158 000
Union of Communication Workers (UCW)	197 000	166 000
Civil and Public Services Association (CPSA)	191 000	140 000
Banking Insurance and Finance Union (BIFU)	157 000	—
National Association of Schoolmasters and the Union of Women Teachers (NAS/UWT)	156 000	—
National Union of Railwaymen (NUR)	143 000	334 000
National Graphical Association (NGA)	134 000	—
Post Office Engineering Union (POEU)	130 000	—
Association of Professional Executive Clerical and Computer Staff (APEX)	100 000	—

[1] Some of the unions listed had different titles in 1960.
Source: Certification Officer, *Annual Report 1984* (HMSO 1985) and TUC, *Annual Report* (TUC 1961)

unions has been to divide them into three traditional types derived from their historical antecedents. By this approach it is suggested that first 'craft' unions emerged, whose membership was strictly confined to those craft workers who had served a recognized apprenticeship. Second, a number of 'industrial' unions were formed in coalmining, docks, railways and gas which aimed recruitment exclusively at workers in these industries. Finally, the 'general' unions were established by amalgamation amongst existing trade unions. These enrolled almost all types of employee regardless of their occupation or industry. Thus we have a seemingly useful threefold category of union types: 'craft', 'industrial' and 'general'. By this traditional classification, we can look at every trade union and ask what features each possesses enabling it to be placed into one of the three categories. Such an approach depends upon there being a pure set of characteristics which enables the classifier to approximate each union to the pure type, and then to label it either craft, industrial or general.

The problems of this particular structural analysis of trade unions quickly emerge, when the classifier attempts to isolate a pure type. If a craft union is defined as one only enrolling specific workers who have served apprenticeships, whilst it refuses membership to all other workers, it soon becomes apparent that only a few small unions qualify as such. These include, for example, those catering for musicians, airline pilots, shuttlemakers, coopers, journalists, and power loom overlookers. Similarly, if attempts are made to find examples of industrial unions, similar problems of definition are encountered. It cannot be claimed that either the NUM or the NUR, for instance, are industrial unions. In both industries several other unions have substantial memberships, such as the Union of Democratic Mineworkers and the National Association of Colliery Overmen, Deputies and Shotfirers, and the Associated Society of Locomotive Engineers and Firemen respectively. Furthermore, there is the problem of defining an industry.

The third category of general unions is perhaps not even a category at all but a residual description covering all the other unions which cannot be easily defined as either craft or industrial organizations. It is not surprising therefore that, lacking even the doubtful definitional rigour of the first two categories, we have least trouble in describing two of the largest British unions, the TGWU and GMBATU, as general unions. These two unions, which were formed out of amalgamations after the first world war, have members drawn from almost every occupation and industry in Britain.

The essential weakness of the craft, industrial and general structural analysis is that it confuses rather than clarifies the problems of definition. It forces each union into a single category, when in fact the overwhelming majority of unions have features common to all three categories. The AUEW for example, has a large number of engineering craftworkers in its membership. But it also recruits foundry workers, construction employees and relatively unskilled workers. Clearly, such a union – one of the largest in Britain – cannot be adequately located within a simple three category model. Moreover, such a structural analysis does not allow for the development of white-collar unionism: either where exclusive white-collar unions exist, or where many so-called craft, industrial and general unions have developed substantial white-collar sections.

One distinguished observer of British trade union structure has rejected the classical categories of classification on the grounds that

> Since certain important classifications of union types have their origin in the slogans of dead ideological debate, rather than in objective description, they neither explain the present morphology of trade unionism nor illuminate its likely behaviour.[10]

He suggests a more fruitful analysis which categorizes unions into those with 'open' and those with 'closed' membership recruitment policies. Traditional craft unions usually restrict their membership to those men and women working at a clearly definable trade which normally involves a formal period of training. Such unions operate a closed recruitment policy in line with their fundamental purpose of representing their members' interests to the exclusion of all other related employees.

Similarly, small skilled cotton textile unions restrict their membership by admitting only a limited number of recruits to their ranks through promotion and time serving at their jobs. Equivalent policies used to be pursued by the train drivers who would only admit members into the Associated Society of Locomotive Engineers and Firemen after many years of service in other railway grades. Even today, train drivers have to serve as 'second men' after their initial instruction before they eventually become 'drivers'. Unions with closed union policies do not seek growth in numbers but aim at security in closed shop situations and strong, if small, organization. Other unions, such as the NUM and the NUR, which might be regarded as typical industrial unions, also follow closed membership policies because they do not recruit members from outside their immediate spheres of influence. In consequence their membership expands or contracts according to the changing manpower levels in their industries.

Open membership policies are usually associated with the big general unions, such as the TGWU, AUEW, ASTMS and NUPE. They seek membership growth almost regardless of their members' jobs or of the industry in which they work. Such unions have to organize their internal structures to cope with diverse membership needs. Yet union growth patterns over a long period of time suggest that whilst unions with open membership policies have grown rapidly, those with closed policies either have remained relatively static in size or have declined as their industry's labour force has diminished. These include, for example, the unions in the coalmining, railways and textile industries.

> This distinction between 'open' and 'closed' unionism is seen as most significant when unions are viewed dynamically – i.e. in relation to membership growth and decline . . . The main growth pattern in evidence is thus one of 'open' unions, with boundaries that are increasingly difficult to define.[11]

Factors other than their relative open or closed nature also influence union growth, structure and organization. These can be divided into external economic and environmental factors and internal union decisions and policies. The first group of factors assumes that unions can do little but adjust to external forces over which they have little control. The second category suggests that the unions which are most successful seek, through leadership policy initiatives and deliberate internal change, to convince existing and potential members that they can effectively challenge and overcome adverse economic and environmental circumstances by adapting proactively to them. Both these views of union growth and structure are far more complicated and problematic than are either the 'craft-industrial-general' or the 'open-closed' theories.

The external economic and environmental factors influencing union growth and structure are the business cycle, the level and rate of change of unemployment, the relationship between pay and changes in the general price level, and the attitudes and policies of employers and government towards union recognition, collective bargaining and trade unionism. The most influential long-term external forces bringing about fundamental change in trade union growth and organization are those structural economic movements causing the decline of certain industries and occupations and the growth and birth of others. Unions are forced to accept the consequences of those forces in the long term, though they may seek to resist or mitigate them in the short term. If a union's membership is based in a declining industry it can do little more than to fight a rearguard action. According to this view, no amount of strong perceptive leadership or changes in internal structures can prevent a steady loss of membership and bargaining power. Examples in recent decades include the steel industry, railways, the docks and coalmining.

Conversely, whilst declining industries and occupations usually result in falling union membership, expanding industries and occupations may present other unions with opportunities for membership recruitment, employer recognition and collective bargaining. In these circumstances the view that dynamic and imaginative union leadership can achieve union growth and reshape the union map has obvious validity. Much, it is argued, depends upon the ability of the unions concerned to exploit opportunities for membership growth by highlighting the fears, discontents and insecurities of employees. Examples are to be found in the growth of ASTMS, NUPE and BIFU.

A detailed analysis of change in trade unions argues that the external agents of change have been overstated and that the ability of unions to change within themselves has been understated. Whilst accepting that external economic and environmental factors play a powerful role in shaping trade unions, internal factors, it is argued, such as dynamic union leadership, the mobilization of membership opinion, worker militancy, rank and file policy participation, the vertical dispersal of union power and new methods of job regulation can, in many cases, offset external forces. It would appear that the process of change in trade unions emerges as the result of the interaction of a wide variety of external and internal factors:

> significant and lasting change depends on the existence of two critical pre-conditions: first,

a more or less united leadership committed to change; second, a decision making structure that is sufficiently receptive to change to enable the leaders to get their way.[12]

A further explanation of how trade union structure is determined concerns the influence of collective bargaining on the character, structure, internal government and membership of trade unions. Because collective bargaining is central to the purposes and objectives of trade unions, it is concluded that it must be the predominant force shaping and changing them. A change in collective bargaining structure, it is argued, is followed by changes in the internal structure and organization of the unions involved.

> Collective bargaining is put forward not only as an influence on other aspects of union behaviour, not just as an important influence, but as the 'main', 'major', 'foremost', or 'principal' influence. These adjectives imply that, where collective bargaining is the predominant method of regulation, its dimensions account for union behaviour more adequately than any other set of explanatory variables can do.[13]

Furthermore, collective bargaining is heavily influenced by the attitudes of employers and the structure of employers' associations which in turn, according to this view, determine trade union membership, structure and internal organization. This explanation of trade union structure and change depends heavily upon the many external economic and institutional factors determining the various types of collective bargaining.

Multiunionism and union mergers

Union structure in Britain has been criticized on the grounds that there are too many unions whose structures lead to competitive membership recruitment and to demarcation conflicts. Even at the turn of the century, the Webbs observed that 'to competition between overlapping unions is to be attributed nine-tenths of the ineffectiveness of the trade union world.'[14] Some 60 years later the Royal Commission on Trade Unions and Employers' Associations asked 'what can be done to reduce multi-unionism?'[15] Yet the TUC adopted resolutions calling for a 'federated union' as early as 1874, and in 1918, 1927 and 1964 it produced further reports suggesting ways to reform the structure of British trade unions and to reduce their number. Although substantial reductions have been made in the number of trade unions from over 1 000 in 1900 to about 400 in the mid 1980s, Britain retains a multiplicity of trade unions, with overlapping memberships and sometimes conflicting policies within the same industry and firms.

Many of the proposals for trade union structural reform, coming from both within and without the trade union movement, focus on the case for large industrial unions. Yet the original trade union impetus for industrial unions was mainly political, since it was rooted in the syndicalist theory that workers should first create industrial unions and then through a general strike take over their industries and establish a socialist society. By such means, it was envisaged, trade unionism would become a revolutionary force, thus avoiding all the alleged weaknesses of the parliamentary road to socialism. Prior to the first world war, for example, the coalminers proposed 'That our objective be, to build up an organization that will ultimately take over the mining industry, and carry it on in the interests of the workers.'[16] Most trade unions, however, ignored this political motive and those which accepted the advantages of industrial unionism did so mainly because it was an obviously tidy form of trade unionism. It closely followed the emerging structure of industry and the developing pattern of national collective bargaining within it.

Many years later, the Report of the Donovan Commission concluded that 'there is no sign of any general evolution towards industrial unionism.'[17] The reasons for this are, first, the preference of British trade unionists has been to form organizations representative of specific occupations or related groups of occupations. This tendency has been reinforced by the inclinication of employees to identify themselves with their occupational interests and with the skills necessary to do their job, rather than with their industry. Second, there is the problem of defining an industry – where, for example, does the engineering industry begin and end? Third, at the beginning of the century when the call for industrial unionism was at its strongest, industry was characterized by large numbers of small and medium sized firms, operating within single industries. Today giant firms, including multinational corporations, straddle several industries and have to deal with more than one industrial union. Finally, even if the theoretical objections could be overcome, the practical problems associated with industrial unionism are probably insuperable.

> However defined, industrial unionism would involve a drastic upheaval in the structure of almost every major union in the country and virtually all expanding unions. It would, for example, mean the dismemberment of craft unions and of both the giant general unions.[18]

The most obvious way of reducing the number of trade unions is through amalgamation or merger. Since the law was changed in 1964, amalgamations are now possible after a simple majority of the votes cast by the members of each union involved. On this basis, a number of significant amalgamations has taken place between various trade unions, such as between the Amalgamated Society of Boilermakers, Shipwrights, Blacksmiths and Structural Workers and the General and Municipal Workers Union in 1982 which formed EMBATU. There has also been a strong tendency for open unions to amalgamate and this has led to the growth of a small number of very large unions. Not all these amalgamations have been for the better, however. Many have taken place for political and organizational reasons with little hope of improving the overall structure of British trade unionism. Furthermore, the growth of large unions through amalgamation has often only transferred the conflict between unions into conflict within the new union.

Trade union mergers or amalgamations do not follow a single definable pattern. It is useful to distinguish between the objectives of different mergers by using a threefold classification. 'Thus we refer to *defensive, consolidating* or *expansionist* mergers, and seek to apply those terms to both the major and minor unions involved in a given merger.'[19] A defensive merger, for example, enables the minor union involved to escape irreversible decline as its membership contracts and its falling finances prevent it from effectively servicing its members. For the major union involved, the same merger could be an expansionist one, since it seeks to expand its membership and activities into new areas of employment. In certain cases, even the major union in a merger could be seeking to protect its position defensively. A good example of a defensive merger took place in 1971 when UCATT was formed by the amalgamation of four building trade unions: the Amalgamated Society of Painters and Decorators; the Amalgamated Union of Building Trade Workers; the Association of Building Technicians; and the Amalgamated Society of Woodworkers. Before the creation of UCATT union membership in the construction industry had been falling rapidly and it was hoped that one large general union would reverse this trend. The formation of UCATT has, in fact, stabilized membership and density within the industry, since union membership at amalgamation in 1971 was 260 000 and in 1982 it was 261 000.

A consolidating merger between trade unions usually takes place 'where the aim of those involved [is] to consolidate a shared position in a given industry or occupational area.'[20] An example of a consolidating merger arose in the engineering industry in 1971, when the Amalgamated Engineering Union (AEU) and the Amalgamated Union of Foundry Workers merged with the Draughtsmen and Allied Technicians Association

(DATA) and the much smaller Construction Engineering Union to form the AEU. This merger consolidated the AEU's membership and bargaining power in the engineering industry. It was not defensive because the two largest unions, the AEU and DATA, had steadily rising memberships between 1961 and 1971, and none of the merging unions was in serious financial difficulties. It reverted to the AEU in 1986.

An expansionist merger takes place when the major union seeks 'the basis for further expansion and development, sometimes into quite new job territories.'[21] Much of the growth and expansion of the TGWU and ASTMS has taken place by merging with many smaller unions over a long period. Between 1969 and 1976, for example, ASTMS was involved as the major union in 17 successful mergers with minor unions or professional associations in many diverse fields of white-collar employment. The TGWU, which was itself formed by the merger in 1922 of 18 unions, has grown considerably by continually seeking mergers with smaller unions. Between 1968 and 1974, for example, the TGWU absorbed into its membership no less than 15 small unions catering mainly for manual workers. In 1981 the National Union of Agricultural and Allied Workers (NUAAW) merged with the TGWU in a purely defensive decision by the NUAAW which can hardly be said to have improved the rationale of British union structure. The minor unions in all these cases were concerned with achieving defensive mergers with the TGWU, whose trade group structure they found attractive. For its part TGWU saw the mergers as an effective way of expanding its membership and penetrating new job territories.

The overall impact of trade union mergers from the late 1960s to the present time has been to complicate the structural rationale of British trade unions rather than to simplify and rationalize it. Most mergers have taken place to satisfy the self-interest of the unions concerned and not to achieve a more coherent trade union structure. The merger movement of the 1960s and 1970s, in short, 'appears as a somewhat random process. Certainly, it appears to lack direction, or movement in any preordained conscious form.'[22] Moreover, 'the government and structure of British unions appear to be more diverse, contradictory and conflicting at the end of [the] period of study [1980] than they were in 1960.'[23]

Another method of coping with multiunionism is the use of trade union federations. A small number of trade union federations remain in Britain. In engineering there are a number of manual and white-collar unions representing some two million trade unionists. These have formed the Confederation of Shipbuilding and Engineering Unions which negotiates directly with the Engineering Employers Federation. Federations also exist for similar purposes in other industries such as teaching and textiles. Such federations have been described as a half-way house to industrial unionism. This is because they bring unions into closer co-operation together in the industry in which they are located.

Other practical devices for overcoming some of the deficiencies of multiunionism include dual membership agreements, the block transfer of members between unions, and agreements between unions that they will not compete for members in the same industries and firms. The Donovan Report suggested 'one union for one grade of work within one factory'[24] as the guiding principle to be agreed between competing unions to improve trade union structure. To date, however, there is little evidence that many unions have adopted this proposal or similar devices for reducing the worst effects of an apparently unreformable trade union structure. Perhaps the greatest practical changes in recent years have come about through the close working relationships created, out of necessity, by shop stewards from many different unions at shopfloor level in order to facilitate workplace bargaining.

5.4   DEMOCRACY AND INTERNAL AFFAIRS

Trade unions emerged in Britain at a time when only a minority of the population was enfranchised, and when representative political democracy was in its infancy. Almost invariably as they were formed trade unions adopted democratic constitutions giving their members, in theory at least, ultimate control over the policy decisions and the organization of their own union. Trade unionists were therefore familiar with democratic political principles, and many of the problems associated with them, whilst Parliament was almost completely unrepresentative of substantial sections of the population. Thus the value of trade union democracy has always extended far beyond that of the individual union.

> In large measure, the chance that the collectivist society which is developing in most countries will be democratic rests on the possibility that trade unions, although supporters of socialist objectives, will maintain their independence of the state, and will act to protect their members and the citizenry in general against the tremendous state power inherent in a collectivist society.[25]

Equally, as a long and detailed comparative study of union democracy in America and Britain has concluded: 'the future of unionism is inseparable from the future of organized society.'[26] By these views, the retention of individual freedoms and collective rights within a pluralist democracy like Britain are inescapably bound up with the problem of trade union internal democracy. The unions are seen to be one of the most powerful collectivist institutions outside the agencies of the state.

Union democracy is not merely an exercise in democratic self-government for its own sake. After all, as organizations, unions are largely concerned with protecting their members' incomes and working conditions. It is arguable that what constitutes their interests should be decided by the members themselves. Union democracy, therefore, has a very instrumental objective requiring practical representative organization. Most union constitutions and rule books emphasize the right of members at local level to debate motions and to advance resolutions which can then be processed through all levels of trade union government up to the highest policy making bodies.

The local union branch, often based on a geographical area rather than the place of work, is the basic and most vital element in the democratic organizational chain. The next level of trade union organization is either the 'district', 'division' or 'region', with the national headquarters, often in London, being the apex of the union's formal authority structure. The geographical and functional levels between the branches and the national office usually possess powerful rights and some degree of autonomy too, as in the mineworkers and among the engineering workers unions. The transport workers union, for example, is divided not only into geographical regions but also into different 'trade groups'. These are largely autonomous groupings, providing an internal structure which helps to ensure that the interests of individual members are not lost within an organization which now has some one and a half million members.

A majority of unions also hold annual conferences, whilst others hold biennial or even triennial conferences, at which local resolutions processed through the branch and regional levels can be debated. In the printing and publishing industry, for example, the National Union of Journalists conference meets annually and that of the National Graphical Association biennially. Branches send delegates to their conferences according to membership distribution, with the delegates often mandated to vote on major policy issues in accordance with the majority view of local members. National executive committees are charged with the efficient and effective running of their unions between conferences and with the carrying out of conference policy decisions. Some unions hold very large conferences with hundreds of official delegates such as the TGWU whilst others, like the AUEW, elect a comparatively small National Committee which has the power to determine union policy on a broad range of collective bargaining and other issues.

Membership participation

It is generally accepted by students of politics that the writing of formal democratic constitutions by no means ensures that democratic principles will be followed by those responsible for administering them. Union democracy cannot flourish when branch meetings are only attended by a fraction of the membership, or if a politically determined and cohesive minority seeks to impose its policies upon an apathetic majority. Neither can it do so where a small number of powerful national officers manipulates the union conference for their own ends in order to retain their own power and authority. Similarly, democracy becomes discredited if union rules are used to prevent the emergence of an effective opposition within a union, by prohibiting particular groups, for example, from disseminating their views in written form. Democracy is also threatened when powerful general secretaries change their union's policies a short time after a union conference on the dubious grounds that the circumstances facing the union have substantially changed.

Some trade unionists, on the other hand, argue that union democracy has little real purpose because it hinders the efficient operation of trade unions in the narrow pursuit of the economic self-interest of their members. Put another way:

> business unionism, as a set of ideas justifying the narrowest definitions of a union's role in society, also helps to legitimate one-party oligarchy, for it implies that union leadership is simply the administration of an organization with defined, undebatable goals: the maximization of the member's income and general welfare.[27]

Attention must therefore be given to those major factors which either enhance or inhibit the development and maintenance of internal union democracy.

Full-time union officers enjoy considerable security of tenure in their jobs. Because of their knowledge of union affairs, continuity in office, bargaining experience and political skills, they usually exercise a very considerable influence over the determination of union policies, resources and organization. 'No king on earth is as safe in his job as a Trade Union official',[28] claims one of Shaw's characters in his play *The Apple Cart*. Whilst this can be regarded as a typical Shavian exaggeration, very few union officers are dismissed or removed from office. The methods of appointing full-time union officers have some bearing upon the influence which they wield within their unions. Some unions, like the engineering workers and the railwaymen for instance, elect their officers in the belief that it ensures that their members will pick the persons best suited for the job as well as helping to encourage democratic control of the union. Elected officers, it is argued, are usually more responsive to the hopes and aspirations of their members than are selected ones. Moreover, if they are subject to periodic re-election, they are conscious that they can be removed from office if they do not satisfy membership needs.

Yet election often reduces the job security of elected officials and it can prevent them from persuading their members to follow necessary but unpopular policies. Evidence also suggests that elected officers usually have to serve for a long period as voluntary office holders before they can expect election to a full-time post. This can result in them being middle-aged before they commence their professional trade union career. This has obvious implications for their training and their role in policy and organizational matters. An alternative method of appointing full-time officers, and one favoured by the majority of unions, is by an internal selection process. This, it is argued, avoids the defects of election and enables the union to secure the services of younger, vigorous and educated professionals. These, if provided with a clear career structure in the union, it is said, will work hard in the interests of the union and of themselves. Job security is improved and vocational training made easier. On the other hand, non-elected officers, who are usually selected by other and more senior full-time officers, are more likely to be answerable to them than to the ordinary union membership to whom they are nominally accountable.

Nearly all unions elect their general secretary, however, and this usually involves a considerable political campaign and a power struggle among various factions in the union. Elections, if they are to have meaning and relevance for union members and thereby break through the apathy barrier, must involve real choice between competing candidates offering different policies, ideologies and styles of leadership. Such candidates are in turn supported by party factions, each fighting to gain support and votes for their candidate. Such a 'party system', it is argued, brings corresponding benefits because 'democracy is strengthened when members are not only related to the larger organization but are also affiliated with or loyal to subgroups within the organization.'[29] Mutually warring factions, on the other hand, are 'a luxury most unions cannot afford.'[30] In recent years the elections of the general secretaries of the AUEW, EEPTU, GMBATU and TGWU, for instance, have been marked by distinct political differences between the major candidates, and vigorous campaigns which were closely covered by the mass media.

Despite the opportunities provided for democratic participation, membership involvement in union affairs has never been high and much attention has been focused upon the small attendances at branch meetings and low polls in union elections. However, little equivalent comment is made about the poorly attended and often perfunctory annual meetings of shareholders, ostensibly responsible for running very large public companies. Nevertheless, attempts have been made by some unions to improve interest in branch meetings by moving them from geographical to workplace or industrial branches where meetings are sometimes held during working hours. Although such arrangements allow shop stewards to take an active part in union activities, there is a continued reluctance by ordinary trade unionists to become involved in union policy making. For most of them, the shop steward is the union rather than the formal union structure. Unions with memberships which are scattered across wide areas of industry or are working in small isolated units, such as in USDAW, NUTGW and the National Union of Seamen, for instance, find it particularly difficult to develop effective branch activities. Here the co-ordinating role of the full-time officers is crucial.

A further factor inhibiting membership participation in union affairs is related to union size. Relatively small, compact, and often closed unions, like the NGA, with elected officers well known to members and with high membership identification with the union and its policies, usually have effective membership involvement. But some large open unions with selected officers, who are increasingly without practical working experience of their members' occupations, suffer from poor branch involvement. Yet general observation can be misleading as much depends upon the structure of the union under examination.

> It is not by itself the size of the major unions that prevents a vigorous and coherent internal process of democratic participation. It is the miscellaneity of so much of the membership composition . . . The problems of external structure and strategy and of internal organisation and democracy meet here.[31]

Union ballots

A great deal of media and political attention has been paid to the fact that in many unions there is a considerable divergence between the views and attitudes of the leadership and those of rank and file members. In most, but not all cases, a situation develops where the union leadership – which usually means the general secretary and executive committee – hold political opinions and attitudes to militant industrial action which do not appear to be held by the majority of their members. Many reasons have been advanced to explain this divergence. A commonly held view is that the vast majority of union members have little interest in their union's internal democratic processes, elections to office or in debating and shaping policy. In the face of such mass apathy, it is argued, a highly motivated political minority can dominate and use, for their own ends, the union's formal democratic processes. They usually act strictly within the confines of the union rule book and obtain office, position and policy control legitimately. A few unions, such as the CPSA, ASTMS and the Technical Administrative and Supervisory Section of the AUEW, have apparently been functioning efficiently for many years with a permanently left-wing leadership and right-wing membership. Examples of the reverse situation are difficult to find.

The usual response to this divergence of opinion and attitude between union leaders and members is to urge the apathetic members to attend their local branch meetings, to take part in union elections and to debate and shape union policy. Such urgings are rarely if ever effective. Considerable political and media attention has been paid to important union elections, such as those for the posts of general secretary or president of the largest unions, with the media and politicians drawing attention to the main candidates' political and ideological convictions. Although media campaigns have created more interest in union elections, the common system of voting at branch meetings or at the workplace appears to have inhibited high turnouts for voting.

One answer to the reluctance of many union members to take part in branch voting is to provide them with a postal ballot. This requires unions to post ballot forms to each member and provide them with a stamped addressed envelope. The member can then make up his or her own mind at home, vote and post the ballot form to the independent counting agency employed. The same balloting system can also be used for other important decisions such as whether to accept or reject pay offers, change union rules, or take industrial action. Only one major British union, the AUEW, has used postal ballots extensively and has claimed government money to cover their costs, though other unions seem likely to do so.

Objectors to these proposals argue that postal ballots further reduce the importance of branch meetings, isolate each member when voting, give considerable influence to the media over how individual members vote and place an unacceptable financial burden on the unions. Above all, they claim, it would be an intolerable interference with the right of individual unions to determine their own internal affairs, rules and democratic procedures. The TUC, largely in response to media pressure and the threat of legislation after 1979, has encouraged affiliated unions to review their democratic procedures and balloting systems. By decision of Congress, though, TUC affiliates were initially forbidden to accept government finance to cover the cost of secret postal and workplace ballots; this policy was subsequently reviewed.

The Trade Union Act 1984, which its supporters claim aims to return the unions to their members, requires trade unions to conduct secret postal ballots, at least once every five years, for the election by all voting members of their principal policy making executive bodies. This legal requirement brings to an end the practice in some unions of electing their national executive committees at their annual conference or at branch meetings. Ballots can be held either at the workplace or on a geographical basis providing that they meet the stringent requirements of the Act. Where the general secretary or president of the union is also a voting member of the union's principal executive committee, he or she must be elected by secret postal or workplace ballot at least once every five years. If existing general secretaries wish to avoid this legal requirement, unions can change their rules to make them non-voting members of their national executive committees.

The 1984 Act also regulates the internal democratic procedures of trade unions by requiring them to hold properly conducted secret ballots before taking official industrial action. Only those members who would be involved in taking industrial action can vote, and a majority of those voting must make it clear that they wish to take part in the action. These requirements have made it necessary for unions to make alterations in their rule books regarding the calling and endorsement of industrial action. The 1984 Act also requires trade unions to hold secret ballots of all their members, at least once every 10 years, on whether they wish the union to have a political fund and to spend it on political objects. Further, the Act closely defines political objects and makes it unlawful for a union which has not successfully balloted its members on a political fund to spend money on these political objects.

Under the Employment Act 1980, independent trade unions can apply to the Certification Officer for refunds of money involved in holding secret ballots. They can also apply for a remedy to an individual tribunal if an employer unreasonably refuses facilities for the holding of secret, workplace ballots.

5.5   RELATIONS BETWEEN UNIONS

In Britain, many different unions represent identical grades or closely related grades of employees in the same industries and even in the same firm. This is an inevitable consequence of the multiunion nature of British trade unionism. Where several trade unions operate in the same industry, such as in engineering, shipbuilding or printing, for example, it is not surprising that there are often conflicts of interest among them which have to be resolved.

Interunion conflict

The problems of multiunionism and interunion conflict are not new. According to the Donovan Commission:

> the TUC should intensify its effort to encourage the unions concerned to adopt closer working arrangements. The TUC should also consider adopting the principle of 'one union for one grade of work within one factory' as a guide for the future development of structure.[32]

Clearly, the complex structure of British trade unionism and interunion conflict are inextricably linked. Yet there are many causes of interunion conflict. The most frequent include: first, competition amongst and between unions for new members; second, the accusation that one union is poaching another union's members or its potential members in its 'sphere of influence'; third, the desire of a union not to lose promoted members to another union; fourth, problems of job demarcation at the workplace; fifth, disagreement amongst and between unions over which of them should have recognition and negotiating rights with particular employers; and sixth, differing policies on pay and conditions of employment towards the employers with which they negotiate.

Most, if not all, trade unions value membership growth as a vital element in their strength in relation to the employers with which they negotiate, and in terms of their influence within the labour movement generally. Large memberships also bring valuable financial economies of scale in providing services to members. The urge to recruit members is therefore an important internal union objective. Similarly, there is evidence to suggest that potential and existing trade unionists are strongly attracted by the protection offered by large, expanding and vigorous unions. Competition amongst unions to recruit members within the same industries and enterprises is therefore inescapable. Only some form of agreed external regulation can effectively limit conflict and disorder between competing trade unions.

Unions with members who are offered promotion can find that they lose them to other unions when they are promoted. In response to this, many open manual unions have developed white-collar, technician and supervisory sections to recruit in the expanding area of white-collar employment and to avoid membership loss by promotion. In recent years, some white-collar unions or unions with white-collar sections have increasingly come into conflict with each other on membership recruitment issues.

Job demarcation has also long been a source of interunion disagreement. This can sometimes express itself in bitter strikes as have occurred in printing, newspaper publishing and shipbuilding. Unions, particularly those catering for skilled employees, for instance, regard certain work, closely related to their members' skills, as 'theirs'. If management, other unions or competing groups of employees attempt to perform 'their' work, they resist this by imposing industrial sanctions against employers and employees alike. The problem is made even more intractable by the tendency for new technology to blur the traditional distinctions among craft workers and between them and other employees. Another major cause of interunion conflict arises out of different policies to pay negotiations and other conditions of employment among trade unions in the same industry. One union, for example, might be willing to accept an offer from an employer which other unions with a similar membership wish to reject. Federations of trade unions and the TUC industrial committees have become the accepted methods of bringing about compromise solutions to such issues.

The Bridlington rules

The TUC has long recognized its responsibility for regulating interunion conflicts amongst those unions affiliated to it. The 1920 Constitution, for example, provided for the establishment of a Disputes Committee for dealing with interunion disputes. In 1924 these disputes had reached such serious proportions that Congress adopted Rule 12 which gave the General Council powers to intervene in interunion disputes involving the alleged poaching of members by rival unions. At the 1939 Congress held at Bridlington, the TUC established a further set of rules and an expected code of behaviour by member unions to regulate interunion competition was agreed. These rules are commonly referred to as the 'Bridlington Principles'. Later Congresses have amended and expanded these principles. For example, in 1976 the TUC revised 'Rules 10, 11, 12 and 13 and the regulations governing procedure in regard to disputes to bring them into line with recent practice', adding that they 'constitute a code of conduct accepted as morally binding by affiliated organisations. They are not intended . . . to be a legally enforceable contract.'[33] This was done because the TUC was understandably anxious to ensure, wherever possible, that interunion disputes are settled by the trade union movement itself rather than by the courts or by other external agencies.

The Bridlington Principles embody the following guidelines. First, they are aimed at encouraging closely related unions and federations of unions to develop specific and general working agreements on 'spheres of influence' among themselves. These include, for example: transfer of members between unions with benefits where appropriate; 'recognition of cards'; fully agreed and clearly understood demarcation arrangements; and recognized procedures for settling disagreements and misinterpretations among themselves. Where practicable, the TUC suggests that closely associated unions should examine the case for mergers or amalgamations among themselves. Second, where employees apply for membership to a union, they are normally expected to be asked which unions they have previously been members of, if they have correctly resigned from their former unions, and whether they are involved in either a union disciplinary matter or an industrial dispute. It also has to be established that they do not owe unpaid membership subscriptions to other unions. Third, the TUC recommends a model application form for trade unions when recruiting new members. In this way the union and the applicant's former union can normally exchange the requisite information within 21 days of a membership application, thereby ensuring full knowledge of the applicant's previous membership history. Fourth, unions are not expected to commence organizing and recruiting at any place of employment until they have confirmed that other unions are not already involved there. Agreements of 'spheres of influence' are of considerable use in avoiding interunion conflicts. Fifth, it is recommended that unions should consider the possibility of dual union membership arrangements where appropriate. Such arrangements enable management, for example, to temporarily transfer workers between jobs without provoking a demarcation dispute. Sixth, in the event of demarcation disputes between unions, industrial action is not expected to take place until the unions and have referred the matter to the TUC.

Where unions cannot regulate their own relationships with each other they can refer the matter, under TUC Rule 12, to a TUC Disputes Committee established by the General Council. In a majority of cases referred to the TUC, settlement is reached without recourse to a Disputes Committee. When a case is put to a Disputes Committee – made up of three members of the General Council – hearings are held, investigations carried out, and either an award or a recommendation is made. An award is usually made in a demarcation issue not involving an employer which could of course ignore it. A recommendation is usually made in those cases involving employers only. Awards and recommendations are binding upon all affiliated unions and they are reported to Congress in its annual report. If a union refuses to accept the verdict of a Disputes Committee, it can, in the first instance, be suspended by the General Council. It can then be subsequently disaffiliated at the next Congress, although there is a right of appeal by the union concerned. Very few unions have actually been disaffiliated by Congress under the Bridlington Principles. Yet in essence, interunion conflicts stem largely from overlapping union membership, competing recruitment activities, and closely related spheres of influence. The TUC Bridlington Principles do not remove the causes of interunion conflict but only deal with their symptoms.

5.6 SUMMARY

In this chapter we suggest that trade unions are basically bargaining agents. The qualitative concept of unionateness as a measure of union character indicates that individual trade unions, whilst having their own unique characteristics, also possess broad similarities in their purposes, in their methods of operating and in their internal organization with other unions. In tracing union membership growth, we define the quantitative concept of union density. It would seem that membership growth is principally related to the changing industrial and occupational distribution of the labour force. But collective bargaining and internal union factors also influence membership distribution. The latter includes innovative leadership, flexible structures and a rule book allowing rapid adjustment to external economic circumstances. Whilst overall union density increased in the 1970s, it has fallen sharply since 1980.

It also seems that long-term membership trends are linked to the decline of manual employment, and to the expansion of white-collar work and the female penetration of the labour market during the post-war period. Many of the problems of trade union structure which persist stem from the multiplicity of union types which have evolved for over a century. The traditional classification of craft, industrial, and general unionism is less adequate for analytical purposes, than the open or closed typologies of union structure. These appear to be a much better explanation of union growth patterns and membership distribution.

As organizations trade unions, in theory at least, are inverted hierarchies run on democratic principles. The power and authority to make binding decisions within them flows from their membership to their leaders rather than from their leaders to rank and file members. There are a series of internal checks and balances within each union to offset the likelihood of trade union office holders or of power cliques getting out of touch with grass roots opinion. The Trade Union Act 1984 is intended to strengthen this process by making secret postal ballots a statutory requirement. The TUC believes, however, that the intention behind these ballots is to weaken traditional union democracy. Although membership participation is relatively low in most trade unions, the ultimate right of dissatisfied trade unionists is to 'vote with their feet'. A high proportion of appointed officers, undue concern for union efficiency, and a business-union ideology, on the other hand, can be inimical to union democracy.

It is clear that interunion disputes result largely from membership competition and poaching, job demarcation and disputes recognition and bargaining rights. Under the TUC's Bridlington rules, the vast majority of interunion disputes have been resolved for many years.

5.7 REFERENCES

1. S. and B. Webb, *The History of Trade Unionism*, (1984), reprinted by Augustus Kelly, New York, 1965, p. 1.
2. R.M. Blackburn and K. Prandy, 'White collar unionisation: a conceptual framework', *British Journal of Sociology*, June 1965, p. 119.
3. *Ibid.*, p. 112.
4. Department of Trade, *Report of the Committee of Inquiry on Industrial Democracy*, HMSO, London, 1977, p. 11.
5. *Ibid.*, pp. 11f.
6. R. Price and G.S. Bain, Union growth revisited 1948–1974, *British Journal of Industrial Relations*, November 1976, p. 350.
7. R. Price and G.S. Bain, Union growth in Britain: retrospect and prospect, *British Journal of Industrial Relations*, Vol. xix, 1983, p. 56.
8. G.S. Bain and P. Elias, Trade union membership in Great Britain: an industrial analysis, *British Journal of Industrial Relations*, Vol. xxi, 1985, pp. 85–6.
9. H.A. Turner, *Trade Union Growth, Structure and Policy*, Allen and Unwin, London, 1962, p. 241.
10. *Ibid.*
11. J. Hughes, *Royal Commission on Trade Unions and Employers' Associations Research Paper 5, (Part 1) Trade Union Structure and Government*, HMSO, London, 1967, p. 1.
12. R. Undy, V. Ellis, W.E.J. McCarthy and A.M. Halmos, *Change in Trade Unions: The Development of UK Unions since the 1960s*, Hutchinson, London, 1981, p. 330.
13. H.A. Clegg, *Trade Unionism under Collective Bargaining*, Basil Blackwell, Oxford, 1976, p. 11.
14. S. and B. Webb, quoted in H.A. Turner, *op. cit.*, p. 241.
15. Royal Commission on Trade Unions and Employers' Associations, *Report*, HMSO, London, 1968, p. 179.
16. *The Miners' Next Step* quoted in Will Paynter, *British Trade Unions*, Allen and Unwin, London, 1970, p. 95.
17. Royal Commission, *op. cit.*, p. 181.

18. *Ibid.*, p. 180.
19. Undy, Ellis, McCarthy and Halmos, *op. cit.*, p. 22.
20. *Ibid.*, p. 167.
21. *Ibid.*
22. *Ibid.*, p. 219.
23. *Ibid.*, p. 23.
24. Royal Commission, *op. cit.*, p. 184.
25. S.M. Lipset, M.A. Trow and J.S. Coleman, *Union Democracy: The Internal Politics of The International Typographical Union*, The Free Press, Illinois, 1956, p. 411.
26. J.D. Edelstein and M. Warner, *Comparative Union Democracy*, Allen and Unwin, London, 1975, p. 339.
27. Lipset, Trow and Coleman, *op. cit.*, p. 406.
28. B. Shaw, *The Apple Cart*, Penguin, Harmondsworth, 1956, p. 47.
29. Lipset, Trow and Coleman, *op. cit.*, p. 15.
30. P. Taft quoted in J. Hughes, *Royal Commission on Trade Unions and Employers' Associations Research Paper 5 (Part 2), Membership Participation and Trade Union Government*, HMSO, London, 1967, p. 67.
31. *Ibid.*, p. 79.
32. Royal Commission, *op. cit.*, p. 271.
33. Trades Union Congress, *TUC Disputes, Principles and Procedures*, TUC, London (n.d.), pp. 4f.

6

Collective Bargaining

Collective bargaining is that method of determining working conditions and terms of employment through negotiations 'between an employer, a group of employers or one or more employers's organisations, on the one hand, and one or more representative workers' organisations on the other, with a view to reaching an agreement'.[1] Collective bargaining is the institutional centrepiece and focal point of British industrial relations. Indeed the Donovan Commission categorically stated 'that collective bargaining is the best method of conducting industrial relations.' It therefore saw wide scope in Britain for extending both the subject matter of collective bargaining and the number of employees covered by it.[2] In the 1980 workplace industrial relations survey, it is calculated that trade unions were recognized for collective bargaining purposes in 67 per cent of the establishments employing 25 or more employees. Establishments in the nationalized industries had 100 per cent and in the public services 94 per cent. In the private sector, unions were recognized in 68 per cent of the private manufacturing establishments but only in 42 per cent of the private service ones. It was size of establishments especially 'and, to a lesser extent, the size of enterprises [which] were strongly associated with the extent of recognition.'[3]

6.1 THE NATURE OF COLLECTIVE BARGAINING

The term 'collective bargaining', like that of 'industrial democracy', was first used by the Webbs. Its precise nature, however, is subject to much academic debate. Put briefly, the Webbs described collective bargaining as an economic institution, with trade unionism acting as a labour cartel by controlling entry into the trade. Allan Flanders has argued, on the other hand, that collective bargaining is primarily a political rather than an economic process and 'that the value of a union to its members lies less in its economic achievements than in its capacity to protect their dignity.'[4] More recently, the Webbs' classical analysis of collective bargaining and trade unionism has been defended against Flanders' criticisms and reappraisal of it on the grounds that it is 'as a bargaining agent' that the union finds its major 'justification in the eyes of its members and that the issues relating to financial reward are still, whether for material or symbolic reasons or both, among its major bargaining preoccupations.'[5] Marxists, by contrast, contend that collective bargaining is merely a means of social control within industry and an institutionalized expression of the class struggle between those owning capital and those selling labour in capitalist societies. By this view, 'an unceasing *power struggle* is therefore a central feature of industrial relations.'[6]

In practice we do not consider the theoretical distinction between collective bargaining as an economic process and collective bargaining as a political process to be conceptually or empirically valid. Indeed collective bargaining can be viewed from at least three perspectives, none of which necessarily conflicts with the others and each of which could well represent different stages in the development of the collective bargaining process. 'These viewpoints are that collective bargaining is (1) a means of contracting for the sale of labor, (2) a form of industrial government, and (3) simply a system of industrial relations.'[7] These three viewpoints have been described as the 'marketing' concept of collective bargaining, the 'governmental' concept, and the 'industrial relations' or 'managerial relations' concept respectively. The marketing concept, for example, views collective bargaining as the means by which labour is bought and sold in the market-place. In this context, collective bargaining is perceived primarily as an economic and exchange relationship. In other words, it is the method of conducting industrial relations which determines the standard terms and conditions of employment by which labour is supplied to an employer either by its present employees or by newly hired workers. This concept of collective bargaining focuses on the substantive content of collective agreements, on the pay, hours of work, and fringe benefits which are mutually agreed between employers and trade union representatives.

The marketing concept of collective bargaining is nearest to the Webbs' analysis. It assumes, correctly in our view, that industrial relations begins in the labour market. This view of collective bargaining is based on the belief that it provides the means to remedy the fundamental bargaining inequalities existing between the strong position of the employer, on the one hand, and the weak position of the individual employee, on the other, in the buying and selling of labour. The individual pay–work bargain between employer and employee, in short, is not regarded as being between equals. Nor is it made voluntarily by an individual worker with the employer but is negotiated out of economic necessity, since most people have to work in order to live. It is this fundamental imbalance of power which collective bargaining is designed to remedy. By using the device of the 'common rule', it is argued, employees can insist collectively that if an employer hires any of their number, it must offer them not only the standard rate of pay but also the standard conditions of employment for the job.

To what extent collective bargaining establishes an equality of advantage between managements and employees is subject to debate. It is even debatable whether collective bargaining has the power in the long term to redistribute real income between pay and profits. However, since a collective agreement may be necessary to both an employer and its employees, whereas under individual bargaining an agreement is of greater concern to the individual employee, then the imbalance of power against employees in the labour market is to some degree mitigated by collective bargaining. This is also a factor which reinforces the very determined defence of collective bargaining by trade unions when it is proposed to restrict or legally control 'free collective bargaining'.

The governmental concept of collective bargaining views the process as a constitutional system or rule making institution determining relations between management and trade union representatives. In this case, collective bargaining is seen as a political and power relationship. Trade unions in other words are regarded as sharing industrial sovereignty with management and, as the representatives of employees collectively, they use that power to advance their members' aspirations and employment interests at work. This view of collective bargaining stresses both the continuity of the management–union relationship and the continuous process of rule making which takes place between management and unions. In this way, the negotiation of substantive agreements on pay and conditions is not an end in itself. The disputes procedure for resolving differences between employers and unions, for example, provides the means of modifying the terms of an agreement when the occasion warrants. Hence in mature collective bargaining, the distinction between disputes arising out of existing collective agreements and those deriving from matters not covered by collective agreements becomes blurred. Similarly, when collective bargaining procedures are agreed so that employment rules can be continually made and applied between employers and trade unions and 'when labor and management deal with labor relations analytically and systematically after such a fashion, it is proper to refer to the system as "industrial jurisprudence." '[8]

The industrial relations or managerial relations concept of collective bargaining proceeds from the governmental concept. It views collective bargaining as a system of 'industrial governance', since through it trade unions join with employers in reaching decisions on matters in which both parties have equal rather than competing interests. The presence of the union in enterprise decision making, in other words, allows representative participation by employees in the determination of those policies most affecting their working lives. In this way collective bargaining involves trade union representatives, whether they like it or not, in organizational and managerial decision making in those areas covered by collective agreement. As the area of joint control expands, so too does the participation of trade unions in the management of the enterprise. Defining authority within the enterprise, for example, involves specifying areas of joint concern within which industrial relations decisions are made by mutual agreement. Underlying the concept of collective bargaining as a process of industrial governance is the principle that those who are integral to the running of an enterprise should have some voice in determining the decisions of most concern to them. This 'principle of mutuality', it is suggested, correlates with the concept of political democracy, so that collective bargaining becomes a means for establishing its equivalent – industrial democracy – at the workplace.

We do not believe that these three perspectives of collective bargaining are contradictory, incompatible or exhaustive.

> All three aspects of collective bargaining can thus be simultaneously maintained, but each provides a different emphasis, stresses a different guiding principle, and can influence the nature of the actions taken by the parties.[9]

The important thing to recognize is that the nature and depth of collective bargaining differs not only between separate negotiating groups but also within any particular negotiating group at different times. As collective bargaining matures between an employer and a particular negotiating group, it can logically progress through the marketing stage, to the governmental stage and ultimately the managerial stage if the parties wish. Clearly, the essence of the collective bargaining process is its representative nature, its power basis, its adaptability and its flexibility to particular circumstances.

What, briefly, are the conditions necessary for collective bargaining to emerge and to survive as an effective means for regulating relations between employers and trade unions? First, the parties must be sufficiently organized. This means, in practice, that freedom of association and of organization amongst employees into independent trade unions are indispensable conditions for the establishment of viable collective bargaining. Unless employees have the freedom to form themselves into stable organizations independent of both employer and state control, unions do not have the power base from which to negotiate effective collective agreements on behalf of their members. Whether employers are collectively organized depends on the levels at which collective bargaining takes place, the strength of the trade unions, and the structure of industrial relations within the industry. Organization on the part of the employers, therefore, is not a necessary but an enabling condition for collective bargaining to take place.

The second and fundamental condition for collective bargaining to emerge is that employers recognize trade unions for bargaining purposes. Yet the history of trade union recognition in Britain has been a long and frequently bitter struggle. In view of the obstacles which trade unions have often had to overcome in the early stages of their growth, including employer opposition, hostile decisions from the courts, and restrictive legislation, it is not surprising that progress in obtaining trade union recognition has been a slow and conflict ridden process. In Britain, which led the way in the nineteenth century in trade union organization, the struggle to win recognition from employers lasted many decades and continues even today. This was epitomized, perhaps, by the dispute over trade union recognition between Grunwick Processing Laboratories and the Association of Professional Clerical and Computer Staffs in the late 1970s.

After union organization and recognition from an employer have been achieved, and for collective bargaining to be successful, it is also necessary that the parties negotiate in good faith and accept the agreements entered into as binding upon each other. But either side, of course, is free at some later date to use the relevant procedural agreement to terminate or to modify existing agreements and to enter into new negotiations.

There are two methods by which the conditions necessary for effective collective bargaining can develop. One is by legal means, the other is voluntarily. In Britain the preference has been for trade union organization, trade union recognition, bargaining in good faith and the mutual observation of collective agreements to be achieved in accordance with the voluntary or abstentionist principle. The legal standing of collective agreements between the parties continues to be that they are 'binding in honour only'. They only become legally enforceable contracts if the parties mutually agree to make them such. Collective bargaining, in short, is not only the major method of conducting industrial relations in Britain. It is also the method in which the parties to it have preferred to build a framework of voluntary rather than compulsory procedural agreements governing their formal relations. These enable them to create a flexible body of substantive rules on pay and conditions which regulate their mutual rights and obligations in the labour market and the workplace. They also regulate day-to-day managerial relations between management, employees and unions at enterprise and establishment level.

6.2   COLLECTIVE BARGAINING REFORM

Collective bargaining reform has been a major policy issue in British industrial relations since the 1960s, especially after the publication of the Donovan Report in 1968. In essence, two main problems stand out in the debate. The first concerns the private sector pay bargaining system. The central issue here is how company or plant bargaining can be reconciled to industry-wide, multiemployer bargaining and, when they exist, to the exigencies of national incomes policies. The second issue concerns public sector pay bargaining. The main issue here is the extent to which the constraints imposed by government financed industry-wide agreements are compatible with the devolution of negotiating machinery in this sector, on the one hand, and with nonintervention by government in the bargaining process within them, on the other.

These two problems, one associated with the private sector and the other with the public sector, although interrelated, are in practice distinct and separate issues. But the suggested solutions to collective bargaining reform in Britain, such as the Donovan Commission's recommendations, have sometimes been proposed as all purpose panaceas rather than as specific prescriptions for highly particular cases.

The Donovan Commission

The first and one of the most influential analyses of collective bargaining in Britain in the post-war period was that of the Donovan Commission which was set up in 1965 and published its Report in June 1968. The central diagnosis of the Royal Commission was that Britain had 'two systems' of industrial relations. One was the 'formal system' embodied in the official institutions of collective bargaining at national level. The other was the 'informal system' based on the actual behaviour of managers, shop stewards, and workgroups at the place of work. In the words of the Commission:

> The formal system assumes industry-wide organisations capable of imposing their decisions on their members. The informal system rests on the wide autonomy of managers in individual companies and the power of industrial work groups.[10]

According to the Royal Commission, these two systems of collective bargaining were in conflict, with the informal system continuously undermining the regulative effect of industry-wide agreements on pay and conditions of employment. Symptomatic of this conflict, the Commission believed, was the increasing gap or 'wage drift' between nationally agreed rates of pay and actual earnings at the workplace; the failure of national disputes procedures to contain unofficial and unconstitutional strikes at factory level; the absence of company personnel policies; and the persistence of restrictive labour practices and low productivity within firms.

> To remedy this, effective and orderly collective bargaining is required over such issues as the control of incentive schemes, the regulation of hours actually worked, the use of job evaluation, work practices, and the linking of pay to changes in performance, facilities for shop stewards and disciplinary rules and appeals.[11]

The Commission did not consider, however, that such matters could be dealt with effectively by national agreements. It recommended instead that whilst industry-level agreements should be limited to those matters which they could effectively determine, comprehensive company agreements could provide 'the remedy'. These could regulate pay within firms, deal with grievances, discipline, and redundancy, and provide facilities for shop stewards at the workplace. Donovan envisaged, in other words, the formalization of a two tier structure of national and company collective bargaining, but not the abolition of national negotiations as such.

The Royal Commission took the view that top managements should initiate the reform of collective bargaining within their own companies. They should do this, the Report recommended, by developing authoritative collective bargaining machinery, comprehensive procedural agreements and the joint discussion of measures to promote health and safety within their firms. Within such a framework, it was argued, management and unions would then be able to negotiate productivity agreements relating pay to output, thereby lowering unit costs of production, raising the pay of employees, stabilizing prices to consumers, and improving company profitability. The Royal Commission, however, was not entirely convinced that corporate management would be generally committed to undertake these policy initiatives. It further recommended, therefore, that an Industrial Relations Act should be passed requiring larger companies, the nationalized industries, and the public services to register their procedural agreements with the Department of Employment and Productivity (DEP). An Industrial Relations Commission (CIR) was also to be established by this Act and, on reference from the DEP, it would investigate and report on cases arising out of the registration of these agreements. It would also consider problems referred to it by the DEP either concerning companies not large enough to be covered by the obligation to register their collective agreements, or disputes over trade union recognition between employers and trade unions. There were, however, to be no penalties for non-compliance by employers to the CIR's recommendations.

The prognosis for collective bargaining change embodied in the majority report of the Donovan Commission was to be voluntary procedural reform between employers and unions at company level. The law, however, was only to be used to prod reluctant companies in the direction of collective bargaining initiatives, rather than to coerce them into it. Through such measures, it was anticipated, collective bargaining structures would be reformed, the principle of joint negotiation would be extended, productivity agreements could be negotiated, and any conflicts between management and unions within firms would be resolved. Donovan, therefore, was 'mini-reformist' in its purposes, aiming at a common approach to collective bargaining change across most industries. As such, it did not really threaten the industrial relations status quo. However, it failed to distinguish between the collective bargaining problems inherent in some private sector industries, such as in engineering and large-scale manufacturing, and those in the rest of private industry and the public sector. It also made very scant and superficial references to the problems of simultaneously devolving collective bargaining from multiemployer to company level, and of managing incomes policy centrally.

In the event, the Labour Government published its white paper, *In Place of Strife*, in January 1969. Whilst embracing most of the recommendations made by the Donovan Commission, it also contained several paragraphs relating to proposed 'cooling-off' periods in the case of unconstitutional strikes and to the holding of strike ballots in certain other instances. These proposals were totally unacceptable to the trade union movement and a General Election was called in 1970 before the Labour Government had time to reconsider its proposals for industrial relations legislation.

The 1970s

The in-coming Conservative Government's approach to the reform of collective bargaining was very different in its emphasis. Indeed it is doubtful whether the reform of collective bargaining was in any sense its major policy objective for industrial relations. Its aim was, rather, to reform and to change trade unionism not collective bargaining *per se*. While the Donovan Commission had in effect concluded that trade unions were too weak and needed strengthening in order to perform their collective bargaining functions adequately, the Conservative Party had already drawn quite contrary conclusions in its pamphlet *Fair Deal at Work*, published in April 1968. It felt that the unions were too strong and that if the Conservative Party's industrial relations objectives were to be achieved to the benefit of the country at large, then trade union power needed weakening by changes in the law on industrial relations.

The Conservatives' stated objectives were aimed at:

1. More responsible collective bargaining to improve the content of agreements and to ensure that, once made, they are kept.
2. The removal of barriers to industrial efficiency, higher productivity and higher real earnings.
3. The achievement of greater co-operation between management, employees and trade unions in securing industrial peace and progress.
4. Providing fair and reasonable protection for the basic rights of individuals – including the right to work in the occupation of their choice and for which they are best qualified.[12]

In contrast to Donovan, and despite its earlier claim that 'collective bargaining by independent trade unions and employers free of State control is one of the hallmarks of liberty in an industrial society',[13] the Conservative Government enacted the Industrial Relations Act 1971. This legislation epitomized the approach of many critics of British collective bargaining at that time. It reflected the view that direct statutory intervention in industrial relations, especially in trade union affairs and in industrial disputes, through 'a fair, relevant and sensible framework of law, while providing no panaceas, can exert stabilising pressures and help to raise general standards in the way men do business together.'[14] Whatever the merits of the new labour law in advancing individual rights at work, the 1971 Act ultimately proved unworkable and had little direct impact on reforming collective bargaining or in integrating it with a viable incomes policy. It is arguable that the enactment of the Industrial Relations Act hindered the reform of collective bargaining subsequently.

Other proposals for the reform of Britain's collective bargaining structure came somewhat later. They included those of the Confederation of British Industry (CBI) in 1977. It believed that:

> The present system of bargaining has failed. It is one major reason why we have not achieved high employment, high growth, high productivity, and high real earnings; it has hindered good industrial relations: and it has made it harder for the UK to compete and earn her way in the world.'[15]

There was little doubt in the CBI's view that one of the major problems facing private industry at that time was the fundamental shift in the balance of bargaining power to the advantage of organized labour. In its opinion, this was compounded by poor productivity, low profitability, inadequate cash flow, the high cost of borrowing and an 'imbalance in the public sector' which 'has had serious repercussions in the private sector, particularly in the last few years.'[16] For these reasons, there had been, in the CBI's view, uneconomic levels of pay bargaining which were not only inflationary but also against the public interest.

To remedy such instability in the collective bargaining structure, and to improve Britain's economic performance, the CBI saw three broad courses of action to be possible: permanent controls by government on pay bargaining; reliance on market forces together with strict control of the money supply; or free collective bargaining within the constraints of monetary discipline and some central influence on the overall level of wage and salary settlements. Having compared these different approaches, the CBI concluded that the most suitable direction of change would 'be a combination of the second and third choices before us – a system based on market forces and monetary discipline, but one in which central guidance influences pay claims and settlements.'[17] In order to achieve bargaining reform and to create the conditions necessary for high economic growth and greater material prosperity, the CBI went on to suggest that any changes in collective bargaining and pay determination would need to be concentrated on four related fronts: first, action by Government as the country's financial controller and as a pay bargainer in its own right; second, the creation of wider understanding of the nation's economic circumstances; third, the reconstruction of collective bargaining arrangements to reduce competitive bargaining between different pay groups; and fourth, the restoration of greater balance in bargaining power between employers and trade unions.

Like other analyses of British industrial relations at that time, the CBI could see no established pattern or discernible order within the collective bargaining arrangements covering that three-quarters of the full-time employed labour force subject to collective agreements in the late 1970s.

> Although in the public sector bargaining on pay is predominantly at national level, in private industry company or plant bargaining plays a significant part. There are thousands of distinct agreements, often with separate settlement dates, and with a large number of agreements operated within a single company.[18]

To remedy these structural deficiencies within which pay was negotiated, and to contain what it regarded as 'inherently inflationary' and 'competitive bargaining', the CBI maintained that the principal initiative for change rested with the employers.

Amongst its proposals, the CBI suggested that there should be a restructuring of bargaining arrangements within individual plants or companies and across industries. It saw no reason, for example, why multitier bargaining should not take place at more than one level, say at industry or national, company or employer and plant or workplace level. It thought it desirable, however, that there should normally be a clear separation of those items of the employment package negotiated at different bargaining levels. There should, for instance, be no item bargained at more than one level, and only those items for which flexibility was required should be bargained at the lower levels. Moreover, 'strict application of the guidelines would be likely to rule out most bargaining at departmental level, because expertise will not be generally sufficiently high to ensure control.'[19] The CBI also considered that there should be a minimum number of bargaining units or negotiating groups consistent with the structure and organization of the industry or company in question.

This move towards fewer and larger bargaining units within plants, companies, or industries, it was felt, should be accompanied, secondly, by collective action amongst employers to synchronize pay settlement dates. There could thus be a compression of the annual pay round into a much shorter period of time within, say, three months or so. It was suggested, too, that within the shorter pay round, there would be some advantage if those groups with the greatest bargaining power negotiated first. Finally, the CBI argued, more attention should be focussed within companies on the development of rational and easily understood pay structures than had previously been the case. In its view, inadequate internal pay structures not only reflected the disorder of Britain's collective bargaining arrangements, but also generated inflationary pressures within the economy. The overriding principles in pay structures should be 'that adequate control can be maintained; and that there should be accepted differentials related to skill, effort and responsibility.'[20] The approach of the CBI, then, was to advocate reform of private sector collective bargaining through employer initiative and tighter monetary discipline and freer market forces, with the latter acting to constrain inflationary pay negotiations between what it regarded as weak employers and strong trade unions.

Another plea for collective bargaining reform came from within a section of the Trades Union Congress (TUC). Its main concern was with the problems and inadequacies of pay determination within the public services, excluding the nationalized industries. The dissatisfactions amongst unions representing civil service, health service, and local authority employees were, by the late 1970s, twofold. First, they felt that decisions on the pay of public sector employees had become too much a matter for political debate and public discussion rather than of responsible collective bargaining. Implicit in this view was the belief that incomes policies had always operated with far greater rigidity towards public sector employees than towards their private sector counterparts. Second, they also considered that public sector pay problems had been made worse by the extremely centralized nature of the negotiating machinery within their industries.

Towards the end of 1977, for example, David Basnett, then General Secretary of the National Union of General and Municipal Workers and Chairman of the TUC at that time, suggested that a new approach towards public service pay bargaining was required and that the impetus for the change must come from the trade union side. It would involve establishing a more comprehensive machinery to bring together 'unions in local government and the health service, and the industrial and non-industrial civil services, to form a new TUC Public Services Committee.'[21] Once established, he argued, this Committee would convene a regular conference of its member unions. There were common objectives which this Committee would seek. These could include: first, more regular contact with Government Ministers to discuss economic policy; second, making further moves towards synchronization of the principal pay settlement dates within the public services; third, replacing one-off emergency inquiries with permanent pay review bodies. Such bodies could thereby establish genuine pay comparisons between public sector and private sector employees and their findings would be made available to negotiators; fourth, the undertaking of regular reviews of pay structures. Then finally, a review of pay negotiating machinery in the public services could be attempted. 'This would give more authority to lower levels of management and local union officials. The more problems that can be solved at local level, the better.'[22] In 1979, a TUC Public Services Committee was formally established but, as outlined below, the change in the political and economic climate after 1980 seriously frustrated most of its objectives.

The 1980s

After the election to power of Conservative Administrations led by Margaret Thatcher after 1979, collective bargaining in Britain was dominated by economic policies aimed at keeping inflation under control by restricting the money supply, by cutting public expenditure and by legal policies which had the effect of weakening trade union bargaining power, especially in trade disputes. In the private sector, pragmatic reform of collective bargaining structures at employer and enterprise levels continued, largely initiated by management. But it was market factors, ability of employers to pay, rising unemployment and a swing in the balance of power in favour of management which largely influenced the collective bargaining process and bargaining outcomes during that period.

Public sector collective bargaining was characterized by three main features after 1979. First, the Government's cash limits policy and tough stances by public sector employers generally resulted in relatively low pay settlements, sometimes below rates of inflation, for many pay groups. Second, there were a series of bitter industrial disputes in the civil service, water supply industry, coal mining, teaching, health service, railways, steel, and the fire services. Third, besides attempting to ban trade unions at the General Communications Headquarters at Cheltenham, the Government set up the Megaw Committee to inquire into the principles and system by which the remuneration of non-industrial civil servants should be determined. It also set up a pay review body for nurses and midwives in the health service.

In outline, Megaw recommended that 'informal collective bargaining' should be instituted in the civil service, providing 'for the reconciliation of national, economic and financial considerations with the cost of the pay settlement.' It also considered that whilst fair-pay comparisons should continue to be used in the civil service, they 'should have a much less decisive influence than in the past.' Evidence on the recruitment and retention of civil service staff was to be taken into account when conducting negotiations, with scope for extending incentive payments to be considered. Finally, whilst rejecting the introduction of productivity bargaining into the service, the Megaw Committee believed that productivity and efficiency questions should take an important place in collective bargaining 'to ensure that a sustained level of co-operation with productivity and efficiency measures is being achieved.'[23]

Collective bargaining reform remains a major policy issue in Britain today for employers, unions and government, although opinions differ in attempting to resolve the practical problems associated with the structural inadequacies of collective bargaining. First, collective bargaining reform is an inherently difficult problem to solve, largely because of its structural complexity and diversity and the vested interests involved. For example, the problems of the private sector differ from those of the public sector, with differences within each of these sectors arising from their technologies, labour force mix, geographical dispersion and employer and union policies. Second, given these factors and others, there is neither a general panacea nor a short cut to effective collective bargaining reform. The difficulty is in devising policies at governmental, employer and union levels enabling managerial and union negotiators to determine those forms and levels of bargaining which effectively integrate employer and/or enterprise negotiations with national or industry-wide agreements, global pay policy and the so called 'public interest'. The major implication is that bargaining reform can only proceed piecemeal rather than comprehensively, slowly, not rapidly, and voluntarily rather than by direct government coercion.

6.3   BARGAINING STRUCTURE

Where collective bargaining has achieved a degree of permanence and stability, it is possible to identify a framework or structure in which negotiations between employers and trade unions take place. The term 'bargaining structure' is used to describe the 'stable or permanent features that distinguish the bargaining process in any particular system'.[24] Four interrelated features within any collective bargaining structure can be identified. 'These may be termed: Bargaining levels, Bargaining units, Bargaining forms and Bargaining scope.'[25]

The concept of 'bargaining levels', for example, describes the levels at which collective bargaining is conducted within an industry or an organization. In much of British industry, private and public, collective bargaining has normally taken place through multiemployer negotiations at national or industry level between employers' associations or other employer representatives, on the one hand, and federations of trade unions on the other. But collective bargaining also takes place at company or employer level and at enterprise or workplace level. In certain industries, agreements may be negotiated at several levels to determine different elements in the employment package. In some private sector industries, such as in chemicals and in engineering, framework agreements on the pay and conditions of manual workers are determined at national level, even though not all employers are 'federated', and are then supplemented by company, workplace, and even workshop agreements on some matters. In engineering, for example, the negotiating pattern for manual workers can comprise: multiemployer and company bargaining as in Lucas industries; single employer agreements as in Fords; establishment or works level agreements within multiplant companies like the General Electric Company; or a combination of both company and workplace agreements in other multiplant companies such as Massey Ferguson. Bargaining levels, in short, may be high, intermediate or low, whilst in some industries there are a number of levels which may or may not be connected to one another.

Closely related to an industry's or an organization's bargaining levels are its 'bargaining units'. This term refers to the specific group or categories of employees covered by a particular agreement or set of agreements. Bargaining units are obviously connected with bargaining levels, but the latter concentrate on the managerial side of the negotiating table, whilst the concept of a bargaining unit is particularly concerned with the representative functions of trade unions. Individual unions or joint panels of unions, for example, act as bargaining agents for employees within given bargaining units. Bargaining units may be wide or narrow in coverage, and bargaining agents may be few or many in number. In chemicals and some textile trades, for example, there are relatively wide bargaining units with comparatively few bargaining agents. In engineering, there is a fairly wide bargaining unit at national level covering all manual workers in a variety of trades but they are represented, through the Confederation of Shipbuilding and Engineering Unions, by a multiplicity of bargaining agents. Teachers in the university sector and senior managerial employees in the electricity supply industry, on the other hand, have fairly narrow bargaining units and a single bargaining agent in each case. Although there are nominally nine bargaining units in the National Health Service, most of these tend to be narrow in their coverage and they comprise a multiplicity of bargaining agents, especially among the professional and technical staff, with about 40 representative bodies. But there are also separate pay review bodies for doctors and dentists and for nurses, midwives and related grades.

Bargaining units can vary from bargaining level to bargaining level, especially in private industry. At company level, for example, negotiations may be conducted in a number of different bargaining units. There may be one set of agreements for craftworkers and skilled employees, another for process workers, and different agreements for supervisors and white-collar workers. Also, agreements on some items like the standard working week and holiday arrangements may apply to all employees within a company and the bargaining unit may be company-wide. However, where piecework payment schemes operate, there may be a multiplicity of small and separate bargaining units at shopfloor level for the purpose of determining piecework prices. In some of these cases, the intraplant bargaining taking place within these workgroup bargaining units has been described as 'largely informal, largely fragmented and largely autonomous.'[26]

The terms 'bargaining forms' and 'bargaining scope' are also closely connected. Bargaining forms focuses on the ways in which an agreement or a set of agreements is recorded, that is whether it is written and formally signed, or unwritten and informal, whilst bargaining scope is used to indicate the range of subjects covered within a particular bargaining unit by its collective agreements. It would seem, generally, that the higher the bargaining level within an industry or organization, the more formalized its agreements. Yet even where national or company agreements are written down and are fairly formal, they may leave some room for manoeuvre and interpretation through negotiation at lower bargaining levels or by custom and practice in the workplace.

Similarly, as new subjects for negotiation are introduced and accepted within a bargaining unit, the range of subject matter in collective bargaining extends. Where bargaining scope ends, the right to manage or managerial prerogative begins. Although trade unions have traditionally pressed for extensions in the scope of collective bargaining, there are always certain subjects which management reserves the right to settle for itself without having to obtain either union or employee agreement. Bargaining forms, in short, may be either written and formal or unwritten and informal, while bargaining scope may be either comprehensive or restricted in its range.

It is clear, therefore, that the structure of collective bargaining in Britain is diverse and heterogeneous, displaying contrasting degrees of formality and informality among, between and within particular bargaining groups. In these circumstances, the concepts of bargaining levels, bargaining units, bargaining forms and bargaining scope are useful analytic tools for comparing different collective bargaining structures. The bargaining structures within the engineering trades, for example, are quite different from those existing in other private sector industries, in the public services, or in the nationalized industries. The engineering industry, for instance, covers a complex group of activities concerned with the manufacture, installation, maintenance and repair of metal goods. It includes work as wide ranging as metal founding and forging, scientific instrument making, motor vehicle assembling, constructional engineering, lamp and electronic manufacturing and so on. There are also a number of closely related industries like cutlery and edge tool manufacturing and lock, latch and key making which have their own negotiating machinery separate from that of the engineering industry.

The practice in engineering, for example, is for negotiations on major pay fluctuations and the main conditions of employment affecting manual workers to be conducted at national or multiemployer level between the Engineering Employers Federation (EEF), representing the employers, and the Confederation of Shipbuilding and Engineering Unions representing the many unions in the industry. Matters affecting the members of one union only, such as the electricians and plumbers, may also be discussed at national level between the EEF and the union concerned. Similarly, issues affecting members of a particular group of unions may also be raised at national level by the unions involved. Such negotiations are conducted on an *ad hoc* basis at special conferences. The normal practice is for the trade unions making a claim to write to the EEF requesting a conference at which to present their case. This is then considered by the employers and a formal reply is given normally at a further conference. Negotiations continue either until agreement is reached or discussions break down. In addition to these arrangements, the EEF conducts national negotiations on conditions of employment with unions representing certain white-collar workers in the industry.

In practice, however, national negotiations on pay and conditions in engineering are increasingly marginal in their impact on the actual earnings of employees and on their conditions of employment at the place of work. This is because the major decisions on these matters are now generally taken at company or plant bargaining levels or at both. In these circumstances, it is local unions which take the initiative in making claims on behalf of their members to managerial representatives at both company and workplace, or either, level. Such negotiations are held on company premises, in company time and may or may not involve full-time trade union officers in the bargaining process. Furthermore, they normally take place over a single period. Whilst there may be only one pay claim per bargaining unit each year, other matters may be dealt with as they arise as the subject of separate agreements of varying degrees of formality. The bargaining scope might include, for instance, holiday arrangements, payment by results schemes, shiftwork allowances, the amount of overtime, its allocation and so on.

Such local negotiations 'or "domestic claims" are the most personalized aspect of negotiations and for much of the time they deal not in economic claims but in disputes as to grievance procedures, dismissals, work practices, etc.[27] In engineering, in short, both the collective bargaining structure and the elements within it are quite complex; bargaining in engineering is highly differentiated not only in its bargaining levels but also in its bargaining units among firms and within them. But there are also wide divergences in bargaining form and scope within the industry. These vary between considerable formality and comprehensive range, on the one hand, and unstructured informality and restricted range, on the other.

By contrast in the water supply industry, there are separate bargaining units for manual workers, white-collar staff and senior managers. These are the National Joint Industrial Council, the National Joint Council, The National Joint Council for Senior Staff and the National Joint Committee for Chief Officers. Apart from the NJC for Senior Staff and the National Joint Committee, a range of unions are represented on these bodies which discuss a wide range of issues affecting both employers and employees. For manual staff there are also a number of Regional Joint Industrial Councils which have been set up to maintain links between bargaining levels and to implement agreements and decisions made nationally. Control of terms and conditions in this sector, therefore, is very much centrally determined rather than at establishment of workplace level.

6.4   PATTERNS OF COLLECTIVE BARGAINING

As outlined in section 6.1 collective bargaining regulates 'managerial relations' as well as 'pay relations' but it is as a system of pay determination that collective bargaining has a central role in British industrial relations. The incidence of collective bargaining varies between employment sectors, occupational status and size of employing estab-

Table 6.1 *Percentage of employees covered by collective agreements by major sectors 1980.*

	All private sector	Private manufacturing	Private services	All public sector	Nationalized industries	Public administration
Manual employees	50	68	35	76	98	73
Union density (%)	(65)	(75)	(39)	(67)	(91)	(58)
Non-manuals	30	32	29	90	94	89
Union density (%)	(31)	(39)	(21)	(61)	(90)	(57)

Source: W.W. Daniel and N. Millward, *Workplace Industrial Relations Survey* (Heinemann, 1983)

lishments. Another distinctive feature of the pattern of pay determination in Britain 'is the diversity and multiplicity of levels at which there is collective bargaining.'[28]

The distribution of collective bargaining

Table 6.1 provides some indication of the variations in collective bargaining arrangements between manual and nonmanual employees and those of the private and public sectors in the early 1980s. These figures – taken from the 1980 workplace industrial relations survey – though they must be interpreted with some caution do indicate the main features of the distribution of collective bargaining arrangements in Britain. First, public sector employers are more likely to recognize and negotiate with trade unions than are private sector employers. There are, however, variations in the public sector, with higher percentages of collective bargaining for manual and non-manual employees in the nationalized industries, which normally have statutory obligations to negotiate and consult with trade unions, than in public administration. Second, collective bargaining is more likely to take place in private manufacturing industry than it is in the private services. Third, collective bargaining is a more normal practice for manual employees than for those in non-manual employment, again with significant differences between the private and public sectors. The major exception is public administration where the proportion of non-manual employees covered by collective bargaining is higher than for manual employees. Collective bargaining is poorly organized for all groups of employees in the private sector by comparison.

Apart from ownership of establishments, establishment size and to a lesser extent enterprise size are strongly associated with the extent of union recognition and collective bargaining. The 1980 workplace survey shows that in the private sector the number of people employed on site and the number of people employed in total by the enterprise of which the establishments were a part 'exercised strong independent influences upon the extent of trade union recognition'.[29] In the public sector, though size of establishment and size of enterprise are important influences on collective bargaining, enterprise ownership tends to be more significant a factor.

Table 6.2 indicates the variety of levels within which collective bargaining over the

Table 6.2 *Basis for most recent pay increase for manual employees 1980.*

Level	Public sector	Nationalized industries	Public administration	Private sector	Manufacturing	Construction	Miscellaneous services
			(per cent)				
National	75	51	80	46	41	34	53
Employer	24	48	18	22	16	45	21
Workplace	—	1	—	30	41	18	21
Others	1	—	2	2	2	3	5
Total	100	100	100	100	100	100	100

Source: W.W. Daniel and N. Millward, *Workshop Industrial Relations Survey* (Heinemann, 1983)

pay for manual employees takes place. Again the figures must be examined with caution but they do show significant differences between the basis of pay increases for manual employees in different employment sectors. In the private sector, for example, employer and workplace bargaining predominate, with national or multiemployer bargaining more likely to operate in the private sector services. In the public sector, by contrast, multiemployer bargaining is the norm. The main exceptions are the nationalized industries where each public corporation, such as British Rail or the National Coal Board, is often the sole or monopolist employer.

The private sector

In the private sector the pattern of collective bargaining is very complex. Several surveys of employing establishments provide useful evidence about the levels of bargaining which influence changes in rates of pay and other conditions of employment. They also attempt to identify the most important bargaining level having the greatest impact on pay rate changes. But there is no general agreement about what determines particular collective bargaining arrangements. 'The available literature on the subject has tended to view it as a decision taken by the parties on the basis of the various costs and benefits of alternative structures.'[30] The debate centres around whether it is employer or union organization which is the major factor. In Britain the 'literature starts from the assumption that management has the predominant influence.'[31]

For analytical purposes collective bargaining can be classified into 'multiemployer bargaining' and 'single employer bargaining', with single employer bargaining further subdivided into 'centralized' and 'decentralized' bargaining. Private sector multiemployer bargaining is where a number of employers reach an industry-wide or national agreement on pay and conditions with the recognized unions in the industry as a whole, although there are a few examples, such as road haulage, where agreements continue to be negotiated at regional or district level. An increasing number of national pay agreements specify minimum hourly rates or minimum weekly earnings rather than standard rates. Even where standard rates are laid down, provision is often made for company level or workplace productivity payments on top of standard earnings. Industries where multiemployer bargaining continues to have an important influence on earnings include: quarrying and construction; clothing and footwear; paper and printing; timber and furniture; textiles and leather; and bricks, pottery, glass and cement.

Single employer bargaining, especially in large multiplant firms, can be either centralized or decentralized. Centralized bargaining takes place at employer level with negotiated agreements applicable to all plants and sites within the company. Examples include the British Sugar Corporation, with separate bargaining units for process and craft workers, and British Leyland (BL) which has five company-wide bargaining groups with a single settlement date. Prior to collective bargaining reorganization in BL during the 1970s, the company had some 130 separate bargaining units, decentralized negotiations and settlement dates throughout the year. Industries where centralized bargaining takes place include: banking and insurance; hotels and miscellaneous services; transport and communication; and instrument engineering – though it is not very strongly organized in the first two sectors, as indicated in table 6.3. Decentralized or workplace bargaining predominates in shipbuilding, mechanical and electrical engineering, metal manufacture, and metal goods and vehicles. Sometimes each workplace or plant has full delegated authority to settle pay claims and all other terms and conditions of employment locally: this is sometimes described as 'local autonomy bargaining'. In other instances negotiations are conducted at workplace level, but within limits set by corporate centre – sometimes known as 'co-ordinated local bargaining'.

In yet other cases, in a cross section of industries, many companies conduct collective

Table 6.3 *The most important level of pay bargaining in private sector industry.*

Industry	Multiemployer agreements	Single employer agreements Centralized	Decentralized	Percentage of industry covered by collective agreements
	%	%	%	
Quarrying and construction	83	6	11	63
Bricks, pottery, glass and cement	67	17	16	93
Clothing and footwear	66	31	3	70
Paper and printing	63	17	20	86
Timber and furniture	58	22	20	72
Textiles and leather	55	26	19	69
Banking and insurance	38	62	0	50
Distribution	31	40	29	52
Hotels	29	46	25	28
Transport and communication	28	49	23	79
Chemicals	25	42	33	45
Food, drink and tobacco	21	29	50	85
Metal goods	13	11	76	86
Metal manufacture	9	8	83	91
Vehicles	8	32	60	87
Electrical engineering	6	34	60	88
Mechanical engineering	5	12	83	77
Instrument engineering	0	52	48	66
Shipbuilding	0	7	93	69
Total private industry	30	26	44	69

Source: W.W. Daniel and N. Millward, *Workshop Industrial Relations Survey* (Heinemann, 1983)

bargaining at a series of levels, as implied from table 6.3. This may be described as 'mixed bargaining'. A multiemployer agreement at national level, for example, establishes a framework of pay and conditions, providing opportunities for further and more detailed bargaining at employer or company level. Company agreements, in turn, can be supplemented by workplace negotiations over particular terms and conditions of employment locally. With mixed bargaining different subjects are negotiated at different levels. Basic pay rates, minimum earnings, standard hours of work and general conditions can be determined nationally, for example, with actual pay levels, productivity and incentive payments, and specific conditions of employment being determined at company or workplace levels or both. What arrangements exist in particular industries or firms depends on a number of factors including economic, technological and representational influences in each case.

For employers, centralized corporate bargaining has a number of advantages. These include: uniform terms and conditions within the company; more predictable labour costs; stable relationships between different negotiating groups; and fewer pay parity claims. Its major disadvantages are: accommodating the conflicting demands deriving from diverse product markets, labour markets and technologies; excessive formalization of collective agreements; extended lines of communications; and how to monitor workplace arrangements effectively. From the trade union viewpoint, centralized bargaining provides more effective and efficient use of union resources and negotiating skills and better co-ordination between bargaining groups. However, company bargaining, unlike workplace bargaining, can weaken the status and power of shop stewards and create tensions in decentralized unions, such as the engineering workers, where considerable autonomy is vested locally. Also smaller unions with full negotiating rights locally can find themselves squeezed out of centralized negotiations where there is often strong competition for places in the union negotiating team because of multiunionism.[32]

Table 6.4 *Major influences on collective bargaining levels.*

	Multiemployer bargaining	Single employer bargaining Centralized	Decentralized
Product market	competitive	homogeneous	heterogeneous
Work organization	labour intensive	capital intensive	capital intensive
Technology	small batch	homogeneous	heterogeneous
Geographic location	concentrated	concentrated	dispersed
Business structure	many firms: small plant size	multiplant: small plant size	multiplant: large plant size
Union structure	centralized: few unions	centralized: various	decentralized: multiunions
Payment system	time payments	job evaluated	payment by results

The advantages of decentralized bargaining for employers include the following: it enhances local managerial authority for industrial relations; it provides shorter lines of communication and aids speedier resolution of disputes; and it enables management to achieve a flexible approach to workplace change. On the other hand, decentralized bargaining often gives rise to claims for pay parity between workplaces and negotiating groups, in addition to complicating the monitoring of labour cost control.[33] For trade unions decentralized bargaining consolidates shop steward power and eases intraplant communications; but it can also weaken the authority of full-time trade union officers and intraunion or interplant solidarity.

Table 6.4 provides an indication of the major factors influencing multiemployer, centralized and decentralized bargaining. It must be repeated that the situation is highly complex and in many industries there are factors influencing employers and unions in more than one direction, as evidenced by the variety of mixed bargaining which takes place. In general, however, multiemployer bargaining is more likely in labour intensive industries which have large numbers of small firms that are geographically concentrated with selling taking place in competitive product markets. Centralized employer bargaining is more likely in capital intensive industries which are either dominated by a single large firm or where there are relatively few firms each with a sizeable market share. Finally, other things being equal, decentralized bargaining is more likely than centralized bargaining where average plant size is high, where there is significant variation in plant size, 'where plants are geographically dispersed, where technology and the product market varies among plants and where the wage payment system relates pay directly to effort.'[34]

The public sector

Collective bargaining in the public sector takes place within central government, local government and the public corporations. As shown in table 6.5 central government is made up of the civil service, National Health Service, universities, UK Atomic Energy Commission and Forestry Commission. Local government consists of a wide range of public services including education, housing, refuse disposal, public health, personal social services, planning, fire services and transport and highways. The public corporations comprise some 15 major industries or public trading bodies which have a substantial degree of financial independence from central government, including the power to borrow within limits and to hold reserves. Table 6.5 includes only those major parts of the public sector with collective bargaining arrangements. Some public sector groups, such as higher civil servants, the police, nurses, midwives and health visitors, doctors and dentists, and the armed services, have their terms and conditions of work determined by government appointed pay review bodies rather than by collective bargaining. None the less, collective bargaining remains the major method for

Table 6.5 *Major public sector collective bargaining groups.*

Sector	Number of bargaining units	Number of[1] employees
Central government		
Civil Service	2	650 000
National Health Service[2]	9	380 000
Universities	5	87 000
UK Atomic Energy Commission[3]	2	14 000
Forestry Commission	4	7 000
Local government		
Manual staff	5	1 000 000
Education	7	600 000
Administrative and technical staff	11	570 000
Fire Services	3	58 000
Passenger Transport Executives	8	47 000
Municipal Buses	2	20 000
Public corporations		
National Coal Board	7	250 000
British Rail	8	200 000
Post Office	5	175 000
Electricity Supply	5	140 000
British Gas[3]	4	100 000
British Steel	4	66 000
London Transport Executive	16	56 000
British Airways[3]	10	55 000
National Bus Company	3	50 000
British Broadcasting Corporation	1	29 000
British Nuclear Fuels	2	16 000
Scottish Bus Group	4	8 000
British Airports Authority[3]	1	7 000
Civil Aviation Authority	1	7 000
British Waterways Board	2	3 000
Water Authorities[3]	4	65 000

[1] approximate numbers only
[2] excludes groups such as doctors, dentists and nurses with their own pay review bodies
[3] likely to be privatized in part or wholly in the future
Source: ACAS, *Industrial Relations Handbook* (HMSO 1980)

determining the pay and employment conditions for the vast majority of public sector employees in Britain.

In general public sector collective bargaining has three main characteristics. First, in contrast to the private sector, 'nationally negotiated agreements continue to be of paramount importance,'[35] though in the largely monopolistic public corporations, which are the sole buyers of labour, national agreements are not multi-employer agreements but single employer ones. Second, most public sector industries or enterprises have collective bargaining machinery for all groups of employees with clearly defined and sometimes large bargaining units. These are often divided into manual, craft, professional and technical, and managerial groups typified, for example, by the electricity supply industry and British local authorities. Third, Whitley bargaining machinery based on the recommendations of the Committee on Relations between Employers and Employees in 1917–18 provides the dominant model for conducting negotiations in most of the public sector.

National bargaining provides the most authoritative pay agreements in central government, local government and the public corporations, but there is still scope for local or establishment negotiations in some parts of the public sector, limited largely to manual employees on productivity or incentive payments. In central and local government, there is no local pay bargaining for manual or non-manual employees in the UK Atomic Energy Commission, the educational services, the fire services or passenger transport executives. The same is true in British Rail, Electricity Supply, British Airways, the British Broadcasting Corporation, British Nuclear Fuels, the British Airports Authority, the Civil Aviation Authority and the British Waterways Board amongst the public corporations. But in most of the remaining public sector, varying local additions to the national pay rates of manual workers are made.

In the industrial civil service, for example, all craft employees receive craft rates of pay determined in the national joint co-ordinating committee and employing departments have no discretion to change them. Nevertheless, they can earn productivity bonuses which vary between establishments. In the health service too despite national agreements some pay flexibility exists for certain manual groups, such as ancillary staff and craft workers, who have locally determined bonuses. These schemes must comply with national guidelines and be self-financing. There are also locally controlled bonus earnings for manual employees in the local authority services. In this sector bonus payments represent some 20 per cent earnings of male manual employees working full-time.

In local government, however, there are conflicting pressures emerging within the collective bargaining system. In the past some individual authorities have made pay settlements independently of national negotiations but the central employer bodies see their collective interests to be best furthered by strengthening national bargaining. Similarly:

> On the trade union side there is rank and file pressure for more decentralised bargaining, whereas the centralised union representatives, while not denying the validity of this claim, have argued for more contact with central government and more integration between unions.[36]

In local government a new balance between central and local negotiations has yet to be worked out.

Certain local negotiations take place in the public corporations. In the National Coal Board (NCB), for example, the establishment of incentive payments for mineworkers in the late 1970s reintroduced an element of locally determined pay in the industry. This scheme is settled nationally but standards are fixed locally so as to result in differential payments between pits and areas. In British Steel (BSC), there are limited national pay negotiations, with a wide range of local and plant bargaining. The items negotiable include performance linked bonuses, job gradings, new technology payments and so on. It has been managerial policy to decentralize collective bargaining in British Rail, emphasizing local productivity agreements at works level. In effect, national agreements in these corporations provide the framework for further negotiations locally. In the electricity supply industry additions to pay for manual employees, such as certain allowances and subsistence payments, are also negotiated at local level.

Typical public sector bargaining units are found in British Rail (BR) and the National Bus Company (NBC). The five main groupings in BR are: salaried and conciliation staff; workshop staff; workshop supervisory staff; professional, technical and research staff; and managerial staff. Each group has its own negotiating machinery at national level, supplemented by regional and local joint committees of management and union representatives. In the NBC there are three bargaining groups: platform, maintenance and service staff; administrative, clerical and supervisory staff; and management staff. These bargaining arrangements are commonly repeated in other parts of the public sector.

It is Whitleyism, however, which provides the central feature of public sector collective bargaining. In outline, Whitleyism is firmly entrenched across the public sector except the universities, schools and further education, the NCB, BSC, the British Broadcasting Corporation (BBC) and British Nuclear Fuels (BNF). The reasons why these sectors are not covered by Whitley negotiating arrangements are largely historical. Collective bargaining for university teachers, for example, is of relatively recent origins and has no Whitley tradition. Bargaining machinery for schools and further education though created much earlier, in 1919, was never modelled on Whitley principles in the first place. Similarly, collective bargaining in the coal and steel industries preceded nationalization. When these industries were taken into public ownership after the second world war, they largely retained existing collective bargaining structures. Lastly, the BBC and BNF are two relatively small and specialist public enterprises with their own internal arrangements and traditions for industrial relations.

Basically, public sector Whitleyism provides a negotiating structure where there is 'a joint negotiating council at the national level for each major occupational grouping within each industry, while below these are councils at the regional, district, local or departmental levels.'[37] The electricity supply industry (ESI) provides a model example of how public sector Whitleyism is organized in practice. The ESI has five Whitley bargaining groups: manual employees; craft workers; professional, administrative, clerical and sales staff; technical, engineering and scientific staff; and higher management. As shown in table 6.6, there are national joint councils (NJIC/NJC/NJB/NJMC) for each bargaining group in the ESI, with district joint councils (DJICs/DJCs/DJBs/ JMCs) and local works and staff committees, except for higher management and craftworkers. The NJIC, for example, determines the main terms and conditions for manual workers, such as rates of pay and conditions of employment, as do the other national negotiating bodies for craft workers, professional and administrative staff, technical and scientific staff and higher management.

Table 6.6 *Whitley machinery in the Electricity Supply Industry.*

Staff group	National machinery	District bodies	Local committees
Manual staff	NJIC	14 DJICs	Works committees
Craftworkers	NJ (B and CE)C	—	—
Professional and administrative	NJC	14 DJCs	Staff committees
Technical, engineering and scientific	NJB	16 DJBs	Technical staff committees
Higher management	NJMC	Area JMCs	—

Source: ACAS, *Industrial Relations Handbook* (HMSO 1980)

For NJIC, NJC and NJB staff, there are district bodies ensuring that the agreements negotiated nationally are applied properly. They also resolve any difficulties arising from the application of national agreements. Beneath district level are local committees which, within the terms of the national agreements, deal with issues such as working hours, shift rotas, schedules and internal grievances. Craft workers in the NJ (B and CE) C do not have formal district or local machinery, though NJMC staff have joint managerial committees to handle local matters at area level. The industry has also agreed procedures for avoiding disputes, with stages at local, district and national levels. There is, moreover, separate consultative machinery in the ESI. This consists of a National Joint Coordinating Council (NJCC) for the industry, with specialist committees on health and safety and on education and training. The tasks of the NJCC include any matters of common interest such as corporate plans, station closures, technological changes and fuel policy. There are also 12 district joint advisory councils and a large number of local advisory committees for consultation at a lower level.

Another feature of public sector Whitleyism is that it operates on common negotiat ing principles, although details vary between sectors. Each joint council, for example, is a standing body which meets regularly and determines its own membership, without necessarily having equal representation from each side. Employer negotiators are normally known as the 'management side' and union negotiators as the 'staff side'. Each side has its 'leader', or chief representative, who is usually responsible for presenting their side's case at joint meetings. The detailed work of Whitley councils is usually carried out by appropriate subcommittees or joint working parties, at national, district or local levels. Largely because of this, the joint secretaries of these bodies play key roles in determining Whitley decisions. Plenary meetings often affirm what has already been agreed in committee.

Another major negotiating principle of Whitleyism is that decisions are 'normally taken by a majority of each side voting separately.' In practice this means that no agreement can be made between the parties unless it is approved by a majority of both the employer and union representatives. This requires agreement within both sides, therefore, and neither side can outvote the other, thus compelling the acceptance of an agreement to which there is opposition. Though, on occasions, this makes joint agreement impossible it has been a useful device for negotiators on both sides facing inflexible opposite numbers. In the past, at least, this convention has prevented 'determined employers from imposing unacceptable settlements upon union representatives against their will.'[38] More recently, however, government cash limit policies have effectively constrained the efficacy of public sector Whitleyism as an acceptable and fair method of pay determination.

6.5   COLLECTIVE AGREEMENTS

Collective agreements are the output or result of the collective bargaining process. First, they provide constitutional frameworks by which the parties to collective bargaining can make, apply and monitor the industrial relations decisions affecting themselves and those on whose behalf they negotiate. Second, they define the market and managerial relations between employers and employees. If they are to be understood and adhered to by the parties, collective agreements need to be written and formalized. This is not to argue that formality of agreements in itself improves industrial relations. Indeed an overformal approach in collective bargaining inducing hairsplitting arguments over the meanings of words is not conducive to effective industrial relations between employers and trade unions or between managers and shop stewards. However, most collective agreements are more formalized than in the past and are put in writing where possible. This contrasts with those earlier 'agreements' in the 1960s and 1970s which were often based on 'shared understandings' and 'custom and practice' between negotiators at workplace level.

Written agreements largely overcome the problems arising in informal and poorly documented industrial relations situations when the main participants change for one reason or another. The continuity between the parties provided by written agreements is vital. Moreover, the stability which they introduce into collective bargaining can contribute to organizational and industrial relations change. But to repeat:

> Formal agreements are not a solution to all industrial relations problems. Their introduction can, however, herald a fresh start and can lead to industrial relations practices which, in the right conditions, should bring order into the working relationship from which could develop a genuine understanding.[39]

This is not to suggest that workers stop bargaining informally with management if they are powerful enough to do this. Indeed, informal practices are likely to be a permanent feature of industrial relations, especially where there are powerful workgroups.

Collective agreements are negotiated at various levels within different industries. They may even be struck at more than one level within an industry. These levels include: multiemployer, national or industry-wide agreements; regional or district agreements; single employer or company agreements; and plant, establishment, workshop or even departmental agreements. Similarly, agreements may be negotiated between a single employer and a single union, as between the Post Office and the Union of Communication Workers for postal grades in the postal services; between one employer and a number of unions, as for manual grades in the Ford Motor Company; between a number of employers and a number of unions, as in the various local authority negotiating groups; between an employers' association and a single union, as in the electrical contracting industry; and between an employers' association and a number of unions, as in the engineering trades. Collective agreements are also negotiated between employer representatives and full-time union officers or between management representatives and shop stewards.

Collective agreements are commonly classified as being either 'procedural' or 'substantive', although it is possible in practice to have both procedural and substantive elements within the same agreement. It has been suggested, for example, that:

> The procedural clauses of these agreements deal with such matters as the methods to be used and the stages to be followed in the settlement of disputes, or perhaps the facilities and standing to be accorded to representatives of parties to the agreement. Their substantive clauses, on the other hand, refer to rates of wages and working hours or to other job terms and conditions in the segment of employment covered by agreement. The first kind of rules regulate the behaviour of parties to the collective agreements – trade unions and employers or their associations, and those who act on their behalf; whereas the second kind regulate the behaviour of employees and employers as parties to individual contracts of employment.[40]

Procedural agreements, in other words, regulate relations between the parties to collective bargaining, define the bargaining units, and determine the status and facilities for trade union representatives in the bargaining process. Substantive agreements, on the other hand, regulate jobs, the pay for them, and the conditions under which they are performed. In practice, however, an agreement on the procedure for training shop stewards which also lays down the substantive payments which they should receive whilst on union business contains both procedural and substantive clauses. There is a tendency for procedural agreements to have a separate and a long term existence. Substantive agreements tend to be altered more regularly to take account of changes in the employment relationship.

Procedural agreements

There are a wide range of procedural agreements in practice. For example:

> There are jointly-agreed procedures for the negotiation of wage settlements, for the resolution of disputes, for settling individual pay and grading issues, for dealing with individual grievances, for handling disciplinary cases, for reaching decisions on dismissals, for recruitment, for training, for redundancy and indeed for any class of business which is brought within the area subject to negotiation.[41]

There is a tendency for the areas coming within the boundaries of collective bargaining to be constantly enlarged, wherever negotiating arrangements have been successfully concluded. The joint procedures governing behaviour and conditions at work are influenced by a number of factors. These include: the industry; its technology; the size and geographical spread of establishments; the quality and style of workplace management; and the extent of trade union organization. They involve all the personal, local, historical and social forces helping to shape the patterns of collective bargaining within the individual industry and workplace.

It has been suggested that 'the cornerstone of collective bargaining in Britain is the procedure agreement'.[42] A procedural relationship between an employer and a trade union is established as soon as the union's right to represent the collective interests of its members is recognized. It is the practice of settling pay and conditions of employment through a negotiating procedure which frequently leads to the development of further joint procedures covering a wide range of areas of common concern to employers, trade unions and their members. In outline, the procedural act of recognition establishing negotiation rights is usually concerned: first, with defining the area in which the representative capacity of the trade unions is acknowledged; second, with indicating the subjects which are to be brought within the scope of joint regulation; and third, with specifying the steps by which agreement is to be sought and the procedure to be followed if there is a failure to agree between the parties. Obviously negotiating procedures do not conform to standard patterns and cannot be readily stereotyped. They vary by industry, the levels at which bargaining takes place, the characteristics and objectives of management and unions and so on. But the recognition agreement is the key one.

In private industry, for example, employers sometimes negotiate a comprehensive set of procedural agreements with trade union representatives at company or enterprise level. The items covered by such agreements include: defining the parties to the agreements; specifying the respective responsibilities of the parties; setting out the general principles of the agreements; and drawing up either a 'status quo' or a 'right to manage' clause or both. The latter deal with how changes in working methods or employment conditions are to be handled. They are predominantly found in the engineering industries. A status quo clause, for example, usually states that when changes in working conditions are to be made by management and when prior agreement has not been reached between management and the unions, the status quo shall prevail. Actions proposed by management, that is, shall not be implemented if objected to by the employees and their representatives, until either agreement has been reached by negotiation or the procedure to avoid disputes has been exhausted. The status quo also requires unions wishing to change working practices to make full use of the procedure for the avoidance of disputes before any departure from existing practices takes place. A right to manage clause, on the other hand, usually reserves the right of management to impose changes in employment or working conditions unilaterally, without negotiation or consultation of any kind. Right to manage clauses usually provide for consultation with the trade unions but not negotiation.

Other clauses in a set of comprehensive procedural agreements at company level might comprise: union membership arrangements; deduction of union contributions at source or the 'check off' system; and the appointment and function of trade union representatives, usually shop stewards, within the procedures. There may also be redeployment and redundancy agreements and a disciplinary code. In the latter case, it is generally held that it is management's duty to maintain discipline within the workplace, whilst it is the union's duty to represent its members within the disciplinary framework. Management is also normally held responsible for taking the initiative and ensuring that there are adequate disciplinary rules and procedures at the workplace, although trade unions are obviously interested in seeing that disciplinary arrangements are used consistently and fairly in the interests of their members.

The most important types of procedural agreement are the individual grievance procedure and the procedure to avoid disputes. 'Expressed in the broadest possible terms, procedures are both treaties of peace and devices for the avoidance of war.'[43] A grievance procedure, for example, is commonly regarded as the means by which individual employees can raise an issue of complaint to management about their pay or conditions of work. It lays down the steps for dealing with such matters. The aim of the grievance procedure is to resolve these issues – the amount of bonus payment received by an employee, the legitimacy or reasonableness of supervisory instructions, or the quantity of overtime allocated to an individual worker, say – as near as possible to the point of the original complaint. It is generally agreed that grievance procedures should be equitable in the ways in which employees are treated, simple to understand and rapid in their operation. Initially a grievance is normally discussed between an employee and his or her immediate superior. If the matter remains unresolved, the employee can then be accompanied at the next stage of the procedure by his or her shop steward. If the issue is not settled at this level, it may then be taken to higher levels of management until either it is resolved, with or without trade union representation, or a 'failure to agree' is recorded.

In the engineering industry, for example, there are both domestic stages and external stages in the procedure for the avoidance of disputes with manual workers. The domestic stage has to be agreed in the establishment concerned and:

> This should cover such matters as the number of stages, the stage at which the shop stewards and, where recognised, the chief shop steward shall be involved, the level of management to be involved at each stage, the procedural level at which matters (whether individual, sectional or general) shall be raised by the party concerned, and the time limits within which different types of question shall be discussed.[44]

It is also agreed that where there is a 'Works Committee', it shall be the final stage in the domestic procedure. However, a works committee's decision on a particular issue does not prevent either party from referring the matter to an external conference for further discussion subsequently.

If an issue is not settled at the final domestic stage of procedure in the engineering industry, it can then be referred on behalf of either party to an external conference. This involves 'representatives of the employers' association and local officials of the trade union(s) concerned, as well as the management representative(s) and the shop steward(s) concerned.[45] Such conferences are supposed to be held within seven working days of receiving a written application from the party wishing to pursue the reference, although usually both parties agree a convenient date to suit their availability. It is also expressly agreed:

> In order to allow for the peaceful resolution of any matter raised by any party, there shall be no stoppages of work, either of a partial or general character, such as a strike, lock-out, go-slow, work-to-rule, overtime ban or any other restrictions, before the stages of procedure provided for . . . have been exhausted.[46]

Only after a 'failure to agree' has been recorded is either side free to take unilateral industrial action against the other. Matters concerning the interpretation or application of national agreements in engineering, on the other hand, are expected to be discussed at national level within seven working days of receipt of a written application.

In practice, individual grievances can give rise to collective disputes thus where trade unions are recognized, individual grievances and collective disputes are often dealt with through the same procedure. Alternatively, where there are separate grievance and disputes procedures, they are sometimes linked so that issues can pass from the grievance procedure into the disputes procedure. Disputes also occur through failure to agree on matters originating in the negotiating procedure. Hence in the event of differences arising between the parties, negotiating procedures commonly provide for these issues to be passed into the collective disputes procedure. The disputes procedure can therefore be a feature or an element in both a grievance and a negotiating procedure. Negotiating and grievance procedures with their associated disputes provisions, in other words, are sometimes kept separate; in other cases the disputes procedure is used to process all matters arising either from general negotiations or from the functioning of the grievance procedure.

If no distinctions are made between a negotiating procedure and a grievance procedure, it is usually in those situations where all the dealings with trade union representatives are regarded as a form of negotiation.

> Where there is a recognised distinction between negotiating and grievance procedures it may not be clear-cut in cases where the negotiating machinery is embodied as a stage in the grievance procedure or where an issue arising as a sectional grievance is adopted as the subject of a formal claim.[47]

The main objects of the machinery for resolving differences between management and trade unionists in Britain are to make, apply and interpret collective agreements, and to deal with grievances affecting either individuals or groups of employees. Typically most industrial relations procedures in Britain do not define the broad issues of rights and duties to be claimed under them in any exact way. Furthermore, it is not usual for a distinction to be made 'between the process of applying and interpreting existing agreements, as against the process of formulating new ones.'[48] The same procedures are used to process disputes of 'right' arising out of existing agreements and disputes of 'interest' arising out of matters not covered by existing agreements. Despite their constitutional diversity, British disputes procedures have three common features: they consist of a number of well-defined procedural stages; they lay down time limits for each stage of the procedure; and they are intended to preclude strikes or other forms of industrial action until all the stages of the procedure have been completed, including sometimes independent arbitration, and a failure to agree has been formally recorded.

Substantive agreements

Substantive agreements vary widely accordingly to the industry or organization in which they are determined. They may be broadly classified as: pay agreements; agreements on working conditions; and agreements on fringe benefits and other payments. Pay agreements for example cover: hourly rates of pay; salaries; pay structures; payment by results; productivity payments; incremental pay scales; minimum weekly earnings; overtime premia; unsocial hours payments; shift-work pay; nightwork payments; maternity pay; holiday pay; call out payments; length of service supplements; sick pay; and so on. Agreements on working conditions are mainly concerned with hours of work, length of the working week, holiday arrangements and annual leave, maternity leave, shift-work rotas, special work clothing, tool allowances and so on. It is much more difficult, however, to specify the precise nature of fringe benefits and other payments. One reason for this is that what is initially regarded as a fringe benefit in an agreement, such as holiday pay or sickness pay, may once negotiated become a standard item in the employment package of the workers concerned. In this way, such benefits are open to continual improvement by further negotiation. More generally, however, fringe benefits include such items as retirement pensions, medical care, housing, social and recreation facilities, travelling and subsistence allowances, low cost loans and so on.

6.6 INDUSTRIAL ACTION

The essence of the employer–employee relationship and the management–union relationship is their power context. The main implications of this are, first, that each party seeks to impose on the other those conditions of employment – in their widest sense – which best suit its own interests. Second, where there is no agreement, consensus, or balance of power between the parties to the employment relationship as to what constitutes fair terms and conditions of employment between them, the stronger party will seek to impose its will unilaterally upon the weaker side. In order to achieve their respective goals, in other words, there is the likelihood of employers ultimately imposing sanctions on their subordinates; and of subordinate employees – either individually or collectively – ultimately imposing their own sanctions against their employers. Such sanctions may generally be described as 'industrial action'. Although industrial action is popularly associated with the use of the strike weapon against employers by trade unions, there is a wide range of industrial sanctions which management, unions and employees can use to further their immediate industrial relations objectives.

Types of action

Historically, the balance of industrial power rested overwhelmingly in favour of the employer. Even the so-called change in the relative balance of industrial bargaining power to the advantage of organized workers in the 1960s and 1970s must not be exaggerated. Although some strategic groups of employees continue to have considerable short term bargaining strength such as some computer operators, gas workers, petrol tanker drivers, and similar groups, this is not the general rule. Most employees do not have much collective strength and ultimately, even in the above named industries, long term industrial power rests predominantly with the employers. Employers and management, in the final resort, can use a variety of industrial sanctions against their workers where they choose to do so. This is especially true where employees are weakly organized.

Managerial sanctions against employees manifest themselves in the form of unco-ordinated and individual actions or organized and collective actions. Unco-ordinated and individual industrial action by management against subordinates, for instance, is typically found in non-union situations. It includes: close supervision; tight works discipline; discriminatory employment practices against certain employees; lay offs; demotions; and the unofficial speeding up of work processes or job tasks. Organized and collective sanctions by management, on the other hand, include: the withdrawal of overtime; mass suspensions; the unilateral changing of work standards or piecework prices; the tactical precipitation of strikes; locking-out; the closing down of enterprises; and the removal of plant and machinery at the workplace.

The withdrawing of overtime or mass suspensions, for example, is sometimes used as a preliminary collective tactic by management to impress its intention on union negotiators that it proposes standing firm on a particular issue during negotiations. Similarly, the unilateral imposition of work standards by management over subordinates might be part of an overall strategy to precipitate a strike situation with the trade unions with which it negotiates. This can happen, for instance, when order books are low but stock levels are high within a firm. In order to avoid having to pay lay off money to its workers, or to prevent further stockpiling of its products, management is sometimes both instrumental and successful in precipitating strike action amongst its own employees. This enables management, first, to run down its stocks, and second to provide sufficient work for its employees, including overtime, when market conditions are more favourable. Precipitating strike action, of course, also makes it possible for management to appear the innocent party to an industrial dispute. In these circumstances, management can imply that it was union action in the first place which caused industrial action to be taken.

Lock-outs by employers, whilst only one elements in a total conflict situation, are in fact often difficult to distinguish from strikes. Yet the question of which party makes an initial declaration to act against the other is in practice immaterial. It seems likely, however, that nowadays employers only use the lock-out tactic very infrequently in order to achieve their industrial relations objectives. First, to do so might adversely affect their public images and inflame public opinion. Second, they can usually obtain the same ends by other means. Whilst employer lock-outs, then, were more common in the past, especially in the private sector and usually when trade union power was weak, they are rare today.

The closing down of factories and offices, and certainly the threat by management to remove plant and machinery from their premises, is a much more likely managerial tactic in current circumstances. Some people would not even view such activities as coming within the ambit of organized industrial action. They would merely see them as legitimate managerial rights, either to liquidate uneconomic enterprises, thus necessitating redundancies, or to coerce unco-operative workers to comply with employer requirements at the workplace. As we show below, managerial actions of this sort on occasions lead to sit ins and work ins by employees.

The categories of potential industrial actions which employees can impose on management are equally wide ranging. As in the case of managerial sanctions, a distinction has to be made between individual and unorganized actions on the part of workers and organized or group sanctions on the other.

> Put simply, in unorganised conflict the worker typically responds to the oppressive situation in the only way open to him *as an individual*. . . . Such reaction rarely derives from any calculative strategy. . . . Organised conflict, on the other hand, is far more likely to form part of a conscious strategy to change the situation which is identified as the source of discontent.[49]

Unorganized industrial action, for instance, manifests itself in several ways. This includes: high labour turnover; bad time keeping; excessive levels of absenteeism; withholding of effort; inefficient working; deliberate time wasting and so on. Other symptoms of unorganized industrial action by individuals include continuous 'complaints, friction, infractions of rules, and similar evidences of low morale and discontent'.[50] A study undertaken in four Lancashire coal mines found that among surface and underground workers 'low morale is associated with a high level of "unorganised" conflict and *vice versa*. On the other hand, we do not assume that high morale and "organised" conflict are necessarily opposed.'[51]

Organized and group industrial action against management is equally diverse and has similarly deep roots. The so-called Luddites or machine breakers, for example, were among the first groups of workers to collectively oppose the unilateral introduction of new technology into their factories by the early textile manufacturers in the nineteenth century. Nowadays, collective opposition by employees to managerial decisions is normally less violent. But it is no less serious, for all that, for management to have to cope with its modern manifestations. At its blandest, organized industrial action by trade unionists can take the forms of working without enthusiasm, non-co-operation with management, going slow, or working to rule, A work-to-rule, for instance, usually involves an interruption of normal work processes by not carrying out what the employees regard as their non-contractual activities. It can entail the carrying out of managerial orders to the letter by the groups in dispute with management. It can result in workers strictly observing the safety or works rules which are normally disregarded by them, even though they are technically in breach of their contracts of employment. It is interesting to note that in working to rule, and where management's orders are obeyed, employees are not generally in breach of their contracts of employment. In deliberately going slow, however, employees are potentially open to action for such a breach, although employers rarely if ever seek legal remedies in such circumstances.

Another type of organized industrial action taken by workers collectively is the overtime ban. From the trade union viewpoint it is a weapon which needs to be used carefully. As a tactical weapon within a broader strategy it has great value. 'As a final weapon with no back-up, its usefulness is less certain, although it may work for less important issues.'[52] An overtime ban has the added disadvantages to trade unionists that it results in loss of pay, with corresponding financial gains for management. A ban on overtime, in other words, is only an 'intermediate' method of taking organized industrial action against employers. It is often used, for instance, to demonstrate to managements that the workforce is united and determined to take further collective action if their negotiating demands are not met. The implication usually is that if the overtime ban fails to elicit the necessary responses from the employer, then tougher industrial sanctions will be imposed by the trade unions and their members.

The ultimate collective sanction used by trade unionists against management is the strike or industrial stoppage. Stoppages of work are normally connected with terms and conditions of employment: when initiated by employees they are described as strikes, when initiated by employers they are lock-outs. Strikes can be official or unofficial and constitutional or unconstitutional. Official strikes are where a union 'officially' supports its members in accordance with union rules during a dispute. A constitutional strike is one taking place after negotiations through the agreed procedure for avoiding disputes have been exhausted and a 'failure to agree' recorded. As shown in figure 6.1 four main categories of strike action are possible.

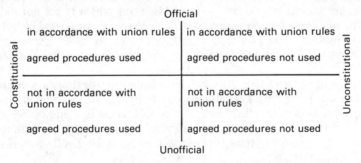

Figure 6.1 Categories of strike action.

Stoppages

Information about the number of stoppages resulting from industrial disputes annually are collected by the Department of Employment's network of unemployment benefit offices. No distinction is made between strikes and lock-outs, with political strikes and small stoppages involving fewer than 10 workers or lasting less than a day excluded, except where the aggregate number of days lost exceeds 100. There is also a possible underrecording of disputes, particularly those near the margins of definition. As shown in table 6.7 there were 1 206 recorded stoppages beginning in 1984, compared with 1 352 in 1983 'and an annual average of 2 002 stoppages for the 10 years 1974–83.'[53]

Because of the recording difficulties relating to numbers of stoppages, another measure – the number of workers involved in stoppages – is a better indicator of the

Table 6.7 *Stoppages in the UK 1964–84.*

Year	Stoppages	Workers involved in stoppages (000s)	Working days lost in stoppages (000s)
	Beginning in year	In progress in year	In progress in year
1964	2 524	883	2 277
1965	2 354	876	2 925
1966	1 937	544	2 396
1967	2 116	734	2 787
1968	2 378	2 258	4 690
1969	3 116	1 665	6 846
1970	3 906	1 801	10 980
1971	2 228	1 178	13 551
1972	2 497	1 734	23 909
1973	2 873	1 528	7 197
1974	2 922	1 626	14 750
1975	2 282	809	6 012
1976	2 016	668	3 284
1977	2 703	1 166	10 142
1978	2 471	1 041	9 405
1979	2 080	4 608	29 474
1980	1 330	834	11 964
1981	1 338	1 513	4 266
1982	1 528	2 103	5 313
1983	1 352	574	3 754
1984	1 206	1 464	27 135

Source: *Employment Gazette* (August 1985)

impact of industrial disputes than is the number of stoppages themselves. The total number of workers involved in stoppages is obtained by aggregating the workers directly and indirectly involved in separate stoppages during that year. Any industrial action not affecting the usual working day, such as works to rule and overtime bans, are excluded, as are overtime working, weekend working which is not normal and public holidays. The number of workers involved in stoppages 'in progress' in 1984 was about one and a half million, compared with some half a million in 1983. There was an average of one and a half million workers involved in stoppages annually 'for the 10 year period 1974 to 1983.'[54]

Another measure of stoppage activity is the number of working days lost in stoppages per year. These are estimates resulting from stoppages at establishments where the disputes occurred. As with other measures a distinction is made between stoppages 'beginning in year' and those 'in progress in year', including those continuing from the previous year. Stoppages beginning in 1984 accounted for 26.9 million working days lost

Table 6.8 *Largest stoppages as proportions of working days lost 1979–84.*

Year	Industry	Working days lost for these industries (millions)	Total working days lost nationally (millions)	Total working days lost nationally (%)
1979	Engineering	16.0		54
	Health and public services	3.2	29.5	11
	Transport and communications	1.0		3
1980	Steel	8.8	12.0	74
1981	Civil service	0.9	4.3	20
1982	Health service and railways	2.3	5.3	43
1983	Electricity, gas and water	0.8	3.8	20
1984	Coalmining	22.3	27.1	82

Source: *Employment Gazette* (August 1985)

that year, with disputes beginning in 1983 but which continued into the following year accounting for the remaining 0.2 million days lost in 1984. The number of working days lost from stoppages 'in progress' in 1984 was 27.1 million, compared with 3.8 million working days lost in 1983. By contrast, the annual average of working days lost in stoppages 'over the 10 years 1974–83' was 9.8 million.[55] Accurate comparisons between years are difficult, however, as the number of working days lost in any one year may be influenced by a small number of large stoppages as shown in table 6.8.

There is no single satisfactory theory explaining stoppage trends in Britain. However, there is a distinct tendency for underlying levels of stoppage activity to have risen in most of the post-war period. A longitudinal study of strikes in Britain by researchers at the Department of Employment draws three broad implications for its analysis. The first is that 'strikes appear to be over fundamental issues, in which economic pressures on participants are very important.' The two most prominent ones are pay and job security. The second implication is that strikes in the main 'are concentrated in a very small proportion of plants, typically the larger ones in certain industries and certain areas of the country'. The third implication is that industries and regions having high average plant size 'tend to experience relatively high rates of strike incidence and relatively high rates of strike frequency as well.'[56] The commonly held view that Britain is especially strike prone is not borne out by the empirical evidence, although the probability of strikes occurring is much higher in a few industries, and markedly in some plants.

Industrial stoppages in the United Kingdom occupy a broadly middle ranking position compared with other countries in the Organization for Economic Cooperation and Development. This is indicated in table 6.9 which shows, for the period 1974–83, that the countries having the highest incidence of working days lost per 1 000 employees were Italy, Greece, Spain, Canada, Ireland and Australia. Those countries recording relatively few days lost per 1 000 employees included The Netherlands, West Germany, Norway, Sweden and Japan. Care must be taken when making detailed comparisons between countries, largely because of differences in methods of recording stoppages and their accuracy, but table 6.9 provides a useful indication of the relative numbers of working days lost through stoppages of work between the countries listed.

Table 6.9 *Industrial disputes: average number of working days lost per 1 000 employees for selected countries 1974–83.*

Country	[1974–78]	[1979–83]	[1974–83]
UK	380	500	440
Australia	690	590	640
Belgium	240	130	210
Canada	990	750	860
Denmark	90	110	100
Finland	490	360	420
France	210	120	170
Germany	60	10	30
Greece	660	1 020	870
Ireland	700	730	720
Italy	1 410	1 190	1 300
Japan	130	20	70
The Netherlands	10	30	20
New Zealand	340	350	340
Norway	70	50	60
Portugal	130	210	190
Spain	1 030	970	1 000
Sweden	30	250	140

Source: *Employment Gazette* (April 1985)

Sit ins and work ins

Sometimes sit ins and work ins are used as alternative tactics to the more traditional forms of industrial action by trade unionists. There are two types of occupation: a redundancy sit in or a work in as protest against the closure of a plant or company; and a collective bargaining sit in to take the place of more traditional forms of industrial action such as working to rule, overtime bans, and all out strikes.

> The defining feature of the work-in is that employees continue production with the aim of demonstrating that the plant is a viable concern. In the case of a sit-in, which often takes place where the production processes make a prolonged work-in impossible, the aim is to protest against a management decision whilst in the case of a proposed closure preventing the transfer of plant and machinery to other factories.[57]

The two main characteristics of sit ins and work ins are the illegal occupation of an employer's premises against its wishes, and the exercising of countervailing control over the establishment by the occupiers. There seem to be three principal reasons why these tactics are favoured in preference to more traditional forms of organized industrial action by trade unionists. First, they offer some degree of control over the establishment being occupied, which is obviously important in redundancy situations where the removal of plant and machinery to other locations is being threatened. Second, since such actions take place on private property, this reduces the likelihood of conflict with the police. Third, by working in or sitting in, employees are better able to maintain their morale and group solidarity. Strikers, for example, often lose contact with their fellow workers, whilst some of them take up other jobs during protracted disputes. Normally employers tend to maintain a fairly low key profile in dealing with trade union tactics of this sort. This is probably because of the long term damage to industrial relationships which might be incurred in evoking the law, 'the cost to the company of the occupation; the effects on employees not involved in the action and the effect of the occupation on the organization's customers.'[58]

6.7 SUMMARY

The central focus of this chapter is collective bargaining, which is the major institutional feature of British industrial relations. Collective bargaining is a complex process, initially with a labour market function. But by challenging managerial prerogative, it is an important means of extending industrial democracy to employees, by enabling them to influence those employment decisions most affecting their daily working lives. Several conditions are necessary for its emergence and survival. These include: freedom of association to organize into trade unions which are independent of employers and the state; employer recognition; bargaining in good faith; and mutual acceptance of the agreements entered into by employers and unions. Of these, trade union recognition by employers has often been both an intractable and a recurrent problem facing trade unionists. The preference of the trade unions has been to obtain recognition from employers by voluntary or coercive means rather than by use of the law.

Collective bargaining reform in Britain has been a major policy issue since the 1960s. The Donovan Commission's prescription for handling the growth of unregulated and informal collective bargaining in private industry was to advocate the negotiation of voluntary comprehensive company agreements between management and trade unions. By such means, it was argued structured bargaining machinery could be established at levels intermediate between national negotiations and workgroup negotiations; bargaining units and especially bargaining agencies might be rationalized; bargaining forms could be documented; and bargaining scope could be extended.

With the rejection of *In Place of Strife*, and with the General Election in 1970, it was the Conservative Party's industrial relations policy, as expressed in *Fair Deal at Work*, which became the legal basis for reforming collective bargaining in the Industrial Relations Act 1971. Later the CBI strongly advocated more structured collective bargaining arrangements in the private sector and the synchronization and compression of the annual pay round. Complementary to these changes the Basnett plan for co-ordinating bargaining in the public sector, including the devolution of negotiating machinery within it, was also considered as a necessary condition for collective bargaining change. Since 1979, pragmatic modifications to collective bargaining have continued in the private sector in conditions of high unemployment and weakened trade union power. In the public sector, collective bargaining has been affected by tough cash limits in pay negotiations and hardening attitudes towards trade unions locally by some employing authorities.

The term 'collective bargaining structure' describes the more stable and permanent features of any particular set of bargaining arrangements. Every bargaining structure comprises four elements: bargaining levels; bargaining units; bargaining forms; and bargaining scope. Bargaining levels, for example, may be multiemployer, single employer, plant or at subplant level. Bargaining units relate to the groups of employees covered by particular bargaining arrangements and collective agreements. A bargaining unit may be wide or narrow in coverage, and may consist of one or more bargaining agents or unions representing employees. In some cases, the breadth of a bargaining unit varies between bargaining levels. Bargaining forms describe whether the agreements are written or formal, or are unwritten and informal. Bargain scope is concerned with the range of subjects covered in particular negotiations. It may be either comprehensive or restricted in coverage.

The incidence of collective bargaining varies between employment sectors and is particularly associated with size of employing establishments. In general, public sector employers are more likely to negotiate with trade unions than are private sector employers, especially in the private services, with bargaining between employers and manual workers more likely than for non-manual workers. In the private sector the pattern of collective bargaining is very complex, where multiemployer and single employer bargaining structures coexist to varying degrees. Single employer bargaining, in turn, may be either centralized or decentralized in multiplant companies. A number of factors are believed to influence the different levels at which collective bargaining takes place. These include: product markets; work organization; technnology; geographic location; business structure; union structure; and payment systems. In the public sector, by contrast, multiemployer national bargaining predominates for most groups of employees, including middle and senior managers, largely within a Whitley framework.

The end products of collective bargaining are collective agreements. They have different degrees of formality and content, are usually written, are signed by the parties and are 'binding in honour' between them. In analytical terms, collective agreements are categorized as either substantive or procedural agreements. Substantive agreements are concerned with terms and conditions of employment, whilst procedural agreements define the relations between the parties to bargaining. Substantive agreements centre on pay, conditions, and fringe benefits associated with particular jobs, with procedural agreements being equally wide ranging. They include negotiating, grievance, disputes, disciplinary, redundancy, dismissal, recruitment, and promotion procedures. Some only apply locally, whilst others are national and industry wide in scope. Procedures, whatever their specific form, provide the ground rules for collective bargaining between employers and management in their dealings with trade unions, trade union representatives and union members.

Where collective bargaining breaks down between employers and unions, usually over fundamental differences between them such as pay, job security and union recognition, a variety of forms of industrial action can be initiated and implemented by either or both parties to the negotiating process. The final sanction used by management and unions against each other is the industrial stoppage. National and international records are kept of work stoppages in Britain and overseas. The major indices used are: number of stoppages; number of workers involved in stoppages; number of working days lost in stoppages; and, for comparative purposes, the number of working days lost through stoppages per 1 000 employees. Such figures are normally collected annually. The commonly held view that British industrial relations is especially strike prone is not supported by the evidence. Though there has been an upward trend in stoppage activity over the past 20 years, the likelihood of strikes or lock-outs is much higher in a few industries, such as coalmining, water transport, motor vehicle assembly, shipbuilding and iron and steel, and more especially in some plants than in others. Since 1979 there have also been a number of large scale and often bitter industrial disputes in the public sector.

6.8   REFERENCES

1. International Labour Office, *Collective Bargaining*, ILO, Geneva 1960, p. 3.
2. Royal Commission on Trade Unions and Employers' Associations, *Report*, HMSO, London, 1968, p. 50.
3. N. Millward, Workplace industrial relations: results of a survey of industrial relations practices, *Employment Gazette*, July 1983, p. 281.
4. A. Flanders, Collective bargaining: a theoretical analysis, in A. Flanders, *Management and Unions*, Faber and Faber, London, 1975, p. 239.
5. A. Fox, Collective Bargaining, Flanders and the Webbs, *British Journal of Industrial Relations*, July 1975, p. 117.
6. R. Hyman, *Industrial Relations*, Macmillan, London, 1975, p. 26.
7. N. Chamberlain and J.W. Kuhn, *Collective Bargaining*, McGraw-Hill, New York, 1965, p. 113.
8. S.H. Slichter, *Union Policies and Industrial Management*, Brookings Institution, Washington, 1941, p. 1.
9. Chamberlain and Kuhn, *op. cit.*, p. 138.
10. Royal Commission, *op. cit.*, p. 36.
11. *Ibid.*, p. 262.
12. Conservative Political Centre, *Fair Deal at Work*, CPC, London, 1968, p. 62.
13. *Ibid.*, p. 56.
14. *Ibid.*, p. 10.
15. Confederation of British Industry, *The Future of Pay Determination*, CBI, London, 1977, p. 5.
16. *Ibid.*, p. 11.
17. *Ibid.*, p. 14.
18. *Ibid.*, p. 25.
19. *Ibid.*, p. 30.
20. *Ibid.*, p. 31.
21. D. Basnett, A way out of warfare over pay, *The Sunday Times*, 4 December 1977, p. 16.
22. *Ibid.*
23. *Committee of Inquiry into Civil Service Pay*, (Chair: Sir J. Megaw) HMSO, London, 1982, pp. 93–7.
24. P.A.L. Parker, W.R. Hawes and A.L. Lumb, *Department of Employment Manpower Papers Number 5, The Reform of Collective Bargaining at Plant and Company Level*, HMSO, London, 1971, p. 3.
25. *Ibid.*
26. A. Flanders, Collective bargaining: prescription for change, in Flanders, *op. cit.*, p. 169.

27. C. Jenkins and B. Sherman, *Collective Bargaining*, Routledge and Kegan Paul, London, 1977, pp. 63f.
28. W.W. Daniel and N. Millward, *Workplace Industrial Relations in Britain*, Heinemann, London, 1983, p. 177.
29. *Ibid.*, p. 25.
30. D.R. Deaton and P.B. Beaumont, The determinants of bargaining structure: some large scale survey evidence, *British Journal of Industrial Relations*, 18, July 1980, p. 203.
31. Advisory Conciliations and Arbitration Service, *Collective Bargaining in Britain: its Extent and Level*, HMSO, London, 1983, p. 24.
32. See Institute of Personnel Management, *Bargaining Strategy*, IPM, London, 1980, pp. 13–15.
33. *Ibid.*
34. ACAS, *op. cit.*, p. 39.
35. A.W.J. Thomson and P.B. Beaumont, *Public Sector Bargaining: A Study of Relative Gain*, Saxon House, Farnborough, 1980, p. 36.
36. K. Walsh, Centralisation and decentralisation in local government bargaining, *Industrial Relations Journal*, vol. 12 (5), 1981.
37. Thomson and Beaumont, *op. cit.*, p. 35.
38. D. Farnham, Sixty years of Whitleyism, *Personnel Management*, July 1978, p. 32.
39. J.C. Ramsey and J.M. Hill, *Collective Agreements*, Institute of Personnel Management, London, 1974, p. 55.
40. A. Flanders, Industrial relations: what is wrong with the system?, in Flanders, *op. cit.*, pp. 86f.
41. N. Singleton, *Industrial Relations Procedures*, HMSO, London, 1975, p. 7.
42. C. Jenkins and B. Sherman, *op. cit.*, p. 24.
43. A.I. Marsh, *Royal Commission on Trade Unions and Employers Associations Research Papers 2 (Part 1) Disputes Procedures in British Industry*, HMSO, London, 1966 p. 4.
44. *Agreement between the Federation and the Trade Unions dated 1st March 1976, operative from 5th April, 1976: Procedure for the Avoidance of Disputes – Manual Workers*, Engineering Employers Federation/Confederation of Shipbuilding and Engineering Unions, London, 1976 para. 9.
45. *Ibid.*, para. 15.
46. *Ibid.*, para. 5.
47. N. Singleton, *op. cit.*, p. 17.
48. A.I. Marsh, *op. cit.*, p. viii.
49. R. Hyman, *Strikes,* Fontana, London, 1972, p. 53.
50. A. Kornhauser, R. Dubin, A.M. Ross (eds.), *Industrial Conflict*, McGraw-Hill, New York, 1954, p. 14.
51. W.H. Scott, E. Mumford, I.C. McGivering, J.M. Kirkby, *Coal and Conflict*, Liverpool University Press, 1963, p. 40.
52. E. Johnston, *Industrial Action*, Arrow Books, London, 1975, p. 25.
53. Stoppages caused by industrial disputes, *Employment Gazette*, August 1985, p. 296.
54. *Ibid.*
55. *Ibid.*
56. C.T.B. Smith, R. Clifton, P. Makeham, S.W. Creigh and R.V. Burn, *Strikes in Britain*, HMSO, London, pp. 89f.
57. Institute of Personnel Management, *Sit-ins and Work-ins*, IPM, London, 1976, p. 2.
58. *Ibid.*, p. 16.

PART THREE

The State and Industrial Relations

7

The Politics of Industrial Relations

Industrial relations in Britain cannot be divorced from party politics. On the one hand, there is the long-established connection between some major trade unions and the Labour Party, with the unions providing the vast majority of Labour Party finance, sponsoring candidates in General Elections and being deeply involved in Party policy making and political activity. On the other hand, there is the Conservative Party which by ideological inclination, social contacts and financial support is closely related to the business community, especially big business. At another political level, we have union and employer pressure groups, notably the Trades Union Congress (TUC) and the Confederation of British Industry (CBI), which seek to influence whichever major political party is in power to follow policies and party programmes which will best serve their members' interests. It is these institutions and traditions which provide an ideological and political framework within which British industrial relations takes place.

7.1 TRADE UNIONS AND THE LABOUR PARTY

Trade unions were created in Britain and developed long before the Labour Party was formed. Unions for skilled workers, for example, and later unskilled workers, developed and grew steadily throughout the nineteenth century and the TUC was established in 1868, more than a generation before the Labour Party. In 1871 the trade unions had gained some protection at law under the Trade Union Act and to some extent the long struggle to prove that they were law abiding, respectable constitutional organizations had been won. The trade union leaders of the time maintained 'a strong presumption in favour of the *status quo*', distrusted innovation and had a liking 'for distinct social classes', with 'each man being secured and contented in his station of life.'[1] They did not want their hard won acceptance by Victorian society to be lost by political adventuring. Up till this time the TUC had been content to use its Parliamentary Committee to protect union interests. It maintained links with the Liberal Party and supported a handful of trade union Members of Parliament to protect and further the interests of the trade unions through specific legislation. Before 1880, however, labour or working-class representation in Parliament was sparse: 'what representation there was was by courtesy of the Liberal Party.'[2]

By the turn of the century, a number of fundamental social changes had occurred which would inescapably involve the unions in political activity from which they would never be able to withdraw. First, there was the gradual extension of the political franchise to almost all adult males. Second, there had been a dissemination of socialist ideas and programmes for political change by groups of social reformers. Third, trade unionists had come to recognize that the law-making powers of Parliament could be used to protect their collective interests and to obtain those other political and social objectives which collective bargaining alone could never achieve. This latter had been emphasized by the threat to union security arising from a series of legal decisions against the unions in the 1890s. Finally, there was the growth of the so called 'new unionism' amongst sections of the relatively unskilled labourers in the docks, gas companies and transport sector from the late 1880s.

It was these developments which led to a demand by the TUC for better representation of labour and working people in Parliament. The outcome was the creation of the Labour Representation Committee (LRC) after a conference called by the TUC in 1900. With the election to the House of Commons of 28 members of the LRC in the 1906 General Election the name of the party was changed and the modern Labour Party was born. The Labour Party and the trade unions have been represented there ever since, albeit with fluctuating fortunes. The logic of these historical and social forces probably made the creation of a broad-based political party representative of working people's interests inevitable. However, once such a party had been formed by the trade unions, and if they were to accept the constitutional constraints of Parliamentary democracy, it followed that the trade unions were creating an organization which they could never completely control. They could only seek to guide, influence and lobby within it. Besides, the unions' chief preoccupation both then and now has always been safeguarding their own existence and their members' incomes, jobs and working conditions. They have also largely financed the Labour Party but:

> the heart of British unionism is still in these jealously revered organizations that stand guard over the collective economic interests of each group – the jobs and the working conditions that go with the jobs.[3]

Many socialists in 1900 would have preferred to have established an independent socialist party free of trade union domination, since they regarded the unions as inherently reactionary and conservative institutions in their social and economic outlooks. Nevertheless, a new political party representing working-class interests could not realistically have been launched without trade union support, finance and organizational strength. As a result there has frequently been an uneasy and tense relationship between the trade unions and the Labour Party, especially with sections of the Parliamentary Labour Party (PLP). The roots of this tension lie essentially in the contradictory desires of the unions. They wish to operate as autonomous and separate economic agents – at first within a free market economy, and latterly within a mixed economy – whilst at the same time wanting to shape a legislative programme for the Labour Party which, at times, has effectively constrained their freedom of economic action on behalf of their members. The necessarily narrower economic objectives of the unions in protecting their members' jobs and employment interests have inevitably conflicted at times with the efforts of the Labour Party to give itself national appeal to win majorities in the House of Commons.

> For the unions the historic connection with the Party provides a political lobby to protect their industrial role: for the Party the connection provides the finance to maintain its political organization.[4]

The 'Labour Movement' in Britain consists of two elements: an industrial wing, the trade unions affiliated to the TUC, and a political wing, the Labour Party, consisting of a coalition of labour interests including party affiliated trade unionists, individual members, the socialist societies such as the Fabians, and the Parliamentary Labour Party (PLP). The theory of the 'Labour Alliance' is that its two wings, the Trade Union Movement and the Party, are interdependent and integral parts of the larger working-class Movement seeking economic, political and social justice for all working-class people and their families, both as workers and citizens. The trade union role is to protect the jobs and to advance the terms and conditions of employment of trade unionists through collective action, as well as funding the Party. The Labour Party's role is:

> To secure for the workers by hand or by brain the full fruits of their industry and the most equitable distribution thereof that may be possible upon the basis of the common ownership of the means of production, distribution, and exchange, and the best obtainable system of popular administration and control of each industry or service.[5]

The genesis and development of the Labour Party as the 'child of the trade union movement' does not only signify a rejection of the view that trade unionism and politics do not mix. It also explicitly accepts that party affiliated unions have interests overriding purely industrial and occupational ones and that the Party is an organization in which union and non-union elements have to live together. The implications of this for the wider Labour Movement and British party politics were less important when the unions were weak economically and numerically, and when the Labour Party had not achieved governmental office. But with the growth in economic power of the unions and the increased political significance of the Labour Party, whether actually in government or as the major opposition party in Parliament, the situation has changed significantly. To quote the TUC:

> Trade unions and political parties do . . . perform quite distinct functions and their preoccupations can be quite different. The growth of the Labour Party to the point where it became the Government of the country has entailed a significant divergence of function. The existence of common roots yet distinct functions is therefore the most important relationship between the trade unions and the Labour Party.[6]

The formal relationship between the affiliated unions and the Labour Party has generally reflected moderate and constitutional thinking among trade unionists, democratic and reformist convictions amongst Labour politicians, and a presumption that the goals of instrumental trade unionism and Parliamentary socialist democracy are compatible. Many however have disputed these views. Fundamentalist socialists have often argued that Parliament is a social and political quagmire where middle-class Labour MPs, time-honoured procedures, constitutionalism and civil service influence effectively inhibit the implementation of genuine socialist policies. Marxists argue, for example, that the election of Labour or Conservative governments makes no difference in the class struggle in capitalist countries like Britain. It is also suggested that Parliamentary alliances, and the need for the Labour Party to present itself as representing the national interest rather than sectional industrial and political groupings, invariably create disillusionment with parliamentary activities amongst its supporters, thus leading militant trade unionists towards direct action instead. However it is analysed the British Labour Movement is a complex social organism incorporating myriad internal tensions and conflicts. 'The Labour Alliance is formally a reality, but its unity is a myth.'[7]

Political funds

The key to understanding the trade union–Labour Party connection is the device of political funds. The Trade Union Act 1913, as amended by the Trade Union Act 1984, enables trade unions or unincorporated employers' associations to include the furtherance of political objects in their rules and to adopt political fund rules providing for expenditure on such objects. The proposal to do so must be endorsed by a simple majority of members in a ballot held under rules approved by the Certification Officer.

The Trade Union Act 1984 requires unions with political funds, and those wishing to continue spending money on political objects, to hold political fund review ballots of their entire memberships at least once every 10 years.

The 1913 Act lays down a number of requirements for union rule books incorporating political funds and objects. First, union expenditure in furthering the political objects set out in the 1913 Act have to be made out of separate political funds, not general funds. Second, any union members giving notice of their objections to political funding in accordance with the Act must be exempt from any obligation of contributing to that fund. In other words they must be free to 'contract out' of paying political contributions or the 'political levy' as it is generally known. Third, exempt members must not be excluded from any benefits of their union, or placed under any disability or disadvantage compared with other members, except in relation to controlling or managing the political fund. Fourth, admission to the union shall not be conditional on paying the political levy.

Union members wishing to claim exemption from contributing to union political funds must give notice of their objection in the form laid down by the 1913 Act. Unless contributions to the political fund are collected by a separate levy, exempt members must be relieved from paying the political element of normal contributions. Union rules must provide for such relief to be given as far as possible to all exempt members when paying their union subscriptions. They must also enable members to know what portion if any of their contributions goes to union political funds. Any union members alleging breaches of political fund rules may complain to the Certification Officer under Section 3(2) of the 1913 Act. Having heard the complainant, and given the union an opportunity to be heard, and if it is considered that a breach of rules has occurred, the Certification Officer may make an order remedying it. Appeals against the Certification Officer's rulings may be made to the Employment Appeal Tribunal on a point of law.

As can be seen from table 7.1, at the end of 1983 there were 57 unions with political funds. They had over seven million members contributing to union general funds, of whom some six million, or 85 per cent, paid political levies. This represented about 57 per cent of trade unionists in unions affiliated to the TUC which, in 1983, had '95 affiliated organisations with a total membership of 10,510,157.'[8] The percentage of members per union contributing to union political funds varies widely. In 25 per cent of these unions, over 90 per cent of their members paid political levies; in 20 unions between 60 and 89 per cent did so; and in the remaining 12 unions less than 59 per cent did so. Only 13 of these unions each had over £100 000 in their political funds at the end of 1983, the two largest funds being those of the National Union of Mineworkers and the General Municipal Boilermakers and Allied Trades Union with over a million pounds each. Since it was an election year, union expenditure of political funds in 1983 rose considerably to over nine million pounds, compared with six million pounds in 1982.

Union political fund expenditure is used for three main purposes: '(1) to affiliate to the Labour Party; (2) to finance parliamentary candidates; and (3) to finance local political activities.'[9] In practice it is only the Labour Party to which trade unions can affiliate, since all other parties are based on individual membership alone. In 1983, for example, the claimed membership of the Labour Party was some seven million members. This consisted of just over six million affiliated trade union members from 49 trade unions, some 600 000 individual members in Constituency Labour Parties (CLPs) and about 60 000 members of socialist societies and co-operative organizations. Union affiliated membership of the Labour Party, therefore, outweighs individual membership by about 10:1, though a small number 'of those who are members through their union's affiliation are individual members as well.'[10] The real significance of union affiliation fees paid by affiliated unions to the Labour Party is that they go to the central

Table 7.1 *Union political funds 1983.*

Union	Number of members contributing to General Funds	Number of members contributing to Political Funds	Per cent contributing to Political Funds
Amalgamated Textile Workers Union	15 237	14 540	95
Amalgamated Union of Engineering Workers – Constructional Section	23 856	17 268	72
Amalgamated Union of Engineering Workers – Engineering Section	735 960	542 584	74
Amalgamated Union of Engineering Workers – Foundry Section	41 287	19 230	47
Amalgamated Union of Engineering Workers – Technical Administrative and Supervisory Section	182 795	113 000	62
Associated Society of Locomotive Engineers and Firemen	23 589	21 954	93
Association of Cinematograph Television and Allied Technicians	19 500	1 666	9
Association of Patternmakers and Allied Craftsmen	6 156	5 000	81
Association of Professional Executive Clerical and Computer Staff	100 177	68 868	69
Association of Scientific Technical and Managerial Staffs	(491 000)	(147 000)	(30)[1]
Bakers Food and Allied Workers Union	37 487	36 558	98
Ceramic and Allied Trades Union	28 873	28 496	99
Confederation of Health Service Employees	222 869	203 730	91
Electrical Electronic Telecommunication and Plumbing Union	383 829	295 254	77
Fire Brigades Union	43 405	26 999	62
Furniture Timber and Allied Trades Union	51 788	35 529	67
General Municipal Boilermakers and Allied Trades Union	875 187	759 856	87
General Union of Associations of Loom Overlookers	1 337	1 337	100
Iron and Steel Trades Confederation	44 296	40 165	91
Liverpool Victoria Section of the National Union of Insurance Workers	2 756	162	6
Musicians Union	38 966	34 108	88
National Association of Colliery Overmen Deputies and Shotfirers	17 079	16 856	99
National Association of Colliery Overmen Deputies and Shotfirers (Durham Area)	1 346	1 346	100
National Association of Colliery Overmen Deputies and Shotfirers (Northumberland Area)	629	622	99
National Association of Colliery Overmen Deputies and Shotfirers (Scottish Area)	1 270	1 270	100
National Association of Colliery Overmen Deputies and Shotfirers (Yorkshire Area)	4 995	4 951	99
National Association of Theatrical Television and Kine Employees	21 123	10 185	48
National Graphical Association (1982)	113 619	59 457	52
National League of the Blind and Disabled	2 995	1 362	46
National Union of Blastfurnacemen Ore Miners Coke Workers and Kindred Trades	5 057	2 330	46
National Society of Metal Mechanics	27 076	24 078	89
National Union of Domestic Appliance and General Metal Workers	3 805	912	24
National Union of Insurance Workers Prudential Section	13 181	9 163	70
National Union of Mineworkers	208 051	200 453	96
National Union of Mineworkers (Durham Area)	11 557	11 496	99
National Union of Mineworkers (Kent Area)	3 724	2 231	60

Table 7.1 *Union political funds 1983. (cont.)*

Union	Number of members contributing to General Funds	Number of members contributing to Political Funds	Per cent contributing to Political Funds
National Union of Mineworkers (Leicester Area)	1 986	1 974	99
National Union of Mineworkers (Northumberland Area)	5 359	5 357	100
National Union of Public Employees	689 046	670 736	97
National Union of Railwaymen	143 404	138 529	97
National Union of Scalemakers	1 210	9	0.7
National Union of Seamen	27 650	22 523	82
National Union of Tailors and Garment Workers	76 130	67 247	88
National Union of the Footwear Leather and Allied Trades	38 115	36 879	97
Post Office Engineering Union	129 950	98 451	76
Power Loom Carpet Weavers and Textile Workers Union	3 200	3 140	98
Rossendale Union of Boot Shoe and Slipper Operatives	4 191	4 154	99
Scottish Carpet Workers Union	1 071	1 068	99
Society of Graphical and Allied Trades 1982	193 710	121 176	63
Society of Shuttlemakers	67	5	7
Society of Telecom Executives	23 005	17 028	74
Tobacco Workers Union	15 165	8 274	56
Transport and General Workers Union	1 547 443	1 517 782	98
Transport Salaried Staffs Association	56 476	46 648	83
Union of Communication Workers	196 426	183 325	93
Union of Construction Allied Trades and Technicians	259 873	171 000	66
Union of Shop Distributive and Allied Workers	403 446	369 547	92
Total of the 57 unions with political funds for 1983	7 131 861	6 097 868	—

[1] 1981 figures
Source: Certification Officer, *Annual Report for 1984* (HMSO 1985)

funds of the Party. They provide the basis of Labour Party financial stability and the leading role which trade union delegates play at Labour Party Conferences through the block voting system, with votes allocated according to numbers of affiliated members, even though the unions do not vote as a single block. Union delegates are also represented on the Party's National Executive Committee.

The second major purpose of union political funds is to promote and maintain parliamentary representation. This expenditure takes two forms:

> There is the making of regular, and, at general election times of what are often large contributions to the Labour Party's election funds, and there is the promotion and maintenance of the union's own direct parliamentary representation.[11]

In the 1979 General Election, for example, 269 Labour MPs were elected. Of these 133 were sponsored by affiliated unions. After the 1983 General Election 209 Labour MPs were returned of whom 112 were union sponsored. In addition to contributing to election expenses, the affiliated unions sometimes supplement the salaries of elected parliamentary representatives. Different methods are used for this. These include: direct annual payments; reimbursement of travelling and other expenses incurred in discharging their parliamentary duties; assistance with constituency expenses and clerical and research assistance. Which methods are adopted depend on union preferences, the local constituency and the specific needs of individual MPs. Naturally the unions prefer sponsoring those candidates likely to be parliamentary winners.

The third main purpose of union political funds is to finance local political activity. These include contributions by union branches to CLPs or local trades councils. Union political funds are also used to support candidates in local authority elections. Sometimes fixed sums are allocated from central funds which are then drawn on by union branches for approved expenditure. In other cases there are established local political funds which union branches use. Occasionally, there are separate local funds to which, by union rules, a fixed proportion of all political funds received must be allocated. Whatever the arrangements, the precise rules defining the scope of local political expenditure 'are likely to be fairly rigid.'[12]

Structure and organization

Figure 7.1 provides an outline of the main structural features of the British Labour Movement. The trade union wing consisted of 49 Labour Party affiliates in 1983, with just over six million trade unionists paying the political levy. In 1983 the TUC had 95 affiliated unions, comprising a total TUC membership of some 10.5 million members, which meant that Labour Party affiliation amongst the major trade unions represented about 57 per cent of TUC membership at that time. Labour Party affiliation enables these unions to send delegates to the Labour Party Conference to influence Party policy; to have representation on the Party's National Executive Committee (NEC) and to sponsor Labour MPs.

The Labour Party consists of the PLP and the extra-Parliamentary party, namely the trade unions, the CLPs and the socialist societies, whose diverse elements only come together at the Party's Annual Conference. In theory, the Annual Conference is the Party's sovereign body. In practice the main power centres are the PLP, the unions and the CLPs, and often bitter conflicts emerge between them in Party debates and on policy issues. It is at Conference that formal Party policy is determined and the NEC is elected. Currently, the NEC consists of 29 members and 'shall, subject to the control and directions of the Party Conference, be the administrative Authority of the Party.'[13] In addition to Party officials and the Party Leader, seats on the NEC are allocated by

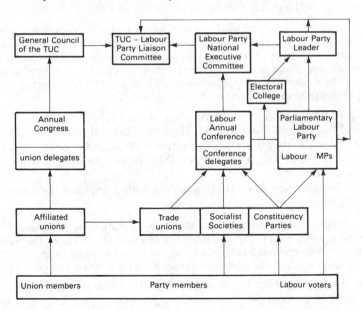

Figure 7.1   Unions and the Labour Party.

election to three main groups: the trade unions, with 12 members; the CLPs, with seven; and women members of whom there are five.

By convention the block voting system is used at the Annual Conference, with the unions accounting for over six million votes and the CLPs some 600 000. This means that the unions have a powerful voice at Conference. They can also 'dominate eighteen of the twenty-nine seats on the NEC if they so wish through their collective voting strength.'[14] More significantly, since the changes in Party Rules in 1981, an Electoral College has been created with the responsibility for electing the Labour Party Leader. The Electoral College meets at Conference, where the votes are divided according to a predetermined formula: 40 per cent to the trade unions and 30 per cent each to the PLP and CLPs. This enabled the unions to play a key role in the election of Neil Kinnock to the Party Leadership after the resounding defeat of the Labour Party in the 1983 General Election and the resignation of the former Leader, Michael Foot.

Finally, trade unions are the main financiers of the Labour Party. According to one authority, '89 per cent of the party's total income is supplied by the unions.' Not all of the income goes to the central bodies. Some goes to the area organizations and local parties but the national Party relies upon union money. One reason why the Labour Party is poorer than the Conservatives 'is that the CLPs are less efficient money-gathering machines than their Conservative counterparts.'[15] Party finance is nevertheless insecurely based, and for many years 'the party's normal activities have been running at a deficit.' This has resulted in 'a continued and heavy borrowing from the bank.'[16] The situation is worsening, since the unions have their financial problems too, with falling memberships, rising costs and squeezes on their financial resources since the late 1970s. Managing the union–Party alliance is delicate enough. Managing its difficult financial position effectively is equally challenging for the Labour Party and its leaders in conditions of change and political uncertainty.

Another institutional device sustaining the union–Labour Party connection is the TUC–Labour Party Liaison Committee linking the General Council, the NEC and the PLP. It was created in the mid 1970s to build closer formal links between the TUC unions and the Labour Party, when relations between them had deteriorated. In 1983, the Committee issued a policy statement declaring its underlying aims:

> Our primary objective is to offer work – and the rights, status and dignity that go with it – to all our people. Our approach is based on a partnership between a Labour Government and the trade union Movement, harnessing into common cause the skills of managers and all those who can help in the drive for full employment and better social provision. Only by creating this new partnership in society can we bring together all resources, talents and expertise to find practical solutions to the problems we face.[17]

Membership of the Liaison Committee comprises 11 senior members of the General Council, 11 of the Labour Party's NEC, 12 of the PLP and joint secretaries from both the TUC and the Labour Party. The Committee meets about seven times a year and has a major 'role in coordinating, wherever possible, the campaigning activities of the TUC and the Labour Party.'[18]

To sum up, British trade unions have gained greatly from their close partnership with the Labour Party:

> Since 1906 this has constantly provided Members of Parliament to defend trade union interests and keep the issues of special interest to trade unionists before the House. When Labour has been in office it has legislated to remedy unwelcome rulings of the courts, repeal obnoxious enactments, or extend the scope of trade union action.[19]

Conversely, the Labour Party has benefited from the trade union connection, by being provided with a very high proportion of its current income for expenditure on its political purposes.

7.2 EMPLOYERS AND THE CONSERVATIVES

Just as there is a strong identity of interest between trade union leaderships and the Labour Party, there is an equally strong political connection between those running private sector businesses and the Conservative Party. Whilst, however, the political connections between trade unionism and the Labour Party are clear cut and overt to everyone, those between private businesses and the Conservatives are more subtle, covert and fragmented. There appear to be three main areas where the interests and activities of employers and the Conservative Party interrelate, overlap and are mutually supportive. These are: their preferred ideologies and economic policies; the social networks existing between big business, the City and Conservative politicians; and the donations provided by some leading employers to the Conservative Party.

Traditionally, the modern Conservative Party has been, and remains, the political party protective of the privately owned enterprise sector and of the market economy as the prime means for allocating and distributing resources in society. As the *Conservative Manifesto* put it in 1983:

> We want to see an economy in which firms, large and small, have every incentive to expand by winning extra business and creating more jobs. This Conservative Government has been both giving these incentives and clearing away obstacles to expansion. . . . Only a government which really works to promote free enterprise can provide the right conditions for that dream to come true.[20]

The manifesto also expressed the necessity of reforming the nationalized industries by continuing 'to expose state-owned firms to real competition', by transferring 'more state-owned business to independent ownership' and by seeking means 'of increasing competition in, and attracting private capital into, the gas and electricity industries.' The Conservatives are supportive, too, of small businesses and claim that the recent 'climate for new and smaller businesses in the UK has been transformed and is now as favourable as anywhere in the world.'[21]

Crouch has argued that in opposition and in the early months of government:

> Conservatives tend to hanker after the abolition of organized structures of government planning and a return to free-market policies. The solution to industrial relations problems is seen as automatically taken care of by the level of unemployment, perhaps backed by legislation that will make strike action more difficult. Industrial relations are then depoliticized; trade unions settle down to a non-political role of industrial bargaining; and the government can revert to a role of occasional consultation in difficult disputes, not having to bother with incomes policy or troublesome tripartite deals that smack of corporatism and concede too much power to the unions.[22]

This contrasts with the alternative strategy favoured by more moderate Conservatives, 'towards which Conservative governments tend to gravitate.' This involves 'some use of free-market policies, but supplemented by corporatist measures for incorporating the unions' into governmental policy making.[23] In practice, of course, these two approaches have been radically reversed since 1979, as successive Conservative Governments have taken explicitly right wing ideological and policy stances on fundamental economic and industrial relations issues, and traditional reformist Conservatives have been virtually excluded from influencing Party policy and Government action. Whichever wing of the Conservative Party predominates, however, 'the vast majority of business executives in Britain support the Conservative Party; the party has also benefited from donations from companies.'[24]

Turning to the social networks between employers and the Conservative Party, we observe here that the evidence is more circumstantial and tenuous, and less rooted in empirical detail. It has to be recognized in the first place, for example, that like the trade

unions and the Labour Party, neither employers nor the Conservatives are homogeneous groupings. Employers may be large or small, manufacturing or non-
manufacturing, whilst the Conservative Party is itself a heterogeneous collection of big
business, City, small business, shopkeeper and landed interests. The social composition
of Conservative MPs reflects this. According to Ball, Conservative MPs 'remain totally
unrepresentative of the electors who vote Conservative and their profile has changed
little.'[25] Table 7.2 is illustrative of the predominantly public school, university, professional and business background of Conservative MPs in the 1979 Parliament, certainly
in comparison with Labour MPs.

Table 7.2 *Social background of Conservative and Labour MPs 1979.*

	Conservative %	Labour %
Professions	45	43
Business	34	5
Public School	73	17
University	68	57
Working class	negligible	35

Source: A. Ball, *British Political Parties*
by permission of Macmillan London and
Basingstoke

The Conservative Party, however, is not exclusively the party of big business, or even
of small business. Electorally, the Conservatives can only win general elections by
attracting lower-middle-class and working-class votes, as well as those of higher business executives, professional workers and City or financial interests. Further, farmers
and landowners have traditionally been a very powerful and influential group in the
Conservative Party and remain so today. The leader of the Conservative Euro-MPs at
Strasbourg in the early 1980s was a former President of the National Farmers Union
(NFU), probably one of the most effective employers' associations and employers'
lobbies in Britain. Also, until 1984, when it rescinded its political fund rules, the NFU
maintained its own political funds. The political funds of the NFU, and those of another
employers' organization the National Association of Shopkeepers of Great Britain and
Northern Ireland, 'totalled £204,900 at the end of 1982.'[26]

Additionally, the British business sector is itself divided, not only between big
business and small business but between manufacturing industry and finance capital. It
is the CBI which purports to speak for the corporate manufacturing and service sectors,
and key public enterprises, but it does not represent Britain's financial institutions and
'it is finance rather than manufacturing which seems the more influential in Britain.'[27]
Further it is finance capital or City interests which now appear to have the closer links
with the Parliamentary Conservative Party. Conservative MPs 'are members of firms in
the City; the numerous lawyers who are Conservative MPs also have closer links with
the City than with the manufacturing industry.'[28] At the end of 1985, for example, it was
disclosed that:

> At least 37 peers and MPs, mostly Conservative, have business ties with companies
> involved in the four consortia fighting for the multi-billion pound Channel Link contract
> . . . [Moreover] more than a third of the peers who spoke in the Lords debate on the
> channel link had a direct business interest in one of the consortia.[29]

Both the Euro Route and Channel Tunnel Groups contained two Conservative MPs,
including two former cabinet ministers, whilst another Conservative backbencher was
Parliamentary adviser to Sea Containers, part of the Expressway consortium. It was

also reported that a Conservative MP had had to apologize to the Speaker of the House of Commons for failing to reveal, in the Commons register of MPs' interests, 'that he was employed by Grayling, a public relations company working for Flexilink',[30] which was an anti-Channel link group of shipping interests.

With the decline in the relative strength of the landed interest in the Conservative Party, as well as those in the Party who were former officers in the armed or colonial services, there has been a significant rise in influence and power of those representing City interests, especially in the Parliamentary Party and in the House of Commons. This has been accompanied by a shift away from the old-fashioned paternalistic Conservatism of past administrations towards the *neo-laissez-faire* ideologies and policies associated with the 'New Right' in the Conservatives which has been ascendent since the mid 1970s. The heavy toll which economic recession has had on manufacturing industry and small businesses in the last few years seems at times to have aroused surprisingly little sympathy amongst the Parliamentary Party. The rise of City interests in the Party partly explains this. Further, the rise of the professional London based Conservative MP 'has reduced even further the influence of local business executives, often the bedrock of local constituency parties.'[31]

Despite changes in its composition in Parliament and amongst its supporters in the electorate, the Conservative Party continues to be the major beneficiary from company political donations. As can be seen in table 7.3, for example, a total of almost £3 million was provided by companies as political donations in 1984, with about £2.25 million going directly to the Conservatives. This represented a fall of 11 per cent over the previous year though some companies only provide Conservative funding in election years. A survey by the Labour Research Department (LRD) examining around 3 000 sets of annual company reports suggests that 'over 50 companies, which accounted for over £280,000 in election year donations, [dropped] out in 1984.'[32] Also some companies boost Conservative donations in election years then cut back the following year.

Table 7.3 also shows that banking and insurance, engineering and the construction sector were the largest contributors to Conservative Party funds in 1984, providing

Table 7.3 *Corporate political donations 1984.*

Sector	No. of companies	Donations to Conservatives £	Per cent change	Total donations £	Per cent change
Mining and quarrying	2	1 400	− 98	11 400	− 84
Food drink and tobacco	33	234 595	+ 11	352 229	+ 3
Chemicals	7	77 500	− 9	91 403	− 19
Metal goods	10	17 370	− 63	32 670	− 40
Engineering	40	364 900	+ 3	449 327	+ 2
Vehicles	4	4 479	− 66	4 754	− 68
Textiles, clothing and footwear	20	51 020	− 25	62 970	− 13
Bricks, pottery and glass	13	46 450	− 45	58 950	− 37
Timber and furniture	5	10 050	− 18	10 150	− 19
Paper, printing and publishing	6	23 250	− 42	45 750	− 17
Other manufacturing	8	63 250	− 22	68 250	− 19
Construction	15	272 775	− 20	306 075	− 19
Transport	12	208 150	− 1	238 862	− 1
Distribution	22	84 175	+170	145 245	+123
Banking and insurance	36	390 675	− 18	504 142	− 27
Investment	52	124 330	− 7	141 887	+ 4
Property	17	94 100	− 7	104 600	− 11
Miscellaneous services	11	153 780	− 5	204 780	+ 23
Totals	313	2 222 249	− 11	2 833 444	− 10

Source: Labour Research Department, *Labour Research*, (August 1985)

£390 675, £364 900 and £272 775 respectively. The only industries to increase their contributions to Conservative central funds in 1984 were the distributive and engineering sectors by 170 per cent and three per cent in turn. Table 7.4 shows the 12 largest corporate donors to the Conservative Party in 1984, headed by British and Commercial Shipping and Racal. These companies gave in total £652 400 which was 'about one third of all donations to the Conservatives' in that year. The Labour Research Department (LRD) also found that 17 donations each exceeding £40 000 were made, 'accounting for 35% (£985,891) of all money donated.' With the exception of the £49 000 provided by the British School of Motoring which went to the Liberals, all of this 'money went to Conservatives and friends.'[33]

Table 7.5 shows that not all major corporate political donations go direct to the

Table 7.4 *Twelve largest corporate donors to Conservative Party funds 1984.*

Company	Donations (£)
British and Commonwealth Shipping	97 900
Racal	75 000
London and Northern Group	57 000
Plessey	55 000
AGB Research	50 000
Distillers	50 000
Hanson Trust	50 000
United Biscuits	49 500
Northern Engineering Industries	45 000
Newarthill	43 000
Trafalgar House	40 000
Trusthouse Forte	40 000
Total	652 400

Source: Labour Research Department, *Labour Research* (August 1985)

Table 7.5 *Seventeen largest corporate donors to Conservative Party funds 1984.*

Company	Donations (£)	(Non-Party Donations)
British and Commonwealth Shipping	101 792	(3 892)
Allied-Lyons	82 000	(80 000)
Racal	75 000	(—)
Plessey	75 000	(20 000)
Taylor Woodrow	63 275	(30 000)
London and Northern Group	57 000	(—)
Marks and Spencer	57 000	(57 000)
Hanson Trust	55 000	(5 000)
Guardian Royal Exchange	53 324	(53 324)
AGB Research	50 000	(—)
Distillers	50 000	(—)
United Biscuits	49 500	(—)
BSM Holdings	49 000[1]	(—)
Northern Engineering Industries	45 000	(—)
Newarthill	43 000	(—)
Trafalgar House	40 000	(—)
Trusthouse Forte	40 000	(—)
Total	985 891	249 216

Source: Labour Research Department, *Labour Research* (August 1985)
[1] went to the Liberal Party

Conservative Party. Out of almost one million pounds donated by the 17 leading political contributors in 1984, about a quarter of this went to non-Party organizations. These political or economic agencies supporting the Conservatives included: the British United Industrialists (BUI); the Centre for Policy Studies (CPS); the Economic League (EL); and Aims of Industry (Aims). BUI is an organization existing in part to raise money for the Conservative Party and it 'launders' donations between companies and the Party; CPS is a 'think tank' for Conservative policy making; whilst EL and Aims are pressure groups dedicated to advancing the causes of private enterprise and the market economy. In 1984, BUI received about £400 000 from 27 companies; the CPS £29 800; EL £176 605 from 32 companies; and Aims '12 corporate donations totalling £15,550.'[34] Whether paid directly to the Party, however, or indirectly to its supportive agencies, corporate donations to Conservative financial viability are vital, since about 'two-thirds of central funds come from company donations.'[35]

Although the bulk of corporate political donations go to the Conservatives, the Liberal–Social Democratic Alliance (LSDA) parties also benefit. One of the largest political donations of £188 000 went to the Liberal Party in 1983. This was made by the British School of Motoring (BSM) and was 'equivalent to half the Liberal's central expenditure in 1983 (excluding a separate general election account).'[36] In 1984 'both Alliance parties continued to be recipients of other company donations.'[37] Thirteen companies were involved, with the largest sum of £49 000 passing from BSM to the Liberals. All the other sums were relatively small, with another of £5 100 going to the Liberals, £9 500 to the Social Democratic Party (SDP) and £14 100 to the LSDA.

In view of the fact that trade unions with political funds are required to hold political fund review ballots at least once every 10 years, it is interesting to observe that the LRD survey found 'only six companies asking for shareholders' consent at the AGM to make donations.'[38] A report by the Constitutional Reform Centre proposes a voluntary code of practice for companies making political donations. It proposes, first, that companies making political donations should obtain shareholder consent at their annual general meetings (AGM). Second, that company boards wishing to make donations should provide shareholders with a statement of why such actions are in the interests of the company and its shareholders, and that they should seek approval of that statement at their AGMs at least once during the life of a Parliament. Third, companies making political donations should do so openly, without using institutional conduits like the BUI.

7.3　THE TRADES UNION CONGRESS

Background

The TUC is one of the longest established political interest groups in Britain, having been founded in Manchester in 1868. Previous but unsuccessful attempts had been made in 1833 and 1845 to establish a central organization to represent the collective interests of working men and of the trade unions. The London Trades Council or the 'Junta', which was established in 1860, had emerged as the representative of the exclusive amalgamated societies of the 'labour aristocracy' but it lacked wider representation, particularly within the new northern industrial cities. The call for a trade union 'Congress' in 1868 reflected the intense concern of existing unions towards the Royal Commission which had been appointed in the previous year to 'inquire into and Report on the Organisation and Rules of Trade Unions'. Representatives of the unions gathered in Manchester and were anxious to present a responsible, constitutional and moderate image of trade unionism to the Royal Commission. They wanted legislation to ensure that trade unions were no longer regarded as criminal conspiracies, and that their funds would be protected from embezzlement by dishonest officials. The first Congress, although poorly attended, agreed upon the necessity of a central trade union body which would meet annually.

The initial and unstable existence of the TUC was transformed by the publication of the Trade Union Bill in 1871. This Bill fell so far short of trade union expectations, still leaving many of their activities potentially criminal, that a new collective determination to protect their interests steadily hardened. At the well-attended Congress of 1871, a Parliamentary Committee of the TUC was established. This was the forerunner of the TUC's modern General Council and was of great influence in the formation of the Labour Party in 1900. From 1871 until the First World War 'the Secretary had only one clerk to assist him in carrying out the work of the Congress; between them they constituted the complete TUC establishment!'[39] The TUC was thus materially ill-equipped to fulfil the duties which the early unions and their leaders expected of it. In 1919 Ernest Bevin, the main architect in the formation of the Transport and General Workers Union, complained that the trade union movement was 'a great shapeless mass, all the time struggling to co-ordinate its efforts, but finding itself without a head to direct.'[40]

Eventually, in 1920, Bevin persuaded Congress to abolish the Parliamentary Committee and to establish a General Council of 30 members representing 17 industrial or trade groups. The first General Council, elected in 1921, possessed much greater power and authority over the policies of the trade union movement than did the former Parliamentary Committee. Increased affiliation fees, for example, were to be used to provide additional staff and better research facilities. It was the General Strike of 1926 and its aftermath, however, which had the most profound effect upon the TUC and its developing General Council.

> The collapse of the 1926 General Strike was of course a landmark in the history of the T.U.C. Immediately it resulted in a severe fall in union membership and morale, but far more than that it meant an urgent need for a reappraisal of the role of Congress and indeed of the movement as a whole.[41]

This 'reappraisal' meant, in the long term, that the TUC turned away from outright political confrontations with governments and capitalist employers. Instead, it concentrated its attentions on extending collective bargaining and on improving the machinery of industrial relations for its member unions. Political reform on a broad front was left to the political wing of the Labour Movement: that is, the Labour Party. But Congress continued to be concerned with securing government policies and amendments to the law benefiting working people and their families. By the Second World War the TUC was playing an active part in promoting the war effort, with Ernest Bevin occupying a vital role in the War Cabinet as Minister of Labour, but there had been very few significant changes in the fundamental structure and organization of the TUC since 1921. The considerable growth of the TUC's power and influence between 1945 and the late 1970s resulted not from changes in its internal organization and structure, but from a growth in trade union membership and from changes in the impact of trade unionism upon the national economy during that period.

Congress also gained from fundamental shifts in industrial and political power in Britain, especially in the 1970s, and from the intervention by successive governments in the private sector of industry.

> The standing of Congress therefore depends on the extent and direction of government intervention in the economy and on the ability of the General Council both to influence the government's actions and to bring the unions along with them.[42]

Certainly until 1979, after the election of the first Thatcher Administration, few post-war governments failed to consult the TUC before taking major policy decisions on economic or social affairs, or before introducing legislation affecting the interests of the Trade Union Movement. Since 1979, however, Conservative ministers and senior civil servants have effectively excluded the TUC from influencing government policy and have rarely sought the opinion of the TUC before taking major policy initiatives.

Nevertheless, the purposes of the TUC remain what they have been since it was first incorporated into the policy making process during the Second World War. These are, first, to act as a voice for affiliated unions and for working people in Britain; second, to advance the interests of affiliated unions and their members by the most appropriate means; and, third, to influence government policy in ways beneficial to affiliated unions and their members. The TUC also seeks a voice in international labour affairs. It was, for example, a founder member of the International Confederation of Free Trade Unions in 1949 and is the British workers' delegate to the International Labour Organization. The TUC also belongs to the European Trade Union Confederation, which deals with issues of interest to European working people both inside and outside the Common Market, and the Trade Union Advisory Committee of the Organization for Economic Cooperation and Development.

The main means used by the TUC to further its aims and objectives include lobbying MPs, government departments and ministers; maintaining close links with the Labour Party and senior Labour MPs; nominating trade union representatives to numerous national, regional and local bodies including statutory committees at all levels; and publishing and disseminating research papers, discussion documents and policy statements. It also uses the media and appropriate public relations techniques to publicize its activities.

Structure and activities

Britain is one of the few countries to have a single trade union confederation representing all major trade unions. In many other industrial nations in the western world, 'trade unions and their national centres are divided on the basis of party politics or on religious grounds.' In others the division is between a national centre for manual workers' unions and one for non-manual unions. 'The trade union Movement in Britain is fortunate in having only one national centre',[43] the TUC. The basic unit is the affiliated union; collectively they provide the TUC with its representative authority and its organizational finance, each union paying an annual affiliation fee based on its total membership. Table 7.6 shows that in 1983 the TUC had 95 affiliated organizations comprising a membership of ten and a half million trade unionists. Between 1979 and 1983, the number of affiliated organizations fell from 112 to 95 and total membership by some 13 per cent. A major reason for the fall in the number of TUC affiliates was the amalgamations and mergers taking place between some unions during these years. These arose largely out of economic necessity especially for those unions which, for various reasons, experienced membership decline and financial pressures on their organizational resources. This influenced the merger of the National Union of Agricultural and Allied Workers with the transport workers union in 1982, for example. The fall in total union membership amongst TUC affiliates after 1980 was a reflection of the increased levels of unemployment at that time, unions lost members as jobs disappeared through redundancy, natural wastage and early retirements, especially in manufacturing industry.

The supreme policy making body of the TUC is its annual Congress which meets at Blackpool on the first Monday in September, remains in session for five days and is presided over by the Chairperson of the General Council. Affiliated unions are entitled

Table 7.6 *TUC affiliated organizations and membership 1979–83.*

Year	Number of affiliated organizations	TUC membership
1979	112	12 128 078
1980	109	12 172 508
1981	108	11 601 413
1982	105	11 005 984
1983	95	10 510 157

Source: TUC, *Annual Reports* (TUC 1979–83)

to send delegates to Congress on the basis of one for every 5 000 members 'or part thereof'. They total over 1 000 and are nominated by individual unions at branch or area level. They are normally mandated to support at Congress those policies democratically determined at their own union conferences. Congress has three main functions: it considers the work done and reported on by the General Council during the previous year; it discusses and takes decisions on motions forwarded to it for the agenda by affiliated unions; and it appoints the General Council for the coming year.

The report of the General Council covers eight key areas: relations between unions; trade union organization and industrial relations; social insurance and industrial welfare; education; international affairs; economic policy; industry committees; and press and information. Policy debates at Congress result from motions submitted for the agenda by affiliated unions. Where several unions submit similar or associated motions they are combined together or 'composited'. Amendments to motions are also submitted by individual unions. Before Congress opens, the General Council meets to determine its position on agenda items. If it agrees with a motion it says so. If it disagrees, a member of the General Council is selected to move its rejection or for it to be 'remitted back' to the General Council for its consideration. This usually means the motion will be lost in all but name. Where the feelings of Congress are clear on a motion, the Chairperson asks for a vote by show of hands. But if there is sufficient demand for a 'card vote' from delegates, the Chairperson normally concedes to it. This means that each trade union leader holds up a card representing its total affiliated membership. The total 'votes' cast are then counted. This is known as the 'block vote' which enables each union to influence voting decisions in proportion to its total membership.

One of the most important functions of Congress is to select the General Council for the forthcoming year. The General Council has a number of duties. For example:

(a) The General Council shall transact the business in the periods between each annual Congress, shall keep a watch on all industrial movements, and shall, where possible, co-ordinate industrial action.
(b) They shall watch all legislation affecting labour, and shall initiate such legislation as Congress may direct.
(c) They shall endeavour to adjust disputes and differences between affiliated organisations.
(d) They shall provide common action by the trade union Movement on general questions, such as wages and hours of labour, and any matter of general concern that may arise . . . and shall have power to assist any union which is attacked on any vital question of trade union principle.[44]

Until 1981–82, the General Council was organized into 18 'trade groups' with an additional group for women. At their 1981 Congress, however, delegates resolved that a new system of determining the composition of the General Council was necessary, since the trade group principle was becoming less relevant to the changing composition of affiliated membership. Since 1982 the General Council consists of three sections. Section A consists of automatic representation for all affiliates with over 100 000 members each. Unions with between 100 000 and 499 999 members have one seat each; those with between 500 000 and 749 999 two seats each; those with between 750 000 and 999 999 three seats each; those with between 1 000 000 and 1 499 999 four seats each; and those over 1 500 000 five seats each. Section B consists of 11 members elected from organizations with less than 100 000 members each and Section C consists of six elected women workers, bringing the total membership of the General Council in 1985 to 44 plus the General Secretary.

Between Congresses the General Council is not merely the custodian of Congress decisions, it also has to respond to events. In this way, it has an inescapable leadership function which has to be exercised cautiously, given the General Council's representative capacity and its responsibility for the trade union Movement as a whole. Sometimes the General Council uses the device of convening special conferences of union national executives where vital policy decisions of national importance to the trade unions have to be made between Congresses. Examples include the TUC's opposition to the Industrial Relations Bill in 1971 and the Employment Bill in 1982, and in 1986 when the TUC convened a special conference to reconsider the Movement's policy towards government funding for trade union ballots.

The General Council meets monthly and is served by seven standing committees one or more of which are attended by General Council members and the General Secretary. These committees are: Finance and General Purposes; International; Education; Social Insurance and Industrial Welfare; Employment Policy and Organization; Economic; and Equal Rights. Each committee is serviced by one or more of the seven departments within the TUC and their professional staff, which in recent years has placed a heavy burden of work on departmental personnel. This has been compounded by having to adjust to continual changes in the economy, the law and government policies. Delegates at Congress regularly urge the TUC to provide more and better services to affiliated unions, to conduct additional research and to provide more information to them, whilst at the same time normally opposing moves to increase affiliation fees proportionally.

The work of the TUC is also assisted by 11 industry committees covering: construction; distribution, food and drink; financial services; fuel and power; health services; hotel and catering; local government; printing; steel; textiles; and transport. These committees bring together all TUC unions with members in these industries and co-ordinate collective bargaining and industrial relations policies amongst them. Some of these industry committees have replaced federations of trade unions which previously acted independently of the TUC. The TUC also has 11 joint committees covering a wide range of activities with external bodies. These are: nationalized industries; public services; arts, entertainment and sport; women; race relations; trades councils; media working group; National Economic Development Council (NEDC); the TUC and CBI; occupational health; and the TUC and the Labour Party. There is also a National Council of Labour representing the TUC, Labour Party and the Cooperative Union.

Despite the fact that the TUC covers the whole of England and Wales – Scotland has its own TUC – it does not possess a strong regional structure. Traditionally, it is local trade councils representing the interests of trade union branches from affiliated unions at local level which provide TUC representation outside London. Trade union branches can affiliate to their local trades council, sending delegates to them according to the size of their branch membership. The trades council is then registered by the TUC. Over 400 trades councils in England and Wales act as local agents for the TUC. Funds are provided from affiliation fees paid by local union branches and trades councils operate model rules, approved by Congress, devised to prevent them from subscribing to the funds of breakaway unions or to the Communist Party and other proscribed organizations.

Many trades councils in the large industrial cities were established long before the TUC itself, and they continue to provide a valuable forum for grass roots union debate on local and regional affairs. The TUC also organizes a conference of trades councils each year and issues an annual report dealing with their activities. Nevertheless, despite TUC supervision many trades councils are taken over by proscribed bodies. In other instances, they follow courses of action which offend declared TUC policies. As a result, they are sometimes suspended. The TUC admits that trades councils are often ignored or poorly supported by trade union branches and that some branches are 'unwilling to become associated with trades councils because of their belief that some trades councils are unrepresentative of the mainstream of the trade union movement and tend towards extremist views.'[45]

The TUC's eight regional councils are based on the government's economic planning regions plus the Wales Trade Union Council. Because of the unwillingness of affiliated unions to pay increased affiliation fees, these councils depend upon voluntary officers to run them, obviously limiting their effectiveness. The TUC has also voiced its concern at the lack of adequate full-time officer support for the regional structure. Hence the TUC is almost unique among national bodies in not having a strong regional organization, 'and it is at least arguable that if such an organization is not developed regional councils may attract the additional attention of unrepresentative fringe bodies.'[46]

Although the TUC's direct impact on the government has diminished since 1979, it is still represented in a variety of important bodies created by government aimed at influencing industrial relations and economic activity. Senior members of the TUC serve, *inter alia*, on the NEDC, the Manpower Services Commission, the Health and Safety Executive, the Equal Opportunities Commission, the Council of the Advisory Conciliation and Arbitration Service, and the boards of public corporations. Service on these nationally important bodies places a considerable burden on the members of the General Council and on the TUC staff who brief and service them. Further, members of the General Council are either general secretaries or national officers of individual unions, with all the heavy work burdens which this involves.

In order to fulfil its wide responsibilities on behalf of the trade union Movement, the TUC continuously seeks a more responsive and representative General Council, and for means of providing better representation for women members. It also accepts the need periodically to review its committee system, its provision of educational services and its internal organization. Its legal, research and information services are regularly updated too. This is in keeping with the TUC's established involvement in the many public agencies created by successive governments. Whilst it seems generally agreed that the TUC reacts only slowly to institutional change, it has nevertheless adapted itself to the varying circumstances facing member unions. Critics believe its central weakness to be its lack of executive authority over affiliated organizations. Its supporters emphasize its considerable moral authority over affiliates. The TUC's political influence on government policy, however, tends to be greater and more effective under Labour governments, under Conservative ones the TUC's impact is generally weaker and tends to fluctuate.

7.4   THE CONFEDERATION OF BRITISH INDUSTRY

The first successful attempt to establish a central organization of employer interests was during the First World War, when the Federation of British Industries was formed in 1916. Its main purpose was to advance the commercial interests of member firms. The formation of earlier organizations had not achieved any permanent or co-ordinated central association of employers in Britain up till that time. But the monopoly interest of the Federation of British Industries was short lived, since immediately afterwards the National Union of Manufacturers – later known as the National Association of British Manufacturers – was formed. Its major focus was the special interests of small manufacturers. In the meantime:

> Some of the employers' organisations, particularly the key Engineering Employers' Federation, were suspicious of the quasi-syndicalist ideas of some of the FBI's leaders and eventually formed a separate organisation to deal with labour matters, latterly called the British Employers' Confederation.[47]

Thus by the end of the First World War, three separate central organizations of employers were claiming to represent the collective interests of private sector businesses in Britain – the Federation of British Industries (FBI), the National Association of British Manufacturers (NABM) and the British Employers' Confederation (BEC).

Since the NABM always had a larger proportion of small firms amongst its members compared with the other two employer organizations, its policies and activities rarely conflicted with those of the other two bodies. However, the separate existence of the Confederation with its main interests focused on industrial relations, and the Federation with its principal concerns centred in commercial affairs, continually provoked difficulties between the two organizations for many years. Furthermore, the interventionist policies of the war-time Coalition Government between 1940 and 1945 and the post-war Labour Government immediately afterwards created new areas in which co-ordinated consultation between government and all major private sector employers was increasingly necessary. Despite attempts to amalgamate these two central organizations of employers during the 1940s, no agreement on terms could be reached between them. In these circumstances, 'the BEC lived a predominantly defensive life, the FBI a largely promotional one.'[48]

The main impetus leading up to the merger between the Confederation, the Federation and the small business manufacturers to form the CBI in 1965 was the renewed interest which took place in economic planning in Britain after 1960. Accordingly, the need for creating more effective and co-ordinated arrangements for the representation of industrial opinion than hitherto became more pressing.

> Thus, in July 1963, the Presidents of the FBI, the BEC and the NABM appointed Sir Henry Benson and Sir Stephen Brown to prepare a report on the way in which the three organisations could be merged into one 'National Industrial Organisation.[49]

As things turned out, the FBI was generally in favour of the Benson–Brown proposals, since the new body was to operate under the Federation's revised charter. Elements within the BEC, however, initially opposed the proposals for a merger among the three bodies. The Engineering Employers Federation, for example, was especially hostile. Amongst other things, its leaders disliked the suggested constitution:

> because it would allow direct membership and representation on the labour committee to individual firms. If companies paid subscriptions to the new body, the Federation argued, they might not also wish to pay to their employers' organisation, particularly if they could exercise influence through the labour committee.[50]

Although in the end the Engineering Federation withdrew its objections because it did not wish to be made the scapegoat for a breakdown in negotiations among the parties it had made its point.

The NABM, on the other hand, proved a much more difficult body to fit into the new organization than its two other constituents. Many of its members felt that the particular interests of smaller businesses could not be defended by the CBI, since it would be predominantly made up of larger employers. They were also opposed to the proposal to admit the nationalized industries into membership. The question of admitting nationalized industries into the CBI was contested on two fronts. First, there were those private sector firms opposed in principle to nationalization. Second, there were those individuals who saw nationalization as a fundamental socialist measure. They were equally opposed to public sector organizations joining a predominantly private sector body. In the event, however, a breakaway organization, the Society of Independent Manufacturers, was formed which later became the Smaller Businesses Association.

The CBI came into being by amalgamation among the three constituent organizations on 30 July 1965. Its initial membership comprised '12,600 firms, the main nationalised industries, 104 employers' organisations and 150 trade associations.'[51] The set of events which tipped the balance in favour of the merger was the approach made by the newly elected Labour Government to British industrial representatives at the end of 1964. The freshly appointed Secretary of State and Minister of Economic Affairs, George Brown, soon made it clear that he wanted to discuss industrial matters and to pursue his productivity policy with only one body of employers, not three. Moreover, the increasing influence of the TUC in economic and political affairs clearly demonstrated to the diehards of private industry that the collective interests of their members and of employers in Britain generally could only be maintained and developed on a unified basis through a common central organization.

Under the terms of its Royal Charter, the principal objects of the CBI are:

(a) to provide for British industry the means of formulating, making known and influencing general policy in regard to industrial, economic, fiscal, commercial, labour, social, legal and technical questions, and to act as a national point of reference for those seeking industry's views;
(b) to develop the contribution of British industry to the national economy;
(c) to encourage the efficiency and competitive power of British industry, and to provide advice, information and services to British industry to that end.[52]

The Confederation's functions on behalf of its member organizations, therefore, are much wider than those in the field of industrial relations alone. Unlike its counterparts in Italy and Sweden for example, the Confederation is not a collective bargaining agency and its main task on behalf of member organizations in industrial relations and other fields is to formulate general employer policy for implementation by its constituent bodies. Its preferred policies are communicated to government, the general public and the TUC. The CBI, therefore, is not only concerned with giving its members an opportunity to voice their opinions, 'it must also ensure that those opinions are aggregated into a policy which is well-informed as well as representative of industrial opinion.'[53]

Membership and organization

The CBI claims to be the 'recognised voice of British business'. It exists primarily:

to voice the views of its members in ensuring that governments of whatever political complexion – and society as a whole – understand both the needs of British business and the contribution it makes to the well-being of the nation.[54]
[Its] task is to ensure that Governments, trade unions, organisations and people of all political complexions fully understand the aims, needs and problems of British business, and to help promote policies for a more effective mixed economy in which both private and public sectors are efficient and financially healthy.[55]

In these roles the CBI is consulted widely by government, the civil service and the media. But it is not solely concerned with major national issues. An important part of its task is to represent business interests at regional and local levels too.

Like most other employer bodies the CBI is made up of corporate members, with membership drawn from many sectors of British business. It claims that well over 10 million people, almost 50 per cent of the employed labour force, work in member firms 'either directly or indirectly through trade organisations or Chambers of Commerce.'[56] Membership comes from three organizational sectors and 'currently represents about 300 000 companies',[57] including those in the industrial, commercial and public sectors, as well as over 200 employers' organizations, trade associations and commercial associations. The industrial and commercial sectors, for example, incorporate some 250 000 public and private companies in extractive, productive and manufacturing industries and the financial, trading and advisory services. Industrial members are recruited amongst others from: agriculture; engineering; printing and publishing; construction; and general manufacturing. The CBI's commercial members include accountants, advertising agencies, architects, bankers, mail order firms, insurance companies, retailers, stockbrokers, solicitors, transport firms and wholesalers. Many of the nationalized industries and public corporations are members, as are over 200 employers organizations, trade associations and commercial associations representing individual manufacturing industries, local trade associations and Chambers of Commerce.

The CBI claims to speak for every size of business 'from the largest to the smallest – around a half of the membership is made up of companies with 200 or fewer employees.'[58] Nevertheless, many small firms continue to see the CBI as an organization dominated by larger firms and are reluctant to join it. Neither does it have local authority and public service members and these employ large numbers of people and organizational resources. Despite its claims, therefore, and despite the fact that it has considerably widened its membership base since 1965, the CBI is largely representative of sections of private manufacturing industry and commerce. Wide gaps in potential membership remain.

Figure 7.2 provides an outline of the CBI's organizational structure. The CBI's governing body is its Council, normally chaired for two years by a President who is elected by the membership. It consists of elected office holders, such as the Deputy President and past Presidents, and the Chairpersons of its 22 Standing Committees. Other representatives on the CBI's Council come from employer, trade and commercial organizations, the pubic sector, its 13 Regional Councils, the Smaller Firms Council and individuals drawn from member organizations of all sizes and activities. All these people are senior professional managers or owner-managers from the private and public sectors. As the ruling body of the CBI, Council takes all policy decisions but in doing so is advised by its Standing Committees. Additionally, the annual National Conference enables delegates to debate policy issues and make their contribution to policy deter mination. CBI policy has two aspects:

> In the long term, the aim is to make a constructive contribution to attitudes and forward thinking on issues affecting business. In the short term, the CBI has to be equipped to react quickly and positively to any proposals by Government or others, which have a bearing on industry and commerce.[59]

Because of its size, Council is too large a body to decide policy details. These are determined by the Standing Committees. The CBI's Standing Committees cover every aspect of business life and are responsible for most of its detailed work on policy making. They put forward ideas, draft policy proposals and present them to Council, drawing on the views of Regional Councils, the Smaller Firms Council and individual members. Each Standing Committee covers a specific area of policy, with the Presi-

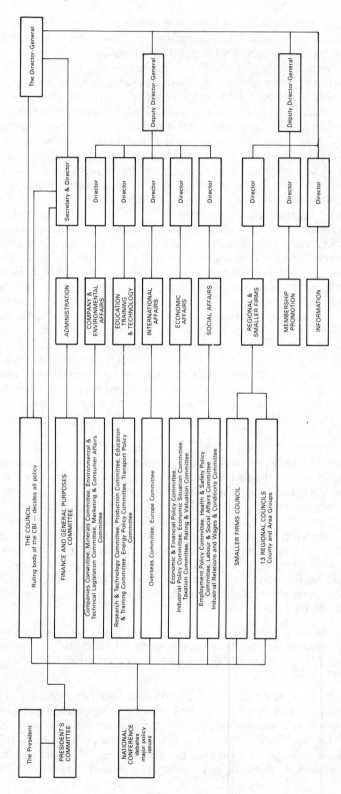

Figure 7.2 CBI organizational structure.

Source: CBI, *Annual Report 1984* (CBI 1985)

dent's Committee having wider terms of reference. It consists of leading CBI figures, including the Chairpersons of key Standing Committees and the Smaller Firms Council. 'Its role is to advise the President on major policy issues and to keep the CBI's public position and overall strategy under constant review.'[60]

The CBI's Standing Committees are important bodies. Some are purely representative and are concerned with obtaining consensus on general policy. Others are specialist committees focusing on particular aspects of policy, whilst others are co-ordinating committees which attempt to keep different policies in line with one another. Each council, committee or group of committees is serviced by one of seven internal directorates. These are: Adminstration; Company and Environmental Affairs; Education, Training and Technology; International Affairs; Economic Affairs; Social Affairs; and Regional and Smaller Firms. Two other directorates are Membership Promotion and Information. The Director-General, assisted by two Deputy Director-Generals, is the CBI's chief executive. The Director-General heads the permanent staff, communicates regularly with the media and the public, and leads negotiations with government and the civil service on specific issues.

The CBI is also divided into 13 regions and regards its regional organization as an important means of keeping headquarters staff, councils and committees in touch with local opinion. Each region has its own Regional Council which acts as a sounding board for membership opinion, whilst facilitating personal contact amongst local members.

> The Regional Councils regularly discuss national issues and the results of these discussions are reported to the CBI Council by their representatives so that regional problems can be taken into account in policy formation.[61]

Regional Councils also provide machinery for consultation with local government and central government officials in their own regions.

Activities

The two major groups of activities in which the CBI is involved are membership services and membership representation. Membership services are wide ranging. The CBI is, for example, an important source of information for daily business needs. It has specialist staff in company law, industrial relations, employment legislation, taxation, education and training, and overseas trade. Members draw on staff expertise thereby keeping themselves up to date on a variety of matters affecting their businesses. The relevant information is communicated by publications, telephone, the Directorates, or the nearest CBI regional office. The Pay Data Bank, for instance, enables member firms to have an accurate and authoritative picture of current pay awards. The Employee Communication Unit draws on wide experience in briefing companies on the best way of ensuring information flows to their workforces, whilst Regional Councils regularly update local trading situations affecting their members.

In representing members' interests, the CBI has extensive contacts in Westminster and Whitehall, locally and internationally. The CBI like the TUC is represented, for example, on NEDC, the Advisory Conciliation and Arbitration Service (ACAS), the Manpower Services Commission, the Health and Safety Commission, the Commission for Racial Equality (CRE) and the Equal Opportunities Commission (EOC). The CBI also lobbies ministers, government departments and MPs. The earlier that government policy making can be influenced the better it is for the CBI and its members. To do this:

> The CBI has to be aware of the thinking of Ministers, the research arms of the political parties, back-bench MPs and civil servants on a continuous basis to ensure its views are put forward at the best possible opportunity.[62]

The process continues as government proposals or consultative documents are published and as bills pass through Parliament. Constructive working relationships are also maintained with the TUC both directly on *ad hoc* issues and through joint membership of public bodies like ACAS, NEDC and so on.

Local issues and local government are equally important target areas for the CBI. Its regional offices and Regional Councillors, for example, are in constant contact with local authorities, MPs and government departments. The CBI also maintains close links with international bodies. These include the European Commission, the European Parliament, the UK Delegation and various European Economic Community institutions through its Brussels office. As the major central organization of employers in Britain, the CBI is a member of the Union of Industrial Federations of the European Community. In more general terms, the CBI seeks to put forward CBI policies to the wider public, both at home and abroad. It therefore maintains close contacts with newspaper, radio and television journalists, with the aim of establishing a better general understanding 'of the wealth-creating role of business and of the opportunities within industry and commerce for satisfying work.'[63]

In its short history, there is little doubt that the CBI has had a major impact on economic and industrial affairs as the major central organization of employers in Britain, even though its views have been less well received by government since 1979. Its members include many of the large manufacturing companies in the country and some important service ones. Moreover, like the TUC, the CBI has a degree of access to governmental decision making, and to appointments on bodies like industrial tribunals and the Council of ACAS, which few other political interest groups can equal. However, it also has its weaknesses. For example, it has not yet extended its membership coverage across the whole of British industry as widely as some of its advocates have suggested. It is strongest among large firms; it is weakest among smaller firms. It has successfully recruited in manufacturing industry; it has been less successful in parts of the service sector. It is also argued that, in comparison with some of its European counterparts, the CBI is under-financed in relation to the wide range of tasks which it attempts to undertake. Finally, the CBI is not a tight and cohesive body but, like the TUC, a coalition interest group with all the advantages and disadvantages which this type of organization brings. According to one authority:

> there is always potential tension in the CBI between those members who would prefer to see the organisation follow a 'strategy of responsibility', cooperating with government in the implementation of its policies in the hope of securing concessions, and those who would like the CBI to engage in more frequent and more outspoken criticisms of government policy even if this impairs the organisation's ability to negotiate concessions from government.[64]

7.5   THE ELECTORATE AND CHANGING POLITICAL ALIGNMENTS

The party political preferences which voters express in Parliamentary elections every four or five years determine the outcome of general elections. The outcome of general elections, in turn, enables the leading party in the House of Commons to take office and to implement its economic, social and industrial relations policies. These policies and governmental programmes have major implications for everyone whether as citizens, workers or trade unionists. As we indicate in this chapter, political divisions in Britain are based largely on social class interests, especially occupational ones. Throughout the immediate post-war period in the 1950s and 1960s, the backbone of Labour Party political support was the manual working class, substantial parts of which were strongly unionized. The backbone of Conservative support was the professional and business middle classes which tended not to be unionized and were generally hostile to trade unionism. Since the 1970s the occupational structure, the distribution of union membership and political allegiances within the electorate appear to be changing. What was predominantly a blue-collar labour force and trade union movement is steadily becoming a white-collar one. And what was predominantly a two party political system seems to be shifting towards a multiparty one. These economic and political changes have important implications not only electorally but also for the politics of industrial relations.

Table 7.7 provides a fivefold occupational classification of the electorate and shows how its class structure changed substantially between 1964 and 1983. The manual working class was the largest occupational group in both years. But whereas in 1964 it constituted nearly a half of the electorate, and was almost three times the size of the salariat of managers, administrators and professional workers, by 1983 the working class and salariat 'were almost of the same size'.[65] Further, whilst the salariat and routine non-manual workers made up 36 per cent of the electorate in 1964, they constituted 51 per cent in 1983. Britain is still divided by social class and occupational differences but 'the shape of the class structure has changed, with important electoral implications particularly for Labour.'[66] In other words, between 1964 and 1983 Britain was transformed from a largely blue-collar workforce to a predominantly white-collar one, with corresponding changes in trade union membership and in the political allegiances of the electorate.

Table 7.8 shows the relationship between class and voting in the 1964 and 1983 General Elections. In 1983 the Conservative vote was lower amongst the salariat and routine non-manual workers than in 1964 but higher amongst supervisors and technicians and the manual working class, whilst the self employed were consistently 'the most Conservative class, and indeed by far the most united class in its politics.'[67] The Labour vote was lower across all classes, particularly amongst supervisors and technicians and the manual working class. The Alliance vote was higher across the classes, notably

Table 7.7 *Class composition of the electorate 1964 and 1983.*

Class	1964 %	1983 %
Salariat	18	27
Routine non-manual	18	24
Self employed	7	8
Supervisors and technicians	10	7
Manual working class	47	34

Source: A. Heath *et al., How Britain votes* (Pergamon 1985)

Table 7.8 *Class and vote 1964 and 1983.*

Party	Salariat 1964	1983	Routine non-manual 1964	1983	Self employed 1964	1983	Supervisors/ Technicians 1964	1983	Manual working class 1964	1983
Conservative	61	54	54	46	74	71	40	48	23	30
Labour	20	14	31	25	12	12	44	26	70	49
Liberal/Alliance	18	31	14	27	13	17	15	25	7	20
Others	1	1	1	2	1	0	1	1	0	1

Source: A. Heath et al, *How Britain Votes* (Pergamon 1985).

amongst the manual working class where it rose from seven per cent in 1964 to 20 per cent in 1983. 'Over the 1964 to 1983 period as a whole the dominant impression is one of "trendless' fluctuation rather than steady dealignment.' Yet if 1964 was the high point of relative class voting, 1983 was remarkable for 'the challenge it posed to the long standing and overwhelming dominance of the Conservative and Labour parties within British electoral politics.'[68]

Table 7.9 shows the political allegiances of trade unionists between 1974 and 1984. In the October 1974 and May 1979 General Elections a majority of trade unionists voted Labour but in June 1983 only 39 per cent did, with 60 per cent voting either Conservative or Alliance. According to opinion polls by June 1984 the Conservatives had slipped to 26 per cent and the Alliance parties to 21 per cent but the 51 per cent of trade unionists claiming that they would vote Labour if an election were held was only a bare majority of all trade unionsts, no more than in May 1979. Put another way about 8.5 million trade unionists voted in the 1983 General Election of whom some 3.3 million voted Labour. Given that there were about six million trade unionists paying the political levy at that time, it seems likely that in 1983 over 'two million members who pay the political levy [failed] to vote Labour.'[69]

Table 7.9 *The politics of trade union members 1974–84.*

Party	October 1974	May 1979	June 1983	June 1984
	%			
Labour	55	51	39	51
Conservative	23	33	31	26
Alliance	16	13	29	21
Others	6	3	1	2
All	100	100	100	100

Source: *The Times* (9 July 1984)

The structure of trade unionism is also changing. Even though white-collar workers are normally more difficult to organize into trade unions than are blue-collar ones, with the major exception of the public sector where union density of both groups is generally high, membership of white-collar trade unions which are TUC affiliates increased almost threefold between 1965 and 1983. This is shown in table 7.10 which also illustrates the absolute and relative decline of blue-collar union membership amongst TUC affiliates between these years. Further, white-collar unions represented about a third of TUC membership in 1983, compared with only 17 per cent in 1965.

There are differences, moreover, in the political allegiances of white-collar trade unionists and blue-collar trade unionists. As can be seen in table 7.11, in both 1983 and 1984, the Conservatives drew stronger political support from white-collar unionists than from blue-collar unionists. Conversely, Labour had weaker political support amongst white-collar unionists than amongst blue-collar unionists. For the Alliance parties, political support was stronger amongst white-collar unionists than it was

Table 7.10 *TUC membership 1965 and 1983.*

Year	White-collar membership	Blue-collar membership	All membership
1965	1 320 554	7 546 968	8 867 522
1983	3 405 865	7 104 292	10 510 157

Sources: TUC, *Trade Unionisn* (TUC 1966) and *Annual Report 1983* (TUC 1983)

Table 7.11 *Political allegiances of trade union members 1983 and 1984.*

Party	White-collar unionists		Blue-collar unionists		All trade unionists	
	%					
	1983	1984	1983	1984	1983	1984
Labour	27	36	46	56	39	51
Conservative	38	39	27	25	31	26
Alliance	33	22	26	16	29	21
Others	2	3	1	3	1	2
All	100	100	100	100	100	100

Source: *The Times* (9 July 1984)

amongst blue collar ones, though it appeared to weaken amongst both groups between 1983 and 1984. It is estimated that the trade unions lost about two million members between 1979 and 1984 but the membership remaining 'is more concentrated than ever among home-owning skilled and white collar people with jobs.'[70] The political parties which to have gained most from these developments so far are the Conservatives and the Alliance; the party which has lost, both electorally and in terms of votes, is Labour.

It is not easy to determine definitively why the Labour Party is less attractive to its traditional voters in general and to trade unionists in particular in recent years. But some tentative reasons can be suggested for its relative electoral decline up to the mid 1980s. First, Labour's traditional support base, the manual working class, has been slowly shrinking in size. It is still the largest social and occupational group in Britain but due to industrial and technological changes and the long term relative decline of the British economy, it is dwindling in number and changing in character. The results have been an increase in the size of the service sector at the expense of the manufacturing sector, an expansion of the routine non-manual workforce relative to manual employment and a contraction of the old staple industries like coalmining, shipbuilding, steel making and so on. All these trends threaten Labour's traditional voting strongholds. Second, the manual working class has never solidly voted Labour anyway. About a third has consistently voted Conservative in general elections. Explanations of this working class Conservatism have emphasized 'either the notion of working-class deference or that of inherited party loyalties.'[71] It seems possible that inherited party loyalties now play a far less significant role in socializing new working-class voters into the party system than they did in the past.

Third, although it is social class which largely determines voting behaviour in Britain, certain non-class cleavages are also important. It has been suggested, for example, that:

> those who depend on the state for employment or for substantial consumption provision tend to subscribe to a 'statist' ideology which has become associated with the Labour Party, while private-sector workers and those who buy their key consumption requirements in the private market tend towards an 'anti-statist' ideology which has become associated with the Conservatives.[72]

A further possible reason, therefore, why Labour support amongst the manual working class has declined recently could be that Labour has been deserted by that part of the manual working class with the least to gain from the extension of state activity in the economy or the expansion of public spending. In both the 1979 and 1983 Elections the Conservatives polled significantly better amongst private sector workers than amongst public sector ones, especially amongst those who were non-unionized. In 1983, 36 per cent of private sector manual workers voted Conservative and 37 per cent voted Labour. Public sector manual workers, by contrast, remained more loyal to Labour, with '46 per cent voting Labour compared with 29 per cent Conservative and 25 per cent Alliance'.[73]

The developments outlined in this section have obvious implications for the political system, industrial relations and the politics of industrial relations. Whether Labour will win back its traditional voters and gain new ones; how the wider Labour Movement will adapt to changes within the social structure, the emerging pattern of trade unionism and its members' political allegiances; the financial relationship between the Conservatives and big business; and whether the third force in British politics – the Liberal–Social Democratic Alliance – will succeed in 'breaking the mould' and changing the politics of industrial relations: all these are key political and industrial relations issues. Their possible outcomes, however, are unlikely to be determined conclusively until the end of the 1980s.

7.6   SUMMARY

The formal political relationship between some of the major trade unions in Britain and the Labour Party is a long-established one. It was the trade unions which were instrumental in forming the LRC in 1900 and a few years later, in 1906, it became the Labour Party. It is the device of union political funds, established under the Trade Union Acts 1913 and 1984, which enables trade unions to establish political fund rules and to raise a political levy from their members to spend on political objects. Members wishing to contract out of the political levy must be allowed to do so and admission to a union most not be conditional on paying the political levy. Union political fund expenditure is used for three main purposes. It enables unions: to affiliate to the Labour Party; to sponsor Labour MPs; and to finance local political activities.

Labour Party-affiliated unions currently provide some six million Labour Party members and the bulk of Labour Party finances. Affiliated unions send delegates to the Party's Annual Conference, influence debates and vote there, have elected members on the Labour Party's NEC, and comprise 40 per cent of the Electoral College which elects the Labour Party leadership. There is also a TUC–Labour Party Liaison Committee, consisting of representatives from the TUC's General Council, Labour's NEC and the PLP including the Party Leader, whose main purpose is to co-ordinate the campaigning activities of both bodies. In the 1983 General Election, 112 union sponsored Labour MPs were elected to the House of Commons. In addition to the normal Parliamentary duties of all MPs the sponsored MPs are expected to promote trade union interests in Parliament and to maintain close links with their sponsoring unions.

Apart from those private sector organizations providing political donations to the Conservative Party, relationships between employers and the Conservatives tend to be less formalized and are based more on personal connections and contacts rather than institutional ones. Many Conservative MPs, for example, sit on company boards, whilst City interests rather than manufacturing interests now appear to have the closer links with the Parliamentary Conservative Party. Other links are provided by common social backgrounds, membership of the same business and social clubs, family connections and informal personal networks. The Conservative Party is also the major beneficiary from corporate political donations which now account for some two-thirds of Conservative central funds. Not all corporate political donations go direct to the Conservatives; some are channelled by conduit bodies such as the BUI, the CPS, the EL and Aims.

The TUC is the only central trade union confederation in Britain representing all major trade unions. In the mid 1980s it had some 90 affiliated unions with a total membership of about 10 million trade unionists. TUC policy is taken at its annual

Congress which meets for a week in Blackpool during September, where affiliated unions send delegates in proportion to their total membership size. The annual Congress also selects the TUC's General Council which implements TUC policy and keeps a watching brief on trade union and labour affairs between Congresses. For the larger unions, membership of the General Council is automatic, for smaller unions and for women members it is by election. The General Council and other TUC Committees are serviced by the TUC's professional staff which are allocated to seven internal departments. Although the TUC's political role has diminished since 1979, it still attends meetings of the NEDC and, like the CBI, is represented on a wide range of public bodies and statutory agencies such as ACAS, the CRE and the EOC.

Compared with the TUC which was established in 1868, the equivalent employers' organization, the CBI, was formed very much later in 1965. During the past 20 years, the CBI has established itself as the central organization representing employers' interests in Britain. It has steadily broadened its membership base and represents business interests to government, unions and the public authorities, whilst at the same time acting as a public relations body for British employers generally. Its membership is drawn from private sector industrial, service and commercial enterprises, major public sector employers, and some 200 employers' associations, trade associations and Chambers of Commerce.

The internal organization of the CBI is fairly complex, with its Council acting as its policy taking centre. Detailed policy proposals, however, are undertaken by the CBI's 22 Standing Committees which are serviced by five internal directorates. The CBI is also organized to deal effectively with local and area issues. To these ends it has a Smaller Firms Council and 13 Regional Councils. These aim to keep in touch with the needs of small firms and local employers and help them solve their day-to-day business problems. The membership services of the CBI are wide-ranging both nationally and locally and are backed up by skilled professional advice from lawyers, accountants, tax specialists and so on. The CBI also lobbies in Westminster, Whitehall and internationally but, again like the TUC, its influence with government has weakened since 1979, though it continues to have representatives on bodies like ACAS and similar public agencies.

During the 1950s and 1960s, Labour Party political support drew heavily from the manual working class, much of which was unionized especially in Labour's industrial heartlands. Similarly, Conservative Party support was focused predominantly amongst the professional and business middle classes, though some third of the working class – the so called 'deferential' vote – regularly voted Conservative in General Elections. Since the 1970s, and especially during the 1980s, significant changes appear to be taking place within the social class and occupational structures as well as within the trade union movement. Although the manual working class remains the largest single class, the salariat, routine non-manual workers and supervisors and technicians now constitute almost 60 per cent of the electorate. Similarly the trade union movement is becoming less a blue-collar one than a white-collar one. These social and industrial developments are apparently being reflected in the changing political allegiances of the electorate. In the 1983 General Election, traditional ties between the Labour Party and some trade union voters seemed to be weakening, as did those between the Conservatives and some of the professional middle classes, with the Alliance parties attracting votes across the occupational and social classes. To what extent these developments result in permanent political changes remains to be tested in future General Elections.

7.7 REFERENCES

1. S. and B. Webb, *Industrial Democracy*, Longmans, London, 1902, pp. 596–9.
2. A. Ball, *British Political Parties*, Macmillan, London, 1981, p. 44.
3. Selig Perlman quoted in I. Richter, *Political Purpose in Trade Unions,* Allen and Unwin, London, 1973, p. 22.
4. D. Farnham, The Labour Alliance: reality or myth?, *Parliamentary Affairs*, Vol. XXIX (1), Winter, 1976, p. 46.
5. Labour Party, *Constitution and Standing Orders of the Labour Party*, London, 1982, Clause IV, (4).
6. Trades Union Congress, *Trade Unionism*, TUC, London, 1966, p. 56.
7. Farnham, *op. cit.*, p. 46.
8. Trades Union Congress, *Report of 115th Annual Trades Union Congress 1983*, TUC, London, 1984, p. 1.
9. B.C. Roberts, *Trade Union Government and Administration in Great Britain*, Bell, London, 1956, p. 373.
10. *Ibid.*
11. *Ibid.*, p. 376.
12. *Ibid.*, p. 380.
13. Labour Party, (1982), *op. cit.*, Clause IX (i).
14. Ball, *op. cit.*, p. 235.
15. *Ibid.*, p. 243.
16. Eric Varley speaking at the Labour Party Conference 1982. See *Report of the Annual Conference of the Labour Party*, Labour Party, London, 1983, p. 34.
17. TUC–Labour Party Liaison Committee, *Policy Statement: Partners in Rebuilding Britain*, TUC–Labour Party, London, 1983, para. 2.
18. TUC (1984), *op. cit.*, p. 243.
19. H. Phelps Brown, *The Origins of Trade Union Power*, Clarendon Press, Oxford, 1983, p. 56.
20. The Conservative Party, *The Conservative Manifesto 1983*, CPC, London, 1983.
21. *Ibid.*, pp. 16f. and 19.
22. C. Crouch, *The Politics of Industrial Relations*, Fontana, London, 1979, p. 133.
23. *Ibid.*, p. 134.
24. G.K. Wilson, *Business and Politics*, Macmillan, Basingstoke, 1985, p. 60.
25. A. Ball, *op. cit.*, p. 219.
26. Certification Officer, *Annual Report of the Certification Officer 1983*, HMSO, London, 1984, p. 24.
27. G.K. Wilson, *op. cit.*, p. 66.
28. *Ibid.*, p. 61.
29. R. Taylor, 'Tories with a stake in the Channel', *The Observer*, 15 December 1985.
30. *Ibid.*
31. G.K. Wilson, *op. cit.*, p. 61.
32. Labour Research Department, 'Fall in company funds to the Tories', *Labour Research*, August 1985, p. 202.
33. *Ibid.*
34. *Ibid.*
35. A. Ball, *op. cit.*, p. 216.
36. Labour Research Department, Company cash for the Liberals, *Labour Research*, May 1985, p. 117.
37. *Labour Research* (August 1985), p. 202.
38. *Ibid.*, p. 203.
39. J. Lovell and B.C. Roberts, *A Short History of the TUC*, Macmillan, London 1968, p. 57.
40. *Ibid.*, p. 59.
41. *Ibid.*, p. 92.
42. H.A. Clegg, *The System of Industrial Relations in Great Britain*, Blackwell, Oxford, 1970, pp. 405ff.
43. TUC (1966), *op. cit.*, pp. 1f.
44. TUC, *Rules and Standing Orders*, Rule 8, 1983.

45. TUC, *Consultative Arrangements within the TUC*, TUC, London (n.d.), p. 20.
46. *Ibid.*, p. 19.
47. W. Grant and D. Marsh, *The Confederation of British Industry*, Hodder and Stoughton, London, 1977, p. 20.
48. S. Blank, *Government and Industry in Britain*, Saxon House, Farnborough, 1973, p. 49.
49. W. Grant and D. Marsh, *op. cit.*, p. 25.
50. E. Wigham, *The Power to Manage*, Macmillan, London, 1973, p. 216.
51. Confederation of British Industry, *Evidence to the Royal Commission on Trade Unions and Employers' Associations*, CBI, London, 1965, p. 7.
52. *Ibid.*
53. W. Grant and D. Marsh, *op. cit.*, p. 87.
54. Confederation of British Industry, *Britain's Business Voice*, CBI, London, 1985, p. 3.
55. Confederation of British Industry, *Isn't it time your voice was heard?*, CBI, London (n.d.), p. 1.
56. CBI (1985) *op. cit.*, p. 5.
57. CBI (n.d.), *op. cit.*, p. 2.
58. CBI (1985), *op. cit.*, p. 5.
59. *Ibid.*, p. 7.
60. *Ibid.*, p. 10.
61. W. Grant and D. Marsh, *op. cit.*, p. 92.
62. CBI (1985), *op. cit.*, p.. 6.
63. *Ibid.*, p. 7.
64. W. Grant and D. Marsh, *op. cit.*, p. 211.
65. A. Heath, R. Jowell and J. Curtice, *How Britain Votes*, Pergamon, Oxford, 1985, p. 35.
66. *Ibid.*, p. 39.
67. *Ibid.*, p. 20.
68. *Ibid.*, pp. 35 and 3.
69. P. Kellner, 'Can the Brothers ever be wooed back to Labour?', *The Times*, 9 July 1984.
70. *Ibid.*
71. J. Dearlove and P. Saunders, *Introduction to British Politics*, Polity Press, Cambridge, 1984, p. 200.
72. *Ibid.*, p. 203.
73. *Ibid.*

8

Public Policy and Industrial Relations

This chapter focuses on the development and growth of the state's industrial relations policies and institutions in the areas of labour market activity, pay determination and conflict resolution between employers and trade unions and employers and employees. The major policies affecting industrial relations are in the labour market and economic management, whilst the state's industrial relations institutions are of two types. First, there are the traditional institutions associated with the creation of trade boards and wages councils and the establishment of state conciliation and arbitration machinery. Second, there are also a number of new institutions. These include the industrial tribunals and the Employment Appeal Tribunal. Other institutional mechanisms, like the National Board for Prices and Incomes, the Pay Board and the Standing Commission on Pay Comparability, have also been created at various times to monitor the pay policies of governments in the post-war period, though each of these bodies was relatively short lived.

8.1 THE STATE AND INDUSTRIAL RELATIONS

The state intervenes in industrial relations in Britain by three main methods: through the law and the courts; its economic policies; and its own industrial relations institutions or agencies. The principal purpose of labour law, for example is 'to regulate, to support and to restrain the power of management and the power of organised labour',[1] though the traditional view of the role of the state and the law in British industrial relations emphasizes the abstentionist or voluntarist tradition. This contends that public or legal interference in the practical conduct of industrial relations rarely benefits the parties concerned. This view, however, is misleading if applied outside the areas of collective bargaining and the freedom to organize which – compared with other countries – continue to enjoy considerable abstention from legal regulation although since 1980 the freedom to strike, and trade union immunities have been effectively narrowed and constrained by legal intervention from the state. The law, government and its agencies have also been interventionist in other aspects of industrial relations for many years. These include: ensurance of safe working conditions in particular industries; regulating employment among young people and female workers; establishment of minimum wage levels in certain trades; and creation of machinery for state intervention in industrial disputes. More recently, laws have been enacted guaranteeing a series of statutory employment rights for individuals against discrimination in their employment on the grounds of race or of sex, against unfair dismissal by their employers and for other purposes.

In considering the role of the state in regulating employment and industrial relations, commentators often forget that the state intervened in the fixing of wages in the reign of Elizabeth I. The development and application of the common law by the judges subsequently resulted in combinations of trade unionists, infringing the so called 'restraint of trade' doctrine, being limited by the law. And it was not until the early stages of the industrial revolution that the doctrine of *laissez-faire* strongly discouraged government interference in economic or industrial affairs. This was on the grounds that if individuals were left to pursue their own self-interest, this would benefit both them and society generally. State interference in business affairs and in industry, it was held, could only lead to the malfunctioning of the market system and to a reduction in the production of goods and real wealth in society. The concept of *laissez-faire* was the predominant social ideology associated with early capitalism and was reflected in the laws of Parliament and the judgments of the courts.

The unregulated growth of the factory system, however, led to horrifying working conditions, intolerable exploitation at work, and disturbing manifestations of human degradation at home and in the early factories. The state, with its moral obligation to ensure the health and prosperity of its citizens, could not for long stand completely aside whilst the working and living conditions of the newly created industrial working classes deteriorated. As a result a series of Parliamentary statutes were passed advancing at least minimum standards of factory safety, industrial welfare and personal morality at work. The consequences of the rigid application of *laissez-faire* principles were clearly incompatible with social and political stability, on the one hand, or with the moral duties of government on the other.

Attitudes to government and state intervention in economic affairs and industrial relations, however, depend largely upon differing philosophies of the state. Those favouring minimum state intervention think that goverment should create only a few of its own institutions and should employ as few people as possible. Less government, by this view, is equated with good government, with the state being regarded as largely neutral in the application of its power. This 'benevolent–neutral' view of state power suggests that government only needs to intervene in industrial relations to protect the employment interests of individuals when no other means are available, or to uphold the wider interests of the society as a whole when these appear to be threatened by particular industrial pressure groups.

Many people reject such a benevolent view of the state. They argue that the state is the political arm of the ruling classes. They believe that state power reflects the political hegemony of the ruling élite, as well as predominantly serving its interests. This view of the state, the 'coercion' view, holds that state intervention in industrial relations, whether by government, law, the courts of the agencies of law enforcement and social order, is mainly designed to ensure that the interests of private capital and the ruling classes are advanced to the detriment of working people and their representative organizations. Yet regardless of which view of the state is correct or acceptable to individuals and citizens, the aim that the roles of government and the state should be small and minimal has not been achieved. Indeed the size and the role of the state have grown ever larger and penetrate almost every aspect of present day social and economic life. by the mid 1980s, for example, almost 30 per cent of the labour force is employed by the public sector, the state controls and utilizes vast capital resources but also has to uphold the interests of its citizens generally. With such a growth in the economic roles of government and of the public sector, the pressures for state intervention in industrial relations have been both cumulative and inevitable.

Until recently, state intervention in industrial relations and the legal regulation of trade union activities in Britain probably owed much more to judicial interpretations of the common law than it did to Acts of Parliament. In the early nineteenth century, for example, judges concluded that trade unions were criminal conspiracies. When the struggles against criminal liablity had been won by the trade unions, and legislation had been passed relieving them from this threat, the judges and the courts subsequently interpreted trade union activities as being liable at civil law. This in turn was remedied by the Trade Disputes Act 1906, which, apart from 1971–74, remained the legal status quo until the late 1970s.

> The Acts of 1871, 1875, and 1906 all aimed largely to remove liabilities which judgements had imposed upon the unions; and that is . . . the reason for their being expressed in a language that establishes formally 'privileges' or 'immunities' in a trade dispute.[2]

Those favouring the benevolent-neutral theory of the state would see the decisions of the judges as being impartial interpretations of the law. Those regarding the state as an instrument of class hegemony and political coercion would see the judges' decisions on labour matters as expressions of the use of the law by the ruling classes as limiting the power of organized labour.

Whatever the truth of these views, it is hard to believe that in making their decisions, judges are not deeply influenced by their own social backgrounds, upbringing, education and perhaps even their political preferences since, 'judges are men, and like other men their decisions are influenced by the social background they have known and the unconscious premises they acquire.'[3] Until the passing of the Industrial Relations Act 1971, and following the repeal of that Act in 1974 and the considerable volume of labour law enacted up till 1979, it is reasonable to conclude that most Parliamentary statutes in the area of collective labour law did little more than to restore to the trade unions and to their members some of the legal rights which had previously been taken away from them by judges' decisions. Indeed trade unionists have often expressed the fear that the rights given to them by new statutes have been reduced or made invalid by the subsequent interpretations of the common law by the courts and by the judges. What Parliament has given to the unions, they argue, the courts have frequently taken away. Since 1979, however, a further series of statutes have been passed by Parliament, weakening trade union bargaining power, organization and activities, whilst other agencies of the state such as the police and the courts have become periodically embroiled in bitter trade disputes and industrial conflict, thus politicizing such events.

The case for continuing the traditional policy of non-intervention in industrial relations by the state and its agencies is no longer practicable or tenable. Indeed in the face of the massive volume of recent individual, collective and protective labour law alone – under the Wilson, Callaghan and Thatcher Administrations in the 1970s and 1980s – it is difficult to maintain the myth that the role of the state is any longer rudimentary in British industrial relations. Perhaps the root of the myth that the state in Britain plays a passive and residual role in industrial relations stems from the fact that there is little legislation in Britain controlling collective bargaining. But this is certainly no longer true in relation to trade union organization or the freedom to strike or take industrial action. However, whenever attempts are made to introduce laws or to impose state regulation over such activities, the trade union movement presents vehement and united oposition against such proposals. Having gained most of its legal rights and collective freedoms after long and difficult struggles against the common law, criminal and civil liability, bitterly hostile employers, and the decisions of judges, many British trade unionists intuitively resist any form of legal or state limitation on their freedom to bargain collectively, on their freedom to take part in industrial action and on their freedom to organize. The role of the state in industrial relations, therefore, remains a problematic one. Where the state's role is perceived to be bipartisan and balanced, it is legitimized and non-controversial. Where it is partisan and explicitly biased, on behalf of employers, unions or the ruling élite, it becomes overtly political and disputable.

8.2   LABOUR MARKET POLICIES

Since the early years of this century governments have taken measures and passed legislation which have either directly or indirectly affected the working of the labour market. Government intervention in the operation of the labour market has fallen into four broad policy areas. These are: first, measures to improve the working of the labour market by bringing the buyers and sellers of labour into closer contact, by improving their knowledge of each other's requirements, and policies designed to influence the level of employment; second, the encouragement of training to provide people with the skills required in the labour market; third, changes in trade union and employment law; and fourth, measures aimed at reducing rigidities in the labour market which restrict the growth of jobs and movements both within and between occupations and industries.

Labour market efficiency and employment

It has always been apparent that labour markets only operate efficiently if the buyers and sellers of labour are aware of each other's needs and of the current pay-rates and conditions of employment being offered. In order to improve the working of the labour market, Parliament passed in 1909 the Labour Exchanges Act. This provided at state expense for centres, usually large unattractive buildings, in industrial towns and urban areas where employers could advertise vacancies and where those seeking employment could find out what jobs were available. One of the principal aims of these labour exchanges was to reduce the level of unemployment by matching the needs of employers with those of the unemployed and by reducing the length of time for which people were unemployed. By the early 1970s labour exchanges had become unfitted for modern needs and expectations so they were transformed into less formal job centres situated in attractive high street premises, where unemployed people and those seeking job changes can look through lists of vacancies and discuss their needs with helpful staff. The need for labour exchanges and job centres has always been obvious and is matched by the large number of state-licensed private employment agencies which specialize in meeting the needs of employers and those seeking employment in certain industries and occupations. Job centres also provide valuable career guidance and training advice. In 1974 job centres came under the control of the Manpower Services Commission (MSC) which has the task of integrating state and private provision for employment and training needs.

The state has had a long and chequered history of intervention aimed at reducing unemployment levels. Such interventions have undoubtedly affected the workings of the labour market. Before 1944, when governments accepted for the first time that they had a prime responsibility for maintaining 'full employment', they claimed that there was little or nothing they could do to alleviate the depression of the 1920s and 1930s for example, governments provided little more than a few minor public works measures that had little lasting impact on the high level of unemployment. After 1945 for a period of over 30 years, governments of all political persuasions sought to maintain high levels of employment through Keynesian demand management methods. These included budgetary stimulation of aggregate demand, the expansion of consumer expenditure and even higher levels of public expenditure. After 1979 this economic strategy was abandoned on the grounds that it was incurably inflationary, resulted in an intolerable burden of taxation and actually created unemployment. Table 8.1 illustrates the fluctuations in unemployment which span these three policy periods.

Table 8.1 indicates clearly that in the 30 year period following 1945 Keynesian policies were very successful in keeping down levels of unemployment in Britain. The same period, however, was one of relative economic stagnation, with persistently high

Table 8.1: *Unemployment as a percentage of the British working population 1921–85.*

Year	Percentage of the working population unemployed
1921	16.6
1931	21.1
1951	1.2
1961	1.5
1971	3.5
1981	10.2
1982	11.2
1983	12.9
1984	13.1
1985	13.1

Sources: W. H. Beveridge, *Full Employment in a Free Society* (Allen and Unwin 1944) and *Employment Gazette* (July 1985)

levels of inflation and low levels of capital investment. The national economic policies pursued since 1979 are aimed, according to their advocates, at enabling Britain to become more competitive, control inflation, lower public expenditure and the burden of taxation, and increase capital investment and the use of new technologies. The period of transition, it is argued, which is marked by high unemployment is regrettable. But this will fall rapidly once a modernized and potentially dynamic economy moves into its expansionary phase. When this will take place, however, is problematic and as yet undetermined.

Unemployment can be categorized in a number of ways, for instance, by: sex; age; occupation; industry; and region. There is little evidence to show, however, that governments have any deliberate policies for dealing with anything other than total unemployment and regional unemployment. Variations in regional unemployment, for example, are pronounced and illustrate the structural problems emerging when traditional industries, employing large numbers of people in clearly delineated geographical areas, go into long-term decline, as outlined in table 8.2. Whilst it is probably true that regional economic policies did little to improve the general position of the depressed regions before their virtual abandonment in the early 1980s, there is very little evidence to show that market forces have improved the prospects for these regions. Despite high

Table 8.2: *Regional unemployment in Britain 1974 and 1984.*

Region	Percentage unemployed 1974	1984
South East	1.5	9.5
East Anglia	1.9	10.1
South West	2.6	11.4
West Midlands	2.1	15.3
East Midlands	2.2	12.2
Yorkshire and Humberside	2.6	14.4
North West	3.4	15.9
North	4.4	18.3
Wales	3.6	16.3
Scotland	3.9	15.1

Source: *Employment Gazette* (July 1975 and July 1985)

levels of unemployment and low cost investment opportunities, employers have shown little inclination to extend their businesses in the depressed regions, preferring instead to locate them in the more prosperous south.

Training

State provision and co-ordination of training, intended to meet the skill and knowledge requirements of the labour market, is used extensively to provide unemployed people with the qualifications or experience which they need to secure jobs. It is also used to enable employed people to retrain in order to move from old industries and occupations to new ones. Training helps the labour market to overcome mismatches between the skills – or lack of them – of the unemployed and those required by employers.

The first effective state-sponsored scheme to improve training came with the creation of the industrial training boards (ITBs) in 1964. By 1978 about 24 ITBs had been formed with the objective of supplying each major industry with properly trained men and women. The costs of such training were spread evenly across employers in the industries covered by ITBs through a compulsory training levy. The 1964 system was modified in 1972 to allow firms to opt out of the levy system if they provided adequate training of their own. In recent years most of the ITBs have been disbanded. In 1973 the Manpower Services Commission was established with responsibility for employment services and training. By the mid 1980s the MSC had secured a dominant position over vocational training provision and its resources.

The principal training objectives of the MSC are: to raise employment and reduce unemployment; to assist the development of national manpower resources; to raise worker morale and job satisfaction; to develop the skill-training of young people; to make training available for all young people under 18 years; and to extend the opportunities for training for adults enabling them to acquire, increase and update their skills and knowledge. The largest training scheme under MSC management is the two-year Youth Training Scheme (YTS) which started in 1983–4 offering all school leavers a combination of training, work experience and education.

> By the end of May 1984 some 375,000 young people had entered the YTS, but only about 238 000 were still attending. This suggests that a significant proportion of school-leavers have been unwilling to join the YTS and that a substantial group of trainees have left the scheme before completion.[4]

Since then the YTS has increased the proportion of registered school-leavers to 339 000 in November 1985. It shows clear signs of becoming a permanent feature of the youth employment scene. Those supporting the YTS believe it is well worth the £1 000 million it costs per year, since it is the only route into permanent and worthwhile employment for very substantial numbers of young people. Those opposing the scheme argue that it is merely a device to reduce the real unemployment figures and provides employers with cheap labour.

In addition to the YTS, the MSC is responsible for a number of special employment and training measures. The Community Industry Scheme provided 8 000 temporary jobs for personally and socially disadvantaged young people by November 1985. The Community Programme is planned to provide 230 000 jobs of up to a year's duration in 1986 for long-term unemployed adults on projects of benefit to the community. The Enterprise Allowance Scheme helps unemployed people wanting to start up businesses by providing them with a flat rate of £40 per week for a maximum of 52 weeks. This is expected to cover 80 000 adults in 1987. The Job Release Scheme makes it easier for older people to give up work early and to release their jobs to unemployed people. This is done by giving them a weekly allowance from the date they leave work until their state pension is paid, providing their jobs are given to unemployed persons. This scheme provided 49 000 jobs for the unemployed in 1985. In addition the Young Workers' Scheme provided 58 000 jobs, the Training in Industry Scheme 1 500 training places and the Job Splitting Scheme 290 jobs. The total number of people covered by these special measures was estimated to be 675 000 at the end of 1985. Without these schemes a high proportion of that number would appear in the unemployment statistics.

Employment law

Changes in the law relating to trade unions, industrial disputes, picketing and employment protection have also affected the labour market since the mid 1970s. It is claimed, for example, that the legal provisions on unfair dismissal have made many employers, particularly small ones, reluctant to take on new employees for fear of the problems they could encounter if they later dismiss them. Similarly, the costs of redundancy payments, fears that women could win pay increases through equal pay claims before industrial tribunals, and the problems of holding jobs open for female employees taking maternity leave have, it is argued, deterred employers from creating more jobs. Whilst there is some research evidence suggesting that employers are unfavourably influenced by current employment protection legislation, it is far from conclusive. In order to meet some of these complaints, the Government increased the qualifying period of continuous employment before individuals can make a claim of unfair dismissal from one year to two in 1985. The regulations governing industrial tribunals were also tightened up so that pre-hearing assessments can reduce the number of doubtful cases going to full hearings. The requirements which female employees claiming maternity leave must fulfil in order to keep their jobs open for their eventual return to work were also tightened up in the employer's favour.

The Employment Acts of 1980 and 1982 and the Trade Union Act of 1984 have reduced the scope of trade union immunities against civil actions arising out of trade disputes or picketing. They also make the granting of court injunctions ordering trade unions to cease industrial action or picketing easier to obtain and enforce. The requirement of the 1984 Act that trade unions must ballot members intending to take strike action has also reduced the freedom of trade union leaders or shop stewards to initiate industrial action. In labour market terms, when seen against a background of high unemployment, these laws could well reduce the ability of trade unions to: increase pay; improve conditions of employment; inhibit the introduction of new technologies and working methods; and maintain unrealistic manning levels. In short, the laws passed between 1980 and 1984 could well reduce the powers of the trade unions to influence the labour market in their favour.

Labour market rigidities

The principal labour market rigidity perplexing government since 1980 is the failure of real wages to move downwards under the influence of high unemployment. Government believes that many more jobs would then be created at lower pay levels. Whilst it is well understood that reductions in money wages rarely if ever take place, the same does not necessarily apply to real wages. For example, real wages fall if money wage increases are less than the rate of inflation. But despite high unemployment, real wages have moved upwards in many sectors of employment since 1980. Indeed, the Treasury has agreed:

> the elasticity of demand for labour with respect to real wages lies between $-\frac{1}{2}$ and -1. The implication is that a cut in real wages of 1 per cent would increase total employment in the UK economy by between 110 000 and 220 000. Thus the Chancellor was able to claim that,

if wages had risen in line with prices in 1981–84, rather than at a rate of 2½–3 per cent faster, perhaps a million and a half extra jobs would have been created.[5]

Movements in real wages, however, might not be as unusual as the Chancellor implies for as the TUC has pointed out 'real wages for white collar workers rose by 16 per cent from 1979 to 1984 while for unskilled workers they fell by 9.9 per cent.'[6]

It remains to be seen whether or not the persistence of high unemployment and reduced trade union power will eventually result in an overall reduction in real wages and a growth in jobs induced by the lower cost of employing people. In order to further assist a fall in real wages and the growth of employment opportunities since 1979 the Government has raised income tax thresholds, increased benefits below the level of inflation, reduced employers' national insurance contributions and abolished the national insurance surcharge. In order to reduce further the upward pressure on the low-wage employment sector, the Government has abolished the Fair Wages Resolution and has limited the powers of wages councils. The net result of these changes after a time-lag of uncertain duration should, it is hoped, be to open up a favourable gap between what unemployed persons receive in benefits and what they could get by taking low paid jobs. It is anticipated that once such a gap appears unemployment will fall rapidly as the economy expands into sustained growth.

Whilst it seems likely that various rigidities in the British labour market have contributed to the persistently high levels of unemployment since 1979, their combined effect is probably negligible compared with deficiency of aggregate demand in the economy and the refusal or inability of the Government to consider reflationary measures. If this view is correct:

> The social and political strife likely to follow a really determined effort to increase [labour market] flexibility by *force majeure* requires more convincing justification than evidence currently on offer.[7]

8.3   STATUTORY PAY REGULATION

Unlike some countries, Britain has never introduced a statutory minimum wage covering all employees. This is not only because of the problem of defining low pay and of administering, inspecting and enforcing national minimum wage provisions, but also because of the apparent lack of trade union enthusiasm for such legislation. Yet the state has long recognized the human and social consequences of allowing intolerably low levels of pay to go unchecked in particular industries. Public opinion in the closing decades of the nineteenth century revealed deep concern at the conditions of many workers in the so called 'sweated trades'. The Committee of the House of Lords which examined these industries in 1889–90 revealed:

> a rate of wages inadequate to the necessities of the workers or disproportionate to the work done; excessive hours of labour; the insanitary state of the houses in which the work is carried on. These evils can hardly be exaggerated. The earnings of the lowest classes of workers are barely sufficient to sustain existence.[8]

These sweated trades existed in most large cities and were concentrated in bootmaking, tailoring, furniture making, chain and nail making, and lace and net production. It was in these trades that the present system of wages councils and wage regulation orders originated .

Wages councils

The first Trade Boards Act was passed in 1909. Its main purpose was to raise wages in a limited number of industries. It was largely an experimental measure which applied to four trades and covered only a minority of workers employed in the sweated trades. These initial trade boards had the strictly limited function of fixing minimum legally binding time rates of wages, although a wages inspectorate was set up to enforce compliance with the legal determinations of the boards. In 1917, the Whitley Committee recommended an extension of trade boards to other trades and industries where employer and trade union organization was weak. This was achieved by the Trade Boards Act 1918 which gave powers to the Minister of Labour to establish further boards 'if he was of the opinion that no adequate machinery existed for the regulation of wages in the trade in question'.[9] It was the hope of the Whitley Committee that the Trade Boards would encourage the development of trade unions and employers' organizations in these industries. This could then lead to the regulation of wages and of conditions of employment in these trades by collective bargaining machinery.

This hope, many times repeated since 1917, has not in the main been fulfilled. By 1938, there were some 50 trade boards – with employer, union and 'independent' members – covering about one and a half million workers. In addition to these trade boards, minimum wage regulation was also achieved in agriculture by the creation of the Agricultural Wages Board for England and Wales in 1924. This was extended to Scotland in 1937 whilst the whole scheme was further strengthened by the Agrcultural Wages Acts of 1948 and 1949. These gave powers to the Agricultural Wages Boards to order wage increases without reference to the Minister of Labour, unlike the existing trade boards which had to obtain that approval.

Subsequent legislation in 1946 and 1959 renamed the trade boards wages councils. Their coverage was extended, with piecework rates, overtime rates, holidays and holiday pay, as well as minimum hourly rates of pay now coming within their scope. The Industrial Relations Act 1971 established the principle that wages councils should move towards their own collective bargaining arrangements where this was possible. To this end, the Commission on Industrial Relations was given the responsibility of examining questions relating to the modification or abolition of wages councils. In total, the Commission looked at wages council industries employing some two million people with a view to encouraging trade unions and collective bargaining within them, although it was not greatly successful in doing this.

The Wages Councils Act 1979 contains several measures making wage councils more effective and more independent of the state. First, representative organizations, such as trade unions nominated by the Secretary of State for Employment, can now appoint their own members to wages councils. Each wages council comprises equal representation of trade unions and employers plus three independent members whose votes can determine decisions. The chairperson of each council is also drawn from the three independent members. Second, the powers of wages councils have been extended to fix most other terms and conditions of employment other than wages, working hours and holidays. Third, wages councils can now make their own wage regulation orders as well as determining their operative date. Finally, the Advisory Conciliation and Arbitration Service (ACAS) now undertakes inquiries into wages council matters on reference from the Secretary of State for Employment. It can recommend, for example, the establishment of statutory joint industrial councils (SJICs) without independent members. The aim of these bodies is to replace wages councils as an intermediate step between statutory pay determination and full collective bargaining between employers and trade unions. As yet none has been established.

By the mid 1980s about 2.75 million employees working in almost 400 000 separate establishments had their pay and conditions of employment determined by about 30 wages councils. These cover a wide variety of industries and trades. They include: licensed residential establishments and licensed restaurants; retail bespoke tailoring;

shirtmaking; the retail food trades; laundries; hairdressing; cotton waste reclamation; and the flax and hemp and lace finishing trades. Some 95 per cent of all workers covered by the wages councils are in the four dealing with retailing, catering, clothing and hairdressing. In a majority of wages council industries, part time female employees predominate. Moreover, although the trade unions have substantial memberships in some of them, collective bargaining has only been established among the larger employers in these sectors. Smaller and scattered employers have yet to be effectively organized by the unions.

Where either trade unions or employers feel that collective bargaining can replace a wages council, they can approach the Secretary of State for Employment requesting that the formal machinery for its abolition should be set in motion. Yet unions are often reluctant to take such a step where their membership levels are low, whilst employers have often:

> feared that without legal enforcement of the rates of pay and hours of work some of the smaller firms might resort to undercutting in both wages and prices, and their organisation would not be able to put a stop to it.[10]

Similarly, where the Secretary of State for Employment feels that ministerial initiative should be taken in abolishing or in rationalizing a wages council, or in abolishing a SJIC, then he or she can make an order which if objected to by those affected can be referred to ACAS for an inquiry and a report. This occurred in the late 1970s, for example, when the Secretary of State referred to ACAS a draft order abolishing nine retail wages councils and establishing two new wages councils in their place. After hearing the objectors' arguments, ACAS recommended that two new wages councils, the Retail Trades (Food) Wages Council and the Retail Trade (non-Food) Wages Council, should be established in this sector. ACAS has also issued reports and recommendations on the fur, toy, button and laundry wages councils.

Once a wages council issues a wage regulation order improving wages and conditions of employment in a wages council industry, a notice is sent to all the employers concerned. It is the legal responsibility of employers not only to display the notice where employees can see it, but also to honour the new employment conditions. If employees are not given the required wage increase, they can make a complaint to the local Wages Inspectorate which has to make immediate enquiries into the case. If a complaint is upheld and the employer accepts that it has not met its legal obligations under the Wages Councils Acts, and it then makes the necessary payments to the employees, the wages inspectors do not usually prosecute that employer. If on the other hand an employer is obstructive, it can be fined. Furthermore, if any employer gives false information, a still larger fine can be imposed. In addition to these fines, the employer must pay arrears of wages due under wage regulation orders. Prosecutions, however, are relatively few as the majority of employers faced by this situation accept the complaint as justified and make the necessary additional payments to the employees involved.

During 1984, the 120-strong Wages Inspectorate undertook inspections of over 41 000 establishments, or some 11 per cent of all wages council establishments. The arrears paid to 18 000 workers following inspection amounted to £2.5 million. About £292 000 was assessed as owing to workers but was not collected because the workers preferred to waive their rights to the arrears. In all cases where underpayments were found, action was taken to ensure future compliance with the statutory minimum and to inform workers of their legal entitlements. Clearly the wages council system of determining minimum wages and conditions in certain industries depends heavily upon the goodwill and the willingness of numerous small employers to accept and to implement wages council awards. There are only 120 inspectors in about 30 wages council industries to enforce wage regulation orders. In July 1985, the Government declared its intention to remove all young people under 21 from any regulation by wages councils and to confine wages councils to setting only a single minimum hourly rate for those over 21 years.

Other regulatory procedures

Although wages councils are obviously the most important element in the state regulation of minimum wages and minimum working conditions in Britain, they have been supported by other legislation fixing terms and conditions of employment in some industries and by such measures as compulsory arbitration and Fair Wages Resolutions of the House of Commons, although the latter were rescinded in 1982. Between 1940 and 1959, for example, compulsory arbitration in industrial disputes was established under Orders 1305 and 1376. This was done initially to cope with the economic and social conditions created by the circumstances of the Second World War. It was extended after 1945 with the agreement of both sides of industry. By it, disputes were referred by the Ministry of Labour to the National Arbitration Tribunal which had been established in 1940. The Tribunal was particularly supported by those trade unions in the public sector which could not easily strike. But an abortive attempt to prosecute the London and Liverpool leaders of a dock strike in 1950 led to the withdrawal of Order 1305 which was replaced by Order 1376. This 'retained certain features of compulsory arbitration, though not the illegality of strikes.'[11] The awards of the National Arbitration Tribunal – or as it was called from 1951 the National Industrial Disputes Tribunal – became compulsory implied terms of employment in the individual contracts of employment of the workers concerned.

In 1959 the Government revoked Order 1376 and replaced it with the Terms and Conditions of Employment Act 1959. Under Section 8 of this Act, either a trade union or an employers' association could claim that an employer was not observing the recognized terms and conditions of employment laid down by the collective agreement for the trade or the industry to which they were a party. If the claim could not be settled by negotiation or conciliation, the case was referred for arbitration to the Industrial Court which took the form of a compulsory award and unilaterally fixed the terms and conditions of employment for the employees concerned. Under the Employment Protection Act 1975, Section 8 of the Terms and Conditions of Employment Act was replaced by Schedule 11 of this Act. It did 'so in terms modelled on the Fair Wages Resolution though with some significant differences in detailed drafting.'[12] In 1980, Schedule 11 was repealed by the Employment Act.

Under this Schedule, the powers of the Central Arbitration Committee (CAC) – which replaced the former Industrial Court – were considerably extended. In addition to claiming for the observance of recognized terms and conditions of employment, settled by agreement or by award, Schedule 11 made it possible to base a claim on the concept of the 'general level' in the trade or industry where there were no recognized terms and conditions. Only those employers' associations or independent trade unions representing a substantial proportion of the employers or employees in the trade or industry could lodge such a claim. The claim was made initially to ACAS which then took steps to obtain a settlement by conciliation. If conciliation failed the claim was then referred to the CAC. Thus Schedule 11 of the 1975 Act was potentially a powerful instrument, since it was capable of being used by the trade unions to impose terms and conditions of employment on those employers paying less than was generally observed in a particular trade or industry. Its powers were clearly in excess of those available under Section 8 of the Terms and Conditions of Employment Act 1959 and for this reason it was repealed by the Conservative Government in 1980.

The objective of the Fair Wages Resolutions of the House of Commons, which were rescinded in 1982, was to obtain generally accepted terms and conditions of employment for those workers employed by firms engaged on public contracts. The first resolution was secured in a limited form in 1891, was amended in 1909, and was strengthened in 1946. Fair Wages Resolutions were not legally enforceable but were statements of intent about basic standards of employment which ought to be binding upon all government and local authority contractors. The resolutions provided that the:

> contractor shall pay rates of wages and observe hours and conditions of labour not less favourable than those established for the trade or industry. . . . The contractor shall recognise the freedom of his workpeople to be members of trade unions [and] must furnish an assurance that he has for the previous three months complied with the Resolution before he is put on the list of tendering firms.[13]

Complaints against employers infringing Fair Wages Resolutions were made to the Department of Employment. If a settlement could not be obtained voluntarily, the case was referred to the CAC for arbitration. Such awards subsequently became incorporated into the employees' individual contracts of employment. The fair wages principle was also incorporated into a number of statutes. Where public money was involved, for instance, a fair wages provision could sometimes be inserted to give employees protection similar to that contained in the Resolution. Examples included the Civil Aviation Act 1949, the Films Act 1960, the Public Passenger Vehicles Act 1981 and the Broadcasting Act 1981. In 1982 the House of Commons accepted the Government's argument that Fair Wages Resolutions prevented competitive tendering for contracts and inhibited the growth of jobs and rescinded them. The cumulative effect of government policy since 1980 has been to reduce the legal protection afforded low-paid workers.

8.4 PAY POLICY

The Keynesian approach

From the industrial revolution to the beginning of the Second World War, it was strongly held by most economists and politicians that the state had no useful part to play in the regulation and promotion of economic activity. It was a period when the doctrines of *laissez-faire* and free trade held great ideological sway. The economic revolution of state regulated aggregate demand and deficit budgeting leading to full employment, which Keynes had advocated in the late 1930s, did not become a political reality until after the cessation of hostilities in 1945. With the introduction of full employment policies, comparative prosperity and the welfare state, new economic problems emerged in Britain, compared with the large-scale unemployment of the inter-war years. Britain's loss of major overseas assets during the war, domestic demand for high volumes of imports, and the loss of many overseas export markets, for example, led to continual balance of payments difficulties after 1950. At the point of comparative full employment, production bottlenecks emerged together with skilled labour shortages. Economic growth lurched forward and then halted, whilst the upward rate of change in prices and money wages forged ahead. At the same time, rising taxation and increased levels of public expenditure began a seemingly unending upward spiral.

It soon became apparent by the mid 1950s that Britain's new economic problems in the post-war era were inflation, balance of payments deficits, economic stagnation, a declining share of world export markets, low productivity, rising taxation, and a weak currency vulnerable to international speculation. The answer to these problems was seen by many economists to be a government regulated system of prices and incomes control aimed at managing inflation, accompanied by economic policies designed to stimulate economic growth, industrial productivity and exports. An incomes policy would keep wages, salaries and prices broadly in line with increases in production and productivity, whilst complementary government economic strategies, it was argued, would encourage economic growth, stimulate investment, introduce technological change and facilitate exports. Through budgetary control of overall demand in the economy and by advancing an appropriate incomes policy, it was argued, government would keep its pledge on full employment as well as being able to manage sterling. These measures, it was thought, would not only control inflation but also prevent recurrent balance of payments and sterling crises. Above all, it was believed, they would allow the level of unemployment to be kept low.

Incomes policy, however, was not without its critics. Some fundamentalists of the right in politics, for example, continually urged a return to the so-called free market economy and a modern form of *laissez-faire* or social market capitalism. They urged, for instance, a higher level of unemployment in order to bring 'discipline' into the labour market and to reduce 'irresponsible' pay demands. They also argued that there was a direct link between the levels of unemployment, on the one hand, and the rate of change of money wages on the other. Hence, from their viewpoint, it was possible to reduce pay demands by increasing unemployment to its 'natural' level. In the face of post-war prosperity and full employment expectations, few politicians dared to put these views to a practical test in the 1950s and 1960s. As incomes policy became unpopular and discredited, however, those claiming that the answer lay in a stricter control over the money supply – monetarists as they are called – were able to challenge Keynesian orthodoxy. They urged, for example, a more balanced budget, greatly reduced levels of public expenditure, a modest public sector borrowing requirement, strict cash limits on public spending, and less reliance by individuals and their families on the welfare state. They also wanted less government interference in the private sector of the economy, a return to freer market forces in economic affairs, the privatization of many public assets, greatly reduced levels of all types of taxation but especially of taxation on personal incomes, and the reform of trade union law.

The political left, on the other hand, has continuously sought greater equality of incomes and of wealth through progressively redistributive taxation, and more nationalization and state ownership of industry. It has also wanted further government intervention in the private sector, and increased levels of public expenditure and taxation. It has advocated, too, state control over investment and prices, planning agreements, import and exchange controls, overseas investment controls and greatly reduced military expenditure. Between these diametrically opposed economic, social and political alternatives, incomes policies could be seen as a democratic search process for a middle way in Britain's political and economic affairs.

The long struggle from the late 1940s to the late 1970s for a durable long-term incomes policy within a democratic framework of government by consent was inevitably a protracted and a difficult process. It was also in the end a failure as the voluntary consent and the sacrifice of self-interest which were indispensable to its success were not forthcoming. Sectional interests representative of both workers and employers sought continually to maintain their established patterns of industrial behaviour and tried to obtain the highest incomes, profits and prices which they could for themselves. When a prices and incomes policy was instituted, it invariably meant that the strongest sectional organizations in the economy could not use their full bargaining strength or market power to their own advantage. They also had to explain either to their union members or to their shareholders that they were doing this in order to further the national interest at the expense of their own short term welfare. Such a process required considerable public debate and economic education if those forgoing their bargaining power or market advantage were to be convinced.

The central idea behind a prices and incomes policy is that, if a stable long term policy backed by public opinion is to be achieved, a 'social contract' between government and the governed has to be forged. In return for public, union and employer acceptance of such a policy, government has to promise equity of treatment among different groups of workers and between employers and unions. It also has: to promote taxation and fiscal policies which do not reduce real incomes after the commencement of the policy; to maintain acceptable levels of employment; and to keep the cost of living stable. If a government cannot allow compensating income increases, then it has to provide a range of essential non-pay and social service benefits to the community. It also has to pursue economic policies which not only contain inflation, but also maintain balance of payments equilibrium and the exchange rate. Additionally, a climate has to be created which encourages economic growth, industrial investment, trade exports and technology. The scope and depth of such a social contract clearly involve considerable governmental power over the various sectors of the British economy. These policies are of such a comprehensive nature, moreover, that it takes a great deal of public awareness to ensure that people are clear both of their obligations and rights under such a social contract.

Britain's first attempt to a peace time incomes policy was in 1948 when Stafford Cripps, the Chancellor of the Exchequer in the post-war Attlee Labour Government, introduced a wages freeze which lasted for almost two years. During what now appears by modern standards to be both a long and rigid wages freeze, wages rose by only some two and a half per cent a year which was well within the rise in national productivity. It was a remarkably successful policy which had the overwhelming support of the TUC.

The Conservative Government of 1951 abandoned the Cripps wages policy in favour of monetary measures designed to control inflation. But rising inflation soon led the Conservative Government to secure TUC support for a policy of voluntary pay restraint. When the TUC refused, the Government sharply deflated the economy which led to a fall in inflation and a rise in unemployment. During the first post-war recession, in 1958, the Government resorted to a quasi-incomes policy by taking a firm line against public sector pay demands. After 1959, the economy moved rapidly towards a boom and in 1961 the Chancellor of the Exchequer, Selwyn Lloyd, introduced a 'pay pause' trying to hold down public sector pay rises. The unions naturally resisted this so the pay pause was not very successful. It was soon replaced by a 'guiding light' policy setting a norm for pay increases which the Government hoped the unions would accept and follow.

After the General Election of 1964, which returned the Labour Party to power after 13 years in opposition, the first Wilson Administration became fully committed to a voluntary prices and incomes policy which at this time had the support of the TUC. The Government, the TUC and the CBI then signed a tripartite 'Declaration of Intent' which promised to establish a long-term voluntary policy of both pay and price restraint in exchange for planned economic expansion, with the parties accepting a three to three and a half per cent pay norm. The National Board for Prices and Incomes (NBPI) was established in 1965 to monitor price and income increases and to advise the Government in these interconnected areas.

In 1966, a severe sterling crisis compelled the Labour Government to drop its voluntary policy and to introduce the first prices and incomes policy in Britain backed by legal sanctions. A six month freeze on pay and prices was introduced, followed by a period of 'severe restraint'. Although the policy obtained only marginal support from the TUC, it was successful in securing confidence in sterling and in reducing inflation to about three per cent a year. But in late 1969 pay controls were abandoned as the unions demanded a return to free collective bargaining. A pay and prices explosion followed as firms and unions scrambled for large increases for themselves after three years of strict income control.

The Conservative Government which was elected to office in 1970 was completely opposed to price and incomes controls in the first instance. It immediately abolished the NBPI, inflation accelerated and unemployment moved towards the one million mark. As in 1958 and in 1961, the Conservative Government tried to impose an 'unofficial' pay policy upon public sector employees alone. But the National Union of Mineworkers forced the Government to drop this approach by striking for and obtaining a 25 per cent pay increase. Other unions followed its example and inflation seemed to be getting out of control. Events then forced the Heath Government to reconsider the need for a formal incomes policy for both pay and prices. The TUC refused to co-operate and in 1972 the Conservatives introduced their first statutory pay policy.

The first stage was a successful six-month freeze followed by a second stage giving four per cent plus £1.00 a week increases per pay group. By this time, the Government had established a Pay Board and a Price Commission to replace the NBPI to monitor its policies. A third stage followed in 1973 giving maximum increases of £2.25 per week or seven per cent for each pay group, whichever was the larger, with a maximum increase of £350 per year. Settlements were to be spaced at 12 months' intervals but threshold agreements were permitted giving an extra 40p per week for every one per cent rise in the retail price index when it had reached six per cent above the level in October 1973.

The Labour Government elected in February 1974 abandoned pay controls, but not price controls. This led to a severe squeezing of industrial profits and to company liquidity problems, thus increasing unemployment and causing the Government to relax price controls in the winter of 1974. It was at this stage that the Labour Government and the TUC introduced their first formal 'Social Contract'. This embodied an agreement reached within the Labour Movement whereby the Government agreed to raise the social wage and to increase taxes on higher incomes and wealth, in exchange for a voluntary pay policy aimed at keeping incomes in line with inflation. It also established a rule that 12 months should be maintained between pay settlements. The Social Contract did little effectively to control inflation which moved rapidly upwards over the 20 per cent level. Eventually, in summer 1975, the Government was forced to take evasive action as the level of inflation began to move towards the 30 per cent mark.

In the event, the Government managed to obtain TUC agreement on a further Social Contract. This included a voluntary pay limit of £6.00 a week as an across the board increase on wages and salaries, with a cut off point of £8 500 per year, to run from August 1975. Early in 1976, talks again took place with the TUC on what should replace this policy in August 1976. After protracted discussions a policy providing for a five per cent increase in total earnings for all hours worked, with a cash minimum of £2.50 and maximum of £4.00 per week, was agreed. The 12-month interval between settlements was also retained. An improvement in Britain's financial circumstances subsequently permitted the Chancellor of the Exchequer to reduce income tax on the assumption that wage and salary increases within the next 12 months would be limited to 10 per cent. Once again, the 12-month rule was retained. For the 12-month period beginning 1 August 1978, the Labour Government announced a five per cent pay guideline which failed to hold. After the so called 'winter of discontent' of 1978-79, it lost the General Election of May 1979, when the Conservatives, elected with a majority, were pledged to a policy of free but 'responsible' collective bargaining for both the private and public sectors.

Experience of the problems of the British economy during the 30-year period up to the late 1970s convinced many that some form of prices and incomes policy was essential if economic growth, balance of payments equilibrium, acceptable levels of employment, and relatively stable prices were to be simultaneously achieved. But trade union commitment to the principle of 'free collective bargaining' in the end overrode government appeals to the national interest and union loyalty to the Labour Party. Any long-term acceptance of an incomes policy as it affects pay implies a fundamental shift in traditional attitudes to collective bargaining by the trade unions and their members, as well as employers.

If an incomes policy is to become a permanent and central feature of managing the national economy, it can only come through convincing the trade unions, employers and the general public by way of experience, debate, and education that there is no alternative strategy for simultaneously obtaining economic stability, industrial growth and national prosperity. The lessons of the Wilson policy in 1966 and the Heath policy in 1972 seem to suggest that a short pay freeze followed by a flexible norm for pay increases stands the best chance of initial success for a viable overall policy. It also appears to be essential that cost of living increases are permitted if trade union co-operation is to be maintained. Normally, unions cannot for long withstand the intolerable internal membership pressures for wage and salary increases when the real living standards of their members are eroded. Pay norms also need to be flexible enough to prevent the erosion of generally accepted pay differentials. Experience suggests, moreover, that if flat rate increases are pursued over too long a period, the end result is an explosion of pay demands to restore traditional pay differences.

If public confidence in the equity and fairness of an incomes policy is to be secured and maintained, experience also indicates that ways must be devised of controlling 'wage drift'. This often gives some workers pay increases considerably in excess of the declared norm. If the commitment to an incomes policy by groups of workers which are unable to exceed the norm through the process of wage drift is to be obtained, then means of measuring and controlling the degree of drift must be devised.

Similarly, where genuine gains in productivity can be secured through changes in working practices, the introduction of new working methods, or the improved utilization of working time, payments in excess of the norm can be justified. But without pay concessions for increased productivity or improved working efficiency, the incentive to raise productivity is probably stifled. The experience of productivity agreements between 1967 and 1970 suggests, nevertheless, that unless they are closely scrutinized by an independent agency they are more likely to be bogus than real. Such agreements are subsequently a source of considerable dissatisfaction about the unfairness of incomes policy among those many groups which are unable to conclude productivity agreements because of the nature of their employment. Similarly, some system of flexibility for price rises must be devised if managerial efficiency is to be reflected in reduced costs contributing to higher profits. Higher prices would also seem to be justified where unavoidable cost increases occur, such as with rising import prices.

Finally, any incomes policy which is intended to endure as a long-term strategy must be able to consider special cases and pay anomalies. Given the bewildering complexity of pay differentials and relative pay rates, together with the fact that the commencement of an incomes policy unfairly affects those groups which have not yet submitted existing pay claims, it is imperative that some means are created to hear complaints about pay anomalies and from those groups pleading that they are special cases. Without such mechanisms, experience of incomes policies suggests that almost every group claims that it is a special case. They do this in the belief that those groups mounting the most professional public relations exercises in defence of their own pay claims stand the best chance of obtaining special treatment for themselves.

Thus nearly all the problems encountered in administering an incomes policy indicate that an independent institution, under the tripartite influence of unions, employers and the government, is indispensable if the policy is to be seen to be fair in its application and realistic in its treatment of anomalies and those pleading a special case. The experience of incomes policy administration by the NBPI between 1965 and its abolition by the Heath Government in 1971, for example, suggests that only a truly independent body representative of the major interest groups in the economy can secure and hold the respect of workers, employers and the general public. Nevertheless, whether past incomes policies have been of long-term benefit to the performance of the British economy, and a means of reconciling full employment with an acceptable level of inflation, is doubtful. Detailed examinations of the workings of incomes policies for the 30 years up to 1979 reveal that:

> Incomes polices can reduce the rate of wage inflation in the short run but no more. Once the policy is off, catch-up increases occur with the result that incomes policies affect the *path* but not the level of wage inflation over time . . . It seems reasonable to conclude therefore that incomes policies have in the past done more harm than good.[14]

This does not necessarily mean that incomes policy will never work effectively but that the ones tried in Britain to date have not done so. The question remains to be answered whether different forms of incomes policies could possibly succeed in the future.

The monetarist approach

The Thatcher Conservative Government, first elected in 1979, was pledged to the complete rejection of incomes policies in favour of strict monetary control measures which, its members believed, would reduce inflation and moderate pay demands and settlements. The Government believed that wage inflation was primarily caused by excessive growth in the money supply. They saw the role of government as controller of the growth in money supply in line with productivity. If that meant higher unemployment, it was an unfortunate short-term consequence which had to be faced. The Government also believed that once strict monetary control had been imposed and inflation reduced, the high level of unemployment – which had been an unavoidable 'side effect' – would drop as real wage levels fell to the point where the labour market was cleared. The policy was apparently successful in reducing inflation which fell from 18 per cent in 1980 to three per cent in 1986. Government policy was also instrumental in causing average earnings to fall from about 21 per cent annually to just over 6 per cent annually during the same period. The level of unemployment however rose from 1.49 million in 1980 to well over three million in 1984 with the underlying trend remaining upward.

It would appear, then, that a combination of monetary policies and rigid cash controls in the public sector had the effect of reducing both inflation and wage increases, but at the cost of high and persistent unemployment. Supporters of monetarist policies argue that the reason for the high level of unemployment was the failure of real wages to fall to the market-clearing level, because of the monopoly power of the unions in the labour market. The Employment Acts of 1980 and 1982 and the Trade Union Act 1984, along with union membership losses and the impact of high unemployment on union bargaining strength, would, it was believed, eventually reduce union power to prevent real wages falling to market-clearing level.

For monetarists, it is all a matter of persisting long enough with monetarist policies until wages reach the point where unemployment is at its 'natural' level and inflation is low and stable. Sustained economic growth will then begin and full employment, low inflation and productivity gains will take place. Control over prices and incomes becomes a function of market forces, and the economic role of government is largely confined to controlling the money supply with public expenditure falling steadily as a percentage of gross domestic product as the economy grows in real terms. The monetarist model is, therefore, one of a self-correcting market system in which any form of state control over incomes and prices becomes both unnecessary and undesirable.

It is not yet possible to say whether or not the monetarist model can achieve what its protagonists predict, nor is it possible to conclude that it will become the new economic settlement which will dominate the future in the way that the Keynesian settlement did for 30 years after 1945. It is very possible, however, that control of inflation by monetarist policies could suffer the same central difficulty experienced by incomes policies which were only successful in the short term. If unemployment begins to fall substantially in a system controlled by monetarists policies, what will then prevent both organized and unorganized labour from forcing up pay levels? On the other hand, if it becomes clear that monetarism can only work with permanently high levels of unemployment, its political and social costs could well be intolerable to an increasing proportion of the electorate.

8.5 CONCILIATION, ARBITRATION AND INQUIRY

Despite the fundamental reluctance of most governments to intervene directly in the regulation of collective bargaining between employers and trade unions, the realities of endemic industrial conflict have compelled the state to provide a permanent system of third party intervention in industrial disputes in Britain. This has taken the forms of conciliation services, arbitration bodies, and facilities for courts of inquiry in particular disputes. Third party intervention by state agencies, especially when apparently intractable industrial conflicts seem to threaten economic and sometimes social stability, has proved to be an effective way of resolving such issues. It is often the only way in which the disputants feel that they can ultimately reach an honourable compromise.

Origins and growth

It is a major principle of third party intervention that the parties to an industrial dispute should first be encouraged to apply their own formal machinery for the settlement of industrial conflict. This usually means exhausting the voluntarily agreed disputes procedure for resolving differences between the parties which both sides are expected to use before engaging in either strikes or lockouts. Such voluntary procedures normally follow a closely defined series of stages which culminate at the national or industry level. By these arrangements, it is the intention of the parties that industrial action will only take place after all stages of the agreed disputes procedure have been formally observed and constitutionally applied. It is only when this final stage has been reached, and when the chances of a negotiated settlement are slender, that third party intervention is usually felt to be appropriate. Such intervention is generally successful because it is believed that the conciliators or arbitrators are as unbiased and impartial as human personality permits and that the political and external influences in settling the dispute are minimized. It is the intention of third party intervention to obtain a settlement acceptable to both sides in conflict, either by bringing them together to resolve their differences, or by suggesting the basis for a settlement or, with the participants' consent, by making an arbitration award.

The origins of conciliation and arbitration in Britain are to be found in the hosiery industry in the middle of the nineteenth century. In 1860 A. J. Mundella, a wealthy Nottingham hosiery manufacturer, called a meeting of local employers to avoid a threatened lock-out by hosiery manufacturers in retaliation for a series of strikes by their workers. He persuaded both sides to establish a permanent Board of Conciliation and Arbitration as a means of settling future disputes between them. This Board was so successful that it was subsequently used as a model by other industries. To the modern observer, it might appear an obvious development. But at that time, it was a considerable step forward in industrial relations 'for employers' and workers' leaders to sit round a table discussing their differences on equal terms.'[15]

These first national conciliation boards not only set the pattern for the settlement of trade disputes through joint regulation in their own trades, but also provided the basis for the future development of national and local collective bargaining machinery in their industries. Mundella, who later became a Liberal MP, strongly advised the political leaders of the day that the state could not willingly stand aside from damaging industrial disputes, if the parties themselves could not resolve their differences. As a result of changes in public opinion, growing numbers of employers, trade unions and workers began to favour the creation of some form of independent conciliation and arbitration machinery which only the state could effectively provide.

It was in 1893 that the Labour Department of the Board of Trade was first established. This followed over a decade of industrial unrest in which Cabinet Ministers, the clergy, and even W. E. Gladstone as Prime Minister, had been forced to intervene as industrial peacemakers. In the same year that Parliament passed its first Fair Wages Resolution, the Royal Commission on Labour under the Chairmanship of the Duke of Devonshire was established. Its main recommendation was that a system of state sponsored conciliation should be provided in those disputes which the parties could not resolve themselves. Accordingly, the Conciliation Act 1896 provided that the Board of Trade might inquire into the causes and circumstances of trade disputes and would make provision for third party conciliation and arbitration if the parties agreed. It was not welcomed by the majority of employers, however, who saw the Act as an unwarranted interference with their established rights over their property and employees. Lord Penrhyn, for example, owner of large slate quarries in North Wales, whose treatment of his striking workers and their families had disturbed late Victorian public opinion, refused a Board of Trade offer of conciliation under the new Act. Like other employers of the time he was firmly of the view that 'my acceptance of it would establish a precedent for outside interference in the management of my private affairs.'[16] Nevertheless, the provisions of the 1896 Conciliation Act gradually became accepted as valuable mechanisms for resolving intractable industrial disputes.

In 1917, the needs and conditions of war led to the creation of the Ministry of Labour which soon collected a wide range of duties and responsibilities in industrial and labour matters. In 1918, the fourth Whitley Report on conciliation and arbitration, while recommending both the extension of conciliation and the introduction of a new 'Standing Arbitration Council', stressed that it should be voluntary in nature. It rejected the imposition of an elaborate system of conciliation and arbitration upon industry, 'in place of the present well-recognised voluntary conciliation and arbitration machinery which exists in so many of the important trades of the country.'[17] In consequence, the Industrial Courts Act 1919 provided a system of voluntary arbitration giving the Minister of Labour powers to refer a trade dispute to arbitration providing that, first, the parties were willing to do this and, second, the relevant disputes procedure had been exhausted. Such arbitration could be provided either by the new Industrial Court or by one or more persons appointed by the Minister. In the latter case, they would act as a board of arbitration chosen by the parties under an independent chairman nominated by the Minister. Under Sections 4 and 5 of the 1919 Act, the Minister could also set up Courts of Inquiry into particular disputes. Thus the Conciliation Act 1896 and the Industrial Courts Act 1919 formed the basis of voluntary third party intervention by the state in trade disputes until the enactment of the Industrial Relations Act in 1971, although between 1940 and 1959 the Minister of Labour could refer a dispute to the Industrial Court for compulsory arbitration under Orders 1305 and 1376.

This system worked tolerably well for many years. Both sides of industry trusted and respected the impartial integrity of the Ministry's panel of arbitrators, on the one hand,

and the skilled services of the Ministry of Labour's conciliation officers on the other. This enviable reputation largely depended upon the absence of overt political interference by government in the state's conciliation and arbitration services. After 1964, however, this independence became more questionable. With the introduction of formal incomes policies, the advice of conciliators and the decisions of arbitrators frequently conflicted with the pay norms and incomes policy guidelines then in operation. Moreover, the system of state intervention in industrial relations became more legally regulated under the provisions of the Industrial Relations Act of 1971, particularly through the agencies of the National Industrial Relations Court and the reformed Commission on Industrial Relations (CIR).

Although the 1971 Act was repealed by the Trade Union and Labour Relations Act in 1974, and a new system of conciliation and arbitration was established under the Employment Protection Act in 1975, the long-established voluntary system of state conciliation and arbitration almost ceased to exist between 1970 and 1975. At the very least, it no longer enjoyed its previous high standing and reputation of being free from direct political influences. In the meantime, in the late 1960s, the Ministry of Labour was renamed the Department of Employment and Productivity. Subsequently, it became the Department of Employment and substantial parts of it were hived off to form the independent Manpower Services Commission with responsibilities for national manpower planning and job training. At the same time, the Employment Services Agency became responsible for the labour exchange services of the Department of Employment. These were renamed as job centres and they also took over the other employment services of the former Ministry of Labour. In 1974, responsibility for industrial health and safety was transferred to the Health and Safety Commission. Lastly, the process of dismemberment of the old Ministry of Labour was largely completed by the establishment of ACAS in 1974. This last measure now finally removed from Ministerial control the state's conciliation and arbitration functions which successive Governments had exercised for over 80 years.

The Advisory Conciliation and Arbitration Service

The origins of ACAS derived during the protracted struggles over the passing of the Industrial Relations Act in 1971. In this and the subsequent period, when the trade unions did all in their power to render that Act unworkable, a body of opinion emerged, representative of both trade unions and employers, which called for the establishment of a conciliation and arbitration service independent of government control and of civil service influence. The result was ACAS, which took up its formal duties in September 1974. Its activities are placed on a recognized legal basis by Sections 1–6 and Schedule 1, Part I, of the Employment Protection Act 1975. Its Chairperson is appointed by the Secretary of State for Employment and it has a council of nine members. One third of these are nominated by the TUC, one third by the CBI and the other one third are independents, mainly academics with special knowledge of industrial relations.

Basically ACAS was created as the embodiment of the voluntary approach to industrial relations. It is charged:

> with the general duty of promoting the improvement of industrial relations and, in particular, of encouraging the extension of collective bargaining and the development and, where necessary, reform of collective bargaining machinery.[18]

It synthesises some of the roles and activities of the old Ministry of Labour, on the one hand, with those of the former CIR, on the other. The Ministry of Labour had mainly concentrated on resolving substantive disputes on pay and conditions arising between employers and trade unions through its conciliation and arbitration machinery. A main concern of the CIR was the development of procedural agreements between the parties to collective bargaining, especially in matters of union recognition.

ACAS provides a wide range of services, but basically they fall into six categories. First, there are its conciliation duties. ACAS can intervene in industrial disputes, for example, at the request of one or more of the parties to a dispute, with a view to bringing about a settlement through collective conciliation between employers and trade unions. Pay and other terms and conditions of employment are usually the most frequent causes of such disputes. But disputes over trade union recognition are also subject to collective conciliation on a voluntary basis. In its collective conciliation work ACAS follows the long-established practice of encouraging the parties to a dispute to use their agreed procedures where they exist. As an independent body, ACAS has continuously maintained that it will not act as an interpreter of incomes policy or government recommended maximum percentage pay increases in the public sector as they affect particular disputes. But it does inquire whether in any particular dispute the parties have taken such policies into account. The collective conciliation service provided by ACAS appears to be valued by employers and unions. Research published in 1983 found:

> Much of the work done by ACAS conciliators is carried out quietly and unobtrusively in the regions. For the most part those employers and trade unions who use conciliation do so to try to settle minor issues rather than major disputes. Moreover, it is only a tiny minority of negotiations that ACAS conciliators are asked by the parties to help. Nevertheless, our survey evidence suggests that when ACAS does intervene both sides have a high regard for the service which it provided and would use it again if a similar issue arose. Thus the general picture which emerges is one of limited demand being met satisfactorily.[19]

ACAS also offers conciliation in cases arising between individual employees and employers. Since the mid 1970s, there has been a considerable extension of statutory employment rights for individuals with their employers. Individual employees who contend that their statutory rights have been infringed can make complaints to industrial tribunals. It is the duty of ACAS conciliation officers to attempt to settle such complaints prior to these being referred to a tribunal. Complaints about unfair dismissal embodied in the Employment Protection (Consolidation) Act 1978 provide the great majority of the cases handled by ACAS conciliation officers. Nevertheless, individual conciliation is also offered in questions of employees' rights embodied in the Equal Pay Act 1970, as amended by new regulations in 1983, the Sex Discrimination Act 1975, the Race Relations Act 1976 and the Employment Acts 1980 and 1982. Some of the individual complaints made under these Acts are eventually heard by industrial tribunals, some are settled by ACAS officers, others are settled privately and the rest are withdrawn.

The second function of ACAS is to provide facilities for arbitration, mediation and investigation into trade disputes. Arbitration is offered at the request of one or more of the parties, but only with the consent of all the parties to the dispute. It is usually done through single arbitrators appointed by ACAS, but it can also take place through boards of arbitration. ACAS can also refer issues for arbitration on a voluntary basis to the Central Arbitration Committee (CAC) which replaced the Industrial Arbitration Board in 1976, which had taken over the duties of the Industrial Court in 1971. The CAC derives its powers from various sources including the Industrial Courts Act 1919 and the Equal Pay Act 1970. Since the revocation of the Fair Wages Resolution in 1982 the CAC has ceased hearing complaints about infringements of that Resolution. The Equal Pay Act, for example, empowers the Committee to amend collective agreements or pay structures which are discriminatory on the grounds of sex. Important additions to the Committee's duties were made by the Employment Protection Act of 1975. Under these provisions, independent trade unions can now obtain in certain instances declarations on disclosure of information from employers. The Committee was responsible for issuing Schedule 11 terms and conditions awards until the Schedule was repealed in 1980.

Other responsibilities of ACAS relate to industry-wide arbitration. It has responsibility, for example: for the Post Office Arbitration Tribunal; for the Railway Staff National Tribunal; and for teachers' arbitration under the Remuneration of Teachers Act 1965. Additionally, ACAS also offers mediation which is a method of settling disputes 'whereby an independent person makes recommendations as to a possible solution leaving the parties to negotiate a settlement.'[20] Mediation is sometimes used where the parties are reluctant to bind themselves in advance to accepting an arbitration award. Having noted an external mediator's recommendations, they then undertake further negotiations between themselves.

The third function of ACAS is advisory work with employers, and to a lesser extent with trade unions and employers' associations. This takes the form of either short advisory visits on specific questions, or longer term in-depth advisory projects and surveys. The subject matter on which advice is sought is wide-ranging. It includes: information relating to general industrial relations matters; grievance, disputes and disciplinary procedures; industrial relations legislation; and contracts of employment. Other advice which ACAS provides is on: pay and payment systems; job analysis; job evaluation and work study; and personnel policies. Although most advisory work is carried out in establishments employing fewer than 300 workers, some National Health Service and local authority employers have also used the facilities of ACAS as an aid to improved industrial relations at local level. Research conducted into the advisory role of ACAS found that a clear majority of those employers and trade unions who sought ACAS advice on a wide range of issues were satisfied with the service.

> To the client group the impartial provision of sound advice appears to be what matters most and to the interested parties group it is the combination of impartiality and independence that primarily attracts clients to ACAS for advice.[21]

Closely related to its advisory work is ACAS's fourth duty, under Section 6 of the Employment Protection Act, to issue codes of practice containing practical guidance for promoting improvement in industrial relations between employers and employees. By the mid 1980s, ACAS had issued three codes. These dealt with disciplinary practice and procedures in employment, disclosure of information for collective bargaining purposes, and time off work for trade union duties and activities. Following approval by the ACAS Council, such Codes are submitted to the Secretary of State for Employment and are laid before Parliament. They are then taken into account in hearings at industrial tribunals.

The fifth major activity of ACAS is to undertake inquiry work aimed at improving industrial relations in particular industries, sectors or firms. Other than inquiries into industrial disputes and questions of trade union recognition, inquiry teams are concerned with two main types of work: inquiries into wages councils on references from the Secretary of State for Employment, and long-term inquiries into companies and industries. The latter derive from the terms of reference of the now defunct CIR.

Inquiries by ACAS, however, are not to be confused with the facilities for *ad hoc* courts or committees of inquiry or investigation into particular industrial disputes provided by the Industrial Courts Act 1919. Committees of Inquiry tend to be used for more general purposes than Committees of Investigation, whilst Committees of Investigation are less formal than Courts of Inquiry. Moreover, unlike Courts of Inquiry, Committees of Investigation have no obligation to lay their reports before Parliament. In each case, these bodies usually comprise a chairperson, an employer and a union representative. The appointment of Courts of Inquiry, for instance, chaired by a judge, is a time honoured method of looking into disputes of a particularly serious and particularly prolonged nature. 'The object of such an inquiry is to establish the facts of the dispute and, by publishing its findings, to focus opinion on the shortcomings of either or both sides.'[22] Courts of Inquiry are appointed by the Secretary of State for Employment and have played a major part in resolving some of this country's most difficult industrial disputes over the last 60 years.

An early and famous example was the 1924 Court of Inquiry into dockers' wages and conditions. It was here that Ernest Bevin's advocacy of the dockers' case earned him the accolade of 'the dockers' KC'. More recent examples include: the Devlin Reports on the docks and port transport industry in the 1950s and 1960s; the Pearson Reports on the electricity supply and the shipping industries in the 1960s; the Wilberforce Report on miners' pay in 1972; and the Scarman Report on the Grunwick dispute in 1977. Such reports prove invaluable:

> where (i) the bulk of workers in the industry is concerned and a national strike is threatened; (ii) where there is a likelihood of strike action which would have a disruptive effect on a wide section of the public; (iii) (occasionally) where an isolated dispute looks like having severe secondary effects; (iv) where persistent disputes reveal the existence of an underlying problem, producing a trouble spot . . . (v) where no further arbitration or negotiation machinery is left.[23]

In recent years, Courts of Inquiry have been little used. On those rare occasions where inquiries have been established, they have normally been under the auspices of ACAS.

Since the early 1980s ACAS has been concerned to play a positive role in helping employers and trade unions to adjust their industrial relations practices and policies in order to meet the challenge of high unemployment, economic recession and new technology. The ACAS annual report for 1984, for example, stressed that new technology requires:

> that the skills required in both older and newer industries will continue to change and that new occupations requiring new aptitudes and experience will arise, bringing with them demands for greater adaptability on the part of managers and workers, greater flexibility in the use of manpower and new approaches to training and retraining.[24]

After observing that the 1980, 1982 and 1984 legislation has changed the legal framework within which industrial relations operates, ACAS also emphasizes that the Service continues to believe 'that the normal processes of discussion, consultation and negotiation – coupled with moves to broaden employee involvement – will and should remain the bedrock of good relations'. On the development of single union agreements and 'straight choice' or 'pendulum' arbitration ACAS counsels caution:

> The Service's experience based on the use of similar arbitration arrangements elsewhere is that their success depends on a high degree of mutual trust between the parties and a substantial interchange of often sensitive information, together with considerable confidence in each others' negotiating skills.[25]

It is obviously a key ACAS function carefully to observe the movements at the frontiers of British industrial relations and advise on the best policies and practices which employers and trade unions can adopt.

8.6 INDUSTRIAL TRIBUNALS

Tribunals of various types provide a predominantly flexible means whereby individuals, preferably without the assistance of lawyers, can obtain redress from administrative decisions or the interpretation of the individual rights which legislation provides for them. The first tribunals in Britain were established in 1911. They were set up to adjudicate on complaints for compensation arising out of the National Insurance Act of that year. Shortly afterwards, during the First World War, an extensive system of tribunals was established to hear cases arising out of the Munitions of War Acts, whilst at the end of the war, a system of War Pension Tribunals was also set up to determine war pension rights. After 1945 further tribunals were created. The measures which they were able to consider included: individual complaints arising out of nationalization legislation; rents; social security matters; national insurance benefits; income tax imposition; and rating assessments.

Such was the proliferation of these administrative tribunals that the Government appointed a Royal Commission to investigate them in 1955. In 1957 its Report recommended the continued use of tribunals as effective, inexpensive, rapid and relatively informal means of settling disputes arising out of legislation affecting the ordinary citizen. The Committee was less satisfied, however, with the operation and proceedings of some tribunals. It suggested that certain operational criteria and safeguards should be followed by all tribunals. Two independent Councils on Tribunals were created to give guidance and to oversee the workings of existing tribunals. But their role was to be supervisory not appellate.

Somewhat surprisingly, 'industrial tribunals' were not created until 1964. They were established in the first instance to hear complaints arising out of the training levies paid by employers under the Industrial Training Act 1964. From the following year, the Redundancy Payments Act 1965 considerably expanded the work load of industrial tribunals, when they began to determine redundancy payments for employees made redundant by their employers. The Industrial Relations Act 1971 extended their jurisdiction still further by giving them the task of determining cases of unfair dismissal brought before them by dismissed employees against their former employers. Even although the Industrial Relations Act was repealed in 1974, the range of statutory rights for employees at work has been considerably widened since 1970. Individual employees can now bring claims to industrial tribunals on a variety of issues arising out of current labour law, as shown in table 8.3.

The statutes regulating the jurisdictions of tribunals include the Equal Pay Act 1970, as amended by the Equal Pay (Amendment) Regulations 1983, the Sex Discrimination Act 1975, the Race Relations Act 1976, the Employment Protection (Consolidation)

Table 8.3 *Main jurisdiction of industrial tribunals.*

Statutory rights of employees	Percentage of applications in 1984
Unfair dismissal	73.0
Redundancy payments	8.6
Employment protection	8.4
Unfair dismissal/redundancy payments	4.6
Race relations	1.8
Equal pay	1.0
Contracts of employment	1.0
Sex discrimination	0.9
Health and safety	0.4
(Industrial training levy[1]	0.1)
Miscellaneous	0.1
	100.0

[1] relates to employers
Source: *Industrial Tribunals in England and Wales Fact Sheet* (March 1985)

Act 1978, the Transfer of Undertakings (Protection of Employment) Regulations 1981, and the Employment Acts 1980 and 1982. Some idea of the growth in the work and in the activities of industrial tribunals can be gauged from the fact that whilst in 1965 these tribunals received about 1 300 cases, this had risen to some 14 000 cases annually by the mid 1980s. Also from employing some 40 staff in two offices in their early days, industrial tribunals were employing over 600 staff in about 25 offices in all parts of the country at an annual cost of about £10 million by this time. In practice, only a minority of applications made to tribunals result in actual hearings and decisions. For example, in 1984 78 per cent of all tribunal applications involved unfair dismissal claims but only one-third were actually heard by tribunals and disposed of. The other two-thirds were settled by agreement between the parties or withdrawn. In most cases conciliated settlements were achieved by officers of ACAS. Of those unfair dismissal cases heard by tribunals in 1984 the applicant was successful in about 32 per cent with only about one per cent of cases resulting in reinstatement or re-engagement for the applicant. In 1983 the percentage of unfair dismissal awards by tribunals of £1 000 or over was 59 per cent, with only 6.8 per cent getting £5 000 or over.

We now turn to the methods and the styles of operation favoured by industrial tribunals and the main regulations governing their procedures. In the first place, they have deliberately sought to establish a reputation for fair and impartial hearings. They do this with as much informality and speed as is consistent with their being courts which apply oaths and administer the laws of the land. Hearings are held in conventional accommodation but ordinary though sober clothing is worn by the chairpersons of tribunals and their staff. The parties bringing and contesting a case are described as the 'applicant' and the 'respondent' respectively. Applicants are normally employees, respondents are usually employers. Each is encouraged to present his own case without the often unnecessary and expensive assistance of solicitors or barristers. In order to assist the lay advocate the atmosphere is as relaxed and as informal as possible. In recent years, however, tribunals have been increasingly criticized for becoming more legalistic with a steadily rising use of solicitors – particularly by employers.

The procedures within industrial tribunals are orderly and everyone has the right and the opportunity to put their own points of view. Each tribunal has a chairperson who is legally qualified with at least seven years' legal experience. The chairperson is advised by two lay advisers, or assessors, each of whom has had considerable experience in industrial relations and of employment matters. One adviser is drawn from a panel nominated by the TUC and the other from a panel nominated by the CBI. It is the chairperson's job to interpret and to apply the law after listening to both sides of the case and to the expert opinions of the two advisers.

Although the tribunal chairperson has considerable discretionary powers over the ways in which an actual tribunal operates, tribunals are obliged to observe the Industrial Tribunals (Rules of Procedure) Regulations 1985. These regulations embody several main rules. Broadly, the general regulations governing industrial tribunals require first of all that applicants make an originating application. This is normally done by completing a standard form – called an IT1 – which is available at most offices and job centres administered by the Department of Employment. This form, which gives basic information identifying the parties and stating the grounds on which relief is sought, is forwarded to the Central Office of Industrial Tribunals, one of which is in London, the other in Glasgow. At this stage a decision is taken whether or not the case comes within the jurisdiction of an industrial tribunal. Care is also taken to ensure that both the applicant and the respondent are correctly identified. In order to reduce the time spent at hearings in establishing the basic facts, current regulations require applicants and respondents to set out their preliminary cases in much greater detail than in the past. Since 1980, a tribunal may in some cases consider, by means of a pre-hearing assessment, the contents of an originating application and a 'notice of appearance'. Its purpose is to discuss whether the case has substance or not. If the tribunal at a pre-hearing assessment believes the case has little chance of succeeding, it can advise either party not to proceed to a full hearing. It cannot, however, prevent either party from proceeding if they ignore its advice. The tribunal can warn them that if they persist they may be liable for costs.

The Central Office subsequently forwards originating applications to the appropriate Regional Office of Industrial Tribunals. The respondent in each case is then informed by the regional office of the contents of the originating application with which it is concerned and is given 14 days to decide whether or not to contest the application. This is termed 'a respondent's notice of appearance', and a respondent not entering an appearance is not normally entitled to take any further part in the proceedings unless called upon as a witness by another person. If conciliation between the parties fails, the tribunal has the power to require written particulars relating to the case to be made available. In addition, the parties may request – in writing to the chairperson – that certain documents relating to the case may be disclosed to the tribunal. This is done by an order for discovery of documents. Finally, the time and place of the hearing are decided and these are communicated to the parties by way of a notice of hearing.

The conduct of a hearing at an industrial tribunal is largely determined by the tribunal chairperson and the case normally takes place in public. He or she can accept written admissions from or on behalf of either of the parties for consideration by the tribunal. Tribunals also have the power to ask for further particulars when they consider this to be necessary. A tribunal can order, at the request of one of the parties, that copies of documents be made for its own use. It is also accepted that both parties have the right to be represented at a tribunal. This is usually done through a manager, a trade union officer, an employers' association representative, a knowledgeable third party, or a lawyer. The chairperson permits each party to make their opening statements, to give evidence, to call witnesses, to cross-examine them, and to address the tribunal. If one of the parties fails to appear or to be represented, the tribunal may dispose of the application in its absence. Tribunals also have the power to dismiss a case when an applicant fails to attend a hearing. Once the evidence has been presented, the chairperson decides, in consultation with the assessors, when to conclude the hearing so that they can make their decision in favour of either the applicant or the respondent.

The decision may be unanimous or a majority one. It is the chairperson who decides on the legal issues and the assessors who contribute their views as to the industrial relations factors involved. The decision is then formally recorded, including the reasons leading to it, and it is conveyed to the parties. This is usually done on the day of the case. In more complex cases, a decision may be reserved and notified in writing later. Such decisions, although not binding on other tribunals, are made available for public inspection. A tribunal may review, revoke or vary its decisions, either where it has committed an error, or where a party did not receive notice of the proceedings, or where a decision was made in the absence of a party or person entitled to be heard. It may also do so when new evidence has become available, or where the interests of justice require such a review. Such instances are rare however. Similarly, a tribunal can review a decision of another tribunal where, because of the death or illness of one of its members for example, it is not practicable to review its own decision.

Industrial tribunals possess powers to determine remedies for employees who are either unfairly dismissed or otherwise discriminated against by employers in violation of labour law. These include the power to order reinstatement, re-engagement, or compensation if the applicant's case is upheld. Although an award in respect of legal costs is not ordinarily made, the general impression is that individuals are not normally deterred from bringing a case before a tribunal for this reason, since witness allowances are made and travelling costs reimbursed. Tribunal cases do not qualify for legal aid but limited legal advice is available for those on low incomes. As noted in table 8.3, the majority of claims brought before industrial tribunals concern: unfair dismissals; redundancy payments; equal pay; maternity leave and maternity payments; and sex discrimination. A few cases involve the determination of contracts of employment; itemized pay statements; time off work for trade union and public duties; protective redundancy awards; discrimination at work in respect of trade union activities; suspension from work on medical grounds; the rights of employees when their employer becomes insolvent; and racial discrimination in employment. As already implied, when an application is made to an industrial tribunal under one or more of these headings, it is the duty of ACAS, which is kept informed of originating applications and of appearance notices, to approach the parties in the first instance. This is done with a view to obtaining an 'out of court' settlement so that the case need not proceed to a tribunal.

The efficacy of ACAS conciliation methods is probably indicated by the fact that about two-thirds of originating applications do not reach a tribunal hearing. It is the task of ACAS conciliation officers to make quick and informal contact with the parties after an appearance notice has been instigated. The aim is to obtain in an unfair dismissal claim, for instance, the reinstatement or re-engagement of the employee. Conciliation officers must be careful not to make value judgments or to adjudicate on the issue. Their purpose is to seek a resolution of the situation which is mutually acceptable to both the parties. ACAS can also take part in discussions between the parties leading to a financial settlement. If this is done, the applicant has to drop the claim against the respondent. Without the skilled services of ACAS conciliation officers, industrial tribunals would become grossly overloaded. Consequently, the backlog of cases would mean intolerable delays before hearings could take place.

One of the most obvious shortcomings of industrial tribunals, from their inception in 1964 until the creation of the National Industrial Relations Court (NIRC) in 1972, was the absence of a court of appeal which could clarify the new labour laws and establish a useful but not inflexible body of case law. From 1972 until 1974, appellate jurisdiction from the decisions of industrial tribunals was available through the NIRC which ceased to exist after the repeal of the Industrial Relations Act 1971 by the Trade Union and Labour Relations Act in 1974. The Employment Appeal Tribunal (EAT) was initially established under the Employment Protection Act 1975. Its present statutory basis is to be found in the Employment Protection (Consolidation) Act 1978 and its jurisdiction and procedures are covered by the Employment Appeal Tribunal Rules 1980. First, it hears appeals on any question of law stemming from the proceedings of an industrial tribunal, with the overwhelming bulk of EAT's work – 90 per cent in 1983 – concerning appeals dealing with unfair dismissal and redundancy, equal pay, contracts of employment, sex and race discrimination and any other individual rights under labour law. Not all matters decided by industrial tribunals can be taken to appeal to the EAT. It does not have jurisdiction, for example, in appeals against improvement or prohibition notices brought under Section 24 of the Health and Safety at Work etc. Act 1974. In all other matters, further appeals from the EAT are possible to the Court of Appeal (or Courts of Session in Scotland) in the first instance and ultimately to the House of Lords.

The second function of the EAT is to hear appeals against the decisions of the Certification Officer on questions of law, or of fact, in relation to the granting of certificates of independence to trade unions under the Trade Union and Labour Relations Act 1974 and Employment Protection Act 1975. The EAT also has appellate jurisdiction on matters of law concerning the political levy and trade union political funds under the Trade Union Act 1913 as amended by the Trade Union Act 1984, and trade union amalgamation under the Trade Union (Amalgamations, etc.) Act 1964.

Appeals can also be made to the EAT on certain trade union ballots arising out of the Employment Act 1980. Since the EAT operates in areas where the NIRC previously made decisions, the latter's law reports remain important legal sources – particularly on matters relating to tribunal procedure. In some respects, the rules of the EAT are identical with those which previously characterized the procedures of the NIRC.

Like the NIRC, the EAT is presided over by a High Court judge. Although it is described as the Employment Appeal Tribunal, it is possible for the EAT to sit in more than one location at any one time. Normally it is centred in London and in Glasgow but it also goes on circuit. The EAT, like the industrial tribunals, comprises a lawyer – in this case a High Court judge – and two non-lawyers appointed for their specialist knowledge of industrial relations. The non-lawyers who are members of the EAT are appointed nominally by the Queen but actually on the joint recommendation of the Lord Chancellor and of the Secretary of State for Employment. In effect, this means that they are nominees of either the CBI or the TUC. The rules of the EAT, moreover permit non-lawyers to argue cases there. In summary, then, the EAT is a court in the fullest sense of the word.

> But declared policy is to maintain its proceedings on as informal a basis as is consistent with efficient, orderly progress. The court will be able to draw on the legal expertise of the lawyer member and the practical knowledge of the other members.[26]

8.7 SUMMARY

This chapter focuses on the role of public policy and state agencies in industrial relations. Whether one views the state as a benevolent neutral in industrial relations or as a coercive representative of vested class interests it is clear that British law, the courts, labour market and economic policy and the state's own industrial relations institutions have all played important parts in regulating relations between employers and employees and between employers and trade unions for many years. Nevertheless, the state's traditional abstentionist role has become an increasingly interventionist one since 1945, especially during the 1970s and 1980s.

Government tries to improve the efficiency and working of the labour market to the benefit of employers and employees by a variety of means. With the all-party commitment for a policy of 'full employment' now at an end, the new policies of Conservative Governments after 1979, whilst apparently succceeding in slowing down inflation, do not appear to be able to solve the economic and social problems associated with steadily rising unemployment since then. Indeed in a period of structural economic change and new technologies, state funded schemes aimed at improving the quality and quantity of industrial training and job skills seem more important than ever. In the area of low pay regulation too, the institutional device of wages councils, although aimed at protecting the low paid and encouraging the development of voluntary collective bargaining machinery, does not appear to have resolved these problems satisfactorily either.

The establishment of viable incomes policies, together with the creation of adequate institutional machinery such as the Prices and Incomes Board to monitor them, was a major policy objective of successive governments from the 1950s until the late 1970s. But no long-term set of guidelines nor a continuously successful application of them was achieved, although various attempts were made by governments to devise voluntary, statutory, unilateral and covert incomes policies in that period. Immediately after 1979, the search for an incomes policy was abandoned and was replaced by an apparently revived belief in the economic and social efficacy of free collective bargaining in the context of a restrictive monetary policy guided by government and new legal constraints on trade unions and employees conducting trade disputes. The net results of these policies were a slowing down in the rates of increase in money wages accompanied by rising unemployment and business bankruptcies, as well as falls in trade union membership and union militancy.

The state's machinery for providing conciliation and arbitration facilities has also been both considerably extended and modified since the Conciliation Act 1896 and the Industrial Courts Act 1919. Since September 1974, ACAS, in continuing the voluntarist tradition embodied in its predecessors at the former Ministry of Labour, the Department of Employment and the early Commission on Industrial Relations, now performs a series of important third party functions as a public but independent industrial relations agency. These include: individual and collective conciliation; arbitration, mediation and inquiry in trade disputes; settlement of trade union recognition claims; advisory work; and the issuing of industrial relations codes of practice.

A number of new state institutions in industrial relations has also emerged in recent years. These derive mainly from the extension of statutory employment rights of individuals since the 1970s. Industrial tribunals, for example, are now deeply involved in deciding claims by employees against employers on such matters as unfair dismissal, redundancy payments, equal pay, and sex discrimination at work. Appeals on the interpretation of this labour law are now possible through the Employment Appeal Tribunal.

8.8   REFERENCES

1. O, Kahn-Freund, *Labour and the Law*, Stevens, London, 1977, p. 4.
2. K.W. Wedderburn, *The Worker and the Law*, Penguin, Harmondsworth, 1971, p. 25.
3. *Ibid.*, p. 26.
4. A. Walker, Policies for sharing the job shortage: reducing or redistributing unemployment? in R. Klein and M. O'Higgins (eds.), *The Future of Welfare*, Blackwell, Oxford, 1985, p. 171.
5. J.R. Shackleton, Is the UK labour market inflexible?, *The Royal Bank of Scotland Review*, September 1985, p. 27.
6. *Ibid.*, p. 32.
7. *Ibid.*, p. 41.
8. Fifth Report from the Select Committee of the House of Lords on the Sweating System (1890) quoted in E.H. Phelps Brown, *The Growth of British Industrial Relations*, Macmillan, London. 1965, p. 197.
9. Ministry of Labour, *Written evidence to the Royal Commission on trade unions and employers' associations*, HMSO, London, 1965, p. 114.
10. H.A. Clegg, *The System of Industrial Relations in Great Britain*, Basil Blackwell, Oxford, 1970, p. 358.
11. K.W. Wedderburn, *op. cit.*, p. 199.
12. Central Arbitration Committee, First Annual Report 1976, HMSO, London, 1977, p. 12.
13. R.W. Rideout, *Principles of Labour Law*, Sweet and Maxwell, London, 1976, p. 421.
14. J.L. Fallick and R.F. Elliott, *Incomes Policies, Inflation and Relative Pay*, Allen and Unwin, London, 1981, pp. 260–1.
15. E. Wigham, *Strikes and the Government 1893–1974*, Macmillan, London, 1976, p. 1.
16. *Ibid.*, p. 13.
17. Ministry of Reconstruction, *Report on Conciliation and Arbitration*, HMSO, London, 1918, p. 3.
18. Advisory Conciliation and Arbitration Service, *Annual Report 1981*, HMSO, London, 1982, p. 6.
19. M. Jones and L. Dickens, Resolving industrial disputes: the role of ACAS conciliation, *Industrial Relations Journal*, 1983, p. 17.
20. Advisory Conciliation and Arbitration Service, *op. cit.*, p. 19.
21. E. Armstrong, Evaluating the advisory work of ACAS, *Employment Gazette*, April 1985, p. 143.

22. R.W. Rideout, *op. cit.*, p. 54.
23. *Ibid.*
24. Advisory Conciliation and Arbitration Service, *Annual Report 1984*, London, ACAS, 1985, p. 8.
25. *Ibid.*, pp. 12 and 16.
26. Industrial Relations Briefing, *The Industrial Tribunals Handbook*, Rabvale, London, 1976, p. 215.

9

Individual Labour Law

In this chapter and the following one on collective labour law, we provide an outline description of the main statutes which, at the time of writing, govern the legal aspects of industrial relations in Britain. It is not the intention in these two chapters to attempt a philosophical explanation of the role of the law in regulating labour relations in an advanced market economy like Britain. Neither is it our intention to provide detailed legal analyses of the law of industrial relations. Those who seek such details can find many more learned expositions of labour law written by members of the legal profession and by academic specialists in the field. What the following two chapters seek to achieve is a concise and introductory guide for students and practitioners of industrial relations to the considerable number of complicated statutes which have been enacted in recent years. In this chapter, we focus on that legislation regulating the individual employment relationship between employers and employees. In chapter 10, we turn to the collective aspects of labour law, such as the law on industrial disputes, trade unionism and collective bargaining.

9.1 THE CONTRACT OF EMPLOYMENT

When it is considered how essential the principle of contract and the legal rights and penalties which this term implies are to an industrial society, it is somewhat surprising that the first specific Act of Parliament covering the contractual relationships between employers and employees was the Contracts of Employment Act 1963. Hitherto, a body of common law had emerged over a long period of time which, to a limited extent, regulated the duties of employees and the responsibilities of employers in their employment relationships. It is not unreasonable to conclude that historically the relative social and economic power of the master or employer far exceeded that of his servants or employees in their contractual relationships. Moreover, although the common law did not alter that fundamental balance of power, it clarified the duties and responsibilities of both parties to the employment contract. The most effective method, however, of redressing the imbalance in power between employer and employee has been trade unionism, not common law or Parliamentary statute. 'As a power countervailing management the trade unions are much more effective than the law has ever been or ever can be.'[1]

As far as the common law is concerned, employees have a duty to be ready and willing to work, to offer personal service to their employer, and to take reasonable care in the exercise of that service. Employees are also required not to wilfully disrupt their employer's undertaking, to obey reasonable orders given by the employer or its agents, and to work for the employer in the employer's time. They are also expected to respect the employer's trade secrets, to safeguard the employer against loss incurred during their service and not to disclose certain information relating to the employer's business. It is becoming increasingly commonplace for employers to write into the contracts of employees a clause forbidding them to disclose confidential information concerning clients or processes to competitors. Many place restrictions on certain employees in order to prevent them from leaving to work for a close competitor or from setting themselves up as competitors. The common law duties of the employee may or may not be contractually specified, but where they are they often derive from custom and practice. The employer in return agrees to pay the agreed wages for the willingness to work and to provide reasonable opportunity to earn the agreed wages, although it appears to be uncertain whether an employer is actually obliged to provide work. Employers have a duty to take reasonable care to ensure their employees' safety, to treat their employees with proper courtesy, and to indemnify them for injury sustained during employment. The importance of these common law requirements, however, has steadily diminished as the former absolute powers of the employer have declined. They have also diminished as the employer's statutory obligations have been more clearly defined and as the law has made specific the employers' responsibilities to their employees.

The Employment Protection (Consolidation) Act 1978 now requires that all those employees who work 16 or more hours per week are given written particulars of the main terms of their employment within 13 weeks of their engagement. Employees who work for less than 16 hours per week are not covered by the legislation unless they have worked for their employer for eight or more hours per week for five years. Whilst the legislation covers apprentices, it does not cover people who are under contract to supply a service such as freelance agents or self-employed persons; neither does it cover dock workers, crown servants or employees normally working abroad. If the employer does not give a written statement within the 13 week period the employee may make a complaint to an industrial tribunal and seek a remedy.

The written particulars must include: the names of the parties to the contract; the date of commencement of employment; any details of continuity of employment where there has been a change of employer; the job title; the details of wage or salary payment; the hours of work; any holiday, sickness and pension scheme arrangements; and the length of notice which employees must give and receive. Further, where a union membership agreement exists, the contract of employment should make it clear that the employee has a legal right to choose either to join or not to join a union. Whilst employees need only give a minimum of one week's notice to terminate their contract, unless it specifies a longer period, employers are required to give employees with four or more weeks' service at least one week's notice, and those with two or more years' service at least two weeks' notice. Employees are then entitled to a minimum of an additional week's notice for each complete year of continuous employment up to 12 years. Where an employer fails to give the legally required minimum notice, *or* payment in lieu of notice, employees can bring a case of 'wrongful' dismissal against their employer, as distinct from 'unfair' dismissal. Where appropriate, employees must also be informed about relevant grievance and disciplinary procedures and any disciplinary rules applying to them.

Two further points need to be made. First, apart from the initial four items listed above, employers can refer employees to any relevant documents incorporating the required information rather than providing it in the written statement itself. It is now increasingly the practice of employers to cover all aspects of employment in a comprehensive company handbook which is issued to all employees. Second, the written statement itself is not the contract of employment. It has no direct legal force at all. It is merely information about what the employer believes to be some of the main terms of the contracts of employment of the individual employees in question.

In statute law, a '"contract of employment" means a contract of service or of apprenticeship, whether it is express or implied and (if it is express) whether it is oral or in writing'[2] between an employer and an individual employee. The express terms of a contract of employment pose few problems. Indeed, the written particulars provided by the employer to each of its employees are the best evidence of the express terms of an employment contract. They normally include the terms and conditions of employment, such as the pay, hours of work, holiday entitlements, pension rights and so on. Although collective agreements between employers and trade unions are not directly legally enforceable unless the parties specifically state so in writing, the terms within collective agreements are normally incorporated into the individual contracts of employment of employees. This is done either by express incorporation or by implied incorporation.

> Even where no express words are used but the normal practice is to pay the wages negotiated by union representatives, there will usually be no difficulty in implying a term that wages are to be paid in accordance with the collective agreement.[3]

Such terms apply to all employees covered by the collective agreements, whether trade unionists or not.

The implied terms of a contract of employment are more complex. Broadly, terms may be implied from the relations between the parties, from custom and practice, and by the law. For example, the courts can decide that certain terms are to be implied into the contracts of employment of workers doing a particular job 'because the judge thinks those terms are essential to the relations between bosses and workers in that industry.'[4] Custom and practice, on the other hand, may only be implied as a term of a contract of employment provided that it is 'reasonable, certain and notorious'. It must, in short, be approved of either by the courts or by industrial tribunals, be capable of reasonably precise definition or description and be well known to the parties.

Although works rules and disciplinary codes are also incorporated into individual contracts of employment, the latter are now regulated to a considerable extent by statute law. Statutory implied terms include, for example: the terms and conditions laid down by wages councils and agricultural wages boards; the equality clauses under the Equal Pay Act 1970; guarantee payments in respect of lost working days: and the terms and conditions imposed by the CAC after an employer has refused to disclose information needed for collective bargaining purposes. These statutory terms governing the contract of employment are rarely if ever expressly incorporated into individual contracts of employment. Employers have a duty to observe them as the law of the land, whilst employees can obtain enforcement of their statutory legal rights by due process of the law. Many of these statutory implied terms in the contract of employment, such as health and safety and unfair dismissal legislation, now effectively supersede the common law requirements.

Under Section 8 of the Employment Protection (Consolidation) Act 1978, employers are obliged to give their employees itemized pay statements. This provides employees with a clear statement of how their gross pay is made up; its methods of calculation; the details of the variable or fixed deductions involved; their net pay; and the method and intervals of payment. Where some deductions are fixed these need not be itemized every time a payment is made provided that employees are given a standing statement of these deductions. This sets out the amount, the intervals between each deduction, and why they are made. Such clear and detailed pay statements are obviously of considerable use in cases taken before industrial tribunals.

Contracts of employment change all the time. Whenever there is a pay increase, a reduction in working hours, a reallocation of work duties, a change in work location, or an agreed move to shiftwork, for example, the conditions of the contract are changed. Where these changes are agreed by trade unions as part of the collective bargaining process, even though both the express and the implied terms of the contract of employment are changed there is no need to issue amended written statements. But there is a statutory obligation to change the written statement when it becomes inaccurate. Where the employment situation is fluid with changing places and hours of work, and where flexible working methods make precise job descriptions extremely difficult to determine, the contract can make specific provisions to cover the requirements of changing work situations. Where the contract specifically permits the employer to require employees to accept geographical and occupational mobility and flexible working hours, for instance, it should be clearly stated.

If employees are dismissed for refusing to accept any change which their contracts clearly require, such as movement to new work sites or a reallocation of duties, it is unlikely that they will be able to contest successfully a case for redundancy payment or unfair dismissal. Where substantial variations in the contract must first be agreed between the parties, this intention should be made quite clear – preferably in writing. With collective bargaining this presents few problems, but without it individual employees must give their consent for any major changes of this sort. If a change takes place and the employees adhere to the new arrangements without protest, it is deemed that they have accepted the change voluntarily. But as one tribunal has pointed out 'voluntary acceptance of new terms must be distinguished from taking Hobson's choice'.[5]

The law relating to changes in the contract of employment and the legal judgments in individual cases suggest that the situation is extremely complex. However, where an employer substantially varies the terms and conditions of employment of its employees, and where their contracts clearly do not permit this to be done, or where it happens in spite of the protests of the employees concerned, that employer is breaking or repudiating the contracts. In such cases, if employees are dismissed for refusing to accept the arbitrary changes made by an employer to their contracts, or where they leave their employment in protest, they might well be able to successfully contest a case of unfair dismissal at an industrial tribunal. However, the courts have decided that where a substantial variation of contract is unavoidable, because of extreme and pressing adverse financial circumstances, employees can be obliged to accept it. In the event of dismissal, the employer would be required to prove to a tribunal that the financial circumstances constituted a dire threat to the organization.

So far we have dealt with contracts of employment of indefinite duration, since most employees and employers expect the contract to continue until one of them decides to terminate it. Many employees, however, commence employment for a fixed period which they understand to be the principal condition of employment. When this is the case, the period of employment should be clearly stated along with the fixed date of termination. Every effort should be made to ensure that employees understand that the job is for a fixed period only. Where a fixed term contract lasts for more than one year, the right of the employee to seek a legal remedy can be waived providing it is in writing. Where the contract is for more than two years the right to redundancy payments can be waived. These restrictions on a legal right, must, however, be clearly stated in the contract. Further, in certain cases where a number of consecutive fixed term contracts have been given to an employee, the courts might decide that the employee's employment was continuous and that he or she should be treated at law as a permanent employee with full legal rights.

9.2 UNFAIR DISMISSAL

At common law, employers have traditionally possessed wide powers to engage and to dismiss their employees at will. Until the Industrial Relations Act 1971, which gave most employees the legal right to claim compensation for 'unfair dismissal', the power of employers to dismiss their employees was only restricted by trade union organization and by collective agreements incorporating established dismissal procedures within them. In theory, any employees who were not given due notice or payment in lieu of notice when dismissed by their employer could sue that employer for 'wrongful dismissal' under their common law rights through the civil courts. But in practice this rarely happened because of the heavy legal costs involved and the generally accepted right of the employer to hire and fire with impunity. Where trade unions were strongly organized, however, they could usually threaten strike action if any of their members was unreasonably dismissed in their eyes. But where trade unionism was weak or non existent, employers possessed virtually unlimited powers of dismissal. The insecurity of employment thus created was, no doubt, acceptable in the nineteenth century but proved completely unacceptable in modern conditions.

It was the Industrial Relations Act 1971 which introduced for the first time the right of legal redress for what it defined in law as 'unfair dismissal'. It also permitted individuals who claimed that they had been dismissed unfairly to bring their cases before an industrial tribunal rather than the common law courts. The comparative informality of industrial tribunals, it was believed, with their emphasis upon common sense and the realities of industrial relations, rather than upon the formality and legal pedantry associated with the civil courts, together with their speed and relative cheapness from the employee's point of view, was a more suitable vehicle for hearing cases involving unfair dismissal.

It is estimated that about half a million dismissals for all reasons might take place each year but only about 30 000 cases are registered annually with industrial tribunals and of these nearly 20 000 are either settled by conciliation or withdrawn. Of the 10 000 or in cases proceeding to a tribunal hearing, about two-thirds are either rejected as being registered beyond the legal time limits or 'out of scope' or – as in most cases – the dismissals are found to be fair and the cases dismissed. Only one-third of the 10 000 or so cases which are heard annually by tribunals are upheld as unfair dismissals and only about one per cent result in the reinstatement or re-engagement of the dismissed employee. The remedy awarded by the tribunals in the majority of cases declared to be unfair dismissals is monetary compensation, with the median award being £1 345 out of 1 752 cases in 1983. By comparison, the median award for cases settled privately by conciliation without a tribunal hearing was £421 out of 9 546 in 1983. These statistics hardly support the popular belief that the unfair dismissal legislation places a heavy burden on employers and deters them from recruiting new employees or dismissing unsatisfactory ones.

With the repeal of the Industrial Relations Act 1971 and the 'consolidation' of the individual rights under the Employment Protection Act 1975, the main body of statute law concerning unfair dismissal is provided by the Employment Protection (Consolidation) Act 1978, as amended by the Employment Acts 1980 and 1982. With the exception of a few classes of employees, all employees with more than two years continuous employment with an employer have a statutory right not to be unfairly dismissed. The qualifying period of continuous employment was raised from six months to twelve months in 1980 and to two years in 1985. This right exists either when they work 16 or more hours per week for their employer or if they have worked 8 or more hours per week for the same employer for at least five years continuously. The excluded categories of employee include: the self-employed; a husband or wife employed by their spouse; registered dock workers; share fishermen; people normally employed outside Britain; those over the employer's normal retirement age, men and women having equal rights; and members of the police and the armed forces. Those employees on fixed term contracts of two years or more, whilst excluded in respect of the expiry of their contract, may bring a case for unfair dismissal unless they have accepted a contract which clearly waives their right to claim a legal remedy for unfair dismissal. Those employees covered by a negotiated dismissal procedure which qualifies for an exclusion order from the Secretary of State are also excluded from the unfair dismissal provisions of the 1978 Act where 'the remedies provided by the agreement . . . are on the whole as beneficial as . . . those provided in respect of unfair dismissal'[7] by Section 65 of the Act.

Between 1980 and 1985 employees working in small firms, which throughout their period of employment had employed 20 or fewer employees, could not make a claim of unfair dismissal if they had not completed two years continuous employment at the time of their dismissal. The requirement of continuous employment for all employees, regardless of the size of the firm employing them, was raised to two years in 1985. This qualifying time period does not apply, however, to dismissals involving certain health and safety requirements or trade union membership and activities. In hearing cases of unfair dismissal in small firms, tribunals are required to take into account the employer's size and administrative resources when considering if the dismissal was carried out fairly.

In cases of unfair dismissal reaching a tribunal, great importance is attached to the reasonableness of the employer's actions and whether or not a satisfactory disciplinary procedure was followed. In 1977, Parliament approved its first code of practice on disciplinary practice and procedures in employment, prepared by the Advisory Concili- ation and Arbitration Service (ACAS), which is due to be updated in the mid 1980s. This gives 'practical guidance on how to draw up disciplinary rules and procedures and how to prepare them effectively.'[8] It is intended as a guide for employers, employees, trade unions and industrial tribunals in establishing and assessing the operation of disciplinary procedures within organizations. The code must be considered by tribunals in determining their decisions, and outlines behaviour which can be interpreted as constituting an offence, enabling tribunals to decide whether an employer has acted reasonably in dismissing an employee.

The code stresses, amongst other things, that disciplinary procedures should be in writing; they should specify to whom they apply; they should provide speedy action; they should indicate the disciplinary actions which may be taken; they should give individuals a chance to state their case; and they should ensure that a sensible system of warnings and a reasonable period of time is provided for employees to improve their behaviour. The code recommends very careful use of the powers of dismissal, empha- sizes the need for an appeals system, and suggests how it should be conducted. The code also stresses the importance of verbal and written warnings, of disciplinary transfers where possible, and of keeping adequate records on disciplinary matters. There is also the need to provide the opportunity to 'wipe the slate clean' for disciplined employees, after a suitable period of good behaviour. Above all, the code emphasizes, there is a need for all employees, including management, to be fully aware of the disciplinary procedure and the possible consequences of infringing it. Where employers have clearly failed to observe the general standards advised in the code, an industrial tribunal usually concludes that their actions have been unreasonable.

The obligation of employers to act in a reasonable manner in disciplining and dismissing employees not only means that employers should follow the ACAS code, it also means that employers should consider whether the situation and the employee's offence merit dismissal, and whether there are mitigating circumstances which 'natural justice' demands should be taken into account when making decisions of this kind. Did the employee understand the rules and warnings received, for example? Did the employee have a chance to explain the conduct in question, and was the actual manner of dismissal satisfactory? The law also requires that an employer should give employees, if requested, written reasons for their dismissal or for the failure to renew a fixed term contract of employment within 14 days of the request being made. Where an employer refuses to do this, or where the reasons for not doing so are believed to be inadequate or untrue, employees may complain to an industrial tribunal. If the tribunal finds an employee's claim to be justified, it can make an award against the employer of two weeks' pay. Where a dismissal letter is given, it can be used as evidence at a hearing before an industrial tribunal.

Section 57 of the Employment Protection (Consolidation) Act 1978 lays down the main grounds on which dismissals can be judged as either 'fair' or 'unfair'. What constitutes fair or unfair dismissal is, of course, a matter of legal and not moral definition. Before the Employment Act 1980, the onus of proof that the employer had acted both reasonably and fairly in dismissing an employee lay with the employer. It is now the responsibility of the tribunal to decide whether the employer acted reasonably given all the circumstances. This change can significantly reduce the burden of proof on the employer when appearing before a tribunal. Apart from 'some other substantial reason', it is only 'fair' to dismiss an employee for a reason which:

(a) related to the capability or qualifications of the employee for performing work of the kind which he was employed to do, or
(b) related to the conduct of the employee, or
(c) was that the employee was redundant, or
(d) was that the employee could not continue to work in the position which he held without contravention (either on his part or that of his employer) of a duty or restriction imposed by or under an enactment.[9]

Dismissal on grounds of incapability means that if employers follow adequate disciplinary procedures and act reasonably, they can fairly dismiss employees even after two years continuous employment on the grounds of an employee's incapability, inadequacy, incompetence or lack of skill in the job. It is essential that employees are allowed a reasonable time in which to improve their performance and, if practicable, are offered suitable alternative employment by their employer. If a case is brought before a tribunal, it can require the employer to produce substantial proof of the employee's lack of capability. Dismissal on grounds of incapability due to sickness, for instance, demands considerable evidence that the employer acted in a reasonable manner. The employer must show that the agreed sick leave arrangements have been exhausted and that every chance has been given to employees to recover sufficiently to undertake their contractual duties. Where absence is continuous over a long period, employees must be warned of the possible consequences. Where necessary, doctors' reports need to be obtained before the process of dismissal is initiated. Where the evidence suggests that an employee is unlikely to be healthy enough to do the existing job again, he or she should if practicable be offered suitable alternative employment and a new contract.

One of the most common reasons for dismissal is on grounds of improper conduct by employees at work. Where misconduct is alleged, the employer must take great care to ensure that an adequate disciplinary procedure has been used, and that all the necessary warnings have been made by the supervisory staff and by management to the employee in question. If the case goes before a tribunal, the employer can be required to produce convincing evidence that misconduct actually took place. An employer also has to show that it acted reasonably in disciplining and in eventually dismissing the employee concerned, and that the employee was given every chance to redeem the conduct. In cases of gross misconduct, however, employees can still be summarily dismissed if they are first given a chance to explain their behaviour. This can sometimes result in evidence being produced which justifies a breach of expected disciplinary standards. This usually happens in cases where employees act very much out of character and where they are clearly suffering from personal stress. In order for an employer to justify dismissal on the grounds of gross misconduct, therefore, it is essential that employees understand exactly what constitutes such behaviour. It is now regarded as good practice to suspend employees immediately when they commit acts of gross misconduct and send them home whilst an enquiry takes place to decide within a few days whether or not to dismiss.

Dismissed employees may also bring cases of unfair dismissal before a tribunal concurrently with claims for redundancy compensation under Part VI of the Employment Protection (Consolidation) Act 1978. In certain circumstances, cases of unfair dismissal may be brought against an employer on the grounds of redundancy. But this is only possible where the employer fails to rebut the presumption both that the dismissal was for redundancy and that it was also unfair. Where an employee is unfairly selected for redundancy on the grounds of personal discrimination by the employer, or where the redundancy selection process is in breach of an agreed redundancy procedure, the employee can also bring a claim of unfair dismissal against the employer. In this case, the aim is to refute the employer's contention that dismissal is entirely on the grounds of redundancy. Where an employer dismisses an employee on clear grounds of redundancy, however, the dismissal is fair under the law.

If dismissal takes place on the grounds that to continue to employ the person involved would result in a breach of statutory requirements, a dismissal is generally regarded as being fair. For example if employees are specifically engaged to drive motor vehicles and they lose their licences through drunken driving, they can be fairly dismissed. Even in these cases, the employer is expected to consider whether the person concerned can be offered alternative work before the decision to dismiss is finally made. Similarly, an employer is permitted to dismiss a person for 'some other substantial reason'.[10] Although this appears to allow employers to escape the main rigours of the legislation on unfair dismissal, in practice this has not been the case. Indeed, tribunals require considerable evidence to be presented by an employer before they uphold cases for fair dismissal on the grounds of 'some other substantial reason'. However, where relevant evidence is produced, fair dismissal can be established on the grounds of economic necessity, commercial security, or because the dismissal took place in order to prevent excessive disharmony at the workplace.

The law also requires that in certain cases dismissal is always unfair. For example, an employer must never dismiss an employee for any 'inadmissible reason', such as for trade union membership, trade union activities, or on the grounds of sex or race. Neither can employees be made redundant when it is the real intention of the employer to dismiss them because of their trade union activities. Where employees believe that they have been dismissed for an inadmissible reason, they can apply to a tribunal for a quick hearing or 'interim relief'. This requires the tribunal to recommend either the person's immediate re-employment or suspension on full pay until the case has been properly heard. Such a recommendation may be made provided the case looks prima-facie reasonable, and that the individual's union supports the claim and gets it to a tribunal within seven days of the dismissal. Moreover, under existing sex and race discrimination legislation, it is also automatically unfair, in most circumstances, to dismiss any employee on the grounds of sex, pregnancy, race, colour and ethnic or national origins.

It is also unfair, in certain circumstances, to dismiss employees for non-membership of a union where a closed shop exists. Until the Employment Act 1982, it was also unfair to dismiss employees for taking part in industrial action if they were unfairly selected for dismissal. Now, however, it is not unfair to dismiss employees for taking part in a strike or other industrial action where an employer, first, has dismissed all those taking part and, second, has not offered re-engagement to any of them within three months of their dismissal.

Finally, dismissal is also unfair if an employer behaves in a way calculated to lead

ventual dismissal of any employees, usually on the grounds of miscon-
e resignation of employees because they find it impossible to remain with
:r. Such enforced dismissals or resignations are said to be 'constructed' by
yer and they are legally described as constructive dismissals. In cases of
.ive dismissal, however, there is a heavy burden on the employee(s) concerned
nt sufficient and substantial evidence that constructive dismissal did in fact take
place. The principal test for constructive dismissal at a tribunal hearing is whether or not
the employer acted in breach of the contract of employment.

In the case of employees dismissed for committing a criminal offence outside their
place and hours of employment, dismissal is only considered fair if the nature of the
offence was such as to hit at the root of the contract of employment. For example, a
conviction for stealing would probably justify the dismissal of an employee whose
honesty and trustworthiness were regarded as essential elements by the employer. The
same type of conviction might not in different circumstances justify dismissal if the
tribunal did not accept that it was fair given the circumstances of the person's
employment. Generally speaking, however, a custodial sentence which prevents
employees from attending their place of work is regarded as 'frustration' of the contract
of employment and may thereby end it.

If a claim for unfair dismissal proceeds to an industrial tribunal, and it becomes
apparent that the employee was actually dismissed, the tribunal usually follows four
broad procedural steps. First, it determines if the application is in order by establishing,
in the first instance, whether the applicant was a full time employee with more than two
years continuous employment and whether the application for a hearing was made
within three months of the dismissal. Second, the tribunal requires the employer as the
respondent to state the principal reason given for the dismissal at issue. Third, the
tribunal considers whether the reason for dismissal was fair or unfair at law and whether
the employer acted reasonably and in accordance with the rules of natural justice.
Lastly, the tribunal determines the remedy which can be awarded if a claim of unfair
dismissal is upheld against an employer.

If a tribunal finds in favour of the applicant, it can order the reinstatement of the
employee into the original job – thus ensuring continuity of service – or re-engagement
into another job of a similar nature with the same employer. In doing this, however, the
tribunal must consider three factors: first, the wishes of the employee; second, whether
the employee contributed to the dismissal; and third, how 'practicable' it is for the
employer to take the employee back. In addition to the remedy of getting the job back, a
tribunal can also award compensation to the dismissed employee or compensation alone.
There are three types of compensation: a basic award; a compensatory award; and an
additional award. The basic award is for the fact of the dismissal and is dependent upon
the age of the employee and years of continuous employment. A compensatory award is
based on the loss of pay and other benefits by the employee. However, if the tribunal
decides that the employee partially contributed to the dismissal, it reduces its assessment
accordingly. Finally, an additional award is payable where an employer fails to comply
with an order to reinstate or to re-engage a dismissed employee. Normally, this amounts
to between 13 and 26 weeks' pay. However, if dismissal was because of the trade union
activities of the employee, then between 26 and 52 weeks' pay can be added to the other
compensation already determined. Awards for unfair dismissals arising out of closed
shop situations are subject to separate criteria and regulations.

9.3   REDUNDANCY RIGHTS

The Redundancy Payments Act 1965 introduced for the first time the principle of a 'property right' in a job. It enabled compensation to be claimed by employees made redundant through no fault of their own.

> Just as a property owner has a right in his property and when he is deprived he is entitled to compensation, so a long-term employee is considered to have a right analogous to a right of property in his job, he has a right to security and his rights gain in value with the years.[11]

This Act was intended not only to bestow a property right in employment, but also to encourage a level of occupational mobility compatible with the needs of an advanced industrial economy. It also sought to discourage overmanning in the older trades and to permit the maximum flow of labour resources to the newer high technology industries.

Redundancy is defined in the 1978 Act as being where an employee, and only an employee, has been dismissed because the employer has ceased or intends to cease business in the place at which the employee was contracted to work. Dismissal on the grounds of redundancy also occurs where an employer has to reduce its labour force because the requirements of the business to carry out work of a particular kind have ceased or diminished. This takes place not only where the business or part of it is closed, but also when the business or work is transferred elsewhere. Redundancy can also take place where a fixed term contract is ended without being renewed, unless the contract was for more than two years and included a waiver clause. Similarly, employees can claim redundancy compensation if they are laid off or put on short time working for four consecutive weeks, or for six weeks in a three-month period. This is so provided the reason for short time working is not due to industrial action. In these circumstances, employees have to serve written notice to the employer of their intention to claim dismissal on the grounds of redundancy within four weeks of the lay-off period.

The best practical test of redundancy is 'has the job disappeared?' If the dismissed employee is replaced by someone else doing the same job, redundancy cannot usually be claimed, although a case of unfair dismissal against the employer on grounds other than redundancy might result. Where a proprietor dies or a business is sold or transferred to other owners without loss of employment, the employees maintain their continuity of employment. Where redundancy takes place within the meaning of the 1978 Act, the principles upon which the amount of compensation is based depend upon the age, length of service and average earnings of the employees. This amounts to: half a week's pay for each year of employment between the ages of 18 and 21; one week's pay for each year between the ages of 22 and 40; and one and a half weeks' pay for each year between 41 and state retirement age. A maximum weekly wage is fixed by the Secretary of State and reviewed annually (£155 in 1986). If an employer wishes to pay in excess of the statutory scheme it is free to do so, but it cannot claim any additional rebate. Redundancy payments are not normally subject to income tax. The rebate scheme for employees was terminated in 1986.

With the major exceptions of crown servants, share fishermen, registered dock workers, domestic servants, employees working abroad, and close relatives of an employer, all employees over the ages of 18 – normally working for more than 16 hours per week and with at least two years continuous employment with the employer – are entitled to redundancy payments if dismissed by their employer on the grounds of redundancy. Alternatively, they can bring their case to an industrial tribunal if they believe that they are entitled to redundancy payments which have not been paid to them. Redundancy payments are not made to those over normal retirement age. Moreover, at the age of 64 for men and 59 for women, redundancy entitlements diminish by one-twelfth with the passing of each month, until at the age of official retirement all redundancy entitlements are lost. Redundancy payments can also be claimed by part time employees working less than 16 hours a week, provided that they have worked eight or more hours a week for the same employer over a continuous period of five years. It is clear, too, that where employees are declared redundant and express the wish to go to another job before their periods of notice expire, they may do so without loss of their redundancy entitlements. This can be done as long as they put their requests in writing to the employer and that the employer agrees to their requests. If an employee leaves the job early without the prior agreement of the employer, on the other hand, redundancy entitlements are forfeited.

When redundancy situations arise, an employer is expected to take every reasonable step to find the employee or employees suitable alternative employment. If the employees do not accept this alternative work, they lose their redundancy entitlements. Obviously whether or not the offer of alternative work is suitable and reasonable depends upon the conditions applying in each case. But generally the offer of alternative work has to be of at least similar status and payment to the previous employment. Where the alternative work is accepted, new contracts of employment have to be agreed.

Under the Employment Protection (Consolidation) Act 1978, an employee can agree to undertake a trial period of not more than four weeks in the new post offered by the employer. At the end of the trial period, both the employee and the employer have to agree that the post is suitable, and then a new contract of employment can be drawn up. Where necessary, the trial period, which might involve formal training, can be extended. Where a four week trial period in a new post is offered and accepted, it is best done in writing. It needs to specify the date of the end of the trial period and the terms and conditions of employment applying after the end of the specified period. If an employee unreasonably refuses an offer of a trial period in a suitable alternative post, any entitlement to redundancy payments may be lost. Contested cases go before industrial tribunals.

Part IV of the Employment Protection Act 1975 lays down the methods and procedures which employers are obliged to observe for handling redundancies when dealing with independent recognized trade unions. These procedures apply to all employees being made redundant regardless of their length of service or of the number of hours they work each week. The employer must also consult the trade unions concerned even if the people being made redundant are volunteers and not trade union members. These procedures, however, do not apply to employers which do not recognize independent trade unions for collective bargaining. Where an employer recognizing independent unions finds the redundancy of some or all of its employees to be unavoidable it must consult with the trade unions and with the Department of Employment 'at the earliest opportunity'. Where more than 10 but less than 100 employees are to be made redundant within a period of 30 days or less, the employer is required to commence consultations with the unions involved at least 30 days before the first intended dismissal. Where more than 100 employees are to be made redundant within a period of 90 days or less, then consultations with the independent unions must take place at least 90 days before the first dismissal occurs.

> The employer must disclose, in writing, to the trade union representatives the reasons for the redundancy, the number it is proposed to dismiss and the number of employees of that description at the establishment in question, the proposed method of selection and the proposed method and period for carrying out the dismissals. It should be noted that he does not have to disclose the precise identity of those it is proposed to dismiss. The employer must consider the representations of the union and give reasons if he rejects any of them.[12]

If an employer fails to observe these consultative requirements before the redundancies take place, only the recognized trade unions can make a claim to a tribunal. If the tribunal upholds the complaint, it can issue a protective award. This protects the employment of those involved for up to a maximum period of 30 days in cases involving more than 10 but less than 100 employees, or 90 days where more than 100 employees are to be made redundant. In those instances involving less than 10 employees, a protective award may be issued for up to 28 days. If the employer does not comply with an award, the employees are entitled to receive pay from the employer for each week of the 28 day, 30 day or 90 day period during which consultations should have taken place. Except in cases involving less than 10 employees, employers are also required to give the same periods of notice of pending redundancies to the Secretary of State for Employment who can call for further information on the matter. If an employer fails to meet these obligations it can be fined on summary conviction. Moreover, where an employer either selects employees unfairly for redundancy, or fails to follow the customary procedures or agreed redundancy agreement, the individuals can bring cases of unfair dismissal against their employer. In these circumstances, a claim for unfair dismissal can run concurrently with a claim for redundancy entitlements.

When employees are given notice of dismissal due to redundancy they are, under the 1978 Act, entitled to reasonable time off with pay to look for another job during working hours or to seek suitable training for future employment. Only those employees with two or more years continuous employment and who work for more than 16 hours per week are entitled to this provision. Complaints concerning the failure of employers to grant reasonable time off are heard by tribunals.

If an employer either fails to pay the required redundancy compensation or rejects the claim that redundancy has taken place, employees can make a claim to an industrial tribunal. The complaint has normally to be made within six months of the effective date of the redundancy. Employers only used to bear a proportion of the total redundancy payment awarded. They can apply to the Department of Employment for a rebate from the Redundancy Payments Fund to offset the cost of redundancy payments. The rebate started at two-thirds in 1965, was later reduced to half, then to 41 per cent in 1977, before falling to 35 per cent in 1985. The Fund was abolished by the Conservative Government in 1986.

Between the enactment of the Redundancy Payments Act in 1965 and the creation of the National Industrial Relations Court in 1971, the lack of an effective system of appeals from the decisions of industrial tribunals led to many inconsistent decisions in redundancy cases. Since 1975, the Employment Appeal Tribunal (EAT) has appellate jurisdiction on matters of law referred to it by industrial tribunals. It has helped to clarify the law of redundancy by guiding the decisions of the tribunals through reference to its appeal cases. When either party to a tribunal decision on redundancy wishes to give notice of an appeal to the EAT, it may do so on a point of law only. As with industrial tribunals, there is a right of representation there by any person, but the EAT does not normally award costs except where the proceedings are considered to be either vexatious or unnecessary.

9.4   EQUAL OPPORTUNITY

Sex discrimination

The Equal Pay Act 1970, the Equal Pay (Amendment) Regulations 1983 and the Sex Discrimination Act 1975 constitute the major legislation protecting employees, mainly women, from being discriminated against on the grounds of their sex or marital status in relation to their terms and conditions of employment. The Sex Discrimination Act 1975, for instance, seeks to prevent discrimination both in employment and in the provision of goods, facilities, services and education on the grounds of sex alone. It is a principal purpose of this legislation to prevent the more obvious types of sex discrimination in employment and to alter fundamentally social attitudes concerning the role of women in society and in the world of work. Indeed, the sex discrimination legislation has been described by one distinguished observer as 'a major attempt to change the social mores of a nation.'[13]

The Equal Pay Act 1970, which came into force with the Sex Discrimination Act on 31 December 1975, is intended to prevent discrimination in the terms and conditions of employment between men and women. Where men and women are employed on 'the same or broadly similar work', both sexes are entitled to the same contractual terms regarding pay, hours of work, holidays, terms of notice, sick pay schemes, and most other conditions of employment. The Act covers all men and women employed in Britain regardless of their hours of work or length of service. It establishes the right of individual employees, regardless of their sex, to equal terms and conditions of employment if they are doing work of the same or broadly similar nature. They also have this right when jobs have been given an equal value under an analytical job evaluation exercise. The Act does not, however, lay any obligation on employers to carry out job evaluation exercises. Furthermore, the law only applies if the terms and conditions of employment of both sexes are determined by a job evaluation rating. Since 1984 claims for equal pay can be heard by tribunals on the grounds that the job evaluation method used was discriminatory on grounds of sex and should be disregarded.

The Equal Pay Act of 1970 does not remove all aspects of discrimination in the terms and conditions of employment. Where the terms of employment of particular employees are affected by compliance with the law – as for example in the restrictions placed upon the hours and time of work for female workers under the various Factories Acts – the 1970 Act does not require the equal treatment of men and women. Similarly, the Act does not require equal terms and conditions 'related to retirement, marriage or death or to any provisions made in connection with retirement, marriage or death.'[14] At the time of writing, however, amendments were being made to sex discrimination law, due largely to important legal decisions made by the European Court.

Initially, a person seeking equal pay and conditions of employment has to take their case to the employer. If the employer denies the claim, the matter may be referred to an industrial tribunal or a county court. There is no minimum period of employment to qualify in claiming this statutory right. To obtain a remedy, however, the employee must have been in the job for at least six months before applying to the tribunal. No claim can be referred to a tribunal more than six months after the job has ended. The Equal Opportunities Commission (EOC) has authority to assist applicants and to provide guidance and advice to the parties in dispute. Where an industrial tribunal finds in favour of the woman or man, it can award pay or damages for up to two years before the date at which proceedings were initiated.

The Equal Pay Act has been modified by Section 8 of the Sex Discrimination Act 1975. This provides that:

> female employees will have an equality clause incorporated expressly or by implication in their individual contract of employment providing for full contractual equality save in those cases where the employer proves that a variation between a woman's terms and those of a man reflect differences in working conditions, job duties, or qualifications, experience, length of service and other personal attributes.[15]

This equality clause has the effect of modifying any less favourable contractual provisions where a woman is employed in like work with a man in the same employment. Where a woman believes that the equality clause, which the law assumes is expressly incorporated into the woman's contract of employment, has been contravened, she may make a claim to an industrial tribunal.

Following a successful claim in 1982 before the European Court of Justice that the Equal Pay Act 1970 did not fully comply with the European directive on equal pay, the British government introduced the Equal Pay (Amendment) Regulations 1983, which came into force in January 1984. These regulations widen the scope of the 1970 Act by permitting industrial tribunals to hear cases based on claims of equal pay for work of 'equal value' between the sexes at the same place of employment or closely connected place of employment. This permits, for example, a qualified female cook to make a claim that her work is of equal value to that of a skilled male craft worker at the same establishment, regardless of the fact that their jobs are very different and not covered by the same job evaluation scheme. Previous to the 1983 Regulations, tribunals could only hear claims involving 'like work' or those employed on 'the same or broadly similar work'. A female making a claim under the amended 1970 Act can obtain the assistance of the EOC.

The employer can resist an 'equal value' claim at a tribunal on the grounds that a genuine 'material factor', presented by the employer, justifies different rates of pay for men and women. Possibly acceptable 'material factors' can involve business and commercial necessities or labour market shortages justifying differences in pay between the sexes. Considerable evidence is required by a tribunal before it accepts that a genuine 'material factor' justifies differences in pay between men and women.

New rules governing the procedures to be followed by industrial tribunals when hearing cases involving the 1983 Regulations have been issued so that a tribunal can, if it feels the case justifies it, appoint an independent expert in job evaluation to measure and compare analytically the job of the female claimant with the job of the male employee with whom she is claiming equality of pay. Before the tribunal finally decides whether or not to accept the independent expert's report and conclusions the report, but not the expert, can be challenged and probed by both the claimant and the employer. The final decision is for the tribunal to make. If it finds in favour of the claimant it can make an award of equal pay which can be back-dated for two years. Appeals against tribunal decisions, on points of law only, are made to the Employment Appeal Tribunal and to the higher courts, with the right to further appeal in certain cases to the European Court of Justice under EEC law.

The Sex Discrimination Act of 1975 largely completes the legal processes aimed at removing sex discrimination in employment begun by the 1970 Equal Pay Act. It extends the prohibition on sex discrimination across the whole field of employment relationships. The 1975 Act covers: employees of all ages; employers with six or more employees; trade unions and employers' organizations; bodies awarding qualifications; the writers and publishers of job advertisements and job descriptions; contractors of outside labour; employment agencies; and crown employees. Those not covered include small firms with five or less employees, private households, the armed services, and the clergy. The 1975 Act distinguishes between direct and indirect sex discrimination. Direct discrimination occurs when an employer treats a man or woman less favourably than it treats or would treat a person of the opposite sex in the same circumstances. Indirect discrimination takes place when an employer applies a job condition equally to both sexes, but in circumstances where the proportion of one sex in the labour force which can comply with it is substantially less than the proportion of the other sex. This can happen, for instance, where an employer requires that employees should normally be of a minimum height or capable of lifting and handling certain objects or weights. Indirect discrimination also occurs when an employer treats either men or women unfavourably on the grounds of their marital or domestic circumstances.

Men and women must also be treated equally under the 1975 Act in respect of job recruitment, the advertisement of vacancies, the selection of candidates, application forms and job interviews. Once employed, men and women have to be treated equally in terms of their promotion opportunities, job transfers, job training, pension rights, age of retirement and fringe benefits. It is unlawful, for example, for an employer to refuse any of these rights on the grounds of a person's sex, or marital status. The law does not apply, however, where the police and prison services stipulate minimum height requirements, or where national security is involved.

The 1975 Act, however, does permit discrimination in favour of married couples where both are required, for example, as wardens of children's homes. The concept of positive discrimination is also established within this Act as a means of permitting certain public bodies, such as colleges of further education, to provide training facilities specifically designed for one sex if the trainees have been out of the labour market for domestic reasons. In the same way, where the work done at a place of employment has traditionally been the exclusive prerogative of one sex, positive discrimination can be exercised as a means of allowing access to the job by the other sex. Single-sex training is legally permissible, for example, where few of that sex were performing the work during the previous year. This could benefit women who want to become apprentice engineering fitters, for instance, or men who want to undertake secretarial training.

Section 7 of the Sex Discrimination Act 1975 also establishes that where sex is a 'genuine occupational qualification for the job' discrimination is lawfully permitted. The 1975 Act very carefully defines such situations. They fall into six main categories. The first is where the essential nature of the job calls for a man or woman for physiological reasons such as for authenticity in entertainment. Second, it is justified for reasons of privacy or decency as in public toilets for example. Third, discrimination is acceptable where single-sex accommodation exists and where sleeping or sanitary facilities are not provided for the other sex and it would be unreasonable to expect the employer to provide them. Fourth, discrimination is permitted in jobs in single-sex hospitals, hostels or prisons, or for people needing special care. Fifth, where jobs in welfare, education or other personal services can more effectively be provided by either a man or a woman, sex discrimination can legitimately take place without breaking the law. Finally, discrimination can occur when advertising jobs abroad, where the laws and customs of the land prevent a man or woman doing a particular job as in some Middle East countries. These exceptions do not apply, however, where the employer is already employing enough people of the same sex and they could be reasonably expected to do the job without undue inconvenience.

When either a man or a woman believes that discrimination has occurred on the grounds of sex, they can take their case to an industrial tribunal or make use of the conciliation services provided by ACAS. The EOC which was set up under the Sex Discrimination Act 1975 also carries out investigations, conducts research, provides education, reviews the legislation, and makes policy recommendations. It is also required to produce an annual report. In addition it can bring complaints to a tribunal, issue nondiscrimination notices, and ultimately obtain injunctions. The EOC also attempts conciliation and helps individuals with their cases. Furthermore, it provides advice to employers. An industrial tribunal upholding a case of sex discrimination against an employer can award compensation to the worker, and it can recommend that the employer takes the necessary steps to reduce or to obviate the discrimination at issue. Contrary to the procedures previously used in cases of unfair dismissal, it is the applicants in sex discrimination cases who are required to produce evidence that discrimination has in fact taken place. It is the employer's responsibility to refute the charge.

Race relations

Britain has acquired a substantial coloured population since the end of the Second World War and the problems of racial discrimination in the hiring of employees, working conditions, job opportunities, training and promotion have become increasingly acute. Until the Race Relations Act 1968, discriminatory practices against racial minorities could only be discouraged through moral and political condemnation. That Act has now been considerably strengthened by the Race Relations Act 1976 and the establishment of the Commission for Racial Equality (CRE). Whilst it is probable that the law can play a positive and influential role in the prevention and correction of racial discrimination in employment, racial discrimination laws – like those concerned with sex discrimination – are primarily intended to modify public attitudes and personal behaviour in this field. The 1976 Act makes it unlawful for any employer in Britain, including the self-employed, to discriminate against a person of a particular racial group on the grounds of colour, race, nationality, citizenship or ethnic orgins. The Act does not, however, make it unlawful to discriminate on grounds of religious or political belief or sexual orientation. The Act covers all employees irrespective of their age, sex, or length of service, although domestic servants in private households, partnerships of five or less, and persons and seamen recruited for employment abroad are specifically excluded from it.

The 1976 Race Relations Act, like the Sex Discrimination Act of 1975, carefully distinguishes between direct and indirect discrimination. Direct discrimination occurs when an employer treats a person on racial grounds less favourably than others in the same circumstances. This can occur, for example, by refusing to train or to promote an employee solely because of that person's colour or race. Indirect discrimination, on the other hand, occurs when an employer applies a condition of employment which adversely affects a particular person or racial group considerably more than it does persons of other racial origins. This could happen, for example, by formally testing an applicant's English language in such a way so as to discriminate indirectly against a racial minority when recruitment takes place. Such testing could result in a smaller proportion of the group passing the test than other persons or groups in the general population. Obviously, indirect discrimination is much more difficult to prove than direct discrimination.

Under the 1976 Act, employers must not discriminate on the grounds of race, colour or nationality when advertising jobs, recruiting, interviewing, selecting, training, transferring, promoting, disciplining or dismissing employees. It is unlawful, for example, to discriminate racially when establishing the terms and conditions of employment. It is also unlawful for an employer to give instructions for subordinates to discriminate racially, or to aid somebody to discriminate racially within an employing establishment. Employment agencies, for instance, must not discriminate on racial grounds in the terms that they offer in jobs or the services they provide their clients. Neither are they permitted to refuse to provide any of their services on racial grounds. Nor does the 1976 Act permit an employer to discriminate when recruiting on the grounds, for example, that it already has a high proportion of coloured employees and that it wishes to preserve a 'balanced' workforce.

Racial discrimination in employment is permitted, however, in a few very closely defined and restricted circumstances. It is allowable, for example, where a person of a particular racial group is needed for authenticity, such as in acting, modelling, or working as a waiter or waitress in an ethnic restaurant. Racial discrimination is also permissible where a certain type of community worker is required to promote the welfare of a particular racial group. It might be necessary, for instance, to appoint a West Indian to run a youth club catering largely for young people of Caribbean origin. Where an employer already has a sufficient number of employees of the specified racial group required to do the job, it must use one of them and not recruit a new employee of that race, if this can be done without undue inconvenience.

Positive or reverse racial discrimination is also permitted by employers or training bodies in certain circumstances. It is permissible, for instance, if they are providing training for a particular racial group or a nationality for the express purpose of enabling that group to take up employment in occupations or areas of employment in which it is under-represented. But it is clearly unlawful under the 1976 Act for anybody to discriminate against individuals, or to bring pressure to bear on them, for seeking to assert their statutory rights under race legislation. Once employees allege that an employer has discriminated against them on grounds of race or of colour, the employer must not victimize those persons. Indeed, the employer may be required to show an industrial tribunal that it did not discriminate against them once the allegation had been made.

Where individuals believe that they have been discriminated against by an employer on the grounds of race, colour or nationality, they may bring a case before an industrial tribunal. As in the other types of hearings determined by tribunals, ACAS first attempts to conciliate and to settle the matter to the mutual satisfaction of both parties. Complaints of discrimination need normally to be made within three months of the date of the discriminatory act. At a tribunal, the applicant may be represented by anyone of their choosing, including a representative of the CRE if that organization agrees. In cases involving direct or indirect discrimination and victimization, the applicant has in the first instance to provide sufficient evidence of the claimed discriminatory act or its circumstances. It is then for the respondent to refute this evidence. It has to be shown in the case of indirect discrimination, for example, either that the employer's action is justifiable within the meaning of the 1976 Act, or that one of the Act's exceptions apply. If the tribunal finds in favour of the applicant, it has to consider what remedies to award. The tribunal can award either an order declaring the rights of the parties, or an order requiring the respondent to pay compensation to the applicant. Alternatively, a recommendation can be made that the respondent takes a particular course of action. Any appeal on a point of law against a decision of a tribunal has to be considered by the Employment Appeal Tribunal.

In 1983 the CRE issued a code of practice aimed at eliminating racial discrimination and promoting equality of opportunity in employment. The CRE issued the code under powers given by Section 47 of the 1976 Act. Whilst the code itself is not legally enforceable, its contents can be used as evidence at tribunals which will take its recommendations into account when hearing claims of racial discrimination in employment. The code gives practical advice to employers, employees, trade unions and employment agencies, not only on how to avoid discriminatory racial practices, but also on the development of positive policies for the enforcement of equality of opportunity. The code declares it to be the responsibility of employers and trade unions to develop equal opportunity policies which are widely understood and accepted by the whole of the workforce within employing establishments.

9.5   UNION MEMBERSHIP RIGHTS

The Employment Protection (Consolidation) Act 1978 provides a statutory right for all employees to belong to an independent trade union of their choice and to take part in its activities. It also provides remedies against employers for any actions short of dismissal which they might take in order to deter or to prevent employees from becoming members of independent unions. Similar remedies are available if employers attempt to discriminate against employees for being members of, or from taking part in appropriate trade union activities. If employees who are trade unionists are dismissed, and they believe that the dismissal arose out of their trade union membership or of their activities as trade union members, they can request 'interim relief' from an industrial tribunal. This must take place within seven days of the incident, and the applicants may be awarded reinstatement or suspension on full pay until a full hearing of the complaint is held. It is, therefore, automatically unfair to dismiss employees on the grounds of their trade union membership or for taking part in appropriate trade union activities. Since the enactment of the Employment Act 1980, it is also regarded as unfair to dismiss an employee who refuses to join a union where a closed shop agreement has been negotiated.

Although the Employment Protection (Consolidation) Act 1978 retains and extends the right originally embodied in the Industrial Relations Act of 1971, which made it unlawful to dismiss or to discriminate against employees for joining, or seeking to join, a registered trade union, the same right is no longer extended to members or potential members of non-independent trade unions. The 1978 Act also seeks to prevent employers from discriminating against employees who, as lay officials of their union, seek time off work for their trade union duties and activities and for training for these purposes. These rights are embodied in Sections 27–28 of the Employment Protection (Consolidation) Act 1978. This means that in practice employers are obliged to allow time off work for shop stewards and other lay officials of independent recognized unions: to negotiate with employer representatives; to hold approved union meetings at the workplace; and to meet full time union officers in working time. Both employers and trade unionists are expected to observe the recommendations of the ACAS code of practice on time off work for trade union duties and activities.

Any employees who consider that their trade union rights have been infringed by an employer may seek a remedy through an industrial tribunal, within three months of the employer's discriminatory act. Such action can be taken by employees regardless of their length of service with an employer. When a tribunal hears cases of discrimination on grounds of trade union membership and activities, the onus of proof is on the employer to show that it has not infringed the employees's rights. If a tribunal finds the employees' complaint to be well founded, it makes a declaration to that effect. It can also award compensation to the employee to be paid by the employer, if the tribunal thinks fit.

9.6 OTHER INDIVIDUAL RIGHTS

Maternity rights

Sections 33–48 of the Employment Protection (Consolidation) Act 1978 provide female employees with the statutory rights: not to be dismissed for reasons related to pregnancy; to receive maternity payments and maternity leave; and to return to their jobs after the birth of a child if they wish, though these provisions are amended by Sections 11–13 of the Employment Act 1980. Section 13, for example, enables a pregnant employee regardless of length of service not to be unreasonably refused time off work for antenatal care and to be paid for this time off. This protection for pregnant employees is an extension of the rights given to women by the Equal Pay and Sex Discrimination Acts of 1970 and 1975. Thus a female employee with at least two years continuous employment may not be 'dismissed at any time primarily because she is pregnant or for any other reason connected with her pregnancy,'[16] and, if she is, she will normally be deemed as having been unfairly dismissed. An employer may dismiss a pregnant woman fairly, however, if her condition makes her work inadequate, or if she becomes incapable of doing the work which she was employed to do. It is fair to dismiss a pregnant woman too, if she cannot continue in her employment without contravening a statutory provision. This may occur, for example, where a female employee is exposed to radiation or to any other health hazards which could endanger her unborn child. But even where the conditions are such that fair dismissal of a pregnant woman is possible, the dismissal can still be unfair if the employer does not make every reasonable endeavour to find suitable alternative work for a pregnant employee during the period leading up to her confinement. Moreover, even if a woman is fairly dismissed whilst pregnant, she is still entitled to paid leave and to her job back. This entitlement is restricted in firms employing less than 20 persons to those pregnant employees with more than two years continuous employment.

Any pregnant woman normally working 16 hours per week or more, and with two years continuous service with her employer, is entitled to maternity payments and to maternity leave, However, the law does not create a statutory right of maternity leave for the pregnant employee. It leaves the issues to be agreed between the employer and the employee under the terms of their contract of employment. To qualify she must work till the beginning of the eleventh week before the expected birth, and she must inform her employer that her anticipated absence is because of her pregnancy. An employer cannot restrict these rights because of any views its managerial agents might hold about pregnancy, morality or marital status. If a pregnant employee works to the eleventh week before her expected confinement, she is then entitled to 11 weeks pre-maternity leave and to six weeks pay at nine-tenths of her normal pay less state maternity allowance. Employers may request employees to apply for their maternity pay and leave in writing, and they are entitled to ask them for a medical certificate providing evidence of pregnancy and of the expected date of confinement. Employers may claim a full refund for any maternity payments which they make from a central Maternity Pay Fund to which all employers contribute.

If a woman wishes to return to work after her confinement, she must inform her employer of her intention to do so in writing at least 21 days before leaving work, or as soon as it is reasonably practical to do so. She is normally expected to return to work within 29 weeks of giving birth, but a four-week extension period is permitted if adequate medical evidence is produced. This means in effect that a woman can be away from work on grounds of pregnancy, confinement, and leave after birth for a total of up to 44 weeks, during which time the employer is obliged to keep her job open for her if she wishes to return to it. Conversely, the employer can delay an employee's return by another four weeks if there are good reasons for doing this. When a woman on maternity leave returns to work, she has the right either to be given back her previous job, or to be given acceptable alternative employment. The latter is required to be a job of similar status and conditions, without any loss of employment benefits. Furthermore, if the employer engages a temporary replacement during the period that a female employee is absent on maternity leave, that person must be informed in writing that he or she will have to leave, if a suitable alternative job cannot be found when the woman on maternity leave returns to work.

The employer can ask the employee, not earlier than 49 days from the date it was given for the birth, to confirm in writing that she intends to return to work. She must give the written confirmation asked for within 14 days or as soon as it is reasonably practicable to do so. Finally, the employee must give written notification to the employer, not later than 21 days before the proposed date of return, that she intends to go back to work. If the employee does not follow these written requirements of notice carefully, she can forfeit her right to return to work.

Any female employee who thinks that her maternity rights have been infringed by an employer may apply for a remedy through an industrial tribunal. These include disputes arising over maternity pay, maternity leave, and reinstatement rights, if they are made within three months of the event. If attempts by ACAS at voluntary conciliation fail, tribunals are then empowered to award compensation to aggrieved female employees and to reinstate them where this is practicable. If a woman is made redundant during pregnancy leave, she is also entitled to redundancy payments and to any other legal rights which she has accumulated under the law.

Where an employer can satisfy a tribunal that it is not practicable to offer the employee her original job back, and that she has unreasonably refused suitable alternative work, her claim for unfair dismissal fails. Further, where an employer satisfies a tribunal that its total number of employees is five or less, and that it is not reasonably practicable to take the female employee back to her original job, or to offer her suitable alternative work, her claim for unfair dismissal also fails.

Guarantee payments

Guarantee wage payments are now available to all those employees who are on short time working or are laid off by their employers. These provisions are covered by Sections 12–18 of the Employment Protection (Consolidation) Act 1978. An employee is entitled, in certain circumstances, to guarantee payments by an employer:

> Where an employee throughout a day during any part of which he would normally be required to work in accordance with his contract of employment is not provided with work by his employer by reason of – (a) a diminution in the requirements of the employer's business for work of the kind which the employee is employed to do, or (b) any other occurrence affecting the normal working of the employer's business in relation to work of the kind which the employee is employed to do.[17]

All employees with more than four weeks continuous employment with their employer who work 16 hours a week or more, or have worked for eight hours or more per week for five years continuously, are entitled to guarantee wage payments. The main excluded categories of employee are those employed for a fixed term of three months or less to perform a specific task, and those whose contracts of employment do not stipulate regular hours of work.

Those employees who are either on short time working or are laid off are not entitled to guarantee payments if they unreasonably refuse an offer of suitable alternative work. Nor are they entitled when the short time working or lay off results from a trade dispute involving other employees of the same or an associated employer. Moreover, payment is only made in respect of each complete working day lost, and guarantee payments are not provided in respect of a day in which some work is provided – even if that work is provided outside normal working hours. Furthermore, there is a maximum entitlement of guarantee payments for five working days per quarter, and these are not cumulative. The calculation of the day's pay depends upon the payment laid down in the individual's contract of employment. It is subject to an upper limit which the Secretary of State for Employment reviews annually. Where employees are covered by a collective agreement which lays down guarantee payments at least as favourable as those of the Act, the parties may jointly apply to the Secretary of State for an exemption from the requirements of the Act. As with the other individual provisions under the 1978 Act, employees not receiving guarantee payments to which they believe they are entitled may bring a case, within three months, to an industrial tribunal. If the complaint is upheld, the tribunal can order the employer to make the appropriate payments.

Medical suspension payments

Employees covered by special occupational health and safety regulations are entitled to receive regular payments from their employer whilst suspended from normal work for medical reasons arising directly from the nature of their work. Sections 19–22 of the Employment Protection (Consolidation) Act 1978 require employers to make weekly payments to any of their employees who are suspended on medical grounds because of the nature of the work which they do. Schedule 1 of the 1978 Act, as amended by the Secretary of State when new occupational hazards are confirmed, lists those compulsory health regulations with which employers are obliged to comply. The Control of Lead at Work Regulations 1980, for example, require employers involved in the manufacture of lead products to suspend employees on medical advice where their health is jeopardized. Suspension is also necessary where illness has already been caused by exposure to lead manufacturing processes. In this and similar cases, employers are obliged to suspend the employees concerned and to provide them with payment for a statutory maximum period of 26 weeks from the day of their suspension.

> It is most important to realise that this right to a certain period of payment of wages does not apply to ordinary absence because of incapacity as a result of sickness. Indeed, it does not apply to any period of absence, even upon a compulsory suspension where the employee is actually incapable of work by reason of sickness or injury.[18]

The right to receive payment during medical suspension applies to all employees with more than four weeks service, providing that they work 16 hours or more per week, or eight hours or more per week with five years continuous service. It operates in those industries and occupations covered by the health orders in Schedule 1 of the 1978 Employment Protection (Consolidation) Act, and to those codes of practice issued under Schedule 16 of the Health and Safety at Work etc. Act 1974. Where an employer dismisses a suspended employee, an award of unfair dismissal can almost certainly be made by an industrial tribunal. If dismissal takes place during medical suspension, a claim of unfair dismissal can be brought by an employee with four weeks service instead of the customary two year qualifying period. Where an employer offers a suspended employee who is capable of doing other work suitable alternative employment, the employee is obliged to accept it. This is provided that a doctor confirms that the employee is medically fit to perform that work. If the employee unreasonably refuses such an offer of suitable alternative employment, he or she may lose entitlement to medical suspension payments. In the case of dismissal for refusing suitable alternative work during medical suspension, a tribunal may decide that fair dismissal has occurred when taking all the factors into account.

Complaints by employees of non-compliance by employers with the medical suspension requirements of the 1978 Act must normally be made within three months of the day of suspension. Where a case is upheld, the tribunal can order the employer to make the necessary payments to the employee. Those employers appointing temporary replacements to do the work of suspended employees must tell the temporary employees that their employment will be terminated on the return to work of the suspended workers. Furthermore, the number of employees currently covered by the health orders, codes of practice and the medical suspension clauses involves only a small minority of the total labour force. But as more health hazards are likely to be identified, the lists of occupations covered by medical suspension orders by the Health and Safety Commission could grow appreciably.

Employer insolvency

If an employer becomes bankrupt or goes into receivership, Sections 121–123 of the Employment Protection (Consolidation) Act 1978, as amended by Schedule 3 of the Employment Act 1982, provide for the payment of those sums owed to the employees by the insolvent firm. The debts which employees can recover include arrears of payments up to a maximum fixed by the Secretary of State for Employment for a period not exceeding eight weeks. These payments include wages, salaries, commissions, guarantee and medical suspension benefits provided under the Employment Protection (Consolidation) Act 1978, remuneration for time off work for trade union duties, and remuneration under a redundancy protective award. Other insolvency entitlements are holiday pay, payment in lieu of notice, and any payments outstanding from a basic award for unfair dismissal made by an industrial tribunal. All employees, including part timers, are entitled to insolvency payments irrespective of their length of continuous service. These rights, however, do not extend to the wife or husband of an employer. Thus the monies owed to employees in the event of their employer's insolvency 'will be treated in the same way as unpaid wages and salaries under existing law – as preferential debts which must be paid in priority to other claims.'[19]

The Employment Protection (Consolidation) Act of 1978 also provides that where employees are covered by an occupational pension scheme, and where due to insolvency the employer has not paid its contributions, these can be paid by order of the Secretary of State for Employment up to certain maxima. Where debts cannot be obtained from a trustee or liquidator, the Secretary of State can also authorize payment from the Redundancy Payments Fund. Those employees wishing to make a claim for debts arising out of their employers' insolvency have to apply to the receiver or liquidator. If payment is not forthcoming after the claim has been made, former employees can refer the matter to the Secretary of State for Employment. If the individuals are not satisfied with the award they receive, they 'may bring a claim against the Secretary of State before an Industrial Tribunal in relation to payments owing [them].'[20]

Time off work for union and public duties

The Employment Protection (Consolidation) Act 1978 establishes five rights for employees to 'reasonable' time off work, time off with pay for industrial relations duties connected with the employer; time off with pay for appropriate industrial relations and health and safety training; time off with pay to look for work in a redundancy situation; time off without pay for certain trade union activities; and time off without pay for public duties. The 1978 Act itself does not give detailed guidance on how the conditions for time off work for employees should apply. It leaves that to a code of practice on time off for trade union duties and activities produced by ACAS in 1977. Although the code provides essential guidance for trade unionists, employers, and industrial tribunals on the time off to which trade unionists are entitled to undertake trade union work, it does not cover time off work either for public duties or to look for jobs in redundancy situations.

Section 27 of the Employment Protection (Consolidation) Act 1978 requires an employer to permit those employees who are officials of independent recognized trade unions to have reasonable paid time off work to carry out appropriate industrial relations duties with their employer or to undergo training which is relevant to these duties. Such training has to be approved by the Trades Union Congress or by the independent trade union of which they are officials. Where these conditions are met and time off is taken, employers are required by the 1978 Act to pay normal earnings to hourly-paid or salaried workers and average earnings to those employees who are paid by results. In practical terms this means that employers are obliged to give shop stewards reasonable time off with pay to deal with industrial relations matters at their place of work and to attend union-approved shop steward and health and safety training courses.

The ACAS code stresses that the basic aim of the present legislation which enables trade unionists to claim time off work is 'to aid and improve the conduct of industrial relations.'[21] It goes on to qualify the right to time off work by stating that trade unions should be aware of the wide variety of circumstances and the different operational requirements to be taken into account in any arrangements for dealing with time off. For example, 'some employers face particular exigencies of production, services and safety in process industries' and 'proper regard will therefore have to be paid to particular operational requirements and obligations of different industries and services.'[22]

It appears, then, that employers can legitimately refuse time off if they feel that it is justified by 'operational requirements'. However, where sufficient notice of time off is given by a trade union, employers need to provide substitute working arrangements in order to release individuals claiming their rights. Members of independent recognized trade unions can also claim time off to take part in the internal activities of their trade unions, such as when attending regional meetings, their national executive, or their union conferences. But the 1978 Act does not require employers to pay such employees for the time they take off. Employers can also refuse time off work for activities which they believe amount to industrial action. But where 'an official is not taking part in industrial action but represents members involved, normal arrangements for time off with pay for the official should apply.'[23] Where employees are members or officials of an independent trade union recognized by the employer and are refused time off work or pay in appropriate circumstances, they can seek a remedy from an industrial tribunal. If such a complaint is not resolved by conciliation through ACAS, the industrial tribunal takes the code of practice into account when hearing the case and making its decision.

The Employment Protection (Consolidation) Act 1978 also provides those persons undertaking certain public duties and those under notice of redundancy to be given time off work which is 'reasonable in all the circumstances'. The public duties relate to those employees who are justices of the peace, members of local government authorities, members of statutory tribunals, members of regional or district health authorities, members of educational governing bodies, and members of water authorities. Employers are obliged to give the holders of such public offices 'reasonable' time off work. There is no legal obligation to pay them, as many of these offices qualify for payment allowances anyway. Where employees are under notice of redundancy, the Employment Protection (Consolidation) Act 1978 gives them the statutory right to reasonable time off with pay during working hours to look for alternative employment. Whilst the act does not stipulate what 'reasonable' time off during notice of redundancy is, an industrial tribunal is only permitted to award a maximum of two-fifths of an employee's weekly pay if a complaint is successfully made to a tribunal.

Rehabilitation of offenders

One of the main objectives of the Rehabilitation of Offenders Act 1974 is to enable certain people who have been convicted of criminal offences to conceal their records when applying for jobs. The aim is to rehabilitate offenders into society by assisting them to obtain jobs whilst at the same time protecting the general public. Before past offenders can claim the protection of the 1974 Act their convictions must be 'spent' –

meaning that a legally determined period free of any further convictions must have followed their original conviction. In other words they must have 'gone straight' for periods closely defined by the Act. If persons with spent convictions apply for jobs the 1974 Act entitles them not to answer any question about previous convictions or to deny that they have ever been convicted. Moreover, if an employer becomes aware that persons in their employment have a spent conviction and dismiss them for failure to disclose a criminal record at the appointment interview, such a dismissal could well be found unfair by an industrial tribunal. Not all jobs and occupations, however, are covered by the Act.

Convictions of life imprisonment or for periods in excess of 30 months can never be spent and are not therefore covered by the 1974 Act. Periods of imprisonment of more than six months, but less than or up to 30 months, are not spent until a conviction-free period of 10 years has passed. A period of imprisonment not exceeding six months requires a conviction-free period of seven years and a fine or other sentence five years. There are also many occupations and employments excluded from the 1974 Act, where rejection for employment or dismissal for failing to disclose a conviction are deemed to be reasonable by employers. The exceptions are specifically listed by Order and include Crown employment, the Post Office, the medical profession, the legal profession, the police, the probation services, teachers, social work, work with people below the age of eighteen and employment in nursing homes.

Statutory Sick Pay

Before the introduction of the Statutory Sick Pay (SSP) scheme in 1983, as amended by the Social Security Act 1985, employees claimed national insurance sick pay from the Department of Health and Society Security (DHSS) on an individual basis which did not directly involve the employer. The SSP scheme transfers a great deal of the responsibility for and the cost of administering and making sick payments for absence from work from the state to the employer, and permits substantial financial savings for the state in terms of money and numbers of civil servants. The SSP scheme also substantially reduces the burden on general practitioners by permitting employees to write their own sick notes – known as self certification – which gives the employer their reasons for being absent from work.

SSP is available to all employees except those on very low earnings, casual workers, those over pensionable age, women receiving maternity benefits and those taking industrial action. Sick pay is not provided for the first three days of sickness which are known as 'waiting days'. Benefit only starts after the fourth qualifying day. It is only after the fourth day of sickness that a 'period of incapacity to work' and the right to payment are established. Payment can only be made for normal working days or 'qualifying days'. The qualifying days have to be clearly designated working days and part of the individual's contract of employment. For the vast majority, but by no means all of the national labour force, the qualifying days are Monday to Friday inclusive. Where there are two or more linked periods of incapacity within a 56 day period – including Saturdays and Sundays – exceeding three days, entitlement to sick pay starts on the fourth day.

When employees are sick they must inform the employer without delay and in accordance with the employer's rules. If they do not do so the employer is entitled to withhold SSP. They must produce, as soon as is practicable, written reasons for their illness. This is generally known as self certification. Only after a period of incapacity for work of seven days do employees have to obtain and produce evidence of sickness from a doctor or any other approved practitioner such as osteopaths and acupuncturists. In the case of illness lasting less than seven days, it is the employer's responsibility to decide whether or not to accept the self certification reasons given by the employee. If, however, the employer rejects or disbelieves the reasons provided by the employee and does not therefore provide sick pay, the employee has the right to appeal against the employer's decision to a DHSS insurance official. In the case of sickness lasting for more than seven days the employer can require the employee to produce further doctor's sick notes at reasonable intervals. The employer then continues to provide sick pay up to a maximum of 28 weeks. After 28 weeks the employee is transferred to the DHSS state sickness scheme which then provides the sick payments.

The rate of sick pay depends upon the employee's average gross weekly earnings but an upper and lower limit, which is reviewed annually, is set by the Secretary of State. The daily rate of SSP is calculated by dividing the weekly rate by the number of qualifying days in the relevant week. The SSP scheme lays a firm obligation on employers to keep adequate records for at least three years of all sickness and sick payments for inspection by the DHSS. The employer is responsible for making all sick payments to employees up to a maximum of 28 weeks, in any one tax year. The employer is entitled to recoup the payments by making deductions each month from the national insurance payments made by both employer and the employees to the Inland Revenue. The SSP scheme can operate alongside an employer financed sick pay scheme but where this is the case it is usually the practice for the agreed daily or weekly sick pay to include the SSP payment.

Disabled persons

The Disabled Persons (Employment) Act 1944, as amended by the 1958 Act, establishes a register of disabled people which is kept by the Manpower Services Commission (MSC). The MSC Disablement Resettlement Officers issue certificates of registration to disabled persons which they can show to employers when seeking work. The 1944 Act requires employers with 20 or more workers to employ a quota of disabled people which is set at three per cent of their total workforce. It is not, however, an offence under the Act to be below the three per cent quota, but when employers are in that position they should not engage anyone other than a registered disabled person without first obtaining a permit to do so from the local job centre. In practice, however, the requirements of the 1944 Act are either ignored or disregarded on an extremely wide scale and very few employers are ever prosecuted or fined.

The 1944 Act also reserves certain designated occupations for disabled persons such as car park attendants and electric lift attendants. The employer must also keep careful records of all the disabled persons employed for inspection by the relevant officials of the MSC. Committees for the Employment of Disabled People were established at local level by the 1944 Act to advise the Secretary of State on matters relating to the employment of disabled persons. They also encouraged local employers to be more conscious of their responsibilities towards the disabled and to fulfil the three per cent quota. The Companies (Directors' Report) (Employment of Disabled Persons) Regulations 1980 require the annual directors' report of firms employing more than 250 people to contain a statement of their policy on the employment, training, career development and promotion of disabled employees. These Regulations, whilst applying to private companies, also impose similar obligations on public sector employers.

Largely because of the ineffectiveness of existing legislation and regulations aimed at protecting and furthering the interests of disabled employees and unemployed disabled persons, in 1984 at the Government's request the MSC produced a code of practice on the employment of disabled people. The code, which was supported by the MSC, the Confederation of British Industry, and the Trades Union Congress, urges employers in both the public and private sectors to accept their social responsibilities for disabled employees and sets out a list of good practices and policies for employing them. Whilst observance of the code is voluntary, it is hoped that employers, trade unions and others will use it as a guide or model when reshaping their policies towards the disabled.

Employee personal data

The Data Protection Act 1984 enables employees to obtain access to personal data held by their employer on computers. The 1984 Act applies only to computer data, however, and not to data stored in written form. The requirements of the 1984 Act are being brought into force by stages and will be fully implemented in 1987. The Act entitles an employee, or data subject, to be informed by the employer, or data user, of any personal data held on computer. The data subject must make a reasoned and reasonable request for the data which must be given in an intelligible and understandable form. The data subject must make the request in writing and where appropriate pay a statutory fee.

From 1987, the data user can only refuse to supply the data subject with a copy of any personal data where the request is not made in writing, the recognized fee is not paid, there is no clear evidence of the applicant's identity, it involves disclosing information about other people without their permission, or the data subject makes too many requests for information. Where these conditions are met, the information must be supplied within 40 days. The data user does not, however, have to explain why the data is being held on computer, or what use it is intended to make of it. All it has to do is to supply a copy of the data information to the data subject.

All computer data users are required by the 1984 Act to register with the Data Protection Registrar and provide the Registrar with the following information: the name and address of the data user; a description of any person(s) it is intended to disclose the personal data to; a description of the data it is intended to hold and for what purposes; a description of the sources it is intended to obtain the personal data information from; and the names of any countries outside the UK it is intended to transfer the data to. From 1987, data users are required to observe a number of basic principles: personal data will only be used for specified and lawful purposes; the data will only be obtained fairly and lawfully; adequate and not excessive data will only be held; and the data user will protect personal data against unauthorized access, alteration, accidental loss or destruction. Those data users failing to observe these principles will be refused registration, deregistered or served with enforcement notices.

Certain types of personal data are exempt from registration or disclosure to data subjects. They include data on how employee pay or pensions are calculated or how and for what reasons deductions from pay are made. Data users can, however, be required to given personal data on employees for use in medical research into occupational health and injury. Users of personal data are also excluded under the Act from disclosing data which involves national security or the prevention or detection of crime. Where a data user, such as an employer, refuses a data subject, such as an employee, access to personal data, the employee can seek a court order to obtain the information. And where a data subject suffers damage or distress due to the use of personal data which is misleading or inaccurate, or where the data has been disclosed or destroyed without proper authorization, the individual may apply to the courts for compensation.

9.7 SUMMARY

In this chapter we examine the ways in which employment legislation regulates the individual relationship between employer and employee. These embrace a range of statutory legal rights including, for example, the right of employees not to be unfairly dismissed and the right of female employees to receive maternity payments and maternity leave from their employers. We also show how individual employees can bring cases before industrial tribunals if such rights are infringed by their employers. In this chapter, we only deal with the rights of individuals under law, since we consider that there are important legal, practical and analytic distinctions between the employment rights of individuals and the collective aspects of labour law dealing with trade unions, the right to strike, and collective bargaining which are described in the next chapter.

In examining the nature of the individual contractual relationship between employers and employees, and the ways in which it has developed, we conclude that the relationship is becoming increasingly regulated by statute. While the common law duties on employers and employees have exercised considerable sway over the thinking and writings of lawyers and of some academic specialists in the field, they are not a very central influence on the day-to-day activities of employers, employees and their representative organizations. In practical terms, the individual labour law enacted since the 1970s has had a great deal more influence over the formalization and regulation of contractual relations between employers and their individual employees than the common law of contract ever did.

There is also convincing evidence to suggest that the importance placed by industrial tribunals upon the written statement setting out the main elements within the contract of employment is leading both employers and trade unions to take the written statement more seriously than hitherto. As our concern here is primarily with the practice of industrial relations rather than with its abstract legal concepts, we have not considered the contract of employment in its wider contexts, although we would concede that it embodies many complex elements. These include the common law duties of the parties and all the personal and collective agreements made between employers and employees and their representatives. However, we accept from a strictly legal, rather than from an empirical industrial relations viewpoint, that the contract of employment comprises all these elements. But in practice employers and employees do not normally see the contract of employment in this legalistic way.

In examining the law of unfair dismissal, we take the view that this is probably the most important of the new statutory rights provided for employees. It has probably been responsible for major improvements in certain employment practices, such as in the recruitment and appointment of employees and in the development of equitable displinary rules and procedures at work. Where employers observe the ACAS code on disciplinary practices and procedures, and where they behave reasonably in disciplining and dismissing offending employees, there is little likelihood of decisions being made against them by industrial tribunals. But, contrary to much popular opinion, there is little evidence to indicate that employers observing sensible standards of recruitment, training and staff discipline are unduly concerned about unsatisfactory employees. Similarly, if an approved disciplinary procedure is followed, employers can still dismiss unsatisfactory or incompetent employees who are in clear breach of their contracts of employment. Conversely, the law of unfair dismissal gives some legal protection to those non-unionized employees likely to be victimized by incompetent or vindictive employers.

In the section on redundancy, we emphasize the purposes of the legislation as being not only to give employees a 'property right' in their jobs, but also to encourage a level of labour mobility within the economy consistent with rapid technological and industrial change. As in the law of unfair dismissal, considerable emphasis is placed on the expectation that employers will behave reasonably when considering redundancies, and that they will make every effort to offer those concerned suitable alternative work where possible. Particular attention needs to be given to the obligations laid upon employers by the Employment Protection Act 1975. Under this Act, employers are required to notify independent recognized unions and the Department of Employment of intended redundancies involving more than 10 employees. Employers are also expected to consult with recognized independent unions over those to be made redundant and how the process of redundancy will be conducted.

Although average weekly earnings of women as a proportion of men's earnings rose from about 55 per cent in 1970 to about two-thirds of men's earnings by the early 1980s, the pay gap between them has continued to remain fairly large. Much depends on the success of the legislation in changing public and personal attitudes towards discrimination and in moderating people's prejudices. In this respect, the education work both of the EOC and of the CRE has a vital role to play. It is also not unreasonable to conclude that the legal rights of trade unionists to be neither dismissed nor discriminated against on the grounds of their union activities is making the victimization of trade unionists less likely but not a totally rare occurrence.

Finally, in examining other individual legal rights at work – including maternity rights, guarantee payments, medical supervision, insolvency of an employer, time off work for trade union and public duties, the rehabilitation of offenders, the employment rights of disabled persons, the statutory sick pay scheme and access by employees to personal computer data – we suggest that these are not likely to be seen by employers and trade unions as being so vital to employment protection as the unfair dismissal, redundancy payments and discrimination provisions. However, the likely financial costs for employers in advancing these rights in practice should not be underestimated.

9.8 REFERENCES

1. O. Kahn-Freund, *Labour and the Law*, Stevens, London, 1977, p. 10.
2. Employment Protection (Consolidation) Act 1978, c. 44, s. 153(1).
3. Incomes Data Services, *Employment Contracts*, IDS London, 1976, p. 7.
4. P. O'Higgins, *Workers' Rights*, Arrow Books, London, 1976, p. 30.
5. IDS, *op. cit.*, p. 65.
6. R.W. Rideout, *Principles of Labour Law*, Sweet and Maxwell, London, 1976, p. 116.
7. Employment Protection (Consolidation) Act 1978, c. 44, s. 65 (2)(d).
8. Advisory Conciliation and Arbitration Service, *Code of Practice. Disciplinary practice and procedures in employment*, HMSO, London, 1977, p. 1.
9. Employment Protection (Consolidation) Act 1978, c. 44, s. 57(2).
10. *Ibid.*, s. 57(1).
11. *Wynes v Southrepps Hall Broiler Farm Ltd.*, (1968), quoted in Rideout, *op. cit.*, p. 176.
12. Rideout, *op. cit.*, p. 205.
13. Kahn-Freund, *op. cit.*, p. 156.
14. Equal Pay Act 1970, c. 41, s. 6(1)(2).
15. Rideout, *op. cit.*, p. 219.
16. *Ibid.*, p. 109.
17. Employment Protection (Consolidation) Act, c. 44, s. 12(1).
18. Rideout, *op. cit.*, p. 107.
19. M. Rubinstein, *A Practical Guide to the Employment Protection Act*, Institute of Personnel Management, London, 1975, p. 47.
20. *Ibid.*, p. 48.
21. Advisory Conciliation and Arbitration Service, *Code of Practice 3. Time off for trade union duties and activities*, HMSO, London, 1977, p. 3.
22. *Ibid.*, p. 3.
23. *Ibid.*, p. 8.

10

Collective Labour Law

The law as a means of regulating industrial relations between employers and unions, unions and their members and unions and the community in a plural society like Britain has only a limited use. In our opinion, it can only attempt to achieve a better balance of power between the parties and should recognize that conflict between their representatives in a market economy is endemic. According to Kahn-Freund:

> The law seeks to restrain the command power of management. How far it succeeds in doing so depends on the extent to which the workers are organised. The law also seeks to restrain the power of the unions. How far it can do so depends on the attitude of the employers.[1]

Moreover, 'any approach to the relations between management and labour is fruitless unless the divergency of their interests is plainly recognised and articulated.'[2] In recent years, however, the law regulating trade unions, collective bargaining and trade disputes, for example, has become more complex and wide-ranging. It is these aspects of the law which are explored here.

10.1   TRADE UNIONS AND THE LAW

Union membership

Internationally it is now widely accepted that employees should be given the right to join free trade unions and to take part in union activities as a fundamental human freedom. This has been embodied in the Universal Declaration of Human Rights, is a Convention of the International Labour Organization, and is in the European Social Charter of the Council of Europe, all of which are acknowledged by Britain. It is one thing to give and to recognize a human freedom in a negative sense by approving a statement of principle. It is quite another matter to ensure that an abstract freedom becomes a reality by providing positive legal guarantees or rights which prevent employers from obstructing their employees from becoming trade union members. Conversely, many countries protect the right of individual employees not to be trade union members. This principle is now incorporated in British labour law in the Employment Act 1982.

In Britain, the struggle to obtain the legal right to organize and join trade unions was long and bitter. The repeal of the Combination Acts in 1824, for instance, whilst making trade unions no longer criminal associations, did not remove the threat that certain of their activities could be construed as criminal conspiracies. Such criminal activities included demanding wage increases and calling and supporting strikes. This uneasy and uncertain state of the law continued until the Conspiracy and Protection of Property Act 1875. Although this statute removed the threat of criminal liability from the act of trade union organization and from certain actions of their members, such as striking, it continued to leave the unions open to possible claims for civil damages from employers. Civil liability for certain torts by trade unionists 'in contemplation or furtherance of a trade dispute' was not finally removed until the Trade Disputes Act 1906.

Although the 1875 and 1906 Acts became the cornerstones of the legal rights of trade unions until the Industrial Relations Act 1971, they only conferred a set of freedoms on trade unionists. There was little that workers could do if their employers sought to dismiss or to victimize them for being members of unions. Neither were they protected if their employers required them to sign a document as a condition of employment stating that they would not become trade union members. It was little use appealing to the law for enforcement of a human freedom, since the courts only normally enforce specific positive rights contained in Parliamentary statutes and common law. Trade unions, therefore, did not look to the law for the protection of what is now internationally recognized as a basic human right. They preferred, instead, strong organization and militant industrial action to achieve their ends. As a result, the traditional trade union attitude towards the law and the courts has been one of hostility and intense suspicion and continues to be the case today.

Because of dissatisfaction with the so-called freedom to join trade unions, some people see the law as an alternative method to ensure positive guarantees of trade union membership and the right of their members to participate in union activities. Legislation introducing the right of employees not to be prevented or deterred from joining a trade union and, where appropriate, from taking part in trade union activities was established in Sections 23 and 58 of the Employment Protection (Consolidation) Act 1978. These rights have now been modified by the Employment Acts 1980 and 1982, where the right to belong or not to belong to a trade union in a closed shop situation is dealt with at law. Similarly, the right of trade unionists to time off work to take part in appropriate trade union activities and to receive relevant training are protected by Section 28 of the 1978 Act.

Trade unionists can exercise these legal rights by applying to an industrial tribunal for a remedy if their employer dismisses them, or takes action short of dismissal, on the grounds of their membership of a trade union or of their legitimate activities connected with it. The law however:

> does nothing to protect an applicant for a job against anti-union discrimination, nothing to prevent an employer from systematically rejecting union members, or, more significant, union members known to be "active", nothing to counteract blacklists.[3]

In short, present legislation only protects those already in employment and not those seeking employment, with the exception of those discriminated against on the grounds of sex or of race.

It is often argued that the positive right to trade union membership should be matched by a reverse right not to be a member of a trade union. This was first embodied in the 1971 Act but it was not retained in either the Trade Union and Labour Relations Act 1974, or the Employment Protection Act 1975, or the Employment Protection (Consolidation) Act 1978. The Trade Union and Labour Relations (Amendment) Act 1976, however, clearly established that employees could be fairly dismissed in closed shop situations, and that they would be unlikely to receive a remedy if they brought a case of unfair dismissal before an industrial tribunal. The position has now been reversed by the Employment Acts of 1980 and 1982. The Employment Act 1980 amends the Employment Protection (Consolidation) Act 1978, so that, short of dismissal, an employer cannot compel employees to join a trade union against their will. The Employment Act 1982 further strengthens the right of employees not to join a trade union by equating at law the negative right not to join a union with the positive right to join. The case for this change was the decision of the European Court of Human Rights in 1981. The dismissal by British Rail of three employees who refused to join a closed shop was deemed in contravention of Article 11 of the European Convention which contains the right to free association and to join a union.

Equating the right to join a trade union with the right not to join has been the subject of much legal, moral and political controversy. Those supporting the two rights as necessarily equal and opposite ones argue, in terms of individual liberties, that the right to join a union must be logically and morally matched by the right not to join. One without the other is perverse. On the other hand, those who support the legal right of employees to join the union of their choice object to the legal right not to join on the grounds that such legislation is really aimed at weakening trade unions and their collective bargaining role. They also see it as further evidence that the law and judges attach undue emphasis to individual employee rights at the cost of the collective rights of employees as represented by trade unions. 'In a collective bargaining system based on the single channel of trade union representation, the legal right to dissociate may be regarded as the equivalent of a right to disorganise the union.'[4]

Union legal status

A great deal of legal interest has centred on the statutory definition of a trade union and on the legal concept of the contract of employment, although in day-to-day industrial relations neither appears to be of any great practical significance. They merely reflect the lawyer's understandable search for conciseness and legal definition which usually play little tangible part in real life industrial relations. The Trade Union Act 1913, in largely following the Trade Union Act of 1871, defined a trade union in law as comprising:

> any combination, temporary or permanent, under the constitution of which the *principal objects* are: *the regulation of the relations between workmen and workmen, masters and workmen, or masters and masters, or the imposing of restrictive conditions on the conduct of any trade union or business.*[5]

The Trade Union and Labour Relations Act 1974 now defines a trade union as any organization which

> consists wholly or mainly of workers of one or more descriptions and is an organisation whose principal purposes include the regulation of relations between workers of that description or those descriptions and employers or employers' associations.[6]

Since the legal definition of a trade union has changed little during more than a century of profound political and industrial change, it can be safely assumed that the real importance of its statutory definition lies in the abstract corporate personality which it confers upon them. In other words, it is a:

> technical device of the law to ensure that a body of individuals can, as an entity, enter into contracts, own property, be liable in contract and tort, sue and be sued in court, be prosecuted for an offence, and be subject to the enforcement of judgements. Whether these practical results are achieved through the techniques of corporate personality or through some other technique is a matter devoid of general interest.[7]

The 1906 and 1974 Acts made it clear, beyond all reasonable doubt, that unions could not be sued as corporate bodies. The 1982 Act, however, partially removes this immunity for liability in tort, making it possible for unions to be sued in their own name.

Of much greater practical importance than any formal legal definition of trade unions and their status are: the requirements they must fulfil to become certificated unions under statute law; and, secondly, their legal obligations to produce annual returns and financial accounts. Trade union registration was first introduced by the Trade Union Act 1871. Under that Act, registration was wholly voluntary and although registration provided very few legal advantages, most unions registered. All the Registrar of Friendly Societies required was a copy of the union rule book and its annual financial returns. The Industrial Relations Act 1971 radically changed the system of registration by making it a necessary condition for unions wishing to use the legal procedures provided by the 1971 Act. Those unions which did not register under this Act lost their entitlement to tax relief on their investment income. The Trade Union and Labour Relations Act 1974 abolishes the method of registration established by the 1971 Act. It requires the Certification Officer to grant certificates of independence only to those trade unions which can demonstrate that they are independent of the control and influence of the employers with which they deal. 'The certificate is conclusive evidence of the independence of the union.'[8]

The Trade Union and Labour Relations Act 1974 also requires every trade union within the definition of the Act to send the Certification Officer details of its annual returns and internal affairs specified in Schedule 2 of the Act. These include: its revenue accounts; balance sheets; current rules; superannuation accounts; and the auditors' report. Trade unions are also required to keep proper accounts and to establish a satisfactory system of control over income, expenditure, receipts and remittances. These detailed financial requirements have probably helped to improve the methods of internal accounting and financial control used by many trade unions. The accounts of all certificated trade unions can now be seen by any member of the public on request.

Whilst positive legal rights now prevent employers from obstructing or compelling employees who wish to join or not to join independent trade unions, corresponding legal rights for those persons refused admittance to a trade union do not exist. Trade unions, like all other voluntary associations, are free to admit or to exclude anyone as long as they keep within their rules governing membership applications. They are not free from legal constraint, however, when disciplining or expelling members. Here they must act within the bounds of the rule book and they must observe the principles of 'natural justice'. Members of a union, in short, possess a 'contract of association' with their fellow members, which can be enforced though the civil courts, and they can only be legitimately disciplined or expelled for an offence specified in the rule book. This can only be done after the member's defence has been heard and all requests for appeals have been considered within the union.

The Trades Union Congress (TUC) requires all affiliated unions to meet certain agreed standards for their rule books in general, and for their disciplinary and expulsion rules in particular. Where an individual member feels that the rule book has been ignored, flouted or misinterpreted, he or she can apply to the civil courts for legal redress. The TUC has also established an Independent Review Body. This hears claims from individual members if they believe that they have been unfairly disciplined or threatened with expulsion by their union in violation of natural justice or the requirements of the rule book. Because most unions have what appears to be satisfactory internal appeals systems, the Independent Review Body hears only a comparatively small number of appeals. Most of these involve membership expulsions in closed shop situations resulting in loss of employment as well as loss of union membership.

Where legal redress is sought, the law protects the democratic rights of trade unionists within their unions. It is through insisting on a strict observance of the union's own rules and the elementary rules of decency which bear the ancient name of 'natural justice' that the courts can and do make up for the lack of a statutory guarantee of an equal opportunity to participate in the making of union decisions.[9]

This means in practice that the courts will uphold the right of individual trade union members: first, to be nominated to stand for all elected union offices; second, to take part in union elections; third, to see that election rules and procedures are adhered to; and fourth, to take part in the process of democratic policy formation within their union. As far as the internal affairs of trade unions are concerned, it is the duty of the law and the courts to uphold the independence and autonomy of trade unions and to defend, on appeal, their members' internal rights. This is done by enforcing the unions' own rule books, the principles of natural justice, and their internal democratic processes through due legal process.

The number of British trade unions has declined from over 1 000 at the turn of the century to about 400 by the mid 1980s. Whilst the decline in the number of trade unions can be partially explained by the extinction of many small trade unions, it is probable that a main reason for their reduction in numbers can be accounted for by amalgamation and mergers. The Trade Union Amendment Act 1876, for example, required the assent of at least two-thirds of the members of each union before amalgamation could take place. The Trade Union (Amalgamation) Act 1917 reduced this by requiring:

> that at least 50 per cent of those entitled to vote should do so and that the votes of those in favour should exceed by at least 20 per cent the votes of those against. Initially this easing of the requirement had a marked effect and a considerable number of smaller unions were absorbed.[10]

This Act probably assisted the creation of the Transport and General Workers Union and other important mergers in the early 1920s.

The Trade Union (Amalgamations etc.) Act 1964 reduced the voting requirement of the 1917 Act still further to a simple majority of those voting in each union. This Act has enabled many more mergers to take place in recent years. Most unions had previously experienced considerable difficulties in getting 50 per cent of their members to vote on amalgamation proposals. Currently, the Certification Officer is responsible for the accuracy and acceptability of amalgamation proposals and for hearing objections and complaints concerning the conduct of ballots. Unions which do not accept his decisions may appeal on a point of law to the Employment Appeal Tribunal. When an amalgamation is satisfactorily completed the Certification Officer registers it.

10.2   TRADE DISPUTES AND LEGAL IMMUNITIES

It is now generally accepted that the freedom of all but a very small minority of employees to withdraw their labour, either as individuals or as members of organized groups, is not only a fundamental human freedom but also an essential condition for the existence of effective collective bargaining. As Lord Wright said in the famous *Crofter* case in 1942:

> Where the right of labour is concerned . . . the rights of the employer are conditioned by the rights of the men to give or withhold their services. The right of workmen to strike is an essential element in the principle of collective bargaining.[11]

If this legal freedom is accepted, it has to be conferred by Parliament, for if the workers could not in the last resort collectively refuse to work, they could not bargain collectively. 'The power of management to shut down the plant (which is inherent in the right of property) would not bet matched by a corresponding power on the side of labour.'[12]

Only totalitarian societies forbid the use of strikes or make striking a criminal offence. Most Western parliamentary democracies accept that the imposition of criminal sanctions, as distinct from civil sanctions, on strikers would violate the European Social Charter. This, however, does not prevent the use either of 'cooling off' periods or 'no strike' clauses in collective agreements. It is also clear that because the freedom to strike is conferred by the law as a basic democratic freedom, it does not follow that all strikes are morally defensible. Indeed, public opinion might be outraged at the use of the strike weapon in certain circumstances where, for example, life or property is deliberately endangered. It is the task of politicians, trade unions, employers' associations and public opinion to establish a social climate and a legal framework of industrial relations which, whilst retaining the freedom to strike, reduces such courses of action to a minimum.

Since the law has not generally proved to be an effective means of reducing strikes, legislation designed to promote good industrial relations practices has been enacted so as to facilitate the activities of the Advisory Conciliation and Arbitration Service (ACAS) and its codes of practice. Furthermore, whilst the freedom to strike is extended to all employees, other than the police, certain civil servants and the crews of ships on the high seas, strikes are often strongly discouraged by the government and public opinion where they obviously damage either the social life of the community or the vital economic performance of the nation.

> Industrial stoppages cause losses to the economy, and hardship to men and women. Everyone, except those on the lunatic fringe, wants to reduce their number and magnitude . . . The important thing to do is to find out why strikes occur, and remove their causes. It is more fruitful to promote collective bargaining . . . than to sharpen the tools of repression.[13]

Such attitudes have only developed in comparatively recent times. Throughout the early nineteenth century by their interpretation of the common law, the courts declared strikes to be criminal until the enactment of the Trade Union Act 1871, which gave unions immunity from the common law doctrine of restraint of trade, and the Conspiracy and Protection of Property Act 1875 which protected trade unions from charges of criminal conspiracy when taking strike action. The courts then exposed trade unions to claims for civil damages when their members engaged in strike activity, until the Trade Disputes Act 1906. The 1875 Act made it quite clear that strikes were not collectively actionable on criminal grounds if such actions were not criminal if done by a single individual. The 1906 Act, which reversed the Taff Vale Judgement of the House of Lords in 1901, protected trade unions from certain civil actions by expressly forbidding the hearing of such cases arising out of trade disputes as defined by that Act. The Industrial Relations Act 1971 largely removed the civil immunities for trade unions and for trade unionists provided by the 1875 and 1906 Acts. It substituted, instead, the statutory and specific wrongs of 'unfair industrial practices'.

When this Act was eventually repealed by the Trade Union and Labour Relations Act 1974, the law effectively reverted to the pre-1971 position by restoring the specific trade union immunities from civil damages given by the 1906 Act. By defining very widely the scope of a trade dispute to include almost any form of industrial action, the 1974 Act effectively restored trade union immunity from civil actions. The legal definition of trade disputes contained in Section 29 of the 1974 Act included all disputes arising out of terms and conditions of employment; engagements, non-engagements, suspension or termination of employment; allocation of work duties between workers or groups of employees; matters of discipline; membership or non-membership of trade unions; facilities for trade union officials; trade union recognition; and disputes arising out of the machinery for negotiation or consultation and other agreed procedures.

This very broad and general definition of trade disputes only prevented trade union industrial action from being the subject of legal claims for civil damages as long as such actions were protected by Section 13 of the 1974 Act. This stated that acts in 'contemplation or furtherance of a trade dispute shall not be actionable in tort'. This legal phrase, which is commonly known as the 'golden formula', renders trade union actions 'immune' from civil proceedings which could take place if the common law was applied. This immunity was closely defined by Section 14 of the 1974 Act. Changes to Section 14, therefore, modify the protection from civil actions largely enjoyed by trade unions since 1906. The key in the 1974 Act to changing and restricting the civil immunities provided in the golden formula lay in the repeal or amendment of Section 14.

Section 15 of the Employment Act 1982 now repeals Section 14 of the 1974 Act. Section 15 of the 1982 Act makes it clear that 'acts in contemplation or furtherance of a trade dispute' are liable to civil damages if they are not covered by the new definitions of trade disputes contained in Section 18 of the 1982 Act. Only trade disputes 'between workers and their employer' now possess the clear protection of the golden formula. Disputes between 'workers and workers' have lost their immunity and, instead of matters being merely 'connected with' the list of defined trade disputes in Section 29 of the 1974 Act, they must now be 'wholly or mainly' related to them. The protection given by the 1974 Act to disputes occurring outside Britain has been more narrowly defined too.

Where proceedings are brought against a trade union for civil damages under the 1982 Act, if the union is to be protected, the law requires that the decision to take industrial action is authorized or endorsed by a 'responsible person' from the union concerned. According to the Act, these include a union's 'general secretary', 'president', 'officials' or 'principal executive committee'. This introduces the legal concept of 'vicarious responsibility' into civil actions arising out of a trade dispute as a result of the 1982 Act. In practice, this means that if a 'responsible person' – as defined by Section 15 of the 1982 Act – repudiates the trade dispute, the claim for damages might fail. Repudiation of the trade dispute by a responsible person representing the trade union, such as its general secretary or president, must take place as soon as it is reasonably practicable to do so. It also requires that the person or persons involved in the dispute are notified in writing of this repudiation as soon as possible. In general terms, this is seen as making trade unions 'responsible' for the actions of their members.

Limitations are placed on the damages the courts can award against a trade union by Section 16 of the 1982 Act. These limits are based on the number of members in the union. Initially, for unions of less than 5 000 members, the limit was £10 000; for unions of between 5 000 and 25 000 the limit was £50 000; for unions between 25 000 and 100 000 the limit was £125 000; and for unions with more than 100 000 members the limit was £250 000. These limits are varied by order of the Secretary of State for Employment. Where damages are awarded, they can only be recovered from certain assets of the union. They cannot be recovered by the courts from 'protected property' such as union provident funds which are used to pay sickness benefit and superannuation to members. Neither can the courts recover damages from union political funds.

The essence of these changes to trade union immunity for civil damages arising out of trade disputes appears to be to retain protection for obvious and genuine disputes between workers and their direct employer and to narrow protection for all other types of dispute. The protections afforded by the 1974 Act to those workers involved in a trade dispute with a Minister of the Crown, because of the political policy he or she is pursuing, appear to lose their immunity under the 1982 Act. Such strikes could be construed as 'political' in their purpose and nature. Nevertheless, the problem of defining other than the most blatant examples of political strikes would appear to be extremely difficult.

The passing of the 1980 and 1982 Acts and the narrowing of trade union immunities in 'contemplation or furtherance' of trade disputes presents British employers with a new situation. Using the law to limit or defeat industrial action was a clear break with the past, where the employers had, in general, accepted that the law was not very constructive in solving industrial relations issues. Employers had little taste for bringing civil law cases before the courts in order to seek damages from unions engaged in industrial action not protected by the 1982 Act. They have, however, found the court injunction a more acceptable and speedy device for stopping a dispute – or making it very expensive for the unions to proceed – without resort to protracted legal wrangles for damages before the civil courts. Employers have also discovered that the courts grant injunctions speedily in the majority of cases and that when they are granted the union's wrath is usually directed against the courts and the judges and not necessarily against the employer. Evidence of this can be found in the use of the court injunction under the 1980 and 1982 Acts in disputes involving British Telecom, provincial newspapers, the motor vehicle industry and in the coalmining industry. Between 1980 and 1984 there were over 30 successful injunctions used in labour disputes.

Injunctions are court orders instructing people or organizations to cease a particular activity or to refrain from following a course of action whilst a civil court hearing of the disputed matters is being processed. Injunctions, therefore, give temporary relief pending a full court hearing. Judges in chambers grant injunctions on the evidence presented by the parties. They grant them when they believe that an arguable case has been made that the party making the application is likely to suffer considerable damage if the activity being objected to is allowed to continue until a full court hearing takes place. This might, indeed, be weeks if not months away. It is always stressed that the granting of an injunction does not prejudice the outcome of the case. Injunctions, if granted, are served on the other party by solicitors and not by the police who are not usually involved in civil law cases. If the injunction is not obeyed the person or organization granted the injunction can return to the court and start contempt of court proceedings against the offending party. If the court agrees, an order of contempt is then issued and, unless the other party obeys the injunction, fines or imprisonment can follow. Appeals can be made against injunctions granted by the High Courts to the Court of Appeal and the House of Lords. Since the passing of the 1980 and 1982 Acts, such appeals have been processed with a speed not usually associated with English courts.

Following contempt proceedings, if the injunction is still not obeyed by the trade unions to whom they are directed, and the industrial action the court has instructed to stop continues, heavy fines can be imposed. If the unions still refuse to pay the fines, the courts can order seizure of their funds and assets by sequestration order. Financial assets of the unions can then be taken from banks and their property sequestrated.

The use of what can now be called the labour injunction has, since the passing of the 1980 and 1982 Acts, become a powerful new tool in the hands of employers seeking to end industrial action which does not enjoy immunity under the new legislation. It is the use of the injunction itself, and not the civil action for damages which might or might not follow, which is decisive. In those cases in recent years where the injunction has been used against unlawful strike action, the successful use of the injunction has not been followed by a court action for civil damages. The injunction, having served its purpose, is not followed by a court action which would merely exacerbate the breakdown in industrial relations between the parties.

10.3   PICKETING

The law relating to the physical conduct of strikes and the rights of strikers to assemble, to communicate information and to persuade others to help or to join them, is commonly referred to as the law of picketing. In most strikes, it is a common practice for the unions to appoint official pickets to stand outside the workplace where the dispute is taking place. This is done to make it clear to employees, management, the public, and other workers delivering or collecting goods and materials there, that a strike is in progress. In furthering their trade dispute, the strikers seek to impose the maximum economic sanctions upon the employer. The law permits them to do this with certain provisions: that physical force is not used; that people and vehicles are not stopped against their will; and that their conduct does not threaten a breach of the peace in the eyes of the police. Picketing is also confined to those employees directly involved in the dispute and to their place of work, or to a clearly connected establishment. Since the Employment Act 1980, secondary picketing is not protected by the law. Within these constraints, pickets remain free to advertise their case and to persuade others of the justice of it. They can do this as long as they do not obstruct and assault others, create a nuisance, trespass, or conspire to commit a breach of the peace. The arbiters of their conduct in each instance are those police who are also there.

Picketing was, by implication, first made legal by the Conspiracy and Protection of Property Act 1875. This permitted pickets to attend a house or a place of work 'in order merely to obtain or communicate information', provided that such activities 'shall not be deemed a watching and besetting'.[14] The intention of this Section of the 1875 Act was to deter and to discover criminal conspiracies rather than to control picketing which did not appear to present any serious law and order problems at that time. The Trade Disputes Act of 1906 extended the protection for picketing by explicitly making it:

> lawful for one or more persons, acting on their own behalf or on behalf of a trade union . . .
> in contemplation of furtherance of a trade dispute, to attend at or near a house or place
> where a person resides or works or carries on business or happens to be, if they do so attend
> merely for the purpose of peacefully obtaining or communicating information, or of
> peacefully persuading any person to work or abstain from working.[15]

Following the enactment of the Employment Act 1980, Parliament issued a code of practice on picketing. This aims to provide practical guidance on picketing in trade disputes for those contemplating, organizing or taking part in a picket and for employers and members of the general public who may be affected by it.

The law on picketing remained largely unchanged from the end of the last century until the Employment Act 1980, despite the revolution which had occurred in road transportation. It was largely because the law was designed to enable pickets peacefully to persuade workers walking to work and those delivering goods by horse drawn vehicles – *not* drivers of cars, buses and heavy lorries – that the law of picketing was claimed by some to be inadequate. It is difficult to persuade and to communicate with people travelling inside modern motor vehicles. Furthermore, the nature of picketing had undergone fundamental changes in the intervening period. It had changed, for example, from the picketing of the producer's premises by those directly involved in a dispute, to the use of large numbers of mobile or 'flying' pickets, picketing consumers of the product made by the strikers. The two national coalmining strikes in the early 1970s saw not the picketing of coalmines, which was plainly unnecessary, but of power stations and coal and coke depots to prevent the generation of electricity and the delivery of fuel to consumers. At the same time, the use of mass picketing by thousands of people, a majority of whom might not even be directly involved in the dispute but merely sympathizers, led to considerable problems for the police who sought guidance from the picketing laws, which were clearly not intended for such situations. A classical example of this was during the long, violent and emotive union recognition dispute at the Grunwick Processing Laboratories in 1977.

The Employment Act 1980, by amending Section 15 of the 1974 Act, brought major changes to the law regulating the conduct of peaceful picketing. The right to picket is clearly retained but lawful picketing is almost exclusively confined to those workers in dispute picketing at or near their own place of employment. So-called 'secondary picketing', mass picketing and flying pickets are not provided with legal protection. Trade union officials can picket any place of work where their members are in dispute and engage in peaceful picketing. Special provisions are made in the 1980 Act to enable those persons whose employment does not provide them with a fixed place of work, for example lorry drivers and commercial travellers, to picket any premises of their employer *from* which they work or *from* where their work is administered.

When pickets behave in a manner judged by the police as likely to cause offence or a disturbance, they can be arrested. Such behaviour includes threatening violence, causing an affray, damaging property, disturbing the peace, using abusive language, obstructing the police in the execution of their duties, criminal trespass or carrying an offensive weapon. Pickets may not obstruct the highway, though they can signal drivers to stop so that they can talk and explain their case. A great deal depends upon the judgement, skill and experience of the police officers involved and on the co-operation they receive from union office holders among the workers in dispute. Any person who wishes to cross a picket line must be allowed to do so.

Where picketing takes place and is not protected by the 1974 and 1980 Acts, and is deemed by an employer to be interfering with its contracts, it may start a civil action for damages against those pickets whom it believes to be responsible. This is done by seeking an injunction – or an interdict in Scotland – from the Courts. These are served on those persons believed to be responsible for the organization of the picketing. On receipt of the injunction, the pickets must cease picketing or possibly place themselves in contempt of court. If the pickets do not obey the injuction, it is the employer's responsibility to commence contempt of court proceedings before continuing with an action for civil damages. In practice, the injunction alone serves the purpose of preventing picketing. It is not the function of the police to be involved with civil actions or to serve a court injunction against pickets. Enforcement of a court order is a matter for the courts and their officers. Whilst the police do not normally assist the employer in identifying pickets or by serving the order themselves, they do assist the officers of the court if they think there might be a breach of the peace.

The code of practice on picketing, issued by Parliament in 1980 to provide practical guidance on the law and on how to ensure peaceful picketing, does not itself impose any legal obligations on pickets. But its provisions are admissible in evidence in proceedings before any court. The code contains guidance on the practical organization of picketing, on the right of any persons to cross a picket line and on allowing the passage of essential supplies and services. It also emphasises the dangers that can result when a large number of pickets are involved. The code recommends that in general the number of pickets should not exceed six, though there are no references to the number of pickets in any Act of Parliament. During the coalmining dispute of 1984–5, however, the High Court ruled that no more than six people could picket at any one colliery gate.

It has long been a practice of workers in dispute to extend their actions to the suppliers and customers of the employer and to persuade workers in related factories to break their contracts of employment. Such secondary action and secondary picketing was protected by Section 13 of the 1974 Act under 'acts in contemplation or furtherance of a trade dispute'. Section 17 of the Employment Act 1980 now removes the immunity of Section 13 for secondary action and secondary picketing. The immunity is retained, however, where the workers of an employer in dispute with that employer seek to persuade other workers in its associated yet geographically distant factories to take sympathetic industrial action, including the 'blacking' of goods and services. From a legal viewpoint, it is now very important that such action is specifically targeted, so that the connections between the primary and secondary actions are obvious and clear. Where the secondary action or picketing are not directly connected, the employer may seek civil damages through the courts.

Where an employer is successful in obtaining a court injunction stopping unlawful picketing and the pickets and their unions ignore it, the employer can commence contempt proceedings. If the pickets and their unions still ignore the injunction the court can order the seizure of their assets and property. An example of the use of an injunction to stop mass secondary picketing is to be found in the dispute between Messenger Newspapers Ltd and the National Graphical Association (NGA) at Warrington in 1983. When the NGA refused to obey the court injunction to stop its members picketing, it was fined for contempt of court.

10.4   THE CLOSED SHOP

In many countries, such as France, West Germany, Italy and Switzerland, the closed shop is either effectively unlawful or severely restricted: the freedom not to organize is put on a par with the freedom to organize. 'If everyone, so it is argued, has the fundamental right to join a union, he has the equally fundamental right not to do so.'[16] While this right is contained in the European Convention on Human Rights, and is the subject of specific legislation in many countries, the closed shop in Britain was neither directly banned nor unduly restricted at law, until the Employment Acts 1980 and 1982. Under these Acts, the right of individual employees not to be unfairly dismissed for refusing to join a trade union or to remain a member in a closed shop situation are protected. Where employees are dismissed for either of these reasons, they can obtain substantial compensation by appealing to an industrial tribunal for a remedy.

Traditionally, closed shops have developed over many years in a number of industries including printing, dock work, coalmining, shipbuilding, and electricity, gas and water supply. Closed shops are concentrated in the public sector and in large establishments employing mainly manual workers. It has been estimated that by the early 1980s nearly one quarter of the working population were in some form of closed shop. A few closed shop agreements between employers and unions – which are now legally described as union membership agreements (UMAs) – are informal understandings that non-union labour will not be employed. It is also understood that employees who leave their union, or lose their membership in some other way, will be dismissed if they do not rejoin the union or if they are not accepted back into its membership. In pre-entry closed shops, it is the normal practice of employers only to engage existing union members, usually with the approval of the union(s) concerned. Where post entry closed shops operate, newly engaged employees are given a set period in which to become members of the specified union(s). In most employment situations where a closed shop exists, the closed shop is the subject of a formal written agreement between the employer and the union(s) concerned. This is done so that the union(s) can make it quite clear to other unions that only their members are to be employed on certain types of work.

Although the closed shop has often been opposed on moral and economic grounds, little attempt has been made in Britain to outlaw it outright. More usually, opposition to it has been either on the grounds of individual freedom not to join a trade union against one's will, or on the consequences of losing one's employment as a penalty for not joining. But such critics, it is argued, miss the real point of the argument, since the case

> for the closed shop can only be made in terms of the need for an equilibrium of power. It cannot be attacked or defended in terms of general ethical sentiments, but only in terms of social expediency . . . It was for reasons of expediency that . . . the Donovan Commission decided not to recommend legislation against it.[17]

This line of reasoning was upheld by the Industrial Relations Act 1971 which, although against closed shops in principle, allowed them to operate in restricted forms known as 'Agency Shop Agreements' and 'Approved Closed Shop Agreements'. Approved closed shops were permitted, for example, to meet the argument that certain unions, such as those covering seamen and musicians, would collapse without them. The opposition to closed shops implicit in the 1971 Act did little or nothing in practice to alter the attitudes of either employers or trade unions towards them. Nor is there evidence that the Act had any appreciable impact upon the scope, content and operation of the closed shop. 'It is a conspicuous example of the failure of a policy and of a failure of the law.'[18]

The Trade Union and Labour Relations Act 1974 did not expressly legalize the closed shop but it withdrew the ineffectual legal controls imposed upon it by the 1971 Act. The situation was complicated by the fact that the 1974 Act, which retained the unfair dismissal provisions first introduced by the 1971 Act, made it clear that an employer could not normally be instructed by an industrial tribunal to reinstate or to re-engage an employee who had been dismissed for leaving or refusing to join a union in a closed shop situation. Nor could a tribunal award compensation for dismissals in such cases, unless the dismissed employee had either religious objections to being a member of any union, or genuine objections on any reasonable grounds to being a member of a particular trade union. The Trade Union and Labour Relations (Amendment) Act 1976 repealed the latter leaving only religious objections as grounds for exclusion. It was because tribunals had to be guided by specific law when dealing with dismissal cases arising out of closed shops that Section 30 of the 1974 Act defined a 'union membership agreement' and 'the conditions under which the dismissal of a conscientious objector who refused to join the union would have to be regarded as unfair despite the closed shop.'[19]

In 1976 a British Rail employee was dismissed as the result of his failure to join a trade union following the introduction of a closed shop agreement in the industry. An industrial tribunal held him to have been fairly dismissed under the Trade Union and Labour Relations (Amendment) Act 1976. He and two others similarly dismissed by British Rail took their case to the European Commission on Human Rights. The Commission declared the 1976 Act to be in breach of the European Convention of Human Rights and this was subsequently upheld by the European Court on Human Rights. These events gave added conviction to the Conservative Government elected in 1979 to introduce legislation which would drastically curtail, though not actually declare void, the operations of the closed shop in Britain. The process was started by the Employment Act 1980 and extended by the Employment Act 1982.

The 1982 Act, for example took the unusual step of providing retrospective compensation out of public funds for those persons who could convince the Secretary of State for Employment, advised by an independent assessor, that they had been dismissed for failure to conform to the requirements of a union membership agreement. He only considered those closed shop dismissals which took place between 16 September 1974 and 15 August 1980. Section 2 and Schedule 1 of the 1982 Act contain procedures whereby applications were made, processed and decided. The principal objective of the closed shop legislation contained in the two Employment Acts and the code of practice on closed shops approved by the House of Commons in 1983 is to provide a rigorous procedure for the establishment at law of union membership agreements. It also aims to provide substantial compensation for cases of unfair dismissal in closed shop situations upheld by tribunals. Employees can bring a complaint before a tribunal that they have had 'action short of dismissal' brought against them by an employer, as well as actual cases of dismissal. Employees can take cases to tribunals regardless of their length of service. But cases need normally be registered within three months of the dismissal. The dismissed employees in closed shop cases can also get 'interim relief' from the tribunal. If it is awarded the contracts of the employees are regarded as unbroken and they are entitled to normal payment pending a full hearing of the unfair dismissal complaint.

Since 1 November 1984, union membership agreements, which meet the legal requirements, must apply to a clearly defined class of employee and be the result of a secret ballot in which not less than 80 per cent of those entitled to vote, or not less than 85 per cent of those who do vote, are in favour of the agreement. A fresh ballot must be held every five years in order to keep the union membership agreement valid in the eyes of a tribunal considering cases of unfair dismissal for non-union membership. Where these ballot arrangements are not observed, there is a very strong likelihood that complaints of unfair dismissal will be upheld by an industrial tribunal. Under a union membership agreement, employees are not required to become trade union members providing: first, they genuinely object on grounds of conscience or other deeply held personal convictions; second, they are opposed to the agreement at the time of the ballot; and third, they were not members before the ballot and did not become members after a successful ballot. Further, employees cannot be fairly dismissed for failing to make payments to a union or other body or person in lieu of union membership.

Where applicants are declared by a tribunal to have been unfairly dismissed for refusing to become or remain a trade union member in an employment situation where a closed shop is enforced, with or without a formally agreed union membership agreement, they can be awarded substantial compensation in excess of awards for other forms of unfair dismissal. The compensation is made up of a 'basic award' a 'compensatory award' and, where the tribunal supports the applicant's claim for reinstatement or re-engagement and the employer refuses the claim, a 'special award'. Based on 1985 figures, compensation could, in exceptional cases, exceed £30 000.

Where an employer argues before a tribunal that the act of dismissal was the result of trade union pressure and took the form of industrial action, or the threat of industrial action, it can use its legal right of 'joinder' and make a request to the tribunal for the trade union to become a party to the proceedings. Where the tribunal finds the employer's claim to be well founded, it can order the joined party to contribute to the compensation. Even where the pressure upon employees to become union members against their beliefs or will stops short of dismissal, they can still bring cases before a tribunal.

Employees also have the right not to be unreasonably expelled or excluded from a trade union in closed shop situations. Where employees feel they have been unreasonably expelled or excluded they can take a complaint to an industrial tribunal. The tribunal will make a decision based on the individual circumstances and merits of each case. The tribunal is guided by the code of practice on closed shop agreements and arrangements. The tribunal takes into account the rules of the union, but does not necessarily base its findings on whether or not the rules were observed. Where a tribunal makes a declaration that an employee was unreasonably expelled or excluded from union membership, that individual is entitled to claim compensation from the union. Such an application for compensation cannot be made before the union has had time to reconsider the case and to admit or re-admit the person involved. This process does not prevent individual members taking a case to the ordinary courts under the common law, if actions taken against them by their trade union are contrary to the union's own rules or in violation of natural justice.

The Employment Act 1982 also introduces a prohibition on union membership requirements in commercial contracts. The objective of these sections is to make unlawful and void any clauses in commercial contracts for goods or services requiring another employer to guarantee that it will only use trade union labour. This form of pressure, whilst still not a common practice, has been growing in recent years. It is usually associated with the printing industry and with strong closed shop situations. The union aim is to prevent an employer placing orders and contracts with firms not employing trade union labour and not operating closed shops. Firms or suppliers must not exclude, or fail to consider, tenders for commercial contracts on the ground that the firm concerned does not employ union members. Conversely, contracts must not contain requirements that only non-union labour is to be used, though conditions of this nature are almost unknown. Trade disputes or any other form of industrial action, or threat of action, to enforce union labour only clauses in contracts are not protected by Section 13 of the 1974 Act and are therefore potentially actionable in tort.

10.5   COLLECTIVE BARGAINING AND THE LAW

Recognition and collective agreements

To some extent the history of collective bargaining in Britain is the history of the struggle for trade union recognition. The classical method used by manual workers during the nineteenth century for this purpose was to increase their level of trade union membership and their strength of organization to the point where they were confident that formal recognition from their employers could not be refused. If their employers agreed, there was no problem. But if the employers decided not to concede recognition, nor to abandon their unilateral determination of pay and conditions of employment, the unions had to decide whether to take strike action or to present a further request for recognition at some later date. This process of attrition was virtually unregulated by law and it continued in slightly modified form until the Industrial Relations Act 1971. This Act provided for the first time a limited legal procedure which could be used by those trade unions, registered under the Act, that wished to obtain formal recognition agreements from their employers.

Recognition disputes remained one of the most bitter and protracted forms of industrial conflict between trade unions and employers well into the twentieth century but their incidence declined as trade union membership grew and as the institution of collective bargaining became firmly established. Government also played a positive role in extending collective bargaining. It did this by recognizing the right of its own employees to belong to trade unions and by negotiating with them. By promoting the development of collective bargaining machinery after the First World War, the Whitley Reports also played a crucial part in persuading many employers to recognize trade unions and to negotiate with them.

The Employment Protection Act 1975 provided, under Sections 11–16, a legal procedure by which independent certificated unions could try to obtain formal recognition agreements from employers without resort to overt industrial conflict. This did not mean, of course, that unions did not continue to use the strike weapon as a means of obtaining recognition if they preferred that method to one of due legal process, or that employers were legally obliged to negotiate recognition agreements. This legal procedure, which involved the Advisory Conciliation and Arbitration Service and the Central Arbitration Committee, was repealed by the Employment Act 1980.

Statute law is not now involved with trade union recognition which is left to be determined voluntarily by the good sense, or otherwise, of trade unions and employers.

This does not mean, however, that the courts do not have to decide whether or not a union is recognized by an employer. In many cases the courts are obliged to settle the question of union recognition in order to decide a union's right to claim such basic legal entitlements as the right to be consulted on impending redundancies, to be consulted about the transfer of an employer's undertaking, to receive bargaining information and to appoint safety representatives. The courts have had to decide the criteria which constitutes union recognition by the employer in order to decide whether or not a union is legally entitled to their statutory rights.

Formal contractual association lies at the heart of all business transactions within market based industrial economies like that of Britain. The law encourages the drawing up of formal business contracts between freely consenting parties, on the assumption that both sides expect the other to meet their contractual obligations with mutual goodwill and acceptance. If either side fails to fulfil its obligations then redress and compensation can be sought by the other party through the civil courts. On this basis, innumerable contracts are agreed daily between producers and wholesalers, for example, between shipbuilders and shipping companies, between local authorities and road construction companies, between housebuilders and house purchasers and so on.

Collective agreements, however, are not legally enforceable between employers and unions because they are not commercial contracts between consenting parties but are highly complex social and economic agreements regulating the working lives of thousands of people in the organizations in which they are employed. Such agreements do not easily meet the general criteria of the law of commercial contract. It is clearly not the intention of the unions or employers in negotiating collective agreements to regard them as legally enforceable contracts, unless they take the highly unusual step of declaring in writing that the collective agreement they have negotiated is intended to be legally enforceable. The voluntary and non-contractual nature of collective agreements was upheld by the civil courts in 1969 in the *Ford Motor Co.* v *Amalgamated Union of Engineering and Foundry Workers* decision. Here it was 'held that an agreement between the Ford Motor Co. and a number of unions could not be enforced as a contract.'[20] The decision was based on the factual finding that there was no contractual intent. Furthermore, the nature and uncertain wording of collective agreements and particularly their aspirational character, it was felt, would 'present grave problems of enforcement.'[21]

Collective agreements, therefore, are better understood, not as legally enforceable commercial contracts, but as 'an industrial peace treaty and at the same time a source of rules for terms and conditions of employment, for the distribution of work and for the stability of jobs.'[22] This view of collective agreements was endorsed by the experience of the Industrial Relations Act between 1971 and 1974, when all collective agreements were presumed to be legally enforceable unless clearly indicated otherwise by the parties. The TUC response was to insist that affiliated unions put clear disclaimers in all the written agreements which they signed. At the same time, employers showed little interest in persuading the trade unions to make collective agreements legally enforceable. One reason was that employers were aware of the impracticability of suing unions or employees for compensation of breach of contract, to say nothing of the damaging effect which such litigation would have on personnel and industrial relations. Thus Section 18(1) of the Trade Union and Labour Relations Act 1974 now states unambiguously that any collective agreement:

> shall be conclusively presumed not to have been intended by the parties to be a legally enforceable contract unless the agreement –
> (a) is in writing, and
> (b) contains a provision which (however expressed) states that the parties intend that the agreement shall be a legally enforceable contract.[23]

The law has also played an important positive role in encouraging and in fostering the growth of voluntary collective bargaining and the development of jointly agreed negotiating machinery in Britain. The historical evidence strongly suggests, for example, that the Trade Union Act 1871, the Conspiracy and Protection of Property Act 1875 and the Trade Disputes Act 1906, powerfully fostered the growth of voluntary collective bargaining machinery in Britain. The Royal Commission on Labour in 1894, which led to the Conciliation Act 1896, along with the influential Whitley Reports which appeared at the end of the First World War, all played considerable parts in encouraging the growth of voluntary collective bargaining as an effective means of determining mutually acceptable terms and conditions of employment between employers and employees. Moreover, the nationalization Acts enacted since 1945, and the growth of public sector employment, have clearly encouraged the growth of voluntary collective bargaining as the principal method of regulating employer-employee relationships.

It has generally been the intention of the legislators, therefore, not to make collective agreements legally enforceable, but to encourage the responsible development of voluntary collective bargaining in Britain. The Whitley Reports, for instance, were implemented in this voluntary spirit by the Ministry of Labour immediately after the First World War. They did much to encourage the development of national collective bargaining machinery through the establishment of joint industrial councils representative of both employers and trade unions during the inter-war period. More recently, ACAS has been given the statutory duty of promoting good industrial relations through encouraging the extension of collective bargaining and joint negotiating machinery in industry. In order to protect its neutral role and independent status in promoting collective bargaining, ACAS has not been called upon to enforce or to advocate any incomes policies devised by successive governments.

Disclosure of information

The trade unions have long argued that employers should disclose certain information to them so that they can negotiate more realistically together. They have wanted this information to check both the veracity of management's financial statements and any claims that their employers cannot afford to meet their pay demands. The unions' requests for information have usually been a claim that management should 'open the books' for inspection. Some employers wishing to foster responsible collective bargaining have voluntarily given union representatives such commercial, financial and production information when this has been requested. Where employers have refused to disclose this information, some unions have proved most resourceful in obtaining the evidence they require. They have obtained this from annual company reports, newspapers such as the *Financial Times*, and stockbroker financial information services. They have also used the trade union research services provided by the Trades Union Congress, Ruskin College at Oxford and the Labour Research Department.

Sections 17 to 21 of the Employment Protection Act 1975 now place a general duty on all employers to disclose information for collective bargaining purposes to independent recognized trade unions. There is also a legal procedure enabling independent trade unions to complain if an employer refuses such information. As a general guide to these Sections of the Act, ACAS issued a code of practice on disclosure of information to trade unions for collective bargaining purposes in 1977, subsequently approved by Parliament, which it is hoped can guide trade unions, employers and the Central Arbitration Committee (CAC) when considering the information that can legitimately be requested for collective bargaining purposes.

The 1975 Act applies to every employer, including the public services and government departments, and lays a general duty on employers to disclose on the request of representatives of independent trade unions:

> all such information relating to his undertaking as is in his possession . . . without which the trade union representatives would be to a material extent impeded in carrying on . . . collective bargaining, and . . . information which it would be in accordance with good industrial relations practice that he should disclose to them for the purposes of collective bargaining.[24]

The trade unions must be independent and recognized by the employer for the purpose of collective bargaining. If the employer rejects the union's claim that it recognizes them, the issue can be determined by conciliation. The information disclosed by the employer has to be in writing or be confirmed in writing. Although the Act is not specific on what information should be disclosed, it clearly states that the ACAS code is to be the general guide for both parties and for the CAC in determining whether or not the employer has complied with the requirements of the Act.

Section 18 of the Employment Protection Act 1975 places certain restrictions on the general duty of employers to disclose information. Information is restricted, for example: where it endangers national security; contravenes another law (such as the Official Secrets Act 1911); breaches confidential sources; relates specifically to individuals without their agreement; or causes substantial injury to the undertaking. The employer needs only to give the information in a form which it believes to be most suitable. It can refuse information 'where the compilation or assembly would involve an amount of work or expenditure out of reasonable proportion to the value of the information in the conduct of collective bargaining.'[25] Where an employer appears to unreasonably refuse to disclose the requested information an independent trade union may present a complaint to the CAC in writing that 'an employer has failed to disclose . . . information which he is required to disclose.'[26] The complaint is usually first referred to ACAS for conciliation but if this fails the CAC hears the complaint and decides whether it is well founded, stating the reasons for its findings. If the CAC finds the complaint well founded, it specifies the information which the employer should disclose and a date by which the employer has to provide the information. If the employer still refuses to disclose the required information, the union can, under Section 20 of the Act, submit a further complaint. This leads to a CAC award making the disclosure of the specified information part of the terms and conditions of each individual employee's contract of employment which can be enforced through the courts.

The ACAS code is not concerned with the legal process whereby the law can be enforced. Its aim is to provide practical guidance on the most reasonable ways in which information can be requested and conceded for the purposes of collective bargaining. The code states that the Act imposes no specific items of disclosure on employers, but leaves it to the code to recommend what actual information should be disclosed in the interests of good industrial relations. Failure to observe the code does not itself render anyone liable to proceedings 'but the Act requires any relevant provisions to be taken into account in proceedings before the Central Arbitration Committee.'[27] The code is clearly a 'relevant provision'.

The code of practice recommends employers to disclose information on pay, conditions of service, manpower levels, company performance and productivity, and on the employer's general financial situation. It suggests, too, that managements formulate a policy on disclosure and make formal joint agreements on disclosure arrangements with the trade unions with whom they negotiate. It advises trade unions to undertake training to ensure that negotiators know what information to ask for and that they are equipped to use the information effectively.

Misunderstandings can be avoided, costs reduced, and time saved, if requests state as precisely as possible all the information required, and the reasons why the information is considered relevant. Requests should conform to an agreed procedure. A reasonable period of time should be allowed for employers to consider a request and to reply.[28]

The Transfer of Undertakings (Protection of Employment) Regulations 1981, issued by Parliament, which put into effect the EEC's Acquired Rights Directive 77/187, gives most but by no means all employees new rights when their employers sell or transfer their businesses. These Regulations, which can into effect in 1982, provide most employees with the automatic transfer of their employment contracts when transfers, sales or mergers take place but not where a business is taken over by purchase of shares. They also require employers, with certain exceptions, to inform and consult recognized trade unions about proposed transfers or mergers and their probable effects upon employees. The Regulations declare that any existing rights of trade union recognition, and the duty to bargain collectively, may be automatically transferred in a merger. Any dismissals arising out of a transfer or merger, or connected with it, are considered unfair unless the employer can show that they were necessary for economic, technical or organizational reasons. If employers involved in transfers or mergers do not comply with these Regulations, recognized trade unions but not individual employees may complain to an industrial tribunal within three months of the completion of the transfer. Where complaints are upheld by a tribunal, it may award up to two weeks pay to each employee. This is an insignificant award compared with that available under the redundancy procedural rights in the Employment Protection (Consolidation) Act 1978.

10.6 UNION BALLOTS

As we have already indicated, individual trade unionists can appeal to the courts for redress if their union treats them in ways which do not accord with the union's rule book. Trade unions must also submit details of their internal organization, methods of operation and accounts to the Certification Officer if they wish to become a certified independent union under the 1974 Act. Until the Employment Act 1980, the question of internal trade union democracy was considered to be their own private business. Sections 1 and 2 of the 1980 Act, however, enable the Secretary of State for Employment to approve public money for independent trade unions to conduct certain secret ballots. Trade unions are not obliged to make use of Sections 1 and 2 and the Secretary of State has discretion in financing such ballots. The objective of these provisions is to enable vital decision taking within trade unions to be determined by secret postal ballots of their memberships and, in theory, to 'improve' internal union democracy.

The ballots qualifying for financial support are those concerned with: the calling or ending of strikes; the election of executive committees; the election of certain union officers; amending the rules of a union; and seeking approval for trade union amalgamations. The scheme only covers secret ballots and the unions must endeavour to send ballot papers to every member. The ballot must be conducted without interference or constraint and the counting of the votes must be above suspicion. The scheme for national union ballots is administered by the Certification Officer and independent trade unions wishing to make use of the statutory provisions apply to him.

Workplace secret ballots of trade union members also qualify for public financial assistance. The 1980 Act makes it obligatory on employers of more than 20 workers to comply with a request from an independent trade union to permit a secret ballot on their premises. The employer is only required to provide facilities for trade unions which are recognized and not for others. The employer is expected to provide all reasonable facilities and opportunities to enable every trade unionist entitled to vote to do so. The detailed arrangements for the conduct of the ballot, including pre-ballot publicity and the provision of polling booths, are the responsibility of the union. Where an employer refuses to co-operate with a trade union request for a workplace secret ballot, the union may make a complaint to an industrial tribunal. If the tribunal upholds the complaint, it may order the employer to pay compensation to the union and make a declaration that the employer has failed to comply with a secret ballot request. Tribunals cannot, however, order employers to allow secret trade union ballots on their premises.

The process begun by the 1980 Act to ensure that vital internal trade union decisions are democratically determined by secret postal or workplace ballots of the whole membership was enlarged by the Trade Union Act 1984. The 1984 Act has four major provisions: secret ballots for the election of trade union leaders and principal executive bodies; secret ballots before taking industrial action; secret ballots for political funds and objects; and public money to trade unions to cover the cost of secret ballots.

Part I of the 1984 Act requires trade unions to elect all voting members of the union's principal executive governing body by secret ballot of the whole membership. Elections must take place at least once every five years. This requirement applies 'notwithstanding anything in the union's rules'. Where, under union rules, members of the union's executive are not elected, for example the general secretary in some cases, that person shall be entitled to attend and speak but not to vote at meetings of the executive body. The 1984 Act lays down the minimum requirements for the conduct of elections to a union's principal executive body. Outgoing members of an executive may remain in office for a hand-over period not exceeding six months. All union members entitled to vote must be given equal voting rights. The union must keep accurate records of all their members' names and addresses and keep them up to date. Unions must have complete and accurate registers of members.

Voting is normally by secret ballot and members must be given every opportunity to vote. Voting must take place without interference from, or constraint imposed by, the union or any of its members, officials or employees and the votes must be fairly and accurately counted. Executive members must not be elected indirectly by conference delegates or regional committees or by any 'block vote' system. All members of the union are entitled to vote but certain exceptions laid down in the union's rules can be made: unemployed members; those in arrears with union dues; new members with less than three months' standing; and apprentices, trainees and students. Where appropriate, a union can divide its membership by geographical area, trade groups, occupation or by clearly separate sections, and elections can take place for executive members by all the union members within these defined divisions.

The 1984 Act requires all union members, except for a small number of members usually excluded by union rules, to be eligible to stand for election to the union's principal executive. Unions may set reasonable lower and upper age limits on candidates or require a minimum period of membership. But they must not stipulate that candidates are required to belong to a particular political party. Any union member who qualifies under the 1984 Act to vote or stand in union elections and is prevented from doing so can make a complaint to the Certification Officer or to the courts. The member can also complain that the union does not keep an adequate register of members. Union members who believe their union has not complied with the Act must make a complaint within one year of the election result being announced. The member makes the complaint to the Certification Officer and need not be involved in any legal expenses. The union member will be required to give specific evidence of election malpractice.

If the Certification Officer determines that the union has broken the Act's requirements, he can make a declaration to that effect. Where such a declaration is made, the member can take the complaint to the courts, unless the union accepts that it has broken the Act's requirements and has put the matter right. However, if the union does not accept the Certification Officer's findings, the member can proceed with a complaint to the courts. Where the courts accept the Certification Officer's declaration, they can order the union to hold a fresh election, take steps to remedy the infringement, such as recounting the votes or updating its membership register, or in cases of minor infringements order the union not to commit the offence again. Where a union refuses to recognize the court's order, or refuses to accept its right to make such an order, the court can declare the union to be in contempt and it may impose a fine, followed possibly by further fines and orders leading eventually to the sequestration of the union's assets.

Part II of the Trade Union Act 1984 requires trade unions to hold secret ballots before authorizing or endorsing official industrial action by their members. Failure to hold ballots before taking industrial action can result in the loss of legal immunity by the union in the event of any action for civil damages. Where union members intend taking industrial action involving a breach of their contracts of employment, they must first hold a secret ballot of those members directly involved in taking the action. The ballot must be held not more than four weeks before the start of the industrial action and a majority of those voting must be prepared to take the action. Where these two conditions are met, the action should be immune from civil actions for damages. Where the union wishes its members to take action short of striking, as well as strike action, a separate question for each must be contained on the ballot paper and immunity for both forms of action depends upon separate majority votes in favour of each.

Where union members take industrial action not authorized or endorsed by the union following a secret ballot, the union will be held responsible unless the action is clearly repudiated by the union's principal executive, the general secretary or the president. The repudiation must be put in writing as soon as possible. The persons or person legally permitted to make the repudiation must not, following the repudiation, behave in a manner which is inconsistent with the repudiation.

Where a union fails to fulfil the requirement to hold secret ballots before taking official industrial action, it loses its immunity in legal proceedings for civil damages. Actions may be brought by employers who can prove that their employees have broken their contracts of employment without first having gone through a successful ballot, or where commercial contracts have been interfered with, and that they have suffered financial loss. Customers and suppliers who can show that their contracts have been interfered with can also bring civil actions. Employers and others affected by the industrial action can also seek injunctions to have the industrial action called off which, if not complied with, can lead to contempt of court fines and the sequestration of union funds and assets. The scale of damages which the courts can award was fixed at an upper limit of £250 000 for the largest unions in 1984. If an employer seeks and obtains an injunction, it does not mean it must proceed with a case for civil damages. Nor is it necessary to seek an injunction before proceeding with a civil action. An employer can seek civil damages against a union, which did not hold the necessary ballot, after the industrial action has been resolved.

The 1984 Act stipulates those union members entitled to vote in a ballot on industrial action and how the ballot should be conducted. Only those members called upon to take such action are entitled to vote. Employees not eligible to take part in the ballot cannot be lawfully asked to take industrial action at a later date without a further ballot. The ballot paper must state specifically that members are being asked to take part either in strike action in breach of their contracts of employment or in industrial action falling short of a strike. The questions must be framed to require a straight 'yes' or 'no' answer. Voting must be in secret and every reasonable opportunity must be given to those entitled to vote to do so, either by post or at the workplace. The votes must be fairly and accurately counted and the results made public to those entitled to vote. The results must declare the total number of votes cast, the number of 'yes' votes, the number of 'no' votes and the number of spoiled or unacceptable ballot papers.

Part III of the 1984 Act introduces a number of changes in the law governing union political funds. The Trade Union Act 1913 permits unions to set up separate political funds and to use the money in those funds for political objects. Monies kept in a union's general fund cannot be used for political purposes. Members who wish to contribute towards the political fund pay a small addition to their basic union subscription known as the political levy. If they do not wish to pay the political levy, they have to 'contract out' in writing. The 1913 Act enables those unions with a political levy to provide the Labour Party with most of its finance as well as providing for expenditure on parliamentary and local government elections involving union sponsored candidates. The 1913 Act originally laid down a number of simple requirements which unions had to comply with in order to establish and use a political fund. The union had first to hold a ballot of its members before a political fund could be established. It was then required to adopt a number of political fund rules which had to be approved by the Registrar of Friendly Societies (now the Certification Officer). Once a successful ballot had been undertaken there was no legal requirement for it to be repeated or confirmed at regular intervals.

The 1984 Act makes a number of important changes to the 1913 Act. It requires, for example, all unions with political funds established under the 1913 Act to hold secret political fund review ballots of their members before 31 March 1986 to confirm that they still want to raise a political levy and have a political fund. Further review ballots must take place at intervals of not more than 10 years after the initial ballot. The review ballots must be conducted in accordance with rules laid down by the Certification Officer. If a union fails to hold the required review ballot, any member of the union may make a complaint to the courts which may then order the union to comply. Failure to obey the courts could lead to contempt of court proceedings. Where a review ballot rejects continuing the political fund, the union must: take immediate steps to stop collecting the political levy; refund levy payments made after the ballot, if so requested by members; stop all expenditure on political objects within six months and transfer the existing monies in the political fund to other funds held by the union. Where a union fails to do these things after a 'no' vote by a majority of the union members in a review ballot, any member of the union may seek a High Court order requiring the union to comply with the Act's requirements.

The 1984 Act also clarifies and updates the definition of 'political objects' contained in the 1913 Act. Only expenditure falling within the Act's definition is lawful. Expenditure is lawful under the Act if it is incurred: for contributions to a political party; for expenses, services and property provided for a political party; for costs involved in the selection and election of candidates for political office; for the support and maintenance of those holding political office; for political meetings or conferences and the expenses of delegates and for producing, publishing and distributing literature, films and advertisements intended to persuade people to vote or not to vote for a candidate or a political party.

Finally, Part IV of the 1984 Act enables ballots held under Parts I and III of the Act to qualify for state financial assistance. Unions wishing to receive financial assistance can apply to the Certification Officer. He is required to follow the rules laid down by the Employment Act 1980 and the Funds for Trade Union Ballots (Amendment) Regulations in coming to a decision. The main purpose of this financial provision is to cover the heavy costs of conducting postal ballots of the full membership of trade unions. Financial assistance is available for secret postal ballots dealing with the following: calling or ending industrial action; electing a union's principal executive body or any other posts provided by the rules; amending union rules; approving or disapproving amalgamation proposals; accepting or rejecting a pay and conditions offer made by an employer; and for political fund review ballots.

The claimed objective of the Trade Union Act 1984 is to 'return trade unions to their members'. The main instrument intended to achieve this is the secret postal ballot, or, where appropriate, carefully conducted workplace ballots. Opposition to the Act is largely a rejection of the arguments that existing trade union rules, balloting systems and internal democratic procedures are faulty in any major way. In opposing the 1984 Act, the TUC initially rejected the use of public funds to pay for trade union elections and unions applying for financial assistance were faced with possible expulsion from the TUC. This policy was subsequently modified however. It will be some years before it is possible to say if the 1984 Act is working as intended and whether the results are more moderate trade union leadership and less militant attitudes to industrial action, as well as reduced involvement with party politics.

10.7   HEALTH AND SAFETY AT WORK

The early factory system which grew out of the industrial revolution during the opening decades of the nineteenth century created wretched working conditions, especially for the many young children and women employed in textile factories and the coalmines. The prevailing economic and political philosophy of *laissez-faire* initially discouraged Parliament from passing protective legislation but the social outcry and shock to Christian conscience at such working conditions eventually led the state to intervene. Thus laws controlling the length of working hours for children were enacted and women were not allowed to be employed in mines 'dragging trucks of coal to which they were harnessed by a chain and girdle going on all-fours, in conditions of dirt, heat and indecency which are scarcely printable.'[29]

Yet the early factory legislation of 1802 and 1833 was not characterized by a concern for the safety of life and limb. It focused, rather, on the excessively long hours worked by women and children in particular industries, and on the morality and religious education of the industrial revolution's new working classes. One of the main problems of this legislation was the enforcement of the standards established by Parliament in the new factories of the north. This led in 1833 to a limited form of state factory inspection which was steadily strengthened by successive Acts of Parliament. Safety legislation throughout the nineteenth century and well into the present century, however, did not develop along coherent and consistent policy lines. It was enacted in a piecemeal manner to deal with public concern and worker agitation over specific matters such as working hours and dangerous conditions of work in factories, mines, railways, shipping, glass manufacture, baking and road transport. This piecemeal approach to safety legislation continued after the Second World War, though greater effort was subsequently made to codify existing legislation along industrial lines and to strengthen the powers of the various inspectorates.

By 1970, there were nearly 30 Acts of Parliament dealing specifically or partially with industrial safety, some 500 legal regulations, and seven separate inspectorates. The principal legislation, still largely in force, was: the Agriculture (Poisonous Substances) Act 1952; the Mines and Quarries Act 1954; the Agriculture (Safety, Health and Welfare Provision) Act 1956; the Factories Act 1961; and the Offices Shops and Railway Premises Act 1963. The responsibility for enforcing safety standards laid down by the various statutes was divided between seven largely autonomous inspectorates: the Factory Inspectorate; the Mines and Quarries Inspectorate; the Agricultural Safety

Inspectorate; the Explosives Inspectorate; the Nuclear Installations Inspectorate; the Radio Chemical Inspectorate; and the Alkali and Clean Air Inspectorate.

During the late 1960s, increasing concern was expressed by the public, the trade unions, and employers about Britain's poor record in industrial health and safety matters. There was also concern about the plethora of disconnected, confusing, overlapping and often antiquated legislation, and the outdated and inadequate systems of inspection and legal enforcement of minimum safety standards. In 1970, the Committee on Safety and Health at Work was appointed under the chairmanship of Alfred Robens. Its terms of reference were: to review the provisions made for securing health and safety at work; to consider what changes were needed in existing legislation; to examine the nature and extent of voluntary action by management and employees in securing safe working conditions; and to state what steps could be taken to protect the safety of the general public as well as of employees.

The Report of the Committee on Safety and Health at Work marked a completely new approach to industrial safety. It stressed the apparently surprising viewpoint that health and safety at work could not be adequately secured by existing legislation or inspectorates. It would be best pursued, it argued, by creating a climate in which government, management and employees were jointly responsible for the voluntary attainment and supervision of adequate safety standards.

> We have stressed that the promotion of safety and health at work is first and foremost a matter of efficient management. But it is not a management prerogative. In this context more than most, real progress is impossible without the full co-operation and commitment of all employees. How can this be encouraged? We believe that . . . workpeople . . . must be able to participate fully in the making and monitoring of arrangements for safety and health at their place of work.[30]

The Report also criticized the volume of overlapping and confusing legislation which dealt piecemeal with the specific safety problems of different industries. It criticized too: the weaknesses of the different small and autonomous inspectorates; the inadequacy of fines and the legal enforcement of safety standards; and the lack of a powerful centralized agency with responsibilities for research, education and the establishment of specific standards of health and safety at work for all employees.

The Health and Safety at Work etc. Act 1974 closely followed the recommendations of the Robens Report. Part I of the Act establishes in broad terms the general duties of employers, the self-employed and employees in achieving acceptable safety standards at work. It states:

(1) It shall be the duty of every employer to ensure, so far as is reasonably practicable, the health, safety and welfare at work of all his employees.
(2) Without prejudice to the generality of an employer's duty under the preceding subsection, the matters to which that duty extends include in particular –
    (a) the provision and maintenance of plant and systems of work that are so far as is reasonably practicable, safe and without risks to health;
    (b) arrangements for ensuring, so far as is reasonably practicable, safety and absence of risks to health in connection with the use, handling, storage and transport of articles and substances;
    (c) the provision of such information, instruction, training and supervision as is necessary to ensure, as far as is reasonably practicable, the health and safety at work of his employees;
    (d) so far as is reasonably practicable as regards any place of work under the employer's control the maintenance of it in a condition that is safe and without risks to health and maintenance of means of access to and egress from it that are safe and without such risks;
    (e) the provision and maintenance of a working environment for his employees that is,

so far as is reasonably practicable, safe, without risk to health, and adequate as regards facilities and arrangements for their welfare at work.[31]

The 1974 Act lays the responsibility on employers for issuing a written policy statement on health and safety within their organizations and for devising means of implementing it. This policy statement has to be brought to the attention of all the workforce. Where safety representatives are appointed by recognized independent trade unions, employers are obliged to consult them on all safety matters. By making these general duties for health and safety applicable to 'every employer', including the self-employed and the controllers of premises, the 1974 Act ensures that no employers are excluded from the general legal obligation of ensuring satisfactory health and safety standards at work. These general duties on employers are also extended to protect members of the public, thereby giving the Act extremely wide application.

Part I of the 1974 Act similarly lays a general duty upon all employees to take 'reasonable care' whilst at work not only for their own health and safety, but also for that of other employees. Employees are required, for example, to co-operate with all those persons in supervisory capacities charged with carrying out the general duties laid upon the employer by the Act. The Act continues the common law practice of holding employees responsible for the observance of necessary safety measures, the avoidance of reckless behaviour, and the interference with or misuse of 'anything provided in the interests of health, safety or welfare in pursuance of any of the relevant statutory provisions.'[32]

Section 6 of the 1974 Act imposes for the first time a general duty on designers, manufacturers, importers and suppliers of certain products to ensure that the articles which they offer for sale are designed, constructed and tested to be safe when properly used. They also have to ensure that information is available about the article, the testing of it, and how it should be correctly used. Finally, they are required to carry out any necessary research to discover, eliminate and minimize any risks to health and safety related to the product which they are designing, manufacturing, importing or supplying.

Sections 10 to 14 of the 1974 Act create a new and centralized Health and Safety Commission (HSC) to direct the general policy of health and safety at work and to implement the many long-term implications of the Act. It comprises a full time independent Chairperson and nine part time Commissioners made up of three union-nominated members, three employer-nominated members, two from the local authorities and an independent member. The Commission has taken over the responsibilities for most occupational, health and safety matters formerly divided among several Government departments. It is also responsible for forming a unified inspectorate, undertaking research, and providing training, education and general information to those requiring it. Control of general policy is in the hands of the mainly part time HSC, the day-to-day responsibility for health and safety matters, the implementation of the HSC's policies and the general administration and enforcement of safety standards at work rests with the Health and Safety Executive (HSE) which is staffed by civil servants. It is a basic duty of the HSC and the HSE to propose ways of consolidating existing and overlapping legislation. They are also expected to issue safety regulations and codes of practice to be observed by employers, employees and the courts. Ultimate control over the HSC and HSE is vested in the Secretary of State for Employment who may 'give to the Commission at any time such directions as he thinks fit with respect to its functions . . . or expedient to give in the interests of the safety of the State.'[33]

Sections 18 to 26 of the 1974 Act provide for the appointment of inspectors by the HSE, with powers to enforce the administration of all safety legislation and the required standards of health and safety at work. It is an offence for any employer or for any other person to obstruct or to prevent the entry of inspectors to premises which they are legally entitled to inspect. The main instruments of enforcement open to the inspectorate are 'improvement' and 'prohibition' notices which can be served on employers by individual inspectors. If inspectors consider that a law has been broken in respect of health and safety at work, they can issue an improvement notice to the responsible person requiring that the contravention be remedied within a certain time. If the necessary action is not taken within the specified time, a prohibition notice may then be issued stopping the particular work operation. Inspectors also possess the power to issue prohibition notices if there is an immediate risk or danger to workers or to the general public.

Employers may appeal against these notices to an industrial tribunal. But until the tribunal makes a decision the prohibition notice applies. Where an inspector thinks there is no immediate risk, a 'deferred prohibition' notice may be served upon an employer giving it time to take the necessary remedial steps without stopping production. Non-compliance with improvement or prohibition notices can lead to fixed maximum fines imposed by magistrates' courts, or unlimited fines by higher courts in the case of trial by indictment and even imprisonment in exceptional cases. The HSC, the HSE and the inspectorates also possess powers under Sections 27 and 28 of the 1974 Act obliging persons and organizations to disclose necessary information relating to health and safety matters to them. These powers may only be used with the consent of the Secretary of State for Employment.

Part II of the 1974 Act establishes the Employment Medical Advisory Service (EMAS) and defines its responsibilities and functions. EMAS is an organization of doctors and nurses whose task is to give advice about occupational health, and to help to prevent ill health caused by bad working conditions. Employers, employees, self-employed persons or accredited trade union representatives can all request the assistance of EMAS with any occupational health problems. It advises individuals on the type of work which best suits them or on the work that they should avoid on health grounds. EMAS also gives advice to the inspectorates and to the HSE on long-term policy recommendations on occupational health. Where certain industrial health regulations are in force, or where people are employed on known hazardous work, EMAS gives medical advice and conducts medical examinations of employees. EMAS is also concerned with the measurements of physical and environmental work hazards such as noise, vibration, dust and mental stress and in setting standards and acceptable levels of exposure to such health hazards. Finally, EMAS carries out long-term research into various aspects of occupational health about which little or nothing might be known.

Part III of the Act makes detailed changes to the building safety regulations to improve health and safety specifically in the building and construction industries which have bad safety records. Lastly, Part IV of the Act deals with other miscellaneous and general matters including, for example, those relating to radiological protection and fire precautions at work.

The safety regulations and codes of practice, issued under the 1974 Act, require the obligatory appointment of employee safety representatives and statutory safety committees at the workplace. The Robens Report clearly stated that predominant reliance on a system of external health and safety inspection had not proved to be particularly successful. This should be strengthened, it recommended, in order to underpin an internal system of regulation, control and inspection by management and employees jointly. This fundamental change in emphasis to the monitoring of health and safety standards at work cannot be stressed too strongly, since the Health and Safety at Work etc. Act 1974 is largely founded on this principle.

We recommend, therefore, that there should be a statutory duty on every employer to consult with his employees or their representatives at the workplace on measures for promoting safety and health at work, and to provide arrangements for the participation of employees in the development of such measures . . . Guidance should, however, be given in a code of practice outlining model arrangements, including advice on joint safety committees and the appointment of employees' safety representatives.[34]

This general duty of management to consult with employees and to recognize the appointment of trade union safety representatives and the formation of safety committees is embodied in Section 2 of the 1974 Act. It is also to be found in the regulations on safety representatives and safety committees and the code of practice on safety representatives approved by the HSC and by the Secretary of State for Employment in 1977. In order to facilitate the emergence of competent safety representatives, the HSC has issued a code of practice on time off for training safety representatives. The regulations and codes became operative in October 1978. Independent recognized trade unions are now given the legal right to appoint safety representatives from among their members at their workplace, without obstruction or interference from the employer. At the written request of any two union appointed safety representatives, an employer is obliged to form a safety committee. Section 116 and Schedule 15 of the Employment Protection Act 1975 abolish the right of employees, other than those who are members of independent recognized unions, to elect safety representatives within the meaning of the regulations and codes.

The code of practice on safety representatives recommends that safety representatives take an overall and general view of their duties, rather than the narrow one of only representing their own union members. The code goes on to advise that the number of representatives appointed within an organization should bear some relationship to several factors. These include: its total number of employees; its variety of occupations; the size of the workplace and its locations; the operation of shiftwork; the types of work activity; and the degree of inherent danger within them. Other factors to be considered when appointing safety representatives are: the rate of change taking place in working conditions; its technology and manpower levels; and the problems of workplaces with high risks such as in steel and in chemicals and those with low risks but with specific danger areas within them. Where possible, safety representatives should have at least two years experience of the workplace or similar workplaces with the same safety problems.

The advised functions of safety representatives include keeping themselves informed of the general legal requirements on health and safety at work and the specific legal hazards facing the employees which they represent. They are expected to know the best precautionary measures available to protect employees. They should conduct regular inspections of the workplace and investigate the circumstances relating to accidents and known high risk work situations. Safety representatives must also be fully aware of their employer's safety policy and should help keep it up to date as well as encouraging cooperation with its objectives by all employees. They are advised to bring all known safety hazards to the attention of the employer and to assist in taking measures designed to reduce such hazards. Where possible, safety representatives are encouraged to keep standard written records and to make them available for inspection by all those concerned with health and safety matters at the workplace.

When Safety Inspectors visit a workplace, management and safety representatives have to be given copies of their reports and of any advice provided. Current safety regulations make it clear that criminal charges cannot be brought against safety representatives when accidents happen or when failures to meet the requirements of any safety legislation occur. According to the HSC:

the Commission have directed that the Health and Safety Executive shall not institute criminal proceedings against any safety representative for any act or omission by him in respect of the performance of functions assigned to him by the Regulations or indicated by the Code of Practice.[35]

The regulations strongly recommend the establishment of voluntary joint management and safety representative committees. If an employer refuses to establish a safety committee, a complaint can be made to an industrial tribunal by the safety representatives of independent recognized trade unions. The tribunal can then issue an award compelling the employer to establish a safety committee within a three month period, after consultation with the safety representatives and union officials. Notices must be published for the attention of all employees, announcing the formation of the safety committee, its membership, the area which it covers and the safety policy that it has to implement. The HSC advises that specific safety committees shall be established and that health and safety matters should not be made a subsidiary or additional responsibility of, say, a works negotiating committee. It also advises the establishment of separate safety committees for clearly distinguishable geographical establishments. In very large workplaces it may be necessary to have more than one safety committee.

The functions of safety committees are largely determined by management and safety representatives. It is suggested that their functions should include the following: a careful statistical study of accidents; health trends; notifiable diseases; known hazards and 'near misses'; and the formulation of precautionary policies to reduce the incidence of accidents. Further functions include: safety audits; joint safety inspections at regular intervals; the consideration of Inspectors' reports on the workplace; the reports arising out of special inspections and investigations by safety representatives; the joint production of works safety rules and safe working systems; the organization of safety training and of visits by health and safety experts; and annual inspections of the complete workplace by the whole safety committee. Lastly, the HSC advises that the composition of safety committees:

> should be settled in consultation between management and the trade union representatives concerned through the use of the normal machinery. The aim should be to keep the total size as reasonably compact as possible and compatible with the adequate representation of the interests of management and all the employees, including safety representatives. The number of management representatives should not exceed the number of employees' representatives.[36]

Under the powers given by the 1974 Act, the HSE has issued a stream of major regulations, codes of practice, guidance notes and consultative documents. Regulations which greatly extend the duties and responsibilities of employers cover such things as: the classification, packaging and labelling of dangerous substances; the transportation by road of dangerous substances; dangerous emissions into the atmosphere; first aid requirements at the workplace; the protection of young people on government training schemes; poisonous agricultural substances; the notification of accidents and dangerous occurrences; and many other matters vital to the safety of working people.

10.8   EMERGENCY POWERS, PUBLIC EMPLOYEES AND POLITICAL STRIKES

Governments have long recognized that extensive and prolonged strikes or strikes which endanger life, essential services and property cannot be permitted to go unchecked. Yet this presents considerable political and legal difficulties in a country where the liberty to strike has been firmly established. Virtually all industrial countries possess some legislative provisions to protect essential services, 'or to deal with the problem of the termination of supplies or the withdrawal of the means of supply by reason of industrial action.'[37] But in Britain the tradition of voluntarism in industrial relations, especially in the right to strike and the process of collective bargaining, certainly until fairly recently, has ensured that government possesses fewer controls in these respects than in most other western industrial countries. Section 5 of the Conspiracy and Protection of Property Act 1875, however, still allows for criminal prosecutions where any workers breaking their contracts of employment are likely to cause serious bodily harm or injury to valuable property. This criminal provision is little used yet it remains on statute.

The Emergency Powers Acts of 1920 and 1964 enable governments faced with severe disruptive industrial action to declare a state of emergency, if it appears:

> there have occurred, or are about to occur, events of such a nature as to be calculated, by interfering with the supply and distribution of food, water, fuel or light, or with the means of locomotion, to deprive the community, or any substantial portion of the community, of the essentials of life.[38]

Such a declaration of an emergency can only be made by Parliament and lasts for one month, although the period can be extended if Parliament so decides. In practice, such emergencies have not lasted very long. During an emergency period, orders in council can be issued to secure the preservation of peace and the maintenance of essential supplies and services. Such orders, giving wide powers to governments, must be laid before Parliament and last for seven days at a time. Such orders, however, cannot forbid strikes or peaceful picketing or require a person to return to work. Moreover, existing criminal law may not be changed and orders seeking to impose fines and imprisonment upon striking employees without trial are not permitted by the Act.

The aim of the 1920 Act is to facilitate direct government action during emergencies without introducing new and arbitrary criminal sanctions against any section of the community. It does not restrict the right of Parliament to control the use of emergency powers and the length of time which they remain in force. The Emergency Powers Act 1964 further extended the powers of the 1920 Act by permitting a government to use the armed forces on 'urgent work of national importance' without any consultation with Parliament. This Act is primarily intended to deal with natural catastrophes. But it could be used in damaging trade disputes, as for example, where the withdrawal of their labour by firemen requires the government to use the armed forces to fight fires and to save lives and property. In fact, emergency powers and orders issued under the emergency power legislation have been used only eight times since 1920 – during: the General Strike of 1926; in three dock strikes; and in strikes involving electricity workers, railwaymen, seamen and mineworkers.

Another area where the government has intervened in strike activity was through the Industrial Relations Act 1971. This gave powers to the Secretary of State for Employment to apply to the National Industrial Relations Court (NIRC) for an order directing those responsible not to organize strike action for a period of up to 60 days. These provisions for a 'cooling off' period were aimed at preventing strikes which could, amongst other things, be 'gravely injurious to the national economy' or 'create serious risk of public disorder'. This Act also permitted the Secretary of State to apply to the NIRC, in similar circumstances, for a compulsory ballot of union members, under the supervision of the Commission on Industrial Relations, asking them if they wished to support a strike called by their union's executive or its leaders. Both these devices were clearly an extension of the powers of the state to prevent damaging strikes. These powers, however, were repealed by the Trade Union and Labour Relations Act 1974.

Perhaps only a minority of people would deny the freedom to strike enjoyed by the vast majority of workers to groups of employees doing essential public service jobs, such as firemen or ambulance drivers. Few, equally, would deny to a government the right to use the armed forces to provide a skeleton service in those areas of employment where life, limb and property are placed in jeopardy by striking workers. It is a question of public opinion and political judgement when to invoke emergency powers whose use could easily exacerbate an already difficult strike situation, on the one hand, but whose absence could equally result in the breakdown of essential public services and public order on the other.

There have also been limitations placed on the freedom to strike of some public sector employees. The Conspiracy and Protection of Property Act 1875, for example, provided criminal sanctions against workers in the water and gas industries who:

> wilfully and maliciously broke a contract of service with that authority knowing or having reasonable cause to believe that the probable consequence of his so doing, either alone or in combination, would be to deprive the inhabitants of the area covered by the authority of the whole or the greater part of their supply of that commodity.[39]

The electricity supply industry was added to this list in 1919. The Merchant Shipping Acts of 1894 and 1970 similarly provided criminal sanctions against striking seamen on board ship, implicitly linking such strikes with the concept of mutiny on the high seas. Seamen can strike, however, providing that 48 hours' notice is given after their ship has reached port in the United Kingdom.

The police also are forbidden to strike by the Police Act 1919 which was enacted following a police strike in that year. This Act made it unlawful for members of the police forces to join a trade union but the Police Act 1964 permits them to join the Police Federations which represent police officers over pay and conditions of service. Whilst not technically trade unions the Police Federations act very much like them. The British armed forces can join a trade union but they cannot take any form of industrial action. Similarly, the Post Office Act 1953 makes it an offence for post office workers to interfere with the delivery of mail for political or sympathetic strike purposes. In this case, it is only the Attorney-General who can initiate a prosecution against postal workers. The Industrial Relations Act 1971 repealed those provisions in the Conspiracy and Protection of Property Act 1875 threatening workers in essential public services with criminal proceedings for taking strike action. It is now only the police therefore, who are explicitly forbidden by law to strike or to take part in other industrial action against their employers.

It is common for some people to try and draw a distinction between 'political', 'economic' and 'ordinary' strikes. Strikes in pursuit of purely economic objectives, such as higher pay or better working conditions, for example, are usually regarded as being normal and even acceptable. However, strikes aimed at social objectives such as those to advance nationalization or to combat racial discrimination are regarded by some as being political, unfair and unconstitutional methods of achieving their ends. Yet it is extremely difficult if not impossible in practice to distinguish between economic and political strikes. An attempt to redistribute income from profits to pay, for example, can be seen as a political activity in much the same way that redistributive changes in income tax are political. Many trade unionists declare that it is impossible to separate economic from political aims in industrial relations.

Furthermore, governments intervene in so many aspects of economic activity today that any attempt to draw a meaningful distinction between politics and economics almost certainly ends in failure. At the same time, some trade unions have long held social objectives such as increased old age pensions, the nationalization of key industries and high levels of public spending on welfare provisions, although these have generally been pursued through the manifesto commitments of the Labour Party rather than by direct industrial action. The question could also be asked whether a strike by employees in pursuit of a pay claim in excess of a maximum stipulated by a government as an essential element of its pay policy is an economic strike or a political one. It would appear, then, that the concept of the political strike owes more to ideological distinctions rather than to any clear analytical separation between what are political ends and means and what are economic ones.

It has often been held, for instance, that general strikes are political because they are aimed at bringing down a constitutionally elected government or designed to make it abandon a legislative course of action. The General Strike of 1926, for instance, was held by the Government to be political, unconstitutional and unlawful, whilst the TUC insisted that it was a sympathetic strike aimed at helping the mineworkers to resist a wage cut caused by the withdrawal of coal subsidies by the Government. After its victory in the General Strike, the Government passed the Trade Disputes and Trade Unions Act 1927 making general and sympathetic strikes unlawful; the Act was repealed in 1946. Other examples serve to illustrate the confusion which exists over what constitutes a political strike. A strike by dock workers in 1970, for example, sought to advance the nationalization of the docks at a time when a Bill for a partial nationalization was before Parliament. In 1966, at the height of the seamen's official strike for higher pay in breach of the Government's current incomes policy, the Prime Minister declared in Parliament that it was a strike against the State by a tightly knit group of politically motivated men. Sporadic strikes occurred during and after the passing of the Industrial Relations Act 1971 by unions and by groups of workers opposed to it. Also after the election of the Thatcher Government in 1979, some trade unions organized strikes, rallies, marches and national days of protest against the Employment Acts of 1980 and 1982, cuts in public expenditure and plans to privatize parts of the nationalized industries.

In all these cases, it would appear that the strikers could not or would not distinguish between the political objectives of these strikes and their own economic self-interest. Whilst political strikes, general strikes and sympathetic strikes in Britain are not criminal, the Employment Act 1982 appears to render political strikes liable to actions for civil damages by redefining a trade dispute in Section 18. This limits lawful trade disputes to those between workers and their employer. Further, a union only possesses legal immunity in a trade dispute which 'relates wholly or mainly to' those matters defined in Section 29 of the 1974 Act, rather than being only 'connected with' them. The general effect of these two changes is to make it possible for employers to bring cases for civil damages in trade disputes where it is claimed that the dispute is not between the employer and its workers, or where the strike is not closely connected with those matters listed in Section 29 of the 1974 Act. Obviously, many of the examples of so called political strikes given above would be potentially open to civil action should employers wish to take it. Equally, these two changes in the legal meaning of a trade dispute make sympathy strikes potentially actionable for civil damages. More importantly, perhaps, these legal changes make it possible for employers to obtain injunctions stopping strike action which they argue is political in its nature and intent. As a practical method of stopping strikes, since 1982 employers have found injunctions more attractive than bitter and protracted court actions. If injunctions serve their purpose of stopping a strike, little is achieved by proceeding with civil actions for damages against the unions.

10.9 SUMMARY

The fundamental requirements for the existence of trade unions and collective bargaining are: the freedom for employees to join trade unions and to take part in their activities; the freedom of trade unionists to strike, picket and peaceably further an industrial dispute; and the recognition of trade unions by employers for collective bargaining purposes. Most of these essential elements of collective bargaining within plural societies are now internationally recognized as being basic human freedoms which characterize parliamentary democracies.

Abstract social principles, however, provide only unenforceable human freedoms unless they are backed by positive laws enabling individuals and collectivities to claim their rights through, for example, state-funded but independent conciliation and arbitration services and labour courts. British labour law now provides, for example, procedures for independent trade unions and their members to seek disclosure of information for collective bargaining purposes from employers. As a means of last resort, the law permits individual trade unionists to seek legal redress if they are unreasonably or unfairly expelled from a trade union, or if they are excluded from any trade union membership activity or benefit to which their union rule book entitles them. However, the law does not enable individuals to claim the absolute right to be admitted to membership of specific trade unions.

The law and the courts also clearly recognize the freedom of employees to strike and to take other non-criminal forms of industrial action, including picketing, in contemplation or furtherance of an industrial dispute. Legislation since 1979, however, has considerably narrowed the legal definition of trade disputes thus making many forms of strike action, which hitherto have been common practice, actionable in the civil courts for damages against the unions concerned. This in turn means that the courts are once again able to issue injunctions against striking workers pending proposed civil action.

It would appear, however, that the use of the law to control or to limit strikes is far less effective than the development of jointly agreed collective bargaining procedures to avoid disputes between employers and trade unions. It remains a basic principle of much of the collective labour law passed since 1974, therefore, that the state should explicitly encourage the development of voluntary collective bargaining and the joint regulation of industrial relations on an agreed basis. ACAS, for example, is charged with the general duty of putting this principle into effect by means of persuasion and collective conciliation between employers and unions.

The legal immunities protecting peaceful picketing have been considerably reduced by the Employment Acts 1980 and 1982. Broadly speaking, with the exception of certain permissible secondary picketing, legal picketing is now confined only to those employees in direct dispute with their employer picketing at their normal place of work. An employer faced with pickets who are not the employees with whom it is in dispute can seek injunctions against them, or their trade unions, as well as bringing a civil action for damages against them. The law relating to criminal offences committed during picketing, or in regard to mass picketing, remains unchanged. Experience of controlling flying pickets, violence and mass picketing during the coalmining dispute of 1984–5 suggests that existing police and court powers are reasonably adequate.

With the brief exception of the three-year period between 1971 and 1974, when the Industrial Relations Act 1971 was in force, collective agreements in Britain have been presumed to be legally unenforceable through the courts. Hence they are not regarded as legally binding contracts by statute law. This view of the essentially voluntary nature of collective agreements, however, has been obliquely breached by the legal requirements now laid upon employers to disclose certain information to trade union representatives for collective bargaining purposes.

Internal trade union democratic procedures are now affected by the secret ballot requirements of the Trade Union Act 1984. Secret postal or workplace ballots are necessary for the election of trade union principal executive bodies, before the authorization or endorsement of official industrial action and for the establishment or continuation of political funds and expenditure on trade union political objects. Where trade unions fail to hold ballots required by the 1984 Act, union members, employers and others can seek court injunctions and civil damages.

The report of the Robens Committee marked a fundamental change in approach to health and safety at work. The Health and Safety at Work etc. Act 1974 has created a powerful and centralized set of representative institutions. It is also intended to codify the piecemeal safety statutes passed over the last 150 years, as well as to form a unified health and safety inspectorate. The most radical intention of the 1974 Act, however, is to shift the principle of enforcement for health and safety at work away from external inspection to internal accountability. This is being done by making management and employees jointly responsible for adequate health and safety standards at work. The legally enforceable devices for advancing this new approach lie in the legal right of independent trade unions to appoint safety representatives at the workplace and to demand the formation of joint safety committees.

Finally, it is clear that governments have had continual difficulties in attempting to regulate industrial action by their own employees who provide essential services to the community, and what appears on occasions to be politicized industrial conflict. In practice, however, it is extremely problematic to define political strikes and to determine their constitutional acceptability.

10.10 REFERENCES

1. O. Kahn-Freund, *Labour and the Law*, Stevens, London, 1977, p. 9.
2. *Ibid.*, p. 15.
3. *Ibid.*, p. 173.
4. R. Lewis, Collective labour law, in G. S. Bain (ed.), *Industrial Relations in Britain*, Basil Blackwell, Oxford, 1983, p. 383.
5. K. W. Wedderburn, *The Worker and the Law*, Penguin Books, Harmondsworth, 1971, p. 410.
6. Trade Union and Labour Relations Act 1972 c. 52, s. 28(1).
7. O. Kahn-Freund, *op. cit.*, p. 220.
8. R. W. Rideout, *Principles of Labour Law*, Sweet and Maxwell, London, 1976, p. 257.
9. O. Kahn-Freund, *op. cit.*, p. 224.
10. R. W. Rideout, *op. cit.*, p. 263.
11. *Crofter Hand Woven Harris Tweed Company Limited* v. *Veitch* (1942), quoted in K. W. Wedderburn, *op. cit.*, p. 340.
12. O. Kahn-Freund, *op. cit.*, p. 225.
13. *Ibid.*
14. Conspiracy and Protection of Property Act 1875 38 & 39 Vict. c. 86, s. 7.
15. Trade Disputes Act 1906 6 Edw. VII c. 47, s. 2.
16. O. Kahn-Freund, *op. cit.*, p. 193.
17. *Ibid.*, p. 199.
18. *Ibid.*, p. 203.
19. *Ibid.*, p. 205.
20. *Ibid.*, p. 127.
21. R. W. Rideout, *op. cit.*, p. 59.
22. O. Kahn-Freund, *op. cit.*, p. 122.
23. Trade Union and Labour Relations Act 1984 c. 52, s. 18(1).
24. Employment Protection Act 1975, c. 71, s. 17(1).
25. *Ibid.*, s. 18(2).
26. *Ibid.*, s. 19(1).
27. Advisory Conciliation and Arbitration Service, *Code of Practice 2. Disclosure of Information for Collective Bargaining Purposes*, HMSO, London, 1977, p. 1.
28. *Ibid.*, p. 4.

29. S. Webb, Introduction to Hutchins and Harrison, *A History of Factory Legislation*, 1903, p. vii, quoted in K. W. Wedderburn, *op. cit.*, p. 241.
30. Report of the Committee, *Safety and Health at Work*, (Robens Report), HMSO, London, 1972, p. 18f.
31. Health and Safety at Work etc. Act, 1974, c. 37, s. 2.
32. R. W. Rideout, *op. cit.*, p. 386.
33. Health and Safety at Work etc. Act 1974, c. 37, s. 12.
34. Robens Report, *op. cit.*, p. 22.
35. Health and Safety Commission, *Safety Representatives and Safety Committees*, HMSO, London, 1977, p. 15.
36. *Ibid.*, p. 39.
37. R. W. Rideout, *op. cit.*, p. 334.
38. Emergency Powers Act 1920, quoted *ibid*. p. 335.
39. *Ibid.*, p. 296.

PART FOUR

Industrial Relations in Practice

11

Management and the Right to Manage

'The right to manage', also known as 'managerial prerogative', 'managerial rights', or 'managerial functions', is at the centre of industrial relations decision making. The right to manage has always been jealously guarded by those managing organizations whether as owner managers or as professional managers of corporate employers. Similarly, trade unions, their representatives and union members have continuously coveted, challenged and sought to share through collective bargaining those managerial prerogatives most affecting employee interests at corporate and workplace level. Having indicated in Chapters Nine and Ten how externally generated labour law has effectively tempered the unilateral right to manage by managers within organizations, we turn in this chapter to examine the nature of managerial prerogative and those areas of enterprise decision making where it remains today.

11.1   THE RIGHT TO MANAGE

The right to manage relates to those areas of corporate and workplace decision making which managements consider to be exclusively theirs and hence are not subject either to collective bargaining with trade union representatives or to legal regulation. Such rights were traditionally taken to include the hiring and firing of employees, promotion, discipline, manning, production control, overtime allocation and other job-related issues. Marsh argues that the notion of managerial prerogative 'carries with it the implication that there are actions or areas for action so essential to management that these must remain unilaterally the property of management if management itself is to continue to exist.'[1] However, since recognized trade unions seek to constrain unilateral managerial control within work organizations, the question arises whether there is any logical limit to the extent to which trade unions can penetrate into the traditional functions of management. Where unions are recognized for collective bargaining purposes, therefore, the right to manage is never absolute. Even where there are no trade unions, works councils and informal customs and practices effectively constrain the right to manage in many areas of job decision making.

Any definitive description of managerial prerogative is problematic, since the term has a number of different meanings. In practice, there is no clear distinction from one industry to another of what exactly constitutes a solely managerial function. The industry where the struggle to retain the so-called right to manage has been most bitterly fought in Britain is engineering. After the national lock-out in the industry in 1897–98 and under the terms of settlement dated 28 January 1898, the federated employers insisted they would 'admit no interference with the management of their business'. They also reserved the right to introduce into any federated workshops, at the option of the employer, any condition of labour operational at the beginning of the dispute. The agreement did not apply, however, to the determination of hours of work or rates of pay. Similarly, in the Managerial Functions Agreement of 1922, the parties agreed that 'The Employers have the right to manage their establishments and the Trade Unions have the right to exercise their functions.'[2]

The reasons why engineering employers have continuously asserted their right to manage are not difficult to identify, although they derive largely from nineteenth century circumstances. The first justification for the right to manage was the claim that private owners of industrial capital, or their appointed agents, had the right to do as they wished with what they owned or were responsible for. More importantly, the insistence by the engineering employers on their managerial functions was also a product of nineteenth century craft trade unionism. The early craft unions in the engineering trades did not wish to negotiate with employers on terms and conditions but wanted to impose their own common rules of the trade upon employers unilaterally. They wanted in other words: to determine union pay rates for the job; to prevent 'de-skilling'; to lay down their own manning levels; to control overtime; and to regulate the supply of apprentices into their trades. They were also opposed to management introducing piecework payment systems. The engineering employers, in short, considered that they were being opposed by craft organizations which would accept no compromises with them. If trade union craft controls were to be rigidly insisted upon, the employers held, then there was no alternative other than to maintain their own exclusive right to manage within their enterprises. It is a tradition remaining strong in engineering and related industries today. A further justification of the right to manage is the 'economic efficiency argument'. This holds that professional managers alone, whether in private or public enterprise, have the necessary expertise and knowledge to make the 'right' decisions within their organizations. According to Storey, since managers are merely taking 'technical' decisions in their enterprises in the best interests of all parties, 'it would be wrong to prejudice their judgement with considerations of a partisan, political nature'.[3]

Seen in these contexts, the doctrine of managerial prerogative is not an easy orthodoxy to view sympathetically today. Yet the struggle to maintain managerial prerogative continues in most work organizations. 'In a very real sense the conflict over managerial prerogatives and functions is part of the struggle . . . for status and recognition'[4] by the employers' managerial élite: an élite based not on property rights, but on its claimed knowledge and skills of management techniques and business administration. The struggle is also part of the conflict between management's need to innovate within enterprises and the employee's need for job security and job control. Ever since the early trade union challenges to management's virtually unrestricted powers in industry over 100 years ago, managers have used the managerial prerogative argument in their own defence against further trade union encroachments into managerial functions and of their responsibility for enterprise efficiency and success. Any restriction on this prerogative, they argue, is bound to result in lower economic performance and loss of managerial control.

Notwithstanding these points, by definition the union role is primarily one of attempting to limit the powers of managements to make decisions unilaterally within both private and public enterprises in matters affecting their members' employment and job interests. By its very nature trade unionism is a device aimed at containing managerial prerogatives. Yet despite the increasing restrictions put on management's right to manage by trade unions, economic performance within work organizations does not seem to have been unduly hampered by their presence. It could be argued in fact, that management's capacity to adapt itself to the conditions imposed by the presence of trade unions is generally underestimated by managers. Indeed, it has been suggested 'that further restrictions on managerial prerogative by the workers would be more likely to improve than to endanger organizational performance'.[5] It is also clear that although many managers continue to assume that there are some prerogatives which trade unions must never be allowed to encroach upon, they are increasingly hazy about their boundaries. Taken to its logical extreme:

> Within a system of management by agreement there would no longer exist any area of management decision-taking where management itself could claim an absolute and uni-lateral right to resist union influence in any form.[6]

Managerial prerogative today, then, may most usefully be defined as 'the residue of discretionary powers of decision left to management when the regulative impacts of law and collective agreements have been subtracted'.[7] Although some unions disclaim any desire to participate in management, just as management contests the right of trade unions to obviate its own functions, the extent to which collective bargaining, in containing managerial prerogatives, becomes participation in management is a matter of degree. Further, since collective bargaining affects so many aspects of organizational decision-making, a form of worker participation in management exists wherever trade unions are recognized for collective bargaining purposes by employers.

In short, although trade union penetration of managerial prerogatives is likely to be greatest in those areas most closely associated with personnel management – such as in pay determination, conditions of employment, job security and methods of working – only practical and ideological considerations place real limits on trade union interest in the technical aspects of present day managerial functions. What were the boundaries of managerial rights in the past are natural areas of collective bargaining today. Further-more, what seem to be the boundaries of managerial rights today might well be natural areas of collective bargaining and participation in the future. Whilst employees do not appear to demand participation in all managerial decisions, it is 'neither practicable nor desirable to draw up a list of decisions which should be for ever exclusively manage-ment's business'.[8]

11.2   WORKS RULES, DISCIPLINE AND DISMISSAL

It is not generally realized the extent to which the growth of early capitalism imposed severe constraints on the daily lives of ordinary working people. These included strict rules on time keeping, regular attendance at work, maintaining standards on the job, obeying unquestioningly the orders of management, and generally conforming to the rules of the workplace. Adjustment to these new circumstances of work did not come easily and one of the early prerogatives imposed by the 'masters' on their 'servants' was a harsh and rigid industrial discipline. Well into this century conditions of employment were strictly regulated in most workplaces and employees were tightly controlled by managerial authority alone. In the railway workshops at Crewe around 1900, for example:

> No smoking was allowed. Suspension was the usual penalty . . . on one occasion a man was dismissed on the spot for knocking out an unlit pipe against a door-post. Employees were not allowed to wash their hands, under pain of instant dismissal. Two visits to the lavatory in one day could mean suspension.[9]

Clearly, the main purpose of disciplinary rules of this sort both to deter and to deal out retribution to recalcitrant workers within a system of rigid managerial control.

Works rules

The old style of industrial discipline derived from the belief that it was solely management's prerogative to make decisions, especially on disciplinary matters, and that there
should be no restrictions on this right, particularly from subordinates. Such a view of
workplace discipline was invariably combined with either an authoritarian or a paternalistic style of management. It often coincided with a set of disciplinary rules harshly
administered, inconsistently applied and arbitrarily enforced. As employing establishments grew in size, and as employers were forced to delegate their disciplinary
authority to lower levels of management, it was first line supervisors who emerged with
almost absolute powers of hiring and firing subordinate workers. The main written
sources of these disciplinary regulations were the so-called 'works rules'. These were
usually a comprehensive code of written rules drawn up unilaterally by the employers to
regulate the behaviour of subordinates in their establishments. They were regarded by
the courts as express terms of the contracts of employment between individuals and
their employers, and infringements of which could result in fines, suspension from duty,
or instant dismissal.

Works rules continue to exist in most establishments today but are no longer the sole
source of disciplinary authority. In law 'works rules seem to have a kind of intermediate
place between the collectively regulated parts of the employment contract and the parts
which are purely individual.'[10] Nowadays, works rules are intended to do a great deal
more than merely to make known to employees an employer's disciplinary
requirements. They are found in a variety of forms. In some cases, they are simply
occasional notices fixed to works notice boards informing employees of general instructions from management. In other cases, the separate instructions are collected together
in a booklet described as the 'Works Rules Book', 'Conditions of Employment', or the
'Employee Handbook'. With successive revisions the text expands to become 'an
amalgam of disciplinary rules, warnings, advice, claims to managerial "rights", pension
fund regulations, information about the firm's welfare benefits, and so on.'[11]

A detailed examination of works rule books in the engineering industry concluded
that they are full of wide-ranging claims of the rights of management and strongly
worded clauses referring to the obligations of employees. They cover five main items at
the workplace: engagement; the employee's duties and the authority of management;
pay and welfare services; explicit rules of workplace behaviour; and suspension or
termination of employment. It is suggested that they serve 'contractual', 'precautionary', 'regulative', 'informative', and 'expressive' purposes. Through the latter, for
instance, managements seek legitimacy for their works rules and for administering
them. 'In the light of these considerations works rule books seem to operate as one of
the most explicit instruments of enterprise government at the workplace.'[12] Some
organizations are now bringing their works rules into the area of joint regulation, by
attaching them to written local agreements negotiated with trade unions.

Disciplinary and dismissal procedures

For a number of reasons disciplinary practices have changed considerably in recent
years. Capital invested in the training of employees, for example, has increased the
value of human resources at work, 'making the indiscriminate use of disciplinary action,
especially dismissal, even more wasteful'.[13] Furthermore, most full time employees
now have a statutory right not to be unfairly dismissed by their employers after two
years of continuous employment. Also, management's powers to take unilateral decisions on disciplinary matters have been severely curtailed by the challenge of trade
union organization. At the very least, where trade unions are recognized, they

normally have the right to represent their members when disciplinary action is taken against them. In these circumstances, the unilateral managerial right to discipline employees is no longer absolute. On the one hand, punitive managerial sanctions against employees suspected of disciplinary infringements have given way to corrective action being taken against them. This is, first, to win their co-operation and, second, to promote self-discipline on their part. On the other hand, most managements now take a less authoritarian approach to disciplinary matters in any case. They do this by not only trying to develop fair and consistent disciplinary policies, but also accepting the legitimacy of trade union involvement in administering them.

Broadly, there are eight main categories of workplace offence which can lead to disciplinary action against employees: negligence; unreliability; insubordination; interfering with the rights of other employees; damaging corporate property; endangering safety; immoral conduct; and theft. Although the works rules and, to a lesser extent, collective agreements constitute the formal sources of management's disciplinary authority, custom and practice or unwritten understandings in the workplace also have an important influence on management's reactions to alleged infringements of works discipline. Two main approaches which management now uses to achieve improved standards of discipline within the workplace are preventative and corrective. Preventative measures, for instance, include effective recruitment, selection and promotion procedures and fitting the person to the job within an organization. Training and communication systems are also important means of preventing disciplinary problems arising amongst employees. New recruits particularly need to be made aware of the standards of workplace discipline required by their employers.

The corrective approach to discipline at work is more common. Its purpose is to give individuals the chance to change and modify their behaviour through a series of warnings and progressively more severe penalties after repeated instances of misconduct. The potential penalties available to management vary in their severity and in their impact. They include verbal and written warnings, fines, suspensions, job transfers and ultimately dismissal. Verbal warnings, for instance, can be either informal or formal and are normally used as a minor penalty. Somewhat more serious is the written warning set down on a special form to ensure that the recipient knows the consequences of repeating the same or worse offences. Amongst unionized workforces, it is common practice for written warnings to be given to employees in the presence of their shop steward. Other sanctions used by management are fines and deductions on employees such as non-payment when an employee is late. In other cases, suspension is used by some managements for more serious offences. Similarly, demotion is occasionally applied in response to proved carelessness in a job, whilst job transfers are used to avoid indiscipline rather than as a penalty against it.

Dismissal is the ultimate sanction available to management in disciplinary cases against employees. Since most employees now have a statutory right not to be unfairly dismissed by their employers, together with the right to challenge such dismissals before an industrial tribunal, though, the development of effective disciplinary rules and procedures within enterprises is vital to management and employees alike. In its code of practice on disciplinary procedures in employment, for example, the Advisory Conciliation and Arbitration Service (ACAS) advises that disciplinary procedures should not be viewed primarily as a means of imposing sanctions upon employees but should be designed to improve their personal conduct. Such procedures should also:

(a) Be in writing
(b) Specify to whom they apply
(c) Provide for matters to be dealt with quickly
(d) Indicate the disciplinary action which may be taken
(e) Specify the levels of management which have the authority to take the various forms of

        disciplinary action, ensuring that immediate supervisors do not normally have the power to dismiss without reference to senior management.

(f) Provide for individuals to be informed of the complaints against them and to be given an opportunity to state their case before decisions are reached

(g) Give individuals the right to be accompanied by a trade union representative, or by a fellow employee of their choice

(h) Ensure that, except for gross misconduct, no employees are dismissed for a first breach of discipline

(i) Ensure that disciplinary action is not taken until the case has been carefully investigated

(j) Ensure that individuals are given an explanation for any penalty imposed

(k) Provide a right of appeal and specify the procedure to be followed.[14]

ACAS strongly recommends that formal, written and recognized disciplinary procedures should be established within enterprises. Management usually initiates the drawing up of such procedures. But, where trade unions are recognized for bargaining purposes, it is essential that they accept the fairness of the disciplinary rules applying to their members. Where management has an agreed disciplinary procedure with the trade unions, it needs to decide whether or not non-unionists have the same rights under it as those employees belonging to the recognized unions. Furthermore, evidence provided by the 1980 workplace industrial relations survey suggests that establishments having recognized unions tend to have disciplinary procedures 'normally agreed with the trade unions and set out in a document signed by both management and unions'.[15]

    Disciplinary procedures, it is suggested, comprise two distinct but inter-related parts. On the one hand, there is the enforcement of discipline by a system of progressively more severe sanctions administered by successive levels of management; this can be called the administrative procedure. 'On the other hand, there is a corresponding series of stages which allows employees recourse to appeal against the disciplinary sanctions imposed; in other words, the *appeals* procedure.'[16] The key features of such procedures are first, that the responsibility for taking disciplinary action rests with management. It is management which investigates the case, sets the penalty to be enforced and informs the employee of this intention. Second, employees have the right not only to be represented by their trade unions at a disciplinary hearing, but also to appeal against any penalty imposed by management if they consider this to be unfair.

    In most disciplinary matters, it is normal practice for the supervisor or first line manager to give a series of verbal warnings to the offending employee. If the employee's behaviour fails to improve, the next stage of a typical procedure is for the supervisor, in consultation with the employee's shop steward, to issue a formal written warning to the employee. After repeated minor offences, or a more serious offence, the employee receives a final written warning from the departmental manager after consultation with the employee's shop steward. Further offences can lead to the suspension of the employee by the departmental manager, following consultation with the senior shop steward and the personnel department. In practice, because of the wide variety of behaviour constituting misconduct, and because of the need for consistency in dealing with these matters, the personnel department often becomes involved at an early stage to avoid disputes and to ensure that the proper procedures are being followed. Finally, where additional infringements of disciplinary rules by the offending employee or gross misconduct occur, the ultimate sanction is dismissal. It is normally the responsibility of senior management to take this decision after it has consulted with the senior shop steward and the personnel department.

    At all stages of the disciplinary procedure, the employee normally has recourse to a parallel appeals procedure. This can either be a separate procedure, or more usually, the grievance procedure through which issues are raised by trade union members and their representatives. At each disciplinary level, an appeal against disciplinary sanctions by management can be taken up by the employee's trade union representative where this is asked for. Such appeals are heard by higher management, culminating with top management.

A typical chain of appeal from supervisory level upwards is through the disciplined employee's shop steward to the departmental manager in the first instance. If this is unsuccessful, it is followed by an appeal to senior line management through the senior shop steward. The last internal appeal is usually made to top line management, again through the senior shop steward. In some cases, final access can also be obtained to independent third party arbitration or to the national disputes procedure – although this is not often used. In a few instances, some organizations have joint appeals procedures. These have equal representation of both managerial and trade union nominees. Usually, such committees are obliged to reach a unanimous decision.

It is clear, then, that the traditional right of management to discipline employees unilaterally is now constrained not only by statute law, but also by the development of appeals procedures within the disciplinary codes as outlined above. There are also a small number of organizations which have even more participative approaches to discipline. They use joint procedures for managing discipline. In these cases, both the administration of discipline and the hearing of appeals are jointly determined. These necessitate shop stewards sitting with managerial representatives on formal joint disciplinary committees. The purpose of these joint committees is to investigate all reported disciplinary cases and, if necessary, to take disciplinary action against offending employees.

Most managers would view the joint approach to discipline as implying either a weakening of their own prerogative to discipline subordinate employees, or reflecting failure on the part of management to manage. Many shop stewards are equally suspicious of joint disciplinary procedures, because they fear that they could become too closely associated and incorporated with management in the workplace. In practice, a joint approach to discipline in both its administrative and its appeals aspects is only normally effective where relations between employers and unions are openly conducted, and where there is mutual trust between them.

11.3 PAYMENT SYSTEMS

In the early days of capitalism, the ways in which workers were paid for their labour services and their pay relationships were usually determined by the master alone. Both the wage payment system and the pay structure within the firm were unilaterally regulated by the owner-managers and were claimed as a managerial prerogative. This is still the case in some parts of private industry today, especially within medium and smaller companies which are not unionized. In general, however, payment systems and pay structures have to be mutually agreed where trade unions are recognized. Pay rates and pay relationships are then jointly determined by managerial and union representatives within the appropriate collective bargaining machinery. But it remains the responsibility of management to administer the payment system and the pay structure in each case. Pay is a reward for employees, on the one hand, and a cost to employers on the other.

> For managers the pay system applied to employees may be seen as an important instrument of management policy; while employees may be more likely to see it in terms of maximising rewards and its impact on standards of living and job security.[17]

In selecting a particular payment system for a group of workers, management usually adopts two main criteria. It seeks that method of payment which gives it the greatest degree of cost control and of supervisory power over subordinate employees, as well as providing the best incentive for efficient job performance by the employees themselves. In essence, management has three choices. It can use a time rate system; it can pay employees by results; or it can combine both methods. A time rate payment system, for example, provides a standard level of pay for a given amount of time spent on the job, whether by the hour, day, month or year. There is normally no direct link between payment received and the effort put into the job by employees on time rate payments systems. Payment by results schemes (PBR), on the other hand, are 'based either on payment per piece produced or on a form of time allowed/time taken basis' which 'have in the past seemed a certain way of ensuring or improving output'[18] from the workforce.

Time rates

The most common straight time rate payment system is the salary. About 40 per cent of Britain's male full time labour force is paid by salary and about 27 per cent 'of full time women workers'.[19] The differences between a wage and a salary are both economic and social. Wage earners, for instance, are normally manual workers who are paid a basic hourly or weekly rate of pay with supplements to their basic rate such as overtime, shiftwork, or bonus payments often negotiated between management and trade unions. The 'hourly paid' are usually paid in cash directly for the work which they do, and the way in which it is done, rather than for what is done.

By contrast, salary earners – or 'the staff' as they are sometimes described – are normally white-collar employees. They receive a fixed flat rate payment weekly, monthly or sometimes quarterly by cheque or credit transfer directly into their bank. Although some salary scales are negotiated for salaried employees, others are not. Even where they are, the point at which salaried employees are placed within these scales when starting employment often depends entirely upon management discretion. Salaried employees may be clerical, professional, technical, or managerial staff who usually have expectations of advancement 'based on age, seniority, qualifications, experience, performance, to higher levels of monetary reward. The wage earner's expectations are much more limited.'[20]

The distinctions between wage and salary payments emerged mainly for historical reasons. With the growth of capitalism in the nineteenth century, wage payment systems provided flexibility for employers in response to fluctuating work loads within their enterprises. In this way, they could relate wage payments to output, to productivity, or to the amounts of overtime worked by subordinates. By varying manning levels in relation to the quantity of orders for their products, employers could control their labour costs and keep them as low as possible. Compared with manual workers, however, the number of white-collar staff within these organizations was fairly small. In return for their loyalty and commitment to the company or to the individual proprietor, these employees were given more favourable hours of work and better working conditions than manual workers. These included security of employment, regular salaries, and better chances of promotion. But they were also expected to work additional hours when necessary with little or no extra payment for it.

Salary payments are characterized:

> by pay progressions, whether published or unpublished, related to increasing experience, quality of performance and career expectations, whether through the use of incremental scales, pay ranges, merit additions or promotions.[21]

A salary system has two main features: first, it comprises a pay structure of differential payments and a related job structure; and second, it provides a set of rules and procedures defining the relationships between the pay and the job structures, the qualities necessary for movement within and between these structures, and the processes by which decisions are made when there is competition for limited promotion opportunities amongst individual employees. The essence of a successful salary system is not only to relate the pay and job structures satisfactorily, but also to ensure that they are administered fairly and equitably.

The main characteristic underlying the administration of many salary payment schemes, which largely distinguishes them from methods of wage payment, is their use of incremental scales – although not all salaries are incrementally based. Salaries which have incremental scales provide a range of annual additions to employee pay. Although these incremental scales are sometimes collectively determined through collective bargaining, as in the public sector for example, they are usually administered under firm employer and managerial control.

> Incremental pay arrangements can be expressed in terms either of scales within definite incremental steps or ranges, and the latter can be 'closed' (i.e. have minima *and* maxima) or 'open-ended' (i.e. have *either* minima *or* maxima, but not both). For the purposes of analysis we have found it useful to classify systems with salary scales as 'fixed' systems and systems based on ranges, whether closed or open-ended, as 'variable'.[22]

Fixed schemes generally allow for some degree of flexibility in their operation, variable schemes place more constraints on managerial options. Furthermore, fixed systems are widely supported in the public sector, whereas private sector employers generally prefer variable systems – especially for senior staff. The fixed-variable dichotomy, however, represents the opposite ends of a spectrum, since there are three sub-divisions within each of the fixed and variable categories. Fixed salary scales may have automatic progression for employees like those engaged in routine clerical work; limited flexibility such as for some professional staff; or automatic progression to a fixed point with controlled discretion beyond it, such as for teachers in higher education. Similarly, variable progression may be through a range of increments according to guidelines; through a range of increments but with no definite guidelines such as for junior managers and technical staff; or through variable progressions without incremental ranges such as for senior managers in the private sector. Recent research suggests that white-collar salary systems vary along the following lines:

- senior management staff – with open ended salary bands, progression through which is discretionary to the employer;
- junior management – with fixed range salary bands, again with discretionary progression, perhaps tied more closely to some form of performance appraisal system;
- clerical and technical staff – with fixed range salary bands, sometimes involving fixed increments to the mid-point of a band, and flexible elements beyond, sometimes based on performance appraisal;
- incremental scales for all staff, through which the individual moves by regular and specified steps. In such cases it is the range in the scale which determines the rate for the particular job.[23]

Three things stand out about salary payments. First, what management expects from its salaried employees is frequently less easy to measure and to monitor than what is required from its wage earners, mainly because of the nature of the work which they do. Second, the choice of salary systems within an enterprise has to be related to a number of organizational characteristics. These include: the nature of its work; its technology; its corporate objectives; its style of management; the role of the pay system in rewarding ability and effort; and the environment in which it operates. Third, the administration of salary systems continues to provide management with a considerable degree of discretion and control in the ways in which they are operated. Thus although salary structures are becoming negotiable, the processes by which decisions are made in placing individuals within a salary range, and in promoting individuals between

incremental scales once they are appointed, invariably remain a managerial prerogative. In other words, both the efficient administration and the equitable application of
most salaries and their job structures rely heavily on effective managerial control and
fairness on management's part. Partly because many manual employees have little
faith in management's ability to fulfil either of these functions equitably, salaries for
manual workers in Britain continue to be the exception rather than the rule.

Wages and payment by results (PBR)

Time rate wage payment systems and salaries for manual employment as explained
above are not the norm. Most wage payment systems for manual employees comprise a
number of elements. The first is the basic hourly rate which is sometimes determined on
an industry-wide basis through national collective bargaining or in other cases by
employer or workplace agreements. A time rate payment system by itself, however,
provides only a limited incentive to improve productivity, efficiency or output. Thus
whilst time rates are widely applied in managerial and non-manual work, in complex
process industries and the service sector, 'in some cases a payment by results element
may be superimposed upon a time rate'.[24] Hence, in addition to the basic time rate for
the job, a manual worker's weekly earnings might include PBR, overtime payments,
shift work allowances, other special premia like seniority increments and – where PBR
does not operate – some kind of payment 'in lieu' of a direct bonus. Obviously,
managerial control over its subordinates' wage payments is much less than over salaried
workers' employment packages, since collective bargaining has made considerable
inroads into managerial regulation of wage payment systems.

The clearest difference between wage payment systems and salary payments is the
scope given within the former for some form of payment by results. Although some
salaried employees, such as sales personnel, are paid by results, PBR 'may be broadly
interpreted to mean any system of wages or salaries under which payment is related to
factors in a worker's performance other than time spent at his employers disposal'.[25]
In 1982 nearly one half (45 per cent) of adult men were paid by results and 30 per cent
of adult females. This compares with about 25 per cent of men in the late 1930s and
about a third in the 1960s. It is estimated that in 1981 only about 18 per cent of
non-manual male workers and 12 per cent of female non-manual workers were paid by
results.

Management's underlying assumption in using PBR schemes, is that where
employees vary the output of their jobs according to effort, this can be related to
payment received. In this way, it is hoped, the prospect of higher earnings results in
greater effort on the part of employees. Payment by results is also attractive to
employers wishing to vary their wages bills as demand for their products changes. There
are various PBR schemes. Moreover, in most PBR schemes the total wage packet is
made up of a number of elements. These may include a fixed basic element, a variable
output bonus and a fall-back provision. The bonus element can be calculated on a daily,
weekly, or monthly basis. In other cases it is paid over an even longer period of time or
of output. Under some PBR schemes, the weekly bonus is paid on the average output of
the previous month or quarter. This aims to reduce the effects of fluctuations in work
output from one week to another on employee earnings.

Basically, there are three types of PBR: individual PBR, group PBR and measured
day work (MDW). Individual PBR comprises two main systems; piecework and incentive bonuses. The oldest of these is straight piecework. This is where an employer pays a
standard price for each piece or unit of output produced by the individual employee.
Under this method, pay and output are directly proportional. Nowadays, most piecework systems also incorporate a time rate element. Fall-back rates guarantee a mini-

mum level of weekly earnings irrespective of output, and 'waiting time' is paid when pieceworkers are held up by interruptions of work beyond their immediate control. Individual piecework earnings may also be supplemented by fixed hourly, daily, or weekly payments to preclude excessive fluctuations in the earning levels.

Where employee effort is measured in terms of the time taken to do a job, rather than in the quantity of output produced, and a standard time is allowed to complete it incentive bonus changes are brought into effect. Although there are a variety of such systems, an incentive bonus scheme is essentially used where an employee is paid a basic time rate with a standard time set for completing the job. A bonus is then paid in relation to the time saved in actually doing the job or to the extra product produced in the time allowed for doing it.

> Under these systems, the fixing of a price for the work to be done and the determination of work-loads for particular tasks are formally separated. A wage is negotiated in terms of units of time and the times allowed for different tasks are then fixed separately.[26]

The main differences among these payment systems lie in the varying relationship between pay and output which they utilize. They comprise: proportional straight line, progressive, geared, stabilized, regressive, or variable schemes. Their aims include encouraging learners, discouraging excessively high performance or safeguarding management against errors in standard setting. All these schemes are based on work study standards. The British Standards Institution employ a scale of performance: 75 performance corresponds with a normal level of effort which an employee on a time rate would achieve. The standard level which employees on PBR would be expected to achieve corresponds with a 100 performance. Under a proportional straight line incentive scheme, for example, guaranteed minimum earnings are normally paid at 75 performance, whilst a 100 performance results in a 33⅓ per cent increase in earnings, with earnings at other performance levels pro rata. Examples of other types of schemes are provided in figure 11.1.

The Taylor Differential Piece Rate system is progressive in that it yields a higher rate of pay for above standard performance. In practice, however, the majority of individual PBR schemes in Britain, whether piece based or time based, tend to be regressive such as the Bedaux scheme, with the effective price per unit of output declining as the worker's output rises. Under such schemes, gross earnings rise at a lower rate than total output. This means that unit labour costs diminish with increased levels of output. Thus employers are protected against rising unit costs resulting from falls in output, whilst employee earnings are less liable to fluctuation than under proportional or progressive schemes.

Individual PBR is most suitable in jobs which have a high manual content, a repetitive nature, short cycle operations, and where there are no marked fluctuations in the product market. Individual PBR works most successfully: where the proportion of average earnings comprising a variable output bonus does not exceed 25 per cent; where performance standards are properly work measured; and where learning and improvement factors are also taken into account when establishing work standards. It is preferable with PBR systems to determine internal differentials by systematic job evaluation and to regularly revise the suitability and administration of the bonus system being used. The work being done needs to be measurable and directly attributable to the individual, whilst the pace of work should be controlled by those doing it rather than by the job technology. Management also needs to ensure that its subordinates receive a steady flow of work, not subject to frequent changes in methods of production or in its use of materials and equipment.

Group PBR operates where the production process makes it difficult to attribute job performance or work output to individual workers. It is also used to encourage

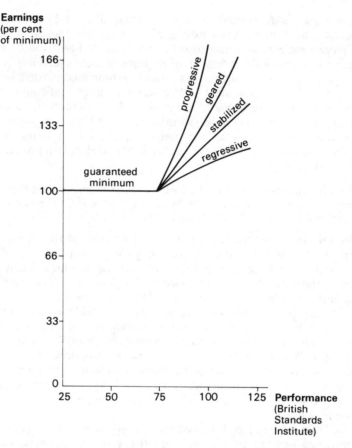

Figure 11.1   Progressive, geared, stabilized and regressive incentive bonus schemes.

workgroups to work co-operatively. In these cases, normal PBR schemes may be applied to groups with bonus payments allocated amongst group members equally or in a predetermined ratio. Workgroup members need to be reasonably competent but the motivational effort of group PBR can diminish as workgroup size increases.

Another incentive payment is the 'lieu' bonus. These are additional payments, in place of bonuses, paid to timeworkers who cannot be employed on PBR directly. They are a form of pay compensation to employees like maintenance workers not able to supplement their weekly earnings by normal PBR. Lieu bonuses are often calculated according to the average bonus of direct workers and are paid in the belief that if total production increases, indirect workers must have contributed to the productivity of the direct workers concerned. In practice, the most common reason for paying lieu bonuses is to prevent any major changes occurring in pay relationships and earnings between skilled timeworkers, on the one hand, and less skilled piecework or bonus workers on the other. Consequently, lieu bonuses are rarely related to effective work measurement.

Measured day work is the generic term given to those wage payment systems occupying a midway position between individual and group PBR, especially with 'banded' ranges of payment, on the one hand, and day rate schemes based on high time rate payments on the other. Under MDW pay is fixed on the understanding that employees 'maintain a specified level of performance, but the pay does not fluctuate in the short term with . . . actual performance'.[27] To work effectively MDW relies heavily on some form of work measurement and job assessment to define the required level of performance by employees and to monitor the levels of job performance. In outline, MDW comprises either a time rate payment for specified job performance; a time rate payment and a bonus payment for a specified performance; or a series of options by which employees maintain one of a series of performance levels to which differing rates of pay apply. The essence of MDW is that a specific effort bargain is struck between employer and employees. By it employers agree to pay an agreed level of wages in return for a specified level of job performance by their employees.

Various reasons are suggested for adopting MDW. These include: the prevention of sectional wage bargaining; the elimination of leap-frogging pay claims; the preclusion of wide fluctuations in employee earnings; and the maintenance of rational pay structures. Changes to MDW from PBR are most commonly conducted when PBR has decayed to such a degree that industrial relations have become seriously affected by it. This is reflected in the increased rejection of job times, in job mobility by employees and by steady loss of managerial control over workplace earnings. Employees may also be concerned at the instability of their earnings and the inequities in practice between their pay rewards and job effort. MDW is then seen as a means by which management can secure standard effort and 'of employees securing stable earnings. It can thus meet the immediate objective of both sides.'[28] It is a mixture of industrial relations criteria, management and employee needs, and technological factors which usually contribute to the introduction of MDW payment systems.

An alternative to standard MDW is the premium pay plan (PPP). This is a stepped or graduated form of MDW requiring detailed work measurement and administrative machinery. It is designed to overcome the major shortcomings of individual or group PBR, whilst allowing individual employees some choice of job performance and of movement between pay bands for themselves. It does not rely solely on financial incentives to ensure high performance but demands high standards of managerial supervision. Under PPP, employees improve their pay in two ways. Either they achieve a higher level of performance over a specified period in their existing jobs, or they move to another job with a higher pay-rate and increased work-performance classifications. The closely specified procedures and highly structured nature of PPP, however, necessitate continuously strict checks by management on employee effort. Its characteristics suggest that operating PPP demands high managerial standards and that management does not abdicate its monitoring responsibilities as so often happens with other forms of PBR.

Pay structures

Payment systems are also related to internal pay structures.

> At any place of work a network of differentials exists between the various occupations or skills and between those who share those same occupations and skills. A wage structure consists of the pay relationships of all the groups or individuals in a firm.[29]

These are connected in turn to a network of external pay relativities varying by occupation, industry and region. There is normally a continual struggle amongst all work groups within an enterprise to maintain their internal differentials and to get them 'right'. In other cases, the structure of differentials within and amongst bargaining groups is reasonably rational and orderly. In many cases it is not so, as pay differentials change in accordance with market and bargaining factors.

Changes in internal differentials are caused by many factors. These include labour market shortages, product market fluctuations, trade union bargaining power and the impact of government policies on existing differentials. Formerly, it was management alone which determined an organization's internal pay differentials in the light of market forces. Whilst in non-union firms this remains a managerial prerogative, internal pay structures are more likely to be determined jointly with unions, frequently in a number of bargaining units. This makes the whose issue of establishing equitable internal differentials a highly inflammatory and extremely contentious one. At least 13 different sequences play some part in producing a given pattern of pay levels within an organization at any one time.

> They are considerations of labour-market rates, career aspirations, beliefs about fair payment, wage-bargaining processes, overtime pay, wage drift, productivity bargains, age increments, merit payments, length-of-service increments, working conditions allowances, attempts to avoid grade distortion and attempts to restore differentials.[30]

Even where job evaluation is used, getting internal differentials 'right' can be a difficult and conflict ridden process.

Company-wide incentives and financial participation

Company or workplace incentive schemes and various forms of financial participation in the private sector, such as profit and gain sharing, have been relatively slow to develop in Britain compared with some countries such as the USA. However, largely because of the taxation provisions of the Finance Acts 1978 and 1980, it is probable that about 250 000 employees had been allocated company shares under some form of profit sharing arrangement by the end of 1982, 'with another 100 000 participating in approved share option schemes'.[31]

Payment by results or measured day work can be successful for individuals or even groups of employees but do not always contribute to overall corporate or plant performance. To offset the weakness of these payment systems, some managements in the private sector have introduced more comprehensive incentive payment systems based upon employee performance in the organization as a whole, or in part of it. For example, a bonus can be paid to employees in relation to the business's total volume of output. Bonuses can also be related to total sales volume during a given period. One particular system, the Scanlon Plan, provides a bonus based on the ratio of wages paid to sales value. Improvements in this ratio are taken to indicate an economic gain to the company and a proportion of the savings made is distributed to the employees.

Another method on which company-wide bonus systems are based is added value (AV). AV consists of the sales revenue of a company less its expenditure on materials and services purchased such as wages, salaries, administrative costs and profits. It represents the value added by the production or other processes within the enterprise. Added value is a useful indicator of corporate economic efficiency, hence any increase in its value demonstrates an improvement in overall performance. The Rucker Share of Production Plan, for example, uses the ratio of wages to AV on which to base bonus payments. Any improvement in this ratio results in the distribution of a bonus to employees. The expectation is that the desire of employees to increase the bonus pool available induces them to accept changes in working methods thus raising overall corporate efficiency. Though the direct effect of company- and plant-wide incentives on individuals is relatively weak, schemes such as the Rucker and Scanlon Plans are cheaper to install and maintain than most PBR and MDW schemes.

In profit sharing employees receive bonus payments or share issues depending upon a firm's profit. Where the bonus is paid in shares, a main purpose is to provide employees with a stake in their firm. Difficulties arise, however, where profits are low and the amount to be shared out is of little or no consequence. Further, most share schemes are limited to companies whose shares are quoted on the Stock Exchange. There are impediments for private companies which wish to create employee shareholding where there is no open market for shares. Employees can even lose their savings under these provisions where their companies go out of business or into receivership. Gain-sharing attempts to involve management, unions and employees in jointly improving a company's productivity and profitability through agreed methods. These include better utilization of labour, capital, materials, energy and other resources affecting corporate output and business performance. Resulting 'gains' are shared between the company and its employees according to a predetermined formula.

Harmonization

The differences in payment systems continuing to exist between white-collar, salaried staff and hourly-paid manual workers derive from largely outdated historical, social and economic factors. Moreover, they are reflected not only in the methods of employee payment but also in the remuneration package in total and in the conditions of employment between the two groups generally. According to ACAS:

> The most significant differences in current terms and conditions are to be found in the coverage and basis of pension and sick pay schemes, the liability of manual workers to lay-off and short time working, basic working hours, and holiday entitlements. In general, most manual workers are still treated considerably less favourably than non-manual workers in all these areas, and full harmonisation would be costly.[32]

Differences are also found in the contribution of overtime and PBR to total pay, fringe benefits, workplace facilities and clocking in.

Harmonization of conditions of employment within organizations and the introduction of staff status for all employees, however, are becoming of increasing interest to management, unions and employees. Although the cost of harmonization is often the main obstacle in introducing staff status for manual workers, the principle is likely to be of growing concern to the parties to industrial relations during the next few years. Experience shows that introducing harmonization can improve not only industrial relations but also corporate efficiency 'provided it has the acceptance of the employees affected – both manual and non-manual, including managers and involves if not single status at least a significant degree of harmonization'.[33]

Where harmonization is introduced it is generally on management initiative. Full and open consultation is normally essential wherever it is contemplated, which is a time-consuming process. In so doing management relinquishes yet another of its prerogatives: rewarding specific employee groups differently. Yet attempts to harmonize conditions of employment produce their own industrial relations problems. In drawing up agreements of this sort the parties have to consider:

> Whether to retain an incentive payment scheme and a guaranteed week, the disparity of hours between blue and white collar employees and the effect on absences and timekeeping. Finally, there is the disparity between what management hope to achieve and what can reasonably be expected in terms of increasing employee involvement.[34]

Moving towards integrating manual and non-manual payment systems and conditions of employment produces its own difficulties, such as staff opposition to losing their relative employment status. Effective harmonization ultimately requires fundamental changes in employee attitudes and in managerial attitudes to the two groups, with sometimes radical changes in working methods.

11.4   NON-UNION FIRMS

Non-union firms are normally found in the private sector. In the public sector, union recognition, collective bargaining and joint consultation are usually standard, if varied, practices. According to the 1980 workplace industrial relations survey, the three strongest influences upon the extent of trade union recognition were 'ownership, the size of establishments and the size of enterprises'. Whilst 100 per cent of the nationalized industry establishments which were surveyed recognized trade unions, as did 44 per cent of those in public administration, only 68 per cent in private manufacturing did, and only 42 per cent of private service enterprises.

Non-union firms are found in a wide variety of private sector enterprises: the partially non-union firm; small and medium-sized firms; and a few large firms. Partially non-union firms, for example, are not uncommon. In practice, many larger firms, whilst recognizing trade unions for their manual and certain grades of non-manual employees, are less willing to do so for salaried workers such as technical and professional staff and middle managers. They operate selective union recognition policies comprising full recognition for production workers, maintenance staff and lower clerical grades combined with a non-recognition policy for all other employees. The 1980 workplace industrial relations survey, for instance, shows that in 37 per cent of the private manufacturing establishments questioned, and in 14 per cent of the private services, unions were recognized for manual employees but not for non-manual ones. There was also a strong tendency for manual unions to be 'more likely to be recognised, the more people were employed on site.'[35]

A number of other studies also show that the larger the employing organization the more likely it is to be unionized and for trade unions to be recognized within it. Research conducted for the Bullock Committee in its inquiry on industrial democracy, for example, shows that the density of union organization in manufacturing enterprises employing over 200 personnel was 77 per cent. When establishments with less than 200 employees were excluded, union density rose to 89 per cent. Taking the private sector as a whole, the Committee concluded that there was 70 per cent union density in those larger enterprises employing 2 000 or more employees, with a density in the order of 20 per cent among smaller enterprises. In the 1980 workplace industrial relations survey, it is shown that the number of people employed on site and the total number employed by an enterprise exercise 'strong independent influences upon the extent of trade union recognition'.[36]

In both small and medium-sized companies, therefore, union recognition for some or all of their employees is less likely to be conceded than in larger firms in both the manufacturing and service sectors. Whether such managerial policies are explicit or not is difficult to determine. More probably, it is an implicit assumption by those owning, directing and managing such enterprises that unions are unnecessary in representing employee interests, for some or all of their employees, and are obstructive to the right to manage. In the smaller firm, close links are often claimed between management and non-managerial employees who sometimes share common unitary perspectives of the enterprise. In other cases both these groups and supervisory staff do not always readily identify with trade unionism and employees can be difficult to organize into union membership. They believe that their employment interests are best advanced by individual effort and compliance with managerial expectations, rather than by collective representation and challenging management's right to manage. Where this is combined with a paternalistic or even *laissez-faire* style of management, employee demand for union representation is weakened and management's claim to the unilateral right to manage without interference is strengthened.

Large non-union firms such as Marks and Spencer PLC and International Business

Machines (UK) Ltd. (IBM UK) are the exception rather than the rule. Large non-union firms are more likely to be American or privately owned, to be involved in non-manufacturing or service activities, to employ predominantly skilled or partially skilled white-collar workers, to be commercially successful in expanding product markets and to have covertly non-union personnel policies. Senior managers within such organizations would argue that their firms are not 'anti-union' but are 'non-union' because they claim that their employees see no real need for union organization or collective representation in employment matters. With enlightened personnel policies and 'people centred' managerial styles, such managers claim, unionization and collective bargaining are irrelevant to organizational success and employee welfare.

The reality is more complex, however, since tight screening in the recruitment and selection of employees, cohesive management control systems, in-company propaganda and training programmes, and attractive employee benefits undoubtedly contribute to employee commitment and loyalty to large non-union employers of this type. This managerial style has been described as 'sophisticated paternalism' and is characterized by 'a deliberate attempt to avoid collective bargaining and often a refusal to recognise trade unions'.[37] A main aim of such companies is to pre-empt industrial relations conflict between management and their employees, not through jointly agreed constitutional procedures, but through the skilful application of proactive personnel management techniques and policies; being successful companies they can normally afford the financial costs in doing this.

Len Peach, when Director of Personnel and Corporate Affairs of IBM UK, claimed, for example, that IBM's personnel relations policy has six key elements conducive to its successful implementation. First, there is the 'practice of Full Employment'. This means that, on the one side, the company offers alternative employment to employees whose jobs are eliminated by economic or technological change. In turn employees must be willing to undertake training, move location and change jobs should the employer deem these to be necessary in the interests of the company. Second, the company is committed to 'Single Status' with all employees under the same conditions of service and with the same employee benefits irrespective of skill. This reflects the willingness of IBM management, it is said, to judge people 'according to their contribution and not to a pre-defined pecking order – which is the essence of a company alert to and willing to change'. Third, the pay system is identical for most employees. It is based on a job evaluation scheme, with a monetary value placed on each job according to the company's policy of paying its employees 'favourably compared with other leading companies – in other words to occupy a high position in the market place'.[38]

The fourth essential feature of IBM's personnel policy is the company's commitment to 'performance assessment and career counselling and planning.' Its main objective is to provide regularly 'a balanced statement of each employee's performance against objectives' assessed by their manager and validated by his or her superior. To this end all IBM managers 'average one week's management training in people skills . . . for every year of their careers.'[39] Fifth, downward communication takes place through such mechanisms as the company newspaper, annual statements, location newspapers, bulletin boards and video tapes of messages from top management. Upward communication is provided through periodic attitude or opinion surveys of employees, with a bienniel survey testing the company's communication processes themselves.

Finally, IBM has two main devices for processing employee grievances and appeals within the company. One is the 'Open Door' system enabling aggrieved employees who are dissatisfied with a managerial decision to appeal against it either through the management hierarchy or by a direct appeal 'to any level of management, by-passing intervening levels.' Twenty-five per cent of these, Peach suggests, are upheld in favour of the employee. The other device is the 'Speak Up' programme allowing individuals – or sometimes groups – to submit anonymous written complaints or requests for more information on a policy question to management and to obtain a formal reply from the person in the company best qualified to answer it. The company apparently receives more than 1 000 'speak ups' per year. These provide, Peach argues, early warnings of problems 'which, unheeded, might cause much distress to both individuals and the company.'[40]

11.5 SUMMARY

In considering the role of management and the right to manage in enterprises, we would argue that in today's industrial relations climate, economic recession notwithstanding, management, with few exceptions, can only manage effectively and successfully with the agreement and consent of subordinate employees. Where trade unions are recognized, there are few prerogatives, rights or functions at the workplace in the payment, deployment or disciplining of labour which remain exclusive to management alone. Even in the engineering trades, where the right to manage has been so vigorously fought for by employer representatives for many years, collective bargaining, or joint regulation, is the predominant method for determining employment conditions for the employees concerned. The right to manage in many enterprises, therefore, continues to rest on the right to initiate organizational and industrial relations change rather than to impose it unilaterally.

The character of works rules has also been modified in recent years. Previously they were a major source of management's disciplinary authority within enterprises. Nowadays, works rule books or employee handbooks serve much wider purposes than the regulation of disciplinary issues alone. These include, for example, advice about the organization's pension funds, its welfare provisions, and other related matters. Disciplinary practices have also been affected by codes of practice, labour law and the growth of trade union membership amongst employees. Increasingly, trade union representatives regard disciplinary matters as not subject to managerial discretion alone. The emphasis generally is on the prevention of disciplinary offences by employees and their correction, rather than on retribution and punishment.

Although dismissal remains the ultimate managerial sanction, disciplinary procedures are more formalized than in the past. Today a series of administrative procedures has normally to be undergone within the disciplinary code before an employee can be dismissed. Within most disciplinary procedures, there is usually a parallel appeals system. This enables those disciplined to appeal against disciplinary actions taken against them by line management, usually through their shop steward or workplace representative.

There has also been a steady diminution of unilateral managerial control over corporate and workplace payment systems recently. Although management continues to have considerable discretion in administering salary payment systems, it frequently has to negotiate salary structures with the unions representing white-collar workers. One of the major distinguishing features of salary payment systems is their use of incremental pay structures. Wage payment schemes, on the other hand, are far less amenable to unilateral managerial regulation, usually they comprise a number of variable elements such as basic rates, shiftwork allowances and overtime payments. Above all, they enable far more scope for the use of payment by results.

The main types of PBR are individual PBR, group PBR and measured day work (MDW). Individual PBR comprises piecework and incentive bonus schemes with most PBR also including a time rate and guaranteed earnings. The variable or bonus element can be regressive, proportional or progressive. MDW is a wage payment system which is intermediate between time rate systems and pure incentive schemes. It guarantees a given payment for a specific output or level of job performance, with the premium pay plan (PPP) offering individuals a choice of job performance and pay bands. Financial participation payment systems, such as profit sharing or share ownership schemes, whilst relatively rare, do appear to be gaining ground in a minority of companies. Move towards harmonizing manual and staff payment systems and working conditions, however, only normally take place where there are fundamental changes in managerial and employee attitudes, combined with sometimes radical changes in working methods.

In the non-union firm, management's right to manage remains relatively unchallenged internally, though constraints are placed on it by externally generated labour law. Further, different managerial philosophies seem to distinguish the small to medium-sized non-union firm from its larger counterpart. In the former, managerial attitudes to union organization are more defensive and even *laissez-faire*, often with no predetermined scheme for union avoidance. In the larger firm, on the other hand, a 'sophisticated paternalist' approach to employee relations is often apparent. This takes the form of more assertive personnel policies and practices specifically aimed at obviating union representation and organization within these enterprises.

11.6 REFERENCES

1. A. Marsh, *Concise Encyclopedia of Industrial Relations*, Gower, London, 1979, p. 186.
2. Quoted in A. Marsh, *Industrial Relations in Engineering*, Pergamon, Oxford, 1965, pp. 250 and 272.
3. J. Storey, *The Challenge to Management Control*, Business Books, London, 1980, p. 45.
4. G.F. Bloom and H.R. Northrup, *Economics of Labor Relations*, Irwin, Illinois, 1965, p. 173.
5. Organization for Economic Cooperation and Development, *Workers' Participation*, OECD, Paris, 1976, p. 42.
6. W.E.J. McCarthy and N.D. Ellis, *Management by Agreement*, Hutchinson, London, 1973, p. 96.
7. J. Storey, *op. cit.*, p. 41.
8. OECD, *op. cit.*, p. 42.
9. K. Hudson, *Working to Rule*, Adams and Dart, Bath, 1970, p. 59.
10. E.O. Evans, Work rule books in the engineering industry, *Industrial Relations Journal*, Summer 1971, p. 57.
11. *Ibid.*, p. 56.
12. *Ibid.*, p. 63.
13. R.T. Ashdown and K.H. Baker, *Department of Employment Manpower Papers Number 6. In Working Order: a Study of Industrial Discipline*, HMSO, London, 1973, p. 5.
14. Advisory Conciliation and Arbitration Service, *Code of Practice. Disciplinary Practice and Procedures in Employment*, HMSO, London, 1977, p. 3.
15. W.W. Daniel and N. Millward, *Workplace Industrial Relations*, Heinemann, London, 1983, p. 290.
16. R.T. Ashdown and K.H. Baker, *op. cit.*, p. 26.
17. D. Grayson, Payment systems for the future, *Employment Gazette*, March 1984, p. 121.
18. B. Conboy, *Pay at Work*, Arrow, London, 1976, p. 6.
19. Advisory Conciliation and Arbitration Service, *Developments in Harmonization*, ACAS, London, 1982, p. 1.
20. T. Lupton and A.M. Bowey, *Wages and Salaries*, Penguin, Harmondsworth, 1974, p. 106.
21. National Board for Prices and Incomes, *Report No. 132. Salary Structures*, HMSO, London, 1969, p. 5.
22. Office of Manpower Economics, *Incremental Payment Systems*, HMSO, London, 1973, p. 4.
23. D. Grayson, *op. cit.*, p. 122.

24. Advisory Conciliation and Arbitration Service, *Advisory Booklet No. 2. Introduction to Payment Systems*, ACAS, London, (n.d.), p. 8.
25. National Board for Prices and Incomes (NBPI), *Report No. 65. Payment by Results*, HMSO, London, 1969, p. 3.
26. *Ibid.*, p. 4.
27. Office of Manpower Economics, *Measured Daywork*, HMSO, London, 1973, p. 8.
28. *Ibid.*, p. 23.
29. B. Conboy, *op. cit.*, p. 57.
30. T. Lupton and A.M. Bowey, *op. cit.*, p. 19.
31. D. Grayson, Shape of payment systems to come, *Employment Gazette*, April 1984, p. 176f.
32. ACAS (1982) *op. cit.*, p. 9f.
33. *Ibid.*, p. 10.
34. Institute of Personnel Management, *Staff Status for All*, IPM, London, 1977, p. 61.
35. W.W. Daniel and N. Millward, *op. cit.*, pp. 17 and 23.
36. *Ibid.*, p. 25.
37. W. Brown and K. Sisson, Industrial relations in the next decade, *Industrial Relations Journal*, vol. 14(1), 1983, p. 11.
38. L.H. Peach, Employee relations in IBM, *Employee Relations*, vol. 5(3), 1983, p. 17f.
39. *Ibid.*, p. 18f.
40. *Ibid.*, p. 19f.

12

The Personnel Function

The essence of the modern personnel function is to enable management to organize the efforts of the people working in enterprises 'to attain the highest levels of efficiency, adaptability and productivity.'[1] In most small organizations the personnel function is exclusively the responsibility of line or functional managers, although there might be someone at senior level 'charged with overall responsibility for personnel matters and who will see that policy and guidelines are agreed and laid down.'[2] In larger organizations, 'managing people' is mainly a line management responsibility but there is normally a specialist personnel management function too. This is staffed by personnel professionals providing policy advice, guidance and support to line managers in their daily dealings with subordinate employees.

Wherever there is an awareness of the importance of people as 'human resources' in their organizations, rather than just as 'economic inputs' or 'wage labour', managers have to concern themselves with the human aspects of management. This gives rise to the need for the expertise and skills of professional personnel managers and has 'led to the establishment of personnel management as a significant and distinct field of management studies.'[3] Personnel management is that part of the function of management arising out of the fact that enterprises employ people, even though the personnel function exists quite independently of whether specialists are employed or not. The focus of this chapter is the professional personnel role within enterprises, its part in policy making and implementation and its relationship with line management.

12.1 THE NATURE OF THE PERSONNEL FUNCTION

The emergence and growth of personnel management within private and public enterprises has been largely shaped by the politico-economic contexts within which personnel policies and practices have developed in Britain. In general, with the economy in recession, the specialist personnel role is weakened, 'hard' and control-centred. With the economy growing, and with skill shortages in the labour market emerging, personnel management is strengthened, 'soft' and welfare-centred. Personnel activity is also affected by government manpower policy, employment law and trade union power. The more interventionist government policy and the stronger trade union power then the greater is the need for professional personnel management.

A major expansion in the professional personnel function took place in many organizations during the 1960s and 1970s. It has been estimated that in 1963, for example, there were about 10–15 000 personnel managers in Britain. By the late 1970s this had risen to a claimed 50 000 personnel specialists.[4] It seems likely that since then the number of personnel practitioners has stabilized, and possibly even declined, with the recruiting, training and developing of human resources within enterprises having shifted to 'assessing, excluding, exiting and retiring them.'[5]

The 1980 workplace industrial relations survey provides some confirmation of this. Only about a quarter of the respondents were personnel managers, fewer than one half spent a major part of their time on personnel work 'and one half of managers who did spend a major part of their time on personnel work were not personnel specialists.' A main finding of this research was the number of establishments and governing bodies still lacking 'personnel specialists despite the growth through the 1970s.' The larger the number of people employed, however, 'the more likely establishments were to have specialist personnel managers and the more likely these managers were to have formal qualifications.' It also appears likely that representation of personnel managers and industrial relations specialists on the governing bodies of organizations is 'strongly associated with the centralisation of pay bargaining'[6] within them.

Perceptions of the personnel function

Perceptions of the personnel management function within enterprises vary widely. Some commentators, for example, are highly critical of specialist personnel management, arguing that in the 1970s, for instance, personnel management began with great promise 'but at the beginning of the 1980s the promise remained unfulfilled.' This critic, Manning, argues that whilst the importance of the efficient and effective managing of human resources within enterprises has not receded, personnel management as a discipline has not made the significant impact in organizations which it should have done. Compared with marketing and production, for example, personnel management has the weakest conceptual base, it is claimed, and the poorest technology in relation to some other managerial functions. 'What is needed is the sort of analytic and creative thinking that has been demonstrated so successfully in disciplines like marketing and finance.' Manning tries to explain the apparent apathy of some line managers towards personnel. To the average manager, he writes, 'personnel all too often seems distant from the immediate problems of achieving his budget and from the wider business needs of the company.'[7]

In the organizations studied by Legge two major points were noted. First, there was a general absence of systematically formulated personnel policies within them. Second, line management tended to neglect the personnel aspects of their decision making roles. She claims that senior management, whilst accepting the need to develop appropriate personnel policies, was often unable to think through and develop consistent personnel strategies. She also found that line managers:

> while recognizing that much of their work was a form of personnel management tended to operate in the area in an *ad hoc* manner, without any clearly thought out and articulated framework to which to relate their activities. As a result, in company decision-making, the personnel management considerations involved in production, marketing and finance decisions were not so much overruled . . . as went by default.[8]

The chairman of Imperial Chemical Industries, John Harvey-Jones, also criticizes the role of personnel professionals. He is not greatly impressed by the ways that some personnel departments are run by those in charge of them. Although personnel managers are the custodians of most of the theory of management, he writes, all too often in his view their activity 'appears to be directed towards offering advice to others, rather than practising within their own house.' He is also doubtful whether prolonged exposure within the specialist personnel function provides an appropriate background for generating 'an all-round businessman with the particular qualities which are required for the highest positions in industry.' Whilst believing that line managers should work in personnel for a period, he does not consider that personnel management should be primarily a specialist activity but 'should be the responsibility of every line manager.'[9]

Other senior executives and corporate leaders are on record as being more supportive of the specialist personnel function and perceiving it in more progressive and proactive terms. The former chairman of British Rail, Peter Parker, for example, views the professional personnel role as the 'agent of change' within the enterprise. He looks to the personnel function to help managers and unions understand the 'different cultures of enterprise and of the community.' The personnel manager's 'new role', he claims, is to be 'the co-ordinator of two cultures', emphasizing the mutuality of the industrial and social purposes of work. Parker argues that the major responsibility of the personnel function is to sustain the effectiveness of an organization's human resources, whilst extending every individual's sense of scope of work. If an enterprise is to achieve its objectives Parker claims, 'I see personnel increasingly involved in the effort to clarify the social policy of an enterprise.' In Parker's analysis, 'industry cannot separate its own working relationships and values from those of the community in which it operates and serves.'[10]

Parker believes that personnel managers should be moved around managerial functions and that line managers should get a feel for personnel work by experiencing it for themselves. Further, the personnel function needs to be fully integrated into organizational structures 'by being absolutely clear about it as supportive of line management.' Parker expects three things from personnel managers: professionalism; to be 'outward looking'; and to operate on two time scales:

> Personnel must develop long-term policies and strategies and it must also be in there pitching when day-to-day problems arise, when tough negotiations are being faced, when line managers need their skill and experience to the full. In a sense, there is the creative philosophical role, the preventive role and the day-to-day role.[11]

Whilst he does not see the personnel department primarily as a 'fire fighting' agency, Parker concedes that even with the best long-term strategies, personnel 'fires' sometimes have to be put out.

A leading senior executive in the private sector, Alex Jarrett, sometime chairman of Reed International, has equally strong views about the importance of the personnel function. For him personnel managers and personnel directors are the people 'with special knowledge and skills about what is the most important asset of our business – the people we employ.' He identifies three issues vitally affecting industrial relations and the success of a company. These are collective bargaining and pay determination, employee involvement, and the career development and remuneration of management. In any company or group of companies, he argues, these are crucial matters on which the business must establish clear policies and strategies. In Jarrett's view the personnel department and its professional staff have, with their specialist knowledge and skills, a major contribution to make to organizational effectiveness. It is individual line managers, however, who carry the prime responsibility for industrial relations in their own departments and the outcome of pay negotiations. Personnel professionals also have a role in developing and implementing appropriate employee involvement policies. In Jarrett's experience, 'both industrial relations and [employee] involvement are matters of good management in which personnel has a vital part to play.'[12]

These few contrasting examples provide some insight into the different perceptions about the personnel function amongst management practitioners and academics. They also show that there is no general agreement as to what constitutes its central thrust and direction, apart from concern with the human aspects of management. This should not be surprising, given the diverse origins and different ideological roots of the personnel role in British management. For example, a major ambivalence within personnel management lies between the so-called 'welfare role' of personnel and the 'management control role', with 'the one paternalistically oriented towards the welfare of employees and the other rationally derived from corporate needs to control.'[13] The welfare role, for example, was the earliest type of personnel activity to emerge in Britain and was associated with the altruistic concern for the corporate and social welfare of their employees by a handful of paternalistic employers such as Rowntrees, Cadburys and W.D. and H.O. Wills at the beginning of the century. These firms were the first to appoint 'factory welfare workers' whose duties included raising standards of factory welfare, ensuring factory legislation was implemented, providing personnel counselling to employees and looking after employee amenities such as canteens, rest rooms and recreation grounds.

Seebohm Rowntree saw factory welfare workers as representatives of their firms and of employees. In representing the employer they were expected to devise improvements in conditions of work and keep the 'personal element' prominent in relations with employees. As representatives of employers, Seebohm wrote:

> it is the duty of the social helpers to be constantly in touch with them, to gain their confidence, to voice any grievances they may have either individually or collectively, to give effect to any reasonable desire they may show for recreative clubs, educational classes, etc and to give advice in matters concerning them personally.[14]

In these twin roles welfare workers were seen as intermediaries between employer and employees but were not to be subordinate to either, even if they were to be seen to serve both. Today the welfare role is largely a residual one and is a relatively minor part of the personnel function. The main exceptions are those non-union employers, often with predominantly female workforces, who adopt paternalistic styles of management. Welfare work has, however, left a marked impact on the image of British personnel management giving some people the generally false impression that personnel managers are 'social workers' in industry.

The management control role, in contrast, is rooted in managerial concern for economic efficiency at work and is probably the dominant one within personnel management today. In its control role, personnel management aims to get the best out of the human resources within organizations, minimizing its unit cost, maximizing its productive output and, where possible, integrating individual employee needs with those of the employing organization and its managerial decision makers. This perception of the personnel function clearly identifies personnel work, whether performed by line managers or personnel specialists, firmly within a managerial and employer frame of reference. Whilst implying a more executive role for personnel managers, the management control role also raises questions about the respective allocation of personnel activities between line and personnel managers. It means in practice 'that personnel managers may become involved in an extremely wide range of activities sometimes executive, sometimes advisory, but always a part of the managerial team.'[15]

Two other perceptions of the personnel function have been identified: the 'third-party role' and the 'professional role.' Just as the personnel manager claims some kind of independent status from that of the employer in carrying out a welfare role by acting as an intermediary between the parties and as a corporate conscience for management, especially in understanding the concerns of employees and their needs, so too does the third-party role of personnel management. With the expansion of employment legislation in recent years, for example, the personnel function becomes an important source for interpreting the law and spelling out its implications for employers and employees. By using this legislation to justify certain personnel policies and practices, personnel managers are adopting a third-party intermediary role, based on their expert knowledge and understanding of the law, with 'an implicit assumption that the law enshrines the values of society as a whole in contradistinction to the immediate self-interest of any particular employer.'[16]

The professional role of personnel management is the one largely advocated by the Institute of Personnel Management (IPM) which is the professional association aiming at improving personnel practice in Britain. The professional role sees personnel managers as managerial resources having specialist knowledge and skills 'but also possessing values and concerns which exist independently of a specified organisation.'[17] By this view, the specialist personnel manager is expected to have a series of transferable occupational skills and a set of professional values enabling both economic efficiency for the employer and social justice for employees to be achieved simultaneously within the employing organization. It differs from the third-party role by being explicitly identified with employer interests and operating only informally as the corporate conscience. 'The range of activities may be considerable, but they could become predominantly advisory rather than executive.'[18]

Another perception of the personnel function is provided by Tyson. He argues that close examination of the social constructs used by personnel managers in dealing with personnel problems reflects organizational cultures rather than occupational norms and beliefs. In his research he identifies similarities in beliefs and values between personnel staff in the same organizations and considerable differences between personnel staff in different organizational settings. The real specialism of personnel management, he claims, 'could be described as the capacity to survive, to be adaptable, and to facilitate senior managerial actions.' In his view the role of the personnel specialist leads to an accommodation between organizational and personal values, partly because it is a processing and facilitating role and partly because personnel specialists represent organizational interests and define its identity and character. He concludes that 'personnel managers could be described as specialists in ambiguity.' Such a role, however, 'clearly limits the possibility of developing a capacity to contribute to managerial strategic thinking.'[19]

Power and authority in personnel

The power and authority in any managerial function are normally related to how its activities and tasks are seen as contributing to enterprise efficiency and effectiveness. Some management functions such as production, finance and marketing find it relatively easy to claim a clear relationship between their activities and enterprise success than does the personnel department. The difficulty arises in part because personnel managers are more concerned 'with means rather than ends and inputs rather than outputs, and in situations where it is difficult in determining the relationship between the two.'[20] As functional specialists, personnel managers are involved with obtaining, maintaining and discharging an organizational resource – people – through which corporate objectives are achieved. They are not concerned with the objectives themselves. Further, the personnel function deals with people as complex, sometimes unpredictable individuals who are not amenable to manipulation like inanimate objects such as finance, technology and other material resources.

Another problem inherent in the personnel role is its concern with providing and maintaining human inputs which are utilized in other parts of the enterprise where they are employed. The organizational outputs which employees generate, in association with capital and other resources, are often seen as achievements of other parts of the enterprise, not of the personnel department. If improved or more efficient employee effort is a product of effective personnel practices, such as successful recruitment, sound training or well-designed remuneration packages, the personnel department seldom receives the credit. Indeed, the specific contribution which professional personnel management makes to enterprise success, it is argued, is normally difficult 'to measure and isolate from effects of market and other organizational factors.'[21]

Another difficulty which the personnel role encounters in gaining organizational power and status is the widespread nature of the function. This presents difficulties in defining the boundaries between personnel management and other managerial activities. 'There is also the problem of arriving at realistic definitions of what the personnel department's unique contribution within an organization is.'[22] Because every managerial activity has personnel elements, it is argued, it is difficult for the personnel department to claim that its specific contributions facilitate organizational success. Even where personnel outputs are quantifiable and measurable, such as low absenteeism, few employee grievances or strike-free industrial relations, they are not necessarily attributable to the professionalism of personnel specialists and are rarely credited to the personnel department.

Where there appear to be few personnel problems within an enterprise, line managers can even claim that they deserve the credit for effective personnel management, not the personnel department; but they can blame the personnel department if things go badly. In either case, the diffusion of the personnel function into line management activities 'sometimes leads line managers to question whether the personnel function needs a specialist presence within an organization at all.'[23] Indeed effective 'people management' by line managers can undermine the status of the specialist personnel role because personnel work does not then appear to be a specific activity requiring professional knowledge, skills and expertise. Further, although the personnel department is often responsible for designing and setting up particular personnel systems, such as payment systems, job evaluation and staff appraisal schemes, it does not normally implement them. This is the responsibility of line and functional and managers whose success or failure in these tasks is removed from the direct control of personnel staff.

Recruitment, for example, is a main area where personnel departments are judged by other managers.

> This usually seems to them to be unfair because they cannot manufacture people, and they frequently feel that their failure to recruit is due more to management's refusal to accept their advice on personnel policy than their own incompetence at recruiting . . . Few aspects of the personnel function show up fundamental weaknesses more clearly than does the problem of recruitment.[24]

Because of these factors, personnel departments can have a low status in the eyes of line management and a 'vicious circle of information denial, lack of support and credibility is set up.'[25] This undermines the authority of the personnel function which in its quest for organizational power and recognition has to devise appropriate strategies aimed at influencing corporate decision making, contingent to organizational circumstances, rather than assuming its role is automatically legitimized by all managerial groups.

Personnel professionalism

Whether personnel management is a profession 'will continue to be debated within the more general discussion of whether any managerial occupation could qualify given the usual template applied.'[26] In the classical sense, that of a high status occupational group with full professional autonomy providing personal services to individual fee paying clients, personnel management is clearly not a profession. If, however, professionalism exists where an occupational group 'makes a claim for power and authority in specified areas of occupational performance, then personnel management can be regarded as a professionalized activity.'[27]

This model of professionalism has two main elements. The first is common occupational interests amongst practitioners, even though the professional group itself is heterogeneous. The second is that its practitioners claim and demonstrate high standards of competence and expertise in carrying out their specialist activities and tasks. The first point is made in Watson's study of personnel managers. He claims that there is a common consciousness among personnel specialists, especially in their concern with gaining status with senior management. In his view there is a coherence within the occupation which is far greater than he expected when carrying out his research.

> To find personnel officers and managers in banks, engineering companies, co-operative societies, council offices and so on, speaking in such similar ways on aspects of their jobs was a considerable surprise to me.[28]

Being professional in their jobs, on the other hand, requires personnel managers to be competent and expert in their organizational roles and to provide tangible evidence that they are contributing positively to the effective managing of human resources. It does not necessarily mean being members of a recognized professional body 'with its underlying assumptions of specialist education and training and high occupational status and prestige.'[29] It requires, rather, the demonstration of specialist skills and expertise in managing the increasingly complex employment relationship between employers and employees in an organizational setting. In this sense experience indicates a strong identification by personnel managers with organizational needs and corporate objectives, rather than with those of employees or the wider society. 'What the notion of professionalism symbolises for the contemporary personnel specialist is . . . competence in the meeting of general managerial goals.'[30] Personnel professionals, in this sense, are seen largely as contributing effectively to the successful management of the enterprise, not as being an élite group of externally accountable practitioners.

12.2 PERSONNEL WORK

The work of the specialist personnel function can be examined in terms of its activities and tasks, its varying roles and its functional organization. The activities and tasks of personnel management, for example, incorporate the specific duties and job skills of personnel practitioners in fulfilling their corporate and operational responsibilities. Their roles cover the executive, advisory or administrative actions which they undertake as experts in personnel management. The functional organization of the personnel department emerges from the ways in which personnel activities, tasks and roles are structured within enterprises in order to achieve personnel objectives and the implementation of personnel policy.

Activities and tasks

There are several ways of classifying the work of personnel specialists. Moxon was the first to attempt a comprehensive classification. He did this in a pamphlet published by the IPM at the end of the Second World War in which he defined personnel management as the 'function of management concerned with what is commonly called the human factor.' He went on to identify six major personnel activities: 'Employment, Wages, Joint Consultation, Health and Safety, Employee Services and Welfare, [and] Education and Training.' He subdivided these activities into 48 separate individual tasks.[31] Since then the scope of personnel work has expanded considerably. Nowadays, according to one practitioner, a typical range of personnel activities encompasses: corporate planning including the integration of the personnel function with other managerial functions to achieve enterprise objectives; organization structure; manpower planning; manpower development; remuneration; industrial relations; and employee services.[32]

A more detailed analysis of current personnel activities and a breakdown into their separate tasks is provided by the London School of Economics (LSE) classification reported by Guest and Horwood. In their study of the personnel role in a manufacturing company with 40 work units and 31 000 employees and a regional health authority (RHA) employing 61 500 health service staff, they identified 12 major personnel activities incorporating 85 separate personnel tasks. The 12 activities were: direction and policy determination; planning and research; industrial relations and collective bargaining; pay and benefits determination; payment administration; organization, in either or both design and development; manpower planning and/or control; personnel information and records; employee development and training; recruitment and selection; employee communications; and health safety and welfare.[33] In this study the researchers also identified 31 out of the 85 personnel tasks within the main activity areas that were 'most commonly undertaken' by over 50 per cent of the personnel respondents. These are summarized in table 12.1 as a guide to what personnel staff normally do.

According to this research, there was a considerable degree of common ground in the tasks undertaken by the personnel staff in both organizations, especially in recruitment and selection. There were, however, also marked contrasts reflecting the greater degree of centralized administrative work in the RHA compared with the manufacturing

Table 12.1 *Most common tasks of personnel staff.*

Personnel Activity and most common tasks.	
Direction and Policy Determination	development of policy proposals
	managing subordinate personnel staff
	development of external relations
Personnel Planning and Research	participating in corporate planning
Industrial Relations	attending negotiating meetings
	applying agreements on terms and conditions
	acting as workplace industrial relations specialist
	providing advice to managers on the law
	participation in disciplinary, grievance and disputes procedures
Payment Administration	initiating pay transactions
	dealing with individual pay complaints
Organizational Design and Development	production of job descriptions
Manpower Planning and Control	maintaining records of manpower numbers
	controlling levels of manpower
Personnel Information and Records	determining personnel records requirements
Training and Development	identifying individual training needs
	instructing/lecturing
Recruitment and Selection	determining selection methods
	defining recruitment requirements
	job advertising
	processing job applications
	interviewing candidates
	taking part in selection decisions
	organizing selection programmes
	making offers of employment
	taking up references
Employee Communications	planning employee communications
	operating communications procedures
Health Safety and Welfare	employee counselling and welfare
	liaison work in company health services
	advice on pensions

Source: D. Guest and R. Horwood, *The role and effectiveness of personnel managers* (LSE 1980).

organization, where personnel staff were 'more concerned with day to day grass roots issues including aspects of industrial relations, communications and welfare.' It was also shown that a much higher proportion of the personnel staff in the manufacturing plants engaged 'in a wide range of tasks related to Pay and Benefits Determination, Training and Development, Industrial Relations and, to a lesser extent, Manpower Planning and Control' than were their counterparts in the RHA. It appears that the personnel function in the RHA retained 'much of the tradition of an administrative staffing activity', with personnel staff in the manufacturing organization being more likely to be 'engaged in a full range of advisory, executive and administrative activities.'[34]

Guest and Horwood make an interesting distinction between the activities performed by personnel managers in the two organizations and their personnel subordinates. They define 'generalist' personnel managers as those in charge of personnel activity reporting to line management, with personnel 'specialists' or 'subordinates' reporting to someone within the personnel function. Personnel generalists, for example, were found to be more 'heavily involved in industrial relations' and in direction and policy determination in both organizations than were subordinates. Generalist personnel managers were also identified as those concentrating on training and development in the manufacturing organization and on recruitment and selection in the RHA. Amongst specialist subordinate staff 'only Recruitment and Selection and Training and Development figure[d] prominently' in the manufacturing organization but, in the health authority, personnel subordinates were also involved 'in Pay Determination and Administration, Training and Development and Recruitment and Selection.'[35]

Another major difference between the activities of generalist personnel managers and specialist personnel subordinates was that the managers were 'involved in a wider variety of types of activity than their specialist subordinates.' Of the 85 personnel tasks on the researchers' checklist 41 were 'undertaken by over 50% of the generalists in the manufacturing company compared with only 19 undertaken by over 50% of the specialists', especially in industrial relations and recruitment and selection. In the health service region, the contrast whilst not so dramatic was 'still very marked'.

Similarly, in the manufacturing organization the generalists did an average of 42 personnel tasks compared with 32 for the specialists, whilst in the RHA the comparable figures were 39 tasks for the generalists and 28 for the subordinates. In short, 'the contrast between generalist and specialist appears to be well founded.'[36]

Roles

There is no generally agreed prescription for the work of personnel managers, the extent of their duties varies 'in practice from one employer to another and depends on several factors.' For analytical purposes it is useful to categorize personnel work into its executive, advisory and administrative roles. But the simplified view of the personnel manager as merely an adviser or as someone doing line management's work for them is 'misleading and inaccurate.'[37] In their executive roles personnel managers take full responsibility for particular aspects of personnel work such as in leading management negotiating teams in collective bargaining or in taking employment decisions. In their advisory roles personnel managers provide guidance to line managers on personnel policy and its implementation, as well as giving practical day-to-day help to line management in its dealings with subordinate employees. The administrative role of personnel managers includes maintaining personnel procedures and systems and monitoring their effectiveness.

Most personnel activities contain elements of the executive, advisory and administrative roles, particularly in manpower planning and control, recruitment and selection, industrial relations and collective bargaining, training and development, and health, safety and welfare. In manpower planning and control, for example, personnel managers sometimes have the executive authority to make manpower forecasts based on information provided by line management. They also play an advisory role aimed at controlling manpower levels and an administrative one of maintaining manpower records. In the area of recruitment and selection the executive role of the personnel manager is to determine selection methods, advertise jobs and to interview, with advice provided to line management in making selection decisions. The administrative role includes organizing selection programmes, taking up references and making offers of employment.

In industrial relations and collective bargaining, personnel staff are involved in a number of tasks. These include acting as negotiators, attending management–union meetings and participating in disciplinary, grievance and disputes procedures, all of which include executive and advisory tasks. They also advise line managers on the provisions and implications of employment law. Further, personnel departments are usually responsible for applying and administering the collective agreements covering the terms and conditions of employment of particular bargaining units. Personnel has to ensure too that collective bargaining procedures are properly and consistently applied 'and that they are audited and reviewed regularly.'[38]

The role of the personnel function in training and development is primarily advisory, though personnel staff have executive responsibility when instructing or teaching in particular training programmes. In helping line managers to define staff training needs, for example, or in designing training schemes to satisfy these needs, the personnel function has essentially an advisory role. However, in maintaining and co-ordinating training programmes, personnel provides an administrative service. By contrast, the executive role of the personnel department in the field of health, safety and welfare is exemplified in employee counselling and welfare, with advice being given on pensions and health and safety at work. It is normally personnel's responsibility to provide the administrative link between employers and external medical and social services.

In the remaining major personnel activities, personnel managers and their subordinates are involved in a variety of roles. In pay and benefits determination, for example, the personnel role is often advisory but with executive elements. Pay administration, by definition, is largely administrative including organizing employee payments and dealing with individual pay complaints. In employee communications personnel staff provide advice in planning communications and in administrating and maintaining communication procedures. Lastly, in collecting personnel information and maintaining manpower records and statistics, the personnel role is largely an administrative one.

Organization

So far we have concentrated on the 'horizontal' activities and tasks of personnel staff, that is on the jobs which they do across personnel departments whether as generalist personnel managers or specialist personnel subordinates. In larger organizations personnel work is also differentiated 'vertically' between personnel managers and their subordinates, with jobs being delimited by levels of responsibility and degrees of discretion in doing them. One classification of personnel activity based on a survey by the IPM suggests that that there are four vertical levels at which personnel managers operate. These are:

1 Operational personnel officer, including those who are primarily concerned with the day to day personnel function carrying out policies determined by others.
2 Senior personnel officer, including those who not only carry out an operational role but also advise others on the implementation of broad policy outlines, and possibly contribute to the evolution of policy.

3 Personnel manager, including those whose role is primarily advisory and carries responsibility for subordinate personnel officers.

4 Senior personnel manager, including those who are primarily responsible for the creation of company personnel policy for approval by the board of directors and for the direction/coordination of personnel activities throughout the organization.[39]

In their study of the manufacturing organization and the RHA, Guest and Horwood suggest that 'the conventional model of organisation structure for large organisations contains four types of personnel role'[40], similar to those of the IPM survey. These are: personnel directors or generalists dealing with all types of personnel issue and policy development; corporate specialists involved with personnel planning and co-ordination; personnel managers responsible for day-to-day personnel activities; and personnel assistants undertaking a narrow range of specialist duties. Yet neither of the organizations studied conformed to this model structure, though the 'manufacturing company came close to it.'[41]

As well as classifying the 85 horizontal personnel tasks into 12 types of activity, these authors provide a vertical classification based on an analysis of personnel work 'according to the degree of "autonomy" implicit in the nature of each task.' This was done to examine the division of labour between different personnel jobs and levels of organizational authority. Five 'autonomy classifications' were identified. These are:

(1) "Strategic" Tasks involving overall direction and leadership of the function.
(2) "Analytical/ Conceptual" Tasks involving research into and development of concepts and policy necessary to support performance of "strategic" tasks.
(3) "Advisory/ Responsive" Tasks involving provision of specialist expertise or professional services in support of line management.
(4) "Instrumental– Active" Tasks involving implementation of policy within broadly prescribed limits but with scope and need for creative input and judgment.
(5) "Instrumental– Passive" Tasks involving implementation of administration systems providing little scope for independent judgment.[42]

In the two organizations studied, the contrast between vertical personnel activities was considerable. In the manufacturing organization, for example, only corporate staff were engaged in strategic personnel activities, with none of this group involved in advisory or instrumental activities. By contrast, in the RHA, involvement in strategic personnel activities was just as heavy below regional level as at regional level. Similarly, personnel staff below corporate level in the manufacturing organization tended to be involved in a fairly wide range of non-strategic personnel activities. These included advisory services and routine implementation of personnel procedures. There also appeared to be a wider range of activities amongst personnel staff in the health region and its lower tiers, compared with their counterparts in the manufacturing company. In summary, in examining the vertical structure of the personnel function in the two organizations, the authors were able to identify 'a link between location in the organization and types of activity for the manufacturing organization but not for the Health Service Region.'[43]

12.3 PERSONNEL STRATEGY AND POLICY

Strategy

Karen Legge suggests that in their search for functional authority within organizations personnel managers need to adapt their behaviour to the situational contexts and constraints facing them. If the personnel department wishes to gain power and influence in corporate decision making, she argues, personnel managers have to derive authority from any of three paths. She calls these 'conformist innovation', 'deviant innovation' and that of the personnel 'problem solver'.

Conformist innovation is defined as the attempts by the personnel manager 'to demonstrate a closer relationship between his activities (means) and organizational success criteria (ends)'. In adopting this approach personnel managers accept the dominant values and bureaucratic structures of their employing organizations and try to show the importance of personnel management activities in advancing corporate goals. In doing this personnel practitioners highlight their role in facilitating, if only indirectly, organizational success. They do this by tackling obstacles to enterprise efficiency and effectiveness. This includes reducing labour turnover, for example, improving staff training or extending management development. Personnel's contribution to enterprise success 'becomes less important than its role in anticipating, preventing or rectifying a range of organizational malfunctions.'[44]

As conformist innovators, personnel managers emphasize their 'auditing' and 'stabilization' relationships with management, not their advisory ones. Auditing relationships evaluate whether particular managerial actions conform with corporate policies and procedures. Stabilization relationships result in approving managerial decisions, on the basis of specialist expertise, taking corporate objectives into account. These aim to cope bureaucratically with problems of control and co-ordination by scrutinizing managerial decisions before, during and after they are taken. Both auditing and stabilization relationships require personnel managers to minimize the costs of potentially inconsistent and inappropriate personnel decisions by line managers.

In adopting the conformist innovation strategy, personnel specialists develop an appreciation 'that their contribution will appear more tangible if presented in financial terms.'[45] Conformist innovators therefore attempt to justify personnel work in cost-benefit terms – including costing labour turnover, evaluating training programmes, estimating the financial benefits of new payment systems and so on. They also encourage human asset accounting and the use of the computer in the personnel function. As conformist innovators, personnel managers accept line management's definition of how organizational activities should be determined and what their priorities should be. They do not seek to change them but to facilitate their efficiency and effectiveness.

Whilst conformist innovators accept their ends and adjust their means in the personnel role:

> the deviant innovator, rather than making his activities conform to the dominant values about what constitutes success, attempts to change this means/end relationship by gaining acceptance for a different set of criteria for the evaluation of organizational success and his contribution to it.[46]

In the role of deviant innovator, in other words, the personnel specialist seeks acceptance of personnel policies and procedures on altruistic grounds as well as utilitarian ones. Personnel managers can argue, for example, that work should satisfy individual ends as well as instrumental organizational ones. In doing this they introduce external reference groups into organizational decision making so as to evaluate the effectiveness and acceptability of particular personnel activities. The personnel manager can even act as the 'interpreter and advocate' of societal norms to the enterprise, showing that its dominant norms and value are not necessarily the same as those held in society as a whole.

Personnel specialists using the deviant innovation strategy base their activities, their professional relationships and their authority more on a third-party consultancy role than on an exclusively managerial one. They define the personnel needs of line managers and then decide how these needs should be met rather than allowing line management to do so. They do this by applying their professional expertise and values to personnel issues in accordance with what they see to be appropriate standards within their enterprises. They expect their managerial clients, in turn, to accept personnel's definition of what activities are to be provided rather than asserting their own right to do so. In practice few personnel managers are able to change dominant organizational values so fundamentally, since these are usually derived from commercial needs. Nor are they normally able to exert control over line management. Some control takes place, however, when personnel managers advise line management on appropriate courses of action arising from the requirements of employment law.

Normally, 'neither of these attempts to gain "professional" authority is fully viable.' Many personnel activities are difficult to quantify and evaluate in economic terms, so it is difficult for conformist innovators to demonstrate personnel's contribution to enterprise success. Similarly attempts by deviant innovators to initiate alternative corporate values are likely to provoke resistance amongst line managers accepting the existing ones. In practice, 'personnel specialists tend to oscillate between these two paths to "professional" authority.' In deflationary conditions conformist innovation strategies are likely to be more acceptable, whilst in periods of boom 'the climate for experimentation of all kinds is likely to be more favourable than at other times.'[47]

Legge concludes that whilst conformist innovation and deviant innovation may be perceived as distinct and separate personnel strategies they may also be regarded as different styles of performing the role of the personnel manager as 'problem solver'. It is in their role as problem solvers, she claims, whether directed towards conformist innovation or deviant innovation solutions that personnel managers are most likely to influence personnel policy effectively. She concludes that 'diagnostic problem solving' requires a contingent approach to personnel management, with the design and implementation of personnel policy matching or contingent upon organizational circumstances. A contingent approach to personnel problem solving, she argues, 'brings with it the combined advantages of flexibility . . . with a sensitivity to the political dimensions of organizational life.'[48]

Policy

An espoused personnel or industrial relations policy is an attempt by management to define its proposed courses of action in dealings with employees and trade unions. Policy in this sense provides a set of guidelines within which management play a positive proactive role in personnel management rather than an *ad hoc* reactive one. Positive personnel policies normally provide links with other policy areas such as production, finance and marketing, as well as forming an integral part of the overall strategy by which senior management seeks to achieve its corporate goals and objectives. An espoused personnel policy, in short, provides a strategic framework by which management takes the initiative and seeks to act consistently in all personnel and industrial relations matters. The main purpose of a defined policy is that it:

> promotes consistency in management and enables all employees and their representatives to know where they stand in relation to the company's intentions and objectives. It further encourages the orderly and equitable conduct of industrial relations by enabling management to plan ahead, to anticipate events, and to secure and retain an initiative in changing situations.[49]

It has been argued that the decision to produce an explicit personnel policy 'leads logically to the sort of written policy which some companies have produced and trained their managers to use.' There are a number of advantages, it is claimed, in producing written policy statements. First, the processes involved in producing such documents focus managerial attention and energies on their purposes and objectives. They clarify intentions and remove uncertainties where reliance would otherwise be placed on custom and practice, improvization or where policy is a matter of surmise. Second, written documents provide clear reference points in communicating policy guidelines to managers, employees and employee representatives. Third, by creating the starting point of policy, written statements provide a basis for policy changes and reviews as circumstances require or permit. By being written it is 'easier to change than policies which are embedded in custom and practice, tradition and precedent.'[50]

The first requirement for formulating a corporate personnel policy is that the organization's governing body and senior management give commitment and attention to the task. It is, after all, they who exert a major influence on it and on its integration with other policy areas. It is also necessary to involve line managers and employees in the policy process, since without the agreement and acceptance of those who implement policy and are affected by it it is unlikely that the policy guidelines will be authoritative. This necessitates effective procedures ensuring that senior management, operational management and employees are kept fully informed about what is happening and that they are able to influence policy determination from the outset.

It is further argued that personnel policy formulation also requires the 'guidance and co-ordination which the industrial relations specialist should supply.'[51] The specialist contribution is based on its functional responsibility for personnel management and industrial relations, the time it can devote to the tasks, and the skills, knowledge and expertise of professional personnel specialists. Those employed within the personnel function should be able to undertake an overall study of corporate needs and consult and involve the people who are required to carry out policy at various levels. They are in a position to produce proposals, ensure their discussion and secure agreement to them. This, of course, argues for the appointment of board level, or equivalent, personnel directors or personnel 'strategists' able to influence and formulate policy at the highest organizational levels; though in practice some organizations still fail to do this.

The processes by which formal personnel policies are created and developed are complex. Top management has a key part to play but its approach is affected by the philosophy and style of management it adopts, as well as by the importance it attaches to particular policy issues. The extent of its activity is also affected by corporate size, organizational structure and other internal factors. It is increasingly recognized, however, that whilst line management, employees and their representatives have distinctive roles to play in determining and applying policy, boards must 'assume final responsibility for authorising policy in industrial relations or in other areas.'[52]

According to the Department of Employment's code of practice on industrial relations, 'the principle aim of management is to conduct the business of the undertaking successfully,' but a major objective should be 'to develop effective industrial relations policies which command the confidence of employees.' The code, which is soundly based and has been in use for many years now, interprets industrial relations in its widest sense, not just confining it to collective bargaining and negotiating machinery. It says that there are two main themes underlying the code:

   i the vital role of collective bargaining carried out in a reasonable and constructive manner between employers and strong representative trade unions; [and]
   ii the importance of good human relations between employers and employees in every establishment, based on trust and confidence.[53]

It therefore stresses the need for policies in both collective employment matters and those directly affecting individual employees in performing their job tasks.

The major policy areas which the code emphasizes are employment policy, communication and consultation, collective bargaining, and grievances and disputes, with disciplinary matters now covered by a separate code of practice issued by the Advisory Conciliation and Arbitration Service. In examining employment policies, for example, the code stresses the importance of establishing good working relationships between management and employees in order to make 'the most effective use of its manpower resources and give each employee opportunity to develop his [or her] potential.' It recommends that management should initiate and accept primary responsibility for these policies. 'But they should be developed in consultation or negotiation, as appropriate, with employee representatives.' Such policies should not be influenced by 'age, sex or other personal factors except where they are relevant to the job.'[54]

The employment issues where management is recommended to pay particular attention in policy determination are: the planning and use of manpower; recruitment and selection; training; payment systems; the status and security of employees; and working conditions. In operating its manpower policies, for instance, management is advised to avoid unnecessary fluctuations in manpower levels and to record information helping it to identify the causes of absenteeism and labour turnover. In recruitment and selection it is expected that management will consider filling vacancies by transfer or promotion from within the enterprise, base selection on suitability for the job and ensure that those who are given the responsibility to make selection decisions 'are competent to do so.'[55] Management is recommended to ensure that new employees are given induction training, with other job training being provided to supplement educational, training and work experience.

Turning to payment systems the code argues that these should be kept as simple as possible, based on some form of work measurement and jointly negotiated with trade unions where these are recognized. They should be kept under review ensuring that they suit current circumstances and 'take account of any substantial changes in the organisation of work' or job requirements. It is also considered necessary to provide stable employment and job security for employees, consistent with operational efficiency, and that fluctuations in the level of employee earnings should be avoided where possible. Further, differences in conditions of employment and employee status, and in the facilities available to them, 'should be based on the requirements of the job', not on personal grounds or for non-economic reasons. Similarly, a redundancy policy for dealing with reductions in the workforce is recommended and 'should be worked out in advance so far as practicable and should form part of the undertaking's employment policies.'[56]

The code believes that communication and consultation are essential in all establishments to promote efficiency, mutual understanding and job involvement, especially in periods of change. The most important method of communication, it argues, is by word of mouth, supplemented by written information and meetings for special purposes. Management particularly needs to ensure that information is provided to employees about their jobs, trade union arrangements, opportunities for promotion, welfare facilities and health and safety. It is suggested that management initiate the setting up and maintaining of consultative arrangements best suited to the circumstances of the establishment, in co-operation with trade unions and their representatives. These arrangements, however, 'should not be used to by-pass or discourage trade unions.'[57]

The code's advice on collective bargaining begins with bargaining units. It recommends that a bargaining unit should cover as wide a group of employees as is practicable, since too many small units make it difficult for related groups of employees to be treated consistently. Whilst the interests of employee groups need not be identical, there 'should be a substantial degree of common interest' amongst them, taking account of minority interests. A number of factors should be taken into account in defining bargaining units: the nature of the work; common interests; employee wishes; location of the work; the matters to be bargained about; and whether separate bargaining units are needed for 'particular categories of employees, such as supervisors or employees who represent management in negotiation.'[58]

When considering trade union recognition, management are recommended to examine the support for the claim amongst employees and the effect of granting recognition on existing bargaining arrangements. After recognition, it is argued, relations between management and unions should be based on jointly agreed industrial relations procedures providing clear rules and a basis for resolving differences between them. Regular contacts between management and unions are recommended, not just when trouble arises. Agreements 'should be in writing and there should be agreed arrangements for checking that procedural provisions have not become out of date.' There is also advantage in agreeing at industry level those pay-work issues covering the industry as a whole. These include: terms and conditions suitable for general application; guidelines for negotiating at lower levels; and a procedure for settling disputes, 'either for the industry as a whole or as a model for individual undertakings to adopt by agreement.'[59]

The code goes on to recommend that management and trade unions should agree the number of shop stewards required in an establishment and the workgroups for which each steward is responsible. To encourage union members to vote in steward elections 'management should offer the trade unions facilities to conduct elections . . . and to publicise the date and details.' Whilst the extent and nature of shop steward facilities can be agreed between management and unions, the code says, other facilities can be provided by management. These include: lists of new employees; accommodation; telephones; and offices. Management and unions can also review the training most appropriate for steward needs 'and take all reasonable steps to ensure that stewards receive the training they require.'[60]

The code states that employees have a right to seek redress for grievances relating to their employment. Accordingly, management is expected to establish with employee representatives arrangements for raising grievances and having them settled fairly and promptly. Such procedures should be in writing, have a number of stages or levels and a right of appeal. Where unions are recognized, management is recommended to establish a procedure for settling collective disputes with them. This should be in writing and:

i state the level at which an issue should first be raised;
ii lay down time limits for each stage of the procedure, with provision for extension by agreement;
iii preclude a strike, lock-out, or other form of industrial action until all stages of the procedure have been completed and a failure-to-agree formally recorded.[61]

12.4 LINE MANAGEMENT AND THE PERSONNEL FUNCTION

As already indicated the nature of the personnel role is the subject of long-standing debate, especially in the managing of industrial relations. In some organizations personnel managers are essentially advisers to line managers, with the latter responsible for executive action affecting industrial relations within their own areas of responsibility. In other organizations full executive authority is given to a senior personnel or industrial relations generalist who has the executive authority to instruct line managers in courses of action either directly or through personnel subordinates. Nevertheless, 'a simple distinction between executive and advisory functions, while useful for analytical purposes, obviously needs to be qualified and is likely to become blurred in practice.'[62] From a managerial viewpoint all managers, line or personnel, need to have a clear understanding of their respective roles and responsibilities in industrial relations.

Line management's job is to ensure that corporate policy is executed in their spheres of responsibility and that output targets and job tasks are achieved. Industrial relations form part of these responsibilities and the line manager's operational effectiveness is diminished where basic personnel and industrial relations decisions are referred to others. Workgroup and industrial relations problems are so interconnected that they cannot be properly separated. There are clear advantages for management in ensuring 'that decisions on everyday problems such as the handling of employees' grievances or disciplinary matters are seen to come from the line manager concerned.'[62] Most day-to-day issues are best settled promptly by the people directly involved, when they occur. Line managers are also in the best position to communicate and consult with employees on matters bearing on industrial relations, thus demonstrating their awareness of industrial relations as an integral part of their job.

Since line managers are so immersed in target dates, operational schedules and budgetary control, they sometimes fail to give full weight to personnel issues and take hasty decisions harmful to industrial relations. 'In this context the personnel manager offers such help and advice as may be necessary to ensure equity and consistency in the application of policy.'[63] The role of first line management or workgroup supervisors in communicating policies and plans to subordinate employees is particularly crucial, since they form management's immediate face to face contact with employees with responsibility for workgroup performance. Given their job tasks, it is good practice to define the responsibilities and authority of supervisors in relation to their subordinates, senior managers, personnel staff and employee representatives. Supervisors can also usefully contribute to developing personnel policy, devising new work methods, handling change and participating in managerial preparations for negotiation. Properly utilized, workgroup supervisors can promote the orderly conduct of industrial relations.

Personnel managers make an important contribution to the conduct of industrial relations by taking an overall view of the function and by using their specialist knowledge and skills. Such skills include planning, negotiating, and problem solving. Personnel managers also provide basic personnel services including: maintaining personnel records; administering recruitment procedures; inducting employees; co-ordinating industrial relations; and monitoring the consistent application of personnel policy. They also support line management by providing advice to top management on formulating policy and corporate plans; to top and middle management on implementing policy and plans; and to line management on the everyday conduct of industrial relations. Another aspect of the personnel manager's job is the educative role – helping line management to understand the concepts and techniques of professional personnel management as they bear on industrial relations. In practice, however, line managers mostly judge personnel managers 'on the extent to which their advice is found to be constructive and helpful in solving problems or preventing their occurrence.' In effect, the task of the personnel manager 'is to make line managers more effective without diminishing their authority.'[64]

In collective bargaining management has to prepare for negotiations, decide the composition and authority of its negotiating team, agree to the conduct of negotiations and ensure that concluded agreements are implemented. Preparatory work is complex and time consuming. Whilst personnel managers provide specialist knowledge and skills, it is also necessary to involve representative cross-sections of line managers at this stage. When bargaining 'a wide variety of practice is found in the leadership, composition and authority of the management negotiating team.' In some cases the lead is taken by a senior personnel manager, with line managers providing advice and support. In other cases a line manager leads with advice obtained from the personnel manager. Alternatively negotiations may be conducted by the personnel manager or line managers exclusively. In general, managerial objectives are most likely to be achieved where 'both personnel and line managers at appropriate levels are represented in negotiating teams.'[65]

Whatever its composition, everyone in the management negotiating team has to be clear about its authority to make and settle agreements over all sorts of issues. Although there is advantage in delegating the maximum authority to settle to the negotiators, some matters are always likely to require reference to or discussion with a higher authority as, for example, where policy affecting other bargaining units is affected. One arrangement is for the board or governing body to define the limits within which negotiators can decide, with consultations taking place between them as necessary. Final authority remains with the negotiators who have the knowledge of relevant circumstances 'and whose commitment to the final settlement is required.'[66]

In implementing collective agreements management negotiators need to ensure that managers, supervisors and employees are fully informed and prepared for the changes being introduced. This can be a large-scale activity, with trade union and employee representatives requiring facilities and assistance to carry out their part in the exercise. This necessitates co-ordinating and monitoring agreements to ensure consistency. This can usefully be done by personnel managers, with line managers implementing the agreements affecting their immediate employees.

Communications and consultation require continual oversight from management. Overall responsibility for communications is sometimes delegated to the personnel department which identifies the methods of communication and decides what shall be communicated and when. This enables employees to be properly informed of all written policies and procedures affecting their jobs, including relevant legal requirements, whilst everyday responsibility for communications normally rests with line managers. It is by face to face communication with their workgroups, however, that line managers provide the opportunity to avoid problem areas and to promote mutual understanding amongst the employees they manage.

Collaboration between personnel and line managers is also required in establishing and operating formal systems of consultation. For example, matters of common concern need to be identified; ways of injecting new ideas into consultative committees have to be considered; means of extending the range of subjects discussed require to be found; and methods of assessing the effectiveness of consultative committees have to be explored. In enterprises with well-established arrangements these tasks are often the responsibility of the senior personnel manager. Line managers normally participate in committee proceedings, though, following up action in their own departments subsequently. The authority of such committees is enhanced considerably where senior line management participate as active members.

In drafting and negotiating procedural agreements and in monitoring their operation, both personnel managers and line managers have roles to play. Personnel managers have the responsibility of drafting management's initial proposals, with line and personnel managers conducting negotiations subsequently. Personnel managers can provide advice and guidance by ensuring that procedures are observed, but line managers are normally responsible for ensuring that procedures are properly used in their areas of responsibility. This includes explaining procedures, rules and standards of conduct to their employees. It is particularly important that first line managers or supervisory managers do this, since it is at this level that breaches of rules and procedures most commonly occur. This happens when supervisors are bypassed and senior line management or the personnel department are directly approached. Where this happens too often, agreed procedures fall into disrepute and lose their authority.

When planning pay policies, management aims to control labour costs, prevent pay anomalies and avoid dissatisfactions which can harm industrial relations. This requires that earnings surveys are carried out, pay comparisons are examined and suitable payment systems devised. Many of these activities are handled by the personnel department but there must be close collaboration with line managers. In designing and operating a payment system, for example, line management can help to determine what the objectives of the system are, making the selection from alternatives provided by the personnel specialist. From that point on it is the line management's task to supervise the application of the payment system within their areas of responsibility, particularly ensuring that employees understand the system and how their pay is made up. The amount of discretion allowed to line managers to determine or make adjustments to an individual's pay varies. It is the personnel manager, though, who is in the best position to advise how 'to maintain a balanced wage structure that does not upset collective agreements and remains equitable as between groups and individuals.'[67]

12.5 EMPLOYEE COMMUNICATION AND INFORMATION

Effective communication between management and employees and the dissemination of relevant information from management to employees are now recognized as necessary conditions in any employer strategy aimed at positively involving employees in the enterprises in which they work. This requires appropriate communication structures and a managerial policy on what information is to be provided to employees either directly or through their representatives. The starting point is a positive commitment from top management which defines in broad terms the objectives being sought, how they are to be achieved and what needs to be communicated. A main aim is to encourage all employees to identify with the enterprise as a whole. In establishing and implementing its policy, management has to take account not only of employee needs but also any constraints placed on the employer. These include protecting confidentiality, balancing openness with secrecy and safeguarding organizational interests.

Communication channels within enterprises are vertical or horizontal. Vertical channels are those from senior management to employees, or from union members to their negotiators. Horizontal channels are those between management and union representatives at various levels of organizational decision making. To be successful, both vertical and horizontal channels need to facilitate two-way exchanges of information between those involved. This enables management to communicate to employees through their supervisors and to receive feedback, union members to communicate to their union negotiators through shop stewards and to receive feedback and managerial and union representatives to communicate with each other.

If trade unions are recognized, it is essential from a managerial standpoint that where information is provided to employees it should be done not only through their shop stewards but also their supervisors, though some managements communicate directly with their workforce. Trade union representatives cannot be expected to communicate management's point of view, since they are elected to represent employee interests not managerial ones. Rather, they are the focal point of upward communication or feedback from employees to management. Stewards have a prime duty to their members and provision must be made for them by management for opportunities to communicate to and with their constituents. It is essential for management to ensure that shop stewards do not receive information before workgroup supervisors. 'Nothing more effectively destroys the morale of junior management than this.'[68]

As indicated in table 12.2 there is a wide variety of information which employers can provide and communicate to employees or their representatives. The most basic information relates to the employee's immediate job. A number of surveys show that information about the individual employee's job and job tasks is what many employees consider to be their most important priority. A comprehensive and integrated employee communication and information strategy requires other corporate information to be made available to all employees, however, including supervisory and

Table 12.2 *Information for employees.*

Types of information	Examples
Job information	Job description, job training, terms and conditions, contractual details, physical environment, relationships with others, promotion prospects, grievance and disciplinary procedures
General information	Management and organizational structures, products, customers, numbers employed, appointments, resignations, promotions, long-service awards, labour turnover, job security
Marketing information	Sales, market shares, exports, competition, trading position, order book
Policies and plans	Manpower, health and safety, training, industrial relations, pay, job evaluation, sickness, savings schemes, investment, new products
Financial information	Income, distribution of income, tax paid, unit costs, profit and loss account, balance sheet, sources and application of funds, added value, productivity

managerial staff. This encompasses such general information about the enterprise as: its structure, products, customers and personnel; marketing information about sales, competitive situation and trading position; corporate policies and plans, especially those covering manpower, investment and new products; and financial information in its widest sense. This assumes that management is able to collect and disseminate such information and is prepared to bear the economic costs of providing and distributing it.

In structuring effective communication and information channels, management has to take account of what is to be communicated, who is to be responsible for communicating it, to whom the information is directed and the most appropriate form in which to present it. As already indicated, employee communication takes place between managers and individual employees or through representatives. Similarly communication can be oral, visual or written. A major factor influencing the choice of means is the number of employees to whom the information is directed. In general, where the number of employees to be given information is relatively small, verbal methods such as briefing groups or departmental meetings are preferable. But, as the number of employees requiring the information increases, either written or visual methods or both become more appropriate. These include: memoranda; minutes; videos; mass meetings; conferences; enterprise newsletters; and annual reports from top management to all employees. Personal letters to each employee from senior management are also used.

Where management and independent unions negotiate it is a statutory duty of employers under the Employment Protection Act 1975 to disclose information to union negotiators 'which it would be in accordance with good industrial relations to disclose.'

> To determine what information will be relevant negotiators should take account of the subject-matter of the negotiations and the issues raised during them; the level at which negotiations take place (department, plant, division, or company level); the size of the company; and the type of business the company is engaged in.[69]

The sort of information which the code of practice says could be relevant includes: pay and benefits; conditions of service; manpower; performance; and financial details. It also recommends that employers and unions jointly should decide how disclosure can be most effectively implemented. 'They should consider what information is likely to be required, what is available, and what could be reasonably be made available.'[70]

12.6 SUMMARY

The personnel function of management is concerned with the managing of people at work and with their relationships within the enterprise. The nature of the personnel function, however, is problematic and the subject of long-standing debate. There is no general agreement about what personnel activities and tasks should be allocated to line managers and to personnel specialists respectively. Nevertheless, whilst the specialist personnel role is long established, and can be traced back in its welfare form to the early years of this century, the number of personnel managers employed in enterprises have increased in recent years. Their power and status vary and no single model of the personnel function is universally accepted.

A number of roles for personnel management have been identified. These include: the welfare role aiming to provide employee well-being within enterprises; the management control role aimed at human resource efficiency; the independent role aimed at autonomy for the personnel specialist; and the professional role aimed at developing relevant occupational skills and values amongst personnel practitioners. Given such contrasting operational interpretations of their function, it is not surprising that personnel specialists sometimes fail to gain the power, authority and status to influence personnel policy and to persuade line managers to adopt professional personnel practices. Functional success in the specialist personnel role is more likely where personnel practitioners adopt an employer frame of reference and contribute, through their professional knowledge and skills, to the effective managing of the contractual relationship between employers and employees.

There are various ways of classifying personnel work. The LSE classification with its 12 'activity classifications', containing 85 separate tasks, and its five 'autonomy classifications' is very useful. It provides an analytical tool for examining how personnel work is structured both horizontally and vertically. It also distinguishes between the activities and tasks of personnel managers and those of personnel subordinates. Generalist personnel managers in charge of the personnel function normally engage in a wider variety of tasks than do their specialist personnel subordinates. They are also more likely to be involved in direction, policy determination and industrial relations than are their subordinates.

Analytically, personnel work can be divided into its executive, advisory and administrative roles, though in practice most personnel activities incorporate elements of each of them. In its vertical organization personnel work falls into 'autonomy' groupings. These are: strategic activities providing leadership of the personnel function; analytical/conceptual activities providing support for strategic tasks; advisory/responsive activities providing professional support for line management; instrumental-active activities providing policy implementation; and instrumental-passive activities administering personnel systems with little scope for independent judgment. This autonomy classification is a more useful analytical device for classifying personnel work by levels of responsibility than are personnel job titles, which vary enormously in their scope and responsibilities.

Three strategies are suggested by which personnel managers can achieve functional authority in organizations. Conformist innovators, for example, accept the dominant utilitarian values of their organizations and attempt to demonstrate the financial benefits of personnel management in achieving corporate efficiency and effectiveness. Deviant innovators, by contrast, seek a more independent role for the personnel specialist by challenging dominant organizational values, and by defining the personnel management needs of line managers and providing the means to satisfy them. Diagnostic problem solving requires a contingent approach to personnel management, using conformist innovation or deviant innovation strategies as appropriate.

Espoused personnel and industrial relations policies provide written guidelines for promoting consistent action amongst line managers, whilst enabling employees and their representatives to know where they stand in personnel issues. They are an integral element in senior management's aim of achieving its corporate goals and objectives. In formulating and applying personnel policies, top management initiative is necessary but it also requires line management, personnel, union and employee involvement if these activities are to be legitimized. A useful checklist for examining personnel and industrial relations policy is provided by the Department of Employment's code of practice. The areas it highlights as deserving particular managerial attention include: employment policy; communication and consultation; collective bargaining; and grievances and disputes; with discipline and dismissal now covered by a separate code.

In managing industrial relations, line managers and personnel managers play complementary but supportive roles without which management is at a tactical disadvantage. Normally line managers are responsible for the application of personnel policies and procedures within their areas of responsibility, with personnel managers providing advice, guidance and services on particular issues. The special contribution which personnel managers make in industrial relations derives from their ability to take an overview of the function and their professional knowledge and skills in negotiating, planning and problem solving. In collective bargaining and the implementation of collective agreements, for example, both line managers and personnel specialists have roles to play. In general, personnel has a co-ordinating and monitoring role and line management an executive one, although there are exceptions. Similarly, collaboration between line managers and personnel managers is essential in establishing and operating effective consultation and communication arrangements. In pay issues personnel normally provides the policy framework and line management supervises the operational details. Ultimately, however, management's responsibility in industrial relations is collective.

Effective communication and information strategies are increasingly recognized as necessary conditions for involving employees in the enterprises in which they work. To be successful they require commitment from top management and the development of appropriate communication structures and information provision. Communication channels may be vertical or horizontal, directed at employees individually or through their representatives. A wide variety of corporate information can be provided by employers including job, general, marketing and financial information and information relating to corporate policies and plans. Communication can be verbal, written and/or visual; non-verbal methods are more likely as the number of employees requiring information increases. Where independent trade unions are recognized, they have a statutory right to information from employers for the purposes of collective bargaining.

12.7   REFERENCES

1. D. Barber, *The Practice of Personnel Management*, Institute of Personnel Management, London, 1982, p. 8.
2. B. Ream, *Personnel Administration: a Guide to the Effective Management of Human Resources*, ICSA, Cambridge, 1984, p. 7.
3. A. Fowler, *Personnel Management in Local Government*, Institute of Personnel Management, London, 1980, p. 18.

4. M. Niven, *Personnel Management 1913–63*, Institute of Personnel Management, London, 1967, p. 152 and H.A. Clegg, *The Changing System of Industrial Relations in Britain*, Blackwell, Oxford, 1979, p. 218.
5. J. Hunt, The shifting focus of the personnel function, *Personnel Management*, February 1984, p. 15.
6. W.W. Daniel and N. Millward, *Workplace Industrial Relations in Britain*, Heinemann, London, 1983, pp. 125f and 286f.
7. K. Manning, The rise and fall of personnel, *Management Today*, March 1983, p. 74ff.
8. K. Legge, *Power, Innovation and Problem Solving in Personnel Management*, McGraw-Hill, London, 1978, p. 37.
9. J. Harvey-Jones, How I see the personnel function, *Personnel Management*, September 1982, p. 26f.
10. P. Parker, How I see the personnel function', *Personnel Management*, January 1983, p. 17f.
11. *Ibid.*, p. 19.
12. A. Jarrett, How I see the personnel function, *Personnel Management*, June 1982, pp. 32–35.
13. G. Thomason, *A Textbook of Personnel Management*, Institute of Personnel Management, London, 1975, p. 26.
14. Quoted in M. Niven, *Personnel Management 1913–63*, Institute of Personnel Management, London, 1967, p. 23.
15. D. Guest and R. Horwood, *The Role and Effectiveness of Personnel Managers: a Preliminary Report*, London School of Economics, London, 1982, p. 11.
16. *Ibid.*, p. 10.
17. *Ibid.*, p. 11.
18. *Ibid.*
19. S. Tyson, Personnel management in its organizational context, in K. Thurley and S. Wood (eds.), *Industrial Relations and Management Strategy*, Cambridge University Press, Cambridge, 1983, p. 156.
20. K. Legge and M. Exley, Authority, ambiguity and adaptation: the personnel specialist's dilemma, *Industrial Relations Journal*, Autumn 1976, p. 54.
21. *Ibid.*
22. D. Farnham, *Personnel in Context*, Institute of Personnel Management, London, 1984, p. 112.
23. *Ibid.*
24. T.P. Lyons, *The Personnel Function in a Changing Environment*, Pitman, London, 1971, p. 37.
25. K. Legge and M. Exley, *op. cit.*, p. 57.
26. G. Thomason, *A Textbook of Personnel Management*, 4th ed., Institute of Personnel Management, London, 1981, p.55.
27. D. Farnham, *op. cit.*, p. 149.
28. T.J. Watson, *The Personnel Managers*, Routledge and Kegan Paul, London, 1977, p. 50.
29. D. Farnham, *op. cit.*, p. 149.
30. T.J. Watson, *op. cit.*, p. 198.
31. G.R. Moxon, *Functions of a Personnel Department*, Institute of Personnel Management, London, 1951, p. 3.
32. D. Barber, *op. cit.*, p. 8ff.
33. D. Guest and R. Horwood, *op. cit.*, p. 18.
34. *Ibid.*, pp. 24, 27 and 28.
35. *Ibid.*, pp. 31 and 37.
36. *Ibid.*, pp. 31–33.
37. A. Fowler, *op. cit.*, p. 25.
38. D. Farnham, *op. cit.*, p. 128.
39. D. Barber, *op. cit.*, p. 10f.
40. D. Guest and R. Horwood, *op. cit.*, p. 37.
41. *Ibid.*, p. 38.
42. *Ibid.*, p. 20.
43. *Ibid.*, p. 41.
44. K. Legge and M. Exley, *op. cit.*, p. 59f.

45. *Ibid.*, p. 60.
46. *Ibid.*, p. 61.
47. *Ibid.*, p. 62f.
48. K. Legge, *op. cit.*, p. 115.
49. Commission on Industrial Relations, *Report No. 34. The role of Management in Industrial Relations*, HMSO, London, 1973, p. 6.
50. *Ibid.*
51. *Ibid.*, p. 12.
52. *Ibid.*, p. 15.
53. Department of Employment, *Industrial Relations Code of Practice*, HMSO, London, 1972, p. 2.
54. *Ibid.*, p. 9.
55. *Ibid.*, p. 10.
56. *Ibid.*, p. 11f.
57. *Ibid.*, p. 16.
58. *Ibid.*, p. 19.
59. *Ibid.*, p. 22.
60. *Ibid.*, pp. 24 and 25.
61. *Ibid.*, p. 26f.
62. CIR, *op. cit.*, p. 16.
63. *Ibid.*, p. 18.
64. *Ibid.*, p. 20.
65. *Ibid.*, p. 21.
66. *Ibid.*
67. *Ibid.*, p. 25.
68. Confederation of British Industry, *Communication with People at Work*, CBI, London, 1977, p. 18.
69. Advisory Conciliation and Arbitration Service, *Code of Practice 2. Disclosure of Information to Trade Unions for Collective Bargaining Purposes*,
70. *Ibid.*, p. 5.

13

Shop Stewards and Workplace Representation

The position of shop stewards in British industrial relations grew in importance between the end of the Second World War and the economic recession of the early 1980s. They are present throughout public and private industry. Wherever trade unions are recognized by employers, trade union representatives often emerge at workplace level to represent their members and the workgroups electing them. They are not just a phenomenon of manual trade unionism alone, since white-collar 'office' or 'departmental' representatives are also commonplace. In the post-war period shop stewards – or workplace representatives whatever their title – moved 'from a somewhat obscure and relatively minor position in industrial relations to one of great prominence and widely acknowledged importance.'[1]

13.1 SHOP STEWARDS

The term 'shop steward' is the title usually given to the unpaid representatives of trade unions at the workplace. Shop stewards exist in most places of work where trade unions are recognized. In this chapter and elsewhere we use the term shop steward to describe those lay representatives of manual and non-manual unions whose duties centre on the workplace. Although the term shop steward is in general use, some unions and industries use other descriptions. In the printing industry, for example, the equivalent to the shop steward is the 'father' or 'mother' of the chapel; amongst draughtsmen it is the 'corresponding member'; in the civil service they are called the 'staff side members of the local Whitley Committee'; and in the iron and steel industry they are described as 'works representatives'. Whatever their title, they represent their union at the workplace and those union members electing them to protect them in dealings with management.

> The general view of the shop steward . . . sees him as essentially a shop floor bargainer using every opportunity available to him to try to satisfy members' demands. . . . His activities, from the Management viewpoint, appear to involve a constant challenge of their prerogatives and authority.[2]

Origins

Trade unionism arose to protect employees and further their interests at the workplace. Although trade unions are established and durable organizations, the original need for workplace representation is as necessary as ever. Shop stewards not only represent unions which often appear to be remote and impersonal bureaucracies in the eyes of the vast majority of their members, they also fulfil the ever present need of the workgroup for familiar and tangible leadership which not only articulates their values and expectations within the workplace, but also is subject to their continuous influence and control. However, the role and behaviour of shop stewards varies enormously. The factors influencing them include: the union and the industry to which they belong, the type of workgroups which they represent and the traditions and attitudes of workers and management. They are also influenced by the type of product or service which the industry supplies, its technology, whether collective bargaining is centralized or devolved, and the economic circumstances of the employers.

Irrespective of these factors, shop stewards seek the best pay and working conditiaons which they can for their members. The universality of shop stewards, their influence and importance in the determination of pay and conditions at work, and their ability in many work situations to pursue courses of action independent of both management and full time trade union officers, ensure them a central place in British industrial relations. But it has not always been so. In terms of the long history of trade unionism and of collective bargaining, the emergence of shop stewards is a comparatively recent phenomenon.

Before 1945, shop stewards with representative negotiating functions were few in number and were limited to a handful of industries such as engineering, shipbuilding and printing. Most union representatives at the workplace were 'collectors' whose main duty was to obtain maximum union membership and to collect weekly membership subscriptions or union dues. They rarely if ever represented members' interests to their employers but called in full time officers when the need arose. An independent estimate of the number of shop stewards in 1960 put their figures at 90 000, with the Trades Union Congress (TUC) estimating that there were 200 000 of them at that time. The Royal Commission on Trade Unions and Employers' Associations in 1968 put the total at about 175 000. Still later, in 1971, a survey by the Commission on Industrial Relations indicated that there were between 250 000 and 300 000 shop stewards plus some 45 000 non-union workplace representatives. The TUC claimed in the early 1980s that the trade unions had about 300 000 shop stewards, 200 000 safety representatives and 100 000 pension trustees. This suggests that there could be as many as 500 000 union workplace representatives, with an estimated annual turnover of 120 000. These figures must be compared with the approximately 3 000 full time union officers whose numbers are likely to grow or decline in proportion to total union membership. It would appear, therefore, that a very large amount of trade union work and activities is carried out by shop stewards and other workplace representatives.

It is since 1945, then, that the number of shop stewards in Britain has increased. This was accompanied by a growth in their bargaining strength and in their ability to represent members' grievances to management at the workplace. Their authority in relation to the formal structure of trade unionism and to the power of full time officers was also substantially strengthened. There are several factors which gave rise to this power base in British industrial relations. These included: the impact of relatively full employment between 1945 and 1979 on workplace discipline and on authority relations between managers and employees; the use of payment by results wage systems; the growth of overtime working; and the decentralization of collective bargaining in favour of company and workplace negotiations, including, in many cases, productivity and efficiency bargaining. Other factors which influenced the growth in power of shop stewards were the reluctance of trade unions to appoint more full time officers, the spread of the closed shop, the development of procedural agreements involving shop stewards and a change of attitude within the trade unions favouring the appointment of workplace representatives. In more recent years, the passing of a considerable volume of employment protection law has also increased the functions of the shop steward at the workplace.

Authority

Despite the important role which shop stewards have played in the development of trade unionism, and the large numbers that now daily represent their union and its members at the workplace, little mention is made of shop stewards in many union rule books. As the Donovan Report observed in 1968:

> Where union rule books mention shop stewards, and many of them do not, they generally say something about method of appointment, and the body to whom the stewards is nominally responsible. They may mention the duties of recruiting and retaining members, and collecting subscriptions. If the business of representing members is touched on, little is said about it.[3]

The Royal Commission went on to recommend that union rules concerning shop stewards in relation to such matters as elections, terms of office, the filling of casual vacancies, 'the bounds of the shop steward's jurisdiction, his relations with other union officials and his place in the union's organisation'[4] should be written into trade union rule books.

Similar conclusions were reached by an independent survey of over 30 union rule books. It concluded that:

> their provisions are sparsely and vaguely worded, though a primary source of reference for all union officers. The failure of some rule books to define realistically a steward's function and responsibilities may reflect the attitude of a union to workplace representatives. Some unions appear to want to play down their significance, others deliberately leave their role relatively undefined to allow enlargement as dictated by local circumstances.[5]

As one of the members of the Royal Commission writing some years after the publication of its recommendations observed: 'most unions have not altered their rules on shop stewards, and rights to representation remain much as they were'.[6] In practice, however, many trade unions issue handbooks and other guidance for shop stewards containing information about union policy and instruction on what the unions believe to be their main duties and responsibilities on behalf of their unions and their members.

It is difficult not to conclude that the majority of unions, whilst accepting the essential role of shop stewards as official representatives of the trade unions, leave them very much alone to get on with their jobs with a minimum of formal regulation. It is reasonable to assume that the situation suits both unions and stewards alike. On the other hand, a detailed study of workplace industrial relations and the activities of shop stewards in a single plant has stressed that 'the divorce between larger union and domestic organization has often been grossly exaggerated', and that 'stewards often place great emphasis upon the importance of the larger union as the embodiment of union principles and as a basis for their self-identity.'[7] The most comprehensive survey of workplace industrial relations carried out since the Donovan inquiry in 1966 came to broadly similar conclusions in 1980. It found that in all types of branches, but especially geographically based ones, 'shop stewards were much more frequent in their attendance than were other branch members. Stewards also commonly held positions on their branch committee.'[8] These findings suggest that too much emphasis is generally placed on the formal structure of trade union power as indicated by the union rule book, and too little attention is paid to the real incidence and distribution of power within trade unions at the workplace.

So, the shop steward has traditionally been seen as the representative of the trade union at the workplace whose first loyalty is to the union and to its policies. Some writers have pointed out, however, that the study of workgroups and of their values and expectations provides an equally important explanation of steward behaviour. This view is reinforced by the evidence that non-unionized workgroups often evolve their own leaders or representatives who put their views to management. One researcher has suggested:

> One of the central features of work is that it is usually done in groups, groups of individuals cooperating under the direction of a leader or leaders . . . The working group is one of the main types of social group, and social interaction at work is one of the main forms of social interaction. Working groups differ from other groups . . . in that they are brought together in order to collaborate over work and the pattern of relationships in the group is primarily determined by the task to be done.[9]

It seems apparent, therefore, that leaders can emerge within any workgroup. These workgroup leaders then express the views and anxieties of the group to management. The shop steward is just such a workgroup leader as well as being a trade union representative.

Much controversy surrounds the question as to what the dominant influences on the steward's role are and whether it is the workgroup or the union which commands the steward's first loyalty. There is considerable evidence to suggest, for example, that where there are divided loyalties or a conflict of interests between their members' aspirations and formal union policy, shop stewards generally side with their workgroups. Similarly, whilst full time union officers can oppose workgroups when they want to take action which is counter to official union policy, they usually do so with relative impunity. A shop steward adopting a similar approach will more often than not be quickly removed from leadership by the workgroup. As an early study of industrial relations in a car plant noted:

> the unrest was on the shop floor. The stewards attempted to act constitutionally . . . When this failed and their members took strike action, they attempted to obtain a return to work. They were under pressure from their members, and their leadership appeared reluctant.[10]

Elections

Some union rule books contain rules broadly regulating the election of shop stewards and the length of time which they serve before re-election. Some merely state that shop stewards will 'be appointed' and in a few cases the district officer or the union executive appoints shop stewards. A small number of rule books fail to mention shop stewards at all. Most unions are aware of the difficulties in enforcing detailed rules for electing shop stewards at the place of work and prefer a flexible approach which helps to ensure that somebody suitable is found to do the job. Many union rule books do not stipulate the precise method of electing shop stewards or the composition of the electorate. Similarly, the qualifications of those eligible to stand for office are often omitted, although some unions stipulate both a minimum period of union membership and a minimum age for those seeking to become stewards. Rule books generally have little to say about the removal of shop stewards if they fail in their duties or break union rules but union executives sometimes have the power to remove stewards if necessary.

The reality of workplace representation is that shop stewards only retain their position and authority so long as they have the confidence and support of the members and of the workgroups they represent. It is because shop steward constituencies are relatively small, and because stewards are usually well known to their fellow workers, rather than because of the existence of carefully worded rule books, that they are likely to conduct themselves as democratic representatives. Comparatively few trade unionists are aware of these rules and few would be willing to enforce them if they had to. 'The members who elect him will regard him essentially as their representative in dealings with the management'. Yet, 'potentially, stewards face conflicting claims on their loyalty, and may encounter problems in reconciling the expectations of constituents with those of the union'.[11]

Surveys suggest that in general the job of the shop steward is not eagerly sought after. Neither are elections, which are usually by show of hands, fiercely contested. A survey conducted for the Donovan Commission in 1967, for example, indicated that 71 per cent of the shop stewards questioned were elected unopposed, 36 per cent whilst wanting the job had had to be asked to do it, and 40 per cent had had to be persuaded to take on the task. Further surveys of workplace industrial relations in 1972 and 1973 confirmed these findings. In 1973, for example, 75 per cent of the shop stewards who were surveyed replied that they had been unopposed in their elections, compared with 78 per cent in 1972; 38 per cent had wanted the job but had had to be asked to take it on; whilst 37 per cent had had to be persuaded to become stewards. 'The remaining quarter wanted the job and did not have to be persuaded.'[12] Somewhat surprisingly, the situation had changed little by 1980 when the workplace industrial relations survey found that the appointment of manual shop stewards was most commonly made by a show of hands at a meeting of union members. 'This remained the case in 1980 and was also evident for non-manual stewards.' Furthermore, 'some method of periodic reappointment was reported in most cases, normally once per year, but in about half the cases there had been no alternative candidate'.[13] It would seem that 'competition for the post of shop steward is thus not very keen and once chosen, shop stewards are fairly secure', although 'the post of shop steward is more attractive than that of branch secretary.'[14]

The size of a shop steward's constituency varies widely accordingly to the trade union and the industry, the size of the employing establishment and the functions of shop stewards. Where large numbers of workers are concentrated in comparatively small working areas, stewards tend to represent more people than in scattered work situations with relatively small workgroups. There is also a tendency for shop stewards of skilled workgroups to represent fewer members than stewards from general unions whose membership is largely unskilled. The survey evidence suggests that the average number of members represented by shop stewards is about 30 but this figure hides very considerable variations between unions and sectors of employment. Senior shop stewards with more clearly defined collective bargaining functions represent an average of about 350 members. During the 1970s there was a remarkable growth in the number of full time shop stewards or conveners who spent all or nearly all their work time on trade union duties connected with their workplace. Before the early 1970s full time shop stewards were a rarity; by the late 1970s, there were many such, especially in large establishments:

> The difference between larger and smaller establishments was most marked in relation to the reported incidence of full time conveners. Full time conveners were rare in workplaces with fewer than 500 people, but nearly two-thirds of establishments with 2,000 or more employees had full time conveners for manual workers.[15]

These senior stewards or conveners are invariably paid by their employers as full time employees. An earlier survey revealed that the average shop steward spent approximately six hours a week on trade union duties and senior stewards about 10 hours. Nowadays, only a very small proportion of stewards lose pay from their employer as a result of their union activities, since the Employment Protection (Consolidation) Act 1978 provides a statutory right for trade unionists to have time off work to undertake their trade union duties and activities.

In most large establishments where trade union organization is strong and many shop stewards are elected, a structure of senior shop stewards and conveners emerges to form a hierarchy of representative authority. Even in moderately-sized workplaces, a small number of senior stewards and a convener are elected so that 'the senior shop steward system – in the sense that some stewards have more influence and facilities than others – is extremely widespread in . . . British industry . . . and may be regarded as the norm rather than the exception'.[16] A convener of shop stewards, as the name suggests, originally existed to call or to convene meetings of shop stewards. Today, the title implies a leadership role normally acquired through election from amongst a group of stewards.

In some multi-union plants, a convener is elected to represent each union, in other cases one steward emerges as the convener because of his or her personal qualities rather than through being the representative of the largest union. The convener, or one of the conveners in some multi-union situations, acts as the chairperson of shop stewards when they form a joint committee.

> Managements often acknowledge that conveners in particular hold influential positions, and they are often given much wider freedom of movement within the factory and special access to senior managers. The work's convener is often an experienced trade unionist, and . . . many of them appear to hold office for long periods . . . [their] knowledge of precedents, previous arrangements and unwritten understandings often give them added influence over individual stewards.[17]

Research also suggests that most managers find it easier to develop better working relationships with senior stewards and conveners than with less accessible full time union officers, since the latter are usually less readily available for contact and they do not possess the conveners' intimate knowledge of domestic working arrangements.

Activities

During the 1960s and early 1970s multi-employer bargaining, modified and restricted by successive incomes policies, determined the basic pay, hours of work, and holidays with pay for the majority of manual employees and to a lesser extent for non-manual employees. Shop stewards rarely took part in these national negotiations. A national survey of workplace industrial relations carried out in 1978 concluded that in manufacturing industry single employer collective agreements had largely replaced multi-employer agreements as the major influence upon the pay of manual workers. This conclusion was supported by the 1980 workplace industrial relations survey which reported that it 'was true for manufacturing industry, and pay determination in manufacturing industry is of major importance'.[18] As shop stewards play an important part in negotiating pay agreements with single employers in manufacturing industry their influence has obviously grown. However, shop stewards play a less important role in public sector and service industry pay negotiations. Also surveys conducted in 1978 and 1980 may not hold good for the mid 1980s after several years where very different economic policies and labour market conditions have prevailed.

Shop stewards normally negotiate on pay matters at domestic level within the constraints of national agreements. They tend to concentrate on piecework prices and other forms of payment by results. They also influence items such as special payments for adverse working conditions, allowance or payments for tools, 'inconvenience' money, travelling time, and 'washing' time. They seek to upgrade jobs through job evaluation and determine the level and distribution of overtime. Stewards also obtain payments in exchange for new working methods or for relinquishing custom and practice and demarcation rules within the workplace. Finally, shop stewards negotiate on other conditions of employment such as the distribution and pace of work; quality control; manning levels; labour flexibility; physical conditions; the introduction of new technology; and job creation.

Stewards have traditionally dealt with safety problems. But the passing of the Health and Safety at Work etc. Act 1974, and the legal obligation laid upon employers to permit the appointment of employee safety representatives on workplace safety committees, has to some extent relieved shop stewards of this vital responsibility. Shop stewards also negotiate with management the distribution of working hours, including starting and finishing times and meal and rest breaks. They are nearly always involved in questions of discipline, suspensions and possible dismissal of their members.

Another of their cardinal duties is representing their constituents, either individually or collectively, when they have a disagreement with an immediate supervisor or other members of management. Such disagreements arise out of disputes over pay, hours of work, working conditions, the pace or volume of work, lateness, absenteeism and the distribution of overtime. Conflict can also occur between employees and management over supervisory orders or instructions, arguments between fellow workers, and over personal conduct at work. Other procedural matters which stewards negotiate include the quality and quantity of work; demarcation arrangements; and infringements by management of established custom and practice. When differences of opinion arise between their members and first line management, shop stewards normally take the complaint through the established grievance procedure.

Most shop stewards also take their basic union duty of recruiting new members very seriously. Union rules sometimes specifically state that it is the principal job of the workplace representative to recruit new starters, inspect union cards, collect membership subscriptions and seek 100 per cent union membership at the place of work. It is estimated that in 1980 some 25 per cent of the work force were covered by closed shop arrangements, compared with about 16 per cent in the 1960s, including 9 per cent of all white-collar workers. Of these about 82 per cent were in post-entry closed shops and the remainder in pre-entry shops. Since 1980 there has been some evidence to suggest that the closed shop is in relative decline under the impact of legislation and changing employer and employee attitudes. Where pre-entry closed shops and union membership agreements exist, employers only offer jobs to those applicants already in the union and approved by it. These are confined to a relatively small number of industries such as printing, dock work, shipbuilding and parts of the engineering trades. More common is the post-entry shop. Here employees start work without being union members, but as a condition of employment, they are required to join a specified trade union within a given time, if they are to continue in their job.

The issue of the closed shop arouses considerable moral feeling, intense political attitudes and strong opinions concerning the freedom of individuals in their employment relationships. Its protagonists, for example, argue that the closed shop justly ensures that all those receiving the alleged advantages of trade union negotiations should join and contribute towards the maintenance of the body which bargains on their behalf. They maintain that the closed shop benefits the employer through the discipline which can be exerted through the union on all the employees covered by the agreements concerned.

> Where trade union control proves effective the closed shop can help in establishing stable and effective organization and some employers see advantages in it as ensuring that they are talking to effectively organized representative bodies; there is the implicit hope that the closed shop can maintain discipline in order to secure the enforcement of agreements.[19]

Those opposed to the closed shop, on the other hand, argue that it restricts the freedom of individuals and in many cases forces them to join trade unions against their will or better judgement. If such employees follow their consciences, it is claimed, this can lead to the loss of their employment. If they are not already union members when applying for employment in a pre-entry closed shop situation, many potential employees cannot even be considered for the job. Similarly, if they fail to join a specified union after starting work in a post-entry closed shop, determined by the ballot requirements laid down in the Employment Act 1982, employees can be dismissed fairly in the eyes of

324 Understanding Industrial Relations

the law. Some writers have argued that the closed shop in newspaper publishing and the docks, for instance, has permitted excessive overmanning and restricted new working methods and the rate of technological change within these industries. Others suggest that in skilled trades the closed shop restricts craft entry and that this leads to manpower shortages in these sectors of employment. It would appear, however, that many shop stewards strongly favour 100 per cent trade union membership through the closed shop. It could well be largely their attitudes and efforts which have led to so many trade unionists in manufacturing being covered by some kind of formal or informal closed shop agreement in recent years, although the majority of such agreements involve post-entry rather than pre-entry requirements.

Attitudes and beliefs

One of the most difficult tasks for those studying industrial relations is to assess the attitudes, aims and values which the different participants to industrial relations bring to the bargaining table. Such behavioural qualities are important because they can influence the approach of the participants to negotiation, the decisions which they make, the actions which follow, and the ideologies which they propagate. The popular image of the shop steward, for example, is that of a noisy, aggressive and left-wing manual worker who has little education, judgement, sophistication or concern for people other than those whom he represents. Yet this image bears as little resemblance to reality as the view that all managers are rapacious 'capitalists' obsessed with the pursuit of company profits or enterprise efficiency, without concern for or interest in their subordinate employees whom they treat merely as 'hired hands' and as impersonal parts of the productive system.

Although both these stereotypes contain some elements of truth, a number of surveys and case study research have shown that shop stewards' attitudes and values are diverse and wide ranging. The Royal Commission's Report of 1968 in drawing heavily upon the first in depth research on shop stewards to be undertaken argued:

> it is often wide of the mark to describe shop stewards as 'trouble makers'. Trouble is thrust upon them. In circumstances of this kind they may be striving to bring some order into a chaotic situation, and management may rely heavily on their efforts to do so . . . Thus shop stewards are rarely agitators pushing workers towards unconstitutional action. In some instances, they may be the mere mouthpieces of their work groups. But quite commonly they are supporters of order exercising a restraining influence on their members in conditions which promote disorder . . . 'For the most part the steward is viewed by others, and views himself, as an accepted, and even moderating influence; more of a lubricant than an irritant.'[20]

Most of the attitudes, norms, and views which people hold are the result of their backgrounds, education, experiences and social conditioning. Shop stewards are not exempt from these social processes. Their attitudes and behaviour are not only influenced by their personal values, social aims, and political beliefs. They are also the result of the pressures brought to bear upon them by a range of external factors. These include their workgroups, management, other shop stewards, their union, the conditions prevailing at the workplace and the state of the local labour market. One survey concluded:

> Though most shop stewards seek and achieve amicable relations with management, motives are mixed. Stewards may not invariably be acting as they would like, but are responding to various pressures. The steward has a difficult political position between the conflicting interests of management and men – answerable to a union outside the immediate conflict and subject to the pressures of the nature and traditions of the workplace.[21]

Other research has emphasized the ideological awareness of shop stewards. It is argued, for instance, that the view of the shop steward as being at the centre of the web of conflicting pressures seeking only to balance them and to conciliate among them is a one sided view. In the words of one shop steward:

> Basically, industry with the work force on one side and the management on the other, is a conflict of interest. Where you have a conflict of interest the work people are going to say, 'Look, what you've got we want; either some of it or all of it.' There's going to be a resistance to this and it's accepted that we go through the haggling process to sort out who's going to have what.[22]

In yet another study, the authors of a detailed and exhaustive single plant analysis of shop steward behaviour in Britain drew an interesting distinction between the attitudes of manual and of white-collar shop stewards:

> On the shop floor, stewards more consistently adopt a conflict image of industry and, along with this, express a stronger and more consistent commitment to union principles. On the staff side, there is a greater degree of ambivalence over the nature of relationships in industry, and a less certain commitment to union principles. Staff stewards, as a group, more readily espouse a belief in industrial harmony and individualism.[23]

It is evident that the forces and influences shaping the attitudes, beliefs, and actions of shop stewards are extremely complicated. However, care should be taken not to assume that shop stewards merely respond to the multiplicity of pressures surrounding them. Some of them at least are influenced by political principles and social beliefs which rarely, if ever, are shared by management. It would be a mistake, nevertheless, to believe that such ideological differences between the participants in industrial relations need necessarily on their own lead to industrial conflict.

13.2 SHOP STEWARD COMMITTEES

In those workplaces where there are a number of shop stewards representing several trade unions, and where informal relationships cannot adequately deal with the problem of representative decision making, shop stewards create their own formal committees where all the stewards sit to determine policy and to make majority decisions. Such committees are rarely referred to in trade union rule books and they often act quite independently of the formal union structure and outside of its control. These committees which are an important expression of shop steward organization and power are usually referred to as 'joint shop stewards' committees' or JSSCs. Only about one-third of workplaces, where shop stewards are well organized, have JSSCs and they are more common in larger establishments than in smaller ones. It is in such committees that union workplace policy is largely determined and a number of representative shop stewards are chosen to negotiate with management, usually through a works committee on which both parties are represented.

The structure of shop steward committees is immensely varied and they depend for their form upon such factors as the needs of shop stewards, the organization of the workplace, its physical layout, and whether or not there is a single plant or multiplant location. Where there is more than one plant the structures created by shop stewards are sometimes called shop steward 'combine committees'. Conversely, in very large workplaces with thousands of employees and many shop stewards, there are separate shop steward committees for different departments or work areas. Each of these sends representatives to a central shop steward committee largely dominated by experienced senior stewards and conveners. Since such large workplaces are usually multi-union establishments, shop stewards from many different unions are represented on these bodies.

These committees are usually under the democratic control of all the shop stewards within the workplace and they are ultimately accountable, in theory at least, to rank and file trade union members. JSSCs make policy and take negotiating decisions often with little external influence by local trade union officers or their formal union hierarchies. Research indicates that JSSCs are often controlled by small groups of senior shop stewards and conveners, some of whom work closely with their union full time officers, whilst others are quite independent of theirs. In general, where the workplace is very large and where bargaining is not closely regulated by national agreements, negotiations are mainly conditioned by relations between a small number of stewards and senior managers. In these circumstances, industrial relations is largely the autonomous product of bargains struck between shop stewards and management. Where such conditions exist, the quality of the stewards' representative committee structure is vital.

Normally, the JSSC has as its chairperson the work's convener or, where several union conveners exist, the one elected to do the job. A secretary and other officers are also elected and, except in very large establishments, all stewards attend JSSC meetings. Where the employing establishment is so large that only a representative group of stewards sit on the JSSC, meetings of all the shop stewards are held at regular intervals. It is then that the JSSC defends its policies and subjects them to the majority approval of the stewards present. Care is taken to ensure that shop stewards on the JSSC, and the negotiating team which bargains with management, are representative of the different elements within the unionized workforce. This means that representation has to be distributed according to union membership, to different work areas and departments and to skill, sex, job status and occupational groupings.

If a well balanced JSSC is to be achieved in an establishment, say, with only a few large departments and a large number of small workgroups, and where a large number of unskilled female employees and a small number of highly skilled craft workers are employed, it is essential that the composition of the JSSC takes these factors into account. Unless this is attempted, common policies commanding support amongst the unions are unlikely to emerge. In many workplaces, it is not possible to establish a JSSC because of the fears of minority sections, such as maintenance workers or other skilled groups, that their interests and negotiating strength will be subordinated to the wishes of the larger less-skilled groups. In consequence, two or more separate bargaining units emerge with which management has to deal separately and amongst whom considerable distrust and antagonism can develop.

Joint shop stewards' organizations, operating on a fairly formal basis and observing the usual rules and firm chairing necessary for effective working are now widespread in British industry, though they are only found in a minority of establishments. They have emerged largely in response to the growth in the numbers of shop stewards and to their expanding representative and workplace bargaining functions. They are usually multi-union bodies which have to take account of all the representational complexities of the workplace. The extent to which they operate independently of the formal trade union structure depends upon a variety of factors. These include: the size of the establishment; the structures of the unions; the availability of full time union officers; the degree of local bargaining; and the attitudes and industrial relations policies of management.

It is the prime function of shop steward committees from all parts of the establishment, and from other establishments in the case of multiplant enterprises, to raise those matters most concerning them and their members. JSSCs are also used by small groups of senior stewards and conveners to determine a variety of industrial relations policy initiatives. These include, for example, the content of pay claims to be presented to management but issues other than pay are obviously of great importance to JSSCs. In recent research

Joint shop stewards' meetings were reported in only a minority of establishments with two or more manual or two or more non-manual unions. They were more likely where the unions negotiated on pay on a joint basis in larger establishments and where there was a full-time convener. However, the weak association with establishment level pay bargaining suggests that the meetings were involved with other issues besides pay.[24]

Many of the matters brought before JSSCs by individual stewards relate to comparatively insignificant complaints concerning only a few employees. If such matters cannot be resolved by the shop stewards, they bring collective pressure upon higher management by taking them to the JSSC.

Many JSSCs meet at least once a month in working hours to consider items placed upon a pre-arranged agenda. These committees rely heavily upon stewards reporting back on policy matters so that they can gauge their members' attitudes and whether or not they are likely to endorse policy initiatives. The system is not a one way flow. Once a JSSC has made a decision, it is up to individual shop stewards to communicate it to their members and to report back their reactions. Some committees publish newsletters, whilst in other cases minutes and reports of JSSC meetings are placed on union notice boards. Additionally, JSSCs sometimes raise money through raffles and levies, independent of union subscriptions which they cannot use. This money is used: to cover secretarial, duplication, travel and other expenses; to purchase publications; and to compensate some shop stewards for loss of earnings.

Where strong and representative JSSCs are established by well-organized shop stewards, and when an experienced and tight knit group of senior stewards and full time conveners with well-thought-out policy proposals begins to emerge, management often has little choice but to accept the situation and to negotiate as best it can. Sometimes it seeks to limit the power and authority of a JSSC by insisting on the presence of full time officers at steward meetings, or on the strict observance of centralized national agreements where this is to management's advantage. Management may also employ 'divide and rule' tactics by trying to split off one group of stewards from the main committee. It might agree, for example, to negotiate separately with a committee of craftworkers which believes that its interests will be lost inside a JSSC dominated by unskilled worker representatives. Conversely, management might adopt an industrial relations policy requiring detailed plant bargaining for its implementation and seeking to limit the influence of national agreements or to abandon them altogether. In this case, management sometimes takes the initiative in encouraging the formation of a JSSC, and in establishing a joint negotiating committee. In this way, it strengthens its personnel and industrial relations structures.

A multiplant works committee, or a works committee in a single plant situation, is a formal arrangement for bringing together the senior stewards and the conveners on the JSSC with the senior management team. Its main purpose is to negotiate enterprise or establishment agreements on pay and conditions of employment and the settlement of major grievances between management and unions. The membership and chairing of a works committee are usually agreed in advance between management and the JSSC along with the agenda. The conduct of such committees is normally formal, with the generally accepted rules of committee procedure applying. Although both sides determine their own negotiating teams, experience suggests that large committees are not conducive to effective bargaining. Since the outcome of negotiations depends entirely upon the relative strengths and abilities of the parties and not upon a voting system, the numbers on each side of the bargaining table are not significant. It is unusual for full time union officers or employers' associations representatives to play an active part in all but the very largest works committees.

The stewards' negotiating team usually keeps the JSSC constantly informed of the negotiations in the works committee and, as already stated, it is the task of individual stewards to convey progress reports to their members and to report back their reactions to the JSSC. Much of the effectiveness of the works committee and JSSC system of domestic bargaining relies upon adequate and responsive communications between stewards and their members. Decision making by steward bodies is relatively meaningless, however, if:

> the membership cannot be persuaded to follow or the policies cannot be implemented in other ways. In general terms . . . this is achieved . . . on the shop-floor at the level of the individual stewards.[25]

It is sometimes contended that the piecemeal development of workplace bargaining, and the emergence of JSSCs and of works committees largely outside of union control, is the result of outdated and inadequate union structures. Union rule books, it is said, have failed to formalize shopfloor developments or to meet the needs of local shop stewards. Yet the common trade union practice of using the branch meeting as the basic unit of trade union organization and democracy is a product of nineteenth century conditions. At that time the locality, area and occupation of trade unionists meant far more than the workplace which was often small and where shop steward representation was largely unknown. As part of its proposals for reforming collective bargaining through company and plant agreements, the Donovan Commission advocated the establishment of workplace union branches which would, it believed, help to integrate shop stewards and plant bargaining more firmly into the unions' formal structures. In the 1980 workplace industrial relations survey important differences were found:

> between trade union branches whose members were drawn from a single workplace and branches encompassing members from several workplaces or employers. Branches based at the workplace were smaller, and meetings were attended by a higher proportion of members. In all types of branch, but especially geographical based ones, shop stewards were much more frequent in their attendance than were other branch members. Stewards also commonly held positions in their branch committee.[26]

How much the development of workplace branches has contributed towards the resolution of the problems caused by multi-unionism at the workplace is very difficult to assess. Workplace branches have probably had little more than a marginal impact upon workplace bargaining where JSSCs and works committees are strongly established.

The Royal Commission also recommended the appointment of many more full time trade union officers to cope with the additional burdens which extensive company and plant bargaining cause for union negotiators. A higher proportion of full time officers, it was argued, would encourage more efficient bargaining and would help to bring shop stewards and their unions into closer working relationships. To date, the trade unions have not significantly improved their officer-to-membership ratios. It is clear, however, that in the larger establishments, the appointment of full time senior stewards or convenors has become commonplace. This trend has undoubtedly led to the independence of many JSSCs and works committees from formal union accountability. Many unions and the TUC, however, have extended the resources for the training of shop stewards. In these courses, trade union principles are stressed along with the need for stewards to see themselves as an essential part of the union and not as isolated representatives of their members and their workgroups at the workplace. The 1980 workplace industrial relations survey concludes:

> In cases where stewards had received training, the very large majority of managers felt that the training was valuable. Eighty-four per cent judged that training did help stewards in their work as representatives . . . It is clear that the large majority of stewards gave the highest rating to training and nearly all felt it was useful.[27]

A detailed survey of 14 local unions found that a continuum of relationships exists between shop steward organizations at the workplace and the local union structure. The continuum ranges from full dependence through various degrees of co-operation to complete independence. But, it pointed out, the rapid development of plant and company bargaining, and of plant pay structures and procedural agreements, has in general been carried out by shop stewards with little real contact and support from their local unions. The study suggested that the position of shop steward organizations, and the degrees to which they were dependent or independent of local union officers, could be explained in terms of the following major influences: the size of the establishment; the degree to which collective agreements were centralized or devolved; and the availability of full time officers. Other factors affecting workplace–union relationships were shop steward experience, their organization at establishment level, the scope of workplace bargaining, and the attitudes to bargaining by both managers and full time officers.

Shifts along the continuum of the shop steward and full time officer relationship take place where changes occur in one or more of these major determining factors.

> The most general influences on dependence is the size of workplace organisation. The larger the workplace organisation the greater the resources at its disposal, and the more independent its behaviour. But size is not the only influence at work. The greater the unity within a workplace organisation, the trade union experience of its members and their status as employees, the larger will be the resources at its disposal, and the more it will tend to act on its own.[28]

This study concluded that unions can encourage or discourage workplace independence 'by promoting or hindering organisation, unity and experience. Managers can also encourage workplace independence.' However, the availability of the full time officer is for the union to determine, and, within limits, 'the lack of a full-time officer to whom its representatives can turn may push a workplace organisation towards independence, whereas the ready availability of a full time-time officer may hold it back'.[29]

13.3   UNION FACILITIES

Shop stewards only emerged in significant numbers during the 1960s and 1970s, with relative economic prosperity and a fundamental shift in the balance of bargaining power in favour of trade unions in certain industries and workplaces. Other factors influencing shop steward autonomy include the growth of workplace bargaining in some sectors, and the restrictions imposed by trade unions and the law on the ability of employers to hire, use and dispose of labour unilaterally and at will. In many industries, shop stewards have faced considerable employer opposition to their emergence, whilst encountering a marked reluctance by some full time officers to allow them to negotiate with their employers. Consequently, left to their own devices and with little support from the employers or the formal union organizations, these stewards have had no recourse to those facilities and formal communications necessary to perform their tasks effectively. These include secretarial assistance, research for collective bargaining and training and educational opportunities.

Support facilities

The Report of the Royal Commission on Trade Unions and Employers' Associations recognized that the reform of company and plant bargaining would involve shop stewards in extensive and important negotiations. They would require improved facilities, better communications and relevant training to undertake their duties successfully. The Commission on Industrial Relations (CIR) was asked to consider these matters and to make recommendations. Its Report on the facilities afforded to shop stewards pointed out that 'the need for facilities arises from the functions performed by stewards' and these 'functions and hence facilities must be considered within the context of varying industrial relations systems at industry, company and establishment level'.[30] The CIR considered that management and shop stewards should carefully analyse the functions of shop stewards before deciding the range and types of facilities which they require. The Report emphasized the importance of adequate shop steward facilities as a necessary condition for the establishment of 'good' industrial relations at workplace level, although these were not regarded as a sufficient condition. It also recommended that industry level agreements 'should cover as far as possible the main functions of the steward together with the broad principles which relate to the provision of facilities'.[31]

The CIR Report also recommended that union rule books should define the duties and responsibilities of shop stewards more closely and that the right of stewards to leave their jobs to conduct union business without loss of earnings should be conceded. It also felt that greater clarity and precision in the manner of shop steward elections were required. It saw the need, too, for: a more orderly approach to the issuing of shop steward credentials; the provision of facilities for trade unions to collect membership dues during works time and where possible by the deduction of dues from the payroll; and the supplying of office accommodation for meetings with other shop stewards and full time union officers. The CIR also argued in favour of access to telephones, notice boards, and typing and duplicating facilities for stewards. This would require training opportunities for stewards appropriate to their needs. Finally, the Report stressed, 'once white-collar trade unionism is established its representatives require the same joint agreements on functions and facilities as their counterparts in the manual unions'.[32]

In the same year as the publication of the CIR Report, the TUC issued its own guide to trade unionists undertaking negotiating duties. It recommended, *inter alia*, that shop stewards needed the following facilities if they were to play their full part in collective bargaining and the improvement of industrial relations:

(a) the provision of a list of new entrants to the appropriate trade union representatives;
(b) facilities on the premises for shop stewards to explain to each new worker the advantages of trade union membership together with the terms of the collective agreements covering the establishment;
(c) facilities to collect union contributions or to inspect members' cards or the operation of a check-off system where this is desired by unions;
(d) a room, or at least a desk, in the workplace (in the case of a senior shop steward a separate office would be desirable) together with adequate facilities for storing correspondence and papers. Ready access to telephone and to typing and duplicating facilities;
(e) the provision of a notice board and the use of an internal post system;
(f) the use of a suitable room for the purpose of consulting and reporting to members when necessary during working hours and for meetings of shop stewards committees; and
(g) sufficient time off, with pay at average earnings, during working hours, for a representative to perform all his union duties which relate to the workplace; to attend training courses related to his duties as a union officer and to attend conferences called by his union. A representative should not have to use his holiday entitlement for this purpose.[33]

With the publication of these reports and guides many trade unions, shop stewards and employers became increasingly conscious of the need to provide stewards with adequate and relevant facilities if they were to fulfil their duties and responsibilities effectively. Although some managements realized that such facilities were essential for the effective conduct of workplace bargaining, it is reasonable to assume that other managements only reluctantly accepted shop stewards, and the range of issues which they sought to negotiate. Other employers continued to resist such claims, on the grounds of cost, especially in terms of pay for time off work and of lost production. Furthermore, these employers feared that in providing a wide range of facilities they would raise the status of shop stewards in the eyes of the manual workforce, white-collar employees and supervisory staff. It is extremely difficult to assess whether the provision of such facilities led to improved industrial relations or whether their absence resulted in contrary tendencies. By 1980 however:

> Substantial majorities of senior stewards for manual workers had access to some office services. Ninety-five per cent had access to a telephone. Nearly three-quarters had secretarial assistance or access to a photo-copier or a typewriter. Seventy-one per cent had at least the use of an office. It appeared that there had been a marked tendency for facilities of all types to be introduced in the previous five years.[34]

Communications

The causes of strikes are varied and complex. But inadequate systems of communication on industrial relations policies, changes in working practices and the introduction of new policies affecting the working lives of employees, whilst perhaps not a direct cause of disputes, can certainly contribute to feelings of insecurity, confusion and resentment among employees. Lack of information from higher level management within the workplace, for example, can lead to the circulation of rumours which are invariably exaggerated. Once established, such rumours become difficult to reject or to rebut. The TUC has therefore argued that:

> Managements should ensure that workers are kept well-informed about issues which affect their interests; in particular the payments system, the procedure for resolving grievances and disputes, safety matters and opportunities for training and promotion. In order to prevent duplication of instructions they should also ensure that all managers are fully aware of their area of responsibility.[35]

Whilst the TUC appears to believe with some justification that good communications are the responsibility of management, the industrial relations code of practice suggests that it is a shared responsibility and that 'Management, employees' representatives and trade unions should co-operate in ensuring that effective communication and consultation take place.'[36] The nature of large-scale industrial organizations, however, indicates that the prime but not the exclusive responsibility for ensuring good communications rests with management. It is management which possesses most of the facts about its business and takes the basic decisions affecting the working lives of its labour force. But the supportive role of the trade unions and shop stewards is undoubtedly important, since they can do much to allay the distrust and suspicion of the employer's motives in many workplace situations.

By associating themselves with the communication of basic information and of industrial relations policies to all employees, shop stewards can often raise the threshold of trust and respect between management and employees. It is often overlooked, however, that people in subordinate positions fail either to 'hear' such information or to heed it. This arises because to 'hear' it from a greater power than themselves implies that they will be influenced by it.

> Talking about improving communications therefore involves losing our fear and suspicion about the use of power. . . . Full communication requires an equalization of power [whilst] a major barrier to communication in organizations and in classrooms . . . is that information comes *down* from superior to subordinate or from high status to low.[37]

The practical steps which can be taken in order to improve communications in industrial relations include the following. First, it is necessary to acknowledge that communication is a two way process with management giving information to employees and shop stewards, and then receiving information back from them. This reverse flow of information from employees to management must inevitably be transmitted by shop stewards where they are recognized. It follows that shop stewards have to be fully aware of their responsibility for discussing industrial relations matters on the shopfloor and reporting back the majority response of their members to management. But as many stewards regard themselves as opinion formers and opinion leaders, rather than as mere representatives, this is sometimes difficult.

Second, it is commonly believed that the most effective means of communication within the workplace is by word of mouth. This form of personal contact can be extremely time consuming yet is often very effective. In fact the most important method of communication is by word of mouth 'through personal contact between each manager and his immediate work group or individual employees, and between managers and employee representatives.'[38] But oral communications need to be supplemented by written information including circulars, notice board memoranda, handbooks and minutes of meetings. New employees can be given induction training which makes them aware of the principal policies of the employer and the unions. This ensures that they are aware of the main aspects of their contracts of employment and working conditions.

Third, management and unions can decide jointly what information on the enterprise and its policies should be disclosed to all employees. Headings in such a list would include: information on future employment and manpower policies; the organization of work; product types and ranges; investment strategies; and the firm's personnel and industrial relations policies. Finally, management and unions need to regard the maintenance of good communications as a professional duty on both their parts. This means, in practice, drawing up a written communication plan and training their representatives in the art of effective and accurate communications with those with whom they come into contact.

Training

As the duties of shop stewards have become more complex and more demands are made upon their knowledge and abilities, and since shop stewards have moved more into the centre of the industrial relations stage in many instances, the greater becomes the need for specific education and training for the role. Whilst it is probably true that able and effective shop stewards are largely the product of selection processes among their fellow employees, and of the hard world of experience, there is little doubt that the growing complexity of the tasks which they face calls for carefully designed training courses.

A small number of training courses for shop stewards was provided in the 1950s. But they catered for only a handful of shop stewards who were usually from large companies in the industrial conurbations. These courses were normally provided by the Workers Educational Association, the extra-mural departments of universities, the technical colleges or by the trade unions themselves. Where courses were provided by public educational institutions they had first to be approved by either individual unions or the Education Department of the TUC. The Donovan Commission emphasized the need for more and better training in industrial relations and the CIR produced a report on future training needs and provision. The CIR revealed the paucity of shop steward and management training in industrial relations in a report which concluded

> that training can play an important part in the achievement and maintenance of effective industrial relations . . . [and that] . . . employers and unions have a joint interest in training to improve the conduct of industrial relations.[39]

The TUC rejected this recommendation for joint responsibility arguing that 'the nature and function of union representatives is in any case a matter solely for the unions to decide as are their training and education needs.'[40]

The TUC in maintaining the sole right of the trade union movement to control the aims, content and nature of shop steward training in consultation with the public education service has pointed to the considerable use of public resources devoted to management education. These, it maintains, are very extensive compared with the much smaller public provision for trade union education and training. It suggests that the unions now have a potential training demand for many lay and full time officers. The union demand for paid time off from work for union training has been met by the approval in Parliament of a code of practice on time off for trade union duties and activities. This gives effect to Section 27 of the Employment Protection (Consolidation) Act 1978 which requires employers to provide paid release for representatives of independent trade unions who want training in industrial relations 'which is (i) relevant to the carrying out of those duties; and (ii) approved by the Trades Union Congress or by the independent trade union of which he or she is an official.'[41]

13.4   SHOP STEWARDS AND WORKPLACE BARGAINING

Workplace or domestic bargaining is conducted between shop stewards and managers. Whilst it is sometimes the practice for first line trade union officers and for employer associations' representatives to be informed of the content of workplace agreements for their formal approval, their active participation in such negotiations is the exception rather than the rule. Workplace bargaining is therefore a largely autonomous process shaped by the traditions, constraints and circumstances peculiar to each of the varied workplace conditions existing in Britain.

Bargaining principles

Some of the underlying principles involved if effective negotiation by shop stewards is to take place include the following:

> An understanding of *trade union principles* is required to give trade union bargaining effort a sense of direction; *bargaining awareness* is the ability to identify issues for bargaining; a knowledge of the realities of industrial *power* is necessary, as is also an awareness of the nature of *bargaining relationships* between unions and management. But clearly, in practice, knowledge and understanding are not sufficient conditions for effective bargaining. A favourable balance of power and favourable bargaining relations are necessary.[42]

An understanding of 'trade union principles' in bargaining is necessary if shop stewards are to mobilize their members' support and gain formal union approval for their bargaining objectives. Not all stewards have had sufficient trade union or bargaining experience to be consciously aware of these principles, though it is unusual for senior stewards and conveners not to have them. Furthermore, most experienced shop stewards see it as their duty to educate their members in union bargaining principles. Where bargaining takes place without reference to trade union principles, it may become ineffective and concerned with trivia. Alternatively, it may become 'unprincipled' in the sense that it concedes unfair advantages to certain workgroups and not to others, thus destroying trade union solidarity. The most important principle in bargaining is the creation and presentation of unity among shop stewards, their members and their unions. This unity of purpose is pursued not only as a union principle, but also because it is commonly agreed that 'unity is strength' and that disunity only benefits management.

In its broadest, idealistic sense, trade union unity involves all the unionized workers in Britain. But in the context of workplace bargaining, it usually involves only those union members forming the bargaining unit.

> The idea of unity also implies a concern with justice, fairness, equality and the protection of the less fortunate. Trade unionism is not, or should not be, solely about helping the relatively well-off become even better off.[43]

Adherence to trade union principles is a matter of moral purpose, but also has a practical function in creating an agreed union ethic. This helps to generate solidarity amongst trade unionists and discourages the pursuit of sectional interests which can make the unions at workplace level the subject of damaging cynicism among their members. It would be unrealistic, however, not to recognize that in many circumstances sectional self-interest overrides principles of solidarity and equity. This is often the case where one group of workers can exploit a labour market advantage not open to other groups. In overtime working, for instance, ethical solidarity can be achieved by referring to the trade union principles of maximum hours of work, equity of treatment for all members and the wider fact that unemployment and overtime working can be viewed as ethically incompatible. But this view will not prevail if the workgroup concerned really wants the additional earnings and can see no advantage to the unemployed by refusing overtime.

The second condition for effective shop steward bargaining is 'bargaining awareness'. Experienced and energetic shop stewards are not content with merely ensuring that management honours and observes collective agreements. Nor are they satisfied with just taking up the routine grievances of their members. They actively seek to expand the areas and the depth of workplace bargaining by taking negotiating initiatives and by extending bargaining into areas traditionally controlled solely by management. Such stewards show a highly developed sense of awareness of the ultimate potentiality of workplace bargaining.

> In principle, therefore, if workers are powerful enough they can increase the range of issues over which they bargain. In practice, the problem the steward faces is whether he and his members are powerful enough and whether he can afford to take the risk of finding out.[44]

Bargaining awareness is, therefore, a matter of perceiving bargaining opportunities and the balance of negotiating power between shop stewards and management.

A vital aspect of bargaining awareness is the recognition by shop stewards that they require adequate knowledge of their members' work content, pay and working conditions, and of the conditions in other, similar workplaces. Stewards also need a continuous flow of information from management on a range of matters including manpower requirements, product design, sales policies, investment proposals, research programmes and so on. Awareness of changes in job allocation, variations in overtime and shiftworking, changes in management structures, and the rates of absenteeism and sickness with their possible causes are also relevant. Armed with such knowledge, shop stewards determined to expand the boundaries of workplace bargaining can develop bargaining initiatives which of necessity impinge upon areas previously under the unilateral control of management. Similarly, stewards can use the findings of research departments or the services of specialized research organizations to advance their bargaining goals.

An understanding by shop stewards of the balance of 'power' between themselves and management is the third essential element for effective workplace bargaining. Historically, the employer has nearly always possessed greater market and economic power than either individual employees or even collective groups of workers. This has been reflected in the bargaining context. No employers have readily abandoned a position which allows them to determine pay and conditions of work unilaterally unless obliged to do so by the collective strength of trade unions. Despite the undeniable shift in the balance of bargaining power towards trade unions and their members and away from employers between 1945 and 1979, the balance of negotiating power ultimately rests with employers. The focus of interest from the workplace viewpoint is the relative shifts in the balance of power affecting the bargaining positions of management and unions. If both sides move towards a strike situation unsure of their relative strengths, for example, they might decide on caution and arrive at a compromise solution. If they do not and a strike ensues, then one side is bound to lose more than the other from the outcome. When work is resumed the balance of power will have changed and that fact will be reflected in future negotiations and relationships between the parties.

The balance of power can change, however, without conflict arising. For example, demand in the labour market may become tighter with unemployment giving a bargaining advantage to the employer. Similarly, shop stewards might increase union membership to the point where they can impose a closed shop on management. Little change will result, however, if the side which benefits from a shift in the balance of power neither recognizes that this is happening nor seizes the bargaining advantages offered by it. In short, movements in the balance of power must be followed or accompanied by a new bargaining awareness on the part of shop stewards and of management. Brief or short-term shifts in the balance of bargaining power offer less in the way of fundamental changes in the bargaining opportunities to either side than any long-term power shift, such as those brought about by heavy and prolonged unemployment accompanied by a diminishing social security threshold.

The factor which above all others appears to reduce the advantages for either side if the balance of power shifts is the quality of the 'bargaining relationships' between them. Its basis is the acceptance by management that trade unions and shop stewards are here to stay and that they cannot be eliminated by conflict and unremitting struggle, even in conditions of high unemployment. Equally, there is the recognition by trade unions that the abolition of private enterprises and of managerial control within them is not a political reality except, possibly, in the very long term. Besides, as many unions in the public sector now recognize, the elimination of the private ownership of productive capital does not mean the removal of management with whom they are obliged to negotiate. With the acceptance of these economic and political realities, experienced managers and shop stewards appreciate the importance of developing and sustaining 'good' bargaining relationships between themselves:

> Both steward and manager, therefore, are in a way dependent upon the other for the general achievement of their goals. If each sees the other as powerful and important, they tend to develop a relationship of trust which helps each to achieve his respective goals. It should be emphasized that this does not necessarily mean that one or the other sells out, although clearly there is a danger. The trust relationship is one of dependence, and rests upon the existence of conflict combined with a recognition that some sort of accommodation is inevitable and that power, over a period is more or less evenly balanced.[45]

If the power of either side or its representativeness changes dramatically, it is likely that established relationships will deteriorate. For example, if a management sees its sphere of control curtailed by growing union power and it seeks to handle this sensitively by fostering good relationships with its shop stewards, it might benefit from radical changes in the labour market or in internal divisions amongst the shop stewards. In such situations, it could well decide that the bargaining relationship no longer reflects the realities of the distribution of power. Accordingly, management might decide to take a harsher stance in its relationships with the shop stewards. Again, much depends upon whether the shift in power is slight and short term, or substantial and long term.

Negotiating skills

Experienced shop stewards with proven bargaining abilities stress, not surprisingly, that negotiating skills are the result of inherent personal qualities rather than of training or instruction. Inherent qualities, they argue, are only marginally enhanced by training compared with actual experience of negotiations.

> In the workplace negotiators come up through the shop stewards' committee. Not every steward turns into a good negotiator, but it's the experience of being on a committee itself that does the real training of negotiators . . . we've gained a great deal from . . . role playing . . . they can give you confidence, but there's no substitute for the experience of the real thing.[46]

Shop stewards often point out that they have first to prove their ability at presenting a case on the joint shop stewards committee before their peers have sufficient confidence in their ability to negotiate with management. Less experienced stewards are allowed to attend negotiations with management as observers of the way in which senior stewards and conveners negotiate. In large workplaces, shop stewards are encouraged to specialize so that their skill and detailed knowledge of, say, payment systems or job evaluation can be used on appropriate occasions. Both managers and shop stewards have much to gain by developing as much mutual respect and trust for each other as can be realistically achieved given the conflict ridden nature of bargaining.

> If you know a particular manager always lies to you well obviously you react differently to him, but if you have a manager who always keeps agreements that he's made and signed, there's a mutual respect . . . I respect some managers even though I know full well we both have different roles to fulfil.[47]

When the joint shop stewards committee meets to prepare a package of claims to be presented to management, it needs to have a clear strategy if it is to be successful. First, it has to establish realizable targets for negotiation and to decide whether or not to demand the impossible or the unrealistic, knowing full well that it will soon move back to a more reasonable position. Alternatively, it has to decide whether it should make a realistic claim and stick to it. Both schools of thought have their devotees but it is essential that the committee decides what its 'sticking' positions are. Having determined its bargaining objectives and tactics, the JSSC then has to prepare a detailed and researched case. In the words of one shop steward:

> If there is a major problem or if it is the kind that's going to become a major issue I'll have to prepare myself very carefully right from the beginning. I've got to work for the long-term principle and I want to be consistent all the way.[48]

Once a case is prepared, and it has been influenced by trade union principles and a realistic assessment of the balance of bargaining power, the next step is to prepare the workforce by informing it of the content of the claim and winning its support and solidarity. 'The most important thing for improvements in conditions is membership pressure. But that pressure is affected by many factors including the lead given by shop stewards.'[49] During negotiations most stewards stress the need for unity of approach and teamwork. If during bargaining with management representatives one or more stewards feel that negotiations are going adrift, they rarely say so openly, but request an adjournment to settle the matter. It is a cardinal rule in workplace bargaining that the two sides do not disagree among themselves in public but sort out their differences in private. Adjournments are also used to ensure the accuracy of what is being negotiated.

> When you're negotiating big deals it becomes very important you get everything right because it's going to set your conditions for a year or so . . . We often have short adjournments, the very important five or ten minutes to make sure that things are right.[50]

Most negotiators on both sides of the bargaining table agree that 'face saving' is essential if either side is to continue effectively after making mistakes, revealing lack of knowledge or inexperience, or demonstrating that it is out of touch with those whom it represents. If a manager or a steward, for example, makes a statement or takes up a position which evidence or experience clearly invalidates, his or her position becomes untenable if the other side relentlessly exposes it. But if the negotiators quietly drop the matter and show that they accept, without ridicule or rancour, explanations, rationalizations, or excuses, no matter how thin they may appear to be, the issue can be forgotten and the individual and the negotiations can be saved. Similarly, flexibility on both sides is essential if they are to reach an agreement. Experienced negotiators do not often get trapped into making statements and taking up positions which prevent them exerting some degree of flexibility and having room for manoeuvre.

It is obviously important for shop stewards to keep their members constantly informed of the progress being made in negotiations but it is not possible to present a final agreement for their approval until the negotiations have been concluded. Experienced stewards usually have a shrewd idea of what their members will accept or reject, and the leadership ability to persuade their members that they should concur. The final agreement can be put to their members orally by shop stewards, either department by department or at a mass meeting where the communicative and verbal skills of the stewards are paramount. Alternatively, as is increasingly the case, the decision whether or not to accept management's final offer can be made by secret workplace ballot. If their members accept the stewards' recommendation, there are no real problems. If they reject them, the stewards must be prepared either to go back and re-open negotiations or resign. As most shop stewards do not finally conclude agreements with management before getting majority membership support, they cannot reasonably be denied the right to re-negotiate. But they usually lose considerable respect and standing in the eyes of management and their members if the agreement which they recommend is rejected.

It is generally agreed that the threat of sanctions by either side harms the process of negotiation and the bargaining relationship, if it is used unwisely or as an empty gesture. Experienced negotiators on both sides are fully aware of the sanctions at their disposal and the realities of their use. To threaten the use of sanctions as a means of forcing the other side to concede more than it is able to is often seen as an empty bluff. This renders the chances of reaching a satisfactory compromise more remote. As one trade union negotiator has suggested:

> there are circumstances where the members have demonstrated their power before we ever get round the negotiating table. Then, it is very much in the mind of the management. If the lads come out on strike and I've persuaded them to go back to work on the basis of negotiations, that puts me in a very strong position.[51]

Disclosure of information

It is now generally recognized that for effective workplace bargaining to take place, management should disclose appropriate information about company activities, its resources, and policies to shop stewards. Trade unions have argued for a long time that management should 'open the books' so that the facts relating to collective bargaining can be more accurately judged. It is the belief of most trade unionists that if the main financial information concerning the enterprise is available for their close inspection, they are in a better position to judge what is a reasonable claim to make to management. Until recently, very few employers were willing to disclose detailed information for bargaining purposes to shop stewards or trade unions. In this respect, the TUC argued that employers should disclose information on:

General ownership and organisation structure; manpower and personnel information; financial information covering sales, costs, incomes, 'performance indicators' and the value of the company's assets; prospects and plans including information on investment, sales and manpower.[52]

The Confederation of British Industry has also advised its members that in order to avoid 'the risk of deterioration in industrial relations', companies need to respond to the pressure for 'more information from the top on what is happening and why', adding that 'satisfactory working relationships will not be achieved if employees feel insecure or suspicious.'[53] It has suggested possible areas of disclosure. These include: details of company organization; financial information including turnover, profits, dividends and directors' remuneration; and a summary of the company's competitive situation and productivity levels. Other items of possible disclosure are future plans, manpower information, and policies on pay and conditions of employment.

It is extremely difficult to assess the impact of the various recommendations on disclosure of information and the appropriate clauses of the Employment Protection Act 1975. This Act establishes a procedure enabling independent trade unions to obtain certain information from employers for the purposes of collective bargaining. At the same time, the Advisory Conciliation and Abritration Service (ACAS) has issued a code of practice on disclosure of information to trade unions for collective bargaining purposes. This gives practical guidance both to employers and trade unions on disclosure of information which 'it would be in accordance with good industrial relations to disclose' and 'without which a trade union representative would be impeded to a material extent in bargaining.'[54]

As a general guide, the ACAS code recommends the disclosure of information on pay and benefits, conditions of service, manpower, company performance and finance. It appears likely that the impact of the ACAS code, and the use made by the trade unions of the disclosure clauses in the Employment Protection Act 1975, has enabled shop stewards to obtain more information which they can use in the bargaining situation than was hitherto the case. The 1980 workplace industrial relations survey, however, came to the conclusion that many managers provided little or no information on the financial position of the establishment or business and there were also indications that failure to provide such information was associated with a generally poorer industrial relations climate. But 'substantial use was made of statutory provisions on disclosure of information as the basis for requests for information in a substantial minority of cases'.[55] This survey also found a considerable expansion had taken place in joint consultative committees and in schemes to promote worker involvement and both these initiatives had greatly increased the flow of information from management to employees and shop stewards.

13.5   DEVELOPMENTS SINCE 1979

The rapid increase in unemployment since the late 1970s has undoubtedly affected the conduct of workplace industrial relations. High unemployment is now seen by many to be a permanent feature of the economy and is believed to have created a fundamental change in the attitude of employers, employees and shop stewards to work, industrial relations and managerial authority. Furthermore, largely due to demographic factors, the British labour force – the number of people in work or seeking work – has grown rapidly in the 1980s. The problems created by massive job losses have been exacerbated by a rapid growth in the number of young people and married women seeking paid employment.

It seems likely that at workplace level high unemployment has brought about a greater feeling of caution amongst employees and their union representatives when negotiating on pay and conditions of employment with management, whilst at the same time weakening opposition to the introduction of job flexibility and reduced manning levels. There is little solid evidence to suggest that more than a small minority of employers have adopted 'macho' management styles and forced fundamental changes upon a fearful and resentful workforce. The large majority of employers have probably quietly accepted the shift in bargaining power towards them as an opportunity to make marginal but important changes in the workplace without creating undue hostility, antagonism and anxiety amongst their employees.

Employers have in many cases reinforced their new bargaining advantage by improving their methods of employee communication, by expanding joint consultative arrangements and by experimenting with employee involvement schemes. All these approaches to varying degrees bypass formal shop steward organizations. Such managerial strategies allow shop stewards, conscious of their bargaining weakness, to conduct realistic rear-guard negotiations without losing face or being unnecessarily humiliated by management. The advantages for management have nevertheless been substantial and their new found confidence and authority have permitted important gains to be made in productivity, unit labour costs, manning levels and, ultimately, on profitability in the private sector and efficiency in the public sector.

Legislation affecting industrial relations and trade unions passed since 1979 has also played a part in changing the climate of workplace industrial relations. The Employment Acts 1980 and 1982 and the Trade Union Act 1984 have effectively reduced trade union scope for unfettered industrial action. Perhaps the most important restriction has been upon the ability of shop stewards and local union officials to call industrial action without first conducting secret ballots of their members. The successful use of court injunctions by some employers to stop industrial action and picketing which could be judged to be unlawful under the Employment Acts 1980 and 1982 has also played a part in strengthening the position of employers and management, and in weakening the position of trade unions and shop stewards.

The exclusion of certain employees and small firms from some of the provisions of the employment protection legislation, the tightening of maternity rights for female employees, the withdrawal of the 'fair wages' resolutions of the House of Commons and the extension of the period of time workers must be employed before they can claim unfair dismissal rights from one to two years have all reduced the cover provided to employees by employment protection legislation. Similarly, the legal restrictions placed on the closed shop by the 1982 Act have stiffened the resolve of some employers not to conclude union membership agreements or to dismiss employees who leave their unions. In a few cases, British Rail for example, employers have given formal notice to the unions that they intend to terminate closed shop agreements of long standing.

In addition to these factors reducing the power and influence of shop stewards at the workplace, there has been a clearly discernible growth in joint consultative arrangements between management and employees and in initiatives to increase employee involvement in decision making. According to the 1980 workplace industrial relations survey:

> Our findings give the impression that there have been substantial developments in Britain on a voluntary basis to promote worker involvement in decision making such as that which exists in many European countries. In addition to our evidence on the growth of joint consultative committees, one quarter of managers and a similar proportion of union representatives reported that there had been some attempt during the previous three years to increase worker involvement in the establishment.[56]

When these developments are seen in conjunction with the growth in workplace quality circles or job improvement committees, health and safety committees, improved methods of direct management, employee communication and 'open' employee assessment and promotion schemes, it becomes clear that the nature of the management–employee relationship at workplace level is becoming more complex and integrated. On the basis of the available evidence at present, it is not unreasonable to speculate that the economic depression has not so much been marked by the growth of 'macho' management, but by the development of what has been called 'sophisticated paternalist' managerial styles.

Further changes to shop steward workplace representation, which developed most rapidly in the 30 years following the end of the Second World War, have been brought about by the increasing fragmentation of the labour market and the isolation of many shop stewards from contact with shop stewards in other workplaces and their unions. The fragmentation of the British labour market has been further marked by other developments. These include: the growth of female part time employment in manufacturing and service industries; the expansion of self-employment and of small firms encouraged by government policy; the rapid decline in traditional heavy industry dominated by strongly unionized, male manual workers; the growth of new employment in the high technology and service sectors; the continuation of the long-term trend towards white-collar employment; and the relative decline in public sector employment.

All these post-1970s trends would appear to have weakened rather than strengthened the position of shop stewards in workplace industrial relations. There is, however, little evidence to suggest that any dramatic long-term changes have occurred. The essential framework of shop steward workplace organization is still very largely intact and a change of government and of national economic policy could radically reverse the trends of recent years. Whilst it is obvious that patterns of workplace industrial relations have changed appreciably since 1979, the degrees of change can easily be overstated.

13.6 SUMMARY

Shop stewards are the unpaid representatives of trade unions at the workplace. In this capacity, they represent their unions and the members electing them, although their specific role depends upon the industry, organization and industrial relations environment in which they operate. The large scale emergence of shop stewards is a fairly recent phenomenon. It is really since 1945 that the number of shop stewards within factories, offices and other workplaces has steadily increased. Several factors contributed to their growth in power and influence including relatively full employment until the late 1970s, and changes in the structure of collective bargaining and payment systems. Somewhat surprisingly, comparatively few trade union rule books rigorously define the shop steward function.

Despite their large numbers, it does not appear that the task of representing union members at the workplace is highly sought after. Nevertheless, shop stewards play a vital role in determining workplace industrial relations in conjunction with management. Essentially they are workplace bargainers negotiating on any issues affecting their members' individual or collective interests. Being the initial and often the only link between the workgroup and the union, shop stewards also play a major role in recruiting new union members and in advancing 100 per cent unionism voluntarily or through the closed shop. The behaviour of shop stewards is clearly influenced by the multiple pressures acting upon them from management, other stewards, their members and their union, and by the attitudes and values which they themselves bring to their industrial relations role.

Shop stewards also develop their own workplace committees to facilitate communications among themselves, to integrate policies between different unions, and to present where possible a united front when negotiating with management. Many joint shop steward committees are multi-union ones, often acting outside formal union hierarchies and trade union rule books. To undertake these tasks, senior stewards and conveners sometimes spend all their working hours on union business, and a good deal of their leisure time too. Although JSSCs are involved in a range of activities, their major function is to determine union policy at the workplace and to bargain with management on behalf of their members. The extent to which such committees and shop steward bodies act independently of local union full time officers varies by size of workplace, the availability of full time officers, and the structure of collective bargaining.

The advent of workplace bargaining and shop steward organization obviously places heavy burdens on shop stewards as workplace representatives. They require adequate facilities and effective communications systems to perform their roles effectively. Increasing recognition of these needs is slowly being achieved. The realities of workplace bargaining also necessitate shop stewards having an understanding of the bargaining climate facing them. This includes a knowledge of trade union principles so that they can achieve their bargaining goals, thereby advancing trade union unity and solidarity within the workplace. Without this, trade union purposes are weakened. Other necessary conditions for effective negotiation by shop stewards are bargaining awareness and the ability to assess negotiating opportunities and the balance of bargaining power between management and themselves.

It is evident that workplace industrial relations have been modified by the very different economic and social climate which has prevailed since 1979. It is extremely hazardous, however, to speculate on the changing nature of workplace industrial relations without the hard evidence which only national surveys can elicit. Nevertheless, a number of pointers are apparent. These include: the greater confidence and authority of management, largely created by the fears generated by high unemployment; the rapid growth in recent years of joint consultative committees and other direct links between management and employees; the impact of changes in labour and trade union legislation; and the increasing fragmentation of the British labour market.

13.7 REFERENCES

1. J. Goodman, The role of the shop steward, in S. Kessler and B. Weekes (eds.), *Conflict at Work*, BBC, London, 1971, p. 53.
2. W. E. J. McCarthy, *Royal Commission on Trade Unions and Employers' Associations Research Papers. 1. The Role of Shop Stewards in British Industrial Relations*, HMSO, London, 1967, p. 4.
3. Royal Commission on Trade Unions and Employers' Associations, *Report*, HMSO, London, 1968, p. 26.
4. *Ibid.*, p. 272.
5. J. Goodman and T. G. Whittingham, *Shop Stewards in British Industry*, McGraw-Hill, London, 1969, p. 40.
6. I. Boraston, H. Clegg, M. Rimmer, *Workplace and Union*, Heinemann, London, 1975, p. 191.
7. E. Batstone, I. Boraston, S. Frenkel, *Shop Stewards in Action*, Basil Blackwell, Oxford, 1977, pp. 179 and 185.
8. W. W. Daniel and N. Millward, *Workplace Industrial Relations*, Heinemann, London, 1983, p. 284.
9. M. Argyle, *The Social Psychology of Work*, Penguin, Harmondsworth, 1974, p. 104.
10. G. Clack, *Industrial Relations in a British Car Factory*, Cambridge University Press, Cambridge, 1966, p. 61.

11. J. Goodman in Kessler and Weekes, *op. cit.*, p. 55.
12. S. Parker, *Workplace Industrial Relations*, HMSO, London, 1975, p. 18.
13. W. W. Daniel and N. Millward, *op. cit.*, p. 284.
14. H. A. Clegg, *The System of Industrial Relations in Great Britain*, Basil Blackwell, Oxford, 1970, p. 14.
15. W. W. Daniel and N. Millward, *op. cit.*, p. 33.
16. W. E. J. McCarthy and S. R. Parker, *Royal Commission on Trade Unions and Employers' Associations Research Papers. 10. Shop Stewards and Workshop Relations*, HMSO, London, 1968, p. 27.
17. J. Goodman in Kessler and Weekes, *op. cit.*, p. 55.
18. W. W. Daniel and N. Millward, *op. cit.*, p. 291.
19. B. M. Cooper and A. F. Bartlett, *Industrial Relations*, Heinemann, London, 1976, p. 54.
20. Royal Commission, *op. cit.*, p. 28f.
21. J. Goodman and T. G. Whittingham, *op. cit.*, p. 99.
22. E. Coker and G. Stuttard (eds.), *Industrial Studies 2: The Bargaining Context*, Arrow Books, London, 1976, p. 44.
23. E. Batstone, I. Boraston, S. Frenkel, *op. cit.*, p. 29.
24. W. W. Daniel and N. Millward, *op. cit.*, p. 285.
25. E. Batstone, I. Boraston, S. Frenkel, *op. cit.*, p. 92.
26. W. W. Daniel and N. Millward, *op. cit.*, p. 284.
27. *Ibid.*, pp. 39–41.
28. I. Boraston, H. Clegg, M. Rimmer, *op. cit.*, p. 187.
29. *Ibid.*, pp. 187 and 188.
30. Commission on Industrial Relations, *Report No. 17. Facilities Afforded to Shop Stewards*, HMSO, London, 1971, p. 44.
31. *Ibid.*, p. 45.
32. *Ibid.*, p. 49.
33. Trades Union Congress, *Good Industrial Relations*, TUC, London, 1971, p. 17.
34. W. W. Daniel and N. Millward, *op. cit.*, pp. 42 and 43.
35. TUC, *op. cit.*, p. 27f.
36. Department of Employment, *Industrial Relations Code of Practice*, HMSO, London, 1972, p. 14.
37. M. Pedler, Learning to negotiate, in E. Coker and G. Stuttard (eds.), *Industrial Studies 2: The Bargaining Context*, Arrow Books, London, 1976, p. 105f.
38. Department of Employment, *op. cit.*, p. 14.
39. Commission on Industrial Relations, *Report No. 33. Industrial Relations Training*, HMSO, London, 1972, p. 52.
40. Trades Union Congress, *Report of the 107th Annual Trades Union Congress*, TUC, London, 1976, p. 201.
41. Advisory Conciliation and Arbitration Service, *Code of Practice 3. Time off for Trade Union Duties and Activities*, HMSO, London, 1977, p. 1.
42. E. Batstone, I. Boraston and E. Frenkel, Principles in workplace bargaining, in Coker and Stuttard, *op. cit.*, p. 20.
43. *Ibid.*, p. 23f.
44. *Ibid.*, p. 26.
45. *Ibid.*, p. 36.
46. Trade union negotiators, *ibid.*, p. 44.
47. *Ibid.*, p. 46.
48. *Ibid.*, p. 48.
49. *Ibid.*, p. 50.
50. *Ibid.*, p. 57.
51. *Ibid.*, p. 63.
52. Commission in Industrial Relations, *Report No. 31. Disclosure of Information*, HMSO, London, 1972, p. 12.
53. Confederation of British Industry, *The Provision of Information to Employees*, CBI, 1975, p. 3f.
54. Advisory Conciliation and Arbitration Service, *Code of Practice 2. Disclosure of Information*

for Collective Bargaining Purposes, HMSO, London, 1977, p. 2.
55. W. W. Daniel and N. Millward, *op. cit.*, p. 289.
56. W. W. Daniel and N. Millward, *op. cit.*, p. 289.

14

Negotiation and Consultation

Negotiation in industrial relations is a power relationship between managerial and trade union representatives. It is an activity by which the two sides make agreements regulating the pay or market relations and managerial or authority relations between them. Consultation, by contrast, is the process whereby managerial representatives discuss matters of common interest with employee representatives, normally but not always trade unionists, prior to negotiating or taking a decision. In this chapter, we concentrate on the content and methods of negotiation as a process of joint job control, rather than its structural features which we describe in Chapter Six. We also examine the nature of joint consultation and its relationship to collective bargaining.

14.1   TRADE UNION RECOGNITION

Some underlying issues

Once a group of employees had decided that it wishes to be represented by a trade union to engage in collective bargaining with its employer, the vital and crucial stage is to seek a recognition and negotiating procedure. There can be no collective bargaining unless employers are willing to recognize trade unions for negotiating purposes. Historically, trade union recognition has been only reluctantly conceded by most employers, and in many instances not until after bitter industrial conflict. In practice it has been government encouragement and favourable economic circumstances which have been significant factors in influencing private sector employers to recognize trade unions. In the public sector, it is generally accepted policy that employers negotiate and consult with representative trade unions. The major exceptions are the armed services, the police service, doctors and dentists, nurses and midwives, and so-called 'top people' such as judges, Members of Parliament and senior civil servants. Union recognition was withdrawn from one public sector group however, the Government and Communications Headquarters (GCHQ) at Cheltenham in January 1984, on the grounds of national security. Under the new arrangements, civil servants at GCHQ are 'permitted in future to belong only to a Departmental Staff Association approved by their Director'[1], not to trade unions.

Until the 1960s, little positive action was taken by government, with the major exceptions of the Whitley Reports, either to encourage employees to join trade unions or to protect them from retaliatory action by their employers for so doing. Although governments encouraged their own employees to belong to trade unions, and public contractors were required to recognize the freedom of their employees to be trade union members through the Fair Wages Resolutions, employers were still legally able to discriminate against employees who were trade unionists. There were no legal obligations on employers requiring them to recognize trade unions when this was fairly and legitimately demanded by employee representatives.

The Donovan Commission recommended that any stipulation in a contract of employment requiring an employee not to belong to a trade union should be void and of no effect in law. It also proposed that an Industrial Relations Commission should be set up to investigate union recognition disputes, with authority to make recommendations for recognition where this was considered to be appropriate. Although the Commission on Industrial Relations was established in 1969 to undertake this task, the Industrial Relations Act 1971 subsequently introduced new rules for recognition, aimed at reducing the disruptive effects of multi-union recognition claims. It provided, for example, that if recognition issues could not be resolved voluntarily between the parties, then trade unions registered under the Act could seek the assistance of the National Industrial Relations Court (NIRC) and the Commission on Industrial Relations (CIR).

The problem of trade union recognition was further exacerbated by the requirement that recognition arrangements should observe one of the basic principles embodied in the Act, namely the right of individual employees to join or not to join a registered trade union. However, in attempting to focus trade union recognition decisions on the importance of determining appropriate bargaining units and effective negotiating agents in each case, the 1971 Act provided a departure from the traditional *ad hoc* methods of conceding recognition. Nevertheless throughout its duration, the legislation and its monitoring agencies, the NIRC and the CIR, were consistently opposed by the TUC and its affiliated organizations.

With the repeal of the Industrial Relations Act by the Trade Union and Labour Relations Act in 1974, the effect broadly was to return to the pre-1971 situation. It now became legally unfair, however, to dismiss an employee by virtue of his or her membership of an independent trade union, whilst the Employment Protection Act 1975 subsequently provided a set of procedures by which independent trade unions might refer recognition disputes with employers to the Advisory Conciliation and Arbitration Service (ACAS) for possible resolution.

Despite this legislation, the general issue of trade union recognition was not definitively resolved. The statutory procedures enabling unrecognized unions to obtain the help of ACAS in conciliating with unco-operative employers were repealed in the Employment Act 1980. Recognition issues were once again largely settled by the power that employers or unions were prepared to apply. It has been estimated, for example, that although there are no major recognition problems in the public sector except GCHQ, or among manual workers in large manufacturing firms, problems continue to emerge in the private sector services, white-collar employment in private manufacturing, among manual workers in smaller firms, and among managers in the private sector. Agriculture also has a recognition problem with no effective collective bargaining having been established in this sector. The general situation, however, has been alleviated by two factors. These are: first, the early work of the CIR and of ACAS in the trade union recognition field; and second, the development of managerial policies on union recognition.

Recognition criteria

One purpose of the Employment Protection Act 1975 was to regularize the procedures by which recognition disputes between employers and independent trade unions could be resolved. In that Act 'recognition' referred to 'recognition of the union by an employer, or two or more associated employers to any extent, for the purpose of collective bargaining', whilst a 'recognition issue' arose 'from a request by a trade union for recognition by an employer, or two or more employers, including . . . a request for further recognition.[2] These definitions extended the scope of recognition from those cases where a union was pressing a claim for representative, consultative, or negotiating rights in the first instance, to those where a claim was being pressed for the subject matter of negotiation to be extended.

The work of the CIR also provides a substantial body of experience on trade union recognition and it clearly influenced the ways in which ACAS operated in the field. A basic criterion which the CIR took into account in determining its recommendations on recognition, for example, was whether the employees concerned wanted to have their pay and conditions of employment determined by collective bargaining. One way in which this was done was through balloting the employees. In more complex cases, attitude surveys were used. A second criterion was the extent of union membership and potential membership if collective bargaining arrangements were to be established.

It was in determining the bargaining unit, or the degree of common interest between employees, and in determining the negotiating agent or the appropriateness of the union, which the CIR considered to be of fundamental importance in making its recommendations. Any lack of clarity in defining a bargaining unit in recognition cases can easily lead to inter-union conflicts, competitive union recruitment and subsequent breakdown of new or existing collective bargaining machinery. The CIR considered that the first issue to be decided in establishing a bargaining unit was the scope of the 'core' negotiating group. There are three possibilities in deciding how far a core group can be expanded: by vertical extension through including employees above or below the core group; by horizontal extension through including employee groups of equal status across the organization; or by incorporation of employees with similar job content and status from different work locations.

In determining the negotiating agent, the CIR established three principal standards to be met by a trade union to be recommended for bargaining purposes. These were: its support as a potential bargaining agent, including its actual membership and the number of employees who would be prepared to join if the union were recognized; its independence from employer influence; and its likely bargaining effectiveness. The CIR viewed organizational independence and negotiating effectiveness as being of high initial priority. If employee organizations fail to achieve these standards, employees can subsequently be left without adequate representation. Lack of independence, for example, can lead to further competitive membership recruitment and to unstable collective bargaining arrangements. Under Section 30 of the Trade Union and Labour Relations Act 1974, an independent trade union is now defined as an organization of workers which is neither under the domination or control of an employer or an employers' association, nor liable to interference in its internal affairs tending towards such control. It is the Employment Protection Act 1975 which lays the duty of determining trade union independence, and of issuing certificates of independence, upon the Certification Officer.

In assessing support for collective bargaining among employee groups ACAS was influenced by the CIR's experience. Although it avoided using any single criterion in determining whether or not to recommend recognition after sounding out employee opinion, ACAS applied a number of criteria when it considered individual decisions. These included: current union membership; the employees' wishes for collective bargaining; the employees' wishes for representation by the referring union; potential union membership in the event of recognition; and the history of support for the union among the employees. None of these factors was necessarily decisive in itself. It was also necessary to consider other factors, such as 'the relevance of existing bargaining arrangements to which the applicant union [was] not a party and whether, in such circumstances, a recommendation would be conducive to good industrial relations.'[3]

Managerial policy

According to the Institute of Personnel Management, employer recognition of a trade union's demand to represent its employees for consultative or bargaining purposes represents a fundamental and irreversible change in the employment relationship. It is not therefore 'a step which should be taken without full consideration of its implications or as an immediate or *ad hoc* response to pressure from employees.'[4] Progressive employers in the private sector are increasingly formulating policies on trade union recognition. These aim not only at ensuring an ordered transition to formalized bargaining relationships with trade unions, but also at mitigating the worst possible problems associated with the proliferation of new unions competing for membership in the same job area or occupational group within their firms. It is not in the employer's interest to recognize too many unions or competing unions.

For employers, recognition policies emerge and develop in four main stages: issues to be taken into account by management prior to a recognition claim being made; considerations in deciding whether or not management should recognize unions for bargaining purposes; factors in determining the nature of the initial agreement providing for formal recognition between the parties; and influences affecting the subsequent development of the relationship between the company and the trade union or unions. Prior to a recognition claim being received, some companies are increasingly aware of the need to establish a decision making framework for dealing with such claims. It is at this stage that employers consider the advisability of providing opportunities for a union to recruit members within their companies.

In responding to recognition claims employers have to take a number of factors into account: whether the employees constitute an appropriate bargaining unit; the level of union membership in the group; the capacity of the union to adequately represent the employees concerned; the extent to which the union demands recognition; the current policy for recognition in the industry; the impact of recognition on existing collective bargaining arrangements, and so on. In doing this, management has to take account of the fact that if a union considers that the company appears to be delaying its request for recognition unduly, either it has recourse to ACAS on a voluntary basis, or it might decide to pursue a policy of direct industrial action against the employer.

Once a decision has been made to recognize trade unions, the initial recognition agreement is of vital concern to both parties. First time recognition can take three main forms: first, the right to representation, that is the right of the union to represent employees usually through union representatives on individual grievances at work; second, the right to consultation, that is the right of the union to be consulted on non-negotiable matters; and third, the right to negotiation, that is the right to represent members fully both in procedural and in substantive matters such as pay and conditions. In most cases, the initial agreement between a company and a trade union usually represents the first stage in a developing relationship and is more usually exploratory rather than comprehensive. However, once full trade union recognition is conceded by employers, the boundaries of collective bargaining become increasingly wide ranging.

14.2 NEGOTIATING SCOPE

Pay, hours and conditions

Substantive collective agreements determine the payments for particular jobs, the methods of calculating such payments, and the relationship of differential salary or wage payments within the job structure. The intervals at which payments are to be made, whether they are weekly, fortnightly or monthly for the hourly paid, or monthly in the case of salaried employees, are also subject to collective agreement. The method of paying employees, such as by cash, credit transfer, or cheque, is normally jointly agreed too, providing that it complies with current wages legislation.

Payment systems vary according to the nature and organization of work, local conditions, technology employed and other factors. They are usually jointly negotiated where trade unions are recognized. There are various payment systems for the parties to choose from. These range from time rate systems including salaries to payment by results schemes which relate the earnings of employees to an assessment of their job performance. Basic time rates, piecework prices, incentive bonus schemes, and 'lieu' bonuses for those not paid directly by results are usually negotiated between employer and union representatives or between individual employees and piecework rate fixers. Guaranteed weekly earnings for the hourly paid are also commonly negotiated to ensure minimum pay for employees, often for the standard work week, if they are subject to short time working or to lay off. They also specify the rates payable to suspended workers and the conditions under which these payment guarantees can be applied or withdrawn.

Pay is also negotiated for work performed in special circumstances. This includes 'London Allowances', 'plus payments' for work undertaken in difficult, dangerous, or unpleasant conditions such as dirt money, danger money, call out payments, and standby duty payments. Holiday pay and maternity pay for an agreed number of days per year are also negotiable, with sick pay increasingly coming within the ambit of joint negotiation too. In this case, agreement has to be reached on what entitlements employees have when sick, the period for which sickness payments – usually based on a sliding time scale – are to be made, the amount of payment in relation to normal earnings, and any arrangements concerning the provision of medical certificates.

Negotiations also cover job evaluation schemes, productivity payments, and merit money for particular groups of workers. Sometimes promotions are jointly regulated by management and unions.

> In some sectors this is done informally, but others have established more formal procedures for joint regulation. These may provide for joint selection panels and give workers who consider they have been overlooked the right to have their case heard by a joint appeals board.[5]

Another item which is negotiable is retirement pensions. Here the parties need to establish whether the scheme is to be contributory or not. Where it is contributory, the relative amounts of the employer's and the employees' contributions have to be determined, as do the age of retirement, the entitlement of dependants if the retired employee dies, arrangements for transferability between schemes, and methods of safeguarding pensions against inflation.

It is common practice to negotiate the standard work week or the number of hours per week which employees are normally expected to work at their place of employment in national-level bargaining. Negotiable locally are stopping and starting times, breaks in working hours for meals and for rest periods, holiday entitlements, flexible working hours and holiday periods. Before 1940 holidays with pay were not general, especially among manual workers. One paid week came in at the end of the Second World War, two weeks in the early 1950s, three weeks in the 1960s, and four weeks paid holiday during the 1970s. By the mid 1980s it is estimated that about 88 per cent of adult men and 85 per cent of adult women in full time employment had holiday entitlements of four weeks or more.[6]

Special rates of pay, or pay premia, for overtime working are normally subject to joint negotiation. Overtime premia, for instance, can be at a time and a quarter, time and a third, time and two fifths, time and a half, or double the standard hourly rate. For non-manual employees there is no great gap between normal hours and actual hours, with non-manuals enjoying relatively short actual hours of work judged by the standards of manual workers. In the case of manual employees, however, and despite the gradual diminution of the standard number of hours per work-week during the post-war period, there has been very little reduction in the actual numbers of hours worked by many adult male manual workers. In some cases, the actual hours worked by male manual workers remains at pre-war levels or at about 48 hours per week. Prior to World War One, for example, normal working hours were generally around 54 per week in manual employment in a six day working week. Hours were reduced to 48 per week by joint negotiation in 1918, and during the inter-war years normal weekly working hours for most manual employees were around 48 hours including Saturday mornings. Soon after the Second World War, the unions succeeded in negotiating reductions in normal working hours to 44 per week and to a five-day working week. Since then, the standard working week has been steadily reduced through negotiation, by stages, to 42½, 40 and – for some groups of white-collar employees – 37½ hours by the early 1980s, though for a few groups it is 35 hours. By the end of 1983 the move away from the basic 40 hour week for manual employees was virtually complete, 'with average basic hours of 39.2, compared with 40.0 in 1978'.[7]

Despite continual reductions in the length of the normal work-week, and rising unemployment, the average levels of overtime for male manual employees, although not for female workers, continue to be high. Such averages conceal wide variations within particular industries, among different sectors of employment, within companies, and by particular groups of workers. Some groups work much higher levels of overtime than the average, whilst others do much less or even none at all. It is characteristic of a lot of overtime working that it is not used to meet the short-term production exigencies of management but is a regular and expected item by employers and employees alike. Although other factors are involved:

> the main reason why workers are willing to work high levels of overtime is clearly to raise their earnings, which would otherwise be much lower; and on the whole workers with lower hourly earnings are readier to work substantial overtime than those whose hourly earnings are higher.[8]

In many cases, there are considerable workgroup pressures not to allow overtime hours to be reduced to levels below those which have become customarily accepted by workers and by line management as being necessary to maintain individual and workgroup earnings. The demand for high levels of overtime paid at premia rates, in short, seems to be primarily influenced by relative pay factors and by the potential earnings expected by workers. To what extent levels of overtime among manual workers are affected by rising unemployment and the demand for more leisure, however, has yet to be demonstrated. Significantly, perhaps, rising unemployment has not generally resulted in less overtime being worked.

A range of other working conditions is also negotiable between management and unions. These include the allocation, pace and quality of work. In manual employment manning, job transfers, demarcation arrangements, general conditions in the workplace, and the introduction of new machinery or new jobs can all be subject to negotiation where management and trade union representatives agree to it.

Trade unions are also vitally concerned to see that safe and healthy working conditions are established and maintained for their members. Although both management and unions have a common interest in advancing safety within the workplace, effective joint procedures are established for dealing with disputes on safety matters and for maintaining good industrial relations within the workplace. 'Final responsibility for safety rests with management, but management cannot discharge its responsibility without a proper system of safety organisation.'[9] Joint safety committees and workers safety representatives are now an integral part of safety organization in many workplaces, as well as being a statutory requirement under the Health and Safety at Work etc. Act 1974. Their function is to promote co-operation between management and employees in achieving high standards of health and safety at work, and to inspect working conditions in the interests of all those employed in factories, shops, offices or elsewhere.

Other employment issues which are negotiated include: the recruitment of new labour; agreements on the numbers of apprentices to be employed; short-time working; redundancy questions; and union membership or closed shop agreements. Agreements are also negotiated for additional allowances like travelling expenses, special clothing and tool allowances, or for disturbance payments for employees required to move their homes when changing their jobs.

Shiftwork

It has long been recognized that shift work can make for the better use of costly fixed capital equipment. It provides output or services on a continuous basis, such as in public transport, hospitals, and electricity generating, for those using them. In continuous process industries, like chemicals and steel making, shiftwork is unavoidable. From the employees' point of view, shiftwork entails working unsocial hours and can include considerable amounts of overtime. For these reasons, it is usual for them to demand not only that working arrangements involving unsocial hours of work carry additional payments, but also that shiftwork systems should be regulated jointly between managerial and union representatives.

Shift premia are paid either proportionally to pay rates or as fixed amounts in addition to basic earnings. Which method is used mainly depends on the shiftwork system in operation. Permanent night shifts, for example, are mostly paid by the proportionate method. Double day shifts, on the other hand, are more frequently expressed as fixed additions. In practice, shift premia may understate the actual premium paid since the basic rate for some occupational categories is increased for those on shiftwork. Some idea of the importance of shiftworking in Britain can be noted from the fact that in manufacturing industry 'the proportion of the workforce on shifts has increased only very slightly since 1968, to about 26 per cent.'[10] If we include non-manual workers, it is probable that about 30 per cent of employees are now engaged on some kind of shiftworking arrangement.

It is the hours a week which a plant or establishment must be operated or a service provided that give a broad indication of the shift system required. The most common method is the 'continuous three shift' system. In this case, four crews are necessary to cover three eight-hour shifts over a seven-day period. Three crews, however, can provide continuous coverage from Monday to Friday through a 'discontinuous three shift' system, thus leaving weekends free. Where two crews operate a morning and night shift of eight hours each, they can give coverage for about 80 hours a week on a 'double day' basis. Two crews operating an alternating 'day and night shift' can cover the same number of hours. 'Permanent nights' are also possible, whilst another arrangement is to employ female workers part time on a 'twilight' shift for about four hours at the end of the normal working day. In some service industries, such as in catering or hospital work, 'split' shifts are used. These alternate work and rest periods.

Most shift systems rotate: this can be anything between a four-day and eight-day cycle. In this way, the popular and unpopular shifts can be shared amongst employees. Furthermore, although eight-hour shifts are the most common, the length of individual shifts varies. This is sometimes because overtime is regularly worked. Employees on an alternating day and night system, for example, may work up to 12 hours on each shift. Whatever the method used, however, employees usually demand a say in the manner in which their shifts are operated and arranged.

Procedures

Procedures and 'supporting agreements provide the framework within which industrial relations business is conducted' between employer and union representatives.[11] In addition to union recognition procedures, steward credential procedures and negotiating procedures, industrial relations procedures cover three major types of issue: discipline and dismissal; individual grievances; and disputes over pay and conditions. In public industry and the public services, procedures tend to be negotiated nationally, though they operate locally. In the private sector, the pattern is variable, with much more scope for local autonomy and for negotiating agreements at employer or establishment level.

There are other procedures which employers and unions use to 'do business' together. Some, for example, establish recruitment guidelines, defining the experience and qualifications needed to do the jobs to be filled. They ensure that no arbitrary conditions are imposed on an applicant's suitability for employment and that no one is discriminated against because of their age, sex, race or their trade union activities. In attempting to protect the jobs of their members, trade unions also negotiate procedures for dealing with redundancies as part of a joint approach to long-term manpower planning. Here management and unions consider how to minimize or avoid employee redundancies by reducing overtime, restricting recruitment, allowing natural wastage or by introducing short-time working when jobs are threatened. Where redundancies are unavoidable, it is normal practice to agree arrangements for retraining, redeploying, resettling, or retiring workers early. Voluntary rather than compulsory redundancy is commonly preferred, with compensatory payments for the loss of jobs involved. Most importantly, the order in which employees are to be made redundant and the criteria for selection have to be agreed. Provision is also made for informing local job centres about the numbers, skills, occupations, and date of availability of redundant workers to assist them to find new jobs.

Negotiation also determines closed shop or union membership agreements, where union membership is a condition of employment. Research shows that major changes in the nature of the closed shop took place in the 1970s. Besides legal requirements, negotiations on closed shops have resulted in increasingly sophisticated agreements which, despite variations in detail, have standardized content and application. It is now common, for example, to exclude existing nonunionists from compulsion to join the union where new agreements are negotiated. Similarly, closed shop procedures incorporating provision for independent arbitrators for dealing with difficulties arising from union membership agreements 'have become a regular, if seldom used feature' of such arrangements.[12]

14.3 THE PAY-WORK BARGAIN

Pay determination is central to the negotiating process. But pay is only one side to the bargaining equation: the other is the amount of work which employees agree to perform for a given payment. In practice, every employment contract consists of two elements: an agreement on the rate of pay (either per unit of time or per unit of output) or a pay rate bargain, and an agreement on the work to be done or an effort bargain. A collective agreement then – or an individual agreement between an employer and an employee –

is a pay–work bargain which fixes the terms of exchange of work done for money payable between the parties. It attempts to define the relationship between the monetary rewards for working and the amount of work expected by employers for the job to be done. Basically, the pay–work bargain takes one of three forms: standard bargaining; effort bargaining; and productivity and efficiency bargaining – although these are not mutually exclusive categories of negotiation.

Standard bargaining

The most typical type of pay–work bargain is standard bargaining. In standard collective bargaining, a specified rate of payment such as an hourly rate or a yearly salary is negotiated between employers and trade unions. This is paid to all employees provided that a minimum standard of work is achieved over the agreed work period. In other words, for the given rate of payment, different employees may produce different amounts and quantities of output or contribute various levels and quantities of effort. In standard bargaining, therefore, there is no direct relationship between pay rewards and work done or between the pay rate and the effort bargain. This does not preclude standard bargaining providing a base rate of pay upon which an effort bargain can subsequently be struck.

Standard bargaining is typical in salaried employment where it is difficult to measure the work being performed or to determine the time required for carrying it out at a defined standard of performance by a qualified worker. Although clerical work measurement techniques may be applied to some categories of clerical employment, it is much more difficult in practice – although not impossible – to measure the effort, output or efficiency of professional groups of employees like teachers, nurses, research workers, or even managers whose work can often only be qualitatively rather than quantitatively assessed.

Certain manual occupations cannot be objectively work measured. In retail selling, in bar keeping and in restaurants, for example, although payment by results is sometimes used, it is extremely difficult in practice to relate job payment to job performance in any precise or equitable way. Standard bargaining tends to be used, therefore, where it is difficult to measure the work being done or where machine technology is the prime determinant of work effort: it merely attempts to establish standard payments for minimum levels of job performance. In these circumstances, the most that can be done to relate pay to performance is to attempt to establish a fair and agreed relationship between payment offered, on the one hand, and the skills, responsibilities, effort and working conditions for the job on the other. The technique sometimes used to achieve this objective is job evaluation. As a management technique, job evaluation seeks to bring about a systematic and rational relationship between jobs and rates of pay. It cannot and should not replace normal collective bargaining. 'A job evaluation exercise should never be regarded as a permanent fixing of differentials.'[13]

Effort bargaining

It is unrealistic to suggest that standard bargaining is a satisfactory method of relating payment to work done in all instances. Indeed, much attention has been devoted towards devising satisfactory means whereby payment can be more closely linked to the output or productivity of workers, especially in manual employment where productivity can be measured and where wage payment systems are used. 'The commonest alternative has been to use the payment system as a means of functionally relating the output of the workers or work-group and the pay received.'[14] The use of payment by results (PBR), whether piecework, incentive bonuses or measured daywork, rests on three assumptions only the first of which can be taken as factually established: that work effort varies in its intensity; that the financial motive at work is the most important one; and that the best way of harnessing this motive to increase work effort by employees is to use PBR. By this view, effort intensity is determined independently of earnings with standard bargaining, so that an increased pay bargain does not on its own change the effort bargain. However:

> If one postulates that more output means more effort, then it is possible to conclude an effort bargain, and this is essentially what a successful financial incentive scheme does. The worker agrees to raise his output in exchange for the guarantee of higher earnings.[15]

What is being purchased by employers under effort bargaining is a supply of labour input for performing varying job tasks. Effort, however, is not easily quantifiable. It is only output or the application of effort which can be effectively measured since effort is purely subjective. It is clear that 'in the absence of an agreement on the effort intensity per unit of time that is being purchased, effort intensity can vary between certain limits.'[16] Under these conditions, employees have an upper limit to the exertion which they expend in their job tasks, whilst employers have a lower limit to the exertion which they expect from subordinates. The purpose of effort bargaining is to determine those levels of output which relate to specific levels of payment, and to ensure equal pay for those employees contributing equal effort. The successful application of PBR requires, therefore, that employees as well as the employer share the same perceptions of what constitutes the right standard of effort for a given job, as well as the correct rate for doing it.

The belief that there is a 'correct' rate for a job is held by both management and employees alike. Where piecework payments are operative, for example, managerial and worker views as to what piecework price represents the correct rate inevitably differ and have to be reconciled by effort bargaining. 'A rate is "correct" if it matches notions of the "right" earnings with notions of the "right" standard of effort, and it is "loose" or "tight" if it does not do so.'[17] What happens in practice is that negotiators argue first about the right earnings for the job – the pay rate bargain – and, second, about the right effort and the right production standards in doing it – the effort bargain. It seems likely that PBR works reasonably well where management and trade union representatives believe in the fairness of the bargain struck and where they behave accordingly. This happens when the bargain represents 'a fair day's work for a fair day's pay' for both sides, with successful operation of PBR depending on mutual skill in effort bargaining. Under effort bargaining, however, wages cannot be explained by labour market competition alone; they are also political phenomena to be understood through political analysis of the processes of collective bargaining, with the product market rather than the labour market having the major impact on piecework pay determination.

Productivity and efficiency bargaining

In one respect, productivity bargaining is like effort bargaining; it is concerned with the problem of relating payment received to work done. Instead of operating through the payment system, however, it seeks to improve productive performance by employees in the pay bargaining process itself. As such:

> It involves the parties to the bargaining process in negotiating a package of changes in working method or organisation, agreeing on the precise contents of the package, their worth to the parties and the distribution of the cost savings between the reward to labour and other alternative destinations such as return to capital and the reduction or stabilisation of the product price.[18]

The term productivity bargaining lacks exact precision but it may broadly be described as an agreement in which advantages of one kind or another, such as higher wages or increased leisure, 'are given to workers in return for agreement on their part to accept changes in working practice or in methods or in organisation of work which will lead to more efficient working'.[19] It is probably best conducted at company or workplace level. Although a productivity bargain is a one-off exercise relating pay increases to productivity increases, it does not preclude a series of bargains being struck over time. Further, the pay-work agreement determined through productivity bargaining contrasts vividly with that negotiated through normal effort bargaining in an important respect. With PBR the pay rewards allocated to wage earners can fluctuate from week to week as output or productivity varies. Under productivity bargaining, they are usually predetermined with fluctuating payments kept to a minimum as far as is possible.

The significance of productivity bargaining is threefold. First, compared with other approaches to the pay-work bargain, productivity bargaining seems to be more successful in tightening up the pay–productivity link within organizations. This has potential benefits for management, unions, employees, consumers, and the national economy. It has been argued from the managerial viewpoint, for example, that productivity bargaining induces greater cost consciousness in management and that it brings management into closer contact with trade union negotiators. For the trade unions, it is suggested, productivity agreements extend the range of subject matter in collective bargaining, whilst employees, it is said, also gain because they can obtain more stable earnings and greater leisure opportunities from productivity package deals.

Second, it is argued, productivity bargaining opens up new sources of untapped productivity potential within an enterprise. This can be done, for instance, by grouping minor changes in working practices into a total productivity deal which then becomes worthy of consideration by both management and unions as a source of higher productivity and of improved wage payments respectively. Alternatively, a joint attack can be made in the negotiating process on problems in the wage payment system, in the working environment, or in both. These are unlikely to be dealt with in standard or effort bargaining, inhibited as they are by custom and practice and traditionally hostile negotiating stances.

The third significance of productivity bargaining is the opportunity provided for improving the climate of industrial relations between management and trade unions at company or establishment level, since effective productivity bargaining necessitates openness and trust between the parties in the negotiation process. Management, for example, has to take a more predictive approach to negotiation than it does in standard or effort bargaining. This requires abandoning defensive or reactive bargaining postures in favour of greater initiative in industrial relations planning and labour utilization, as well as being 'open' in their approach to union representatives. Trade union negotiators, on the other hand, also need to modify their traditional bargaining stances if productivity bargaining is to succeed. They have to accept, for example, greater involvement in those areas of decision making which are traditionally regarded as being within managerial discretion alone. Compared with other types of collective bargaining, union negotiators have to be prepared to accept more participation by rank and file workers in formulating and applying the pay-work rules regulating employee behaviour.

In short, a joint problem-solving approach is required in genuine productivity negotiations since it involves the better use of labour and the more effective use of capital equipment within the workplace. The sorts of issues bargained about include: removal of excessive overtime; increased flexibility in the use of labour among skilled trades and between skilled and less-skilled workers; changes in manning levels; and reductions in the labour force. Negotiations also focus on greater flexibility in the movement of labour within the enterprise; flexible working hours; the cutting out of time wasting practices and non-working time; introducing new technology and so on. In return for concessions on matters of these sorts, and for contributions by their members towards cost savings, trade union negotiators correspondingly demand a wide range of benefits for their members. These include:

> higher earnings, greater stability of earnings and increases in holiday and sick pay; shorter hours of work; better fringe benefits; better promotion prospects; security against redundancy; and other tangible benefits, e.g. increased interest in the job.[20]

Since there are many employees who are not directly engaged in productive output, the term 'productivity bargaining' is inapplicable to those non-manual workers for whom it is inappropriate to specify quantitative changes in working practices in exchange for higher payments. Productivity bargaining is also a dubious description for those pay-work bargains negotiated for 'manual workers who have previously conducted agreements specifying changes in working practices but for whom such agreements are no longer appropriate.'[21] It was the National Board for Prices and Incomes which first coined the phrase 'efficiency agreements' for those negotiations having the underlying aim of constantly raising efficiency 'on the basis of close and continuing co-operation between managements and workers so as to achieve and maintain the highest standards in the use of both equipment and manpower.'[22] Productivity bargaining can be used in those situations in which specific changes in working practices are agreed in return for direct improvements in pay and conditions. Efficiency bargaining, on the other hand, covers those circumstances in which improvements in pay and non-pay benefits are linked to forecasted and costed gains within the enterprise, resulting from co-operation between management and the workforce in organizational change and technological innovation.

The classical phase of productivity bargaining was the 1960s. Indeed, it was a deliberate government policy to support productivity agreements within the framework of successive incomes policies in that period. However, in deteriorating economic circumstances and with rising unemployment since the 1970s, productivity bargaining has become a less acceptable means of conducting pay negotiations for most trade union negotiators, since it often involves redundancies and job losses. Standard bargaining with its emphasis on the pay rate bargain rather than on the effort bargain or the productivity bargain once again is the dominant trade union approach to negotiation. Less emphasis is now placed on the pay-productivity link in negotiations, although managements sometimes enforce changes in working methods unilaterally, and more attention is focused on cost-of-living arguments by union negotiators or claims to restore eroded pay differentials. As unemployment has risen, and management has sought productivity improvements, these too have often been imposed unilaterally, sometimes by consultation but often without negotiation.

It would be wrong to consider productivity bargaining as a new concept. Productivity agreements have been much more widespread and are of much longer standing than is sometimes assumed. Even the so-called pathfinding Fawley Productivity Agreements at the Esso Petroleum Company's oil refinery near Southampton in the early 1960s were by no means as unique as some commentators have implied. Their novelty lay in the range and depth of their coverage rather than in the conception of productivity bargaining as such. At all events, large numbers of organizations, both large and small, in the private sector and in the public sector, practised productivity bargaining in the 1960s. These included Alcan Industries, Dunlop Rubber, the Central Electricity Generating Board, Imperial Chemical Industries and the London Transport Executive. Four main types of productivity bargaining were made during this period: national negotiations into which a productivity element was injected; national negotiations aimed at establishing a framework for company bargaining; small-scale bargaining at plant level or below; and full scale and comprehensive productivity package deals.

Productivity bargaining has not always received the full support of either union or managerial negotiators. In the first place, productivity bargaining can have severe disadvantages for the workers and trade unions concerned. For example, it may threaten redundancy, affect some workers' earnings adversely, result in inconvenient hours of work, and generally cause a sense of anxiety and disturbance amongst employees. Similarly, difficulties are sometimes encountered by employers from those other employees, normally white-collar workers, who are outside the scope of productivity bargaining. These employees often feel that they are being treated unfairly because their productivity cannot be measured, or because they are already co-operating fully with management in their methods of working. More importantly, there are those trade unionists and their supporters who, because of their ideological perceptions, believe productivity bargaining to be 'part of a major offensive by the employing class of this country to shift the balance of forces in industry permanently in their direction.'[23] On these grounds, it is argued, productivity bargaining must be resisted and opposed by all rank and file trade unionists in their own interests.

14.4   THE NEGOTIATION PROCESS

Negotiation is defined as 'a process for resolving conflict between two . . . parties whereby both modify their demands to achieve a mutually acceptable compromise.'[24] Industrial relations negotiation is the interactive activity by which representatives of management and unions make decisions on matters of joint concern to them and those whom they represent. Both parties are then jointly responsible for the mutually agreed decisions. Substantive bargaining normally seeks to resolve conflicts of interest between the parties, grievance bargaining conflicts of right. There are, it would seem, at least three basic elements in the negotiation process. The first is that negotiation involves social relations between those individuals and groups which are party to collective bargaining; the second is the representative and communicative functions of negotiation; and the third is that differences in power exist between those represented in the negotiation process, employers and employees.

The social contexts

Each management–union negotiation or set of negotiations is unique. Whilst situations can repeat themselves in different negotiations, they never repeat themselves exactly. Nevertheless, three main sets of factors seem to be of major influence in determining the climate of any particular negotiation; its institutional background; its behavioural contexts; and the ideologies of the negotiators. The institutional factors which have an impact on negotiation include the level of procedure within which negotiations take place, the type of claim under discussion, the balance of bargaining power between management and unions, and the degree of formality or informality in particular negotiations. The ways in which a shopfloor grievance over shiftwork allowances might be resolved between the production manager and the senior shop steward within a low technology food canning factory, for example, would be quite different from negotiating a company-wide productivity agreement and package deal for process workers in a highly profitable multi-plant chemical company.

The behavioural contexts of negotiation are also important in determining the climate of bargaining between the parties. These include, for example, the size of the negotiating groups, the interests which they represent, the personalities involved and their negotiating skills. At one extreme, negotiation takes place at the interpersonal level, between two people – a single managerial representative and one trade union negotiator. Most collective bargaining, however, involves inter-party negotiations. These range from fairly small groups on each side of the bargaining table to 20 or more representatives from management and a similar number of trade unionists representing different trade unions. Negotiations in the latter case are likely to be far more formal, protracted and difficult to resolve than when only two individuals are directly involved in, say, a relatively small scale workplace issue. With larger groups there is a greater need for an ordered format to channel individual effort and synchronize the efforts of group members. 'This discourages a free and informal sort of individual participation and minimises the prospects of developing meaningful relationships within the group.'[25]

Bargaining is also likely to be affected by the ideologies and skills of the respective negotiators. As one full-time trade union officer in the Midlands is reported to have remarked:

> If a manager is so anti-union it hurts him to sit and talk with the union official, and it shows in his actions, I don't show him any mercy. I'll do my best to grind him into the ground as quickly as I can. Every deal will be an expensive one and then if someone more senior comes along to me and says 'What's with you and this bloke?' 'Well, I'm afraid we just don't get on. He hates us, and as long as he's in that position there'll be trouble in the firm.'[26]

Similarly, negotiations are also influenced by the relative experience and skills of the negotiators. In practice, there is probably no substitute for the experience of the give and take of real-life negotiation. 'We can learn a lot from education and training courses,' it has been said, 'but there's no substitute for the experience of the real thing.'[27]

Distributive and integrative bargaining

Another significant influence on the bargaining climate is the type of negotiation between the parties. The two pure types which exist are described as 'distributive' or 'competitive' bargaining and 'integrative' or 'co-operative' bargaining. Distributive bargaining occurs where management and unions are in a situation of basic conflict over the ways in which something might be divided or decided between them. There is, for instance, an inevitable conflict between management and unions when pay and profits have to be distributed between them. More pay for employees usually means less profit for the company, whilst more profit for the company normally means less pay for the employees. Similarly, in the public sector, conflicts emerge between employers seeking more efficient working methods from their employees, such as a rise in productivity or by less recruitment, and employees opposing these moves. Distributive bargaining, in other words, is essentially a conflict-resolving process and a zero-sum game – a gain for one side must mean equal loss for the other. It typically aims to enable the parties to reach a compromise over how either fixed or limited resources may be allocated between them.

In integrative bargaining, by contrast, both sets of negotiators recognize that they may have one or more common problems which require mutual resolution between the two sides. Compared with distributive bargaining, integrative bargaining is more a problem-solving process and a positive-sum game with benefits for both parties. It takes place, for example, in the development and negotiation of productivity agreements. Unlike distributive bargaining, genuine integrative bargaining aims to increase the size of the resources for distribution between the two sides rather than just dividing it between them. Integrative bargaining occurs, for instance, when a company is faced with a marked downturn in business. Either management or unions can use an integrative bargaining approach by identifying common goals for determining methods of dealing with possible reductions in hours, potential lay offs, likely redundancies and so on. If they fail to do this, bargaining will be purely distributive because of its win-lose implications for each party. This heightens conflict between them and a mutual sense of distrust emerges in the negotiation process.

It is quite clear that both the content and the styles of distributive and integrative bargaining differ. In the former, the parties are directly competing with each other and are in overt conflict over the distribution of fixed resources. In distributive negotiations one side's gain is the other side's loss. Similarly, the attitudes of the respective parties to the negotiating process in distributive bargaining are likely to be hostile, suspicious and lacking in openness towards each other. In purely integrative bargaining, on the other hand, however rare it might be in practice, the parties need to co-operate to achieve their perceived common ends. There has to be considerable mutual trust and openness of communication between them for co-operative bargaining to take place. As a process, integrative bargaining is a much more tentative and exploratory method of negotiation than is distributive bargaining. More time is required to carry it out, whilst the pace of negotiations may be slower than in distributive bargaining. Similarly, the negotiators have to be willing to talk about the goals at which they are really aiming.

Distributive and integrative bargaining, in short, have different objectives, their content differs, and the negotiators involved in the two processes perceive themselves and their opponents in different ways. The real-life problems facing negotiators, however, are complicated by the fact that much bargaining in which they are involved is 'mixed' bargaining, being partly distributive and partly integrative. To shift from one type of negotiation to the other is a difficult task. What negotiators reveal to assist in joint problem-solving situations, for example, can weaken their bargaining position when it comes to distributing the resource gains which have been made and their problems resolved.

The negotiating continuum

Negotiation aims at reaching 'accommodations, often of a temporary nature, between different interests and expectations.' In industrial relations, it involves regulating the parties different interests and pursuing their complementary objectives, although it is also part 'of a wider relationship of employment which is essentially collaborative.'[28] Negotiators, therefore, normally want to reach agreement. In every negotiation, there is a negotiating continuum, as shown in figure 14.1, incorporating the 'bargaining range' of each side. An effective negotiation enables each party to identify the 'bargaining parameters' between them and to reach an agreed settlement within these parameters. 'Having discovered the possibility of a settlement, it is about securing that settlement at least cost and agreeing to its implementation.'[29]

As can be seen in figure 14.1, management's bargaining range in a given negotiation runs from its ideal settlement point to its resistance point, with a target point of favourable *and* realistic expectation in an intermediate position between the two. The unions also have a bargaining range, but running in the opposite direction. The bargaining parameters lie between the resistance points of each side. A negotiated settlement is normally achieved within these parameters. In distributive bargaining it is the skill of the negotiators to probe each other's divergent target and resistance points in order to move towards a mutually acceptable compromise. The more skilled the negotiators, and the more equal the balance of bargaining power between them, the more likely it is that the final agreement and settlement will lie between each side's target points. Where bargaining power is unequal the stronger side is likely to achieve its bargaining objectives with little resistance from the other side.

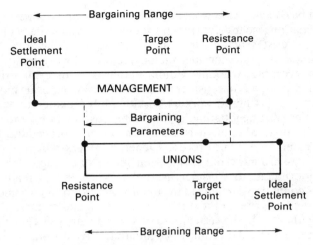

Figure 14.1 The negotiating continuum.

Negotiation phases

Negotiations proceed through a number of phases before managerial and union representatives can reach a mutually acceptable compromise and agreement. Unless agreement is reached in the negotiating process, there is the likelihood that either party will force the other one to accept its demands by some form of industrial action or coercive means. Effective industrial relations negotiations are aimed at preventing disputes arising between the parties and at reaching mutually acceptable agreements benefiting both sides represented at the negotiating table. This does not mean that each side 'wins' the negotiation, it means that each side achieves something in the negotiation which enables it to keep face with those whom it represents.

In practice a negotiating cycle proceeds through three main phases: preparation, negotiation and implementation. Preparation involves, for example, 'objective setting' and 'strategy determination'. Deciding bargaining objectives is not an easy task, since conflicts often develop within each side before negotiation commences. It is not unusual before negotiations and even during them for intra-group disagreements to emerge within the negotiating groups. The important thing is for neither party to weaken its bargaining position by showing less than a united front to its opponents. Each side's negotiating goals are determined by a process of 'intra-organizational' bargaining. This takes place among the bargaining teams prior to the commencement of negotiations. This enables them to show a common front to the opposing negotiating team. In this respect:

> intra-organizational bargaining within the union is particularly interesting. While it is true that for both parties to labor negotiations many individuals not present in negotiations are vitally concerned about what transpires at the bargaining table, the union negotiator is probably subject to more organizational constraints than his company counterpart.[30]

Having assessed their relative bargaining power and decided their respective bargaining objectives and bargaining range, management and unions are then able to prepare their cases prior to presenting them. In examining their strategy determination before negotiating, each side is seeking for ways to adjust the outlook and expectations of their opponents in the negotiating process. This is a vital step in the negotiating cycle. It includes assessing the strength and weaknesses of the case, the likely counter arguments to it, what might be conceded but what must be achieved, and its order of presentation. Strategy determination also involves making judgements about the likelihood of having to threaten or to resist sanctions in order to achieve one's bargaining objectives. Unions, for example, have to consider the possibilities of working to rule, restricting output, banning overtime, working without enthusiasm, or even striking. Management, on the other hand, has to consider the possibilities of imposing more supervision, withholding overtime, laying-off workers, or ultimately locking-out employees.

When the parties start negotiating, although it is customary for the trade unions to present their case first, whether it is a substantive or a procedural claim, and for management to respond to it, the process is generally reversed in productivity bargaining. The union's case in a pay claim having been made, for example, management often requests an adjournment to consider its reply. When this is ready, management responds with its counter arguments to the unions, the unions then sometimes requests a further adjournment prior to them making a revised and counter claim. After the parties come together again they attempt to determine a final agreement which usually takes several meetings to achieve unless negotiations break down.

The negotiation phase normally proceeds through four subsidiary stages. They are not necessarily clearly delineated, and often the parties move backwards and forwards amongst the stages rather than proceeding smoothly towards final agreement. These negotiating stages are variously described as the 'initial' or 'arguing' stage, the 'exploratory' or 'proposing' stage, the 'consolidating' or 'bargaining' stage, and the 'decision' or 'agreeing' stage. The initial or arguing stage comprises opening statements from either side of their initial bargaining positions and their reasons for pursuing them as well as rejecting each other's claim or demands. This stage is in effect a 'safety valve' for each negotiating team. It enables each set of negotiators to 'let off steam' and establish the broad parameters within which it is prepared to negotiate with its opponents. It is characterized by listening, questioning and testing the commitment of each side to its initial and seemingly inflexible initial bargaining position.

After the initial bargaining positions of the two sides have been established, negotiations enter an exploratory or proposing stage. At this point each party tries to find out where the other group really stands. External clues in pay bargaining, for example, come from knowledge of recent settlements elsewhere, the willingness and ability of the union to call and finance strike action, the state of the order book of the company, market conditions, shopfloor attitudes and traditions, likely support from other unions or other employers and so on. There are also a series of internal clues which can be discerned from around the negotiating table itself. Negotiators, for example, have to draw their own conclusions about the bargaining positions of their opponents by their behaviour across the bargaining table. Are they sincere, trustworthy, determined, flexible, receptive to pressure and so on? To do this, they ask direct questions, try out proposals, make demands and offers, 'they threaten and sometimes abuse, they bring in time pressures and show impatience, all in the hope that their opponent might reveal and possibly move his target and resistance points.'[31] This is often a time-consuming and frustrating process. The proposals each side makes are highly conditional: 'if you do this, we could do that'. They provide, however, the basis for moving into the next negotiation stage.

This is the consolidating or bargaining stage. The parties now concentrate on convergent rather than divergent issues thus minimizing conflict between them. Negotiators seek to avoid contentious matters and act on the understanding that everyone around the bargaining table wishes to move towards a final agreement. This stage of the negotiating cycle is about exchange, the central core of the bargaining process. Each side aims to gain something from the other for a concession on their part: 'if you do this, we will do that'. It is here that tactical adjustments are made by both parties in their aim to motivate the other side away from an unacceptable position to a mutually agreeable 'contract zone'.

Negotiation then moves rapidly into the decision or agreeing stage. It becomes increasingly apparent to the negotiators at this point that only a compromise settlement is attainable. Final concessions and trade-offs are made between the parties and 'a detailed summary of each item in the package must be read and agreed between the negotiators'.[32] The details are normally put in writing and a final settlement which on balance is adequate for both sides rather than ideal for either is the prime objective. With the negotiation phase of the negotiating cycle completed, it is the joint responsibility of both parties to implement and monitor their agreement. Each side then normally evaluates its bargaining outcomes with its objectives, its negotiating performance and its future plans. Whatever the outcome however:

> You learn negotiating skills by experience and observation. You know how far they will go, they know how far you will go and there are certain steps which both sides can take to resolve the problem. But the two sides can misjudge each other. You can't be 100 per cent sure that you've judged your case rightly or you've judged their reactions rightly.[33]

14.5   JOINT CONSULTATION

Joint consultation has a chequered history in British industrial relations. It seems to have enjoyed three periods of popularity during the last 50 years: throughout the Second World War, the late 1940s and since the late 1970s. In the intervening period, the 1950s and 1960s, a decline in joint consultation set in in most sectors, though as the 1960s drew to an end it seems that joint consultative machinery had continued to exist in some sectors 'but that it generally did little which caught the imagination of the parties.'[34]

Types of consultation

One of the problems of examining joint consultation is that there is no generally agreed definition of the term. In practice joint consultation normally takes place at employer or enterprise level and there seem to be three approaches to it. These may be described as pseudo-consultation, classical consultation and integrative consultation. Pseudo-consultation exists where management takes a decision and informs employees of that decision through employee representatives. It is a system of consultation through which management merely communicates predetermined decisions with employee representatives. In this case management either passes information to employees or receives information from them. Employees have no power to influence managerial decisions and their representatives are not normally union members. Indeed, it is arguable that the express intention of such an approach is to prevent the emergence of employee-based power centres in non-union firms. Although this type of consultation is less common today than it was in the past, there are still sections of private industry, where trade unionism is weak, which use this bland form of consultation or, more accurately, information-giving of the employer to employee representatives. As a method of industrial relations, it merely seeks to maintain management's right to manage, neither to challenge it nor to legitimize managerial authority.

Classical consultation, as defined by the Institute of Personnel Management, is a method of:

involving employees through their representatives in discussion and consideration of relevant matters which affect or concern those they represent, thereby allowing employees to influence the proposals before the final management decision is taken.[35]

Classical consultation has four main characteristics. First, it focuses on matters of common interest to employers and employees, specifically excluding areas of potential conflict between them such as terms and conditions of work. Second, joint consultative machinery is normally kept separate from negotiating machinery. Third, it remains management's responsibility to take and implement the final decisions arising from the consultative process. Fourth, it involves all employees, including non-union employees such as supervisors and managerial staff. Classical consultation therefore involves a paradox, it is assumed 'that management should only agree to share responsibility on controversial and conflicting subjects like wages' as in collective bargaining, 'on common interest issues it cannot do more than consult'.[36]

Integrative consultation, by contrast, is not an instrument of management so much as a means of advancing employee participation within enterprises by 'settling democratically the purposes of industrial undertakings, purposes which managers themselves serve.'[37] Under these conditions the artificial distinctions between the subject matter of negotiation and consultation are blurred. Integrative consultation in other words enlarges the area of joint decision making between managerial and employee representatives. Management and unions discuss and explore matters which are their common concern such as increasing productivity or changing working methods. Often this is approached in a problem-solving manner with a view to coming to a joint decision. It is a process more akin to integrative bargaining than to classical consultation or distributive bargaining. Indeed, if joint consultation is to mean anything 'it must give employees a genuine influence on important decisions – it must have teeth.'[38]

Clearly there is some debate about the aims of negotiation and consultation and the relationship between them. Some view them as separate but related processes. Others contend that 'there is no absolute dividing line that constitutes a universal separation between them.'[39] This means that in practice managerial and employee representatives need to consider carefully how to link the two:

> It may often be advantageous for the same committee to cover both. Where there are separate bodies, systematic communication between those in the two processes is essential.[40]

In developing appropriate consultative machinery, management and employee representatives also have to consider the levels at which representative systems are most likely to be effective and how they can be linked horizontally and vertically. Problems can arise in multi-union situations, for example, or in integrating non-union and managerial staff into a consultative system where there is strong union organization amongst other employee groups.

Subject matter and determinants of consultation

Table 14.1 indicates the main areas in which consultation between managerial representatives and union representatives typically takes place. The empirical material is taken from the Department of Employment's survey of company organization and worker participation in the late 1970s. The most popular matters raised at these consultative committees were welfare matters and physical conditions of work which were discussed in over 90 per cent of the companies surveyed. These were followed by safety matters, the companies' current trading position, changes in production methods, hours of work and disciplinary procedures. These took place in between 70 per cent and 89 per cent of the companies examined. The least popular issues for joint consultative meetings were capital investment and redundancy.

Table 14.1 *Subject matter covered by joint consultative machinery.*

Subject	Per cent	Rank
Welfare matters	94	1
Physical conditions of work	91	2
Safety matters	89	3
Current trading position	87	4
Major changes in production methods	77	5
Hours of work	74	6
Disciplinary procedures	71	7
Redundancy	65	8
Capital investment	56	9

Source: *Employment Gazette* (April 1980)

A number of explanations have been advanced to account for the incidence and growth of joint consultation within enterprises. One study, for example, suggests that the larger the size of a plant, 'the greater the likelihood of its having a [joint consultative] committee.' Multi-unionism also appears to be associated with the creation of joint consultative committees, as are plants where there is single employer bargaining. The conclusions of these researchers are not only that joint consultation has increased in Britain since the late 1970s but also that consultative committees 'are becoming increasingly heterogeneous in nature, both in terms of the characteristics of the plants where they are established and in terms of their performance as viewed by management.'[41]

Another study claims that there are three theses explaining fluctuations in the extent of joint consultation in Britain. Its authors describe them as: the 'McCarthy thesis'; the 'accommodation thesis'; and the 'external threat thesis'. The McCarthy thesis suggests that there is an inverse relationship between trade union power and joint consultation: when union power is strong joint consultation is weakened, when union power is weak joint consultation is strengthened. The accommodation thesis, by contrast, characterizes joint consultation as 'a management strategy to maintain its authority when challenged by rising trade union power'. Finally, the external threat thesis 'argues that an acute development of external pressure is required for the two sides to co-operate in joint consultation', since normally neither side wishes to collaborate openly with the other.[42] Whilst inclining towards the external threat thesis, these authors believe that the time 'is long overdue for a greater refinement in our theories of joint consultation, especially in respect of the variation in its extent over time'.[43]

14.6 SUMMARY

Negotiation is a voluntary activity providing employers and unions with autonomy in making industrial relations decisions. The willingness of employers to recognize trade unions for representational purposes is the crucial first step in establishing negotiating machinery. Although historically there have been no direct legal obligations on employers to recognize trade unions, the Employment Protection Act 1975 provided, before their repeal in 1980, a set of procedures by which independent trade unions could seek the assistance of ACAS in obtaining recognition agreements from employers refusing to recognize and negotiate with union representatives in the first instance. In ascertaining the demand for recognition and the extent of actual or potential trade union membership amongst employee groups, ballots or surveys became one, but not the only, established method which enabled ACAS to make recommendations on recognition claims. Underlying this structured approach to determining recognition is the need for the parties to define appropriate bargaining units, bargaining levels and bargaining agents in each case.

The range and scope covered by negotiation are extensive. Rates of pay, hours of work, holiday and sickness payments, and retirement pensions figure prominently in the negotiation process. But working conditions, disciplinary matters and other substantive and procedural issues are also negotiable. The standard work-week, holiday allowances and overtime premia, for example, are determined for many workers by joint negotiation, with systematic overtime continuing for many adult male workers as a means of increasing their weekly earnings, despite the gradual reduction of the standard working week and rising unemployment. Shiftwork allowances are another form of additional payment jointly determined for employees working on a variety of shift systems. Manning levels, grievances, short-time working, and redundancy issues are also open to negotiation between employer and trade union representatives.

Central to joint negotiation is the pay–work bargain. It comprises two elements: the pay rate bargain and the effort bargain. In standard bargaining there is no direct relationship between pay received and work done. In effort bargaining attempts are made to relate employee or workgroup output to the wage payment system, with a successful PBR scheme depending upon fair effort bargaining. Productivity and efficiency bargaining seek to improve employee performance within the negotiation process itself. This has advantages for both management and unions. To be successful, productivity and efficiency bargaining necessitate a favourable bargaining climate between negotiators. Productivity deals, however, are not always acceptable to trade union representatives, especially when their members are threatened by loss of employment due to external economic factors beyond their control.

Negotiation is basically a power relationship. There are a variety of institutional, behavioural and negotiating factors determining the bargaining climate of any negotiation. One of the most important influences is whether the issues between the parties can be resolved by distributive or integrative means. Distributive bargaining is a competitive bargaining situation and a conflict-resolving process conducted on a win–lose basis. Integrative bargaining is a co-operative bargaining situation and a problem-solving process. In either case or in mixed bargaining, the strategies and tactics of negotiation vary. Before joint agreements are concluded, negotiations usually proceed through a number of stages: these are the initial or arguing stage, the exploratory or proposing stage and the consolidation or bargaining stage. The parties then have to implement and monitor the collective agreements jointly arrived at.

Joint consultation is a more diffuse activity and has a more fluctuating history than negotiation. Three types of consultation exist: pseudo-consultation, classical consultation and integrative consultation. Its subject matter includes employee welfare, physical conditions, safety, and changes in production and working methods. There is also evidence to suggest that where it complements negotiation, joint consultation tends to be associated with large plant size, multi-unionism and single employer bargaining.

14.7   REFERENCES

1. Society of Civil and Public Servants, *GCHQ: the Campaign so Far*, CSU and SCPS, London, 1985, p. 3.
2. Employment Protection Act 1975, c. 71, s. 11(2) and 11(3).
3. Advisory Conciliation and Arbitration Service, *Annual Report 1977*, ACAS, London, 1978, p. 47f.
4. Institute of Personnel Management, *Trade Union Recognition*, IPM, London, 1977, p. 24.

5. Trades Union Congress, *Good Industrial Relations*, TUC, London, 1971, p. 18.
6. Pattern of holiday entitlement, *Employment Gazette*, vol. 89(12), December 1981, p. 534.
7. Recent changes in hours and holiday entitlements', *Employment Gazette*, vol. 92(4), April 1984, p. 173.
8. National Board of Prices and Incomes, *Report No. 161. Hours of Work, Overtime and Shiftworking*, HMSO, London, 1970, p. 51.
9. TUC, *op. cit.*, p. 18.
10. C. Fudge, Night and day, *Employment Gazette*, vol. 88(10), October 1980, p. 1120.
11. J. Muir, *Industrial Relations Procedures and Agreements*, Gower, Aldershot, 1981, p. 177.
12. J. Gennard, S. Dunn and M. Wright, The content of closed shop agreements, *Department of Employment Gazette*, vol. 87(11), November 1979, p. 1092.
13. J. Powell, *Work Study*, Arrow Books, London, 1976, p. 70.
14. R.B. McKersie and L.C. Hunter, *Pay, Productivity and Collective Bargaining*, Macmillan, London, 1973, p. 4.
15. H. Behrend, The effort bargain, *Industrial and Labor Relations Review*, July 1957, p. 506.
16. *Ibid.*, p. 505.
17. *Ibid.*, p. 508.
18. R.B. McKersie and L.C. Hunter, *op. cit.*, p. 4f.
19. Royal Commission on Trade Unions and Employers' Associations, *Research Papers 4. 1 Productivity Bargaining, 2 Restrictive Labour Practices*, HMSO, London, 1967, p. 1f.
20. *Ibid.*, p. 27.
21. National Board for Prices and Incomes, *Report No. 123. Productivity Agreements*, HMSO, London, 1968, p. 38.
22. *Ibid.*
23. T. Cliff, *The Employers' Offensive*, Pluto Press, London, 1970, p. 3.
24. G. Kennedy, J. Benson and J. McMillan, *Managing Negotiations*, 2nd ed., Business Books, London, 1984, p. 12.
25. B. Kniveton and B. Towers, *Training for Negotiating*, Business Books, London, 1978, p. 63.
26. Quoted in E. Coker and G. Stuttard (eds.), *Industrial Studies 2: The Bargaining Context*, Arrow Books, London, 1976, p. 46.
27. *Ibid.*, p. 44.
28. P.D. Anthony, *The Conduct of Industrial Relations*, London, IPM, 1977, pp. 227–8.
29. G. Kennedy, J. Benson and J. McMillan, *op. cit.*, p. 20.
30. R.E. Walton and R.B. McKersie, *A Behavioral Theory of Labor Negotiations*, McGraw-Hill, New York, 1965, p. 6.
31. P. Warr, *Psychology and Collective Bargaining*, Hutchinson, London, 1973, p. 24f.
32. G. Kennedy, J. Benson and J. McMillan, *op. cit.*, p. 122.
33. Quoted in Coker and Stuttard, *op. cit.*, p. 58.
34. W.R. Hawes and C.C.P. Brookes, Change and renewal: joint consultation in industry, *Employment Gazette*, vol. 88(4), April 1980, p. 356.
35. Institute of Personnel Management, *Practical Participation and Involvement. 2 Representative Structures*, IPM, London, 1981, p. 8.
36. W.E.J. McCarthy, *Royal Commission on Trade Unions and Employers' Associations Research Papers 1. The Role of Shop Stewards in British Industrial Relations*, HMSO, London, 1968, p. 36.
37. H.A. Clegg and T.E. Chester, Joint consultation in A. Flanders and H.A. Clegg (eds.), *The System of Industrial Relations in Great Britain*, Blackwell, Oxford, 1967, p. 324.
38. J. Henderson, *The Case for Joint Consultation*, Industrial Society, London, 1970, p. 18.
39. IPM (1981), *op. cit.*, p. 105.
40. Department of Employment, *Code of Industrial Relations Practice*, DE, London, 1972, p. 17.
41. P.B. Beaumont and D.R. Deaton, Joint consultative arrangements in Britain, *Journal of Management Studies*, vol. 18(1), 1981, pp. 62 and 68.
42. P. Joyce and A. Woods, Joint consultation in Britain: results of a recent survey during recession, *Employee Relations*, 6(3), 1984, p. 2.
43. *Ibid.*, p. 6.

PART FIVE

Conclusion

15

Industrial Relations and the Changing Balance of Power

This final chapter draws some tentative but brief conclusions about the main trends in British industrial relations and their wider economic, political and social implications. We do this by focusing initially on the maturing of Britain's industrial relations institutions up to 1979. We then briefly explore the impact of the economic and political changes which have taken place in Britain since 1979 on employers and unions.

Britain has experienced two distinct periods in the development and growth of its industrial relations institutions and practices since the end of the Second World War. The first period was one of comparative economic prosperity, relatively low unemployment and broad political consensus between 1945 and the election of the Conservative Thatcher Government in 1979. It was characterized by two main features. First, there was a maturing and institutionalization of industrial relations practices focused on workplace and employer bargaining and the establishment of procedures in industrial relations. Second, it was underpinned by aggressive, reactive and powerful trade unions which were periodically incorporated into government policy making.

Between the end of the Second World War and 1979, the strength of the British labour movement expanded generally and the power of the trade unions increased particularly. This growth in union power was demonstrated by a number of clearly observable trends. First, there was a substantial growth in trade union membership amongst manual workers, white-collar employees, public sector employees and middle and lower managers, reflected in some cases by the extension of the closed shop. By the late 1970s, for example, trade union density had passed the 50 per cent level. Second, there was an extension of collective bargaining in employing organizations and at workplace level. This in turn led to a decrease in managerial power to make decisions unilaterally without at least obtaining some degree of trade union co-operation and consent. Third, this period also saw a very substantial growth in the number of workplace trade union representatives and their increasing participation in managerial decision making and day-to-day administration at the workplace. Fourth, there was a growth of governmental intervention in almost every aspect of the national economy which closely involved the trade unions. Also, for nearly three decades, the TUC exercised a powerful influence over most national economic policies. It became possibly the most important organization to be influenced if attempts at establishing workable and lasting incomes policies were to succeed. Fifth, after the repeal of the Industrial Relations Act by the Labour Government in 1974, employment laws were enacted which were clearly advantageous to the trade unions collectively and to trade unionists and workers individually.

The 'new industrial relations' in the relatively short period since 1979 have been epitomized by more assertive management, 'union realism' and government hawkishness, with, paradoxically, a depoliticizing of industrial relations in which the economic market-place has become more important, only temporarily perhaps, than the political market-place. At the same time, union power has become greatly weakened, industrial relations initiatives have swung towards management, and the unions have been effectively excluded from influencing governmental policy making and threatened by economic recession. Indeed, the period since 1979 could possibly mark a turning point in Britain's economic and political situations with their obvious implications for industrial relations. Indications of this recent shift in direction include: declining prosperity and low economic growth; falling real wages for many groups; high unemployment; reductions in public expenditure; and a changing balance of power in industrial relations away from employees and their trade unions in favour of employers and management. Clearly, these changes could be short-lived and a return to the pattern of economic events and industrial relations characterizing the 1950s, 1960s and 1970s could follow a change in government or of economic policy. On the other hand, Britain could be entering a new and distinct period of economic, industrial and social change from which there is no turning back. If this is so, then it will have a profound impact on Britain's future pattern of industrial relations.

15.1   THE MATURATION OF BRITISH INDUSTRIAL RELATIONS

The maturation of British industrial relations in the post-war period up to 1979 was exemplified by three main features: first, the evolutionary and conservative nature of its institutions; second, the increasing complexity and diversity of its practices; and third, the growing specialization of its organizations and participants. During these years the development of British institutions and practices such as collective bargaining, managerial behaviour, trade unionism and governmental agencies was deeply influenced by their history.

Unlike other industrialized countries, Britain has had over 300 years of comparative internal political stability and over 200 years of continuous industrial change. Parallel to these developments was a series of occupational and social changes. These were initiated piecemeal in the context of nineteenth century liberal political economy but they matured within the contrasting circumstances of mid twentieth century welfare state capitalism.

In the middle of the nineteenth century, for instance, local and district collective bargaining between employers and trade unions originated and developed on a fragmented basis in a number of craft trades, such as engineering and shipbuilding, and in other non-craft industries like coalmining and cotton textiles. In response to the inter-war economic depression, local bargaining gave way in most cases to national level or industry-wide bargaining between national employers' associations and federations of trade unions. But with changing economic circumstances in the 1950s and 1960s, company and workplace bargaining between managers and shop stewards increasingly became the standard practice for determining actual pay and conditions in much of manufacturing industry. During the mid 1970s, centrally determined incomes policies, and 'Social Contracts' struck between Governments and the Trades Unions Congress (TUC), effectively neutralized collective pay determination at national employer and local levels, although it was only short lived.

Union growth in Britain has also emerged pragmatically from different occupational and industrial bases. The early locally based craft societies, for example, became nationally organized by the mid nineteenth century in response to the industrial, economic and social changes facing them. Some of these unions, such as the engineering and building workers, continued to increase in size by opening up their membership boundaries and by subsequently amalgamating and merging amongst themselves, especially after the 1920s. More recently, in the 1960s and 1970s, white collar unionism spread amongst new groups of employees, such as clerical and administrative workers, that had no deep traditions of trade union membership or workgroup solidarity. Such pragmatic and evolutionary changes within the institutions of collective bargaining and trade unionism reflected not only their inherent stability but also their essential traditionalism. They also revealed the distrust of radical innovation in industrial relations practices amongst its participants.

The complexity of post-war industrial relations within a plural society like Britain was shown by the variety of views which permeated it and by the contrasting practices which characterized it. The Marxist perspective of industrial relations, for example, is as different from the unitary perspective as the latter is from the pluralist position. Industrial relations policy making therefore – whether at governmental level, within companies, or within trade unions – has been continuously bedevilled by policy and ideological conflicts amongst individuals and groups with differing perceptions concerning the nature and scope of industrial relations decision making in British society. However, the multiplicity of economic, legal, political, and social forces which have impinged on industrial relations participants and their organizations make simplistic and purely ideological explanations of industrial relations practices and phenomena inadequate. Moreover, despite the wide range and scope of industrial relations practices which continue to exist – such as different collective bargaining structures, specific procedures, and contrasting trade union types – their adaptation to particular circumstances has varied enormously.

The maturation of industrial relations, certainly up to 1979, was also reflected in the increasing specialization of its organizations and in the growing professionalization of industrial relations roles. Both trade unions and employers' associations, for example, developed increasingly wide ranging services to their members including research, legal, information and training facilities. The rapidly accepted functions of bodies such as the Advisory Conciliation and Arbitration Service (ACAS) and industrial tribunals also illustrated the growing fragmentation and specialization of industrial relations institutions. Equally, the increasing numbers of personnel managers, safety officers, shop stewards and industrial relations officers appointed during the 1960s and 1970s were further indicators of the growing complexity of industrial relations decision making and of role specialization within it.

One of the major changes affecting employers and management in industrial relations during this period was the growing size of employment units. This led to the standardization of employment practices between some larger companies and public sector organizations. The consistent application of employment policies and industrial relations procedures within such enterprises and their workplaces had some positive benefits for management, employees and workgroups. But it was sometimes offset by the disadvantage of inflexibly applying policies and procedures in particular cases. Indeed, the bureaucratization of industrial relations policy making and its application, it is claimed, sometimes raised the level of industrial conflict between management and subordinate employees rather than reduced it. It certainly increased the propensity for subordinate employees to unionize.

Growing interest was also shown by some higher level managements in the organization and administration of industrial relations within their enterprises. The major impetus for this change in managerial emphasis almost certainly derived from the impact of the labour law enacted during the 1970s. One result of this legislation and the presence of industrial tribunals was the increasing pressure on top management to devise appropriate personnel policies and industrial relations procedures at employer level so as to comply with legal requirements, particularly affecting the recruitment, selection, payment, disciplining, and dismissal of subordinate employees. Closely related to management's growing concern with industrial relations professionalism was the emergence of specialist personnel managers within private sector and public sector enterprises. These were recruited to advise on the development and execution of effective personnel policies within their employing organizations.

At a time when line management was showing a preference for dealing with shop stewards and shopfloor representatives at the workplace, it was paradoxical that some lower level managerial employees were themselves becoming trade union members. This created a dilemma for top management as to whether to recognize such unions for negotiating purposes. It also raised the question for managerial trade unionists where their first loyalties lay: was it with their unions or with management? The overall picture which emerged, therefore, was of the steady liberalization of the employer-employee relationship. Moreover, until the end of the 1970s, with the slow challenge to the right to manage, with the growth of joint regulation, and with increased job security for employees resulting from labour law and trade union strength, there seemed to be a falling off in managerial confidence and in management control in parts of private and public industry. These trends, in part, were underpinned by the growing interest shown by some politicians and trade union leaders in industrial democracy and worker participation in board level decision making.

During the 1960s and 1970s, the trade union movement also had to adapt itself to change and external pressures. Union density increased and trade unions grew in membership size by amalgamation and merger. It was the emergence and growth of white collar trade unionism which was one of the most outstanding trade union developments of the 1960s and 1970s. Nevertheless, substantial non-unionized areas of employment, especially in the small-scale private sector and private services, remained. Another trend within the trade unions was the steady expansion in the numbers and activities of shop stewards and safety representatives at the workplace. Moreover, important new legal rights could be claimed by independent trade unions and their members which further strengthened the power base of trade unionism in industry and in society.

Increasing union size, however, did nothing to mitigate the industrial relations problems associated with multi-unionism and internal union democracy. Continual technological change and the changing structure of employment highlighted the widening incongruence between the rapidly evolving structure of industry, on the one hand, and the ossified structure of British trade unionism on the other. The advent of fewer large unions, therefore, did not in itself improve inter-union relations at the workplace. It was the pragmatic and *ad hoc* structures initiated by shop stewards within factories and offices which provided the day-to-day means for inter-union co-operation at the place of work, and for grassroots democracy within the trade union movement. At the same time, there is little evidence to suggest that shop stewards were generally integrated into their official trade union hierarchies. Nor was the branch normally the focal point of rank and file union activity. For most trade unionists, the shop steward was 'the union' which partly explains the conflict existing between the official union movement and some of its rank and file activists during these years.

As far as collective bargaining of pay and working conditions was concerned, the major trend during the 1960s and 1970s was the preference amongst practitioners for employer and workplace bargaining. To what extent pay bargaining at employer and workplace level was compatible with near permanent incomes policies at that time is questionable. Indeed, there is little doubt that part of the large scale reaction by trade unionists against the centrally regulated incomes policies of the middle and late 1970s derived from the threat which continual pay restraint posed both to decentralized pay bargaining outcomes and to traditional pay differentials. Nevertheless, the growth of domestic and local bargaining was facilitated by the negotiation of local procedures on the lines recommended by the Donovan Commission. Similarly, greater formalization of workplace industrial relations practices took place partly through the encouragement of ACAS and by the services which it provided for managements and trade unionists at enterprise level. Also important were ACAS's codes of practice and the disclosure of information and time off provisions embodied in the 1975 and 1978 Employment Protection Acts.

Other areas of industrial relations which became increasingly regulated by collective agreement included: health and safety at work; closed shop agreements; productivity-pay links; pension schemes; sick pay; maternity leave and maternity pay; flexible working hours; time off for trade union duties and training; and a slowly widening range of fringe benefits. Because of continuous pay policies and inflation, however, the pay bargaining process was frequently constrained by a variety of incomes policies. One result of this was that pay differentials were often squeezed, thus accelerating the reduction of pay differences between skilled and less-skilled workers which had been continuous since the last war.

Whether collective bargaining during these years became more sophisticated than hitherto is arguable. At the same time, where employees and workgroups were strongly organized, custom and practice remained a major method of workgroup control against managerial authority. Overall, however, the increasing scope of collective bargaining and of the subject matter covered by it clearly challenged established managerial prerogatives during this period. The main implication for managers was their growing willingness to develop a style of management by agreement with employees and their unions. For the unions, such developments necessitated higher levels of expertise and training among their workplace representatives, which they proceeded to provide.

Although the combined effect of changes in the balance of industrial and political power between employers and unions in the period 1945–79 must not be exaggerated, the trade union position at the bargaining table was greatly enhanced in relative terms by economic prosperity and government policy. Nevertheless, government and employers still possessed a clear dominance of economic and social power over organized labour if they chose to use it. They did not do so probably because of the prevailing social ethos and the political circumstances of the time. These reflected the general view that the trade union movement was approaching the peak of its power and that it would use this power both wisely and unselfishly in the national interest. By the end of the 1970s, however, many doubted if this was actually taking place. Furthermore, some were expressing the contrary view that the involvement by government, powerfully supported by national organizations of employers and trade unions, in almost every aspect of the national economy would lead to a corporate state or one controlled by government in association with the powerful interests of society, giving individual citizens very little control over their daily lives. Added to this, there was growing concern that the interventionist endeavours of successive governments to improve the performance, productivity and competitiveness of British industry and the economy had achieved very little. The standard of living enjoyed by the inhabitants of our major competitive trading nations continuously outstripped that of Britain's, for example, whilst governmental intervention, Keynesian economic policy and trade union power, it was claimed, had apparently not found the key to sustained economic prosperity and growth. These themes were sucessfully exploited by the Conservative Party, led by Margaret Thatcher, at the 1979 General Election.

15.2   DEVELOPMENTS SINCE 1979

The Conservative Government elected to office in May 1979 expounded a totally different set of economic and social ideologies from that of previous post-war administrations. The largely, if somewhat patchy, consensus politics of the previous 35 years was to be severely modified. The 'new' Conservatism challenged the concept and the expansion of the welfare state, the operation of Keynesian economic controls to secure full employment, high levels of public expenditure and governmental intervention in the 'supply side' of the economy. The impact of these fundamental changes on industrial relations, trade unions and the employer-employee relationship was to be considerable. Anxieties about the previously emerging corporate state soon vanished, and new fears about the social and political consequences of the emergence of this new *laissez-faire* capitalism began to emerge.

The new economic ideology and its policies were based upon the theory that inflation and industrial decline were the result of the 'old economics' of the post-war period. This 'monetarist' approach to economic policy making claimed that Britain's economic ills resulted from a number of factors. These included: decades of Keynesian 'mis-management' of the economy; inadequate control of the money supply; high levels of public expenditure; trade union restrictive practices at the workplace; overmanning; overpriced wages; increases in money wages not matched by productivity; poor price and quality competitiveness; too much reliance on subsidies from government; and too much governmental intervention in the economy. Radical economic policies and new employment legislation which it was believed would help reverse Britain's inflation and relative industrial decline were introduced after 1979, such as the Employment Acts 1980 and 1982 and the Trade Union Act 1984. Further, the public was told that the Government's policies would not be relaxed despite any anguish or suffering that would follow. Indeed, the Government claimed, a long period of difficult and painful economic and industrial readjustment might have to be endured before a genuine recovery began.

The results of these new policies soon emerged: unemployment rose to over three million with young people, women and black people disproportionately represented within it; the number of bankruptcies increased sharply; manufacturing industrial capacity fell markedly as firms closed down or reduced both manpower and output; interest rates were held at previously unknown levels in order to facilitate the Government's monetary policy; and levels of provision fell in education, the social services, health care and many other areas as public and social expenditure was reduced. All this was accompanied by slowly falling inflation; greatly increased compe-titiveness in the labour market; steadily falling money wage settlements; loss of trade union membership as unemployment increased; a weakening of union bargaining power; an increase of employee work loads; and greater labour flexibility as producti-vity generally improved. These changes also coincided with the introduction of the new technology of microelectronics into some sectors of the economy which threatened many conventional jobs. Evidence of deep social stress began to emerge in the inner city areas and amongst the more vulnerable members and weaker groups of society. Whilst the Government drew attention to the world wide recession against which the new policies were being implemented, and repeatedly claimed that evidence of Britain's slow economic recovery was clearly discernible, this optimistic view was never shared by the Confederation of British Industry, the TUC, major investors or the majority of independent economic forecasters.

Against this background of almost bewilderingly rapid political, economic and legal change, the nature of industrial relations between employers and unions, and manage-ment and employees, began a period of readjustment which has continued till the present time. The major influences on private sector employers were market forces, government economic policy, the new technologies and a rising pool of unemployed labour. For those manufacturing firms selling and competing in international markets, the pressures were particularly intense, with many losing business, shedding labour and some going into receivership. Further, government economic policy based on high interest rates, tight control of the money supply and cutbacks in real levels of public spending put additional strains on the ability of marginal firms to survive in increasingly difficult economic circumstances as national output and aggregate demand fell.

Because of these radical changes in the economic environment, employers became very cost conscious seeking to reduce total and unit labour costs, to maintain their national and international market positions and to ensure the economic and financial survival of their companies. Managements, in general, began at first to halt and then to reverse the influence which shop stewards and trade unions had earlier exerted over managerial policy decisions and the day-to-day running of factories and offices. They also began: to reduce manpower by a combination of redundancy and natural wastage; to change working methods; to alter job descriptions; to introduce new plants and machinery; to increase work loads and work speeds; and to tighten up workplace discipline. Some managers also re-established their unitary views of the enterprise by adopting traditional authoritarian methods of employee control again, as well as resisting the pay and procedural claims of trade union officers, shop stewards and militant workgroups. Against a background of so-called 'macho' management, abrasive government policies, new employment legislation and rising unemployment, the trade unions and their members either fought unconvincing industrial action or retreated carefully step by step from further industrial confrontation.

The swing in the balance of bargaining power back to private sector employers away from the trade unions and employees was not only reflected in the re-emergence of tougher styles of management. There was a general reassertion of managerial confidence and of the right to manage in many firms. Some employers, especially in the private sector, became increasingly unwilling to recognize trade unions, whilst a few others even sought derecognition policies by adopting 'union busting' tactics imported from North America. Employers were also more likely than in the past to create communication channels which bypassed the trade unions and their representatives, by using briefing groups, quality circles, and 'direct' communication techniques including videos, personal 'chats' from managing directors and letters sent straight to the homes of employees. By minimizing the importance of formal trade union lines of communication, some managements were capitalizing on the perceived weakness of trade unions and the fears of further job losses by their members.

If many private sector employers adopted the 'short circuiting' approach to employees and their unions, public sector employers took, in general, a much more assertive and aggressive line. After 1979 a series of bitter and often protracted industrial disputes took place in the public sector. Some of the areas affected were: the steel industry; the National Health Service; the railways; the civil service; coalmining; and school teaching. These arose in essence out of radical changes in government policy towards the objectives, financing, organization and managing of public sector enterprises, initiated by the administrations led by Margaret Thatcher after the elections of 1979 and 1983. The main measures taken by government affecting industrial relations between public sector employers, their employees and their unions included: cuts in levels of public spending; cash limits within which pay was to be determined; privatization and the abolition of certain public authorities such as the metropolitan county councils; and the introduction of general management practices into public service organizations such as the National Health Service. All these measures resulted, to varying degrees, in conflict between public sector employers and the unions representing their members, as well as a decline in morale and motivation amongst public sector workers at all levels.

Technological changes affecting work processes and relations between employers and their workforces also took place at this time. Electronic data processing by mainframe computers had been followed by the development of microelectronic integrated circuits (MICs) cramming the processing power of large computers onto very small devices at very low costs. This made it possible to modify any product or process involving elements of measurement, control, data processing, storage or recall. Increasingly, MICs were used to create new products; modify existing ones; control manufacturing processes; increase the versatility of design processes; and process, store and analyse data automatically sensed and stored. Such technology resulted, amongst other things, in better machine control; better and quicker information; improved machine programming; and reduced labour costs. Preliminary evidence suggests that most managements adopting the new technologies made little attempt to manage the resultant changes proactively – they were just expected to happen. The focus was largely on their technological aspects, leaving problems affecting work organization and the human aspects of change to be dealt with later.

The continuous introduction of new technology called into question the need for traditional occupational skills. In much of manufacturing and service industry the increasing use of computerized technology led to widespread debate about how the natural fears of employees about its effects on their working lives could be accommodated without loss of economic efficiency. In many instances, especially where major changes such as closures or changes in skill mixes were involved, the interests of employers and employees were not easily reconcilable and are unlikely to be so in the future. The skills required in both older industries and new ones continued to change, with new occupations requiring different aptitudes and experience. They brought with them demands for greater adaptability by managers and employees, for greater flexibility in the use of manpower and for new approaches to training and retraining.

Overall, it would appear, the period after 1979 provided both opportunities and costs for management. On the one hand, it claimed back the right to manage and its decision making authority in those areas where this had been eroded and weakened. In doing this it reasserted control and leadership within its enterprises. On the other hand, the often radical economic, technological and organizational changes resulting from these managerial initiatives seemed to do little to improve genuine employee motivation and morale or whole-hearted commitment to corporate goals and objectives. A silent resentful acceptance of these changes was probably more common, with some convergence of private sector and public sector industrial relations practices. It is certainly doubtful whether public sector employers could any longer uphold their previous claim and policy of being 'model employers'. The harsh economic and political realities of the period had effectively changed this.

For the unions, the post-1979 period was also a very difficult one. They suffered large membership losses of some two million members between 1979 and 1985, resulting from economic recession and rising unemployment, often hostile and assertive managerial behaviour and forceful government economic and legal policies. Reductions in union income put pressure on smaller unions to merge with larger ones and were instrumental in making unions undertake cost cutting exercises and reappraisals of their financial management procedures. Internal financial pressures also led some unions, such as the engineers, the electricians and plumbers and some smaller organizations, to force the TUC to reconsider its policy of requiring affiliates not to accept government cash to fund membership postal ballots.

Changes in employment legislation also promoted modifications to union rule books, such as those covering elections to union governing bodies and the role of secret ballots in union policy making. One byproduct of the extension of membership participation in some unions was increased factionalism amongst different political groupings, with first one faction then another taking control of their union's decision making bodies. Changes in the law relating to political fund rules, however, resulted in substantial majorities in each case for retaining existing provisions, thus reinforcing links between the Labour Party and its affiliated organizations. Increased attention was also paid within some unions to the legal provisions requiring secret ballots before industrial action and the periodic reapproval of closed shop agreements.

Union leadership in the 1980s vacillated between outright confrontation to the 'new' industrial relations, such as tougher managerial styles and the new employment laws, and a 'new realism' which was pragmatic, moderate and realistic in its outlook. Most of the younger generation of union leaders emerging at this time belonged to the latter rather than to the former school. They were anxious to protect and defend their members' jobs and employment interests by skilful persuasion and caution rather than by outright militancy and obduracy. Certainly there was a change in the balance of power within the unions, with the shop steward role becoming weakened and atomized and power moving to the organizational centre of most trade unions. Additionally, with fear of unemployment and further job losses, many union members became less willing to take collective industrial action against their employers and adopted conciliatory negotiating stances in collective bargaining.

The underlying trend in industrial relations after 1979 was change – in economic and legal policy affecting industrial relations; in technological developments; in employer, union and employee attitudes; and in managerial–union relations. By the mid 1980s, the economic recession gripping British industry since the late 1970s continued to influence most employment sectors. Unemployment which affected about one in 30 of the working population in the mid 1970s was the experience of one in seven of the working population 10 years later. By the mid 1980s, employment in manufacturing industries was 20 per cent below that of 1980 and was the sector which had borne the brunt of economic hardship during the intervening period. By 1986, there were few signs that any major increase in employment in the economy as a whole was likely; parts of Britain such as the older manufacturing centres were particularly hard hit.

A major feature of the new employment laws created in 1980, 1982 and 1984 was the way in which they provided for the organizations and individuals directly affected by them, rather than government or the state, to initiate legal actions against those failing to meet their provisions. By the mid 1980s it was noticeable that there was growing awareness both by some employers and some unions of the ways in which collective labour law might affect their actions. There appeared to be a significant increase in the volume of legal actions about industrial relations brought by employers, unions and individuals. Employers were often successful in the courts, especially when seeking injunctions, whilst certain trade unions sought the protection of the courts against managerial actions threatening the terms and conditions of their members or their union membership rights. Whether these developments further undermined the spirit of industrial relations 'voluntarism' remains to be seen, but after 1979 Parliament's introduction of a complex series of new statutory provisions significantly changed the framework of the law within which managements and unions operated.

In private sector pay bargaining, the economic problems facing larger companies continued to lead many of them to devolve negotiations to establishment level, where closer links between pay and unit performance could be established. Although multi-employer arrangements continued to be significant in some sectors, the focus of bargaining and consultation moved generally to local level within companies and plants. Whilst some employers continued to expand consultative arrangements with their employees, more radical extensions of employee involvement in corporate decision making were distinctly absent. In the public sector, increasing divergence with levels of pay settlement in the private sector caused constant frustration and dissatisfaction amongst public sector employees, with progress towards bargaining reform slow and protracted.

Hours of work were also widely discussed. Whilst the unions wanted substantial reductions in the length of the working week, employers wanted any reductions to be offset by improvements in output and cost effectiveness, with compensating increases in labour flexibility. Industrial relations procedures, notably in grievance handling, discipline and dismissal, were however extended in their application and scope after 1979. Another development was that of sole bargaining or single union agreements between some employers and a few unions. These provided sole negotiating rights for the union and joint procedures for the avoidance of industrial action through a commitment by both parties to binding arbitration in the event of disputes between them. They were mainly negotiated in the new technology industries, often when employers recognized unions for the first time. Some interest was also expressed in agreements involving 'pendulum' or 'straight choice' arbitration in which an independent arbitrator is required to make a clear choice between competing claims put forward by the parties.

If these are the major changes which took place after 1979, the question remains how permanent they are and whether or not they are reversible should a new and very different government come to power. It is, of course, possible that what one government has done, another can undo by changing the law and by returning to a pattern of economic policy making and a climate of industrial relations negotiating such as prevailed until the late 1970s. Should the present very high level of unemployment persist, however, it would be extremely difficult to challenge the renewed confidence of managements in their dealings with employees and unions. This would continue to reduce the influence and bargaining power of shop stewards and trade union officials, whilst increasing that of employers and management. Continuing changes in the structure of the economy could further weaken trade union organization. Such conditions could well sustain the 'new industrial relations' which emerged between employers and employees after 1979, rather than reverse them.

Select Bibliography

Advisory Conciliation and Arbitration Service (Annual), *Annual Report*, London, ACAS.

Advisory Conciliation and Arbitration Service (1977), *Code of Practice. Disciplinary practice and procedures in employment*, London, HMSO.

Advisory Conciliation and Arbitration Service (1977), *Code of Practice 2. Disclosure of information for collective bargaining purposes*, London, HMSO.

Advisory Conciliation and Arbitration Service (1977), *Code of Practice 3. Time off for trade union duties and activities*, London, HMSO.

Advisory Conciliation and Arbitration Service (1980), *Industrial Relations Handbook*, London, HMSO.

Anthony, P. D. (1977), *The Conduct of Industrial Relations*, London, Institute of Personnel Management.

Armstrong, P. J., Goodman, J. F. B., and Hyman, J. D. (1981), *Ideology and Shop-floor Industrial Relations*, London, Croom Helm.

Ashdown, R. T., and Baker, K. H. (1973), *Department of Employment Manpower Papers Number 6. In Working Order: a study of industrial discipline*, London, HMSO.

Bain, G. S. (1970), *The Growth of White-Collar Unionism*, Oxford, Oxford University Press.

Bain, G. S. (ed.) (1983), *Industrial Relations in Britain*, Oxford, Blackwell.

Bain, G. S., and Price, R. (1980), *Profiles of Union Growth: a Comparative Statistical Portrait of Eight Countries*, Oxford, Blackwell.

Barnes, D., and Reid, E. (1980), *Governments and Trade Unions*, London, Heinemann.

Barrett, B., Rhodes, E., and Beishon. J. (ed.) (1975), *Industrial Relations and the Wider Society*, London, Collier Macmillan.

Batstone, E., Boraston, I., and Frenkel, S. (1977), *Shop Stewards in Action*, Oxford, Blackwell.

Batstone, E., Boraston, I., and Frenkel, S. (1978), *The Social Organization of Strikes*, Oxford, Blackwell.

Batstone, E., Ferner, A., and Terry, M. (1984), *Consent and Efficiency*, Oxford, Blackwell.

Beaumont, P. (1981), *Government as an Employer: Setting an Example*, London, Royal Institute of Public Administration.

Blackaby, F. (ed.) (1980), *The Future of Pay Bargaining*, London, Heinemann.

Boraston, I., Clegg, H. A., and Rimmer, M. (1975), *Workplace and Union*, London, Heinemann.

Bradley, K., and Gelb, A. (1983), *Worker Capitalism: the New Industrial Relations*, London, Heinemann.

Brewster, C., and Connock, S. (1985), *Industrial Relations: Cost Effective Strategies*, London, Hutchinson.

Brown, H. P. (1983), *The Origins of Trade Union Power*, Oxford, Oxford University Press.

Brown, W. (ed.) (1981), *The Changing Contours of British Industrial Relations*, Oxford, Blackwell.

Central Arbitration Committee (Annual), *Annual Report*, London, HMSO.

Certification Office for Trade Unions and Employers' Associations (Annual), *Annual Report of the Certification Officer*, London, HMSO.

Child, J. (ed.) (1973), *Man and Organization*, London, Allen and Unwin.

Clegg, H. A. (1971), *How to Run an Incomes Policy*, London, Heinemann.

Clegg, H. A. (1979), *The Changing System of Industrial Relations in Britain*, Oxford, Blackwell.

Clegg, H. A., Fox, A., and Thompson, A. F. (1964), *A History of British Trade Unions since 1889*, Oxford, Oxford University Press.

Coates, K., and Topham, T. (1980), *Trade Unions in Britain*, Nottingham, Spokesman.

Commission on Industrial Relations (1972), *CIR Study 1. Employers' Organisations and Industrial Relations*, London, HMSO.

Commission on Industrial Relations (1973), *Report No. 34. The Role of Management in Industrial Relations*, London, HMSO.

Commission on Industrial Relations (1974), *Report No. 85. Industrial Relations in Multi-plant Undertakings*, London, HMSO.

Confederation of British Industry (1977), *In Place of Bullock*, London, CBI.

Confederation of British Industry (1977), *The Future of Pay Determination*, London, CBI.

Confederation of British Industry (1979), *Pay: The Choice Ahead*, London, CBI.

Confederation of British Industry (1980), *Trade Unions in a Changing World*, London, CBI.

Creedy, J. (ed.) (1981), *The Economics of Unemployment in Great Britain*, London, Butterworth.

Creedy, J., and Thomas, R. B. (ed.) (1982), *The Labour Market in Britain*, London, Butterworth.

Crouch, C. (1979), *The Politics of Industrial Relations*, London, Fontana. ·

Crouch, C. (1982), *Trade Unions: The Logic of Collective Action*, London, Fontana.

Currie, R. (1979), *Industrial Politics*, Oxford, Clarendon.

Daniel, W. W., and Millward, N. (1983), *Workplace Industrial Relations in Britain*, London, Heinemann.

Department of Employment (1972), *Industrial Relations Code of Practice*, London, HMSO.

Department of Employment (1980), *Code of Practice on Closed Shop Agreements and Arrangements*, London, HMSO.

Department of Employment (1980), *Code of Practice on Picketing*, London, HMSO.

Department of Trade (1977), *Report of the Committee of Inquiry on Industrial Democracy*, London, HMSO.

Dunlop, J. T. (1958), *Industrial Relations Systems*, Carbondale, Southern Illinois University Press.

Dunn, S., and Gennard, J. (1984), *The Closed Shop in British Industry*, London, Macmillan.

Durcan, J., *et al.* (1983), *Strikes in Post-War Britain*, London, Allen and Unwin.

Ellis, V. (1981), *The Role of Trade Unions in the Promotion of Equal Opportunities*, Manchester, Equal Opportunities Commission.

Evans, A. (1979), *What next at Work?* London, Institute of Personnel Management.

Fallick, J., and Elliott, R. F. (1981), *Incomes Policies, Inflation and Relative Pay*, London, Allen and Unwin.

Farnham, D. (1984), *Personnel in Context*, London, Institute of Personnel Management.

Flanders, A. D. (1970), *Management and Unions: The Theory and Reform of Industrial Relations*, London, Faber.

Fox, A. (1971), *A Sociology of Work in Industry*, London, Collier Macmillan.

Fox, A. (1974), *Man Mismanagement*, London, Hutchinson.

Fox, A. (1985), *History and Heritage*, London, Allen and Unwin.

Friedrichs, G., and Schaff, A. (eds.) (1982), *Microelectronics and Society*, London, Pergamon.

Gennard, J. (1977), *Financing Strikers*, London, Macmillan.

Goodman, J. F. B., and Whittingham, T. G. (1969), *Shop Stewards in British Industry*, London, McGraw-Hill.

Grant, W., and Marsh, D. (1977), *The Confederation of British Industry*, London, Hodder and Stoughton.

Guest, D., and Fatchett, D. (1974), *Worker Participation: Individual Control and Performance*, London, Institute of Personnel Management.

Guest, D., and Horwood, R. (1980), *The Role and Effectiveness of Personnel Managers*, London, London School of Economics.

Guest, D., and Horwood, R. (1982), *Success and Satisfaction in Personnel Management*, London, London School of Economics.

Guest, D., and Kenny, T. (eds.) (1983), *A Textbook of Techniques and Strategies in Personnel Management*, London, Institute of Personnel Management.

Hawkins, K. (1976), *British Industrial Relations 1945–1975*, London, Barrie and Jenkins.

Hawkins, K. (1981), *Trade Unions*, London, Hutchinson.

Hepple, B., and O'Higgins, P. (1981), *Employment Law*, (4th ed.), London, Sweet and Maxwell.

Hunter, L. C., and Mulvey, C. (1981), *Economics of Wages and Labour*, London, Macmillan.

Hyman, R. (1972), *Strikes*, London, Fontana.

Hyman, R. (1975), *Industrial Relations: A Marxist Introduction*, London, Longmans.

Hyman, R., and Brough, I. (1975), *Social Values and Industrial Relations*, Oxford, Blackwell.

Jenkins, C., and Sherman, B. (1977), *Collective Bargaining*, London, Routledge and Kegan Paul.

Kahn-Freund, O. (1977), *Labour and the Law*, London, Stevens.

Kahn-Freund, O. (1979), *Labour Relations: Heritage and Adjustment*, Oxford, Oxford University Press.

Keenoy, T. (1984), *Invitation to Industrial Relations*, Oxford, Blackwell.

Kennedy, G., Benson, J., and McMillan, J. (1984), *Managing Negotiations*, London, Business Books.

Legge, K. (1978), *Power, Innovation and Problem Solving in Personnel Management*, London, McGraw-Hill.

Lewis, D. (1983), *Essentials of Employment Law*, London, Institute of Personnel Management.

Lewis, R., Davies, P., and Wedderburn, K. W. (1979), *Industrial Relations Law and the Conservative Government*, London, Fabian Society.

Lewis, R., and Simpson, B. (1981), *Striking a Balance? Employment Law after the 1980 Act*, Oxford, Martin Robertson.

Lockyear, J. (1979), *Industrial Arbitration in Great Britain*, London, Institute of Personnel Management.

Lovell, J., and Roberts, B. C. (1968), *A Short History of the TUC*, London, Macmillan.

McCarthy, W. E. J., and Ellis, N. D. (1973), *Management by Agreement*, London, Hutchinson.

Marchington, M. (1982), *Managing Industrial Relations*, Maidenhead, McGraw-Hill.

Marsh, A. I. (1966), *Royal Commission on Trade Unions and Employers' Associations Research Papers. 2 (Part 1) Disputes Procedures in British Industry*, London, HMSO.

Marsh, A. I. (1979), *Concise Encyclopaedia of Industrial Relations*, London, Gower Press.

Marsh, A. I. (1982), *Employee Relations Policy and Decision Making*, Aldershot, Gower.

Martin, R. M. (1980), TUC, *The Growth of a Pressure Group 1868–1976*, Oxford, Clarendon.

Moran, M. (1977), *The Politics of Industrial Relations*, London, Macmillan.

Morley, I. E., and Stephenson, G. M. (1977), *The Social Psychology of Bargaining*, London, Allen and Unwin.

Musson, A. E. (1972), *British Trade Unions 1800–1875*, London, Macmillan.

Muir, J. (1981), *Industrial Relations Procedures and Agreements*, London, Gower.

Parker, P. A. L., Hawes, W. R., and Lumb, A. L. (1971), *Department of Employment Manpower Papers Number 3. The Reform of Collective Bargaining at Plant and Company Level*, London, HMSO.

Poole, M., *et al.* (1984), *Industrial Relations in the Future: Trends and possibilities in Britain over the next decade*, London, Routledge and Kegan Paul.

Purcell, J. (1981), *Good Industrial Relations: Theory and Practice*, London, Macmillan.

Purcell, J., and Smith, R. (eds.) (1981), *The Control of Work*, London, Macmillan.

Ramsey, J. C., and Hill, J. M. (1974), *Collective Agreements*, London, Institute of Personnel Management.

Richter, I. (1973), *Political Purpose in Trade Unions*, London, Allen and Unwin.

Royal Commission on Trade Unions and Employers' Associations, (1968), *Report*, London, HMSO.

Singleton, N. (1975), *Industrial Relations Procedures*, London, HMSO.

Smith, C. T. B., Clifton, R., Makeham, P., and Burn, R. V. (1978), *Manpower Paper No. 15: Strikes in Britain*, London, HMSO.

Stephenson, G. M., and Brotherton, C. J. (eds.) (1979), *Industrial Relations: A Social Psychological Approach*, Chichester, Wiley.

Storey, J. (1980), *The Challenge to Management Control*, London, Business Books.

Storey, J. (1983), *Managerial Prerogative and the Question of Control*, London, Routledge and Kegan Paul.

Taylor, R. (1980), *The Fifth Estate: Britain's Unions in the Modern World*, London, Pan.

Thomason, G. (1981), *A Textbook of Personnel Management*, (4th ed.), London, Institute of Personnel Management.

Thomason, G. (1984), *A Textbook of Industrial Relations Management*, London, Institute of Personnel Management.

Thomson, A. W. J., and Beaumont, P. B. (1978), *Public Sector Bargaining: A Study of Relative Gain*, Farnborough, Saxon House.

Thurley, K., and Wood, S. (eds.) (1982), *Industrial Relations and Management Strategy*, Cambridge, Cambridge University Press.

Torrington, D., and Chapman, J. (1983), *Personnel Management*, (2nd ed.), London, Prentice Hall.

Trades Union Congress (Annual), *TUC Report*, London, TUC.

Trades Union Congress (1966), *Trade Unionism*, London, TUC.

Turner, H. A. (1962), *Trade Union Growth, Structure and Policy*, London, Allen and Unwin.

Turner, H. A., Roberts, G., and Roberts, D. (1977), *Management Characteristics and Labour Conflict*, Cambridge, Cambridge University Press.

Undy, R., Ellis, V., McCarthy, W. E. J., and Halmos, A. M. (1981), *Change in Trade Unions*, London, Hutchinson.

Walton, R., and McKersie, R. (1965), *A Behavioural Theory of Labor Negotiations*, New York, McGraw-Hill.

Webb, S., and B. (1920), *Industrial Democracy*, London, Longmans.

Wedderburn, K. W., Lewis, R., and Clarke, J. (eds.) (1983), *Labour Law and Industrial Relations: Building on Kahn-Freund*, Oxford, Oxford University Press.

Weekes, B., Mellish, M., Dickens, L., and Lloyd, J. (1975), *Industrial Relations and the Limits of the Law*, Oxford, Blackwell.

Wigham, E. (1973), *The Power to Manage*, London, Macmillan.

Index